THE SUNDANCE READER

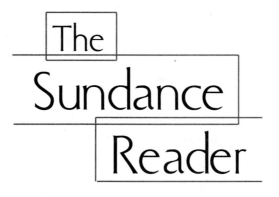

The Sundance Reader

THIRD EDITION

Mark Connelly

Milwaukee Area Technical College

THOMSON

HEINLE

Australia Canada Mexico Singapore Spain United Kingdom United States

The Sundance Reader, Third Edition
Mark Connelly

Publisher: *Michael Rosenberg*
Acquisitions Editor: *Dickson Musslewhite*
Development Editor: *Christine Caperton*
Production Editor: *Diana Baczynskyj*
Marketing Manager: *Ken Kasee*
Director of HED Marketing: *Lisa Kimball*
Senior Print Buyer: *Mary Beth Hennebury*

Compositor: *G & S Typesetters*
Project Manager: *Gretchen Otto*
Photo Manager: *Sheri Blaney*
Cover Designer: *Dutton & Sherman Design*
Printer: *Maple Vail*

Cover Photo: Daniel D. Morrison / Index Stock Imagery

Printed in the United States of America.
1 2 3 4 5 6 7 8 9 10   06 05 04 03 02

For more information contact Heinle, 25 Thomson Place, Boston, MA 02210 USA,
or you can visit our Internet site at http://www.heinle.com

0-15-505940-8 (Student Text)
0-8384-6061-5 (Student Edition w/ InfoTrac®)

Library of Congress Cataloging-in-Publication Data

The sundance reader / Mark Connelly.--3rd ed.
        p. cm.
    Includes index.
    ISBN 0-15-505940-8 (pbk.)
    1. College readers. 2. English language--
        Rhetoric—Problems, exercises, etc.
        3. Report writing—Problems, exercises, etc.
        I.Connelly, Mark

PE1417.S87 2002
808'.0427—dc21

2002068739

To Stanley Felber

Contents

2 | Narration: Relating Events   41

Instead of lecturing, a famous scientist repeats a simple command to his new student—"look, look, look."

A young doctor learns that to avoid the threat of a lawsuit, the next time he sees an accident victim, he should "drive on."

A minor traffic incident reveals the tenuous existence of undocumented aliens in America.

Entering an integrated school, the author of *Makes Me Wanna Holler* receives his first lesson in racism.

A social activist returns to Boston's Irish ghetto where four of his brothers died.

In 1976 a new deadly virus claimed its first victim. Ebola was not AIDS, but it foreshadowed the deadly epidemic to come.

3 | Description: Presenting Impressions   110

Blending the Modes

Writing Beyond the Classroom

4 | Definition: Establishing Meaning

5 | Comparison and Contrast: Indicating Similarities and Differences

6 | Analysis: Making Evaluations   281

Blending the Modes

Writing Beyond the Classroom

Writing Beyond the Classroom

8 | Process: Explaining How Things Work and Giving Directions

Blending the Modes

Writing Beyond the Classroom

9 | Cause and Effect: Determining Reasons and Predicting Results

Blending the Modes

Opposing Viewpoints: The "Abuse Excuse"

Opposing Viewpoints: Global Warming

Writing Beyond the Classroom

10 | Argument and Persuasion: Influencing Readers

Blending the Modes

Opposing Viewpoints: Reparations for Slavery

Opposing Viewpoints: Cultural Identity

Writing Beyond the Classroom

Appendix: Writer's Guide to Documenting Sources

Thematic Contents

ART AND ENTERTAINMENT

AUTOBIOGRAPHY

BIOGRAPHY

BUSINESS AND ECONOMICS

CHILDHOOD

CIVIL RIGHTS

| COMMUNITY AND CULTURE

| CRITICAL THINKING

| DIVERSITY

| EDUCATION

| ENVIRONMENT

| HEALTH AND MEDICINE

HISTORY

JOB INTERVIEWS

LANGUAGE

LAW AND CRIME

| NATURE

| POLITICS

| PSYCHOLOGY AND HUMAN BEHAVIOR

SCIENCE AND TECHNOLOGY

SOCIOLOGY

VALUES

WOMEN AND MEN

WORK AND CAREER

WRITING

Preface

The Sundance Reader contains more than ninety readings drawn from a range of academic disciplines and professions. The collection of essays and articles, organized by rhetorical modes, includes both classic and contemporary authors such as George Orwell, E. B. White, Chris Hedges, Anna Quindlen, Scott Simon, Ellen Goodman, and Maya Angelou. In addition to writing from the disciplines of law, medicine, and science by writers such as Alan M. Dershowitz, Oliver Sacks, and Carl Sagan, *The Sundance Reader* offers students practical advice on résumé writing and job interviews. Applied readings at the end of each chapter demonstrate how writers use the rhetorical modes beyond the classroom. Entries such as "The Reconstructed Logbook of the Titanic," "Interrogation of Lee Harvey Oswald," and "Cleaning Battery Terminals" illustrate various writing tasks students will face in future courses and in their careers.

The Sundance Reader's wide variety of topics on the environment, culture, social issues, and business make the textbook suitable for thematic courses. Individual chapters include self-contained units on current issues, and the thematic table of contents lists a number of topics that can be explored in depth.

With its wealth of readings and four-part questioning strategy following each entry, *The Sundance Reader* provides students a unique perspective on how writing is shaped in different contexts.

The Sundance Reader has several features that make it a useful teaching tool for college instructors:

- *A range of readings* Each chapter opens with brief, readable entries that clearly demonstrate the rhetorical mode, followed by longer, more challenging essays. Many of the essays are short enough to be read in class and used as writing prompts, reducing the need for handouts. Other, longer essays provide opportunities for extended analysis and class discussion. In short, instructors have flexibility in assigning readings best suited to their student populations.

- *A "Blending the Modes" reading* Each chapter highlights a model "blended mode" showing how writers often use several methods of development to tell a story or explain a process.
- *Writing beyond the classroom* Each chapter includes a section illustrating how writers use the modes in "the real world." Advertisements, brochures, government documents, and a résumé introduce elements of business and technical writing to composition students. In addition, several of the entries taken from academic and professional journals are reproduced with full documentation.
- *An emphasis on writing* *The Sundance Reader* moves students from *reading* to *writing*. Chapters open with reading questions and conclude with writing strategies and lists of suggested topics. Each chapter ends with a **"Rhetorical Checklist"** of common writing problems.
- *Writers on writing* The readings include William Zinsser's "The Transaction" and Peter Elbow's "Desperation Writing," which examine writing as both a process and a product. In "Resumes That Rate a Second Look," Anne Weisbord demonstrates the importance of writing skills to job seekers.
- *An emphasis on critical thinking* *The Sundance Reader* stresses critical thinking by including James Austin's article about the role of chance in scientific research. Samuel Scudder's essay "Take This Fish and Look at It" dramatizes the importance of detailed observation. Darrell Huff's "How to Lie with Statistics" heightens student awareness of how statistics are misused and manipulated.
- *Opposing viewpoints entries* Instructors have found that presenting essays with opposing viewpoints can stimulate class discussions and prompt writing activities. *The Sundance Reader* presents pairs of pro and con articles on four critical issues: the "abuse excuse," global warming, slavery reparations, and cultural identity.
- *Focus on diversity* More than a third of the selections are written by women. African-American, Hispanic, Native-American, and Asian writers are represented. In addition to social commentaries by Anna Quindlen and Martin Luther King Jr., women and minorities are featured in nontraditional areas such as business and technology.
- *Writing across the curriculum* *The Sundance Reader* demonstrates how each mode is developed by writers working in several disciplines, including law, medicine, psychology, history, law enforcement, and business.
- *Collaborative writing* Writing suggestions following the readings include directions for collaborative writing activities. The introduction provides useful guidelines for successful group writing.
- *Advice on the job search* *The Sundance Reader* contains articles offering students practical advice on writing résumés, succeeding in job interviews, and evaluating job offers. Other articles provide recommendations for entrepreneurs and business managers.

NEW IN THIS EDITION

- *InfoTrac® College Edition*   Students are directed to explore the huge world of research possibilities with *InfoTrac® College Edition* search cues. *InfoTrac® College Edition* contains dependable, familiar publications that cover a broad spectrum of disciplines and topics. Provided **free** with every copy of the text, *InfoTrac® College Edition* provides on-line access to hundreds of journals and periodicals. The easy-to-use database of reliable, full-length articles from top academic journals and popular sources is ideal for launching lectures, igniting discussions, and opening whole new worlds of information and research for students. (Exclusive to Thomson Learning. Available only to North American college and university students. Journals subject to change.)

- *Twenty-five new essays*   New selections include "A Doctor's Dilemma" by **James Dillard**; "Returning to Southie" by **Michael Patrick MacDonald**; "Letter from Ground Zero" by **Jonathan Schell**; "Gaza Diary" by **Chris Hedges**; "The Company Man" by **Ellen Goodman**; "TV Addiction" by **Marie Winn**; "What Is Terrorism?" from *The Economist;* "Men vs. Women over Walking at Night" by **Bob Levey**; "Irish and Blacks" by **Michael Barone**; "Two Ways to Belong to America" by **Bharati Mukherjee**; "One Internet, Two Nations" by **Louis Gates Jr.**; "The Skinny" by **Richard Brookhiser**; "What's Wrong with This Picture?" by **James Poniewozik**; "What They Saw at the Holocaust Memorial Museum" by **Philip Gourevitch**; "Friends, Good Friends—and Such Good Friends" by **Judith Viorst**; "Propaganda Techniques in Today's Advertising" by **Ann McClintock**; "How to Mark a Book" by **Mortimer Adler**; "Why Blacks Are Returning to Their Southern Roots" by **Maya Angelou**; "The Effects of the Telephone" by **John Brooks**; "Why Schools Don't Educate" by **John Taylor Gatto**; "Black Men and Public Space" by **Brent Staples**; "Why Even Pacifists Support This War" by **Scott Simon**; "Uncle Sam and Aunt Samantha" by **Anna Quindlen**; "An Idea Whose Time Has Come" by **Manning Marable**; and "A Childish Illusion" by **Shelby Steele**.

- *Visual writing prompts*   A section on visual writing prompts in Chapter 1 asks students to write responses to three photos.

- *An annotated essay in each chapter*   The first essay used to introduce each mode is annotated to guide students through its construction.

- *Writer's Guide to Documenting Sources*   This new appendix provides examples on how to apply the MLA and APA rules for documenting sources.

- *Companion Web site*   *The Sundance Reader* Web site (http://sundance.heinle.com) provides students with sample essays, tips on writing in each mode, suggested topics, help with common grammar problems, information about the writing process, and interactive exercises.

Above all, *The Sundance Reader* has been designed to encourage students to read and develop confidence as writers.

Acknowledgments

I would like to thank the following reviewers for their critiques and recommendations for this edition:

James Baskin, *Joilet Junior College*
Sheryl Chisamore, *Ulster County Community College*
Rita D. Costello, *University of Louisiana–Lafayette*
Thomas E. Fish, *Cumberland College*
Roxanna Pisiak, *SUNY–Morrisville*
Margaret Black Tatum, *Kirtland Community College*
Patricia Van Osterhoudt, *Mt. San Antonio College*

I also want to acknowledge reviewers who provided recommendations for the second edition:

Michael A. de Benedictus, *Miami Dade Community College–Kendall Campus*
David Elias, *Eastern Kentucky University*
Frederick Gracobazzi, *Kirkland Community College*
Joyce Marie Miller, *Collin County Community College*
Peggy J. Pavlisin, *Lincoln Land Community College*
Harry R. Phillips, *Central Piedmont Community College*

All books are a collaborative effort. My special thanks go to Michael Rosenberg, publisher; Dickson Musslewhite, acquisitions editor; and Christine Caperton, developmental editor, for their continued support, vision, and enthusiasm for *The Sundance Reader*. I would also like to thank the talented Heinle production and marketing team: Diana Baczynskyj, production editor; Mary Beth Hennebury, senior print buyer; Lisa Kimball, director of higher education marketing; Ken Kasee and Katrina Byrd, marketing managers; Sheri Blaney, photo researcher; John McHugh, vice president of sales and marketing; Elise Kaiser, vice president of production; and Karen

Judd, director of development. The staff at G&S Typesetters has been extremely helpful, especially Yvonne Ramsey, copyeditor and indexer; Amy Simpson, proofreader; Alison Rainey, project editor; and Gretchen Otto, production coordinator. I am also very grateful for the efforts of Tom Hartman in creating and updating the companion Web site.

1

Introduction

HOW WE WRITE

In the summer of 1939 scientist Leo Szilard was worried. As Americans enjoyed the New York World's Fair, the exiled physicist followed events in Europe with growing anxiety. His experiments proved that a nuclear chain reaction could create an atomic bomb. German scientists had split the atom, and the Nazis had seized rich deposits of uranium in Czechoslovakia. As a Jew who had escaped on the last train out of Nazi Germany, Szilard was horrified at the prospect of Hitler obtaining nuclear weapons. Now living in New York, he tried to warn the American government, but officials in Washington were unwilling to fund atomic research. A refugee without resources or political contacts, Szilard sought help from his old friend Albert Einstein, a Nobel Prize winner with an international reputation. Szilard hoped the government would listen to Einstein. Although the idea of a nuclear chain reaction had never occurred to him, Einstein quickly grasped its implications and suggested writing to President Roosevelt. Einstein dictated a letter and asked Szilard to revise it. Szilard wrote a new version then telephoned Einstein, who requested another meeting. Accompanied by fellow physicist Edward Teller, Szilard met Einstein at a summer cottage to discuss the letter. The scientists soon became frustrated. Einstein realized their abstract theories would be difficult to explain to a nonscientist. Equally frustrating was the fact that English was a second language to all three scientists. Einstein dictated a new draft to Edward Teller in German. Leo Szilard wrote two more letters in English and mailed them to Einstein. After reviewing them carefully, Einstein selected the longer version and signed it. Just eight paragraphs long, the letter began with a simply worded declaration of Einstein's concerns:

Sir:
   Some recent work by E. Fermi and L. Szilard, which has been communicated to me in manuscript, leads me to expect that the element uranium may

1

be turned into a new and important source of energy in the immediate future. Certain aspects of the situation which has arisen seem to call for watchfulness and, if necessary, quick action on the part of the Administration. I believe therefore that it is my duty to bring to your attention the following facts and recommendations. . . .

This letter (see page 596 for the full version) was presented to President Roosevelt and helped launch the Manhattan Project and the nuclear age.

The story behind Einstein's letter demonstrates important elements about writing. Writing is a complex process and does not occur in a vacuum. It takes place in a *context* formed by three factors:

1. The writer's purpose and role
2. The knowledge base, attitudes, needs, expectations, and biases of the reader
3. The conventions, history, and culture of a particular discipline, profession, organization, publication, situation, or community

Writing, as the creation of Einstein's letter shows, is often *collaborative*, the product of a group activity. Writing may reflect the ideas of more than one person. Einstein's letter also illustrates a common dilemma writers face in a technological society. Experts frequently have to communicate with readers outside their discipline, people with little understanding or appreciation of the writers' subjects.

Context explains why a newspaper article about an airplane crash differs from a Federal Aviation Administration (FAA) report or the airline's condolence letter to the victims' families. Stated simply and printed in narrow columns for easy skimming, a newspaper account briefly describes current events for general readers. An FAA report detailing the causes of a plane crash runs hundreds of pages and includes extensive data and testimony of witnesses and survivors. Directed to aviation safety experts, the report is stated in technical language largely incomprehensible to the average reader. The airline's letter to victims' families addresses people enduring confusion, grief, and anger. Carefully worded, it attempts to inform readers without appearing callous or falsely sympathetic.

You may have noticed how context affects your own writing. The notes you take in class for personal use look very different from the in-class essay you submit for a grade. The words you choose when adding a line to a birthday card for your seven-year-old cousin differ from those used on a job application or in a note to your roommate. Almost unconsciously, you alter the way you write depending on your purpose, reader, and circumstances. To be an effective writer in college and in your future career, it is important to increase your understanding of the three elements that form a writing context.

1. Can you recall writing situations where you had difficulty expressing your ideas because you were unsure how your reader would react? Did you have problems finding the right words or just "getting your thoughts on paper"?
2. Have you found that teachers and professors have different attitudes about what constitutes "good writing"? How is writing a paper in English literature different from writing a paper in psychology or economics?
3. Have you observed that magazines often have strikingly different writing styles? What do articles in *Cosmopolitan, Car and Driver,* or the *Wall Street Journal* reveal about their intended readers?

THE WRITER

All writing has a goal. A shopping list serves to refresh your memory. A memo informs employees of a policy change. Research papers demonstrate students' knowledge and skills. Résumés encourage employers to call applicants for job interviews. Even essays written for self-expression must contain more than random observations. To be effective an essay must arouse interest, provide readers with information they can understand, and offer proof to support the writer's thesis.

The Writer's Purpose

Students and professionals in all fields face similar writing tasks. The way they present their ideas, the language they use, and even the physical appearance of the finished document are determined in part by their purpose. Although every writing assignment forms a unique context, most writing tasks can be divided into basic modes or types:

narration *To relate a series of events, usually in chronological order.* Biographies, histories, and novels use narration. Business and government reports often include sections called *narratives* that provide a historical overview of a problem, organization, or situation. Letters to friends usually consist of narratives detailing recent events or experiences.

description *To create a picture or impression of a person, place, object, or condition.* Description is a basic element in all writing and usually serves to provide support for the writer's main goal. Descriptions may be wholly factual and objective, as in an accident report or parts catalog. Others may contain personal impressions emphasizing what the writer saw, thought, or felt. A novelist describing a city is more likely to focus on his or her "feel" of the streets and people rather than on statistics and census figures.

definition *To explain a term, condition, topic, or issue.* In many instances definitions are precise and standard, such as a state's definition of second-degree murder or a biology book's definition of a virus. Other definitions, such as that of a good parent or an ideal teacher, may be based on a writer's personal observation, experience, and opinion.

comparison/contrast *To examine the similarities and differences between two or more subjects.* Textbooks often employ comparison/contrast to discuss different scientific methods, theories, or subjects. Comparisons can be made to distinguish topics or to recommend one subject as superior to others. Consumer magazines frequently use comparison to highlight differences among competing products.

analysis *To evaluate a subject and identify its essential elements, impact, effectiveness, or qualities.* Writers of a formal analysis can follow a standard method. Stockbrokers, medical examiners, building inspectors, archaeologists, botanists, criminologists, and other professionals generally use uniform methods of studying subjects and presenting their conclusions. Essayists and newspaper columnists, on the other hand, analyze issues from an entirely personal perspective, relying on anecdotal evidence and individual observation. A reviewer's column about a new movie, a sports writer's column about a coach's performance, and a pollster's view on the president's popularity are examples of personal analysis.

division *To name subgroups or divisions in a broad class.* Writers seek to make a large or complex topic understandable or workable by dividing it into smaller units. Insurance can be divided into life, health, homeowner's, and auto policies. A zoology text divides animals into fish, birds, mammals, and reptiles.

classification *To place objects into different classes or levels according to a single measurement.* Writers classify with a scale to grade subjects. Homicides are classified as first-, second-, or third-degree according to circumstances and premeditation. Burns are classified as first-, second-, or third-degree based on the severity of tissue damage.

Like analysis, division and classification can be based on professional standards or personal evaluation. A financial adviser might rate mutual funds by risk and performance using commonly accepted criteria. A movie critic, however, could grade films on a one-to-five-star scale based solely on his or her tastes.

process   *To explain how something occurs or to demonstrate how to accomplish a specific task.* A nuclear power plant, the human heart, and inflation can be described as processes. By examining each stage, a writer can make a complex mechanism or event easier to understand. A recipe, the owner's manual of a computer, and a first-aid book offer step-by-step instructions to complete specific tasks.

cause and effect   *To trace the reasons for or results of an occurrence.* A writer can list causes for an increase in crime, for the return of an endangered species, or for the success or failure of an advertising campaign. Similarly, he or she could list the effects crime has on a community, the response to rescued wildlife, or the impact of television commercials. Physicians refer to medical books that explain the causes of disease and the effects of drugs.

persuasion and argumentation   *To influence reader opinion, attitudes, and actions.* Writers persuade with logical appeals based on factual evidence, with ethical appeals based on values or beliefs, or with emotional appeals that arouse feelings to support their views. A fund-raising letter persuades readers to donate money to a charity. An engineer's report presents an argument why a building should be condemned or an engine redesigned. Essayists and columnists try to influence readers to accept their opinions on topics ranging from abortion to welfare reform.

QUESTIONS

1. Consider how you have organized papers in the past. Did any assignments lend themselves to one of the modes? Could following one of these methods make it easier to present and organize your ideas?

2. Do you use modes such as *comparison, classification,* or *cause and effect* in organizing your thoughts and solving problems? Do you *compare* apartments before deciding which one to rent or *classify* courses you want to take next semester by difficulty or desirability?

The way writers achieve their goals depends greatly on the other two elements of context: their readers and the discipline. Each chapter of *The Sundance Reader* focuses on one of these modes, illustrating how writers use it in different contexts.

A Note about Modes

Modes refer to the writer's basic goal. Often writing cannot be neatly labeled. Few writing tasks call for the use of a single mode. A dictionary entry is pure definition, and a parts catalog offers simple product descriptions. But a movie review *analyzing* a new release will first *describe* the film and possibly *compare* it to the director's previous work. It might use *narration* to explain elements of the plot and *classification* to rank it with other films in its genre. Some writing can easily fit two or more categories. The Declaration of Independence, for instance (page 532), is an example of both *cause and effect* and *persuasive writing.*

Visual Writing Prompts: Thinking in the Modes

The modes are not abstract academic devices. We think in the modes when we make decisions or respond to ideas. For example, you use *narration* to tell a story to a friend, *comparison* to determine whether you should buy or lease a new car, and *process* to teach someone how to prepare a meal. In responding to events and ideas, we find ourselves thinking in the modes.

After looking at each of the following photographs, use one or more of the modes to write a brief response.

Description: *Describe* your first reactions to the picture of Seattle street kids. Did you feel anger, pity, fear, disgust? What kind of young people are drawn to guns? *Describe* the problems these boys represent.

Process: Briefly outline the steps it would take for a youth program to intervene with street kids and prevent violence. What *process* is needed to turn their lives around?

Argument: *Persuade* readers to accept your view of stronger gun control laws. Would stricter gun laws lessen crime and violence, or would they fail? Write an editorial clearly stating your views.

Definition: *Define* the term "role model." What are role models and how do they affect the way we shape our lives? Does the photograph of Joan Collins and her daughter depict a role model at work? Why or why not?

Seattle street kids with gun, 1983.   © Mary Ellen Mark

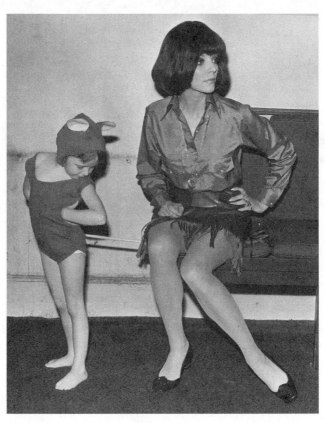

Joan Collins and daughter, 1968.   Hulton Getty

Suicide, 1942. I. Russell Sorgi Photograph from the Buffalo Courier Express Library, Collection, courtesy of E. H. Butler Archives, Buffalo State College.

Comparison: *Contrast* the way boys and girls are raised. How do parents, society, and popular culture influence our ideas about gender roles? What does this picture reveal to you about girls and the way they come to view their bodies?

Classification: *Classify* in order of importance the influences that shaped your view of gender roles. What were the strongest forces that guided your childhood development?

Narration: Write a narrative about the photograph of a suicide. Invent any details to create a fictional suicide letter, newspaper account, or police report.

Cause and Effect: Explain the *causes* of suicide. What drives people to end their lives? Detail *effects* that a suicide has on surviving friends and family.

Analysis: *Analyze* the composition of the suicide photograph. Does this fleeting image seem to tell a story? Note the policeman entering the hotel, the men in the window, the signs in the window.

Analyze the social or psychological impact of this image. What do you see in the suicide of a woman in 1942, when millions of people were trying to avoid death in combat and concentration camps? Is the woman's act ironic, selfish, or pathetic?

The Writer's Role

An important aspect of context is the writer's role. As a student your role is much like that of a freelance writer. Your essays, reports, and research papers are expected to reflect only your own efforts. In general, your work is judged independently. A low grade on a first paper should not affect your chances of earning a higher grade later in the semester. What you write in psychology has no influence on your grades in English. Your comments on controversial issues are not likely to be raised at future job interviews.

Outside of academics, however, your role is more complicated. Often you act as an agent of a larger organization, corporation, or profession. Business letters, memos, and reports are assumed to express the views of the employer, not a single employee. Expressing personal views that conflict with corporate practices or administrative policy can jeopardize your position. Frequently, you will have an ongoing relationship with your readers. Comments made in one letter or report affect how readers will respond to your ideas in the future.

Probably the most obvious aspect of a writer's role concerns *perspective*, or the writer's position in the paper. Writing in a newspaper's sports section, a columnist may be free to offer personal opinion: "Given poor ticket sales and the age of the stadium, I predict this town will lose its ball club within two years." A front-page article, however, would be weakened by the use of first person. A reporter would express the same view in more objective terms: "The decline in ticket sales and the age of the stadium indicate the city is in danger of losing its baseball team."

When writing as a member of a group or as an agent of an organization, remember that the ideas you express will be considered the ideas of the group. Refrain from stating anything that would alienate other members or expose your organization to liability. If you state personal views, make sure you clearly identify them as being your opinions.

In many instances your profession will dictate a role that will greatly shape what is expected in your writing. Police officers and nurses, for example, are required to provide objective and impersonal records of their observations. Fashion consultants, decorators, and advertising executives, who are esteemed for their creativity, are more likely to offer personal insights and make first-person statements.

QUESTIONS

1. Consider the jobs you have had and the businesses you have worked for. What writing style would be appropriate for professionals in these fields? Is objective reporting required, or are employees free to offer personal impressions and suggest innovations?
2. What type of writing do you expect to confront in your career? How does writing in engineering and accounting differ from writing in public relations, sales, or nonprofit charities? Does your future profession demand adherence to governmental regulations and industry standards, or does it allow for individual expression?

THE READER

Writing is more than self-expression; it is an act of communication. To be effective your message must be understood. The content, form, and tone of your writing are largely shaped by the needs and expectations of your readers. A medical researcher announcing a new treatment for AIDS would word an article for *Immunology* very differently from one for *Newsweek* or *Redbook*. Each magazine represents a different audience, a different knowledge base, and a different set of concerns. Fellow immunologists would be interested in the author's research methods and would demand detailed proof of his or her claims. Readers of *Immunology* would expect to see extensive data and precise descriptions of experiments and testing methods. Most readers of nonmedical publications would require definitions of scientific terms and would expect brief summaries of data they would be unable to evaluate. Readers of *Newsweek* could be concerned with issues such as cost, government policy, and insurance coverage. Subscribers to a women's magazine such as *Redbook* might wonder if the treatment works equally well for both sexes or if the treatment would be suitable for pregnant women with HIV.

Audiences often differ within a discipline. The medical researcher writing for the *New England Journal of Medicine* would be addressing practicing physicians, not laboratory researchers. Doctors would be interested in the practical aspects of the treatment. What drugs does it interact with? What are the side effects? Which patients should receive the drug and in what doses? An article in *Nursing* would focus on the concerns of nurses who closely monitor patients for reactions. What effect does the treatment have on a patient's physical and psychological well-being? Are there special considerations for patients with unrelated disorders, such as hypertension and diabetes?

As a writer you will have to determine how much knowledge your readers have about your subject. Do technical terms have to be defined? Does your writing include historical or biographical references requiring explanation? Do you use concepts that general readers might misunderstand or find confusing? In addition to your readers' level of understanding, you must consider your readers' needs and expectations in relation to your own goal. What information do your readers want from you? Is your audience reading for general interest, curiosity, or entertainment, or do they demand specific information in order to make decisions or plan future actions?

It is also important to take into account how your readers will respond to your ideas. Is your audience likely to be favorable or hostile to you, your ideas, or the organization you might represent? Defense attorneys and prosecutors have different attitudes toward illegally obtained evidence. Environmentalists and real estate developers have conflicting philosophies of land use. Liberals and conservatives have opposing concepts of the proper role of government regulation. When presenting ideas to audiences with undefined or differing attitudes, you will have to work hard to overcome their natural resistance, biases, and suspicions.

Individual Readers

The papers you write in high school and college are usually read by a single teacher or professor who is evaluating your work in the context of a particular course. Instructors form a special audience because they are counted on to read your work and remain objective. Beyond the classroom, however, you may have to persuade someone to read your résumé or proposal. Few of these readers will even attempt objectivity. Unlike the papers you write for instructors, your reports and letters seek more than a grade. In many instances, you will ask an employer for a job or attempt to persuade a client to buy a product. In accepting your ideas, your reader may be investing substantial resources on your behalf, conceivably placing his or her career in your hands. In writing to these individuals, you will have to analyze their needs and concerns very carefully.

Extended Readerships

Many contexts involve two audiences: the immediate person or persons who receive your document and a second, extended readership. When you write as a student, most of your work is returned to you. In most jobs your correspondence, reports, and publications are retained for future reference. The safety inspection report you write in April may be routinely skimmed by your supervisor, filed, and forgotten. But if a serious accident occurs in May, this report will be retrieved and closely examined by state inspectors, insurance investigators, and attorneys. If you engage in a dispute with a customer or another employee, your writing may be reviewed by a supervisor or, in the case of litigation, introduced into court as evidence. Many professionals practice "defensive writing," precisely wording their thoughts and observations, understanding that whatever they write may be examined by adversaries. In court, police officers and physicians are often asked to explain and defend comments they wrote months or years before.

When you write outside of academics, bear in mind who else may see your writing. This is a critical consideration whenever you are writing as an employee or agent of others. Think carefully before making remarks that might be misunderstood out of context.

The Perceptual World

To learn how readers respond to ideas, it is helpful to understand what communications researchers call the *perceptual world,* the context in which people perceive new information and experiences. As individuals or groups, readers base their reactions on a number of factors that have varying significance and often operate simultaneously.

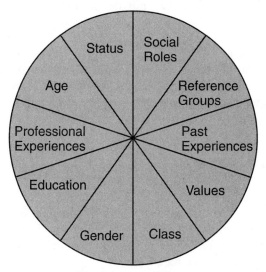

The Perceptual World

- **Past experiences** influence how people respond to new information and situations. Readers who have lost money in the stock market will be more skeptical of an investment offer than those who have enjoyed substantial returns. A labor union with a harmonious relationship with management will view contract offers differently from a union with a history of stalled talks, bitter negotiations, and strikes.
- **Education,** both formal and informal, affects people's reading ability, background knowledge, and understanding of terminology. Training in specific disciplines will also influence how readers evaluate the evidence writers present as support. Scientists and mathematicians may be more skeptical of advertising claims using statistics than the general public.

- **Professional experience,** along with training and job responsibilities, shapes people's attitudes. An economics professor with tenure may exhibit a greater ability to be objective about a new tax policy than a small-business owner struggling to meet a weekly payroll. Police officers and emergency room doctors may be less sympathetic to drunken drivers than people who rarely see the harm they cause.
- **Status** or amount of investment influences people's response to potential change. An entry-level employee is less likely to be concerned about a change in pension plans than is one nearing retirement. Homeowners have more invested in their neighborhoods than renters and may show greater interest in crime or pollution.
- **Values,** whether religious, political, or cultural, help shape readers' responses. Often these values are unspoken but deeply held. People's attitudes about money, sexual conduct, drug use, child rearing, the role of government, and many other issues affect how they react to new ideas.
- **Reference groups** include people or institutions readers respect and to whom they defer. A physician who is unsure about prescribing a new drug may base his or her decision on the opinion of the American Medical Association. A student thinking of changing his or her major might seek advice from parents and friends.
- **Social roles,** such as being a parent, civic leader, or property owner, influence how a person evaluates ideas. A thirty-year-old with two small children will have different concerns from someone of the same age without children. A shop steward plays a special role and may be expected to react differently than other employees.
- **Age** affects reader attitudes in two ways. People are products of the times they have lived through. Men and women who came of age during World War II have different views than those who grew up during the Vietnam War. In general, older readers have more invested in existing institutions than younger readers and may be more cautious about change.

Other aspects of the perceptual world include gender, ethnic background, and income. In determining your readers' perceptual world, it is important to avoid basing assumptions on common stereotypes. Not all older people are conservative, and not all African Americans endorse affirmative action. Many elements of the perceptual world are unconscious and cannot be easily ascertained. No doubt you have been surprised by the reactions of friends you believed you knew very well.

QUESTIONS

1. How would you describe the perceptual world of your parents, coworkers, or friends? How do their common experiences, values, roles, and educa-

tion affect their attitudes? How would they respond to a letter urging them to donate money to the homeless, to support a handgun ban, or to picket an abortion clinic? Which issues would be difficult to present to them? Why?

2. Have you ever tried to understand someone you hoped to influence in some way? In practicing a presentation, preparing for a job interview, or seeking the right words to discuss a difficult issue with a friend or family member, did you consider how that person might react? Is understanding people's perceptual worlds something we engage in every day?

THE DISCIPLINE

The communication between writer and reader occurs within a particular discipline, setting, culture, publication, or situation. Each academic discipline has a unique history. Some disciplines, such as literature and mathematics, have slowly evolved over thousands of years. Students still read *Oedipus* and study Euclid's principles of geometry. In contrast, the fields of computer science and bioengineering are so new that many of their founders are still actively developing the nature of the discipline.

Every discipline has its own communications style and methods of measuring data, weighing results, and presenting conclusions. In the humanities, research is generally oriented to examining specific works. Whether the researcher is studying Bach, Shakespeare, or Georgia O'Keeffe, the artist's work is the central focus. Disciplines often contain several schools of thought or types of criticism. In literature, for example, some scholars interpret a novel in light of the author's life and thoughts. Other critics would analyze the book in terms of its historical position or political message. Some critics specialize in feminist or Marxist interpretations of literature. But no matter what their approach, literary critics essentially present an educated opinion based on interpretations of the text.

In the sciences, such as biology, chemistry, and physics, scholars base their evaluations on the principles of laboratory research and experiments. Scholars making new assertions in these fields must demonstrate where they obtained their data and prove that other scientists can repeat their experiments and obtain the same results. Although the sciences can seem exact, personal opinion can play a significant role in setting up experiments and interpreting data.

The social sciences of psychology, sociology, criminology, political science, and economics blend some of the features of the humanities and sciences. Although psychologists and criminologists can conduct experiments and often use scientific evidence, many of their conclusions are based on data that can be collected and interpreted in a number of ways.

As a college student you can appreciate the nature of each discipline by examining your textbooks, particularly introductory chapters that often provide a history of the field.

Each profession forms its own context of historical experience, technical training, areas of concern, responsibilities, and political and social outlooks. Corporate executives charged with obtaining investor capital for expansion and research develop different attitudes toward capital gains taxes than social workers assisting low-income families. The medical profession has a strict tradition of relying on standardized treatment and research methods. Physicians tend to be skeptical of anyone claiming to have a cure for a disease unless the claims can be clearly supported by research and not simply by anecdotal endorsements. Professions measure success differently, praising creativity, sales, or communications skills. Law enforcement officers approach a case of suspected child abuse with the goal of determining if evidence indicates a crime has been committed. A mental health professional is more interested in the child's well-being, whether the situation meets the definitions of legal abuse or not. A therapist would treat even an imagined incident seriously if it caused the child distress.

The discipline, profession, or situation creates different methods of using and looking at writing. David Ogilvy, a noted advertising executive, devoted his career to writing ad copy, coming up with snappy, creative, innovative ways of grabbing consumers' attention and boosting sales of his clients' products. For him, writing is a tool to project an image, gain attention, and, above all, sell:

> Always try to inject *news* into your headlines, because the consumer is always on the lookout for new products, or new ways to use an old product, or new improvements in an old product.
>
> The two most powerful words you can use in a headline are FREE and NEW. You can seldom use FREE, but you can almost always use NEW—if you try hard enough.

Fran Martin, a nurse who serves as an expert witness in medical malpractice trials, offers a very different kind of writing advice to nurses. Unlike ad writers whose success depends on creativity or originality, nurses are counted on to maintain precise records:

> You communicate with other health care providers through the chart and, obviously, incorrect data doesn't give an accurate picture of your patient's condition. That could lead to life-threatening errors. It also raises the specter

of fraud, which could make your actions appear not just negligent, but also criminal.

Writing Contexts

The contexts in which writers operate are limitless, but a few general patterns follow:

1. **Expert to general reader:** Most books and articles are written by experts to people reading for information or enjoyment. An attorney preparing a university brochure on date rape would have to anticipate that most student attitudes have been largely formed by the media. He or she might have to dispel common misconceptions and explain terms and legal procedures.
2. **Expert to expert within a discipline:** Law reviews, medical journals, and trade magazines are largely read by professionals within a specific field. Writers for these periodicals can assume readers will understand basic concepts and terminology. Advanced textbooks in biology or criminal law rarely provide the introductory material found in first-year books. The letters, reports, and documents generated within a corporation or government agency may adopt a unique style and format that almost become a code few outsiders can understand. But writers in these situations should always keep an extended readership in mind. An audit, budget review, or investigation could circulate as a memo or letter to a wider audience.
3. **Expert to expert in different disciplines:** This is perhaps one of the most challenging contexts writers face. Einstein's letter to Roosevelt is a classic example of this context—a world-famous scientist attempting to explain a discovery to a powerful leader with minimal knowledge of physics. How does an engineer explain the practical difficulties to a designer interested in style and creativity? How does an economist persuade a politician facing reelection to raise taxes or cut benefits? In communicating with professionals in different disciplines, it is important for writers to establish trust, to address their readers' concerns, and to explain unfamiliar concepts clearly.

THE WRITING PROCESS

Writing is a process as well as a product. Good writing respects each of the three elements of context. When you plan a writing project, determine your purpose, evaluate your readers, and follow the conventions of your discipline. Many college instructors provide requirements for writing assignments. In a professional situation you can benefit from examining samples of the writing tasks you are undertaking.

Prewriting

Writing is not only a means of preparing a finished document but is also a way of thinking and exploring. You can use a number of planning techniques to discover topics, define your thesis, and list needed items.

Freewriting records thoughts and impressions without interruption and without any concern for spelling, grammar, or punctuation. Freewriting should not be confused with writing a rough draft. Freewriting is like talking to yourself. It may have no direction, it may skip from topic to topic, and it may contradict itself. Freewriting is a bit like making a series of fast sketches before determining the subject matter of a large painting. The goal of freewriting is not writing a "paper" but simply discovering possible topics.

Overhearing a claim that the government was behind the influx of drugs in the inner city, a student sat at her computer and rapidly recorded a stream of thoughts on the topic of conspiracy theories:

The CIA is behind the drug epidemic. The US government pays South Koreans to set up grocery stores in the inner city. Every president since Nixon has lied about MIA's held captive in Southeast Asia. The airforce lies about UFO sitings. The number of conspiracy theories is limitless. The lumber industry is against legalizing marijuana because hemp makes better paper than woodpulp. Roosevelt knew the Japanese were going to bomb Pearl Harbor but let it happen. Conspiracies are endless. They are populair. They sell a lot of newspapers and create a lot of TV shows & employ an army of theoriests who move from talk show to talk show touting their books and their latest proof that the CIA or blacks or the Fortune 500 is responsible for some horrible deed or social threat. No doubt some mad scientist in a govt lab created AIDS and loosed it on the world. No doubt someone has cured cancer and has been kidnapped or killed so millions of doctors and thousands of drug companies won't go out of business. Why? Why do people love these theories?

Some people to need to believe that no lone assassin could have killed JFK. They cling to this belief, no matter what the evidence. Why? Maybe we need to believe in conspiracy theories. It makes the evil in the world less frightening. We are not victims of random chaos, but evil people who can theoretically be located and exposed. To abandon conspiracy theories means accepting chaos. Also it allows us to escape blame. If we blame all our problems on mysterious forces beyond our control, then we can dodge personnal responsibility.

Although this freewriting is loose, repetitive, and misspelled, it moves from listing conspiracy theories to speculating about why people need to believe in them. The student now has something to focus on and a possible title: "Why We Need Conspiracy Theories."

Brainstorming is another prewriting process that can help you generate ideas and identify possible topics for further writing. As in freewriting, list your ideas as quickly as possible. Do not bother to worry if your ideas are repetitive or irrelevant. Again, your purpose is not to outline a paper but simply to develop ideas.

Brainstorming can be used to discover a topic for an essay or to help a professional identify details that need to be included in a business letter or report. A composition student assigned a comparison/contrast essay might list as many ideas as possible in hopes of discovering a topic:

```
high school teachers/college professors
male/female attitudes about first dates
American/Japanese ideas about privacy
Puerto-Ricans vs. Mexican-Americans
Mexican-born vs. 1st generation Mex-Americans
English only vs. Bilingual
Mexican-born English/1st gen. Mex-Am attitudes
```

Through brainstorming or listing, the student has run through a number of ideas before focusing on a topic suited for a short paper comparing the attitudes of Mexican-born Americans and their children toward English.

Even when the topic is defined, brainstorming can help writers identify what they should include. The third-shift supervisor of a warehouse who is planning a report following a forklift accident could use brainstorming to make sure he or she produces a complete report that managers can use to examine the firm's legal liability, safety policies, employee training, and equipment use:

```
time/date/location of accident.
Injured personnel--Alex Bolton, Sara Lopez
     (Medical Status)
911 call--get time from dispatcher
Bolton's forklift--last inspection (service log)
forklift load--stability (check manual)
Use of helmets, earplugs
surveillance cameras (tapes)
accident witnesses
```

From this list, the supervisor identifies the information needed to meet the needs of the readers.

WRITING ACTIVITIES

1. *Freewriting:* Select one of the following topics, and write for at least ten minutes. Do not worry about making sense or maintaining logical connec-

tions between ideas. Remember, this is not the rough draft of a paper but an attempt to develop ideas and discover topics.

your worst job	blind dates	television talk shows
job interviews	marriage	capital punishment
recycling	censorship	student loans
campus housing	car repair	media images of women

2. *Brainstorming:* Select one of the columns of ideas and build on it, adding your own ideas. Jot down your thoughts as quickly as possible. Do not worry if some of your ideas are off the topic.

men/women	success/money	vacation plans
dating	careers	plane/car
expectations	salary/income	hotel/meals
conflicts	risk/reward	budget/costs

Clustering represents a more visual method of developing ideas. Instead of complete sentences or listed ideas, topics are grouped in circles and boxes. Visual markers such as arrows, question marks, and ink color can be used to organize and link ideas. A student writing about the information superhighway clustered the following topics:

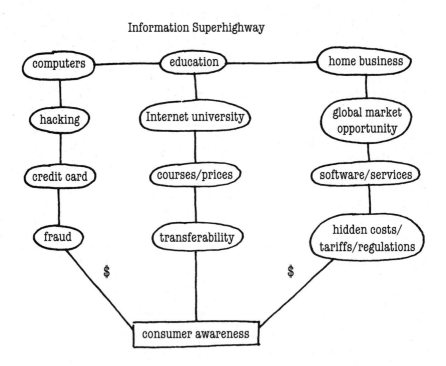

Information Superhighway

Drawing clusters helps the student focus on a topic: consumer awareness and the Internet.

Asking questions is a method used by reporters and investigators to help identify critical information. For generations newspaper reporters have been trained to ask the "Five Ws": Who? What? When? Where? Why? Asking questions can help you identify topics and narrow your focus. A student considering writing a paper about Arthur Miller's *Death of a Salesman* might list the following questions to help identify a topic for a short analytical paper:

Death of a Salesman

What are Willy's values?
Is Willy a victim of society or of his own delusions?
What role does Uncle Ben play?
Is Willy's suicide caused by despair or a last attempt at success?
What impact does Willy's infidelity have?
Biff steals a suit and a fountain pen. What do these objects represent?
Linda knows Willy has lost his salary but does not confront him about it. Why?
Why does Miller pose Willy and Biff next to Uncle Charlie and Bernard?
Is the play an attack on the American dream?
Why does Willy refuse to take a job from Charlie?
This play is world famous but the hero is abusive, selfish, and short-tempered. Why is
     the play so popular?
What is the purpose of the requiem at the end? How would the play be different
     without it?

By posing lists of questions, you can often identify key issues and provoke critical thinking that will lead to developing a thesis.

WRITING ACTIVITIES

1. *Clustering:* Select one of the following topics. Use a large piece of paper to record and arrange your ideas. Group related ideas with circles or squares. Use arrows to connect ideas. You may use different colors, switch from pen to pencil, or mark major ideas with a highlighter. Whatever method you use, do not allow your artwork to overshadow your goal of developing ideas for a paper.

year-round school	computer hacking	nutrition
gay rights	the American dream	women in combat
airports	working out	childless couples
aging	being laid off	divorce

2. *Asking questions:* Select one of the following topics, and write a list of questions. Write as quickly as possible, and do not worry about being repetitive. Try to ask as many questions as you can to explore as many avenues as possible.

recent hit movie	gangs	television violence
day care	welfare reform	suburbs
role models	teen pregnancy	corporate downsizing
labor unions	singles' bars	drunk driving

Moving from Topic to Thesis

A paper is never "about" something; it must make a clear statement. The student who begins writing "about *Death of a Salesman*" may either find himself or herself facing an endless number of issues or end up creating nothing more than a plot summary. Writing should have a focus, a direction. The word *thesis* refers to the writer's main idea. A good thesis makes a clear point that is supported by the body of the writing. In some writing the thesis is the central idea or controlling statement. In argumentative writing the thesis is clearly articulated. In descriptive or narrative writing the thesis can be implied. A writer who offers a powerful description of the homeless may assume readers will be moved to take action.

A thesis makes a strong statement about a topic:

Topic: Consumers and the Internet
Thesis: Users of the Internet unknowingly expose themselves to consumer fraud.

Topic: Conspiracy theories
Thesis: Like ancient mythology, today's conspiracy theories serve to explain the unexplainable and reduce fear of chaos.

Topic: *Death of a Salesman*
Thesis: Willy Loman commits what psychologists call altruistic suicide.

Once you have determined your thesis, you can begin writing. Writers work in many different ways. Some make elaborate outlines and carefully write a draft, perfecting each paragraph or section until they complete a text ready for proofreading. Others make few plans but write several complete drafts, writing and revising key areas over and over again.

Many writers go through a five-stage process that helps improve their writing and save time. As a beginning writer you can benefit from following these guidelines. With experience, you can personalize your method of writing.

HOW TO WRITE AN ESSAY

1. **Plan—establish context.** Once you have established your goal and thesis, determine how you will develop your paper in light of your readers' needs and the conventions of the discipline. Develop an outline listing the items needed to achieve your goal. Your opening should attract attention, announce the topic, and prepare readers for main ideas presented in the body of the work. The conclusion should bring the paper to a logical end, using a final observation, quote, or question to make a strong impression.

2. **Write—get your ideas on paper.** After reviewing your plans, write as much as possible without stopping. Writing the first draft can be considered controlled freewriting. As you write, new ideas may occur to you. Record *all* your thoughts. Do not pause to check spelling or look up a fact because it may break your train of thought. Underline words you think are misspelled or sentences that contain grammatical errors. Leave gaps for missing details. Place question marks next to items you want to double-check.

3. **Cool—put your writing aside.** It is difficult to evaluate your work immediately after writing because much of what you wish to say is still fresh in your mind. Set your work aside. Work on other assignments, read, watch television, or take a walk to clear your mind. Afterward, you can return to your writing with greater objectivity.

4. **Revise—review your writing in context.** Before searching your paper for misspelled words or grammatical errors, examine it holistically. Review your goal and plan. Examine any instructions you have received. Then read your paper. Does it clearly express your goal and support your thesis? Is it properly directed to your audience? Does it violate any principles in the discipline? Revision can mean rewriting the entire paper or merely reworking certain details.

5. **Edit—correct mechanical errors and polish style.** When you have a completed paper, examine your writing for missing words, grammatical errors, and misspelled words. In addition, review your diction. Eliminate wordy phrases and reduce repetition. Make sure ideas flow evenly and smoothly. *Reading a paper aloud can help identify errors and awkward sentences.*

These five stages are not neatly isolated. Writing, according to current research, is *recursive*—the steps overlap and occur simultaneously. As you write you will find yourself brainstorming, editing, correcting, spelling, and freewriting.

Each writing assignment is unique. For example, a narrative requires attention to chronology, while a division paper demands clear organization, and persuasion depends on the skillful use of logic. Each discipline represents a distinct discourse community. In literature courses students are expected to provide original interpretations of literary works such as plays and novels. Students in the sciences are required to follow strict standards for gathering data, analyzing results, and presenting conclusions. Undoubtedly, you may find some papers more challenging than others. Because it is often difficult to determine how hard a particular assignment may be, it is advisable to start writing as soon as possible. Just ten minutes of prewriting will quickly reveal how much time and effort you need to devote to any paper.

Strategies for Creating a Composing Style

1. **Review your past writing.** Consider how you have written in the past. Which papers received the highest and lowest grades in high school? Why? What can you recall about writing them? What mistakes have you made? What comments have teachers made about your work?
2. **Experiment with composing.** Write at different times and places, using pen and paper or a computer. See what conditions enhance your writing.
3. **Study returned papers for clues.** Read your instructors' comments carefully. If your papers lack a clear thesis, you should devote more attention to prewriting and planning. If instructors fill your papers with red ink—circling misspelled words and underlining fragments—devote more time to editing.

WRITING THE WHOLE COMPOSITION

The stages of the writing process are illustrated here by a student developing a paper for a freshman composition class. Having read and discussed several essays concerning criminal justice, the class was instructed to turn in a short commentary debating the merits of a current legal issue.

Prewriting

The student began by exploring topics through prewriting. Note that her work blends several techniques, including brainstorming, freewriting, and clustering:

Topics: Criminal justice (issues)
          capital punishment pro/con
          gun control
          Courtroom TV
          What is the impact of televised trials?
          Do TV trials educate the public?
          How does media attention affect juries?
          Victims and crime—are they forgotten?
          Who speaks for victims?
          Do prosecutors properly speak for victims?

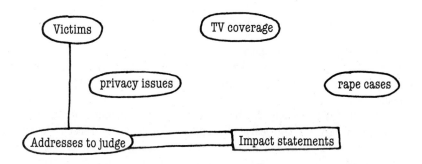

Victim impact statements are increasingly a feature of modern trials as people are allowed to state their feelings about the crime and the criminal after he/she is convicted. Judges can consider the impact of the crime on the victim in sentencing. Sometimes victims ask for harsh punishment and sometimes they even ask for leniency and give the criminal, especially a young person a 2nd chance........

Who is most impressive?
What about victims who can't speak well or don't know English?
What about families of homicide victims?
Victims without mourners? Less important?

Topic: Victim impact statements
Thesis: Although victim impact statements are supposed to empower the victims of
          crime, they may serve only to further marginalize the most helpless among us.

Planning

Victim Impact Statements

INTRO: Background of impact statements
          Definition

PRO: -- empowers victims who feel forgotten
         -- helps heal victims by addressing criminal
         -- helps people regain control over their lives & move on
         -- makes the human cost of a crime part of the sentencing decision.

CON: Question?
         Whose impact is more effective?
         Middle class professional vs. Welfare mom

END: Question, helpful or hurtful to victims?

First Draft

Across America today more and more victims of crime are being allowed to address the court in terms of making what is called a victim impact statment. This written or oral presentation to the court allows victims to express their feelings to the judge after someone has been convicted of a crime.

Advocates of victim impact statements point to key advantages. First, these statements give victims' a voice. For years, victims have felt helpless. Prosecutors represent the state, not the crime victim. Victims have been dismayed when prosecutors have aranged plea bargains without their knowledge. Some victims are still recovering from their injuries when they learn the person who hurt them has plead to a lesser charge and received probation.

Therapists who work with victims also say that being able to adress the court helps with the healing process. Victims of violent crime can feel powerless and vulnerable. Instead of suffering in silence, they are given the chance to address the criminal, to clear their chests, and get on with the rest of their lives.

Impact statements allows judges to consider what sentences are appropriate. In one case a judge who planned to fine a teenager for shoplifting accepted the store owner's suggestion of waving the fine if the defendant completed his GED.

But giving victims a chance to speak raises some issues. What about the victim who is not articulate, who doesn't even speak English? In murder cases the victim's relatives are given a chance to speak? Does this mean that a middle class professional victim with a circle grieving friends and family members will be granted more significance than the homeless murder victim who leaves no one behind?

Victim impact statements may help empower victims who are educated, personally impressive, and socially promient. But they may also allow forgotten victims to remain voiceless.

After completing the first draft, the student set the paper aside for several hours before returning to examine it. As a rough draft it clearly captured the writer's main ideas, but it could be improved to make a greater impression on readers. Note the student's marginal comments; "SP" refers to a misspelling. The editing process is still incomplete in this stage.

Revision

Across America today more and more victims of crime are being allowed to address the   wordy
court in terms of making what is called a victim impact statment. This written or oral pre-   SP
sentation to the court allows victims to express their feelings to the judge after someone
has been convicted of a crime.

Advocates of victim impact statements point to key advantages. First, these statements give victims\a voice. For years, victims have felt helpless. Prosecutors represent the
state, not the crime victim. Victims have been dismayed when prosecutors have aranged   SP
plea bargains without their knowledge. Some victims are still recovering from their injuries when they learn the person who hurt them has plead to a lesser charge and received   SP
probation.

Therapists who work with victims also say that being able to adress the court helps   SP
with the healing process. Victims of violent crime can feel powerless and vulnerable. Instead of suffering in silence, they are given the chance to address the criminal, to clear
their chests, and get on with the rest of their lives.   cliché

Impact statements allows judges to consider what sentences are appropriate. In one
case a judge who planned to fine a teenager for shoplifting accepted the store owner's suggestion of waving the fine if the defendant completed his GED.   SP

But giving victims a chance to speak raises some issues. What about the victim who   weak
is not articulate, who doesn't even speak English? In murder cases the victim's relatives
are given a chance to speak? Does this mean that a middle class professional victim with
a circle of grieving friends and family members will be granted more significance than the
homeless murder victim who leaves no one behind?

Victim impact statements may help empower victims who are educated, personally
impressive, and socially promient. But they may also allow forgotten victims to remain   SP
voiceless.

Revision Notes

Needs better opening -- needs attention-getter
Sharper definition
Clearer examples
Tighter conclusion

Second Draft

The courtroom scene was riveting. One by one, the survivors of a deadly commuter-train
shooting took the stand and addressed the man who had maimed them. Their voices quiv-
ering with emotion, they told the court how the gunman's actions changed their lives for-

ever. Spouses and parents of the dead spoke of loss. There were tears, moments of intense anger, and quiet despair. Victim impact statements have become a common feature of criminal proceedings. Spoken in court or submitted in writing, these statements provide an opportunity for victims to be heard before sentencing.

Advocates of victim impact statements believe these declarations give victims a voice, an opportunity to be heard. Traditionally, victims have appeared in court only as witnesses subject to cross-examination. Prosecutors, victims soon learn, represent the state and not individuals. Still hospitalized after a brutal beating, a New Jersey restaurant owner learned from reading a newspaper that his assailants had plea-bargained to a lesser charge and received probation. Joining with other victims, he became an advocate for victims' rights, including impact statements.

Therapists who counsel victims of crime believe that addressing the court and taking an active role in the legal process instead of remaining a passive witness helps people recover from a sense of helplessness and regain a measure of self-respect.

Impact statements allow judges to consider appropriate sentences. In a Florida case, a judge who intended to fine a teenager for shoplifting agreed with the store owner's suggestion that the fine be waived if the defendant completed his GED.

But giving victims a chance to speak has led to ugly courtroom scenes which seem inappropriate in a democracy. In Milwaukee a sister of a young man murdered by Jeffrey Dahmer wailed and shrieked in contortions of pure rage. The relative of another murder victim shouted that he would execute the killer himself. Bailiffs had to restrain him as he begged the judge, "Just gimme five minutes with him!" Defense attorneys argue these harangues are unnecessary. What need is there to heap abuse upon a person about to lose his or her life or liberty? Can anger and harassment be considered healing?

But even restrained, well-reasoned impact statements raise troubling questions. What about the victim who is too impaired, too frightened, or too wounded to speak? Is his or her absence judged as indifference? What about those whose English is limited? What of those without friends or family? Should the drunk driver who kills a young professional missed by friends, family, and colleagues receive a tougher sentence than the drunk driver who kills a homeless man who dies unmourned, unmissed, and uncounted? Do we really want our courts and society to suggest that some lives are more significant than others?

Victim impact statements may help empower victims, especially the educated, the personally impressive, and the socially prominent. But these statements, unintentionally, may also further marginalize the most helpless among us, allowing forgotten victims to remain voiceless.

QUESTIONS

1. What have you found most challenging or difficult about writing? Discovering ideas? Getting started? Revising?
2. What comments have instructors made about your writing? Does a pattern exist? Have they suggested areas for improvement?

3. What writing habits do you have? What could aid you in improving your work and meeting deadlines? What ideas in this chapter might you adopt to write more effectively?

WRITING ON A COMPUTER

If you have never written on a computer, take advantage of whatever opportunities your campus offers to learn word processing. Modern computer programs are user-friendly, and learning to utilize them will make your college career easier as well as prepare you for your future profession. Almost every career today requires computer literacy. If you find yourself overwhelmed by technology, as many professional writers do, consider taking a computer course. Many colleges offer one-credit courses or free seminars. If no course is available, ask a friend or classmate to show you how he or she uses a computer to write.

Strategies for Writing on a Computer

1. **Appreciate the advantages and limitations of using a computer.** Computers can speed up the writing process, allow you to add ideas, correct spelling, and delete sentences without having to retype an entire page. Computers will not automatically make you a better writer, however. They cannot refine a thesis, improve your logic, or enhance critical thinking. *Don't confuse the neatness of the finished product with good writing.* An attractively designed document must still achieve all the goals of good writing.
2. **Learn the features of your program.** If you are unfamiliar with writing on a computer, make sure you learn how to move blocks of text, change formats, check spelling, and, most importantly, master the *print* and *save* functions. *Find out if your program has an* Undo *function. This can save the day if you accidentally delete or "lose" some of your text.* This function simply undoes your last action, restoring deleted text or eliminating what you just added.
3. **Write in single space.** Most instructors require that papers be double-spaced, but you may find it easier to compose your various drafts in single space so you can see more of your essay on the screen. You can easily change to double space when you are ready to print the final version.
4. **Save your work.** If your program has an automatic save function, use it. Save your work to a floppy disk or hard drive. If you are working on a college or library computer and do not have a disk, print your work after a writing session. Don't let a power shortage or a keystroke error cause you to lose your work!
5. **Label your files clearly.** Because many programs limit the number of characters you can use in a file title, choose your names carefully. Develop a clear no-

tation system such as ENG1 or PSYCH2. If you wish to save a new version of your first English essay you can name it ENG1A.

6. **Print drafts of your work as you write.** Computer screens usually allow you to view less than a page of text at a time. Although it is easy to scroll up and down through the text, it can be difficult to revise on the screen. You may find it easier to work with a hard copy of your paper. Consider double or even triple spacing before you print, so you will have plenty of room for handwritten notations.

7. **Keep backup disks of your work.** Floppy disks are fragile. Store them in a case and keep them clear of dust and debris. Do not leave them near a television or stereo as electrical fields can disturb the data you have stored. *Store important data on more than one disk or save printed copies.*

8. **Make use of special features.** Most word processing applications allow you to count the number of words, check spelling, and use a built-in thesaurus. Some programs will aid you with grammar and usage rules.

9. **Use spell and grammar checks but recognize their limitations.** Spell checking will go through your document and flag words it does not recognize, quickly locating many mistakes you might overlook on your own. *Spell checks do not locate missing words or recognize errors in usage, such as confusing* there *and* their *or* adopt *and* adapt. *Grammar checks sometimes offer awkward suggestions and flag correct expressions as errors.* Reading your text aloud is still the best method of editing.

COLLABORATIVE WRITING

Writing often occurs in groups. Even when produced by a single person, writing may have to reflect the views of many people. Thomas Jefferson wrote the Declaration of Independence, but a committee including Jefferson, John Adams, Benjamin Franklin, and two others made forty-seven changes. Franklin replaced Jefferson's original phrase (in italics) "we hold these rights to be *sound and undeniable*" with "*self-evident.*" More changes occurred when the declaration was presented to the entire Continental Congress. Jefferson's impassioned attack on slavery was eliminated to appease southern representatives. In all, eighty-seven alterations were made to Jefferson's declaration before it was unanimously accepted. By the time John Hancock stepped forward to sign the Declaration of Independence, a quarter of Jefferson's original draft had been changed or deleted.

As a college student, you may be called on to work in a writing group. More and more professors are teaching collaborative writing because writing in groups is common in business and industry. Most professionals work in groups or committees. The partners of a small software company seeking a new personnel director have to agree on the wording of a want ad. The sales team introducing a new product must determine what language to use in its brochures. Volunteers seeking government funding for a day care center must work together on a proposal.

Working in groups poses additional challenges in the writing process. The writing must express the ideas of different people. Viewpoints and personalities may clash. Even scheduling time for the group to meet may be challenging. Because people regard their writing as personal expression and are accustomed to working alone, it can be difficult for them to accept criticism.

But whether you are writing alone or in a group, the basic process remains the same. The writing must address the issue, meet the needs of the readers, and respect the conventions of the discipline or discourse community. To be effective, writing groups must achieve the "Three Cs" of group dynamics: *cohesion, cooperation,* and *compromise.* Members must have a clearly defined goal or task. They must be willing to meet and to work outside the group. Finally, and often most difficult, individuals must be willing to accept that their opinions may not prevail and be willing to drop or alter ideas they greatly value.

Strategies for Collaborative Writing

1. **Work to establish cohesion by stressing the goals, intended readers, and requirements of the writing project.** It is important for members of a writing group to feel trust so they can share ideas. In addition, they must be willing to offer and accept criticism.
2. **Keep the group focused on the task by creating a timeline.** People enjoy talking. Discussions can easily become generalized forums for spirited debate or the latest gossip. A target timeline can help keep the group on track by outlining expected outcomes and reminding members of the deadline. The timeline should reflect stages in the writing process.
3. **Make meetings productive by setting goals and assigning tasks.** Meetings can easily degenerate into a series of discussion sessions, which, though interesting, may not help produce the needed writing. Members should be assigned specific responsibilities: gathering research, conducting interviews, writing sample drafts. Each meeting should open with a goal statement of what is to be achieved. Meetings should end with a summary of what has been completed and an announcement of what must be accomplished at the next meeting.
4. **Designate one member to serve as a moderator or recorder.** One member of the group should serve as chair or recorder to document the progress of the group and serve as secretary to exchange messages between meetings.

5. **Avoid personalizing disagreements.** It is important to discuss opposing viewpoints in neutral terms. Avoid attaching ideas to individuals, which can lead to "*us* against *them*" conflicts.
6. **Take advantage of technology.** Students often have trouble finding common times to meet for social activities, let alone assignments. Consider how the group can maintain links through telephone conferences, fax machines, and the Internet.

WRITER'S BLOCK

At some time almost everyone experiences writer's block, the inability to write. With a paper due in a few days, you may find yourself incapable of coming up with a single line or even unable to sit at your desk. You can feel frustrated, nervous, bored, tired, anxious. The more time passes, the more you think about the upcoming assignment, the more frustrated you can become.

Even professional authors sometimes find themselves unable to write. There is no magic cure for writer's block. But although there is nothing that will make your writer's block disappear, there are some tactics you can try.

Strategies for Overcoming Writer's Block

1. **Recognize that writer's block exists.** When you have the time to write, write. Don't assume if you have two weeks to complete an assignment that you will be able to write well for fourteen days. Get as much writing as possible done when you can. If you delay work, you may find yourself unable to write as the deadline nears.
2. **Review your assignment.** Sometimes the reason you feel that you have nothing to say is that you have not fully understood the assignment. Read it carefully and turn the instructions into a series of questions to spark your thinking.
3. **If you are having trouble selecting a topic, review the assignment for key words and search the Internet.** See what Web pages these key words produce. If you don't have access to the Internet, look for these words in a dictionary or encyclopedia. Even wholly unrelated references can sometimes spark your imagination and help you develop ideas.
4. **Write anything.** The longer you delay writing, the harder it will be to start. If you have trouble focusing on your assignment, get into the mood for writing by sending an e-mail or a letter to a friend. Use an on-line chat room to get into the rhythm of expressing yourself in writing.

5. **Talk to a friend and discuss your assignment or goal.** Talking with a friend can often boost your confidence and reduce your anxiety about an assignment. A spirited discussion can spark free associations about your topic, helping you to view your subject from new angles.

6. **Force yourself to write for five minutes.** Sit down and write about your topic for five minutes nonstop. Let one idea run into another. If you have trouble writing about your topic, write about anything that comes to mind. Even writing nonsense will help you break the physical resistance you may have to sitting down and working with a pen or keyboard. Try to steer your experimental writing to the assigned task. If your draft is going nowhere, save your work and stop after five minutes. Take a walk or run some errands, then return to your writing. Sometimes seeing a word or phrase out of context will lead to significant associations.

7. **Lower your standards.** Don't be afraid to write poorly. Write as well as you can, making notes in the margin as you go along to remind yourself of areas that need revision. Remember that writing is recursive and even badly written statements can form the foundation of a good paper.

8. **Don't feel obligated to start at the beginning.** If you find yourself unable to develop a convincing opening line or a satisfactory introduction, begin writing the body or conclusion of the paper. Get your ideas flowing.

9. **Switch subjects.** If you are bogged down on your English paper, start work on the history paper due next month. Writing well on a different subject may help you gain the confidence you need to return to a difficult assignment.

10. **Record your thoughts on tape or note cards.** If you find writing frustrating, consider talking into a tape recorder or listing ideas on index cards. You may find working with nonwriting materials an effective method of getting started.

11. **Try writing in a different location.** If you can't work at home because of distractions, go to the library or a quiet room. If the library feels stifling and intimidating, move to a less formal environment. You may discover yourself doing your best work while drinking coffee in a noisy student union.

12. **If you still have problems with your assignment, talk to your instructor.** Try to identify what is giving you the most trouble. Is it the act of writing itself, finding a topic, organizing your thoughts, or developing a thesis?

WRITING ACTIVITIES

1. Choose one of the following topics and use the five-step method described in this chapter to draft a short essay. *As you write, note which stages of the process pose the greatest challenges. Alter your composing style in any way that improves your writing.*

roommates	mandatory courses	televised trials
step-parents	campus security	buying a car

current fashion   "outing" gays   personal privacy
the insanity defense   college sports   favorite television
                                              show/band/film

2. Select an upcoming assignment and write a rough draft. Use this experi-
    ence to identify topic areas that require the most attention. *Save your notes
    and draft for future use.*
3. Write a letter or e-mail to a friend about a recent experience. Before send-
    ing it, set the letter aside, letting it "cool." After two or three days, exam-
    ine your draft for missing details, awkward or confusing phrases, mis-
    spelled words, or repetitious statements. *Notice how revision and editing can
    improve your writing.*

READING CRITICALLY

As a student you are accustomed to reading to gain information. Cramming
for a history exam, you read a textbook, hoping to extract the dates, facts,
and concepts that will appear on the test. Reading a novel, you may allow
yourself to be swept away by an exciting plot or an intriguing character. But
as a writer, you need to read critically; you need to read with a "writer's eye."

While most diners simply savor a new gourmet item, a cook wants to
know the recipe. Visitors to a new office tower may marvel at the atrium, but
an architect analyzes the support structure. Moviegoers gasp at an exciting
car chase as film students review the director's editing technique. As a writer,
you need to look at writing in much the same way. In addition to determining
what an essay says, it is important to note *how* it is organized, how the writer
overcame problems, and how language and detail contribute to its effect.

Strategies for Critical Reading

When you pick up a magazine, you rarely read every article. You flip through
the pages, letting your eyes guide you. A headline, a photograph, a chart, or
a familiar name makes you pause and begin reading. If bored, you skip to
the next article. While reading your textbooks, you often skim, moving over
familiar material so you can devote more time to items that are new to you.
If you read *The Great Gatsby* in high school, for a college literature course
you will probably find yourself reviewing it rather than reading it.

In this course, however, you should read *all* the assigned selections
carefully. Reading with a writer's eye, you will examine familiar works dif-

ferently than readers seeking information. Critical reading, like writing, occurs best in stages.

1. **Look ahead and skim entries.** Do not wait until the night before to examine assigned readings. Check your syllabus and skim through future readings to get a general impression. Often, if you think about the authors and their issues, you can approach an essay more critically. The more you bring to the reading, the more effective your analysis will be.

2. **Study the headnote and introduction.** Consider the author, the issue, and the context of the reading.

3. **For the first reading, read the entire work.** Just as in writing the first draft, it is important to complete the entire essay. Do not bother to look up unfamiliar words. Instead, try to get the "big picture" and understand the writer's main goal.

4. **Read with a pencil or pen in your hand.** Make notes and underline sentences that strike you as interesting, odd, offensive, or troubling. Reading while holding a writing tool will prompt you to write, to be an active reader rather than a passive consumer of words.

5. **For the first reading, focus on understanding the author's meaning.** Summarize, in your own words, what the essay is about. Identify the thesis and the main types of support.

6. **For the second reading, begin with the questions following the essay.** Considering the questions can help you focus on a closer, analytical reading of the work. The questions are arranged in three groups:

   Understanding Meaning　What is the author's purpose? What is the thesis? What is the author trying to share with his or her readers?
   Evaluating Strategy　How does the author make his or her point? What support is used? How does the writer organize ideas?
   Appreciating Language　How does the writer use words? What does the language reveal about the intended reader? Does the language reflect the writer's attitudes?

7. **Summarize your responses in a point or two for class discussion.** Consider how you will express your opinions of the essay to fellow students. Be prepared to back up your remarks by citing passages in the text.

8. **Most important, focus on what this essay can teach you about writing.** How can this writer's style, way of organizing ideas, or word choice enrich your own writing? Though you may not want to imitate everything you see, you can pick up techniques to broaden your personal array of skills.

9. **Think of how writers wrestle with the same problems you face.** If you have trouble making an outline and organizing ideas, study how the essays in

this book are arranged. If your instructor returns papers with comments about vague theses and a lack of focus, examine how the writers in this book state their theses.

10. **Above all, read to learn.**

Read the following essay by Cornel West, and study how it has been marked during a critical reading. West is a highly organized writer who blends the use of several modes in this comparison essay on the current state of African-American political leadership.

CORNEL WEST

Cornel West was a religion professor and Director of Afro-American Studies at Princeton University before he was appointed to the faculty at Harvard University. The author of Keeping Faith, Prophetic Fragments, *and other books, West has specialized in writing on race in America.*

Black Political Leadership

OVERVIEW: *"Black Political Leadership" appeared in West's best-selling 1994 book* Race Matters. *In this section, West compares the current generation of black political leaders with leaders of the Civil Rights era. Although West's purpose is to compare, he uses a number of modes to develop his ideas.*

Black political leadership reveals the tame and genteel face of the black middle class. The black dress suits with white shirts worn by Malcolm X and Martin Luther King Jr., signified the seriousness of their deep commitment to black freedom, whereas today the expensive tailored suits of black politicians symbolize their personal success and individual achievement. Malcolm and Martin called for the realization that black people are somebodies with which America has to reckon, whereas black politicians tend to turn our attention to *their* somebodiness owing to *their* "making it" in America.

    This crude and slightly unfair comparison highlights two distinctive features of black political leaders in the post–Civil Rights era: the relative lack of authentic anger and the relative absence of genuine humility. What stood out most strikingly about Malcolm X, Martin Luther King Jr., Ella Baker, and Fannie Lou Hamer was that they were almost always visibly upset about the condition of black America. When one saw them speak or heard their voices, they projected on a gut level that the black situation was urgent, in need of immediate attention. One even gets the impression that their own stability and sanity rested on how soon the black predicament could be improved. Malcolm, Martin, Ella, and Fannie were angry about the state of black America, and this anger fueled their boldness and defiance.

    In stark contrast, most present-day black political leaders appear too hungry for status to be angry, too eager for acceptance to be bold, too self-invested in advancement to be defiant. And when they do drop their masks and try to get mad (usually in the presence of black audiences), their bold rhetoric is more performance than personal, more play-acting than heartfelt. Malcolm, Martin, Ella, and Fannie made sense of the black plight in

Margin annotations:

1 thesis/ opening

clothes as symbolic

compare

note use of italics

2 division

provides examples

3 shift/ transition

use of repetitive wording for emphasis

contrast

a poignant and powerful manner, <u>whereas</u> most contemporary black political leaders' oratory appeals to black people's sense of the sentimental and sensational.

4

supplies personal definition

Similarly, Malcolm, Martin, Ella, and Fannie were examples of humility. Yes, even Malcolm's aggressiveness was accompanied by a common touch and humble disposition toward ordinary black people. <u>Humility is the fruit of inner security and wise maturity.</u> To be humble is to be so sure of one's self and one's mission that one can forego calling excessive attention to one's self and status. And, even more pointedly, to be humble is to revel in the accomplishments or potential of others—especially those with whom one identifies and to whom one is linked organically. The relative absence of humility in most black political leaders today is a symptom of the status-anxiety and personal insecurity pervasive in black middle-class America. In this context, even a humble vesture is viewed as a cover for some sinister motive or surreptitious ambition.

cause and effect

5
division

definition

<u>Present-day black political leaders can be grouped under three types: race-effacing managerial leaders, race-identifying protest leaders, and race-transcending prophetic leaders.</u> The <u>first type</u> is growing rapidly. The Thomas Bradleys and Wilson Goodes of black America have become a model for many black leaders trying to reach a large white constituency and keep a loyal black one. This type survives on sheer political savvy and thrives on personal diplomacy. This kind of candidate is the lesser of two evils in a political situation where the only other electoral choice is a conservative (usually white) politician. Yet this type of leader tends to stunt progressive development and silence the prophetic voices in the black community by casting the practical mainstream as the only game in town.

6
analysis

The <u>second type</u> of black political leader—race-identifying protest leaders—often view themselves in the tradition of Malcolm X, Martin Luther King Jr., Ella Baker, and Fannie Lou Hamer. Yet they are usually self-deluded. They actually operate more in the tradition of Booker T. Washington, by confining themselves to the black turf, vowing to protect their leadership status over it, and serving as power brokers with powerful non-black elites (usually white economic or political elites, though in Louis Farrakhan's case it may be Libyan) to "enhance" this black turf. It is crucial to remember that even in the fifties, Malcolm X's vision and practice were international in scope, and that after 1964 his project was transracial—though grounded in the black turf. King never confined himself to being solely the leader of black America—even though the white press attempted to do so. And Fannie Lou Hamer led the National Welfare Rights Organization, not the Black Welfare Rights Organization. In short, race-identifying protest leaders in the post–Civil Rights era function as figures who white Americans must appease so that the plight of the black poor is overlooked and forgotten. When such leaders move successfully into elected office—as with Marion Barry—they usually become managerial types with large black constituencies, flashy styles, flowery rhetoric, and Booker T. Washington–like patronage operations within the public sphere.

Race-transcending prophetic leaders are rare in contemporary black America. Harold Washington was one. The Jesse Jackson of 1988 was attempting to be another—yet the opportunism of his past weighed heavily on him. To be an elected official and prophetic leader requires personal integrity and political savvy, moral vision and prudential judgment, courageous defiance and organizational patience. The present generation has yet to produce such a figure. We have neither an Adam Clayton Powell Jr., nor a Ronald Dellums. This void sits like a festering sore at the center of the crisis of black leadership—and the predicament of the disadvantaged in the United States and abroad worsens.

7
examples

final effects

USING THE SUNDANCE READER

The Sundance Reader is organized into nine chapters focusing on writers' goals. The readings in each section illustrate how writers achieve their purpose in different contexts. Each chapter opens with an explanation of the goal or mode. The first few readings in each chapter are brief, clear-cut examples of the mode and can serve as models for many of your composition assignments. The middle readings are longer and more complex and demonstrate writing tasks in a range of disciplines and writing situations. Each chapter ends with samples of applied writings taken from business, industry, and government to illustrate how writing is used beyond the classroom.

When reading entries, keep these general questions in mind:

1. **What is the writer's purpose?** Even writers pursuing the same goal—to tell a story or explain a process—have slightly different intentions. What is the purpose of the story—to raise questions, to motivate the reader to take action, or to change his or her point of view?
2. **What is the writer's thesis?** Does a clear thesis statement exist that you can highlight, or is it implied? Can you restate the thesis in your own words?
3. **Who are the intended readers?** Note the source of the article. What does it tell you about the readers? Does the writer direct it to a specific group or a gen-

eral audience? What assumptions does the writer seem to make about the reader? What terms or references are defined? What knowledge does the writer expect his or her audience to possess?

4. **What evidence does the writer use to support the thesis?** Does the writer provide personal observation, statistics, studies, or the testimony of others to support his or her views?

5. **What is the nature of the discipline, profession, or writing situation?** What discipline is the writer addressing? Is he or she working within a discipline or addressing readers in another discipline? Is the writer addressing general readers? Do special circumstances guide the way the writer develops the thesis, presents ideas, and designs the physical appearance of the writing?

6. **How successful is this writing—in context?** Does the writer achieve his or her goals while respecting the needs of the reader and the conventions of the discipline or situation? Do special circumstances explain why some aspects of the writing appear to "break" the rules of what most English courses consider "good writing"?

 Companion Web Site

Throughout *The Sundance Reader* companion Web site, **http://sundance.heinle .com,** provides links to on-line support, offering additional information, answers to common questions, and help for writing each mode.

 InfoTrac® College Edition

For additional reading go to InfoTrac College edition, your on-line research library, at **http://infotrac.thomsonlearning.com.**

- Enter the search terms "writing process" using the Subject Guide.
- Enter the search terms "collaborative writing"using Keywords.
- Enter the search terms "brainstorming"using Keywords.

2

Narration

WHAT IS NARRATION?

Narration seeks to answer the basic question "What happened?" The goal of narration is to tell a story. The Bible, Greek myths, Native American fables, novels, short stories, diaries, autobiographies, and history books are examples of narration. Narrative writing forms the heart of most newspaper articles. Narration is also one of the most common types of professional writing. Physicians write narration to record a patient's history or outline a course of treatment. Attorneys use narrative writing to relate the details of a crime or explain the rationale for a lawsuit. Government reports, grant proposals, sales brochures, and business plans generally include a section labeled "narrative" that provides the history of an organization or a summary of a current project.

The Writer's Purpose

Narration can be subjective or objective, depending on the writer's goal and context. Subjective narration focuses on personal impressions, thoughts, insights, and feelings. Often the writer is at the center of the narrative, either as a principal character or key witness. In "The Lesson" (page 61) Nathan McCall relates his first encounter with racism while attending a previously segregated school:

> It was the beginning of my sixth-grade school year, and I was walking down the hall, searching for my new class, when a white boy timed my steps, extended his foot, and tripped me. The boy and his friends nudged each other and laughed as I stumbled into a locker, spilling books and papers everywhere. "Hey, nigger," the boy said. "You dropped something."

McCall's purpose is to share a deeply personal experience of pain and humiliation, impressing readers with what he thought and felt. His emotional reactions form the core of the narrative:

> I was sitting on the gym floor with the rest of the student body, watching a school assembly program, when a group of rowdy white upperclassmen began plucking my head and ridiculing me. I got confused. *What should I do?* To turn around and say something to them would start another fight. To get up and leave would require me to wade through a sea of hostile white students to reach the nearest exit. With nowhere to go, I sat there and took the humiliation until I broke. Tears welled in my eyes and started running, uncontrollably, down my face. I sat silently through the remainder of the assembly program with my vision blurred and my spirit broken. That was the only time, then or since, that I've been crushed so completely.

Objective narration, on the other hand, is usually stated in the third person to give the writer's views a sense of neutrality. In objective narration, the author is not a participant but a collector and presenter of facts. In "Ebola River" (page 73) Richard Preston chronicles the outbreak of a deadly virus in Sudan:

> It hit the hospital like a bomb. It savaged patients and snaked like chain lightning out from the hospital through patients' families. Apparently the medical staff had been giving patients injections with dirty needles. The virus jumped quickly through the hospital via the needles, and then it hit the medical staff. A characteristic of a lethal, contagious, and incurable virus is that it quickly gets into the medical people. In some cases, the medical system may intensify the outbreak, like a lens that focuses sunlight on a heap of tinder.

Authors do use first person in objective narration, particularly when they have directly participated in or witnessed events. However, unlike Nathan McCall, who focused on his *internal reactions* to situations, a scientist like Oliver Sacks stresses *external events*, making professional rather than personal judgments. In "The Man Who Mistook His Wife for a Hat" (page 86) Sacks relates his experience with Dr. P., a highly talented professor of music who had begun exhibiting bizarre symptoms. Recounting his initial examination, Sacks objectively records his findings:

> I stilled my disquiet, his perhaps, too, in the soothing routine of a neurological exam—muscle strength, coordination, reflexes, tone. . . . It was while examining his reflexes—a trifle abnormal on the left side—that the first bi-

zarre experience occurred. I had taken off his left shoe and scratched the sole of his foot with a key—a frivolous-seeming but essential test of a reflex—and then, excusing myself to screw my ophthalmoscope together, left him to put on the shoe himself. To my surprise, a minute later, he had not done this.

"Can I help?" I asked.

"Help what? Help whom?"

"Help you put on your shoe."

"Ach," he said, "I had forgotten the shoe," adding, *sotto voce*, "The shoe? The shoe?" He seemed baffled.

"Your shoe," I repeated. "Perhaps you'd put it on."

He continued to look downwards, though not at the shoe, with an intense but misplaced concentration. Finally his gaze settled on his foot: "That is my shoe, yes?"

Did I mis-hear? Did he mis-see?

"My eyes," he explained, and put a hand to his foot. "*This* is my shoe, no?"

"No, it is not. That is your foot. *There* is your shoe."

"Ah! I thought that was my foot."

Was he joking? Was he mad? Was he blind? If this was one of his "strange mistakes," it was the strangest mistake I had ever come across.

I helped him on with his shoe (his foot), to avoid further complication. Dr. P. himself seemed untroubled, indifferent, maybe amused. I resumed my examination. His visual acuity was good: he had no difficulty seeing a pin on the floor, though sometimes he missed it if it was placed to his left.

Though mystified by the patient's odd behavior, Sacks focuses less on his personal responses than on his professional evaluations as a doctor and scientist. When he mentions himself in the narrative, the commentary is limited to explaining his role in conducting a medical examination.

In an effort to create a greater sense of objectivity, many writers avoid using the first person by documenting personal actions in passive voice. Instead of stating, "I took photographs of the crash site," they report, "Photographs of the crash site were taken." Rhetoricians, English instructors, and editors often object to passive voice because it is wordy and less precise. Passive voice deletes the actor from the action, in this case failing to state who took the photographs. Still, many writers insist on using passive voice to deliberately avoid personalizing their narratives.

Focus

Related to the writer's purpose is the narrative's focus. A biography of Abraham Lincoln can be a general account of his entire life or a psychological study of his problem with depression during the Civil War. A book about World War II could concentrate on military activities or on the role of women in the defense industry. An article on recycling may provide a survey of national trends or an in-depth study of a single city's program.

Focus determines the kinds of details the writer includes in the narrative and the types of evidence on which he or she relies. In writing a popular history about the sinking of the *Titanic*, Walter Lord based much of his narrative on memories of the survivors. This gave his book human interest and created a tense series of dramas as he recounted the ship's last hours. A nautical engineer writing a technical article explaining the sinking of the "unsinkable" luxury liner would pay attention to mechanical details, specific measurements, and statistics.

Chronology

Chronology, or time, is a central organizing element in narrative writing. Writers do not always relate events in a straight timeline. A biography, for instance, does not have to begin with birth and childhood. Writers often alter the time sequences of their stories to dramatize events or limit their topic. A biographer of Franklin D. Roosevelt might choose to highlight a key event or turning point in his life. The narrative might open with his polio attack, flash back to his childhood and early political career, then flash forward to his recovery and election to the presidency. Other writers find it more dramatic to begin a narrative at the end and then explain what led to this final event. The first chapter of a book about Czar Nicholas II could describe his execution and then flash back to the events leading to his downfall and death.

Each method of organizing a narrative has distinct advantages and disadvantages:

- **Beginning at the beginning** creates an open-ended narrative, providing readers with little direction to later events. Writers who relate complex stories with many possible causes can use a straight chronology to avoid highlighting a single event. Using a direct beginning-to-end approach is the most traditional method of telling a story. One of the difficulties with this method can be determining exactly when the narrative should start. Often the beginning of a story consists of incidental background information that readers may find uninteresting.
- **Beginning at the middle or at a turning point** can arouse reader interest by opening with a dramatic scene. This method of organization can focus the chain of events, persuading readers to concentrate on a particular issue. This is a com-

mon pattern in nonfiction articles, biographies, and histories written for a general readership. Critics, however, can view this alteration of chronology as distorting. Not all historians, for instance, may agree that Roosevelt's illness was the "turning point" of his life. Some biographers might feel that focusing on his physical disability ignores his intellectual development or downplays his political role.

- **Beginning at the end** serves to dramatize the final event. When everything is presented in flashback, readers see events, actions, and thoughts in hindsight. The elements of suspense and randomness are removed, providing a stronger sense of cause and effect. Some readers will object to this method because it implies the final outcome was inevitable, when, in fact, events just as easily could have led to alternative endings.

STRATEGIES FOR READING NARRATION

When reading the narratives in this chapter, keep these questions in mind.

Meaning

1. What is the author's narrative purpose—to inform, enlighten, share a personal experience, or provide information required by the reader?
2. What is the writer's role? Is the author a participant or direct witness? Is he or she writing in a personal context, focusing on internal responses, or in a professional context, concentrating on external events?
3. What readership is the narration directed toward—general or specific? How much knowledge does the author assume readers have?
4. What is the nature of the discipline, discourse community, or writing situation? Is the narration objective or subjective? Does the original source of the narrative (newsmagazine, scientific journal, or government document) reveal anything about the context?

Strategy

1. What details does the writer select to highlight? Are some items summarized or ignored?
2. What kind of support does the writer use—personal observation or factual documentation?
3. What is the sequence of events? How is the narration organized? Does the writer begin at the beginning, the end, or a midpoint?
4. Does the writer use flashbacks and flash-forwards?

5. What transitional devices does the writer use to advance the narrative? Does the author use time references such as "later that day" or "two months later"?

Language

1. What does the level of language suggest about the writer's role, intended readers, and the nature of the discipline or writing situation?
2. How does the writer use words to create tone and style? What do word choices suggest about the writer's attitude toward the subject?

S A M U E L   S C U D D E R

Samuel Scudder (1837–1911) was born in Boston and attended Williams College. In 1857 he entered Harvard, where he studied under the noted professor Louis Agassiz. Scudder held various positions and helped found the Cambridge Entomological Club. He published hundreds of papers and developed a comprehensive catalog of three centuries of scientific publications in mathematics and the natural and physical sciences. While working for the United States Geological Survey, he named more than a thousand species of fossil insects. Although later scientists would question some of his conclusions, much of Scudder's work is still admired for its attention to detail.

Take This Fish and Look at It

OVERVIEW: *Today educators stress critical thinking, which begins with close observation. In this famous essay, Scudder relates the lesson in observation he learned under Professor Agassiz, whose teaching method was simple. Instead of lecturing, he directed his young student to "look again, look again." Note that Scudder omits details such as dates, addresses, even Professor Agassiz's appearance.*

It was more than fifteen years ago that I entered the laboratory of Professor Agassiz, and told him I had enrolled my name in the Scientific School as a student of natural history. He asked me a few questions about my object in coming, my antecedents generally, the mode in which I afterwards proposed to use the knowledge I might acquire, and, finally, whether I wished to study any special branch. To the latter I replied that, while I wished to be well grounded in all departments of zoology, I purposed to devote myself specially to insects. [1] *intro sets time / brief summary / uses dialogue*

"When do you wish to begin?" he asked. [2]

"Now," I replied. [3]

This seemed to please him, and with an energetic "Very well!" he reached from a shelf a huge jar of specimens in yellow alcohol. "Take this fish," he said, "and look at it; we call it a haemulon; by and by I will ask what you have seen." [4]

With that he left me, but in a moment returned with explicit instructions as to the care of the object entrusted to me. [5]

"No man is fit to be a naturalist," said he, "who does not know how to take care of specimens." [6]

I was to keep the fish before me in a tin tray, and occasionally moisten the surface with alcohol from the jar, always taking care to replace the stopper tightly. Those were not the days of ground-glass stoppers and elegantly [7] *gives directions*

47

shaped exhibition jars; all the old students will recall the huge neckless glass bottles with their leaky, wax-besmeared corks, half eaten by insects, and begrimed with cellar dust. Entomology was a cleaner science than ichthyology, but the example of the Professor, who had unhesitatingly plunged to the bottom of the jar to produce the fish, was infectious; and though this alcohol had a "very ancient and fishlike smell," I really dared not show any aversion within these sacred precincts, and treated the alcohol as though it were pure water. Still I was conscious of a passing feeling of disappointment, for gazing at a fish did not commend itself to an ardent entomologist. My friends at home, too, were annoyed when they discovered that no amount of eau-de-Cologne would drown the perfume which haunted me like a shadow.

8

first
impression

In ten minutes I had seen all that could be seen in that fish, and started in search of the Professor—who had, however, left the Museum; and when I returned, after lingering over some of the odd animals stored in the upper apartment, my specimen was dry all over. I dashed the fluid over the fish as if to resuscitate the beast from a fainting fit, and looked with anxiety for a return of the normal sloppy appearance. This little excitement over, nothing was to be done but to return to a steadfast gaze at my mute companion.

emphasizes
boredom

Half an hour passed—an hour—another hour; the fish began to look loathsome. I turned it over and around; looked it in the face—ghastly; from behind, beneath, above, sideways, at three-quarters' view—just as ghastly. I was in despair; at an early hour I concluded that lunch was necessary; so, with infinite relief, the fish was carefully replaced in the jar, and for an hour I was free.

9

On my return, I learned that Professor Agassiz had been at the Museum, but had gone, and would not return for several hours. My fellow-students were too busy to be disturbed by continued conversation. Slowly I drew forth that hideous fish, and with a feeling of desperation again looked at it. I might not use a magnifying-glass; instruments of all kinds were interdicted. My two hands, my two eyes, and the fish: it seemed a most limited field. I pushed my finger down its throat to feel how sharp the teeth were. I

discovers
by
drawing

began to count the scales in the different rows, until I was convinced that was nonsense. At last a happy thought struck me—I would draw the fish; and now with surprise I began to discover new features in the creature. Just then the Professor returned.

10

"That is right," said he; "a pencil is one of the best of eyes. I am glad to notice, too, that you keep your specimen wet, and your bottle corked."

11

With these encouraging words, he added: "Well, what is it like?"

12

He listened attentively to my brief rehearsal of the structure of parts whose names were still unknown to me: the fringed gill-arches and movable operculum; the pores of the head, fleshy lips and lidless eyes; the lateral line, the spinous fins and forked tail; the compressed and arched body. When I finished, he waited as if expecting more, and then, with an air of disappointment:

"You have not looked very carefully; why," he continued more earnestly, "you haven't even seen one of the most conspicuous features of the animal, which is plainly before your eyes as the fish itself; look again, look again!" and he left me to my misery.   13

I was piqued; I was mortified. Still more of that wretched fish! But now I set myself to my task with a will, and discovered one new thing after another, until I saw how just the Professor's criticism had been. The afternoon passed quickly; and when, towards its close, the Professor inquired: 14 *initial reaction*

"Do you see it yet?"   15

"No," I replied, "I am certain I do not, but I see how little I saw before."   16

"That is next best," said he, earnestly, "but I won't hear you now; put away your fish and go home; perhaps you will be ready with a better answer in the morning. I will examine you before you look at the fish."   17

This was disconcerting. Not only must I think of my fish all night, studying, without the object before me, what this unknown but most visible feature might be; but also, without reviewing my discoveries, I must give an exact account of them the next day. I had a bad memory; so I walked home by Charles River in a distracted state, with my two perplexities.   18

The cordial greeting from the Professor the next morning was reassuring; here was a man who seemed to be quite as anxious as I that I should see for myself what he saw.   19

"Do you perhaps mean," I asked, "that the fish has symmetrical sides with paired organs?"   20

His thoroughly pleased "Of course! of course!" repaid the wakeful hours of the previous night. After he had discoursed most happily and enthusiastically—as he always did—upon the importance of this point, I ventured to ask what I should do next.   21 *asks for help*

"Oh, look at your fish!" he said, and left me again to my own devices. In a little more than an hour he returned, and heard my new catalogue.   22

"That is good, that is good!" he repeated; "but that is not all; go on"; and so for three long days he placed that fish before my eyes, forbidding me to look at anything else, or to use any artificial aid. "Look, look, look," was his repeated injunction.   23 *repeated command*

This was the best entomological lesson I ever had—a lesson whose influence has extended to the details of every subsequent study; a legacy the Professor had left to me, as he has left it to so many others, of inestimable value which we could not buy, with which we cannot part.   24 *thesis/ value of lesson*

25
flash
forward to
humorous
incident
A year afterward, some of us were amusing ourselves with chalking outlandish beasts on the Museum blackboard. We drew prancing starfishes; frogs in mortal combat; hydra-headed worms; stately crawfishes, standing on their tails, bearing aloft umbrellas; and grotesque fishes with gaping mouths and staring eyes. The Professor came in shortly after, and was as amused as any at our experiments. He looked at the fishes.

26   "Haemulons, every one of them," he said; "Mr. _____ drew them."

27   True; and to this day, if I attempt a fish, I can draw nothing but haemulons.

28   The fourth day, a second fish of the same group was placed beside the first, and I was bidden to point out the resemblances and differences between the two; another and another followed, until the entire family lay before me, and a whole legion of jars covered the table and surrounding shelves; the odor had become a pleasant perfume; and even now, the sight of an old, six-inch worm-eaten cork brings fragrant memories.

29   The whole group of haemulons was thus brought in review; and, whether engaged upon the dissection of the internal organs, the preparation and examination of the bony framework, or the description of the various parts, Agassiz's training in the method of observing facts and their orderly arrangement was ever accompanied by the urgent exhortation not to be content with them.

30
conclusion
"Facts are stupid things," he would say, "until brought into connection with some general law."

31   At the end of eight months, it was almost with reluctance that I left these friends and turned to insects; but what I had gained by this outside experience has been of greater value than years of later investigation in my favorite groups.

Understanding Meaning

1. What is the purpose of Scudder's narrative? What is he trying to impress on his reader? What makes this essay more than a simple "first day of school" story?
2. Why did the professor prevent Scudder from using a magnifying glass? What did Professor Agassiz mean when he said "a pencil is one of the best of eyes"?
3. What did Scudder find frustrating about Dr. Agassiz's teaching method?
4. *Critical Thinking:* How effective was Professor Agassiz's nineteenth-century teaching method? By directing a new student to "look again, look again," did he accomplish more than if he had required Scudder to attend a two-hour lecture on the importance of observation? Is close observation a discipline most of us lack? Can you consider detailed observation the first level of critical thinking?

Evaluating Strategy

1. How does Scudder focus his narrative? What details does he leave out?
2. Do his personal reactions to the smell and his frustrations dramatize an extremely passive event? How can a writer create action in a story where the events are mental or emotional?
3. How does Scudder re-create his sense of boredom and frustration?
4. *Other Modes:* How does Scudder use *description* of the fish, the specimen bottles, and the smells to provide readers with a clear impression of the laboratory?

Appreciating Language

1. Review Scudder's narrative. How much scientific language does he use in relating his story? What does this say about his readers?
2. This story has little action. Essentially, it is a story about a man interacting with a dead fish. What words add drama or humor to the narrative?

Connections across the Disciplines

1. Scudder is a scientist writing to a general reader. How do you compare his writing style and vocabulary with Oliver Sacks's (page 86)?
2. *Critical Thinking:* Consider Professor Agassiz's statement, "Facts are stupid things until brought into connection with some general law." What does this say about instructors who teach facts and give multiple-choice tests based on rote memory?

Writing Suggestions

1. Apply Professor Agassiz's technique to a common object you might use every day. Spend five minutes carefully examining a clock radio, your watch, or a can of your favorite soft drink. Then write a brief *description* of what you have observed. List the features you have never noticed before.
2. Professor Agassiz gave his student little direction beyond a simple command. Write an essay relating an experience in which a parent, teacher, superior officer, or boss left you to act on your own. What problems did you encounter? Were you frustrated, afraid, or angry? Was it a learning experience?
3. *Collaborative Writing:* Working with three or four other students, select an object unfamiliar to the group. Allow each member to study the object and make notes. *Compare* your findings, and work to create a single *description* of it. Pay attention to the words you select to create an accurate, objective picture of the object. Notice the details you overlooked that others observed.

JAMES DILLARD

James Dillard is a physician who specializes in rehabilitation medicine. In this narrative, first published in the "My Turn" column in Newsweek, *he relates an incident that nearly ended his medical career.*

A Doctor's Dilemma

OVERVIEW: *As you read this narrative, keep in mind how most people expect physicians to respond in a life-threatening emergency.*

1   It was a bright, clear February afternoon in Gettysburg. A strong sun and layers of down did little to ease the biting cold. Our climb to the crest of Little Roundtop wound past somber monuments, barren trees and polished cannon. From the top, we peered down on the wheat field where men had fallen so close together that one could not see the ground. Rifle balls had whined as thick as bee swarms through the trees, and cannon shots had torn limbs from the young men fighting there. A frozen wind whipped tears from our eyes. My friend Amy huddled close, using me as a wind breaker. Despite the cold, it was hard to leave this place.

2   Driving east out of Gettysburg on a country blacktop, the gray Bronco ahead of us passed through a rural crossroad just as a small pickup truck tried to take a left turn. The Bronco swerved, but slammed into the pickup on the passenger side. We immediately slowed to a crawl as we passed the scene. The Bronco's driver looked fine, but we couldn't see the driver of the pickup. I pulled over on the shoulder and got out to investigate.

3   The right side of the truck was smashed in, and the side window was shattered. The driver was partly out of the truck. His head hung forward over the edge of the passenger-side window, the front of his neck crushed on the shattered windowsill. He was unconscious and starting to turn a dusky blue. His chest slowly heaved against a blocked windpipe.

4   A young man ran out of a house at the crossroad. "Get an ambulance out here," I shouted against the wind. "Tell them a man is dying."

5   I looked down again at the driver hanging from the windowsill. There were six empty beer bottles on the floor of the truck. I could smell the beer through the window. I knew I had to move him, to open his airway. I had no idea what neck injuries he had sustained. He could easily end up a quadriplegic. But I thought: he'll be dead by the time the ambulance gets here if I don't move him and try to do something to help him.

An image flashed before my mind. I could see the courtroom and the   6
driver of the truck sitting in a wheelchair. I could see his attorney pointing
at me and thundering at the jury: "This young doctor, with still a year left
in his residency training, took it upon himself to play God. He took it upon
himself to move this gravely injured man, condemning him forever to this
wheelchair . . ." I imagined the millions of dollars in award money. And all
the years of hard work lost. I'd be paying him off for the rest of my life. Amy
touched my shoulder. "What are you going to do?"

The automatic response from long hours in the emergency room kicked   7
in. I pulled off my overcoat and rolled up my sleeves. The trick would be to
keep enough traction straight up on his head while I moved his torso, so
that his probable broken neck and spinal-cord injury wouldn't be made
worse. Amy came around the driver's side, climbed half in and grabbed his
belt and shirt collar. Together we lifted him off the windowsill.

He was still out cold, limp as a rag doll. His throat was crushed and   8
blood from the jugular vein was running down my arms. He still couldn't
breathe. He was deep blue-magenta now, his pulse was rapid and thready.
The stench of alcohol turned my stomach, but I positioned his jaw and
tried to blow air down into his lungs. It wouldn't go.

Amy had brought some supplies from my car. I opened an oversize in-   9
travenous needle and groped on the man's neck. My hands were numb, covered with freezing blood and bits of broken glass. Hyoid bone—God, I
can't even feel the thyroid cartilage, it's gone . . . OK, the thyroid gland is
about there, cricoid rings are here . . . we'll go in right here . . .

It was a lucky first shot. Pink air sprayed through the IV needle. I   10
placed a second needle next to the first. The air began whistling through it.
Almost immediately, the driver's face turned bright red. After a minute, his
pulse slowed down and his eyes moved slightly. I stood up, took a step back
and looked down. He was going to make it. He was going to live. A siren
wailed in the distance. I turned and saw Amy holding my overcoat. I was
shivering and my arms were turning white with cold.

The ambulance captain looked around and bellowed, "What the   11
hell . . . who did this?", as his team scurried over to the man lying in the
truck.

"I did," I replied. He took down my name and address for his reports. I   12
had just destroyed my career. I would never be able to finish my residency
with a massive lawsuit pending. My life was over.

The truckdriver was strapped onto a backboard, his neck in a stiff collar.   13
The ambulance crew had controlled the bleeding and started intravenous
fluid. He was slowly waking up. As they loaded him into the ambulance, I
saw him move his feet. Maybe my future wasn't lost.

14   A police sergeant called me from Pennsylvania three weeks later. Six days after successful throat-reconstruction surgery, the driver had signed out, against medical advice, from the hospital because he couldn't get a drink on the ward. He was being arraigned on drunk-driving charges.

15   A few days later, I went into the office of one of my senior professors, to tell the story. He peered over his half glasses and his eyes narrowed. "Well, you did the right thing medically of course. But, James, do you know what you put at risk by doing that?" he said sternly. "What was I supposed to do?" I asked.

16   "Drive on," he replied. "There is an army of lawyers out there who would stand in line to get a case like that. If that driver had turned out to be a quadriplegic, you might never have practiced medicine again. You were a very lucky young man."

17   The day I graduated from medical school, I took an oath to serve the sick and the injured. I remember truly believing I would be able to do just that. But I have found out it isn't so simple. I understand now what a foolish thing I did that day. Despite my oath, I know what I would do on that cold roadside near Gettysburg today. I would drive on.

Understanding Meaning

1. What was Dillard's goal in publishing this narrative in a national news magazine?
2. Does this narrative serve to contrast ideals and reality? How does Dillard's oath conflict with his final decision?
3. Does the fact that the victim was drinking have an impact on your reactions to the doctor's actions? Does Dillard seem to show contempt for his patient?
4. *Critical Thinking:* Does this essay suggest that there is an undeclared war between doctors and lawyers? Do medical malpractice suits improve or diminish the quality of medicine? Are lawyers to blame for the author's decision to "drive on" next time?

Evaluating Strategy

1. *Other Modes:* Does this narrative also serve as a persuasive argument? Is the story a better vehicle than a standard argumentative essay that states a thesis and presents factual support?
2. Does this first-person story help place the reader in the doctor's position? Is this a more effective strategy than writing an objective third-person essay about the impact of malpractice suits?

3.   Why does Dillard mention that the patient later disobeyed his doctor's orders and left the hospital so he could get a drink?
4.   How do you think Dillard wanted his readers to respond to the essay's last line?

Appreciating Language

1.   What words does Dillard use to dramatize his attempts to save the driver's life? How do they reflect the tension he was feeling?
2.   What language does Dillard use to demonstrate what he was risking by trying to save a life?
3.   What kind of people read *Newsweek*? Do you find this essay's language suitable?

Connections across the Disciplines

1.   How does Dillard's practical experience contrast with the scientific lesson Samuel Scudder learned in academia (see page 47)?
2.   Compare Dillard's experience with that of George Orwell in "Shooting an Elephant" (see page 78). Are both narratives about people torn by conflict between what they believe is the right thing to do and their professional obligations?

Writing Suggestions

1.   Relate an emergency you experienced or encountered. Using Dillard's essay as a model, write an account capturing what you thought and felt as you acted.
2.   Write a letter to the editor of *Newsweek* in response to Dillard's essay. Do you find his position tenable? Are you angry at a doctor who vows not to help accident victims? Or do you blame the legal community for putting a physician in this position?
3.   *Collaborative Writing:* Discuss Dillard's essay with a number of students and list their reactions. Write a division paper outlining their views.

Ramon "Tianguis" Pérez is an undocumented alien and does not release biographical information.

The Fender-Bender

OVERVIEW: *This narrative, taken from Pérez's book* Diary of an Undocumented Immigrant, *illustrates how even a minor incident can affect the precarious existence of an undocumented alien. For Pérez, a few pieces of paper stand between a life in America and deportation.*

1   One night after work, I drive Rolando's old car to visit some friends, and then head towards home. At a light, I come to a stop too late, leaving the front end of the car poking into the crosswalk. I shift into reverse, but as I am backing up, I strike the van behind me. Its driver immediately gets out to inspect the damage to his vehicle. He's a tall Anglo-Saxon, dressed in a deep blue work uniform. After looking at his car, he walks up to the window of the car I'm driving.

2   "Your driver's license," he says, a little enraged.

3   "I didn't bring it," I tell him.

4   He scratches his head. He is breathing heavily with fury.

5   "Okay," he says. "You park up ahead while I call a patrolman."

6   The idea of calling the police doesn't sound good to me, but the accident is my fault. So I drive around the corner and park at the curb. I turn off the motor and hit the steering wheel with one fist. I don't have a driver's license. I've never applied for one. Nor do I have with me the identification card that I bought in San Antonio. Without immigration papers, without a driving permit, and having hit another car, I feel as if I'm just one step away from Mexico.

7   I get out of the car. The white man comes over and stands right in front of me. He's almost two feet taller.

8   "If you're going to drive, why don't you carry your license?" he asks in an accusatory tone.

9   "I didn't bring it," I say, for lack of any other defense.

10   I look at the damage to his car. It's minor, only a scratch on the paint and a pimple-sized dent.

"I'm sorry," I say. "Tell me how much it will cost to fix, and I'll pay   11
for it; that's no problem." I'm talking to him in English, and he seems to
understand.

"This car isn't mine," he says. "It belongs to the company I work for.   12
I'm sorry, but I've got to report this to the police, so that I don't have to pay
for the damage."

"That's no problem," I tell him again. "I can pay for it."   13

After we've exchanged these words, he seems less irritated. But he says   14
he'd prefer for the police to come, so that they can report that the dent wasn't
his fault.

While we wait, he walks from one side to the other, looking down the   15
avenue this way and that, hoping that the police will appear.

Then he goes over to the van to look at the dent.   16

"It's not much," he says. "If it was my car, there wouldn't be any prob-   17
lems, and you could go on."

After a few minutes, the long-awaited police car arrives. Only one offi-   18
cer is inside. He's a Chicano, short and of medium complexion, with short,
curly hair. On getting out of the car, he walks straight towards the Anglo.

The two exchange a few words.   19

"Is that him?" he asks, pointing at me.   20

The Anglo nods his head.   21

Speaking in English, the policeman orders me to stand in front of the   22
car and to put my hands on the hood. He searches me and finds only the car
keys and my billfold with a few dollars in it. He asks for my driver's license.

"I don't have it," I answered in Spanish.   23

He wrinkles his face into a frown, and casting a glance at the Anglo,   24
shakes his head in disapproval of me.

"That's the way these Mexicans are," he says.   25

He turns back towards me, asking for identification. I tell him I don't   26
have that, either.

"You're an illegal, eh?" he says.   27

I won't answer.   28

"An illegal," he says to himself.   29

"Where do you live?" he continues. He's still speaking in English.   30

I tell him my address.   31

"Do you have anything with you to prove that you live at that address?"   32
he asks.

I think for a minute, then realize that in the glove compartment is a let-   33
ter that my parents sent to me several weeks earlier.

34   I show him the envelope and he immediately begins to write something in a little book that he carries in his back pocket. He walks to the back of my car and copies the license plate number. Then he goes over to his car and talks into his radio. After he talks, someone answers. Then he asks me for the name of the car's owner.

35   He goes over to where the Anglo is standing. I can't quite hear what they're saying. But when the two of them go over to look at the dent in the van, I hear the cop tell the Anglo that if he wants, he can file charges against me. The Anglo shakes his head and explains what he had earlier explained to me, about only needing for the police to certify that he wasn't responsible for the accident. The Anglo says that he doesn't want to accuse me of anything because the damage is light.

36   "If you want, I can take him to jail," the cop insists.

37   The Anglo turns him down again.

38   "If you'd rather, we can report him to Immigration," the cop continues.

39   Just as at the first, I am now almost sure that I'll be making a forced trip to Tijuana. I find myself searching my memory for my uncle's telephone number, and to my relief, I remember it. I am waiting for the Anglo to say yes, confirming my expectations of the trip. But instead, he says no, and though I remain silent, I feel appreciation for him. I ask myself why the Chicano is determined to harm me. I didn't really expect him to favor me, just because we're of the same ancestry, but on the other hand, once I had admitted my guilt, I expected him to treat me at least fairly. But even against the white man's wishes, he's trying to make matters worse for me. I've known several Chicanos with whom, joking around, I've reminded them that their roots are in Mexico. But very few of them see it that way. Several have told me how when they were children, their parents would take them to vacation in different states of Mexico, but their own feeling, they've said, is, "I am an American citizen!" Finally, the Anglo, with the justifying paper in his hands, says goodbye to the cop, thanks him for his services, gets into his van and drives away.

40   The cop stands in the street in a pensive mood. I imagine that he's trying to think of a way to punish me.

41   "Put the key in the ignition," he orders me.

42   I do as he says.

43   Then he orders me to roll up the windows and lock the doors.

44   "Now, go on, walking," he says.

45   I go off taking slow steps. The cop gets in his patrol car and stays there, waiting. I turn the corner after two blocks and look out for my car, but the cop is still parked beside it. I begin looking for a coat hanger, and after a

good while, find one by a curb of the street. I keep walking, keeping about two blocks away from the car. While I walk, I bend the coat hanger into the form I'll need. As if I'd called for it, a speeding car goes past. When it comes to the avenue where my car is parked, it makes a turn. It is going so fast that its wheels screech as it rounds the corner. The cop turns on the blinking lights of his patrol car and leaving black marks on the pavement beneath it, shoots out to chase the speeder. I go up to my car and with my palms force a window open a crack. Then I insert the clothes hanger in the crack and raise the lock lever. It's a simple task, one that I'd already performed. This wasn't the first time that I'd been locked out of a car, though always before, it was because I'd forgotten to remove my keys.

Understanding Meaning

1. How serious is the accident?
2. Why does the van driver insist on calling the police?
3. What makes this incident a dangerous one for Pérez?
4. How does Pérez attempt to prevent the van driver from summoning the police?
5. Pérez answers the Chicano patrolman in Spanish. Was this a mistake? How did the officer treat Pérez?
6. *Critical Thinking:* Pérez implies that Chicanos have been offended when he has alluded to their Mexican roots; they insist on being seen as American citizens. What does this say about assimilation and identity? Does the Chicano officer's comments about Mexicans reveal contempt for immigrants? Have other ethnic groups—Jews, Italians, the Irish—resented the presence of unassimilated new arrivals from their homelands?

Evaluating Strategy

1. Why is a minor incident like a fender-bender a better device to explain the plight of the undocumented immigrant than a dramatic one?
2. How does Pérez use dialogue to advance the narrative?

Appreciating Language

1. What words does Pérez use to minimize the damage caused by the accident?
2. What word choices and images stress the importance of paper documents in the lives of aliens?

Connections across the Disciplines

1. Compare Armando Rendón's attitude (page 586) toward his Spanish heritage with that of the Chicanos Pérez describes. How are they different? How common is the issue of embracing or rejecting one's ethnic origins?
2. How does Pérez's situation differ from Nathan McCall's (page 61)?

Writing Suggestions

1. Write a short narrative essay detailing a minor event that provided insight into your life or social conditions. Perhaps you discovered our dependence on energy when your apartment lost power and you could not use your computer, watch television, or even open the garage door to get your car. A simple interaction with a homeless person may have caused you to question your assumptions about the poor.
2. *Collaborative Writing:* Working with a group of students, discuss your views on immigration and undocumented or "illegal" aliens. Take notes and write a brief statement outlining your views. If major differences of opinion exist, split the group into subgroups, and draft pro and con opinion statements.

NATHAN MCCALL

Nathan McCall grew up in Portsmouth, Virginia, where he attended both black and integrated public schools. In 1975 he was convicted of armed robbery and sentenced to eight years in prison. After serving three years, McCall was released and studied journalism at Norfolk State University. He became a reporter for the Virginian Pilot-Ledger Star *and later moved to the* Atlanta Journal-Constitution. *He covered the 1988 Republican National Convention in New Orleans and accompanied Andy Young on a European trade mission. In 1989 he joined the staff of the* Washington Post. *McCall's autobiography* Makes Me Wanna Holler *was published in 1995 and a collection of essays,* What's Going On, *in 1997.*

The Lesson

OVERVIEW: *In this passage of his autobiography, McCall relates his experience as one of the first African-American students bused to a previously all-white public school in Virginia. His goal in this narrative is to share with readers the emotional trauma caused by racial hatred.*

My harshest introduction to the world of white folks came in September 1966, when my parents sent me to Alford J. Mapp, a white school across town. It was the beginning of my sixth-grade school year, and I was walking down the hall, searching for my new class, when a white boy timed my steps, extended his foot, and tripped me. The boy and his friends nudged each other and laughed as I stumbled into a locker, spilling books and papers everywhere. "Hey, nigger," the boy said. "You dropped something." 1

The word sounded vile coming from his white mouth. When I regained my footing, I tore into that cat and tried to take his head off. Pinning him against a locker, I punched him in the face and kept on punching him until his two buddies jumped in to help him out. While other white students crowded around and cheered them on, we scuffled there in the hall until the bell rang, signaling the start of the next class period. Like combatants in a prizefight, we automatically stopped throwing punches and separated at the sound of the bell. The white boys went their way down the hall, calling me names along the way and threatening to retaliate. I gathered my papers, straightened my clothes, and reeled toward my next class, dazed, trying to figure out what had just happened to me. 2

My parents sent me to Mapp in 1966 because that was the first year that blacks in Portsmouth were able to attend school wherever they wanted. The U.S. Supreme Court had long before ruled against the notion of separate but equal schools; still, Virginia, one of the states that had resisted de- 3 segregation, was slow in putting together a busing plan. Without a plan to ship black students to schools across town, over the years blacks and whites in Portsmouth had simply remained in separate schools. I could have gone to W. E. Waters, a junior high school that had just been built in our neighborhood, but, like many blacks then, my parents figured I could get a better education at the white school across town.

4   I was proud of their decision and held it out teasingly to my brothers as proof that I was the smart one in the family, that I held more academic promise than them. Billy had flunked the second grade, and Dwight and Junnie never showed much interest in books. My less studious brothers would attend their regular, all-black high school, but I was going to a *white* school, which made me feel special.

5   My parents didn't talk with me beforehand about the challenge I would face as one in the first wave of blacks to integrate Mapp. We had all seen TV news footage of police in riot gear escorting black students through hostile, jeering crowds to enroll in all-white high schools and colleges across the country, but for various reasons my parents saw no cause for alarm at Mapp. It was only a junior high school, which seemed far less menacing than the racially torn high schools and college campuses we heard about. Besides, there were no warning signals in Portsmouth to tip off my parents, no public protests by white citizens or high-profile white supremacist politicians like Alabama governor George Wallace threatening to buck the school integration plan.

6   At Mapp, I was the only African-American in most of my classes. When I walked into one room and sat down, the students near me would get up and move away, as if my dark skin were dirty and hideous to them. Nobody talked directly to me. Instead, they shot daggers to each other that were intended for me. "You know, I hate niggers," they would say. "I don't understand why they're always following white people everywhere. We can't seem to get away from them. Why don't they just stay in their own schools?"

7   It wasn't much better dealing with white teachers. They avoided eye contact with me as much as possible and pretended not to see or hear white student hecklers. It was too much for an eleven-year-old to challenge, and I didn't try. Instead, I tried to become invisible. I kept to myself, remained quiet during class discussions, and never asked questions in or after class. I kept my eyes glued to my desk or looked straight ahead to avoid drawing attention to myself. I staggered, numb and withdrawn, through each school day and hurried from my last class, gym, without showering so that I wouldn't miss the only bus headed home. Students who missed the first school bus had to walk through the white neighborhood to the main street

to catch the city bus. Mapp was located in a middle-class section of town called Craddock, where the whites were as hateful as the poor whites in Academy Park.

The daily bus ride home brought its own set of fears. A group of white 8 boys got on our bus regularly for the sole purpose, it seemed, of picking fights. I was scared to death of them. With older brothers to fight at home, I was confident I could whip any white boy my age and size, but many of the white guys who got on that bus were eighth graders, and they looked like giants to me. Others were older, white, leather-jacket-wearing hoods who I was certain were high school dropouts.

When we boarded the bus, blacks automatically moved to the rear, as if 9 Jim Crow laws were still in effect. The white boys would board last, crowd into the aisles, and start making racial slurs when the bus pulled away from school. "I hate the smell of niggers. They sure do stink. Don't you think niggers stink, Larry?"

"They sure do, man. They smell bad." 10

Before long, fists flew, girls screamed, and people tussled in the aisles. 11 Few of the black guys on the bus were big and bad enough to beat the tough white boys, who outnumbered us seven to one. I never joined in to help the black guys out. I huddled in the far corner at the rear of the bus, tense, scared as hell, hoping the fighting wouldn't reach that far before the driver broke it up.

Children have an enormous capacity to adapt to insanity. I took my 12 lumps in school and tried as much as possible to shrug it off when I went home. Billy, Dwight, and Junnie came home most days full of stories about the fun they were having at pep rallies and football games at their all-black high school. I envied them because I couldn't match their stories with tales of my own about fun times at Mapp. I savored every minute of my week-nights at home and used weekends to gather the heart to face Mapp again. Monday mornings, I rose and dutifully caught the school bus back to hell.

The harassment never let up. Once, when my English teacher left the 13 room, a girl sitting near me drew a picture of a stickman on a piece of paper, colored it black, scribbled my name below it, and passed it around the class-room for others to see. I lost my temper, snatched it from her, and ripped it up. She hit me. I hit her back, then the whole class jumped in. When the teacher returned, I was standing up, punching one guy while another was riding my back and hitting me in the head. The teacher demanded, "What's going on here?"

The white kids cried out in unison, "That *black* boy started a fight 14 with us!"

15   Without another word, the teacher sent me to the principal's office and I was dismissed from school. The week-long suspension alerted my parents that something was wrong. Mama sat me down and tried to talk to me about it. "Why were you fighting in school?"

16   "It wasn't my fault, Mama. That girl drew a picture of me and colored it black."

17   "That's no reason to fight. What's the matter with you? Your grades are falling and now you get into a fight. Don't you like your school?"

18   I tried to explain, then choked up and broke down in tears. Seeing that, my parents sought and got approval to transfer me to the neighborhood school, W. E. Waters.

19   But it wasn't over yet. One day, before the transfer went through, I was sitting on the gym floor with the rest of the student body, watching a school assembly program, when a group of rowdy white upperclassmen began plucking my head and ridiculing me. I got confused. *What should I do?* To turn around and say something to them would start another fight. To get up and leave would require me to wade through a sea of hostile white students to reach the nearest exit. With nowhere to go, I sat there and took the humiliation until I broke. Tears welled in my eyes and started running, uncontrollably, down my face. I sat silently through the remainder of the assembly program with my vision blurred and my spirit broken. That was the only time, then or since, that I've been crushed so completely. When it was over, I collected myself, went to the boys' bathroom, and boo-hooed some more.

20   There was no greater joy than that last bus ride home from Mapp. I sat near a window and stared out, trying to make sense of those past few months. Everything that had happened to me was so contrary to all I'd been taught about right and wrong. Before Mapp, every grudge I had ever held against a person could be traced to some specific deed. I couldn't understand someone hating me simply for being black and alive. I wondered, *Where did those white people learn to hate so deeply at such a young age?* I didn't know. But, over time, I learned to hate as blindly and viciously as any of them.

Understanding Meaning

1. Why did McCall's parents send him to a white school?
2. How did the white students respond to his presence?
3. How was McCall treated by the white faculty?

4. What impact did the students' reactions have on the author?
5. Why did McCall envy his brothers, who attended an all-black school?
6. What lesson did McCall learn?
7. *Critical Thinking:* McCall makes the observation that "Children have an enormous capacity to adapt to insanity." Can you think of current incidents or examples from your own life that support this view? Is this a universal phenomenon?

Evaluating Strategy

1. How does McCall blend a series of separate incidents into a single narrative?
2. What objective facts does McCall introduce into the narrative? Why are they important?
3. *Other Modes:* How does McCall use *description* and *comparison* to develop his narrative?

Appreciating Language

1. McCall uses the terms *black* and *African-American* interchangeably. Does this appear inconsistent, or does it simply help the writer avoid repetition?
2. McCall states that the word *nigger* sounded "vile" coming from a white student. Is he suggesting that the race of the user determines the meaning of a word most people view as a term of contempt?
3. *Critical Thinking:* At one point McCall states that he wished to be "invisible." Why does this word have special meaning for African-Americans?

Connections across the Disciplines

1. Consider Carl T. Rowan's account of his black teacher in "Unforgettable Miss Bessie" (page 137). Does McCall's account suggest that many students are better served in black schools with black teachers?
2. How does McCall's experience compare to that of Ramon Pérez (page 56)? Do their experiences give them a sense of being alien?

Writing Suggestions

1. Write a short essay about an incident in which you learned something about your status in society. Think of a time in which people responded to you not as an individual but as a member of a group. Have you ever been seen as one of *them* and labeled by others who have a fear or hatred for people who are differ-

ent? What occurred, and how did people's reactions make you feel? Choose words carefully to express how the incident made you feel.

2. *Collaborative Writing:* Discuss McCall's narrative with a group of students. Ask members of the group to respond to McCall's "lesson." Work together to write a brief *description* of how children learn to hate others.

MICHAEL PATRICK MACDONALD

Michael Patrick MacDonald (1966–) was born in Boston and grew up in South Boston's Old Colony housing project located in one of the country's poorest white urban communities. He helped launch Boston's gun buy-back program and founded the South Boston Vigil Group, and he works with many anti-violence programs. In 1999 he published his autobiography All Souls, *which received the American Book Award.*

Returning to Southie

OVERVIEW: *As you read this section from* All Souls, *note how MacDonald's Boston Irish neighborhood reflects social problems generally associated with other ethnic communities. Consider the role violence and drugs had in shaping MacDonald's childhood.*

I was back in Southie, "the best place in the world," as Ma used to say before the kids died. That's what we call them now, "the kids." Even when we want to say their names, we sometimes get confused about who's dead and who's alive in my family. After so many deaths, Ma just started to call my four brothers "the kids" when we talked about going to see them at the cemetery. But I don't go anymore. They're not at the cemetery; I never could find them there. When I accepted the fact that I couldn't feel them at the graves, I figured it must be because they were in heaven, or the spirit world, or whatever you want to call it. The only things I kept from the funerals were the mass cards that said, "Do not stand at my grave and weep, I am not there, I do not sleep. I am the stars that shine through the night," and so on. I figured that was the best way to look at it. There are seven of us kids still alive, and sometimes I'm not even sure if that's true.

I came back to Southie in the summer of 1994, after everyone in my family had either died or moved to the mountains of Colorado. I'd moved to downtown Boston after Ma left in 1990, and was pulled one night to wander through Southie. I walked from Columbia Point Project, where I was born, to the Old Colony Project where I grew up, in the "Lower End," as we called it. On that August night, after four years of staying away, I walked the streets of my old neighborhood, and finally found the kids. In my memory of that night I can see them clear as day. *They're right here,* I thought, and it was an ecstatic feeling. I cried, and felt alive again myself. I passed by the outskirts of Old Colony, and it all came back to me—the kids were joined in my mind by so many others I'd last seen in caskets at Jackie O'Brien's Funeral Parlor. They were all here now, all of my neighbors and friends who

1

2

67

had died young from violence, drugs, and from the other deadly things we'd been taught didn't happen in Southie.

3   We thought we were in the best place in the world in this neighborhood, in the all-Irish housing projects where everyone claimed to be Irish even if his name was Spinnoli. We were proud to be from here, as proud as we were to be Irish. We didn't want to own the problems that took the lives of my brothers and of so many others like them: poverty, crime, drugs—those were black things that happened in the ghettos of Roxbury. Southie was Boston's proud Irish neighborhood.

4   On this night in Southie, the kids were all here once again—I could feel them. The only problem was no one else in the neighborhood could. My old neighbors were going on with their nightly business—wheeling and dealing on the corners, drinking on the stoops, yelling up to windows, looking for a way to get by, or something to fight for. Just like the old days in this small world within a world. It was like a family reunion to me. That's what we considered each other in Southie—family. There was always this feeling that we were protected, as if the whole neighborhood was watching our backs for threats, watching for all the enemies we could never really define. No "outsiders" could mess with us. So we had no reason to leave, and nothing ever to leave for. It was a good feeling to be back in Southie that night, surrounded by my family and neighbors; and I remember hating having to cross over the Broadway Bridge again, having to leave the peninsula neighborhood and go back to my apartment in downtown Boston.

5   Not long after, I got a call at Citizens for Safety, where I'd been working on antiviolence efforts across Boston since 1990. It was a reporter from *U.S. News & World Report* who was working on an article about what they were calling "the white underclass." The reporter had found through demographic studies that Southie showed three census tracts with the highest concentration of poor whites in America. The part of Southie he was referring to was the Lower End, my own neighborhood at the bottom of the steep hills of City Point, which was the more middle-class section with nicer views of the harbor. The magazine's findings were based on rates of joblessness and single-parent female-headed households. Nearly three-fourths of the families in the Lower End had no fathers. Eighty-five percent of Old Colony collected welfare. The reporter wasn't telling me anything new—I was just stunned that someone was taking notice. No one had ever seemed to believe me or to care when I told them about the amount of poverty and social problems where I grew up. Liberals were usually the ones working on social problems, and they never seemed to be able to fit urban poor whites into their world view, which tended to see blacks as the persistent

dependent and their own white selves as provider. Whatever race guilt they were holding onto, Southie's poor couldn't do a thing for their consciences. After our violent response to court-ordered busing in the 1970s, Southie was labeled as the white racist oppressor. I saw how that label worked to take the blame away from those able to leave the city and drive back to all-white suburban towns at the end of the day.

Outsiders were also used to the image, put out by our own politicians, that we were a working-class and middle-class community with the lowest rates of social problems anywhere, and that we wanted to keep it that way by not letting blacks in with all their problems. Growing up, I felt alone in thinking this attitude was an injustice to all the Southie people I knew who'd been murdered. Then there were all the suicides that no one wanted to talk about. And all the bank robberies and truck hijackings, and the number of addicts walking down Broadway, and the people limping around or in wheelchairs, victims of violence.

The reporter asked me if I knew anyone in Southie he could talk to. He wanted to see if the socioeconomic conditions in the neighborhood had some of the same results evident in the highly concentrated black ghettos of America. I called some people, but most of them didn't want to talk. We were all used to the media writing about us only when something racial happened, ever since the neighborhood had erupted in antibusing riots during the seventies. Senator Billy Bulger, president of the Massachusetts Senate, had always reminded us of how unfair the media was with its attacks on South Boston. He told us never to trust them again. No news was good news. And his brother, neighborhood drug lord James "Whitey" Bulger, had liked it better that way. Whitey probably figured that all the shootings in the nearby black neighborhood of Roxbury, and all the activists willing to talk over there, would keep the media busy. They wouldn't meddle in Southie as long as we weren't as stupid and disorganized as Roxbury's drug dealers. And by the late eighties, murders in Southie had started to be less visible even to us in the community. Word around town was that Whitey didn't allow bodies to be left on the streets anymore; instead, people went missing, and sometimes were found hog-tied out in the suburbs, or washed up on the shores of Dorchester Bay. The ability of our clean-cut gangsters to keep up appearances complemented our own need to deny the truth. Bad guy stuff seemed to happen less often within the protected turf of South Boston. Maybe a few suicides here and there, or maybe an addict "scumbag," but that was the victim's own problem. Must have come from a bad family—nothing to do with "Our Beautiful World," as the *South Boston Tribune* was used to calling it, above pictures of church bazaars, bake sales, christenings, and weddings.

8   I agreed to take the reporter on a tour through Southie. We stayed in the car, because I was too nervous to walk around with an "outsider" in a suit. It was bad enough that I was driving his rented sports car. People in Southie usually drove big Chevys, or when they were in with "the boys," as we called our revered gangsters, they'd upgrade to an even bigger Caddy or Lincoln Continental. I wore sunglasses and a scally cap, the traditional local cap once favored by hard-working Irish immigrants and longshoremen, and more recently made popular by tough guys and wannabes. I disguised myself so I wouldn't be identified collaborating with an outsider. Everyone knew I was an activist working to reduce violence and crime. But when they saw me on the news, I was usually organizing things over in Roxbury or Dorchester, the black places that my neighbors thanked God they didn't live in. "That stuff would never happen in Southie," a mother in Old Colony once told me. Her own son had been run over by gangsters for selling cocaine on their turf without paying up.

9   When I rode around the Lower End with the reporter, I pointed to the landmarks of my childhood: St. Augustine's grammar school, where Ma struggled to keep up with tuition payments so we wouldn't be bused to black neighborhoods; the Boys and Girls Club, where I was on the swim team with my brother Kevin; Darius Court, where I played and watched the busing riots; the liquor store with a giant green shamrock painted on it, where Whitey Bulger ran the Southie drug trade; the sidewalk where my sister had crashed from a project rooftop after a fight over drugs; and St. Augustine's Church, down whose front steps I'd helped carry my brothers' heavy caskets. "I miss this place," I said to him. He looked horrified but kept scribbling notes as I went on about this being the best place in the world. "I always had a sense of security here, a sense of belonging that I've never felt anywhere else," I explained. "There was always a feeling that someone would watch your back. Sure, bad things happened to my family, and to so many of my neighbors and friends, but there was never a sense that we were victims. This place was ours, it was all we ever knew, and it was all ours."

10   Talking to this stranger, driving through the streets of Southie, and saying these things confused me. I thought about how much I'd hated this place when I'd learned that everything I'd just heard myself say about Southie loyalty and pride was a big myth, one that fit well into the schemes of career politicians and their gangster relatives. I thought about how I'd felt betrayed when my brothers ended up among all the other ghosts in our town who were looked up to when they were alive, and shrugged off when they were dead, as punks only asking for trouble.

I didn't know now if I loved or hated this place. All those beautiful   11
dreams and nightmares of my life were competing in the narrow littered
streets of Old Colony Project. Over there, on my old front stoop at 8 Patterson Way, were the eccentric mothers, throwing their arms around and
telling wild stories. Standing on the corners were the natural-born comedians making everyone laugh. Then there were the teenagers wearing their
flashy clothes, "pimp" gear, as we called it. And little kids running in packs,
having the time of their lives in a world that was all theirs. But I also saw
the junkies, the depressed and lonely mothers of people who'd died, the
wounded, the drug dealers, and a known murderer accepted by everyone as
warmly as they accepted anything else in the familiar landscape. "I'm
thinking of moving back," I told the reporter.

Understanding Meaning

1. What kind of neighborhood is Southie? How would you describe it?
2. What happened to MacDonald's brothers?
3. Why did MacDonald feel uncomfortable returning to the neighborhood with
   an outsider?
4. What positive elements did MacDonald see in his old community?
5. *Critical Thinking:* How much of MacDonald's essay is a story of denial by whites
   on welfare who insist they are working class and by white liberals who assume
   that only African-Americans experience pervasive poverty, drugs, and gang
   violence?

Evaluating Strategy

1. What impact does the first line have? Why would MacDonald's mother call this
   neighborhood the "best place in the world"?
2. How does MacDonald use riding around Southie with a reporter as a device to
   advance the essay?
3. What does MacDonald's final statement reveal about his attitude toward his
   community? What draws him back to a neighborhood that claimed the lives of
   four brothers and a sister?

Appreciating Language

1. Why does MacDonald's family come to refer to the four lost sons as "the kids"?
   What does this generic term suggest about their loss?

2. In Southie gangsters are called "the boys." Does this term indicate an acceptance or even affection?

3. MacDonald tells the reporter he always felt a sense of security in Southie. What kind of security is found in a neighborhood of drugs, violence, and murder?

Connections across the Disciplines

1. Consider essays by Nathan McCall (see page 61) and Luis Alberto Urrea (see page 129). Do many people assume that only minorities endure life in communities marked by drugs, gangs, poverty, and violence? Why do liberal social reformers ignore the whites of Southie?

2. Do you see similar elements in N. Scott Momaday's story (see page 142) of returning to his homeland? Are there universal elements in returning to the place where you grew up? Do we always have nostalgia for our childhood homes, even if they contained negative elements?

Writing Suggestions

1. Write a brief narrative about returning to a place that shaped your life—an old school, the first place you had a job, a friend's home, your first apartment. Rather than focusing on physical details, concentrate on what the location meant to you.

2. *Collaborative Writing:* Discuss this essay with a group of students and list reasons why society seems to overlook the plight of poor whites. Why do both liberals and conservatives appear to deny that white neighborhoods share many of the problems that plague minority communities?

RICHARD PRESTON

Richard Preston is a journalist who frequently contributes to the New Yorker. *In 1987 he published a book about astronomy,* First Light, *which won the American Institute of Physics Award. His next book,* American Steel, *examined the Nucor Corporation's plan to build a revolutionary steel mill. In 1994 he published* The Hot Zone *documenting the outbreak and spread of the deadly Ebola virus. His most recent book,* The Cobra Event, *is a suspense thriller about bioterrorism.*

Ebola River

OVERVIEW: *In this passage from* The Hot Zone, *Preston details the initial appearance of the Ebola virus in Sudan. Although written in the third person and focusing on objective observation, Preston's use of factual detail creates a chilling drama.*

On July 6, 1976, five hundred miles northwest of Mount Elgon, in southern Sudan, near the fingered edge of the central-African rain forest, a man who is known to Ebola hunters as Yu. G. went into shock and died with blood running from the orifices of his body. He is referred to only by his initials. Mr. Yu. G. was the first identified case, the index case, in an outbreak of an unknown virus.

Mr. Yu. G. was a storekeeper in a cotton factory in the town of Nzara. The population of Nzara had grown in recent years—the town had experienced, in its own way, the human population explosion that is occurring throughout the equatorial regions of the earth. The people of that area in southern Sudan are the Zande, a large tribe. The country of the Zande is savanna mixed with riverine forest, beautiful country, where acacia trees cluster along the banks of seasonal rivers. African doves perch in the trees and call their drawn-out calls. The land between the rivers is a sea of elephant grass, which can grow ten feet high. As you head south, toward Zaire, the land rises and forms hills, and the forest begins to spread away from the river and thickens into a closed canopy, and you enter the rain forest. The land around the town of Nzara held rich plantations of teak and fruit trees and cotton. People were poor, but they worked hard and raised large families and kept to their tribal traditions.

Mr. Yu. G. was a salaried man. He worked at a desk in a room piled with cotton cloth at the back of the factory. Bats roosted in the ceiling of the room near his desk. If the bats were infected with Ebola, no one has been able to prove it. The virus may have entered the cotton factory by some unknown route—perhaps in insects trapped in the cotton fibers, for example, or in rats that lived in the factory. Or, possibly, the virus had nothing to do with the cotton factory, and Mr. Yu. G. was infected somewhere else. He did not go to a hospital, and died on a cot in his family compound. His family gave him a traditional Zande funeral and left his body under a mound of stones in a clearing of elephant grass. His grave has been visited more than once by doctors from Europe and America, who want to see it and reflect on its meaning, and pay their respects to the index case of what later became known as Ebola Sudan.

4   He is remembered today as a "quiet, unremarkable man." No photograph was taken of him during his lifetime, and no one seems to remember what he looked like. He wasn't well known, even in his hometown. They say that his brother was tall and slender, so perhaps he was, too. He passed through the gates of life unnoticed by anyone except his family and a few of his co-workers. He might have made no difference except for the fact that he was a host.

5   His illness began to copy itself. A few days after he died, two other salaried men who worked at desks near him in the same room broke with bleeding, went into shock, and died with massive hemorrhages from the natural openings of the body. One of the dead men was a popular fellow known as P. G. Unlike the quiet Mr. Yu. G., he had a wide circle of friends, including several mistresses. He spread the agent far and wide in the town. The agent jumped easily from person to person, apparently through touching and sexual contact. It was a fast spreader, and it could live easily in people. It passed through as many as sixteen generations of infection as it jumped from person to person in Sudan. It also killed many of its hosts. While this is not necessarily in the best interest of the virus, if the virus is highly contagious, and can jump fast enough from host to host, then it does not matter, really, what happens to the previous host, because the virus can amplify itself for quite a while, at least until it kills off much of the population of hosts. Most of the fatal cases of Ebola Sudan can be traced back through chains of infection to the quiet Mr. Yu. G. A hot strain radiated out of him and nearly devastated the human population of southern Sudan. The strain burned through the town of Nzara and reached eastward to the town of Maridi, where there was a hospital.

6   It hit the hospital like a bomb. It savaged patients and snaked like chain lightning out from the hospital through patients' families. Apparently the medical staff had been giving patients injections with dirty needles. The virus jumped quickly through the hospital via the needles, and then it hit the medical staff. A characteristic of a lethal, contagious, and incurable virus

is that it quickly gets into the medical people. In some cases, the medical system may intensify the outbreak, like a lens that focuses sunlight on a heap of tinder.

The virus transformed the hospital at Maridi into a morgue. As it 7
jumped from bed to bed, killing patients left and right, doctors began to notice signs of mental derangement, psychosis, depersonalization, zombie-like behavior. Some of the dying stripped off their clothes and ran out of the hospital, naked and bleeding, and wandered through the streets of the town, seeking their homes, not seeming to know what had happened or how they had gotten into this condition. There is no doubt that Ebola damages the brain and causes psychotic dementia. It is not easy, however, to separate brain damage from the effects of fear. If you were trapped in a hospital where people were dissolving in their beds, you might try to escape, and if you were a bleeder and frightened, you might take off your clothes, and people might think you had gone mad.

The Sudan strain was more than twice as lethal as Marburg virus—its 8
case-fatality rate was 50 percent. That is, fully half of the people who came down with it ended up dying, and quickly. This was the same kind of fatality rate as was seen with the black plague during the Middle Ages. If the Ebola Sudan virus had managed to spread out of central Africa, it might have entered Khartoum in a few weeks, penetrated Cairo a few weeks after that, and from there it would have hopped to Athens, New York, Paris, London, Singapore—it would have gone everywhere on the planet. Yet that never happened, and the crisis in Sudan passed away unnoticed by the world at large. What happened in Sudan could be compared to the secret detonation of an atomic bomb. If the human race came close to a major biological accident, we never knew it.

For reasons that are not clear, the outbreak subsided, and the virus vanished. 9
The hospital at Maridi had been the epicenter of the emergence. As the virus ravaged the hospital, the surviving medical staff panicked and ran off into the bush. It was probably the wisest thing to do and the best thing that could have happened, because it stopped the use of dirty needles and emptied the hospital, which helped break the chain of infection.

There was another possible reason why the Ebola Sudan virus vanished. 10
It was exceedingly hot. It killed people so fast that they didn't have much time to infect other people before they died. Furthermore, the virus was not airborne. It was not quite contagious enough to start a full-scale disaster. It traveled in blood, and the bleeding victim did not touch very many other people before dying, and so the virus did not have many chances to jump to a new host. Had people been coughing the virus into the air . . . it

would have been a different story. In any case, the Ebola Sudan virus destroyed a few hundred people in central Africa the way a fire consumes a pile of straw—until the blaze burns out at the center and ends in a heap of ash—rather than smoldering around the planet, as AIDS has done, like a fire in a coal mine, impossible to put out. The Ebola virus, in its Sudan incarnation, retreated to the heart of the bush, where undoubtedly it lives to this day, cycling and cycling in some unknown host, able to shift its shape, able to mutate and become a new thing, with the potential to enter the human species in a new form.

Understanding Meaning

1. What is known about Mr. Yu. G.? What made him important to science?
2. What effect does the Ebola virus have on people? How does it kill?
3. How does the virus spread from one person to another?
4. Why did this outbreak kill only a few hundred people and not spread across the world like AIDS?
5. *Critical Thinking:* What implications do Ebola and similar viruses have in a world where jet travel would make it easy for a single patient to spread the disease to people thousands of miles from the outbreak?

Evaluating Strategy

1. How does Preston organize the chain of events? What chronological pattern does he use?
2. How does Preston assemble scientific facts to create a dramatic story? Can an objective narrative have an emotional impact on readers? Can facts truly "speak for themselves"?
3. In paragraph seven, Preston places his readers into the events by using second person, "If you were trapped in a hospital . . ." What impact does this have? Is this an effective strategy?

Appreciating Language

1. How would you characterize Preston's level of diction? Does the lack of medical terminology weaken the narrative's scientific value? What does it say about the intended audience?
2. Underline those phrases that dramatize the events. How effective are they?

3. What words does Preston use to describe the virus? How does he emphasize its lethality?

Connections across the Disciplines

1. Preston is writing about people threatened by an invisible virus. How does this confrontation differ from the dramas related by Nathan McCall (page 61) and Ramon Pérez (page 56)? Does Preston have to personalize the action of the virus to heighten the narrative's drama?
2. Consider Samuel Scudder's "Take This Fish and Look at It" (page 47). How important is detailed observation in Preston's account?

Writing Suggestions

1. Write a short essay *analyzing* what threats the Ebola and related viruses could pose in the future. What would happen if the virus broke out in a city like New York or Las Vegas?
2. Write a brief factual but dramatic narrative about an event you experienced or witnessed. Select details that create strong impressions, but avoid exaggerating or distorting facts.
3. *Collaborative Writing:* Working with at least three other students, draft a short persuasive letter to the White House arguing that the military should be equipped to rapidly respond to biomedical disasters. You may use Einstein's letter to President Roosevelt (page 596) as a model. Use Preston's account to support your thesis.

George Orwell was the pen name of Eric Blair (1903–1950), who was born in India, the son of a British official. Blair graduated from the prestigious Eton school but joined the Indian Imperial Police instead of attending a university. After four years of service in Burma, he left to pursue a writing career. His first book, Down and Out in Paris and London, *explored the plight of the poor and homeless during the Depression. His later books included* Animal Farm *and* Nineteen Eighty-Four.

Shooting an Elephant

OVERVIEW: *As you read Orwell's narrative, consider what message about imperialism he was trying to communicate to his British readers. What is his implied thesis?*

1   In Moulmein, in Lower Burma, I was hated by large numbers of people—the only time in my life that I have been important enough for this to happen to me. I was sub-divisional police officer of the town, and in an aimless, petty kind of way anti-European feeling was very bitter. No one had the guts to raise a riot, but if a European woman went through the bazaars alone somebody would probably spit betel juice over her dress. As a police officer I was an obvious target and was baited whenever it seemed safe to do so. When a nimble Burman tripped me up on the football field and the referee (another Burman) looked the other way, the crowd yelled with hideous laughter. This happened more than once. In the end the sneering yellow faces of young men that met me everywhere, the insults hooted after me when I was at a safe distance, got badly on my nerves. The young Buddhist priests were the worst of all. There were several thousands of them in the town and none of them seemed to have anything to do except stand on street corners and jeer at Europeans.

2   All this was perplexing and upsetting. For at that time I had already made up my mind that imperialism was an evil thing and the sooner I chucked up my job and got out of it the better. Theoretically—and secretly, of course—I was all for the Burmese and all against their oppressors, the British. As for the job I was doing, I hated it more bitterly than I can perhaps make clear. In a job like that you see the dirty work of Empire at close quarters. The wretched prisoners huddling in the stinking cages of the lock-ups, the grey, cowed faces of the long-term convicts, the scarred buttocks of the men who had been flogged with bamboos—all these oppressed me with an intolerable sense of guilt. But I could get nothing into perspective. I was young

and ill-educated and I had had to think out my problems in the utter silence that is imposed on every Englishman in the East. I did not even know that the British Empire is dying, still less did I know that it is a great deal better than the younger empires that are going to supplant it. All I knew was that I was stuck between my hatred of the empire I served and my rage against the evil-spirited little beasts who tried to make my job impossible. With one part of my mind I thought of the British Raj as an unbreakable tyranny, as something clamped down, in *saecula saeculorum*, upon the will of prostrate peoples; with another part I thought that the greatest joy in the world would be to drive a bayonet into a Buddhist priest's guts. Feelings like these are the normal by-products of imperialism; ask any Anglo-Indian official, if you can catch him off duty.

One day something happened which in a roundabout way was enlight- 3 ening. It was a tiny incident in itself, but it gave me a better glimpse than I had had before of the real nature of imperialism—the real motives for which despotic governments act. Early one morning the sub-inspector at a police station the other end of the town rang me up on the phone and said that an elephant was ravaging the bazaar. Would I please come and do something about it? I did not know what I could do, but I wanted to see what was happening and I got on to a pony and started out. I took my rifle, an old .44 Winchester and much too small to kill an elephant, but I thought the noise might be useful *in terrorem*. Various Burmans stopped me on the way and told me about the elephant's doings. It was not, of course, a wild elephant, but a tame one which had gone "must." It had been chained up as tame elephants always are when their attack of "must" is due, but on the previous night it had broken its chain and escaped. Its mahout, the only person who could manage it when it was in that state, had set out in pursuit, but he had taken the wrong direction and was now twelve hours' journey away, and in the morning the elephant had suddenly reappeared in the town. The Burmese population had no weapons and were quite helpless against it. It had already destroyed somebody's bamboo hut, killed a cow and raided some fruit-stalls and devoured the stock; also it had met the municipal rubbish van, and, when the driver jumped out and took to his heels, had turned the van over and inflicted violence upon it.

The Burmese sub-inspector and some Indian constables were waiting 4 for me in the quarter where the elephant had been seen. It was a very poor quarter, a labyrinth of squalid bamboo huts, thatched with palm-leaf, winding all over a steep hillside. I remember that it was a cloudy stuffy morning at the beginning of the rains. We began questioning the people as to where the elephant had gone, and, as usual, failed to get any definite information.

That is invariably the case in the East; a story always sounds clear enough at a distance, but the nearer you get to the scene of events the vaguer it becomes. Some of the people said that the elephant had gone in one direction, some said that he had gone in another, some professed not even to have heard of any elephant. I had almost made up my mind that the whole story was a pack of lies, when we heard yells a little distance away. There was a loud, scandalised cry of "Go away, child! Go away this instant!" and an old woman with a switch in her hand came round the corner of a hut, violently shooing away a crowd of naked children. Some more women followed, clicking their tongues and exclaiming; evidently there was something there that the children ought not to have seen. I rounded the hut and saw a man's dead body sprawling in the mud. He was an Indian, a black Dravidian coolie, almost naked, and he could not have been dead many minutes. The people said that the elephant had come suddenly upon him round the corner of the hut, caught him with its trunk, put its foot on his back and ground him into the earth. This was the rainy season and the ground was soft, and his face had scored a trench a foot deep and a couple of yards long. He was lying on his belly with arms crucified and head sharply twisted to one side. His face was coated with mud, the eyes wide open, the teeth bared and grinning with an expression of unendurable agony. (Never tell me, by the way, that the dead look peaceful. Most of the corpses I have seen looked devilish.) The friction of the great beast's foot had stripped the skin from his back as neatly as one skins a rabbit. As soon as I saw the dead man I sent an orderly to a friend's house nearby to borrow an elephant rifle. I had already sent back the pony, not wanting it to go mad with fright and throw me if it smelled the elephant.

5   The orderly came back in a few minutes with a rifle and five cartridges, and meanwhile some Burmans had arrived and told us that the elephant was in the paddy fields below, only a few hundred yards away. As I started forward practically the whole population of the quarter flocked out of their houses and followed me. They had seen the rifle and were all shouting excitedly that I was going to shoot the elephant. They had not shown much interest in the elephant when he was merely ravaging their homes, but it was different now that he was going to be shot. It was a bit of fun to them, as it would be to an English crowd; besides, they wanted the meat. It made me vaguely uneasy. I had no intention of shooting the elephant—I had merely sent for the rifle to defend myself if necessary—and it is always unnerving to have a crowd following you. I marched down the hill, looking and feeling a fool, with the rifle over my shoulder and an ever-growing army of people jostling at my heels. At the bottom, when you got away from the

huts, there was a metalled road and beyond that a miry waste of paddy fields a thousand yards across, not yet ploughed but soggy from the first rains and dotted with coarse grass. The elephant was standing eighty yards from the road, his left side towards us. He took not the slightest notice of the crowd's approach. He was tearing up bunches of grass, beating them against his knees to clean them and stuffing them into his mouth.

I had halted on the road. As soon as I saw the elephant I knew with perfect certainty that I ought not to shoot him. It is a serious matter to shoot a working elephant—it is comparable to destroying a huge and costly piece of machinery—and obviously one ought not to do it if it can possibly be avoided. And at that distance, peacefully eating, the elephant looked no more dangerous than a cow. I thought then and I think now that his attack of "must" was already passing off; in which case he would merely wander harmlessly about until the mahout came back and caught him. Moreover, I did not in the least want to shoot him. I decided that I would watch him for a little while to make sure that he did not turn savage again, and then go home.

But at that moment I glanced round at the crowd that had followed me. It was an immense crowd, two thousand at the least and growing every minute. It blocked the road for a long distance on either side. I looked at the sea of yellow faces above the garish clothes—faces all happy and excited over this bit of fun, all certain that the elephant was going to be shot. They were watching me as they would watch a conjuror about to perform a trick. They did not like me, but with the magical rifle in my hands I was momentarily worth watching. And suddenly I realised that I should have to shoot the elephant after all. The people expected it of me and I had got to do it; I could feel their two thousand wills pressing me forward, irresistibly. And it was at this moment, as I stood there with the rifle in my hands, that I first grasped the hollowness, the futility of the white man's dominion in the East. Here was I, the white man with his gun, standing in front of the unarmed native crowd—seemingly the leading actor of the piece; but in reality I was only an absurd puppet pushed to and fro by the will of those yellow faces behind. I perceived in this moment that when the white man turns tyrant it is his own freedom that he destroys. He becomes a sort of hollow, posing dummy, the conventionalised figure of a sahib. For it is the condition of his rule that he shall spend his life in trying to impress the "natives" and so in every crisis he has got to do what the "natives" expect of him. He wears a mask, and his face grows to fit it. I had got to shoot the elephant. I had committed myself to doing it when I sent for the rifle. A sahib has got to act like a sahib; he has got to appear resolute, to know his own mind and do definite things. To come all that way, rifle in hand, with two thousand people marching at my heels, and then to trail feebly away, having done nothing—no, that was impossible. The crowd would laugh at me. And my whole life, every white man's life in the East, was one long struggle not to be laughed at.

8   But I did not want to shoot the elephant. I watched him beating his bunch of grass against his knees, with that preoccupied grandmotherly air that elephants have. It seemed to me that it would be murder to shoot him. At that age I was not squeamish about killing animals, but I had never shot an elephant and never wanted to. (Somehow it always seems worse to kill a *large* animal.) Besides, there was the beast's owner to be considered. Alive, the elephant was worth at least a hundred pounds; dead, he would only be worth the value of his tusks—five pounds, possibly. But I had got to act quickly. I turned to some experienced-looking Burmans who had been there when we arrived, and asked them how the elephant had been behaving. They all said the same thing: he took no notice of you if you left him alone, but he might charge if you went too close to him.

9   It was perfectly clear to me what I ought to do. I ought to walk up to within, say, twenty-five yards of the elephant and test his behaviour. If he charged I could shoot, if he took no notice of me it would be safe to leave him until the mahout came back. But also I knew that I was going to do no such thing. I was a poor shot with a rifle and the ground was soft mud into which one would sink at every step. If the elephant charged and I missed him, I should have about as much chance as a toad under a steam-roller. But even then I was not thinking particularly of my own skin, only the watchful yellow faces behind. For at that moment, with the crowd watching me, I was not afraid in the ordinary sense, as I would have been if I had been alone. A white man mustn't be frightened in front of "natives"; and so, in general, he isn't frightened. The sole thought in my mind was that if anything went wrong those two thousand Burmans would see me pursued, caught, trampled on and reduced to a grinning corpse like that Indian up the hill. And if that happened it was quite probable that some of them would laugh. That would never do. There was only one alternative. I shoved the cartridges into the magazine and lay down on the road to get a better aim.

10   The crowd grew very still, and a deep, low, happy sigh, as of people who see the theatre curtain go up at last, breathed from innumerable throats. They were going to have their bit of fun after all. The rifle was a beautiful German thing with cross-hair sights. I did not then know that in shooting an elephant one should shoot to cut an imaginary bar running from ear-hole to ear-hole. I ought therefore, as the elephant was sideways on, to have aimed straight at his ear-hole; actually I aimed several inches in front of this, thinking the brain would be further forward.

When I pulled the trigger I did not hear the bang or feel the kick—one   11
never does when a shot goes home—but heard the devilish roar of glee that
went up from the crowd. In that instant, in too short a time, one would have
thought, even for the bullet to get there, a mysterious, terrible change had
come over the elephant. He neither stirred nor fell, but every line of his
body had altered. He looked suddenly stricken, shrunken, immensely old,
as though the frightful impact of the bullet had paralysed him without
knocking him down. At last, after what seemed a long time—it might have
been five seconds, I dare say—he sagged flabbily to his knees. His mouth
slobbered. An enormous senility seemed to have settled upon him. One
could have imagined him thousands of years old. I fired again into the same
spot. At the second shot he did not collapse but climbed with desperate
slowness to his feet and stood weakly upright, with legs sagging and head
drooping. I fired a third time. That was the shot that did for him. You could
see the agony of it jolt his whole body and knock the last remnant of
strength from his legs. But in falling he seemed for a moment to rise, for as
his hind legs collapsed beneath him he seemed to tower upwards like a
huge rock toppling, his trunk reaching skyward like a tree. He trumpeted,
for the first and only time. And then down he came, his belly towards me,
with a crash that seemed to shake the ground even where I lay.

I got up. The Burmans were already racing past me across the mud. It   12
was obvious that the elephant would never rise again, but he was not dead.
He was breathing very rhythmically with long rattling gasps, his great
mound of a side painfully rising and falling. His mouth was wide open—
I could see far down into caverns of pale pink throat. I waited a long time
for him to die, but his breathing did not weaken. Finally I fired my two remaining shots into the spot where I thought his heart must be. The thick
blood welled out of him like red velvet, but still he did not die. His body
did not even jerk when the shots hit him, the tortured breathing continued
without a pause. He was dying, very slowly and in great agony, but in some
world remote from me where not even a bullet could damage him further. I
felt that I had got to put an end to that dreadful noise. It seemed dreadful to
see the great beast lying there, powerless to move and yet powerless to die,
and not even to be able to finish him. I went back for my small rifle and
poured shot after shot into his heart and down his throat. They seemed to
make no impression. The tortured gasps continued as steadily as the tick-
ing of a clock.

In the end I could not stand it any longer and went away. I heard later   13
that it took him half an hour to die. Burmans were arriving with dahs and
baskets even before I left, and I was told they had stripped his body almost
to the bones by the afternoon.

14   Afterwards, of course, there were endless discussions about the shoot-ing of the elephant. The owner was furious, but he was only an Indian and could do nothing. Besides, legally I had done the right thing, for a mad ele-phant has to be killed, like a mad dog, if its owner fails to control it. Among the Europeans opinion was divided. The older men said I was right, the younger men said it was a damn shame to shoot an elephant for killing a coolie, because an elephant was worth more than any damn Coringhee coo-lie. And afterwards I was very glad that the coolie had been killed; it put me legally in the right and it gave me a sufficient pretext for shooting the ele-phant. I often wondered whether any of the others grasped that I had done it solely to avoid looking a fool.

Understanding Meaning

1. What is Orwell's goal in relating this incident? What does this event symbolize?
2. What role does Orwell play in the narrative? How does his behavior as a police officer conflict with his personal views?
3. What are Orwell's attitudes toward the Burmese?
4. Orwell's readers were primarily British. What was he trying to impress upon them?
5. *Critical Thinking:* Consider Orwell's statement, "With one part of my mind I thought of the British Raj as an unbreakable tyranny . . . with another part I thought that the greatest joy in the world would be to drive a bayonet into a Buddhist priest's guts." What does this admission reveal?

Evaluating Strategy

1. Orwell opens the essay with the statement, "I was hated by large numbers of people." What impact does this have on readers? Does it accomplish more than simply attracting attention?
2. How does Orwell balance his role between narrator and participant?
3. *Other Modes:* Where does Orwell use *description, comparison, analysis,* and *per-suasion* within his narrative?

Appreciating Language

1. What metaphors does Orwell use in telling the story?
2. Underline the figurative language Orwell uses on page 83 to describe the labored death of the elephant. What images does he use to create a sense of horror?

3. Orwell calls the Burmese "natives," "coolies," and "Burmans." He describes their huts as "squalid" and the rice paddies as a "miry waste." What does this suggest about his view of Asia?

Connections across the Disciplines

1. How does Orwell's first-person narrative about an event differ from Richard Preston's third-person account? How does the writer's presence in the drama affect the focus of the essay?
2. Review Yi-Fu Tuan's "Chinese Space, American Space" (page 233) and Kenna and Lacy's "Communications Styles: Taiwan" (page 272). What do these writers reveal about the differences between Asians and Europeans? Can they shed light on the conflict Orwell encountered?

Writing Suggestions

1. *Critical Thinking:* Orwell relates an incident in which his role conflicted with his personal beliefs. Write a brief narrative about an event that placed you in a similar situation. Have your roles as parent, employee, manager, student, or friend caused you to act against your values? Have you ever been compelled to lie on behalf of others? In relating the story, clearly distinguish between the actions you took and your better judgment.
2. *Collaborative Writing:* Work with other students to create a short statement analyzing Orwell's message about political power and the nature of abusive governments. Have each member write a draft then work together to combine ideas into a single statement. If there are major differences, develop a comparison or division paper to contrast or list opinions.

BLENDING THE MODES

OLIVER SACKS

Oliver Sacks (1933–) was born in London and studied in Oxford before coming to the United States to complete his education. A professor of neurology, he has written several accounts of his patients who suffer from baffling and often disturbing neurological disorders. His 1974 book Awakenings *told the stories of patients recovering from comas and served as the basis of a motion picture. This section, taken from a book of the same title, tells the story of Dr. P., who developed prosopagnosia, an inability to connect perceptions with understanding.*

The Man Who Mistook His Wife for a Hat

OVERVIEW: *In this "tale"—a term he uses to describe his patients' histories—Sacks first describes a set of odd symptoms exhibited by a professor of music. He then recalls his own astonishment as the highly educated artist found it difficult to identify common objects. As you read notice how Sacks uses* comparison, analysis, definition, *and* cause and effect *to develop his narrative.*

1   Dr. P. was a musician of distinction, well-known for many years as a singer, and then, at the local School of Music, as a teacher. It was here, in relation to his students, that certain strange problems were first observed. Sometimes a student would present himself, and Dr. P. would not recognize him; or, specifically, would not recognise his face. The moment the student spoke, he would be recognised by his voice. Such incidents multiplied, causing embarrassment, perplexity, fear—and, sometimes, comedy. For not only did Dr. P. increasingly fail to see faces, but he saw faces when there were no faces to see: genially, Magoo-like, when in the street he might pat the heads of water hydrants and parking meters, taking these to be the heads of children; he would amiably address carved knobs on the furniture and be astounded when they did not reply. At first these odd mistakes were laughed off as jokes, not least by Dr. P. himself. Had he not always had a quirky sense of humour and been given to Zen-like paradoxes and jests? His musical powers were as dazzling as ever; he did not feel ill—he had never felt better; and the mistakes were so ludicrous—and so ingenious—that they could hardly be serious or betoken anything serious. The notion of there being "something the matter" did not emerge until some three years later,

when diabetes developed. Well aware that diabetes could affect his eyes, Dr. P. consulted an ophthalmologist, who took a careful history and examined his eyes closely. "There's nothing the matter with your eyes," the doctor concluded. "But there is trouble with the visual parts of your brain. You don't need my help, you must see a neurologist." And so, as a result of this referral, Dr. P. came to me.

It was obvious within a few seconds of meeting him that there was no   2
trace of dementia in the ordinary sense. He was a man of great cultivation and charm who talked well and fluently, with imagination and humour. I couldn't think why he had been referred to our clinic.

And yet there *was* something a bit odd. He faced me as he spoke, was   3
oriented towards me, and yet there was something the matter—it was difficult to formulate. He faced me with his *ears*, I came to think, but not with his eyes. These, instead of looking, gazing, at me, "taking me in," in the normal way, made sudden strange fixations—on my nose, on my right ear, down to my chin, up to my right eye—as if noting (even studying) these individual features, but not seeing my whole face, its changing expressions, "me," as a whole. I am not sure that I fully realised this at the time—there was just a teasing strangeness, some failure in the normal interplay of gaze and expression. He saw me, he *scanned* me, and yet . . .

"What seems to be the matter?" I asked him at length.   4

"Nothing that I know of," he replied with a smile, "but people seem to   5
think there's something wrong with my eyes."

"But *you* don't recognise any visual problems?"   6

"No, not directly, but I occasionally make mistakes."   7

I left the room briefly to talk with his wife. When I came back, Dr. P.   8
was sitting placidly by the window, attentive, listening rather than looking out. "Traffic," he said, "street sounds, distant trains—they make a sort of symphony, do they not? You know Honegger's *Pacific 234*?"

What a lovely man, I thought to myself. How can there be anything se-   9
riously the matter? Would he permit me to examine him?

"Yes, of course, Dr. Sacks."   10

I stilled my disquiet, his perhaps, too, in the soothing routine of a neu-   11
rological exam—muscle strength, coordination, reflexes, tone. . . . It was while examining his reflexes—a trifle abnormal on the left side—that the first bizarre experience occurred. I had taken off his left shoe and scratched the sole of his foot with a key—a frivolous-seeming but essential test of a reflex—and then, excusing myself to screw my ophthalmoscope together, left him to put on the shoe himself. To my surprise, a minute later, he had not done this.

12   "Can I help?" I asked.

13   "Help what? Help whom?"

14   "Help you put on your shoe."

15   "Ach," he said, "I had forgotten the shoe," adding, *sotto voce*, "The shoe? The shoe?" He seemed baffled.

16   "Your shoe," I repeated. "Perhaps you'd put it on."

17   He continued to look downwards, though not at the shoe, with an intense but misplaced concentration. Finally his gaze settled on his foot: "That is my shoe, yes?"

18   Did I mis-hear? Did he mis-see?

19   "My eyes," he explained, and put a hand to his foot. "*This* is my shoe, no?"

20   "No, it is not. That is your foot. *There* is your shoe."

21   "Ah! I thought that was my foot."

22   Was he joking? Was he mad? Was he blind? If this was one of his "strange mistakes," it was the strangest mistake I had ever come across.

23   I helped him on with his shoe (his foot), to avoid further complication. Dr. P. himself seemed untroubled, indifferent, maybe amused. I resumed my examination. His visual acuity was good: he had no difficulty seeing a pin on the floor, though sometimes he missed it if it was placed to his left.

24   He saw all right, but what did he see? I opened out a copy of the *National Geographic Magazine* and asked him to describe some pictures in it.

25   His responses here were very curious. His eyes would dart from one thing to another, picking up tiny features, individual features, as they had done with my face. A striking brightness, a colour, a shape would arrest his attention and elicit comment—but in no case did he get the scene-as-a-whole. He failed to see the whole, seeing only details, which he spotted like blips on a radar screen. He never entered into relation with the picture as a whole—never faced, so to speak, *its* physiognomy. He had no sense whatever of a landscape or scene.

26   I showed him the cover, an unbroken expanse of Sahara dunes.

27   "What do you see here?" I asked.

28   "I see a river," he said. "And a little guest-house with its terrace on the water. People are dining out on the terrace. I see coloured parasols here and there." He was looking, if it was "looking," right off the cover into mid-air and confabulating nonexistent features, as if the absence of features in the actual picture had driven him to imagine the river and the terrace and the coloured parasols.

29   I must have looked aghast, but he seemed to think he had done rather well. There was a hint of a smile on his face. He also appeared to have de-

cided that the examination was over and started to look around for his hat. He reached out his hand and took hold of his wife's head, tried to lift if off, to put it on. He had apparently mistaken his wife for a hat! His wife looked as if she was used to such things.

I could make no sense of what had occurred in terms of conventional   30
neurology (or neuropsychology). In some ways he seemed perfectly preserved, and in others absolutely, incomprehensibly devastated. How could he, on the one hand, mistake his wife for a hat and, on the other, function, as apparently he still did, as a teacher at the Music School?

I had to think, to see him again—and to see him in his own familiar   31
habitat, at home.

A few days later I called on Dr. P. and his wife at home, with the score of   32
the *Dichterliebe* in my briefcase (I knew he liked Schumann), and a variety of odd objects for the testing of perception. Mrs. P. showed me into a lofty apartment, which recalled fin-de-siècle Berlin. A magnificent old Bösendorfer stood in state in the centre of the room, and all around it were music stands, instruments, scores. . . . There were books, there were paintings, but the music was central. Dr. P. came in, a little bowed, and, distracted, advanced with outstretched hands to the grandfather clock, but, hearing my voice, corrected himself, and shook hands with me. We exchanged greetings and chatted a little of current concerts and performances. Diffidently, I asked him if he would sing.

"The *Dichterliebe!*" he exclaimed. "But I can no longer read music. You   33
will play them, yes?"

I said I would try. On that wonderful old piano even my playing sounded   34
right, and Dr. P. was an aged but infinitely mellow Fischer-Dieskau, combining a perfect ear and voice with the most incisive musical intelligence. It was clear that the Music School was not keeping him on out of charity.

Dr. P.'s temporal lobes were obviously intact: he had a wonderful musi-   35
cal cortex. What, I wondered, was going on in his parietal and occipital lobes, especially in those areas where visual processing occurred? I carry the Platonic solids in my neurological kit and decided to start with these.

"What is this?" I asked, drawing out the first one.   36
"A cube, of course."   37
"Now this?" I asked, brandishing another.   38
He asked if he might examine it, which he did swiftly and systemati-   39
cally: "A dodecahedron, of course. And don't bother with the others—I'll get the icosahedron, too."

Abstract shapes clearly presented no problems. What about faces? I took   40
out a pack of cards. All of these he identified instantly, including the jacks,

queens, kings, and the joker. But these, after all, are stylised designs, and it was impossible to tell whether he saw faces or merely patterns. I decided I would show him a volume of cartoons which I had in my briefcase. Here, again, for the most part, he did well. Churchill's cigar, Schnozzle's nose: as soon as he had picked out a key feature he could identify the face. But cartoons, again, are formal and schematic. It remained to be seen how he would do with real faces, realistically represented.

41   I turned on the television, keeping the sound off, and found an early Bette Davis film. A love scene was in progress. Dr. P. failed to identify the actress—but this could have been because she had never entered his world. What was more striking was that he failed to identify the expressions on her face or her partner's, though in the course of a single torrid scene these passed from sultry yearning through passion, surprise, disgust, and fury to a melting reconciliation. Dr. P. could make nothing of any of this. He was very unclear as to what was going on, or who was who or even what sex they were. His comments on the scene were positively Martian.

42   It was just possible that some of his difficulties were associated with the unreality of a celluloid, Hollywood world; and it occurred to me that he might be more successful in identifying faces from his own life. On the walls of the apartment there were photographs of his family, his colleagues, his pupils, himself. I gathered a pile of these together and, with some misgivings, presented them to him. What had been funny, or farcical, in relation to the movie, was tragic in relation to real life. By and large, he recognised nobody: neither his family, nor his colleagues, nor his pupils, nor himself. He recognised a portrait of Einstein because he picked up the characteristic hair and moustache; and the same thing happened with one or two other people. "Ach, Paul!" he said, when shown a portrait of his brother. "That square jaw, those big teeth—I would know Paul anywhere!" But was it Paul he recognised, or one or two of his features, on the basis of which he could make a reasonable guess as to the subject's identity? In the absence of obvious "markers," he was utterly lost. But it was not merely the cognition, the *gnosis*, at fault; there was something radically wrong with the whole way he proceeded. For he approached these faces—even of those near and dear—as if they were abstract puzzles or tests. He did not relate to them, he did not behold. No face was familiar to him, seen as a "thou," being just identified as a set of features, an "it." Thus, there was formal, but no trace of personal, gnosis. And with this went his indifference, or blindness, to expression. A face, to us, is a person looking out—we see, as it were, the person through his *persona*, his face. But for Dr. P. there was no *persona* in this sense—no outward *persona*, and no person within.

I had stopped at a florist on my way to his apartment and bought myself   43
an extravagant red rose for my buttonhole. Now I removed this and handed
it to him. He took it like a botanist or morphologist given a specimen, not
like a person given a flower.

"About six inches in length," he commented. "A convoluted red form   44
with a linear green attachment."

"Yes," I said encouragingly, "and what do you think it *is*, Dr. P.?"   45

"Not easy to say." He seemed perplexed. "It lacks the simple symme-   46
try of the Platonic solids, although it may have a higher symmetry of its
own. . . . I think this could be an inflorescence or flower."

"Could be?" I queried.   47

"Could be," he confirmed.   48

"Smell it," I suggested, and he again looked somewhat puzzled, as if I   49
had asked him to smell a higher symmetry. But he complied courteously,
and took it to his nose. Now, suddenly, he came to life.

"Beautiful!" he exclaimed. "An early rose. What a heavenly smell!" He   50
started to hum *"Die Rose, die Lillie . . ."* Reality, it seemed, might be conveyed by smell, not by sight.

I tried one final test. It was still a cold day, in early spring, and I had   51
thrown my coat and gloves on the sofa.

"What is this?" I asked, holding up a glove.   52

"May I examine it?" he asked, and, taking it from me, he proceeded to   53
examine it as he had examined the geometrical shapes.

"A continuous surface," he announced at last, "infolded on itself. It ap-   54
pears to have"—he hesitated—"five outpouchings, if this is the word."

"Yes," I said cautiously. "You have given me a description. Now tell me   55
what it is."

"A container of some sort?"   56

"Yes," I said, "and what would it contain?"   57

"It would contain its contents!" said Dr. P., with a laugh. "There are   58
many possibilities. It could be a change purse, for example, for coins of five
sizes. It could . . ."

I interrupted the barmy flow. "Does it not look familiar? Do you think it   59
might contain, might fit, a part of your body?"

No light of recognition dawned on his face.[1]   60

No child would have the power to see and speak of "a continuous sur-   61
face . . . infolded on itself," but any child, any infant, would immediately

---

[1] Later, by accident, he got it on, and exclaimed, "My God, it's a glove!" This was reminiscent of Kurt
Goldstein's patient "Lanuti," who could only recognise objects by trying to use them in action.

know a glove as a glove, see it as familiar, as going with a hand. Dr. P. didn't. He saw nothing as familiar. Visually, he was lost in a world of lifeless abstractions. Indeed, he did not have a real visual world, as he did not have a real visual self. He could speak about things, but did not see them face-to-face. Hughlings Jackson, discussing patients with aphasia and left-hemisphere lesions, says they have lost "abstract" and "propositional" thought—and compares them with dogs (or, rather, he compares dogs to patients with aphasia). Dr. P., on the other hand, functioned precisely as a machine functions. It wasn't merely that he displayed the same indifference to the visual world as a computer but—even more strikingly—he construed the world as a computer construes it, by means of key features and schematic relationships. The scheme might be identified—in an "identi-kit" way—without the reality being grasped at all.

62   The testing I had done so far told me nothing about Dr. P.'s inner world. Was it possible that his visual memory and imagination were still intact? I asked him to imagine entering one of our local squares from the north side, to walk through it, in imagination or in memory, and tell me the buildings he might pass as he walked. He listed the buildings on his right side, but none of those on his left. I then asked him to imagine entering the square from the south. Again he mentioned only those buildings that were on the right side, although these were the very buildings he had omitted before. Those he had "seen" internally before were not mentioned now; presumably, they were no longer "seen." It was evident that his difficulties with leftness, his visual field deficits, were as much internal as external, bisecting his visual memory and imagination.

63   What, at a higher level, of his internal visualisation? Thinking of the almost hallucinatory intensity with which Tolstoy visualises and animates his characters, I questioned Dr. P. about *Anna Karenina*. He could remember incidents without difficulty, had an undiminished grasp of the plot, but completely omitted visual characteristics, visual narrative, and scenes. He remembered the words of the characters but not their faces; and though, when asked, he could quote, with his remarkable and almost verbatim memory, the original visual descriptions, these were, it became apparent, quite empty for him and lacked sensorial, imaginal, or emotional reality. Thus, there was an internal agnosia as well.[2]

---

[2] I have often wondered about Helen Keller's visual descriptions, whether these, for all their eloquence, are somehow empty as well? Or whether, by the transference of images from the tactile to the visual, or, yet more extraordinarily, from the verbal and the metaphorical to the sensorial and the visual, she *did* achieve a power of visual imagery, even though her visual cortex had never been stimulated, di-

But this was only the case, it became clear, with certain sorts of visuali-   64
sation. The visualisation of faces and scenes, of visual narrative and
drama—this was profoundly impaired, almost absent. But the visualisation
of *schemata* was preserved, perhaps enhanced. Thus, when I engaged him in
a game of mental chess, he had no difficulty visualising the chessboard or
the moves—indeed, no difficulty in beating me soundly.

Luria said of Zazetsky that he had entirely lost his capacity to play   65
games but that his "vivid imagination" was unimpaired. Zazetsky and Dr. P.
lived in worlds which were mirror images of each other. But the saddest
difference between them was that Zazetsky, as Luria said, "fought to regain his lost faculties with the indomitable tenacity of the damned,"
whereas Dr. P. was not fighting, did not know what was lost, did not indeed
know that anything was lost. But who was more tragic, or who was more
damned—the man who knew it, or the man who did not?

When the examination was over, Mrs. P. called us to the table, where   66
there was coffee and a delicious spread of little cakes. Hungrily, hummingly,
Dr. P. started on the cakes. Swiftly, fluently, unthinkingly, melodiously, he
pulled the plates towards him and took this and that in a great gurgling
stream, an edible song of food, until, suddenly, there came an interruption:
a loud, peremptory rat-tat-tat at the door. Startled, taken aback, arrested
by the interruption, Dr. P. stopped eating and sat frozen, motionless, at the
table, with an indifferent, blind bewilderment on his face. He saw, but no
longer saw, the table; no longer perceived it as a table laden with cakes. His
wife poured him some coffee: the smell titillated his nose and brought him
back to reality. The melody of eating resumed.

How does he do anything? I wondered to myself. What happens when   67
he's dressing, goes to the lavatory, has a bath? I followed his wife into the
kitchen and asked her how, for instance, he managed to dress himself. "It's
just like the eating," she explained. "I put his usual clothes out, in all the
usual places, and he dresses without difficulty, singing to himself. He does
everything singing to himself. But if he is interrupted and loses the thread,
he comes to a complete stop, doesn't know his clothes—or his own body.
He sings all the time—eating songs, dressing songs, bathing songs, everything. He can't do anything unless he makes it a song."

While we were talking my attention was caught by the pictures on   68
the walls.

---

rectly, by the eyes? But in Dr. P.'s case it is precisely the cortex that was damaged, the organic prerequi-
site of all pictorial imagery. Interestingly and typically he no longer dreamed pictorially—the "message"
of the dream being conveyed in nonvisual terms.

69   "Yes," Mrs. P. said, "he was a gifted painter as well as a singer. The School exhibited his pictures every year."

70   I strolled past them curiously—they were in chronological order. All his earlier work was naturalistic and realistic, with vivid mood and atmosphere, but finely detailed and concrete. Then, years later, they became less vivid, less concrete, less realistic and naturalistic, but far more abstract, even geometrical and cubist. Finally, in the last paintings, the canvasses became nonsense, or nonsense to me—mere chaotic lines and blotches of paint. I commented on this to Mrs. P.

71   "Ach, you doctors, you're such Philistines!" she exclaimed. "Can you not see *artistic development*—how he renounced the realism of his earlier years, and advanced into abstract, nonrepresentational art?"

72   "No, that's not it," I said to myself (but forbore to say it to poor Mrs. P.). He had indeed moved from realism to nonrepresentation to the abstract, yet this was not the artist, but the pathology, advancing—advancing towards a profound visual agnosia, in which all powers of representation and imagery, all sense of the concrete, all sense of reality, were being destroyed. This wall of paintings was a tragic pathological exhibit, which belonged to neurology, not art.

73   And yet, I wondered, was she not partly right? For there is often a struggle, and sometimes, even more interestingly, a collusion between the powers of pathology and creation. Perhaps, in his cubist period, there might have been both artistic and pathological development, colluding to engender an original form; for as he lost the concrete, so he might have gained in the abstract, developing a greater sensitivity to all the structural elements of line, boundary, contour—an almost Picasso-like power to see, and equally depict, those abstract organisations embedded in, and normally lost in, the concrete. . . . Though in the final pictures, I feared, there was only chaos and agnosia.

74   We returned to the great music room, with the Bösendorfer in the centre, and Dr. P. humming the last torte.

75   "Well, Dr. Sacks," he said to me. "You find me an interesting case, I perceive. Can you tell me what you find wrong, make recommendations?"

76   "I can't tell you what I find wrong," I replied, "but I'll say what I find right. You are a wonderful musician, and music is your life. What I would prescribe, in a case such as yours, is a life which consists entirely of music. Music has been the centre, now make it the whole, of your life."

77   This was four years ago—I never saw him again, but I often wondered about how he apprehended the world, given his strange loss of image, visuality, and the perfect preservation of a great musicality. I think that music,

for him, had taken the place of image. He had no body-image, he had body-music: this is why he could move and act as fluently as he did, but came to a total confused stop if the "inner music" stopped. And equally with the outside, the world . . .[3]

In The World as Representation and Will, Schopenhauer speaks of music as "pure will." How fascinated he would have been by Dr. P., a man who had wholly lost the world as representation, but wholly preserved it as music or will.   78

And this, mercifully, held to the end—for despite the gradual advance   79
of his disease (a massive tumor or degenerative process in the visual parts of his brain) Dr. P. lived and taught music to the last days of his life.

Understanding Meaning

1. How does Sacks *describe* Dr. P.'s initial symptoms? What led Dr. P. to seek medical help?
2. What is prosopagnosia? How does Sacks demonstrate its effects?
3. What is Sacks trying to tell readers about how the brain connects perceptions to meaning? Does he use the plight of one patient to demonstrate how our brains operate normally?
4. What did the glove test reveal about Dr. P.'s condition?
5. How does Sacks explain how a person who failed to distinguish his hat from his wife or his shoe from his foot could continue to teach a complex subject like music?
6. *Critical Thinking:* On page 90 Sacks presented "with some misgivings" family pictures for Dr. P. to identify. Why was he reluctant to administer this test? Does this suggest that even doctors, like family members, prefer to deny the seriousness of a patient's condition?

Evaluating Strategy

1. Sacks organizes his writing in a format standard to scientific and medical discourse. He *describes* symptoms, and then provides an analysis. Is this method easy for general readers to follow?
2. What role does Sacks play in the narrative?

---

[3] Thus, as I learned later from his wife, though he could not recognise his students if they sat still, if they were merely "images," he might suddenly recognise them if they *moved*. "That's Karl," he would cry. "I know his movements, his body-music."

3. *Other Modes:* What parts of the narrative include *description, comparison, analysis, definition,* and *cause and effect?* What does the use of these modes reveal about the scientific methods Sacks employs to examine a patient and determine his condition?

Appreciating Language

1. What reaction did you have to Sacks's level of language? Did you find his use of scientific terminology a barrier to meaning, or could you understand much of it through context?
2. Look up the words *dementia, parietal lobe, ophthalmologist, gnosis,* and *persona.*
3. Can a reader understand the *thesis* of Sacks's narrative without knowing the definitions of *ophthalmoscope, fin-de-siècle,* or *empirical?*
4. In explaining some of Dr. P.'s baffling observations, Sacks describes them as being "Martian." How does this metaphor help a general reader grasp the effect of this disorder?

Connections across the Disciplines

1. How does Sacks's role as doctor compare to the role George Orwell plays in "Shooting an Elephant" (page 78)? Do they both strive to objectively observe their subjects?
2. What role does close observation play in the narrative? How does Sacks embody the "look again, look again" approach described by Samuel Scudder (page 47)?

Writing Suggestions

1. Write a few paragraphs relating an incident in which you observed or encountered someone's puzzling behavior. Use detailed observations to share with readers the actions and statements you found intriguing, bizarre, or frightening.
2. *Critical Writing:* Sacks tells his patient he cannot find out what is wrong and urges him to accept what is right and make music the whole of his life. Did Sacks fail as a physician because he could not "cure" Dr. P.? Write a short paper in response to the assertion that people expect too much from doctors.
3. *Collaborative Writing:* Work with other students to generate a one-paragraph *definition* of prosopagnosia based on the information provided in Sacks's article. Read the paragraph aloud to the group, and have each member comment on its accuracy.

WRITING BEYOND THE CLASSROOM

FEDERAL BUREAU OF INVESTIGATION

At 12:30 p.m. on November 22, 1963, President John F. Kennedy was assassinated in Dallas, Texas. An hour and a half later a twenty-four-year-old man named Lee Harvey Oswald was arrested following a scuffle in a movie theater. Oswald was suspected of murdering the president and a Dallas police officer. Witnesses reported seeing Oswald taking a long package into the Texas School Book Depository, the building where he was employed, overlooking the site of the assassination. In the early hours of November 23, Oswald was charged with murder and interrogated by Federal Bureau of Investigation (FBI) agents.

Interrogation of Lee Harvey Oswald

OVERVIEW: *This FBI report records statements made by Lee Harvey Oswald in response to questions and summarizes his account of his movements on November 22. Notice that the writer uses simple, direct language free of figurative expressions or personal responses to create an objective, fact-driven account.*[1]

LEE HARVEY OSWALD was interviewed by Captain J. W. FRITZ, Homicide and Robbery Bureau, Dallas Police Department. OSWALD was advised of the identity of SA JAMES W. BOOKHOUT, and his capacity as a Special Agent of the Federal Bureau of Investigation. He was informed of his right to an attorney, that any statement he might make could be used against him in a court of law, and that any statement which he might make must be free and voluntary. He furnished the following information in the presence of T. J. NULLY, U.S. Secret Service; DAVID B. GRANT, Secret Service; ROBERT I. NASH, United States Marshall; and Detectives BILLY L. SENKEL and FAY M. TURNER of the Homicide and Robbery Bureau, Dallas Police Department.

1

Following his departure from the Texas School Book Depository, he boarded a city bus to his residence and obtained transfer upon departure

2

---

[1] This document contains neither recommendations nor conclusions of the FBI. It was recorded by Special Agent James W. Bookhout in Dallas, Texas on November 23, 1963 and dictated on November 24, 1963.

from the bus. He stated that officers at the time of arresting him took his transfer out of his pocket.

3 OSWALD advised that he had only one post office box which was at Dallas, Texas. He denied bringing any package to work on the morning of November 22, 1963. He stated that he was not in the process of fixing up his apartment and he denied telling WESLEY FRAZIER that the purpose of his visit to Irving, Texas, on the night of November 21, 1963, was to obtain some curtain rods from MRS. RUTH PAINE.

4 OSWALD stated that it was not exactly true as recently stated by him that he rode a bus from his place of employment to his residence on November 22, 1963. He stated actually he did board a city bus at his place of employment but that after about a block or two, due to traffic congestion, he left the bus and rode a city cab to his apartment on North Beckley. He recalled that at the time of getting into the cab, some lady looked in and asked the driver to call her a cab. He stated that he might have made some remarks to the cab driver merely for the purpose of passing the time of day at that time. He recalled that his fare was approximately 85 cents. He stated that after arriving at his apartment, he changed his shirt and trousers because they were dirty. He described his dirty clothes as being a reddish colored, long sleeved, shirt with a button-down collar and gray colored trousers. He indicated that he had placed these articles of clothing in the lower drawer of his dresser.

5 OSWALD stated that on November 22, 1963, he had eaten lunch in the lunch room at the Texas School Book Depository, alone, but recalled possibly two Negro employees walking through the room during this period. He stated possibly one of these employees was called "Junior" and the other was a short individual whose name he could not recall but whom he would be able to recognize. He stated that his lunch had consisted of a cheese sandwich and an apple which he had obtained at MRS. RUTH PAINE'S residence in Irving, Texas, upon his leaving for work that morning.

6 OSWALD stated that MRS. PAINE receives no pay for keeping his wife and children at her residence. He stated that their presence in MRS. PAINE'S residence is a good arrangement for her because of her language interest, indicating that his wife speaks Russian and MRS. PAINE is interested in the Russian language.

7 OSWALD denied having kept a rifle in MRS. PAINE'S garage at Irving, Texas, but stated that he did have certain articles stored in her garage, consisting of two sea bags, a couple of suitcases, and several boxes of kitchen articles and also kept his clothes at MRS. PAINE'S residence. He stated that all of the articles in MRS. PAINE'S garage had been brought there about September, 1963, from New Orleans, Louisiana.

OSWALD stated that he has had no visitors at his apartment on North   8
Beckley.

OSWALD stated that he has no receipts for purchase of any guns and   9
has never ordered any guns and does not own a rifle nor has he ever possessed
a rifle.

OSWALD denied that he is a member of the Communist Party.   10

OSWALD stated that he purchased a pistol, which was taken off him by   11
police officers November 22, 1963, about six months ago. He declined to
state where he had purchased it.

OSWALD stated that he arrived about July, 1962, from USSR and   12
was interviewed by the FBI at Fort Worth, Texas. He stated that he felt
they overstepped their bounds and had used various tactics in interviewing him.

He further complained that on interview of RUTH PAINE by the FBI   13
regarding his wife, that he felt that his wife was intimidated.

OSWALD stated that he desired to contact Attorney ABT, New York   14
City, indicating that ABT was the attorney who had defended the Smith
Act case about 1949–1950. He stated that he does not know Attorney ABT
personally. Captain FRITZ advised OSWALD that arrangements would be
immediately made whereby he could call Attorney ABT.

OSWALD stated that prior to coming to Dallas from New Orleans he   15
had resided at a furnished apartment at 4706 Magazine Street, New Orleans,
Louisiana. While in New Orleans, he had been employed by WILLIAM B.
RILEY Company, 640 Magazine Street, New Orleans.

OSWALD stated that he has nothing against President JOHN F. KEN-   16
NEDY personally; however in view of the present charges against him, he
did not desire to discuss this phase further.

OSWALD stated that he could not agree to take a polygraph examina-   17
tion without the advice of counsel. He added that in the past he has refused
to take polygraph examinations.

OSWALD stated that he is a member of the American Civil Liberties   18
Union and added that MRS. RUTH PAINE was also a member of same.

With regard to Selective Service card in the possession of OSWALD   19
bearing photograph of OSWALD and the name of ALEX JAMES HIDELL,
OSWALD admitted that he carried this Selective Service card but declined
to state that he wrote the signature of ALEX J. HIDELL appearing on same.
He further declined to state the purpose of carrying same or any use he has
made of same.

OSWALD stated that an address book in his possession contains the   20
names of various Russian immigrants residing in Dallas, Texas, whom he
has visited with.

21   OSWALD denied shooting President JOHN F. KENNEDY on November 22, 1963, and added that he did not know that Governor JOHN CONNALLY had been shot and denied any knowledge concerning this incident.

Understanding Meaning

1. What is the writer's goal in this narrative?
2. Does the writer seek to imply Oswald's guilt in any way? What attitude, if any, does the writer project toward his subject?
3. *Critical Thinking: Analyze* this report in light of your own knowledge of the Kennedy assassination. How is looking at an actual document different from reading a narrative written by a historian or journalist?

Evaluating Strategy

1. How does the writer structure the narrative?
2. What does the agent do to create as much objectivity as possible?
3. *Other Modes:* Where does the agent use *description* in his report to create a picture of Lee Harvey Oswald? How objective is it?
4. *Critical Thinking:* How is writing an internal document to a specific reader different from addressing a general audience in a book or magazine article?

Appreciating Language

1. At first glance this report appears to break all the "rules" of good writing. It is flat, colorless, and repetitive. Why is this kind of writing acceptable in this context? Why would the use of lively, colorful imagery defeat the purpose of the report?
2. *Critical Thinking:* Examine this report the way a prospective defense attorney might, looking for evidence of prejudice against the accused. Can you find any examples?

Connections across the Disciplines

1. In "The Man Who Mistook His Wife for a Hat" (page 86) a professional records observations about his subject. Would Sacks's notes or academic reports to colleagues likely read much like this one?
2. How does the text of this report by a law enforcement officer differ from the observations made by George Orwell in "Shooting an Elephant" (page 78)?

Writing Suggestions

1. Imagine you are writing a highly factual novel based on the Kennedy assassination. Rewrite a passage from this report using dialogue, gestures, descriptions. Add the agent's tone of voice, describe Oswald's facial expression, tell readers about the furniture in the room, and create a sense of tension, fatigue, or anger.

2. *Collaborative Writing:* Working with three or four students, write a purely objective report of the incident Nathan McCall describes during the assembly in "The Lesson" (page 61). Imagine your report will be read by the school board and several attorneys. Eliminate McCall's personal reflections, and state simply and directly in objective terms what occurred. Read the text aloud, and ask group members to identify statements that are subjective or make judgments without proof.

WALTER LORD

Walter Lord (1917–2002) was born in Baltimore and studied history at Princeton University. He entered Yale Law School, but his studies were interrupted by World War II. After serving with the Office of Strategic Services, he returned to law school. He served as editor in chief of a business information service but soon turned to writing history. He tracked down and interviewed the sixty-three living survivors of the Titanic *and studied the ship's records to produce* A Night to Remember, *a minute-by-minute account of the doomed luxury liner. Lord's style of blending fact with tense human drama made his book a best-seller. His later books include* Day of Infamy, *about the Japanese attack on Pearl Harbor, and* Incredible Victory, *which tells the story of the Battle of Midway.*

The Reconstructed Logbook of the Titanic

OVERVIEW: A Night to Remember *tells the dramatic story of the famous liner that sank on its maiden voyage in 1912. Considered "unsinkable" by its builders, the* Titanic *had only twenty lifeboats for its 2,207 passengers. Rescuers located 705 survivors, many of them picked up in half-empty boats. To assist readers in following the chronology of events, Lord placed a reconstructed logbook of the ship in the appendix of his book.*

1   *April 10, 1912*

 12 noon | Leaves Southampton dock; narrowly escapes collision with American liner *New York.*

 7:00 P.M. | Stops at Cherbourg for passengers.

 9:00 P.M. | Leaves Cherbourg for Queenstown.

April 11, 1912

 12:30 P.M. | Stops at Queenstown for passengers and mail. One crewman deserts.

 2:00 P.M. | Leaves Queenstown for New York, carrying 1316 passengers and 891 crew.

April 14, 1912

 9:00 A.M. | *Caronia* reports ice Latitude 42°N from Longitude 49° to 51°W.

10 1:42 P.M. | *Baltic* reports ice Latitude 41°51′N from Longitude 49°52′W.

 1:45 P.M. | *Amerika* reports ice Latitude 41°27′N, Longitude 50°8′W.

 7:00 P.M. | Temperature 43°.

 7:30 P.M. | Temperature 39°.

 7:30 P.M. | *Californian* reports ice Latitude 42°3′N, Longitude 49°9′W.

 9:00 P.M. | Temperature 33°.

 9:30 P.M. | Second Officer Lightoller warns carpenter and engine room to watch fresh water supply—may freeze up; warns crow's-nest to watch for ice.

 9:40 P.M. | *Mesaba* reports ice Latitude 42°N to 41°25′N, Longitude 49° to 50°30′W.

10:00 P.M.	Temperature 32°.
10:30 P.M.	Temperature of sea down to 31°.
11:00 P.M.	*Californian* warns of ice, but cut off before she gives location.
11:40 P.M.	Collides with iceberg Latitude 41°46′N, Longitude 50°14′W.

20

April 15, 1912

12:05 A.M.	Orders given to uncover the boats, muster the crew and passengers.
12:15 A.M.	First wireless call for help.
12:45 A.M.	First rocket fired.
12:45 A.M.	First boat, No. 7, lowered.
1:40 A.M.	Last rocket fired.
2:05 A.M.	Last boat, Collapsible D, lowered.
2:10 A.M.	Last wireless signals sent.
2:18 A.M.	Lights fail.
2:20 A.M.	Ship founders.
3:30 A.M.	*Carpathia's* rockets sighted by boats.
4:10 A.M.	First boat, No. 2, picked up by *Carpathia*.
8:30 A.M.	Last boat, No. 12, picked up.
8:50 A.M.	*Carpathia* heads for New York with 705 survivors.

30

Understanding Meaning

1. What is the goal of presenting events in a timeline?
2. How does this log help readers to follow events in a complex story such as a disaster involving hundreds of people?
3. Why would this log be valuable to a board of inquiry investigating the disaster?
4. *Critical Thinking:* According to the log, it took forty minutes to launch the first lifeboat. Although the crew had more than two and one-half hours to evacuate the ship, fifteen hundred people were lost. Do these facts alone raise suspicion of incompetence?

Evaluating Strategy

1. Can such a log as this distort events by emphasizing time relationships instead of causal relationships?
2. How does a writer deal with events that do not have a clear time reference?

Appreciating Language

1. Why is word choice important in brief notations such as those in a log?
2. Can you locate any words that are not objective?

Connections across the Disciplines

1. How is Lord's timeline similar to the FBI report on Lee Harvey Oswald?
2. Would a timeline assist readers in understanding narratives such as Richard Preston's "Ebola River" (page 73)? Why or why not?

Writing Suggestions

1. Reconstruct a log of the actions you took yesterday. Consider the problems that arise in attempting to explain events that did not occur in a specific time frame.
2. *Collaborative Writing:* Working with a group of students, read the log and discuss your impressions. Should a luxury liner be able to safely evacuate its passengers in two hours? Write a paragraph summarizing your group's discussion.

STRATEGIES FOR WRITING NARRATION

1. **Determine your purpose.** Does your narrative have a goal beyond simply telling a story? What details or evidence do readers need to accept your point of view?

2. **Define your role.** As a narrator you can write in first person, either as the major participant in or a witness to events. You can use third person for greater objectivity, inserting personal opinions if desired.

3. **Consider your audience.** What are your readers' needs and expectations? How much background material will you have to supply? Which events will the audience find most impressive?

4. **Review the discipline or writing situation.** If you are writing a narrative report as an employee or agent of an organization, study samples to determine how you should present your story.

5. **Identify the beginning and end of your narrative.** You may find it helpful to place background information in a separate foreword or introduction and limit comments on the ending to an afterword. This can allow the body of the paper to focus on a specific chain of events.

6. **Select a chronological pattern.** After reviewing the context of the narrative, determine which pattern would be most effective for your purpose—using a straight chronology, opening with a mid- or turning point, or presenting the final events first.

7. **Make use of transitional statements.** To prevent readers from becoming confused, make clear transitional statements to move the narrative. Statements such as "later that day" or "two weeks later" can help readers follow the passage of time. Clear transitions are important if you alter chronological order with flashbacks and flash-forwards.

SUGGESTED TOPICS FOR WRITING NARRATION
General Assignments

Write a narrative on any of the following topics. Your narrative may contain passages making use of other modes, such as definition or comparison. Choose your narrative structure carefully, and avoid including minor details that add little to the story line. Use flashbacks and flash-forwards carefully. Transitional statements, paragraphing, and line breaks can help clarify changes in the chronology.

1. Your first job interview
2. Moving into your first dorm room or apartment

3. The events that led you to take a major action—quit a job, end a relationship, or join an organization
4. A sporting event you played in or observed—you may wish to limit the narrative to a single play
5. A first date
6. An event that placed you in danger
7. An experience that led you to change your opinion about a friend or family member
8. A typical day at school or your job
9. The worst day of your college career
10. An accident or medical emergency—focus on creating a clear, minute-by-minute chronology

Writing in Context

1. Imagine you are participating in an experiment. Psychologists ask you to write a journal recording your experiences in college. Specifically, the researchers are interested in measuring stressors students face—deadlines, lack of sleep, conflicts with jobs, financial pressures. Write a diary for a week, detailing instances when you experience stress. Be as objective as possible.
2. Write a letter to a friend relating the events of a typical day in college. Select details your friend will find humorous or interesting.
3. Preserve on paper a favorite story told by your grandparents or other relatives. Include background details and identify characters.
4. You are accused of committing a crime last Tuesday. To establish an alibi, create a detailed log to the best of your recollection of the day's events and your movements.

STUDENT PAPER: NARRATION

This paper was written in response to the following assignment:

> Write a 350- to 500-word narrative essay based on personal experience or observation. Limit your topic, select details, and use figurative language to recreate the sights, sounds, smells, and moods you experienced.

Spare Change

As I stepped off the San Diego Trolley, I knew that I was going to embark on a great adventure. Tijuana. As I neared the entrance to cross the border there was a priest with a plastic bowl and a picture of some kids. The caption on the picture said, "feed Tijuana's homeless children." Yeah, right, I thought to myself, just another scam, this guy probably isn't even a priest. [1]

Tijuana. Just the name of the city brings back a distinct smell. A smell that you will only know if you have been there. It only takes one time and you can relate to what I am saying. A smell that will permeate my olfactory senses forever. A thousand different scents compounded into one. The smell of fast food, sweat, sewage, and tears. [2]

As you cross the border the first thing that hits you is the smell I mentioned earlier. Then you witness the first of many human sufferings you will encounter. The man with no legs begging for money, the woman with her children huddled around her with an old grease stained wax cup hovering in the air waving at you with the eyes of poverty, the children dressed in Salvation Army hand-me-downs, ripped pants and mismatched shoes surrounding you, begging for money. Their hands searching your pockets for change, a wallet, anything that will get them food for the night. [3]

Once I got past the few blocks of human suffering and handed out all I could, I wandered upon a busy little plaza. This place is reasonably clean and clear of trash, you hear the deafening sounds of the music from the nearby clubs, and see dozens of young drunken Americans stumbling around. A lot of tourists are carrying what seems like five bags each and a distressed look, the kind you get when you have [4] been shopping all day long. The children, a score of them holding out these little packs of colored Chiclets, a local gum, sold to you at any price you can haggle them down to. It's pretty pathetic that you should feel the need to haggle over the price of gum with a child, but this is Tijuana. Americans and tourists have come from all over the world to haggle here. That is just the way it is, the way it always will be.

5   As I continued my journey, I reached a bridge. The bridge was horrible. Along the sides there was trash and rubbish. Towards the midspan of the bridge, I experienced one of the most touching moments of my life, one of those happy ones where you don't know if you should shed a tear from happiness or out of despair. There was this little child playing the accordion and another one playing a guitar. He was singing a Spanish song, well actually it sounded like he was screaming as his compadre was strumming the guitar. He had a little cup in front of him, and I threw a coin into it. He just smiled and kept singing. I turned around and left, but this time as I passed the priest I filled his plastic bowl with the rest of my money.

Questions for Review and Revision

1.   This student was assigned a 350- to 500-word narrative in a composition class. How successfully does this paper meet this goal?
2.   How does the student open and close the narrative? Does the opening grab attention? Does the conclusion make a powerful statement?
3.   What devices does the student use to advance the chronology?
4.   Most writers focus on visual details. This student includes the senses of sound and smell as well. How effective is this approach?
5.   The narrative switches from first person ("I") to second person ("you")— should this be corrected? How does it affect the focus of the narrative?
6.   Read the paper aloud. What changes would you make? Can you detect passages that would benefit from revision or rewording?

Writing Suggestions

1.   Using this essay as a model, write a short narrative about a trip that exposed you to another culture. Try to recapture the sights, sounds, smells that characterized the experience.

2. *Collaborative Writing:* Ask a group of students to assign a grade to this essay then explain their evaluations. What strengths and weaknesses does the group identify?

NARRATION CHECKLIST

Before submitting your paper, review these points.

1. Does the narrative have a clear focus?

2. Can readers follow the chronology of events?

3. Do you write in a consistent tense or time? Does your paper contain illogical shifts from past to present?

4. Does the narrative flow evenly, or is it bogged down with unnecessary detail?

5. Does your narrative maintain a consistent point of view? Do you switch from first to third person without reason?

6. Does your narrative suit your purpose, reader, discipline, or situation?

 Companion Web Site

See **http://sundance.heinle.com** for information on writing narration.

 InfoTrac® College Edition

For additional reading go to InfoTrac College edition, your online research library, at **http://infotrac.thomsonlearning.com.**

- Enter the search term "narration" using Keywords.
- Enter the name of an author you read in this chapter using Keywords.
- Enter a theme or idea your class discussed using Keywords.

3

Description

WHAT IS DESCRIPTION?

Description captures the essence of a person, place, object, or condition through sensory details. Nearly all writing requires description. Before you can narrate events, compare, classify, or analyze, you must provide readers with a clear picture of your subject. Dramatists open plays with set and character descriptions. Homicide detectives begin reports with descriptions of crime scenes. Before proposing expanding an airport, the writers of a government study must first describe congestion in the existing facility.

The way writers select and present details depends on context. Carl T. Rowan's article "Unforgettable Miss Bessie" (page 137), published in *Reader's Digest,* describes an influential teacher to a general audience reading for human interest:

> She was only about five feet tall and probably never weighed more than 110 pounds, but Miss Bessie was a towering presence in the classroom. She was the only woman tough enough to make me read *Beowulf* and think for a few foolish days that I liked it. From 1938 to 1942, when I attended Bernard High School in McMinnville, Tenn., she taught me English, history, civics—and a lot more than I realized.

Rowan's description includes details about the teacher's height and weight, the courses she taught, and the name of the school. But Rowan's focus is her "presence" and the impact she had in shaping his life. Writing in the first person, Rowan places himself in the essay to build rapport with his readers.

This intimate portrait contrasts sharply with the description of Lee Harvey Oswald included in an FBI report:

> OSWALD was advised questions were intended to obtain his complete physical description and background. Upon repetition of the question as to his present employment, he furnished same without further discussion.

Race	White
Sex	Male
Date of Birth	October 18, 1939
Place of Birth	New Orleans, Louisiana
Height	5'9"
Weight	140
Hair	Medium brown, worn medium length, needs haircut
Eyes	Blue-gray

Aside from noting that Oswald needed a haircut, the FBI agent never offers personal impressions and presents his observations in cold, factual statements. Unlike Rowan, who is writing to a general audience reading for entertainment, the FBI agent is preparing a report for a specialized reader who will use this information in a criminal investigation. The writer's statements will be scrutinized by investigators and attorneys. The introduction of any personal impressions or colorful phrases would be unprofessional and subject to challenge.

The differences between the descriptions of Miss Bessie and Lee Harvey Oswald illustrate the differences between *objective* and *subjective* description.

Objective and Subjective Description

The purpose of *objective* description is to inform readers by accurate reporting of factual details. Its language attempts to provide photographic realism of what people, places, things, and conditions are like. Research papers, business and government reports, and newspaper accounts of current events are objective. Objective description is effective when the writer's purpose is to present readers with information required to make an evaluation or decision. In many instances, it does not attempt to arouse a reader's interest since it is often written in response to reader demand.

Objective description focuses on facts and observable detail. *The New Illustrated Columbia Encyclopedia*, for example, offers readers this description of Chicago:

The second largest city in the country and the heart of a metropolitan area of almost 7 million people, it is the commercial, financial, industrial, and cultural center for a vast region and a great mid-continental shipping port. It is a port of entry; a major Great Lakes port, located at the junction of the St. Lawrence Seaway with the Mississippi River system; the busiest air center in the country; and an important rail and highway hub.

In contrast to objective description, *subjective* description creates impressions through sensory details and imagery. Short stories, novels, essays, and opinion pieces use highly personal sensory details to create an individual sense of the subject. Instead of photographic realism, subjective description paints scenes, creates moods, or generates emotional responses. Providing accurate information is less important than giving readers a "feel" for the subject. In a subjective description of a car, the color, shape, ride, and the memories it evokes for the writer are more important than facts about horsepower, base price, and fuel efficiency.

Attempting to capture his view of Chicago, John Rechy compares the city to an expectant mother:

> You get the impression that once Chicago was like a constantly pregnant woman, uneasy in her pregnancy because she has miscarried so often. After its rise as a frontier town, plush bigtime madams, adventurers, and soon the titanic rise of the millionaires, the city's subsequent soaring population—all gave more than a hint that Chicago might easily become America's First City. But that title went unquestionably to New York. Brazenly, its skyscrapers, twice as tall as any in the Midwest city, symbolically invaded the sky. Chicago, in squat self-consciousness, bowed out. It became the Second City . . .

Rechy uses imagery and unconventional syntax to create a highly personalized view of the city. In the context of this essay written for a literary magazine, impression is more important than accuracy. Exact number and date statistics are irrelevant to his purpose. The writer's purpose in subjective description is to share a vision, not provide information.

Many writers blend the realism of objective description with the impressionistic details of subjective description to create striking portraits, such as Russell Miller's depiction of Chicago's State Street:

> Summer 1983. State Street, "that great street," is a dirty, desolate, and depressing street for most of its length. It runs straight and potholed from the Chicago city line, up through the black ghettos of the South Side, an aching wasteland of derelict factories pitted with broken windows, instant slum apartment blocks, vandalized playgrounds encased in chain-linked fencing, and vacant lots where weeds sprout gamely from the rubble and from the rusting hulks of abandoned automobiles. Those shops that remain open are protected by barricades of steel mesh. One or two men occupy every doorway, staring sullenly onto the street, heedless of the taunting cluster of skyscrapers to the north.

In this passage, details such as "vandalized playgrounds" are interwoven with expressions granting human emotions to inanimate objects, so wastelands are "aching" and skyscrapers "taunting." Blended descriptions such as this one are useful in strengthening subjective views with factual details. This style of writing is used by journalists and freelance authors writing to audiences who may be reading for both enjoyment and information.

Whether objective or subjective, all descriptive writing communicates through detail—through a careful selection and clear presentation of facts or impressions that serve the writer's purpose and impress readers.

The Language of Description

Words have power. The impact descriptive writing makes depends on *diction*, the writer's choice of words. Whether your description is objective, subjective, or a blend, the words you select should be accurate, appropriate, and effective. In choosing words, consider your purpose, readers, and discipline.

Use Words Precisely

Many words are easily confused. Should a patient's heart rate be monitored "continually," meaning at regular intervals such as once an hour, or "continuously," meaning without interruption? Is the city council planning to "adapt" or "adopt" a handgun ban? Some of the numerous pairs of frequently misused words follow:

allusion   An indirect reference
illusion   A false or imaginary impression

infer   To interpret
imply   To suggest

conscience   A sense of moral or ethical conduct
conscious   To be awake or aware of something

principle   Basic law, rule, or concept
principal   Something or someone important, as in school principal

When writing, consult a dictionary or review the usage section of a handbook to ensure you are using the correct word.

Use Concrete Words

Concrete words are direct and understandable. They communicate more information and make clearer impressions than vague, abstract words:

ABSTRACT	CONCRETE
motor vehicle	pickup truck
modest suburban home	three-bedroom colonial
human resources contingent	employees
protective headgear	helmet
residential rental unit	apartment

Eliminate Unnecessary Words

Avoid cluttering your description with words that add little or no meaning:

WORDY	IMPROVED
at this point in time	now
few in number	few
consensus of opinion	consensus
strike situation	strike
thunderstorm activity	thunderstorms
winter months	winter

Avoid Diluted Verbs

Verbs convey action. Do not dilute their meaning by turning them into wordy phrases that weaken their impact and obscure the action they describe:

DILUTED VERB	IMPROVED
achieve purification	purify
render an examination of	examine
are found to be in agreement	agree
conduct an analysis	analyze

Avoid Clichés and Inflated Phrases

Description uses figurative language such as *similes* (comparisons using *like* or *as*) and *metaphors* (direct comparisons). To be effective, figurative language should create fresh and appropriate impressions. Avoid *clichés* (overly used expressions) and inflated phrases that distort through exaggeration:

CLICHÉ/INFLATED	IMPROVED
crack of dawn	dawn
pretty as a picture	attractive
straight from the shoulder	direct
as plain as day	obvious
terrible disaster	disaster
in the whole world today	today

Understand the Roles of Denotation and Connotation

All words *denote* or indicate a particular meaning. The words *home, residence,* and *domicile* all refer to where a person lives. Each has the same basic meaning or denotation, but the word *home* evokes personal associations of family, friends, and favorite belongings. *Domicile,* on the other hand, has a legalistic and official sound devoid of personal associations.

Connotations are implied or suggested meanings. Connotations often reflect the writer's purpose and opinion. A resort cabin can be described as a "rustic cottage" or a "seedy shack" depending on a person's point of view. The person who spends little money and shops for bargains can be praised for being "frugal" or ridiculed for being "cheap."

The following pairs of words have the same basic meaning or denotation, but their connotations create different impressions:

young	inexperienced
traditional	old-fashioned
brave	reckless
casual	sloppy
the homeless	bums
residential care facility	nursing home
unintended landing	plane crash

Connotations shape meaning and, in many contexts, can be used to express opinion and influence readers. Depending on your point of view, graffiti can be seen as a "prank" or an "act of vandalism."

Be Conscious of Ethical Issues with Connotation   Words can be selected to dramatize or minimize an event or situation. This raises ethical issues. Because words such as *accident* and *explosion* might alarm the public, nuclear regulations substitute the terms *event* and *rapid disassembly*. When the space shuttle *Challenger* exploded in midair, the National Aeronautics and Space Administration (NASA) referred to a "major malfunction." Writers in all disciplines have to weigh the moral implications of the words they choose.

STRATEGIES FOR READING DESCRIPTIONS

While reading the descriptions in this chapter, keep these questions in mind.

Meaning

1. What is the author's goal—to inform, enlighten, share personal observations, or provide information demanded by others? What is the writer's role? Is he or she writing from a personal or professional perspective?
2. What is the intended audience—general or specific readers? How much knowledge does the author assume his or her readers have? Are technical terms defined? Does the description appear to have a special focus?
3. What is the nature of the discipline, discourse community, or writing situation? Is the description objective or subjective? Does the original source of the description (newsmagazine, scientific journal, or government document) reveal something about context?

Strategy

1. What details does the writer select? Does he or she seem to ignore or minimize some details?
2. Does the description seek to establish a dominant impression? Which details support this impression?
3. How are details organized? Does the author use a particular method of grouping observations?

Language

1. What level of language does the writer employ? Are technical terms used without explanation?
2. Does the language include connotations that shade reader reaction to the subject?

JONATHAN SCHELL

Jonathan Schell is a journalist and antinuclear activist who has written extensively about atomic weapons and the problems of nuclear proliferation and disarmament. In 1981 he published The Fate of the Earth, *which called for the abolition of nuclear weapons. His other books include* The Time of Illusion *and* The Gift of Time. *Schell was living six blocks from the World Trade Center when it collapsed on September 11, 2001.*

Letter from Ground Zero

OVERVIEW: *This essay appeared in* The Nation *a month after terrorists struck Manhattan. As you read Schell's narrative, consider how this experience must have affected a journalist who had spent decades warning the public about the threat of weapons of mass destruction.*

Of course there can be no such thing as a literal letter from ground zero— neither from the ground zeros of September 11 nor from the potential nuclear ground zero that is the origin of the expression. There are no letters from the beyond. (By now, "zero" has the double meaning of zero distance from the bombardier's assigned coordinates and the nothingness that's left when his work is done.) As it happens, though, I live six blocks from the ruins of the north tower of the World Trade Center, which is about as close as you can be to ground zero without having been silenced. My specific neighborhood was violated, mutilated. As I write these words, the acrid, dank, rancid stink—it is the smell of death—of the still-smoking site is in my nostrils. Not that these things confer any great distinction—they are merely the local embodiment of the circumstance, felt more or less keenly by everyone in the world in the aftermath of the attack, that in our age of weapons of mass destruction every square foot of our globe can become such a ground zero in a twinkling. We have long known this intellectually, but now we know it viscerally, as a nausea in the pit of the stomach that is unlikely to go away. What to do to change this condition, it seems to me, is the most important of the practical tasks that the crisis requires us to perform. [1]

It takes time for the human reality of the losses to sink in. The eye is quick but the heart is slow. I had two experiences this week that helped me along. It occurred to me that I would be a very bad journalist and maybe a worse neighbor if, living just a few blocks from the catastrophe, I did not manage to get through the various checkpoints to visit the site. A press pass was useless; it got me no closer than my own home. A hole in the storm-fence [2]

1 introduction/ definition of "ground zero"

sets place

graphic details of site

117

describes
what he saw/
TV vs
reality

circling the site worked better. I found myself in the midst of a huge peace-able army of helpers in a thousand uniforms—military and civilian. <u>I was somehow unprepared by television for what I saw when I arrived at ground zero. Television had seemed to show mostly a low hillock of rubble from which the famous bucket brigade of rescuers was passing out pieces of de-bris. This proved to be a keyhole vision of the site. In fact, it was a gigantic, varied, panoramic landscape of destruction, an Alps of concrete, plastic and twisted metal, rising tier upon tier in the smoky distance.</u> Around the pe-rimeter and in the surrounding streets, a cornucopia of food, drinks (thou-sands of crates of spring water, Gatorade, etc.) and other provisions contrib-uted by well-wishers from around the country was heaped up, as if some main of consumer goods on its way to the Trade Center had burst and dis-gorged its flood upon the sidewalks. The surrounding buildings, smashed but still standing, looked down eyelessly on their pulverized brethren. The pieces of the facade of the towers that are often shown in photographs—gigantic forks, or bent spatulas—loomed surprisingly high over the scene with dread majesty. Entry into the ruins by the rescue workers was being accomplished by a cage, or gondola, suspended by a crane, as if <u>in some in-fernal ski resort.</u> When I arrived at the southern rim, the rescuers were all standing silent watching one of these cages being lifted out of the ruins. Shortly, a small pile of something not shaped like a human being but cov-ered by an American flag was brought out in an open buggy. It was the remains, a solemn nurse told me, of one of the firemen who had given his life for the people in the building. And then the slow work began again. Al-

describes
his reaction

though the site was more terrible even than I had imagined, seeing was somehow reassuring. Unvisited, the site, so near my home, had preyed on my imagination.

3   A few days later—one week after the catastrophe—I took my dog for a walk in the evening in Riverside Park, on the upper West Side. Soft orange clouds drifted over the Hudson River and the New Jersey shore. In the dim, cavernous green of the park, normal things were occurring—people were out for walks or jogging, children were playing in a playground. To the south, a slender moon hung in the sky. I found myself experiencing an instant of

contrasting
images of
normal
life

surprise: So it was still there! It had not dropped out of the sky. That was good. After all, our local southern mountain peaks—the twin towers—had fallen. The world seemed to steady around the surviving moon. "Peace" became more than a word. It was the world of difference between the bot-tom half of Manhattan and the top. It was the persistence of all the wonder-ful, ordinary things before my eyes.

Understanding Meaning

1. What motivated Schell to visit the disaster site?
2. How did seeing the site in person differ from seeing it on television? What sights had the greatest impact on Schell?
3. What does Schell mean by the statement that the "eye is quick but the heart is slow"?
4. *Critical Thinking:* Schell states that though the site was more horrible than he imagined, seeing it was somehow comforting. How did visiting the World Trade Center make the disaster less troubling for him?

Evaluating Strategy

1. What senses besides sight does Schell use in creating his description?
2. What visual details does Schell include to impress readers with the scope of the disaster?
3. What role does the moon play in the final paragraph?

Appreciating Language

1. Schell humanizes the damaged buildings so that they "looked down eyelessly on their pulverized brethren." What impact does this image have?
2. What words does Schell use to dramatize the size of the rubble that seems on television to be only a "low hillock"?
3. Schell is a political journalist. How does the tone, style, and diction of this narrative differ from the type of objective reporting you might expect in a newspaper article?

Connections across the Disciplines

1. How does Schell's attention to visual detail mirror the eyewitness reporting by Chris Hedges in "Gaza Diary" (page 121)?
2. Compare Schell's imagery with that of Luis Alberto Urrea's "Border Story" (page 129). Is a key part of writing effective description the ability to place your readers into the scene by using striking images they can relate to?

Writing Suggestions

1. Write a description of a disaster scene you have visited—an auto accident, a fire, a flood, or a blizzard. Use images to help readers visualize the extent of the damage. Remember that your description can include narrative elements such as action and dialogue.

2. *Collaborative Writing:* Working with a group of students, review Schell's article and write a one- or two-paragraph objective description based on his eyewitness testimony.

CHRIS HEDGES

Chris Hedges, a reporter for the New York Times, *was the Middle East bureau chief for the* Dallas Morning News *and was based in Jerusalem from 1988 to 1990. He served as the* New York Times' *Middle East bureau chief based in Cairo in the 1990s. He wrote extensively about the Gulf War and was among the first American journalists to enter Kuwait. Hedges also wrote extensively about the ethnic conflicts in the Balkans in the 1990s. "Gaza Diary" appeared in* Harper's *in October 2001. This article was based on an extensive tour of Palestinian refugee camps.*

Gaza Diary

OVERVIEW: *This section from "Gaza Diary" describes a single Palestinian refugee camp that has been home to Palestinian refugees for decades. Surrounded by Jewish settlements, these refugee camps have been the scenes of violent clashes between Arabs and Israelis.*

Friday afternoon, June 15, Khan Younis

Khan Younis is a dense, gray, concrete shantytown, the black waters from 1 sewers running in thin rivulets down the middle of alleys. There are no gardens or trees. There is no place for children to play, other than the dunes in front of the neighboring Israeli settlements. Vendors in small, dingy stalls sell roasted corn on the cob or falafel. Hunks of meat hang on giant hooks, alongside wooden tables piled with tomatoes, potatoes, green peppers, and green beans. During the rains the camp floods with wastewater. Crude septic tanks, called percolating pits, lie outside homes, covered only by a thin layer of sand. When the pits overflow, the dirty water may slosh into the dwellings. The drinking water, which often does not flow for more than a couple of hours each day, is brackish and brown. It has left many in the camp with kidney problems. Only the lonely minarets, poking up out of the clutter, lend a bit of dignity to the slum.

The latest intifada erupted in September 2000, when Ariel Sharon, 2 then the Israeli opposition leader and now the prime minister, visited the al-Aqsa Mosque, one of the holiest sites in Islam, with about 1,000 Israeli police. Arafat pleaded with then prime minister Ehud Barak to help stop the visit, fearing the violence that would surely erupt, but Barak could do nothing. Since then nearly 500 Palestinians have been killed, along with 100 Israelis and a dozen Israeli Arabs.

3   Khan Younis is one of eight refugee camps in Gaza. It is surrounded on three sides, like a horseshoe, by Israeli military positions. The soldiers there fire down on the roofs of the concrete shacks—asbestos mostly, held down by piles of rocks, cement blocks, and old tires. Bands of Palestinian gunmen, who often initiate the shooting, fire back.

4   A blistering white sun beats down on the camp. Our shirts become damp. Our shoes are soon covered with dust. We walk in single file through the concrete maze, jostling our way past groups of Palestinians. Finally we are afforded a look at the dunes hugging the camp. They are dotted on top with Israeli gun emplacements, sandbagged bunkers, large concrete slabs, and a snaking electric fence. Armored green jeeps and tanks roar and clank along the fence's perimeter, throwing up clouds of dust. Knots of nervous Palestinians stand gazing in the direction of the behemoths until they pass out of sight.

5   The walls of the houses facing the settlements, especially in the El Katadwa neighborhood, on the western edge of the camp, are pockmarked with bullet holes. Jagged chunks of masonry have been ripped away by tank fire. Barrels filled with sand and stacked one on top of the other—for me, an eerie reminder of the Balkans—deny Israeli snipers a view of the streets.

6   Beyond the fence we can see a mobile crane, from which dangles a yellow metal box draped with camouflage. It lumbers inside the Israeli compound like a jerky robot. I am told that the snipers fire down from the box while suspended over the camp.

7   We turn down a crowded alley and come upon a group of older men seated on chairs in a patch of sand, playing backgammon. A black plastic water tank and a TV antenna loom over them. A radio, perched on a window ledge behind metal bars, plays Arabic music. At dusk these men, and the families that live along the perimeter, will move deeper into the camp to seek safety with relatives and friends. Bands of Palestinian gunmen will creep up to shoot at the Israeli positions, and the crackle of automatic fire will punctuate the night air.

Understanding Meaning

1. What are the most striking images of the refugee camps? What physical details are most impressive?
2. What impact does the desolation of these camps have on Hedges? On the residents?

3. Do the details about gun emplacements, bunkers, and electric fences make the camp seem more like a prison?
4. What social and political problems can camps such as this create?
5. Does this description lead you to understand why these camps can become breeding grounds for political extremism and terrorism?

Evaluating Strategy

1. How does Hedges use narrative elements, such as walking through the camp, to prevent his essay from being a still, static description?
2. *Critical Thinking:* When a journalist explores one scene of a conflict, does he or she risk creating propaganda by covering only one side? Can even objective descriptions be used by others to support a political point of view? Would an objective description of German civilian casualties issued by the German military in World War II have been seen by Germany's enemies as Nazi propaganda?

Appreciating Language

1. Can you detect any political bias toward or against the Arabs or Israelis in Hedges's reporting?
2. Would your view of Khan Younis be different if Hedges called it a "detention center" or a "prison" instead of a "shantytown" or a "slum"?
3. Consider the word "refugee camp." Does this suggest temporary or emergency housing rather than permanent residences? Does it suggest that those living there will or should be moved elsewhere in the future?

Connections across the Disciplines

1. Compare this essay with Luis Alberto Urrea's "Border Story" (page 129). Can one describe conditions of human suffering without implying that some action should be taken?
2. In "Returning to Southie" (page 67) a former slum resident is drawn back to his neighborhood, recalling a sense of security and belonging despite the poverty and violence. Can you imagine a Palestinian wanting to return to Khan Younis?

Writing Suggestions

1. Describe a depressed area you have seen firsthand and write an objective account. Avoid using generalized or abstract terms such as "poor" and "crowded," and provide specific visual details as Hedges does.
2. *Collaborative Writing:* Working with a group of students, write a brief division paper listing either the social problems such refugee camps create or proposed solutions to improve the quality of life of the residents.

TRUMAN CAPOTE

Truman Capote (1924–1985) was born in New Orleans and first gained prominence as a writer of short stories. At age twenty-four he produced his first novel, Other Voices, Other Rooms, *which achieved international attention. His other works include* Breakfast at Tiffany's *and* A Tree of Night. *In 1965 he published* In Cold Blood, *which became an immediate best-seller. Based on extensive research and interviews,* In Cold Blood *told the story of the 1959 mass murder of a Kansas farm family and the fate of the killers. Although nonfiction, Capote's book read much like a novel.* In Cold Blood *helped shape a new school of journalism that uses the stylistic touches of fiction to relate wholly factual events.*

Out There

OVERVIEW: *The opening pages of* In Cold Blood *describe the small town of Holcomb, Kansas, where the murders occurred. Capote spent a great deal of time in Holcomb and describes it almost as if it had been his own hometown.*

The village of Holcomb stands on the high wheat plains of western Kansas, a lonesome area that other Kansans call "out there." Some seventy miles east of the Colorado border, the countryside, with its hard blue skies and desert-clear air, has an atmosphere that is rather more Far Western than Middle West. The local accent is barbed with a prairie twang, a ranch-hand nasalness, and the men, many of them, wear narrow frontier trousers, Stetsons, and high-heeled boots with pointed toes. The land is flat, and the views are awesomely extensive; horses, herds of cattle, a white cluster of grain elevators rising as gracefully as Greek temples are visible long before a traveler reaches them.

Holcomb, too, can be seen from great distances. Not that there is much to see—simply an aimless congregation of buildings divided in the center by the main-line tracks of the Santa Fe Railroad, a haphazard hamlet bounded on the south by a brown stretch of the Arkansas (pronounced "Arkan-sas") River, on the north by a highway, Route 50, and on the east and west by prairie lands and wheat fields. After rain, or when snowfalls thaw, the streets, unnamed, unshaded, unpaved, turn from the thickest dust into the direst mud. At one end of the town stands a stark old stucco structure, the roof of which supports an electric sign—DANCE—but the dancing has ceased and the advertisement has been dark for several years. Nearby is another building with an irrelevant sign, this one in flaking gold on a dirty

window—HOLCOMB BANK. The bank closed in 1933, and its former count-
ing rooms have been converted into apartments. It is one of the town's two
"apartment houses," the second being a ramshackle mansion known, because a good part of the local school's faculty lives there, as the Teacherage.
But the majority of Holcomb's homes are one-story frame affairs, with front
porches.

3   Down by the depot, the postmistress, a gaunt woman who wears a raw-
hide jacket and denims and cowboy boots, presides over a falling-apart post
office. The depot itself, with its peeling sulphur-colored paint, is equally
melancholy; the Chief, the Super Chief, the El Capitan go by every day,
but these celebrated expresses never pause there. No passenger trains do—
only an occasional freight. Up on the highway, there are two filling stations,
one of which doubles as a meagerly supplied grocery store, while the other
does extra duty as a café—Hartman's Café, where Mrs. Hartman, the pro-
prietress, dispenses sandwiches, coffee, soft drinks, and 3.2 beer. (Holcomb, like all the rest of Kansas, is "dry.")

4   And that, really, is all. Unless you include, as one must, the Holcomb
School, a good-looking establishment, which reveals a circumstance that
the appearance of the community otherwise camouflages: that the parents
who send their children to this modern and ably staffed "consolidated"
school—the grades go from kindergarten through senior high, and a fleet of
buses transport the students, of which there are usually around three hundred and sixty, from as far as sixteen miles away—are, in general, a prosper-
ous people. Farm ranchers, most of them, they are outdoor folk of very varied stock—German, Irish, Norwegian, Mexican, Japanese. They raise cattle
and sheep, grow wheat, milo, grass seed, and sugar beets. Farming is always
a chancy business, but in western Kansas its practitioners consider themselves "born gamblers," for they must contend with an extremely shallow
precipitation (the annual average is eighteen inches) and anguishing irrigation problems. However, the last seven years have been years of drought-
less beneficence. The farm ranchers in Finney County, of which Holcomb
is a part, have done well; money has been made not from farming alone but
also from the exploitation of plentiful natural-gas resources, and its acquisi-
tion is reflected in the new school, the comfortable interiors of the farm-
houses, the steep and swollen grain elevators.

5   Until one morning in mid-November of 1959, few Americans—in fact,
few Kansans—had ever heard of Holcomb. Like the waters of the river, like
the motorists on the highway, and like the yellow trains streaking down the
Santa Fe tracks, drama, in the shape of exceptional happenings, had never

stopped there. The inhabitants of the village, numbering two hundred and seventy, were satisfied that this should be so, quite content to exist inside ordinary life—to work, to hunt, to watch television, to attend school socials, choir practice, meetings of the 4-H Club. But then, in the earliest hours of that morning in November, a Sunday morning, certain foreign sounds impinged on the normal nightly Holcomb noises—on the keening hysteria of coyotes, the dry scrape of scuttling tumbleweed, the racing, receding wail of locomotive whistles. At the time not a soul in sleeping Holcomb heard them—four shotgun blasts that, all told, ended six human lives. But afterward the townspeople, theretofore sufficiently unfearful of each other to seldom trouble to lock their doors, found fantasy re-creating them over and again—those somber explosions that stimulated fires of mistrust in the glare of which many old neighbors viewed each other strangely, and as strangers.

Understanding Meaning

1. How much of Capote's description can be considered objective, and how much appears subjective?
2. Capote includes a great deal of factual detail—names of highways, the number of students in the high school, and Holcomb's population. What do these facts add to the description?
3. What does Capote attempt to capture in his description of Holcomb?

Evaluating Strategy

1. *Critical Thinking:* A key goal in the opening of any book is to get people's attention and motivate them to continue reading. How does Capote generate interest in describing a nondescript town?
2. What responses do the closing lines in this section of the story create?

Appreciating Language

1. How does the language of Capote's description differ from that of an encyclopedia or newspaper article?
2. *In Cold Blood* has sold millions of copies. What elements in Capote's style make his story about a crime in a small Kansas town so popular? What phrases strike you as being colorful or interesting?

Connections across the Disciplines

1. How does Capote's description of a small town compare with Luis Alberto Urrea's "Border Story" (page 129)? What attitudes do the writers have toward their subjects? What "feel" do they give the landscapes they describe?
2. Does N. Scott Momaday's "The Way to Rainy Mountain" (page 142) suggest a different view of nature and open spaces than Capote's "Out There"?

Writing Ideas

1. Rewrite a recent article from the local newspaper, adding subjective details to arouse human interest for a national audience. Include details about your community to give readers a feel for the location.
2. Using Capote's description of Holcomb as a resource, write a purely objective, one-paragraph description of the town. Include as much factual detail as possible.

LUIS ALBERTO URREA

Luis Alberto Urrea was born in Tijuana to a Mexican father and American mother. He grew up in San Diego and attended the University of California. After graduation and a brief career as a movie extra, Urrea worked with a volunteer organization that provides food, clothing, and medical supplies to the poor of northern Mexico. In 1982 he taught writing at Harvard. His most recent novel, In Search of Snow, *was published in 1994, and he published a collection of poems,* Ghost Sickness, *in 1997.*

Border Story

OVERVIEW: *In this description of the Mexican-American border from* Across the Wire: Life and Hard Times on the Mexican Border *(1993), Urrea uses the device of second person to place his reader in the scene. By making "you" the "illegal," he seeks to dramatize and humanize the plight of the poor seeking a new life in the United States.*

At night, the Border Patrol helicopters swoop and churn in the air all along 1 the line. You can sit in the Mexican hills and watch them herd humans on the dusty slopes across the valley. They look like science fiction crafts, their hard-focused lights raking the ground as they fly.

Borderlands locals are so jaded by the sight of nightly people-hunting 2 that it doesn't even register in their minds. But take a stranger to the border, and she will *see* the spectacle: monstrous Dodge trucks speeding into and out of the landscape; uniformed men patrolling with flashlights, guns, and dogs; spotlights; running figures; lines of people hurried onto buses by armed guards; and the endless clatter of the helicopters with their harsh white beams. A Dutch woman once told me it seemed altogether "un-American."

But the Mexicans keep on coming—and the Guatemalans, the Salvado- 3 rans, the Panamanians, the Colombians. The seven-mile stretch of Interstate 5 nearest the Mexican border is, at times, so congested with Latin American pedestrians that it resembles a town square.

They stick to the center island. Running down the length of the island 4 is a cement wall. If the "illegals" (currently, "undocumented workers"; formerly, "wetbacks") are walking north and a Border Patrol vehicle happens along, they simply hop over the wall and trot south. The officer will have to drive up to the 805 interchange, or Dairy Mart Road, swing over the overpasses, then drive south. Depending on where this pursuit begins, his detour could entail five to ten miles of driving. When the officer finally reaches the group, they hop over the wall and trot north. Furthermore, because freeway arrests would endanger traffic, the Border Patrol has effectively thrown up its hands in surrender.

5   It seems jolly on the page. But imagine poverty, violence, natural disasters, or political fear driving you away from everything you know. Imagine how bad things get to make you leave behind your family, your friends, your lovers; your home, as humble as it might be; your church, say. Let's take it further—you've said good-bye to the graveyard, the dog, the goat, the mountains where you first hunted, your grade school, your state, your favorite spot on the river where you fished and took time to think.

6   Then you come hundreds—or thousands—of miles across territory utterly unknown to you. (Chances are, you have never traveled farther than a hundred miles in your life.) You have walked, run, hidden in the backs of trucks, spent part of your precious money on bus fare. There is no AAA or Travelers Aid Society available to you. Various features of your journey north might include police corruption; violence in the forms of beatings, rape, murder, torture, road accidents; theft; incarceration. Additionally, you might experience loneliness, fear, exhaustion, sorrow, cold, heat, diarrhea, thirst, hunger. There is no medical attention available to you. There isn't even Kotex.

7   Weeks or months later, you arrive in Tijuana. Along with other immigrants, you gravitate to the bad parts of town because there is nowhere for you to go in the glittery sections where the *gringos* flock. You stay in a run-down little hotel in the red-light district, or behind the bus terminal. Or you find your way to the garbage dumps, where you throw together a small cardboard nest and claim a few feet of dirt for yourself. The garbage-pickers working this dump might allow you to squat, or they might come and rob you or burn you out for breaking some local rule you cannot possibly know beforehand. Sometimes the dump is controlled by a syndicate, and goon squads might come to you within a day. They want money, and if you can't pay, you must leave or suffer the consequences.

8   In town, you face endless victimization if you aren't streetwise. The police come after you, street thugs come after you, petty criminals come after you; strangers try your door at night as you sleep. Many shady men offer to guide you across the border, and each one wants all your money now, and promises to meet you at a prearranged spot. Some of your fellow travelers end their journeys right here—relieved of their savings and left to wait on a dark corner until they realize they are going nowhere.

9   If you are not Mexican, and can't pass as *tijuanense*, a local, the tough guys find you out. Salvadorans and Guatemalans are routinely beaten up and robbed. Sometimes they are disfigured. Indians—Chinantecas, Mixtecas, Guasaves, Zapotecas, Mayas—are insulted and pushed around; often

they are lucky—they are merely ignored. They use this to their advantage. Often they don't dream of crossing into the United States: a Mexican tribal person would never be able to blend in, and they know it. To them, the garbage dumps and street vending and begging in Tijuana are a vast improvement over their former lives. As Doña Paula, a Chinanteca friend of mine who lives at the Tijuana garbage dump, told me, "This is the garbage dump. Take all you need. There's plenty here for *everyone!*"

If you are a woman, the men come after you. You lock yourself in your 10 room, and when you must leave it to use the pestilential public bathroom at the end of your floor, you hurry, and you check every corner. Sometimes the lights are out in the toilet room. Sometimes men listen at the door. They call you "good-looking" and "bitch" and "*mamacita*," and they make kissing sounds at you when you pass.

You're in the worst part of town, but you can comfort yourself—at least 11 there are no death squads here. There are no torturers here, or bandit land barons riding into your house. This is the last barrier, you think, between you and the United States—*los Yunaites Estaites.*

You still face police corruption, violence, jail. You now also have a wide 12 variety of new options available to you: drugs, prostitution, white slavery, crime. Tijuana is not easy on newcomers. It is a city that has always thrived on taking advantage of a sucker. And the innocent are the ultimate suckers in the Borderlands.

Understanding Meaning

1. Urrea has called the border a "battlefield." How does his description illustrate this view?
2. What problems do the undocumented aliens face in their attempt to cross the border?
3. How are non-Mexican refugees treated in Tijuana?
4. What is the plight of refugee women on the border?
5. *Critical Thinking:* Urrea quotes a Dutch woman who used the term "un-American" to describe the border patrols. What is un-American about fences and helicopter patrols? Does this response to immigration clash with the Statue of Liberty's promise to welcome the tired and poor?

Evaluating Strategy

1. How effective is the use of the second person? Does it really put "you" in the scene? Does it help dramatize the plight of people many readers might choose to ignore?

2. What details does Urrea use to dramatize conditions along the border?

Appreciating Language

1. Throughout the description, Urrea uses lists—"beatings, rape, murder, torture, road accidents. . . ." How effective are they? Can listing words become tedious?
2. Select the words that create the most powerful images of the border. Why do they make strong impressions?

Connections across the Disciplines

1. How does Urrea's attempt to introduce his reader to the border compare with Truman Capote's description of Holcomb (page 125)?
2. Do the poverty and violence immigrants face in Mexico suggest a reason why some of their descendants, such as the Chicano police officer in "The Fender-Bender" (page 56), reject their heritage?

Writing Suggestions

1. Write an essay describing a place that highlights a social problem. Select a location of which you have personal knowledge, and try to convey the conditions residents face through lists of details.
2. *Collaborative Writing:* Ask a group of fellow students to respond to Urrea's account. Consider the issues his description of the border raises. Ask members to suggest how conditions could be improved, and then draft a short *persuasion* essay outlining your ideas.

JOSÉ ANTONIO BURCIAGA

José Antonio Burciaga (1940–1996) grew up in a synagogue in El Paso, where his father worked as a custodian. Burciaga served in the U.S. Air Force and then attended the University of Texas, where he earned a fine arts degree. Pursuing both art and literature, Burciaga was also active in Chicano affairs. His artwork was first exhibited in 1974. Two years later he published a collection of poetry called Restless Serpents, *followed by a variety of other publications.*

My Ecumenical Father

OVERVIEW: *This essay, which first appeared in* Drink Cultura, *describes Burciaga's father, a man who maintained his ties to Mexican culture while taking pride in his American citizenship and developing a fierce devotion to the Jewish faith.*

¡Feliz Navidad! Merry Christmas! Happy Hanukkah! As a child, my season's greetings were tricultural—Mexicano, Anglo and Jewish. 1

Our devoutly Catholic parents raised three sons and three daughters in the basement of a Jewish synagogue, Congregation B'nai Zion in El Paso, Texas. José Cruz Burciaga was the custodian and *shabbat goy*. A shabbat goy is Yiddish for a Gentile who, on the Sabbath, performs certain tasks forbidden to Jews under orthodox law. 2

Every year around Christmas time, my father would take the menorah out and polish it. The eight-branched candleholder symbolizes Hanukkah, the commemoration of the first recorded war of liberation in that part of the world. 3

In 164 B.C., the Jewish nation rebelled against Antiochus IV Epiphanes, who had attempted to introduce pagan idols into the temples. When the temple was reconquered by the Jews, there was only one day's supply of oil for the Eternal Light in the temple. By a miracle, the oil lasted eight days. 4

My father was not only in charge of the menorah but for 10 years he also made sure the Eternal Light remained lit. 5

As children we were made aware of the differences and joys of Hanukkah, Christmas and Navidad. We were taught to respect each celebration, even if they conflicted. For example, the Christmas carols taught in school. We learned the song about the twelve days of Christmas, though I never understood what the hell a partridge was doing in a pear tree in the middle of December. 6

We also learned a German song about a boy named Tom and a bomb—
O Tannenbaum. We even learned a song in the obscure language of Latin, 7

133

called "Adeste Fideles," which reminded me of, *Ahh! d'este deo,* a Mexican pasta soup. Though 75% of our class was Mexican-American, we never sang a Christmas song in *Español.* Spanish was forbidden.

8   So our mother—a former teacher—taught us "Silent Night" in Spanish: *Noche de paz, noche de amor:* It was so much more poetic and inspirational.

9   While the rest of El Paso celebrated Christmas, Congregation B'nai Zion celebrated Hanukkah. We picked up Yiddish and learned a Hebrew prayer of thanksgiving. My brothers and I would help my father hang the Hanukkah decorations.

10   At night, after the services, the whole family would rush across the border to Juarez and celebrate the *posadas,* which takes place for nine days before Christmas. They are a communal re-enactment of Joseph and Mary's search for shelter, just before Jesus was born.

11   To the posadas we took candles and candy left over from the Hanukkah celebrations. The next day we'd be back at St. Patrick's School singing, "I'm dreaming of a white Christmas."

12   One day I stopped dreaming of the white Christmases depicted on greeting cards. An old immigrant from Israel taught me Jesus was born in desert country just like that of the West Texas town of El Paso.

13   On Christmas Eve, my father would dress like Santa Claus and deliver gifts to his children, nephews, godchildren and the little kids in orphanages. The next day, minus his disguise, he would take us to Juarez, where we delivered gifts to the poor in the streets.

14   My father never forgot his childhood poverty and forever sought to help the less fortunate. He taught us to measure wealth not in money but in terms of love, spirit, charity and culture.

15   We were taught to respect the Jewish faith and culture. On the Day of Atonement, when the whole congregation fasted, my mother did not cook, lest the food odors distract. The respect was mutual. No one ever complained about the large picture of Jesus in our living room.

16   Through my father, leftover food from B'nai B'rith luncheons, Bar Mitzvahs and Bat Mitzvahs, found its way to Catholic or Baptist churches or orphanages. Floral arrangements in the temple that surrounded a Jewish wedding *huppah* canopy many times found a second home at the altar of St. Patrick's Cathedral or San Juan Convent School. Surplus furniture, including old temple pews, found their way to a missionary Baptist Church in *El Segundo Barrio.*

17   It was not uncommon to come home from school at lunch time and find an uncle priest, an aunt nun and a Baptist minister visiting our home at the same time that the Rabbi would knock on our door. It was just as natural to find the president of B'nai Zion eating beans and tortillas in our kitchen.

My father literally risked his life for the Jewish faith. Twice he was as-   18
saulted by burglars who broke in at night. Once he was stabbed in the hand.
Another time he stayed up all night guarding the sacred Torahs after anti-
Semites threatened the congregation. He never philosophized about his ecumenism, he just lived it.

Cruz, as most called him, was a man of great humor, a hot temper and a   19
passion for dance. He lived the Mexican Revolution and rode the rails during the Depression. One of his proudest moments came when he became a
U.S. citizen.

September 23, 1985, sixteen months after my mother passed away, my   20
father followed. Like his life, his death was also ecumenical. The funeral
was held at Our Lady of Peace, where a priest said the mass in English. My
cousins played mandolin and sang in Spanish. The president of B'nai Zion
Congregation said a prayer in Hebrew. Members of the congregation sat
with Catholics and Baptists.

Observing Jewish custom, the cortege passed by the synagogue one last   21
time. Fittingly, father was laid to rest on the Sabbath. At the cemetery, in a
very Mexican tradition, my brothers, sisters and I each kissed a handful of
dirt and threw it on the casket.

I once had the opportunity to describe father's life to the late, great   22
Jewish American writer Bernard Malamud. His only comment was, "Only
in America!"

Understanding Meaning

1. What is a *shabbat goy?*
2. How did the author's family show respect to the congregation?
3. How did the author's family manage to blend respect for several cultures?
4. Burciaga points out that though he learned German and Latin songs in school,
   he was not allowed to sing in Spanish. What does this reveal about the educational system?
5. Why is the description of his father's funeral central to Burciaga's story?
6. *Critical Thinking:* What values does the ecumenical father represent? Are these
   values rare in our society? What lesson could this essay teach?

Evaluating Strategy

1. Would Bernard Malamud's comment, "Only in America," make a good title for
   this essay? Why or why not?

2. Burciaga offers an explanation of Hanukkah. What does this suggest about his intended audience?
3. *Other Modes:* Can this *description* be seen as an extended *definition* of *ecumenical?*

Appreciating Language

1. How did Burciaga's father define "wealth"?
2. Read through Burciaga's description and highlight his use of non-English words and phrases. How does he define them? What impact do all these unfamiliar words have?

Connections across the Disciplines

1. How does Burciaga's multicultural upbringing differ from the childhood described by Nathan McCall (page 61)?
2. How does Burciaga's description of a person he admired compare to that of Carl T. Rowan's account of Miss Bessie (page 137)? Do they use similar techniques? How do they bring their characters to life? What details do they include?

Writing Suggestions

1. Burciaga builds his description largely through details about his father's actions and behavior. Write a few paragraphs describing a person you know well. Try to capture what you consider the person's principal attributes by describing actions that reveal their values.
2. *Collaborative Writing:* Discuss this essay with a group of other students. What do readers find most striking about this Mexican immigrant? Are his attitudes valuable to society? Is multiculturalism a trend today? Have each member write a few paragraphs explaining the significance of this essay. Read the responses aloud, and work to blend as many as possible in a short *analysis* of this essay.

CARL T. ROWAN

Carl T. Rowan (1925–2000) was born in Tennessee and received degrees from Oberlin College and the University of Minnesota. He worked for years as a columnist for the Minneapolis Tribune *and the* Chicago Sun Times, *expressing his views on a variety of issues, especially race relations. Rowan also served as the director of the United States Information Agency and was the ambassador to Finland.*

Unforgettable Miss Bessie

OVERVIEW: *This article describing a schoolteacher originally appeared in* Reader's Digest, *where Rowan serves as an editor. Rowan's account is personal, and much of his description focuses on the impact this teacher had on him and other disadvantaged students.*

She was only about five feet tall and probably never weighed more than 110 1
pounds, but Miss Bessie was a towering presence in the classroom. She was
the only woman tough enough to make me read *Beowulf* and think for a few
foolish days that I liked it. From 1938 to 1942, when I attended Bernard
High School in McMinnville, Tenn., she taught me English, history, civ-
ics—and a lot more than I realized.

I shall never forget the day she scolded me into reading *Beowulf*. 2

"But Miss Bessie," I complained, "I ain't much interested in it." 3

Her large brown eyes became daggerish slits. "Boy," she said, "how 4
dare you say 'ain't' to me! I've taught you better than that."

"Miss Bessie," I pleaded, "I'm trying to make first-string end on the 5
football team, and if I go around saying 'it isn't' and 'they aren't,' the guys
are gonna laugh me off the squad."

"Boy," she responded, "you'll play football because you have guts. But 6
do you know what *really* takes guts? Refusing to lower your standards to
those of the crowd. It takes guts to say you've got to live and be somebody
fifty years after all the football games are over."

I started saying "it isn't" and "they aren't," and I still made first-string 7
end—and class valedictorian—without losing my buddies' respect.

During her remarkable 44-year career, Mrs. Bessie Taylor Gwynn 8
taught hundreds of economically deprived black youngsters—including my
mother, my brother, my sisters and me. I remember her now with gratitude
and affection—especially in this era when Americans are so wrought-up
about a "rising tide of mediocrity" in public education and the problems
of finding competent, caring teachers. Miss Bessie was an example of an informed, dedicated teacher, a blessing to children and an asset to the nation.

9   Born in 1895, in poverty, she grew up in Athens, Ala., where there was no public school for blacks. She attended Trinity School, a private institution for blacks run by the American Missionary Association, and in 1911 graduated from the Normal School (a "super" high school) at Fisk University in Nashville. Mrs. Gwynn, the essence of pride and privacy, never talked about her years in Athens; only in the months before her death did she reveal that she had never attended Fisk University itself because she could not afford the four-year course.

10   At Normal School she learned a lot about Shakespeare, but most of all about the profound importance of education—especially, for a people trying to move up from slavery. "What you put in your head, boy," she once said, "can never be pulled out by the Ku Klux Klan, the Congress or anybody."

11   Miss Bessie's bearing of dignity told anyone who met her that she was "educated" in the best sense of the word. There was never a discipline problem in her classes. We didn't dare mess with a woman who knew about the Battle of Hastings, the Magna Carta and the Bill of Rights—and who could also play the piano.

12   This frail-looking woman could make sense of Shakespeare, Milton, Voltaire, and bring to life Booker T. Washington and W. E. B. DuBois. Believing that it was important to know who the officials were that spent taxpayers' money and made public policy, she made us memorize the names of everyone on the Supreme Court and in the President's Cabinet. It could be embarrassing to be unprepared when Miss Bessie said, "Get up and tell the class who Frances Perkins is and what you think about her."

13   Miss Bessie knew that my family, like so many others during the Depression, couldn't afford to subscribe to a newspaper. She knew we didn't even own a radio. Still, she prodded me to "look out for your future and find some way to keep up with what's going on in the world." So I became a delivery boy for the Chattanooga *Times*. I rarely made a dollar a week, but I got to read a newspaper every day.

14   Miss Bessie noticed things that had nothing to do with schoolwork, but were vital to a youngster's development. Once a few classmates made fun of my frayed, hand-me-down overcoat, calling me "Strings." As I was leaving school, Miss Bessie patted me on the back of that old overcoat and said, "Carl, never fret about what you *don't* have. Just make the most of what you *do* have—a brain."

15   Among the things that I did not have was electricity in the little frame house that my father had built for $400 with his World War I bonus. But because of her inspiration, I spent many hours squinting beside a kerosene

lamp reading Shakespeare and Thoreau, Samuel Pepys and William Cullen Bryant.

No one in my family had ever graduated from high school, so there was 16 no tradition of commitment to learning for me to lean on. Like millions of youngsters in today's ghettos and barrios, I needed the push and stimulation of a teacher who truly cared. Miss Bessie gave plenty of both, as she immersed me in a wonderful world of similes, metaphors and even onomatopoeia. She led me to believe that I could write sonnets as well as Shakespeare, or iambic-pentameter verse to put Alexander Pope to shame.

In those days the McMinnville school system was rigidly "Jim Crow," 17 and poor black children had to struggle to put anything in their heads. Our high school was only slightly larger than the once-typical little red schoolhouse, and its library was outrageously inadequate—so small, I like to say, that if two students were in it and one wanted to turn a page, the other one had to step outside.

Negroes, as we were called then, were not allowed in the town library, 18 except to mop floors or dust tables. But through one of those secret Old South arrangements between whites of conscience and blacks of stature, Miss Bessie kept getting books smuggled out of the white library. That is how she introduced me to the Brontës, Byron, Coleridge, Keats and Tennyson. "If you don't read, you can't write, and if you can't write, you might as well stop dreaming," Miss Bessie once told me.

So I read whatever Miss Bessie told me to, and tried to remember the 19 things she insisted that I store away. Forty-five years later, I can still recite her "truths to live by," such as Henry Wadsworth Longfellow's lines from "The Ladder of St. Augustine":

The heights by great men reached and kept 20
Were not attained by sudden flight.
But they, while their companions slept,
Were toiling upward in the night.

Years later, her inspiration, prodding, anger, cajoling and almost osmotic 21 infusion of learning finally led to that lovely day when Miss Bessie dropped me a note saying, "I'm so proud to read your column in the Nashville *Tennessean*."

Miss Bessie was a spry 80 when I went back to McMinnville and visited 22 her in a senior citizens' apartment building. Pointing out proudly that her building was racially integrated, she reached for two glasses and a pint of bourbon. I was momentarily shocked, because it would have been scandalous in the 1930s and '40s for word to get out that a teacher drank, and nobody had ever raised a rumor that Miss Bessie did.

23   I felt a new sense of equality as she lifted her glass to mine. Then she revealed a softness and compassion that I had never known as a student.

24   "I've never forgotten that examination day," she said, "when Buster Martin held up seven fingers, obviously asking you for help with question number seven, 'Name a common carrier.' I can still picture you looking at your exam paper and humming a few bars of 'Chattanooga Choo Choo.' I was so tickled, I couldn't punish either of you."

25   Miss Bessie was telling me, with bourbon-laced grace, that I never fooled her for a moment.

26   When Miss Bessie died in 1980, at age 85, hundreds of her former students mourned. They knew the measure of a great teacher: love and motivation. Her wisdom and influence had rippled out across generations.

27   Some of her students who might normally have been doomed to poverty went on to become doctors, dentists and college professors. Many, guided by Miss Bessie's example, became public-school teachers.

28   "The memory of Miss Bessie and how she conducted her classroom did more for me than anything I learned in college," recalls Gladys Wood of Knoxville, Tenn., a highly respected English teacher who spent 43 years in the state's school system. "So many times, when I faced a difficult classroom problem, I asked myself, *How would Miss Bessie deal with this?* And I'd remember that she would handle it with laughter and love."

29   No child can get all the necessary support at home, and millions of poor children get *no* support at all. This is what makes a wise, educated, warmhearted teacher like Miss Bessie so vital to the minds, hearts and souls of this country's children.

Understanding Meaning

1.   What is Rowan's purpose in describing Miss Bessie? What makes this teacher significant to a middle-aged man?
2.   What qualities of Miss Bessie does Rowan admire?
3.   Does Rowan offer Miss Bessie as a role model? How does he demonstrate that she is an "asset to the nation"?

Evaluating Strategy

1.   Rowan opens his essay with a physical description of Miss Bessie. Why are these details important to his purpose?

2. Why would this article appeal to readers of *Reader's Digest*? What values does it reinforce?
3. *Critical Thinking:* Would some people object to Rowan's article as being sentimental? Why or why not? Does this article suggest simple solutions to complex problems? Would a Miss Bessie be able to succeed in a modern urban high school?

Appreciating Language

1. Study the words Rowan uses in describing Miss Bessie. Which words have the most impact?
2. Rowan includes dialogue in his article. What do you notice about Miss Bessie's language? What does this add to the description?

Connections across the Disciplines

1. Consider William Raspberry's article "The Handicap of Definition" (page 287). Would Miss Bessie be a figure that resists such a handicap?
2. *Critical Thinking:* Compare Rowan's experience in a black high school with Nathan McCall's experience in "The Lesson" (page 61). Do African-American students from disadvantaged communities benefit from integration or from participation in black schools with black teachers like Miss Bessie?

Writing Suggestions

1. Write a brief description of a teacher, employer, or coworker who greatly influenced your development. Provide specific examples of the lessons you learned.
2. *Collaborative Writing:* Working with three or four other students, discuss Miss Bessie's statement, "What you put in your head, boy, can never be pulled out by the Ku Klux Klan, the Congress or anybody." Use this quote as the headline of a poster urging people to read. Keep your message short. Read it aloud to hear how it sounds.

N. SCOTT MOMADAY

Navarre Scott Momaday (1934–) was born in Oklahoma and graduated from the University of New Mexico in 1958. He received a doctorate in English from Stanford University. Momaday is a literature professor, poet, artist, and frequent contributor to the New Yorker. A Native American, he has published a collection of Kiowa folktales and edited American Indian Authors. *His other books have included* The Gourd Dancer, *an illustrated children's book, and* House Made of Dawn, *a novel that received a Pulitzer Prize.*

The Way to Rainy Mountain

OVERVIEW: *This essay first appeared in the* Reporter. *Momaday later revised it and used it as an introduction to a book of the same title.*

1   A single knoll rises out of the plain in Oklahoma, north and west of the Wichita Range. For my people, the Kiowas, it is an old landmark, and they gave it the name Rainy Mountain. The hardest weather in the world is there. Winter brings blizzards, hot tornadic winds arise in the spring, and in summer the prairie is an anvil's edge. The grass turns brittle and brown, and it cracks beneath your feet. There are green belts along the rivers and creeks, linear groves of hickory and pecan, willow and witch hazel. At a distance in July or August the steaming foliage seems almost to writhe in fire. Great green-and-yellow grasshoppers are everywhere in the tall grass, popping up like corn to sting the flesh, and tortoises crawl about on the red earth, going nowhere in the plenty of time. Loneliness is an aspect of the land. All things in the plain are isolate; there is no confusion of objects in the eye, but *one* hill or *one* tree or one man. To look upon that landscape in the early morning, with the sun at your back, is to lose the sense of proportion. Your imagination comes to life, and this, you think, is where Creation was begun.

2   I returned to Rainy Mountain in July. My grandmother had died in the spring, and I wanted to be at her grave. She had lived to be very old and at last infirm. Her only living daughter was with her when she died, and I was told that in death her face was that of a child.

3   I like to think of her as a child. When she was born, the Kiowas were living that last great moment of their history. For more than a hundred years they had controlled the open range from the Smoky Hill River to the Red, from the headwaters of the Canadian to the fork of the Arkansas and Cimar-

ron. In alliance with the Comanches, they had ruled the whole of the southern Plains. War was their sacred business, and they were among the finest horsemen the world has ever known. But warfare for the Kiowas was preeminently a matter of disposition rather than of survival, and they never understood the grim, unrelenting advance of the U.S. Cavalry. When at last, divided and ill-provisioned, they were driven onto the Staked Plains in the cold rains of autumn, they fell into panic. In Palo Duro Canyon they abandoned their crucial stores to pillage and had nothing then but their lives. In order to save themselves, they surrendered to the soldiers at Fort Sill and were imprisoned in the old stone corral that now stands as a military museum. My grandmother was spared the humiliation of those high gray walls by eight or ten years, but she must have known from birth the affliction of defeat, the dark brooding of old warriors.

Her name was Aho, and she belonged to the last culture to evolve in   4
North America. Her forebears came down from the high country in western Montana nearly three centuries ago. They were a mountain people, a mysterious tribe of hunters whose language has never been positively classified in any major group. In the late seventeenth century they began a long migration to the south and east. It was a long journey toward the dawn, and it led to a golden age. Along the way the Kiowas were befriended by the Crows, who gave them the culture and religion of the Plains. They acquired horses, and their ancient nomadic spirit was suddenly free of the ground. They acquired Tai-me, the sacred Sun Dance doll, from that moment the object and symbol of their worship, and so shared in the divinity of the sun. Not least, they acquired the sense of destiny, therefore courage and pride. When they entered upon the southern Plains, they had been transformed. No longer were they slaves to the simple necessity of survival; they were a lordly and dangerous society of fighters and thieves, hunters and priests of the sun. According to their origin myth, they entered the world through a hollow log. From one point of view, their migration was the fruit of an old prophecy, for indeed they emerged from a sunless world.

Although my grandmother lived out her long life in the shadow of   5
Rainy Mountain, the immense landscape of the continental interior lay like memory in her blood. She could tell of the Crows, whom she had never seen, and of the Black Hills, where she had never been. I wanted to see in reality what she had seen more perfectly in the mind's eye, and traveled fifteen hundred miles to begin my pilgrimage.

Yellowstone, it seemed to me, was the top of the world, a region of deep   6
lakes and dark timber, canyons and waterfalls. But, beautiful as it is, one might have the sense of confinement there. The skyline in all directions is

close at hand, the high wall of the woods and deep cleavages of shade. There is a perfect freedom in the mountains, but it belongs to the eagle and the elk, the badger and the bear. The Kiowas reckoned their stature by the distance they could see, and they were bent and blind in the wilderness.

7   Descending eastward, the highland meadows are a stairway to the plain. In July the inland slope of the Rockies is luxuriant with ax and buckwheat, stonecrop and larkspur. The earth unfolds and the limit of the land recedes. Clusters of trees and animals grazing far in the distance cause the vision to reach away and wonder to build upon the mind. The sun follows a longer course in the day, and the sky is immense beyond all comparison. The great billowing clouds that sail upon it are shadows that move upon the grain like water, dividing light. Farther down, in the land of the Crows and Blackfeet, the plain is yellow. Sweet clover takes hold of the hills and bends upon itself to cover and seal the soil. There the Kiowas paused on their way; they had come to the place where they must change their lives. The sun is at home in the plains. Precisely there does it have the certain character of a god. When the Kiowas came to the land of the Crows, they could see the dark lees of the hills at dawn across the Bighorn River, the profusion of light on the grain shelves, the oldest deity ranging after the solstices. Not yet would they veer southward to the caldron of the land that lay below; they must wean their blood from the northern winter and hold the mountains a while longer in their view. They bore Tai-me in procession to the east.

8   A dark mist lay over the Black Hills, and the land was like iron. At the top of a ridge I caught sight of Devil's Tower upthrust against the gray sky as if in the birth of time the core of the earth had broken through its crust and the motion of the world was begun. There are things in nature that engender an awful quiet in the heart of man; Devil's Tower is one of them. Two centuries ago, because they could not do otherwise, the Kiowas made a legend at the base of the rock. My grandmother said:

9   Eight children were there at play, seven sisters and their brother. Suddenly the boy was struck dumb; he trembled and began to run upon his hands and feet. His fingers became claws, and his body was covered with fur. Directly there was a bear where the boy had been. The sisters were terrified; they ran, and the bear after them. They came to the stump of a great tree, and the tree spoke to them. It bade them climb upon it, and as they did so, it began to rise into the air. The bear came to kill them, but they were just beyond its reach. It reared against the tree and scored the bark all around with its claws. The seven sisters were borne into the sky, and they became the stars of the Big Dipper.

10   From that moment, and so long as the legend lives, the Kiowas have kinsmen in the night sky. Whatever they were in the mountains, they could be

no more. However tenuous their well-being, however much they had suffered and would suffer again, they had found a way out of the wilderness.

My grandmother had a reverence for the sun, a holy regard that now is   11
all but gone out of mankind. There was a wariness in her, and an ancient
awe. She was a Christian in her later years, but she had come a long way
about, and she never forgot her birthright. As a child she had been to the
Sun Dances; she had taken part in those annual rites, and by them she had
learned the restoration of her people in the presence of Tai-me. She was
about seven when the last Kiowa Sun Dance was held in 1887 on the Washita River above Rainy Mountain Creek. The buffalo were gone. In order to
consummate the ancient sacrifice—to impale the head of a buffalo bull
upon the medicine tree—a delegation of old men journeyed into Texas,
there to beg and barter for an animal from the Goodnight herd. She was ten
when the Kiowas came together for the last time as a living Sun Dance culture. They could find no buffalo; they had to hang an old hide from the sacred
tree. Before the dance could begin, a company of soldiers rode out from
Fort Sill under orders to disperse the tribe. Forbidden without cause the essential act of their faith, having seen the wild herds slaughtered and left to
rot upon the ground, the Kiowas backed away forever from the medicine
tree. That was July 20, 1890, at the great bend of the Washita. My grandmother was there. Without bitterness, and for as long as she lived, she bore
a vision of deicide.

Now that I can have her only in memory, I see my grandmother in the   12
several postures that were peculiar to her: standing at the wood stove on a
winter morning and turning meat in a great iron skillet; sitting at the south
window, bent above her beadwork, and afterwards, when her vision had
failed, looking down for a long time into the fold of her hands; going out
upon a cane, very slowly as she did when the weight of age came upon her;
praying. I remember her most often at prayer. She made long, rambling
prayers out of suffering and hope, having seen many things. I was never
sure that I had the right to hear, so exclusive were they of all mere custom
and company. The last time I saw her she prayed standing by the side of
her bed at night, naked to the waist, the light of a kerosene lamp moving
upon her dark skin. Her long, black hair, always drawn and braided in the
day, lay upon her shoulders and against her breasts like a shawl. I do not
speak Kiowa, and I never understood her prayers, but there was something
inherently sad in the sound, some merest hesitation upon the syllables of
sorrow. She began in a high and descending pitch, exhausting her breath to
silence; then again and again—and always the same intensity of effort, of
something that is, and is not, like urgency in the human voice. Transported
so in the dancing light among the shadows of her room, she seemed beyond

the reach of time. But that was illusion; I think I knew then that I should not see her again.

Understanding Meaning

1. How does Momaday describe Rainy Mountain? How do its physical characteristics differ from its importance to the Kiowas?
2. How does Momaday describe his grandmother? What were the dominant features of her life and her home?
3. What is the significance of the Kiowa legend about the seven sisters?
4. *Other Modes:* How does Momaday use *narration* and *comparison* to develop his description?
5. *Critical Thinking:* Momaday states that he did not speak his grandmother's language and did not understand her prayers. Does this loss of an ancestral language by a man interested in his past illustrate Jamaica Kincaid's observation that Americans are "impatient with memory"?

Evaluating Strategy

1. Most descriptions focus on visual images. How does Momaday use sounds to describe his subject?
2. How does Momaday introduce historical background into a highly personal essay? What transitions does he use?

Appreciating Language

1. Momaday discusses his grandmother's reverence for the sun. What connotation does the word *sun* have?
2. Focus on Momaday's word choices. How does he refer to the beliefs of the ancient Native Americans? What do his connotations reveal about his attitudes toward their faith?

Connections across the Disciplines

1. How does Momaday's role as tribal member returning home compare to Armando Rendón's discovery of his roots in "Kiss of Death" (page 586)? Does a difference exist between immigrant and Native American cultures? Is one harder to maintain or preserve?

2. How does Momaday's description of people and places compare with Truman Capote's in "Out There" (page 125)? Do they pay similar attention to detail? Are their attitudes different? Does one writer seem more of an outsider?

Writing Suggestions

1. Write an essay describing an ancestral figure in your own past. Choose a relative, family friend, or neighbor who embodied a sense of your family, community, or culture. Choose words carefully to share with readers your attitudes toward this person.
2. *Collaborative Writing:* Discuss the role of grandparents in current society with several students. Select observations you agree on, and write a few paragraphs presenting your main points. Has the role of grandparents changed? On the one hand, are they discredited because our society emphasizes youth? On the other hand, are they often more influential since many take an active role in raising grandchildren?

BLENDING THE MODES

E. B. WHITE

Elwyn Brooks White (1899–1985) was born in Mount Vernon, New York, and attended Cornell University. He was a regular contributor to the New Yorker *and* Harper's *magazine for fifty years. His articles achieved a reputation for their wit and style. White assisted Edmund Strunk in revising his popular book on writing,* Elements of Style. *He also gained popularity as a writer of children's literature. His books* Stuart Little *and* Charlotte's Web *have become classics.*

Once More to the Lake

OVERVIEW: *First published in* Harper's *in 1941, "Once More to the Lake" describes White's nostalgic return to a boyhood vacation spot. As you read the essay, notice how White uses* comparison *and* narration *in developing his description.*

August 1941

1 One summer, along about 1904, my father rented a camp on a lake in Maine and took us all there for the month of August. We all got ringworm from some kittens and had to rub Pond's Extract on our arms and legs night and morning, and my father rolled over in a canoe with all his clothes on; but outside of that the vacation was a success and from then on none of us ever thought there was any place in the world like that lake in Maine. We returned summer after summer—always on August 1 for one month. I have since become a salt-water man, but sometimes in summer there are days when the restlessness of the tides and the fearful cold of the sea water and the incessant wind that blows across the afternoon and into the evening make me wish for the placidity of a lake in the woods. A few weeks ago this feeling got so strong I bought myself a couple of bass hooks and a spinner and returned to the lake where we used to go, for a week's fishing and to revisit old haunts.

2 I took along my son, who had never had any fresh water up his nose and who had seen lily pads only from train windows. On the journey over to the lake I began to wonder what it would be like. I wondered how time would have marred this unique, this holy spot—the coves and streams, the hills that the sun set behind, the camps and the paths behind the camps. I was

sure that the tarred road would have found it out, and I wondered in what other ways it would be desolated. It is strange how much you can remember about places like that once you allow your mind to return into the grooves that lead back. You remember one thing, and that suddenly reminds you of another thing. I guess I remembered clearest of all the early mornings, when the lake was cool and motionless, remembered how the bedroom smelled of the lumber it was made of and of the wet woods whose scent entered through the screen. The partitions in the camp were thin and did not extend clear to the top of the rooms, and as I was always the first up I would dress softly so as not to wake the others, and sneak out into the sweet outdoors and start out in the canoe, keeping close along the shore in the long shadows of the pines. I remembered being very careful never to rub my paddle against the gunwale for fear of disturbing the stillness of the cathedral.

The lake had never been what you would call a wild lake. There were 3 cottages sprinkled around the shores, and it was in farming country although the shores of the lake were quite heavily wooded. Some of the cottages were owned by nearby farmers, and you would live at the shore and eat your meals at the farmhouse. That's what our family did. But although it wasn't wild, it was a fairly large and undisturbed lake and there were places in it that, to a child at least, seemed infinitely remote and primeval.

I was right about the tar: it led to within half a mile of the shore. But when 4 I got back there, with my boy, and we settled into a camp near a farmhouse and into the kind of summertime I had known, I could tell that it was going to be pretty much the same as it had been before—I knew it, lying in bed the first morning, smelling the bedroom and hearing the boy sneak quietly out and go off along the shore in a boat. I began to sustain the illusion that he was I, and therefore, by simple transposition, that I was my father. This sensation persisted, kept cropping up all the time we were there. It was not an entirely new feeling, but in this setting it grew much stronger. I seemed to be living a dual existence. I would be in the middle of some simple act, I would be picking up a bait box or laying down a table fork, or I would be saying something, and suddenly it would be not I but my father who was saying the words or making the gesture. It gave me a creepy sensation.

We went fishing the first morning. I felt the same damp moss covering 5 the worms in the bait can, and saw the dragonfly alight on the tip of my rod as it hovered a few inches from the surface of the water. It was the arrival of this fly that convinced me beyond any doubt that everything was as it always had been, that the years were a mirage and that there had been no years. The small waves were the same, chucking the rowboat under the chin as we fished at anchor, and the boat was the same boat, the same color green and the ribs broken in the same places, and under the floorboards the same fresh-water leavings and debris—the dead hellgrammite, the wisps of moss, the rusty discarded fish-hook, the dried blood from yesterday's catch. We stared silently at the tips of our rods, at the dragonflies that came and went. I lowered the tip of mine into the water, tentatively, pensively dislodging the fly, which darted two feet away, poised, darted two feet back, and came to rest again a little farther up the rod. There had been no years between the ducking of this dragonfly and the other one—the one that was part of memory. I looked at the boy, who was silently watching his fly, and it was my hands that held his rod, my eyes watching. I felt dizzy and didn't know which rod I was at the end of.

6   We caught two bass, hauling them in briskly as though they were mackerel, pulling them over the side of the boat in a businesslike manner without any landing net, and stunning them with a blow on the back of the head. When we got back for a swim before lunch, the lake was exactly where we had left it, the same number of inches from the dock, and there was only the merest suggestion of a breeze. This seemed an utterly enchanted sea, this lake you could leave to its own devices for a few hours and come back to, and find it had not stirred, this constant and trustworthy body of water. In the shallows, the dark, water-soaked sticks and twigs, smooth and old, were undulating in clusters on the bottom against the clean ribbed sand, and the track of the mussel was plain. A school of minnows swam by, each minnow with its small individual shadow, doubling the attendance, so clear and sharp in the sunlight. Some of the other campers were in swimming, along the shore, one of them with a cake of soap, and the water felt thin and clear and unsubstantial. Over the years there had been this person with the cake of soap, this cultist, and here he was. There had been no years.

7   Up to the farmhouse to dinner through the teeming, dusty field, the road under our sneakers was only a two-track road. The middle track was missing, the one with the marks of the hooves and the splotches of dried, flaky manure. There had always been three tracks to choose from in choosing which track to walk in; now the choice was narrowed down to two. For a moment I missed terribly the middle alternative. But the way led past the tennis court, and something about the way it lay there in the sun reassured me; the tape had loosened along the backline, the alleys were green with plantains and other weeds, and the net (installed in June and removed in September) sagged in the dry noon, and the whole place steamed with midday heat and hunger and emptiness. There was a choice of pie for dessert, and one was blueberry and one was apple, and the waitresses were the same country girls, there having been no passage of time, only the illusion of it as

in a dropped curtain—the waitresses were still fifteen; their hair had been washed, that was the only difference—they had been to the movies and seen the pretty girls with the clean hair.

Summertime, oh summertime, pattern of life indelible, the fade-proof 8 lake, the woods unshatterable, the pasture with the sweetfern and the juniper forever and ever, summer without end; this was the background, and the life along the shore was the design, their tiny docks with the flagpole and the American flag floating against the white clouds in the blue sky, the little paths over the roots of the trees leading from camp to camp and the paths leading back to the outhouses and the can of lime for sprinkling, and at the souvenir counters at the store the miniature birch-bark canoes and the postcards that showed things looking a little better than they looked. This was the American family at play, escaping the city heat, wondering whether the newcomers in the camp at the head of the cove were "common" or "nice," wondering whether it was true that the people who drove up for Sunday dinner at the farmhouse were turned away because there wasn't enough chicken.

It seemed to me, as I kept remembering all this, that those times and 9 those summers had been infinitely precious and worth saving. There had been jollity and peace and goodness. The arriving (at the beginning of August) had been so big a business in itself, at the railway station the farm wagon drawn up, the first smell of the pine-laden air, the first glimpse of the smiling farmer, and the great importance of the trunks and your father's enormous authority in such matters, and the feel of the wagon under you for the long ten-mile haul, and at the top of the last long hill catching the first view of the lake after eleven months of not seeing this cherished body of water. The shouts and cries of the other campers when they saw you, and the trunks to be unpacked, to give up their rich burden. (Arriving was less exciting nowadays, when you sneaked up in your car and parked it under a tree near the camp and took out the bags and in five minutes it was all over, no fuss, no loud wonderful fuss about trunks.)

Peace and goodness and jollity. The only thing that was wrong now, re- 10 ally, was the sound of the place, an unfamiliar nervous sound of the outboard motors. This was the note that jarred, the one thing that would sometimes break the illusion and set the years moving. In those other summertimes all the motors were inboard; and when they were at a little distance, the noise they made was a sedative, an ingredient of summer sleep. They were one-cylinder and two-cylinder engines, and some were make-and-break and some were jump-spark, but they all made a sleepy sound across the lake. The one-lungers throbbed and fluttered, and the twin-cylinder ones purred and purred, and that was a quiet sound, too. But now the campers all had outboards. In the daytime, in the hot mornings, these motors made a petulant, irritable sound; at night, in the still evening when the afterglow lit the water, they whined about one's ears like mosquitoes. My boy loved our rented outboard, and his great desire was to achieve single-handed mastery over it, and authority, and he soon learned the trick of choking it a little (but not too much), and the adjustment of the needle valve. Watching him I would remember the things you could do with the old one-cylinder engine with the heavy flywheel, how you could have it eating out of your hand if you got really close to it spiritually. Motorboats in those days didn't have clutches, and you would make a landing by shutting off the motor at the proper time and coasting in with a dead rudder. But there was a way of reversing them, if you learned the trick, by cutting the switch and putting it on again exactly on the final dying revolution of the flywheel, so that it would kick back against the compression and begin reversing. Approaching a dock in a strong following breeze, it was difficult to slow up sufficiently by the ordinary coasting method, and if a boy felt he had complete mastery over his motor, he was tempted to keep it running beyond its time and then reverse it a few feet from the dock. It took a cool nerve, because if you threw the switch a twentieth of a second too soon you would catch the flywheel when it still had speed enough to go up past center, and the boat would leap ahead, charging bull-fashion at the dock.

11   We had a good week at camp. The bass were biting well and the sun shone endlessly, day after day. We would be tired at night and lie down in the accumulated heat of the little bedrooms after the long hot day and the breeze would stir almost imperceptibly outside and the smell of the swamp drift in through the rusty screens. Sleep would come easily and in the morning the red squirrel would be on the roof, tapping out his gay routine. I kept remembering everything, lying in bed in the mornings—the small steamboat that had a long rounded stem like the lip of a Ubangi, and how quietly she ran on the moonlight sails, when the older boys played their mandolins and the girls sang and we ate doughnuts dipped in sugar, and how sweet the music was on the water in the shining night, and what it had felt like to think about girls then. After breakfast we would go up to the store and the things were in the same place—the minnows in a bottle, the plugs and spinners disarranged and pawed over by the youngsters from the boys' camp, the Fig Newtons and the Beeman's gum. Outside, the road was tarred and cars stood in front of the store. Inside, all was just as it had always been, except there was more Coca-Cola and not so much Moxie and root beer and birch beer and sarsaparilla. We would walk out with the bottle of pop apiece and sometimes the pop would backfire up our noses and hurt. We explored

the streams, quietly, where the turtles slid off the sunny logs and dug their way into the soft bottom; and we lay on the town wharf and fed worms to the tame bass. Everywhere we went I had trouble making out which I was, the one walking at my side, the one walking in my pants.

One afternoon while we were there at that lake a thunderstorm came 12 up. It was like the revival of an old melodrama that I had seen long ago with childish awe. The second-act climax of the drama of the electrical disturbance over a lake in America had not changed in any important respect. This was the big scene, still the big scene. The whole thing was so familiar, the first feeling of oppression and heat and a general air around camp of not wanting to go very far away. In mid-afternoon (it was all the same) a curious darkening of the sky, and a lull in everything that had made life tick; and then the way the boats suddenly swung the other way at their moorings with the coming of a breeze out of the new quarter, and the premonitory rumble. Then the kettle drum, then the snare, then the bass drum and cymbals, then the crackling light against the dark, and the gods grinning and licking their chops in the hills. Afterward the calm, the rain steadily rustling in the calm lake, the return of light and hope and spirits, and the campers running out in joy and relief to go swimming in the rain, their bright cries perpetuating the deathless joke about how they were getting simply drenched, and the children screaming with delight at the new sensation of bathing in the rain, and the joke about getting drenched linking the generations in a strong indestructible chain. And the comedian who waded in carrying an umbrella.

When the others went swimming my son said he was going in, too. He 13 pulled his dripping trunks from the line where they had hung all through the shower and wrung them out. Languidly, and with no thought of going in, I watched him, his hard little body, skinny and bare, saw him wince slightly as he pulled up around his vitals the small, soggy, icy garment. As he buckled the swollen belt, suddenly my groin felt the chill of death.

Understanding Meaning

1. What is White's purpose in describing the resort? What lessons or observations does this journey reveal to him?
2. What are the key features of the lake? How much of it had changed in forty years?
3. White comments in the last line that he "felt the chill of death." How does viewing his son give White a sense of his mortality?
4. *Critical Thinking:* What role does time play in this description? What is White saying about the passage of time, the passage of life? How does watching a child grow affect a parent?

Evaluating Strategy

1.   How does White use his son as a device for recalling his own youth?
2.   Descriptions of places can become tedious lists of geographical details. How does White create action and bring the lake to life?
3.   Writers usually rely on visual details to develop a description of a place. Locate places where White uses other sensory impressions. How effective are they?
4.   *Other Modes:* Locate passages where White uses *comparison* and *narration.* How do they develop the essay? Could you classify this essay as *narration?*

Appreciating Language

1.   White uses figurative language associated with nonnatural objects to describe the lake. For instance, he describes the lake as having the "stillness of a cathedral" and uses references to musical instruments—"the kettle drum, then the snare, then the bass drum and cymbals"—to capture the sound of a storm. What do these word choices suggest about his audience?
2.   White uses brand names throughout his essay. What effect do references to Moxie, Fig Newtons, and Coca-Cola have?

Connections across the Disciplines

1.   How does White's remembrance of his childhood at the lake compare to Michael Patrick MacDonald's attitude toward Southie (page 67)? What role does nostalgia have in describing both a placid lake and a violent slum?
2.   Review John Ciardi's essay "What Is Happiness?" (page 189). Does White's journey to a boyhood retreat suggest an attempt to find happiness in the security of the past?

Writing Suggestions

1.   Write an essay describing a place you revisited after a considerable lapse of time. Comment on what has and has not changed. Use as many sensory details as you can.
2.   *Collaborative Writing:* Work with a group of students who share a common memory of a historical event or recent campus incident. Have each member write a brief narrative. Read each paper aloud to see how people recall and interpret events differently.

WRITING BEYOND THE CLASSROOM

FRANK PILIPP AND
CHARLES SHULL

Abstracts are brief summaries describing articles and reports. The fields of chemistry, biology, law, medicine, literature, and psychology each have specialized abstracts that serve as a valuable source to students and researchers. Most abstracts are now available online. This abstract describes an article analyzing how the subject of AIDS has been treated by TV movies. Other abstracts describe articles on everything from solar power to plastic surgery. As you review this entry, consider how abstracts can help students locate sources for research papers and skim current scholarship. See page 323 for the full article.

TV Movies of the First Decade of AIDS (Abstract)

Database: Expanded Academic Index   1
Subject: AIDS (disease) in motion pictures

TV movies of the first decade of AIDS. (American Values and Images)   2

Journal of Popular Film and Television, Spring 1993 v21 n1 p19(8).   3

Author: Frank Pilipp and Charles Shull   4

Abstract: The decade of 1983–1993 has produced several full-length fea-   5
ture films which respond to the AIDS epidemic. Three of them, 'As Is,'
'Andre's Mother,' and 'An Early Frost' undoubtedly portray the virus as
non-partisan when it comes to gender, color, or sexual orientation, although
they fail to destroy the image of AIDS as being a purely homosexual disease. The disease instead is viewed as punishment inflicted on the main
characters and their families for their violation of middle-class norms and
values.

Subjects: Gays—Portrayals, depictions, etc.   6
Motion pictures—Criticism, interpretation, etc.
AIDS (disease) in motion pictures—Criticism, interpretation, etc.

7   Features: illustration; photograph

8   AN: 14558418

Understanding Meaning

1. What information is contained in the abstract? How helpful would it be if you were researching the way television has responded to AIDS?
2. Is the abstract objective?

Evaluating Strategy

1. What problems does an abstract writer have in reducing an eight-page article to a single paragraph?
2. Should an abstract writer inject subjective opinion?

Appreciating Language

1. How objective is the language of the abstract?
2. Should an abstract be devoid of figurative language?

Connections across the Disciplines

1. At the library locate abstracts in your field and review summaries of several articles. How would they be helpful in doing research?
2. Read the full article (page 323). How successfully does this abstract summarize Pilipp and Shull's article?

Writing Suggestions

1. Select one of the articles in this book and draft an abstract. Try to capture the writer's thesis and main support in a single paragraph.
2. *Collaborative Writing:* Discuss this abstract with a number of students who have read the full article. How effective is this summary? What points do students feel have been omitted?

Want ads describe the ideal candidate for a job opening. This ad, which appeared in the New Orleans Times-Picayune, *presents a job description for a sales representative.*

3M Pharmaceutical Sales Representative Want Ad

3M Sales Representative
Pharmaceutical Products

3M Pharmaceuticals has an immediate need for an experienced sales professional to represent our products to physicians, pharmacies, hospitals and managed care facilities. These products include prescription medications related to the treatment of arthritic, cardiovascular and pulmonary conditions. This position will be based in New Orleans and will require overnight travel.

We prefer a college degree and 2+ years successful outside sales experience. Medical sales experience is preferred. Excellent communications and interpersonal skills are required. We provide base salary plus bonus, company car, complete business expenses and an attractive benefits package.

For confidential consideration, send <u>two (2)</u> copies of your resume to the below address by August 16, 1994. Candidates selected for consideration will be notified by September 2, 1994. No telephone inquiries or employment agency referrals please.

NAS REPLY SERVICE
Dept #7MP1089   One Appletree Square   Minneapolis, MN 55425
We Are An Equal Opportunity Employer M/F/D/V

Understanding Meaning

1. What are the requirements for this position?
2. What does this ad suggest about the reader 3M hopes to reach?
3. *Critical Thinking:* What are the limits of any want ad? Can a job be fully described in a few paragraphs? Why can't employers address all their interests and concerns?

Evaluating Strategy

1. Why does the ad first describe the job and then list the requirements?
2. Why is it important for an employer to promise applicants "confidential consideration"?

Appreciating Language

1. What words does the ad use to describe the ideal candidate?
2. Some ads promise applicants "huge commissions" and demand "hard charging" people. What does the absence of this kind of language suggest about this employer?

Connections across the Disciplines

1. Study want ads in your local newspaper. What common words stand out? How do employers describe the positions and the desired candidates? Do you see trends in the job market?
2. Consider points made by Charles Jamison in "Why My Business Failed" (page 464). How important would a well-written résumé be for an applicant to impress a goal-oriented business owner?

Writing Suggestions

1. Write a want ad for a job you once had. Try to model yours after ones you have seen in the newspaper. Keep your ad as short as possible.
2. *Collaborative Writing:* Work with a group of students and write a want ad together. Imagine you are hiring a part-time employee to act as secretary for your writing group. Determine the skills needed, the major duties, and how the ad should be worded. If members have differences of opinion, craft more than one ad, and ask other students to choose the most effective ad.

Monica Ramos was born in New Orleans and worked as a nurse before entering advertising sales. Although she has never sold pharmaceuticals, she prepared this résumé to apply for the position advertised by 3M (page 157). Given her sales ability and experience working in a hospital, Ramos feels she is qualified for the position. Notice that her résumé uses bulleted lists of specific accomplishments to provide details that are easily read or skimmed.

The Résumé of Monica Ramos

MONICA RAMOS
1455 Josephine Street #12
New Orleans, Louisiana 70118
(504) 524-6580
                                                                            1

OBJECTIVE   Pharmaceutical Sales   2

OVERVIEW   Three years experience in outside sales.   3
             Proven ability to secure new accounts in
             competitive markets. Five years experience
             in cardiac and pulmonary patient care.
             Knowledgeable in cardiac medications.
             Skilled in communicating with physicians
             and hospital staff.

EXPERIENCE   CRESCENT CITY MAGAZINE,   4
1993–Present New Orleans, LA
             <u>Account representative</u> selling advertising
             space in upscale magazine with 50,000
             circulation.
             * Developed 300 active accounts including
               hospitals, nursing homes, HMO's, clinics,
               and drug stores.
             * Personally developed restaurant/
               entertainment section, selling ads to
               100 area restaurants worth $200,000
               annually.

* Consistently rank in top 3 of 15 sales reps.
* Generated 65 new accounts in first three months.
* Directly assisted vice president of Charity Hospital in design of four-page insert.

5 1989–1993   TULANE UNIVERSITY MEDICAL CENTER, New Orleans, LA
Nurse in 25-bed intensive care unit specializing in critical cardiac and pulmonary care.
* Worked directly with physicians, cardiologists, and cardiovascular surgeons.
* Administered full range of cardiac medications.
* Attended in-service seminars presented by pharmaceutical representatives.
* Represented hospital on regional and state planning committees.

6 EDUCATION   LOUISIANA STATE UNIVERSITY MEDICAL CENTER—NEW ORLEANS B.S. Nursing, 1989

7 SALES TRAINING 1994–1995   SALES MANAGEMENT INSTITUTE, New Orleans, LA
* Attended seminars on networking, presentation skills, and closing strategies.

8 VOLUNTEER WORK   GREATER NEW ORLEANS YWCA
Conduct cardiac health/stress management workshops

9   References Available on Request

Understanding Meaning

1. Compare this résumé to the 3M want ad (page 157). Does it address the employer's needs?

2. What skills and experiences does Monica Ramos highlight? What are her important attributes?

Evaluating Strategy

1. One study revealed that the average executive devotes nine seconds to each résumé on initial screening. Does this résumé communicate its main points in a few seconds? Would it make a reader stop skimming and start reading?
2. How is the information arranged? Is it clear and easy to follow?

Appreciating Language

1. What is the tone of the résumé? How do the words portray the applicant?
2. What device does Monica Ramos use to convey a sense of action?

Connections across the Disciplines

1. Review this résumé after reading the article "Resumes That Rate a Second Look" (page 452). How does this résumé rate?

Writing Suggestions

1. Write your own résumé, either a current one or one as if you were prepared to graduate this semester.
2. *Collaborative Writing:* Meet with a group of students and have each member supply a résumé. Discuss the merits of each résumé you review. Talk about problems you have encountered. Take notes to improve your own résumé. Your library or placement office may offer guides and computer programs to help you develop your résumé.

STRATEGIES FOR WRITING DESCRIPTION

1. **Determine your purpose.** What is your goal—to entertain a general audience or to provide information to colleagues, employees, superiors, or customers? What are the most important details needed to support your purpose?

2. **Define your role.** If you are expressing personal opinion, you are free to add subjective elements to your writing. You may wish to include yourself in the piece of writing by making personal references and writing in the first person. If you are writing as a representative of a larger body, objective language is usually more appropriate.

3. **Consider your audience.** Which type of description would best suit your readers—subjective impressions or objective facts? What needs and expectations does your audience have? What details, facts, statistics, or descriptions will influence readers the most?

4. **Review the discipline or writing situation.** Determine if you should use technical or specialized terminology. If you are writing for a profession, academic discipline, government agency, or corporation, use standard methods of developing ideas.

5. **Select details.** Having determined the context, select details that emphasize your purpose, impress your audience, and follow any guidelines in your discipline. Descriptions should have focus. Eliminate details that may be interesting in themselves but do not serve your purpose.

6. **Organize details in an effective manner.** Good description is more than a collection of details. To be effective, your writing should be logically organized. You may organize details spatially by describing a house room by room or a city neighborhood by neighborhood. You may organize details in order of importance. If you use objective and subjective description, these details can alternate or be placed in separate sections.

7. **Avoid unnecessary detail or mechanical organization.** Descriptions have focus. A description of your apartment does not have to list every piece of furniture, explain how each room is decorated, or provide dimensions. In general avoid writing descriptions that draw unnecessary attention to mechanical arrangements:

    > *On the left-hand wall* is a bookcase. *To the right of the bookcase* is a stereo. *Around the corner of the stereo* stands an antique aquarium filled with tropical fish. *Above the aquarium* is a large seascape painting. Model ships line the window sill. A cabinet *to the right of the window* is filled with seashells.

8. **Allow details to create a dominant impression.** A subjective description of a room can focus on a single theme:

    > Although I live hundreds of miles from the ocean, my apartment has a seagoing motif. Beneath a sweeping seascape, a large antique aquarium dominates the liv-

ing room, its colorful tropical fish flashing among rocks and shells I collected in Florida. Miniature schooners, windjammers, and ketches line the windowsill. The ornate glass cabinet intended for china houses my prize collection of Hawaiian seashells.

SUGGESTED TOPICS FOR DESCRIPTIVE WRITING
General Assignments

Write a description on any of the following topics. Your description may contain passages demonstrating other modes, such as comparison or cause and effect. Select details carefully. Determine whether your description should rely on factual, objective support or subjective impressions. In choosing diction, be aware of the impact of connotation.

- Your first apartment
- The people who gather in a place you frequent—a coffee shop, store, tavern, library, or student union
- Your boss or professor
- The most desirable/least desirable place to live in your community
- The most dangerous situation you have faced
- The type of man/woman you find attractive
- The type of relationship you find most desirable
- The most serious environmental problem in your area
- The most interesting or most unconventional person you have met in the past year
- The best/worst party you have attended

Writing in Context

1. Imagine that your college has asked you to write a description of the campus for a brochure designed to recruit students. Your depiction should be easy to read and create a favorable impression.
2. Assume you write a column for an alternative campus newspaper. Develop a sarcastic description of the campus, the college administration, the faculty, or the student body.
3. Write an open letter to the student body of your high school describing what college life is like.
4. Imagine you are trying to sell your car. Write two brief ads, one designed for a campus flyer and the other for a newspaper.

This is the second version of a descriptive paper a student wrote in response to an assignment calling for "a brief description of a person, place, or thing." In the first draft, the student attempted to provide an overall view of New Orleans' French Quarter. Dissatisfied with its superficiality, he decided to concentrate on a single feature of the city.

Cities of the Dead

1   From the freeway the tombs look like a collection of children's playhouses. The white mausoleums mimic spired churches, porticoed mansions, neo-classic banks, Greek temples. The more elaborate tombs are arranged in neat rows and are adorned with flowers. Humbler tombs, resembling concrete dog houses, are jammed haphazardly together like lost luggage.

2   Few graveyards are as famous as New Orleans' above-ground cemeteries. In the 1700s the city's earliest settlers buried their dead along the banks of the Mississippi. As the population grew, the city selected a plot of land near Rampart Street as a burial ground. The traditional practice of burying the dead caused problems in Louisiana's tropical climate and watery soil. The water table was so high that grave diggers frequently struck water after two feet. Coffins bobbed to the surface and had to be sunk. Decaying bodies posed a major health threat, especially in summer. As a result, the dead had to be interred above ground in "vaults."

3   Unlike tombs in other cities, the vaults of New Orleans are reusable. Following a burial, the coffin is sealed in the vault until the body decomposes. Later the remaining bones are removed and placed in a lower crypt, leaving space for a new coffin. This way a single vault can serve a family for generations. Many civic organizations offered their members a cheaper alternative to the family vault by building attached tombs. Often several stories tall, these "apartment buildings" provided rows of tombs called "ovens."

4   Those resting in the three cemeteries, St. Louis Nos. one, two, and three, reflect the city's colorful history. Among the bankers and for-

mer mayors lie the remains of Dominique You, a pirate; the chess
player Paul Morphy; and Alexander Milne, a noted philanthropist.

But perhaps the most famous and mysterious tomb belongs to   5
Marie Laveau, still revered by many as the Voodoo Queen. Loyal fol-
lowers of Marie Laveau enact elaborate graveyard rituals to curry favor. Seeking her blessing, they turn around three times, tap the slab
of the tomb three times, and make a cross with the edge of a brick
kept atop the tomb. Visitors leave flowers and light votive candles,
while others place "hoodoo money"—two pennies or a dime and a
penny—in the flower holders flanking the tomb of one of the most
famous residents in the City of the Dead.

Questions for Review and Revision

1. How effective is the title?
2. The student describes the tombs by comparing them to Greek temples
   and dog houses. How effective is this device? Would the essay benefit
   from including more of the tombs' physical details?
3. What method does the student use to organize the essay? How important
   are paragraph breaks?
4. How effective is the ending? Would you like to see a more developed
   conclusion?
5. Throughout the essay the student places specialized terms like "ovens"
   and "hoodoo money" in quotation marks. How effective are his definitions? Are they clearly stated?
6. Read the paper aloud. What revisions would you make?

Writing Suggestions

1. Write a brief description of a feature unique to your hometown. Is there
   a piece of local history that visitors overlook or find puzzling? Present as
   many sensory details as possible.
2. *Collaborative Writing:* Discuss this essay with a group of students. Have
   each member volunteer opinions on its strengths and weaknesses. Do
   members suggest revisions or a need for added detail?

DESCRIPTION CHECKLIST

Before submitting your paper, review these points.

1. Have you limited your topic?

2. Do your supporting details suit your context? Should they be objective, subjective, or a blend?

3. Is your description focused and clearly organized, or is it only a random list of facts and observations?

4. Have you avoided including unnecessary details and awkward constructions?

5. Does sensory detail include more than sight? Can you add impressions of taste, touch, sound, or smell?

6. Do you avoid overly general terms and focus on specific impressions? Have you created dominant impressions?

7. Do you show rather than tell? Can you add action to your description to keep it from being static?

8. Do you keep a consistent point of view?

9. Read your paper aloud. How does it sound? Do any sections need expansion? Are there irrelevant details to be deleted or awkward expressions to be revised?

 Companion Web Site

See **http://sundance.heinle.com** for information on writing description.

 InfoTrac® College Edition

For additional reading go to InfoTrac College edition, your online research library, at **http://infotrac.thomsonlearning.com.**

- Enter the search term "description" using Keywords.
- Enter the name of an author you read in this chapter using Keywords.
- Enter a theme or idea your class discussed using Keywords.

4

Definition

ESTABLISHING MEANING

WHAT IS DEFINITION?

E ffective communication requires that writers and readers have a shared language. Words and ideas must be *defined* clearly to eliminate confusion and misinterpretation. Definitions limit or explain the meaning of a term or concept. As a college student you have probably devoted much of your time to learning new words and their definitions. Fields such as chemistry, psychology, sociology, economics, law, and anatomy have technical terms that must be mastered in order to communicate within the discipline.

Clearly stated definitions play a critical role in professional and business writing. In order to prevent confusion, conflict, and litigation, many union contracts, insurance policies, sales agreements, and leases include definitions so all parties will share a common understanding of important terms. Government documents and business proposals contain glossaries to familiarize readers with new or abstract terms. Failing to understand a definition can be costly. A tenant who does not understand a landlord's definition of "excessive noise" may face eviction. The car buyer who misinterprets the manufacturer's definition of "normal use" can void his or her warranty.

The term *definition* leads most people to think of a dictionary. But defining entails more than looking something up. Definitions are not always precise or universally accepted. Distinctly different types of definitions exist. To be an effective writer in college and your future profession, it is important to appreciate the range of definitions:

- **Standard definitions** are universally accepted and rarely subject to change. Words such as *tibia, dolphin, uranium, felony, turbine,* and *rifle* have exact meanings that are understood and shared by scholars, professionals, and the general public. Doctors, nurses, paramedics, and football coaches, for example, all recognize *tibia* as a specific bone in the body. Though different state legislatures might disagree on which specific crime constitutes a *felony*, they all accept its general concept.

- **Regulatory definitions** are officially designated terms and are subject to change. The National Football League, Internal Revenue Service (IRS), Federal Aviation Administration, Federal Communications Commission, school boards, labor organizations, the Catholic Church, and insurance companies issue definitions to guide policy, control operations, and make decisions. The IRS definition of *deductible meal allowance* can change yearly. One health insurance company may pay for a liver transplant while another carrier refuses, defining the procedure *experimental*. Regulatory definitions may be universally accepted, but they can change or be limited to a specific region or discipline. The building codes of New York and San Francisco may have varying definitions of what buildings are *structurally sound*. The medical definition of *insanity* varies greatly from the court-accepted, legal definition.

- **Evolving definitions** reflect changes in community attitudes, social values, governmental policy, and scientific research. In the nineteenth century corporal punishment was a routine feature of public school discipline. Today the same actions would be defined as *child abuse*. The term *date rape* defines incidents that generations ago would not be viewed as criminal assaults. Decades ago medical and psychology texts defined *homosexuality* as a mental disorder. Evolving definitions track social change and rarely shift as abruptly as regulatory definitions.

- **Qualifying definitions** limit meanings of words or concepts that are abstract or subject to dispute. How does one define an *alcoholic?* At what point do doctors label a patient *obese* or *senile?* Which young people are labeled *juvenile delinquents?* How does one define *genius?* In some fields organizations provide definitions. The American Medical Association may offer a definition of *alcoholism*. But unlike a regulatory term, physicians and researchers are free to dispute it and apply a different meaning altogether. Some definitions are hotly debated. Researchers, politicians, and social commentators continually argue about whether drug addiction and alcoholism should be defined as *disabilities*, which would entitle people to receive benefits.

- **Cultural definitions** are shaped by the history, values, and attitudes of a national, ethnic, or religious group. Just as evolving definitions alter over time, cultural definitions differ from group to group. In some countries it is customary to offer cash gifts to officials as a *tribute*. In the United States the same action would be defined as an illegal *bribe*. People around the world embrace *freedom* but define it very differently. For most Americans *freedom* is defined in personal terms, meaning freedom of individual movement and expression. In other countries, people may define *freedom* in national terms, as protecting the independence and security of their homeland even if it means censorship and restricted personal liberties.

- **Personal definitions** are used by writers to express individual interpretations of words or ideas. Your concept of a good parent would be a personal definition. A writer can frame an entire essay in terms of a personal definition, such as John Ciardi's "What Is Happiness?" (page 189), or simply establish a series of personal definitions at the outset of a narrative or persuasive paper. Writers often use personal definition as a method of stating their opinions.

Methods of Definition

Definitions can be established using a number of techniques:

1. **Defining through synonyms** is the simplest method of providing meaning for a word. Glossaries and dictionaries customarily define technical terms or foreign words with synonyms. *Costal* refers to *ribs*. A *siesta* can be translated as a *nap*. A *casement* can be explained as a *window*.
2. **Defining by description** provides details about a word or subject and gives readers a sense of what it might look, feel, taste, smell, or sound like. Defining a *costrel* as *a small flask with a loop or loops that is suspended from a belt* provides readers with a clear picture. Descriptive definitions also can demonstrate how something operates. An *airbag* can be defined as *a rapidly inflated cushion designed to protect automobile passengers in a collision.*
3. **Defining by example** provides specific illustrations to establish meaning. A *felony* can be defined as *a serious crime such as murder, rape, or burglary.* Examples can establish meaning through identification. Telling a fourth-grade class that an *adjective is a word that modifies a noun* will not be as effective as providing examples children can easily recognize—*red, fast, tall, silly, old-fashioned, hot.* Complex or abstract concepts are easier to comprehend if defined by example. Income tax instructions include numerous examples to define what is and is not deductible.
4. **Defining by comparison** uses analogies readers can understand to provide meaning to something less familiar. A television reporter covering a space mission defined NASA terminology using comparisons viewers would readily understand. To explain the term *power down*, she remarked that the astronauts were *conserving power by turning off nonessential electrical devices, much like switching off the radio and windshield wipers on a car.* Because they can oversimplify complex ideas, comparative definitions must be used carefully.
5. **Extended definitions** qualify or limit the meaning of abstract, disputed, or highly complex words or concepts. Words such as *sin, love,* and *racism* cannot be adequately explained through synonyms, brief descriptions, or examples. A full description may require several paragraphs. The *yucca* can be defined as a *spear-leafed desert plant,* but, to explain its significance to the Navajo, Terry Tempest Williams writes an entire essay (page 202).

The Purpose of Definition

Definitions generally serve to establish meaning, to provide a common or shared understanding. But they also can be persuasive. Evolving definitions frequently indicate a break with past beliefs and suggest alternative interpretations. The first psychiatrists who defined *homosexuality* in terms of *sexual orientation* rather than as *deviancy, mental disorder,* or *sexual perversion* were clearly trying to persuade their readers to change their attitudes.

To transform public attitudes, writers frequently urge readers to redefine something, to change their perceptions and see striking a child as *abuse* instead of *spanking* or to accept graffiti as *street art* and not *vandalism.* Definitions can play a critical role in shaping opinions and making arguments. Drug addicts, for instance, can be defined in legalistic terms and viewed as *criminals* who should be imprisoned or depicted in medical terms as *sufferers* needing treatment.

Definition in Context

The way writers define subjects depends greatly on context. In defining *depression* for a marketing brochure, a psychotherapist directs an explanation to prospective clients:

> Depression is an internal state—a feeling of sadness, loss, "the blues," deep disappointment. *When it is more severe, you may have feelings of irritability, touchiness, guilt, self-reproach, loss of self-esteem, worthlessness, hopelessness, helplessness, and even thoughts of death and suicide.*

The definition is addressed to the reader, using the word "you," and focuses on personal "feelings" stated in general terms. In contrast, Jessica Kuper's *Encyclopedia of Psychology* offers a definition for mental health professionals:

> *Depression* is a term used to describe a mood, a symptom, and syndromes of affective disorders. As a mood, it refers to a transient state of feeling sad, blue, forlorn, cheerless, unhappy, and/or down. As a symptom, it refers to a complaint that often accompanies a group of biopsychosocial problems. In contrast, the depressive syndromes include a wide spectrum of psychobiological dysfunctions that vary in frequency, severity, and duration.

The inclusion of words such as "affective disorders" and "biopsychosocial" indicate that this definition is intended for a specialized audience familiar with technical terms.

STRATEGIES FOR READING DEFINITIONS

In reading the definition entries in this chapter, keep these questions in mind.

Meaning

1. Which type of definition is the author developing—standard, regulatory, evolving, qualifying, cultural, or personal?
2. What is the author's purpose—to provide a definition to establish common ground, to explain a complex issue, or to persuade readers to alter their opinions?
3. What audience is the writer addressing—a general reader or a specialist? Does the audience need to know the definitions in order to base decisions or guide future actions?
4. What is the nature of the discipline or writing situation? Is the writer working within a strictly regulated profession or the general marketplace of ideas?

Strategy

1. How does the writer define the word, object, or concept—through synonyms, descriptions, examples, or comparisons?
2. Is the definition limited to a specific incident or context, or can it be applied generally? Is the writer defining a particular person or a personality trait that could be shared by millions?
3. Does the writer supply personal examples, or does he or she rely on official sources to establish the definition?

Language

1. What role do word choice and connotation play in establishing the definition?
2. What do the tone and level of language reveal about the writer's purpose and intended audience?

EILEEN SIMPSON

Eileen Simpson is a psychotherapist who struggled for years to overcome dyslexia, a reading disorder that affects more than 20 million Americans. She is the author of several books, including Poets in Their Youth, *a memoir of her marriage to the poet John Berryman. Other books based on her personal experiences explored problems of children growing up without parents. This section comes from her 1979 book* Reversals: A Personal Account of Victory over Dyslexia.

Dyslexia

OVERVIEW: *Simpson provides a standard definition of an existing term by examining its Greek and Latin roots and then demonstrates the effects dyslexia has on its victims. Notice that she supplies examples to help readers fully appreciate the implications of a widely misunderstood disorder.*

1

opens with
definition

<u>Dyslexia (from the Greek, *dys*, faulty + *lexis*, speech, cognate with the Latin *legere*, to read), developmental or specific dyslexia as it's technically called, the disorder I suffered from, is the inability of otherwise normal children to read.</u> Children whose intelligence is below average, whose vision or hearing is defective, who have not had proper schooling, or who are too emotionally disturbed or brain-damaged to profit from it belong in other diagnostic categories. They, too, may be unable to learn to read, but they cannot properly be called dyslexics.

describes
what dyslexia
is not

2

background

For more than seventy years the essential nature of the affliction has been hotly disputed by psychologists, neurologists, and educators. It is generally agreed, however, that it is the result of a neurophysiological flaw in the brain's ability to process language. It is probably inherited, although some experts are reluctant to say this because they fear people will equate "inherited" with "untreatable." <u>Treatable it certainly is: not a disease to be cured, but a malfunction that requires retraining.</u>

3

explains why
reading
is difficult

Reading is the most complex skill a child entering school is asked to develop. What makes it complex, in part, is that letters are less constant than objects. A car seen from a distance, close to, from above, or below, or in a mirror still looks like a car even though the optical image changes. The letters of the alphabet are more whimsical. Take the letter *b*. Turned upside down it becomes a *p*. Looked at in a mirror, it becomes a *d*. Capitalized, it becomes something quite different, a *B*. The *M* upside down is a *W*. The *E* flipped over becomes Ǝ. This reversed *E* is familiar to mothers of normal children who have just begun to go to school. The earliest examples of art work they bring home often have I LOVƎ YOU written on them.

Dyslexics differ from other children in that they read, spell, and write letters upside down and turned around far more frequently and for a much longer time. In what seems like a capricious manner, they also add letters, syllables, and words, or, just as capriciously, delete them. With palindromic words (was-saw, on-no), it is the order of the letters rather than the orientation they change. The new word makes sense, but not the sense intended. Then there are other words where the changed order—"sorty" for story—does not make sense at all.

4 explains how dyslexics see letters

The inability to recognize that g, *g*, and *G* are the same letter, the inability to maintain the orientation of the letters, to retain the order in which they appear, and to follow a line of text without jumping above or below it—all the results of the flaw—can make of an orderly page of words a dish of alphabet soup.

5

Also essential for reading is the ability to store words in memory and to retrieve them. This very particular kind of memory dyslexics lack. So, too, do they lack the ability to hear what the eye sees, and to see what they hear. If the eye sees "off," the ear must hear "off" and not "of," or "for." If the ear hears "saw," the eye must see that it looks like "saw" on the page and not "was." Lacking these skills, a sentence or paragraph becomes a coded message to which the dyslexic can't find the key.

6

It is only a slight exaggeration to say that those who learned to read without difficulty can best understand the labor reading is for a dyslexic by turning a page of text upside down and trying to decipher it.

7

While the literature is replete with illustrations of the way these children write and spell, there are surprisingly few examples of how they read. One, used for propaganda purposes to alert the public to the vulnerability of dyslexics in a literate society, is a sign warning that behind it are guard dogs trained to kill. The dyslexic reads:

8

a Wurring
Guard God
Patoly

9 example #1 demonstrates dyslexia

for

Warning
Guard Dog
Patrol

10

and, of course, remains ignorant of the danger.

11   Looking for a more commonplace example, and hoping to recapture the way I must have read in fourth grade, I recently observed dyslexic children at the Educational Therapy Clinic in Princeton, through the courtesy of Elizabeth Travers, the director. The first child I saw, eight-year-old Anna (whose red hair and brown eyes reminded me of myself at that age), had just come to the Clinic and was learning the alphabet. Given the story of "Little Red Riding Hood," which is at the second grade level, she began confidently enough, repeating the title from memory, then came to a dead stop. With much coaxing throughout, she read as follows:

12   Grandma you a top. Grandma [looks over at picture of Red Riding Hood].
example #2   Red Riding Hood [long pause, presses index finger into the paper. Looks at
of dyslexia   me for help. I urge: Go ahead] the a [puts head close to the page, nose almost touching] on Grandma

for

13   Once upon a time there was a little girl who had a red coat with a red hood. Etc.

14   "Grandma" was obviously a memory from having heard the story read aloud. Had I needed a reminder of how maddening my silences must have been to Miss Henderson, and how much patience is required to teach these children, Anna, who took almost ten minutes to read these few lines, furnished it. The main difference between Anna and me at that age is that Anna clearly felt no need to invent. She was perplexed, but not anxious, and seemed to have infinite tolerance for her long silences.

15   Toby, a nine-year-old boy with superior intelligence, had a year of tutoring behind him and could have managed "Little Red Riding Hood" with ease. His text was taken from the *Reader's Digest's Reading Skill Builder,* Grade IV. He read:

16   A kangaroo likes as if he had but truck together warm. His saw neck and head do not . . . [Here Toby sighed with fatigue] seem to feel happy back. They
example #3   and tried and so every a tiger Moses and shoots from lonesome day and
of dyslexia   shouts and long shore animals. And each farm play with five friends . . .

17   He broke off with the complaint, "This is too hard. Do I have to read any more?"

18   His text was:

A kangaroo looks as if he had been put together wrong. His small neck and   19
head do not seem to fit with his heavy back legs and thick tail. Soft eyes, a
twinkly little nose and short front legs seem strange on such a large strong animal. And each front paw has five fingers, like a man's hand.

An English expert gives the following bizarre example of an adult   20
dyslexic's performance:

An the bee-what in the tel mother of the biothodoodoo to the majoram or   21
that emidrate eni eni Krastrei, mestriet to Ketra lotombreidi to ra from treido   *example #4*
as that.   *of dyslexia*

His text, taken from a college catalogue the examiner happened to have   22
close at hand, was:

It shall be in the power of the college to examine or not every licentiate, pre-   23
vious to his admission to the fellowship, as they shall think fit.

That evening when I read aloud to Auntie for the first time, I probably   24
began as Toby did, my memory of the classroom lesson keeping me close to
the text. When memory ran out, and Auntie did not correct my errors, I began to invent. When she still didn't stop me, I may well have begun to im-
provise in the manner of this patient—anything to keep going and keep up
the myth that I was reading—until Auntie brought the "gibberish" to a halt.

Understanding Meaning

1. What basic definition does Simpson provide? What misinterpretation does she
   note can occur if a condition is considered "inherited"?
2. How does Simpson summarize controversies in the field of research? What do
   scientists from different disciplines agree on?
3. What is the implication to dyslexics and their parents that dyslexia is "not a
   disease to be cured, but a malfunction that requires retraining"?
4. *Critical Thinking:* How can this disorder affect a child's development if it is not
   detected?

Evaluating Strategy

1. Why is it effective to provide an etymology of the word *dyslexia* at the opening?
   Does this help satisfy reader curiosity about a term many people have heard
   but do not fully understand?

2. How does Simpson's introduction of personal experience affect the definition? Does this add a human dimension to her definition, or does it detract from its objectivity? Would the inclusion of personal experience be appropriate in a textbook?

3. Do the examples of dyslexic reading dramatize the effects of this disorder? Would an explanation alone suffice to impress readers with the crippling effects of a reading disorder?

4. *Other Modes:* How does Simpson use *description* and *narration* to develop her definition? What role can stories or case studies provide readers seeking to understand a complex subject?

Appreciating Language

1. Simpson is defining a complex disorder. How does her language indicate that she is seeking to address a general audience? Would the vocabulary differ in a definition written for psychology students?

2. Simpson cites an example of a dyslexic reading a warning sign as "propaganda." Does the use of this word weaken her argument that dyslexia is a serious condition? Why or why not?

3. How does Simpson define the term "palindromic"?

Connections across the Disciplines

1. Simpson describes a disorder from the standpoint of a patient. How does her account differ from Oliver Sacks's account as a physician (page 86)?

2. How does Simpson's task of defining an existing term differ from the task of defining a newly invented term like "Spanglish" (page 177)?

Writing Suggestions

1. Write a concisely worded definition of dyslexia in your own words.

2. *Critical Writing:* Write an essay expressing your view on how dyslexics should be graded in college. Should students with dyslexia be allowed more time on essay tests, be offered special tutorial services, or be given alternative assignments and examinations? Can students with disabilities be accommodated while maintaining academic standards?

3. *Collaborative Writing:* Working with several other students, craft a brief explanation of dyslexia to be incorporated into a brochure for parents of children with learning impairments. Keep your audience in mind, and avoid making negative comments that might upset parents.

JANICE CASTRO, DAN COOK, AND CRISTINA GARCIA

Janice Castro (1949–) is a journalist who became Time *magazine's first health-policy reporter. In 1994 she published* The American Way of Health: How Medicine Is Changing and What It Means to You. *In addition to writing about medicine, she has published articles on topics ranging from pension plans to home-shopping. This essay appeared as part of a* Time *cover story about Hispanics.*

Spanglish

OVERVIEW: *In this essay the writers invent a term to define a blend of English and Spanish spoken by a growing number of Americans. As you read their article, notice how they use* description, example, *and* comparison *to develop their definition.*

In Manhattan a first-grader greets her visiting grandparents, happily exclaiming, "Come here, *siéntate*!" Her bemused grandfather, who does not speak Spanish, nevertheless knows she is asking him to sit down. A Miami personnel officer understands what a job applicant means when he says, "*Quiero un* part time." Nor do drivers miss a beat reading a billboard alongside a Los Angeles street advertising CERVEZA—SIX PACK!

This free-form blend of Spanish and English, known as Spanglish, is common linguistic currency wherever concentrations of Hispanic Americans are found in the U.S. In Los Angeles, where 55% of the city's 3 million inhabitants speak Spanish, Spanglish is as much a part of daily life as sunglasses. Unlike the broken-English efforts of earlier immigrants from Europe, Asia and other regions, Spanglish has become a widely accepted conversational mode used casually—even playfully—by Spanish-speaking immigrants and native-born Americans alike.

Consisting of one part Hispanicized English, one part Americanized Spanish and more than a little fractured syntax, Spanglish is a bit like a Robin Williams comedy routine: a crackling line of cross-cultural patter straight from the melting pot. Often it enters Anglo homes and families through the children, who pick it up at school or at play with their young Hispanic contemporaries. In other cases, it comes from watching TV; many an Anglo child watching *Sesame Street* has learned *uno dos tres* almost as quickly as one two three.

4   Spanglish takes a variety of forms, from the Southern California Anglos who bid farewell with the utterly silly "*hasta la* bye-bye" to the Cuban-American drivers in Miami who *parquean* their *carros*. Some Spanglish sentences are mostly Spanish, with a quick detour for an English word or two. A Latino friend may cut short a conversation by glancing at his watch and excusing himself with the explanation that he must "*ir al* supermarket."

5   Many of the English words transplanted in this way are simply handier than their Spanish counterparts. No matter how distasteful the subject, for example, it is still easier to say "income tax" than *impuesto sobre la renta*. At the same time, many Spanish-speaking immigrants have adopted such terms as VCR, microwave and dishwasher for what they view as largely American phenomena. Still other English words convey a cultural context that is not implicit in the Spanish. A friend who invites you to a *lonche* most likely has in mind the brisk American custom of "doing lunch" rather than the languorous afternoon break traditionally implied by *almuerzo*.

6   Mainstream Americans exposed to similar hybrids of German, Chinese or Hindi might be mystified. But even Anglos who speak little or no Spanish are somewhat familiar with Spanglish. Living among them, for one thing, are 19 million Hispanics. In addition, more American high school and university students sign up for Spanish than for any other foreign language.

7   Only in the past ten years, though, has Spanglish begun to turn into a national slang. Its popularity has grown with the explosive increases in U.S. immigration from Latin American countries. English has increasingly collided with Spanish in retail stores, offices and classrooms, in pop music and on street corners. Anglos whose ancestors picked up such Spanish words as *rancho*, *bronco*, *tornado* and *incommunicado*, for instance, now freely use such Spanish words as *gracias*, *bueno*, *amigo* and *por favor*.

8   Among Latinos, Spanglish conversations often flow more easily from Spanish into several sentences of English and back.

9   Spanglish is a sort of code for Latinos: the speakers know Spanish, but their hybrid language reflects the American culture in which they live. Many lean to shorter, clipped phrases in place of the longer, more graceful expressions their parents used. Says Leonel de la Cuesta, an assistant professor of modern languages at Florida International University in Miami: "In the U.S., time is money, and that is showing up in Spanglish as an economy of language." Conversational examples: *taipiar* (type) and *winshi-wiper* (windshield wiper) replace *escribir a máquina* and *limpiaparabrisas*.

10   Major advertisers, eager to tap the estimated $134 billion in spending power wielded by Spanish-speaking Americans, have ventured into Spanglish to promote their products. In some cases, attempts to sprinkle Spanish

through commercials have produced embarrassing gaffes. A Braniff airlines ad that sought to tell Spanish-speaking audiences they could settle back *en* (in) luxuriant *cuero* (leather) seats, for example, inadvertently said they could fly without clothes (*encuero*). A fractured translation of the Miller Lite slogan told readers the beer was "Filling, and less delicious." Similar blunders are often made by Anglos trying to impress Spanish-speaking pals. But if Latinos are amused by mangled Spanglish, they also recognize these goofs as a sort of friendly acceptance. As they might put it, *no problema.*

Understanding Meaning

1. What is Spanglish? Can you define it in a single sentence?
2. How does the concept of "Spanglish" differ from "broken English"?
3. Who uses Spanglish? What does it indicate about the growing Hispanic influence in the United States?
4. *Critical Thinking:* Many Americans advocate "English only" and oppose bilingual education. What does the emergence of Spanglish reveal about the status of English in America? Is there any danger that immigrants will fail to master English?

Evaluating Strategy

1. How do the authors use examples to create their definition?
2. How do the authors organize details to build a coherent essay?
3. How effective are the opening and closing paragraphs?

Appreciating Language

1. What do the tone and style of the essay suggest about the authors' attitude toward their subject?
2. *Critical Thinking:* The writers call Spanglish "slang." What is slang to you? Would you consider it an appropriate label for Spanglish?

Connections across the Disciplines

1. How does defining an invented term like *Spanglish* differ from defining an established concept like dyslexia? How does this article differ from Eileen Simpson's (page 172)?

2. Janice Castro shows us a lighthearted aspect of Hispanic life. How does this differ from the experiences described by Luis Alberto Urrea (page 129) and Armando Rendón (page 586)?

Writing Suggestions

1. Invent a word to represent something you have observed and support your definition with details. You might define "blind datism" or "recycling phobia" or "cable television withdrawal."
2. *Collaborative Writing:* Ask three or four students to identify a special kind of language they have encountered. Discuss samples and list examples, then write a short definition of "campus-ese," "first-date euphemisms," "parent-ese," or "on-line slang," for example.

ELLEN GOODMAN

Ellen Goodman (1941–) was born in Massachusetts and graduated from Radcliffe College. She worked for Newsweek *and the* Detroit Free Press *before joining the* Boston Globe *in 1967. Her column "At Large" has been widely syndicated since 1976. As an essayist and television commentator, Goodman has discussed feminism, changes in family life, sexual harassment, and male and female relationships. Her essays have been collected in several books, including* Close to Home, At Large, *and* Turning Points.

The Company Man

OVERVIEW: *Instead of using a number of illustrations to develop a definition, Goodman presents a single, extended example of a person who fits her personal view of a workaholic.*

He worked himself to death, finally and precisely, at 3:00 A.M. Sunday morning.

1

The obituary didn't say that, of course. It said that he died of a coronary thrombosis—I think that was it—but everyone among his friends and acquaintances knew it instantly. He was a perfect Type A, a workaholic, a classic, they said to each other and shook their heads—and thought for five or ten minutes about the way they lived.

2

This man who worked himself to death finally and precisely at 3:00 A.M. Sunday morning—on his day off—was fifty-one years old and a vice-president. He was, however, one of six vice-presidents, and one of three who might conceivably—if the president died or retired soon enough— have moved to the top spot. Phil knew that.

3

He worked six days a week, five of them until eight or nine at night, during a time when his own company had begun the four-day week for everyone but the executives. He worked like the Important People. He had no outside "extracurricular interests," unless, of course, you think about a monthly golf game that way. To Phil, it was work. He always ate egg salad sandwiches at his desk. He was, of course, overweight, by 20 or 25 pounds. He thought it was okay, though, because he didn't smoke.

4

On Saturdays, Phil wore a sports jacket to the office instead of a suit, because it was the weekend.

5

He had a lot of people working for him, maybe sixty, and most of them liked him most of the time. Three of them will be seriously considered for his job. The obituary didn't mention that.

6

7   But it did list his "survivors" quite accurately. He is survived by his wife, Helen, forty-eight years old, a good woman of no particular marketable skills, who worked in an office before marrying and mothering. She had, according to her daughter, given up trying to compete with his work years ago, when the children were small. A company friend said, "I know how much you will miss him." And she answered, "I already have."

8   "Missing him all these years," she must have given up part of herself which had cared too much for the man. She would be "well taken care of."

9   His "dearly beloved" eldest of the "dearly beloved" children is a hard-working executive in a manufacturing firm down South. In the day and a half before the funeral, he went around the neighborhood researching his father, asking the neighbors what he was like. They were embarrassed.

10   His second child is a girl, who is twenty-four and newly married. She lives near her mother and they are close, but whenever she was alone with her father, in a car driving somewhere, they had nothing to say to each other.

11   The youngest is twenty, a boy, a high-school graduate who has spent the last couple of years, like a lot of his friends, doing enough odd jobs to stay in grass and food. He was the one who tried to grab at his father, and tried to mean enough to him to keep the man at home. He was his father's favorite. Over the last two years, Phil stayed up nights worrying about the boy.

12   The boy once said, "My father and I only board here."

13   At the funeral, the sixty-year-old company president told the forty-eight-year-old widow that the fifty-one-year-old deceased had meant much to the company and would be missed and would be hard to replace. The widow didn't look him in the eye. She was afraid he would read her bitterness and, after all, she would need him to straighten out the finances—the stock options and all that.

14   Phil was overweight and nervous and worked too hard. If he wasn't at the office, he was worried about it. Phil was a Type A, a heart-attack natural. You could have picked him out in a minute from a lineup.

15   So when he finally worked himself to death, at precisely 3:00 A.M. Sunday morning, no one was really surprised.

16   By 5:00 P.M. the afternoon of the funeral, the company president had begun, discreetly of course, with care and taste, to make inquiries about his replacement. One of the three men. He asked around: "Who's been working the hardest?"

Understanding Meaning

1. How does Goodman define a workaholic? Why does she assert that Phil's heart attack was directly related to his career?
2. What does Goodman's definition imply about the quality of Phil's life? What does she suggest that it was lacking?
3. What, if anything, seemed to have driven Phil?
4. Goodman mentions that Phil provided well for his widow. Is Phil, a hard-working vice-president who cares about his family, an ideal man in the eyes of many women? If Phil were African-American or Hispanic, would he be viewed as a "role model"? Would a "company woman" be seen as a feminist?
5. *Critical Thinking:* Americans have long admired hard workers. Franklin, Edison, Henry Ford, and Martin Luther King Jr. became legendary for their accomplishments. On the other hand, Americans long for more leisure time. Is there a double standard? Do we want to spend more time with our friends and family but expect our doctors, lawyers, contractors, and stockbrokers to work overtime for us, meet our deadlines, and always be a phone call away?

Evaluating Strategy

1. Would Goodman's definition be stronger if she included more than one example?
2. What impact does the final paragraph have? How does this reinforce her point?

Appreciating Language

1. Goodman places certain phrases in quotation marks— "well taken care of" and "dearly beloved." What is the effect of highlighting these terms?
2. What does the term "company man" suggest? Would "church man" or "advocacy man" provoke different responses?

Connections across the Disciplines

1. Does Goodman's use of the fictional Phil make her definition more effective than the less personalized examples offered by Jonathan Ritter in "The World View of a Computer Hacker" (page 185)?
2. Consider Liz Grinslade's article "Evaluating a Job Opportunity" (page 459) and Charles N. Jamison Jr.'s "Why My Business Failed" (page 464). Do such articles suggest that Americans tend to identify themselves with their careers? Do people sometimes have trouble separating themselves from work, allowing a job to define their lives?

Writing Suggestions

1. Develop your own definition of a *workaholic*. Can it be defined in hours worked or by the degree of stress a job creates? Does an actor or writer working eighty hours a week to rehearse a play or write a novel fit the category of *workaholic*? Is a mother with young children by definition a workaholic?

2. *Collaborative Writing:* Speak with fellow students, and write a short statement in response to the question, "What do we owe our employers?"

J O N A T H A N   R I T T E R

Jonathan Ritter (1965–) is a technical writer. After completing his studies at the University of Alberta, Ritter worked as a consultant, computer salesman, and engineer in Canada and Australia. Ritter now edits a community newspaper and develops software programs. Among his greatest interests is the role computers play in shaping society.

The World View of a Computer Hacker

OVERVIEW: *As you read this article, consider what definition you would ascribe to a computer hacker. Can some hackers be deemed "terrorists," "blackmailers," or "vandals"?*

The dawn of the electronic age has brought a new breed of individual to 1
life: the computer hacker. A distant cousin of the weekend hobbyist or casual enthusiast, the hacker regards computers and their employment as the single most defining element of his being. He derives both physical and spiritual fulfillment from their use.

Viewing *data* as weapons and *programs* as their delivery system, the 2
hacker considers himself a privateer of the modern era. He likens his computer to a vessel, a battleship for him to cruise the world's computer networks, assailing the weak and subverting the unsuspecting. To his prying fingers, no data base is sacred. He is the underdog, a David against an army of Goliaths, and he fantasizes about bringing big corporations and, indeed, entire governments, to their knees.

Periodically having to detach himself for such things as going to work or 3
gathering food, the computer hacker is decisively in his element when perched in front of a computer terminal in his basement or attic. Once he has dispensed with his dinner of Alphabits and cheese toast, secured a plentiful supply of Coke and cleaned the previous night's tobacco dust from his screen, the hacker will ready himself for another night's computing session. Consoled by the soothing hum of his machine's cooling fan, he will bask momentarily in the warm glow of the monitor before easing forward, after a few minutes of quiet concentration, to quickly, but gently and with precision, tap out a string of keystrokes. He has targeted his prey.

The computer hacker is not a social animal. He struggles with small 4
talk and has difficulty communicating with technically uninformed people, and his introversion confines him to a tightly knit circle of friends. Arriving

unescorted at a party, he will drift about making perfunctory conversation before gravitating to the basement (or garage) to happily chat away in technobabble with two or three like-minded people. At the party's breakup, he will offer genuine thanks to the host, not so much for the Chivas, but for the chance to meet a fellow developer of self-propagating, autonomous computer programs. A sporadic user of alcohol, the computer hacker breaks his prolonged dry spells with feverish bouts of whisky drinking with other hackers, who invariably spend the evening contriving a plot to destabilize the overseas currency market.

5   The computer hacker's bizarre fixations and peculiar habits are telling signs of his breed. He will, for example, operate all of his computers with the covers removed, partly because he relishes the sight of raw electronics, and partly because he is regularly installing and removing components. He will speak lustily of the "techno-aroma" of new equipment and will regularly place his nose next to the cooling fan to inhale the scents of jet-moulded plastic metal and printed circuit boards. An amorous relationship exists between the hacker and his computers. He can often be found slinking away from a late-night computing session, physically drained and smoking a cigarette.

6   The hacker will often display perplexing and astonishing behavior when associating with mainstream society. When planning to move from one dumpy apartment to another, for instance, the hacker will ask the landlord questions about reliable power and "clean" telephone lines, and his eyes will expertly scan the dwelling for an abundance of AC outlets. In a consumer-electronics shop, the "candy store" for the hacker, he will do such things as program VCRs and ask to look *inside* television sets. He typically knows exactly what he wants before he shops, having studied the 600-page *Computer Shopper's Guide* and memorized product evaluations from *Byte Magazine*. Fluent in at least three computer languages, the hacker commonly leaves people bewildered by his speech. He does this unintentionally, absentmindedly forgetting to include English in his conversation.

7   Friends and family who seek advice or help from the hacker frequently regret the decision. Humour is often of a vocational nature to the hacker, who is likely to regard as extremely funny the suggestions to a co-worker that she look "behind the desk" for a missing computer file, or that perhaps a document that didn't get printed is somehow "stuck in the cable."

8   The hacker's preferences, predictably, reflect his personality. He regards Radio Shack as a store for amateurs and any equipment not meeting U.S. military specifications as "Fisher Price playthings." He spends an inordinate amount of his income on gadgetry, keeps a spare computer around

just in case, and is interested in cellular car phones only for the possibility of using them with his laptop computer.

To the hacker, a job is only a source of income [with] which he is able to purchase more computing implements. He will usually disguise himself as a white-collar worker and function as a support or development person, burrowing himself away in a back office to work on obscure projects unknown and incomprehensible to most of his co-workers. The anonymity of his circumstances is deliberate, as he loathes the idea of a more public position and does not like people to know of his extracurricular activities. He derides IBM for setting the industry standard—stiffened white shirt, plain tie and dark blazer—and will habitually show up for work wearing the same corduroy jacket, pop-stained tie, untucked shirt and beltless trousers. When the temperature drops, he will simply add layers of mismatched clothing as needed.

His company's computer system is almost certainly regarded with disdain, as it rarely matches the power and flexibility of his home system(s). When his management refuses to authorize the purchase of the computer equipment he has asked for, he contemptuously, but briefly, considers sabotaging the company's computer network, or at least crippling it enough to justify his requisition.

Politically, the hacker is attracted to the Reform Party, solely because of its promise to pour millions into lengthening the information highway. Conversely, he is suspicious of the NDP for its "Luddite thinking," and instinctively would never vote for a party whose literature was printed on cheap, dot-matrix printers. Bill Clinton gets praise from the hacker for advertising himself as the first president who can be reached by electronic mail.

The computer hacker can be seen as a manifestation of a society surrounded and enthralled by technology. He is awed by its magnitude, inspired by its possibilities and anxious about its future. He can be likened to his ancestors 10,000 years ago, who rubbed two sticks together and changed the course of the world forever.

Understanding Meaning

1. How does Ritter define hackers? Are they misfits in your view?
2. What role does ego or professional pride play in the world of computer hackers?
3. What attitude does Ritter have toward hackers?
4. *Critical Thinking:* At one point Ritter calls hackers "a distant cousin of the weekend hobbyist" but later states they spend evenings plotting to "destabilize the overseas currency market." Do you see a conflict between these views?

Is the hacker harmless or threatening? Do you see hackers as potential "techno-terrorists"?

Evaluating Strategy

1. What methods does Ritter use to define the world of the hacker?
2. Ritter never mentions the damage hackers have inflicted and could continue to inflict on individuals, corporations, and governments. Is this a serious omission? What does it reveal about his attitude?

Appreciating Language

1. Examine the words Ritter uses to describe hackers. What connotations do they have?
2. How would you characterize Ritter's tone?
3. *Critical Thinking:* Ritter uses the male pronoun "he" throughout the article. Do you see this as an oversight or as a deliberate choice to emphasize his view that hackers are exclusively men?

Connections across the Disciplines

1. Consider the points Carl Sagan makes in his article "Why We Need to Understand Science" (page 563). Do you think many Americans are unable to comprehend how computer hackers could affect society?
2. Review Louis Mizell Jr.'s article, "Who's Listening to Your Cell Phone Calls?" (page 312). What do Ritter and Mizell reveal about how technology can be used by criminals? Do you think most people are aware of how vulnerable they are?

Writing Suggestions

1. Define a personality type you have observed—the male chauvinist, the compulsive shopper, the smoker, the party animal. Your essay should include numerous examples and may be serious or humorous in tone.
2. *Collaborative Writing:* Discuss hackers with several students and write a counter-definition, highlighting the threat hackers can pose to national security, personal privacy, and law enforcement.

JOHN CIARDI

John Ciardi (1916–1986) was a poet, literary critic, and translator. After teaching at Harvard, Rutgers, and the University of Kansas, he left academics to pursue a full-time literary career. As poetry editor for the Saturday Review *for two decades, he attempted to make poetry accessible to a wide audience. Ciardi's most ambitious work was a translation of Dante Alighieri's work, which took him sixteen years. As a poet, critic, and professor, Ciardi was a student of language. For many years he was a guest commentator on National Public Radio, where he offered listeners interesting and amusing anecdotes about the origins and histories of everyday words.*

What Is Happiness?

OVERVIEW: *In this essay, which first appeared in* Saturday Review, *Ciardi tries to define the elusive concept of happiness. In developing his definition, Ciardi analyzes the role of advertising and the nature of materialism in American life.*

The right to pursue happiness is issued to Americans with their birth certificates, but no one seems quite sure which way it ran. It may be we are issued a hunting license but offered no game. Jonathan Swift seemed to think so when he attacked the idea of happiness as "the possession of being well-deceived," the felicity of being "a fool among knaves." For Swift saw society as Vanity Fair, the land of false goals. [1]

It is, of course, un-American to think in terms of fools and knaves. We do, however, seem to be dedicated to the idea of buying our way to happiness. We shall all have made it to Heaven when we possess enough. [2]

And at the same time the forces of American commercialism are hugely dedicated to making us deliberately unhappy. Advertising is one of our major industries, and advertising exists not to satisfy desires but to create them—and to create them faster than any man's budget can satisfy them. For that matter, our whole economy is based on a dedicated insatiability. We are taught that to possess is to be happy, and then we are made to want. We are even told it is our duty to want. It was only a few years ago, to cite a single example, that car dealers across the country were flying banners that read "You Auto Buy Now." They were calling upon Americans, as an act approaching patriotism, to buy at once, with money they did not have, automobiles they did not really need, and which they would be required to grow tired of by the time the next year's models were released. [3]

Or look at any of the women's magazines. There, as Bernard DeVoto once pointed out, advertising begins as poetry in the front pages and ends [4] as pharmacopoeia and therapy in the back pages. The poetry of the front matter is the dream of perfect beauty. This is the baby skin that must be hers. These, the flawless teeth. This, the perfumed breath she must exhale. This, the sixteen-year-old figure she must display at forty, at fifty, at sixty, and forever.

5   Once past the vaguely uplifting fiction and feature articles, the reader finds the other face of the dream in the back matter. This is the harness into which Mother must strap herself in order to display that perfect figure. These, the chin straps she must sleep in. This is the salve that restores all, this is her laxative, these are the tablets that melt away fat, these are the hormones of perpetual youth, these are the stockings that hide varicose veins.

6   Obviously no half-sane person can be completely persuaded either by such poetry or by such pharmacopoeia and orthopedics. Yet someone is obviously trying to buy the dream as offered and spending billions every year in the attempt. Clearly the happiness-market is not running out of customers, but what is it trying to buy?

7   The idea "happiness," to be sure, will not sit still for easy definition: The best one can do is to try to set some extremes to the idea and then work in toward the middle. To think of happiness as acquisitive and competitive will do to set the materialistic extreme. To think of it as the idea one senses in, say, a holy man of India will do to set the spiritual extreme. That holy man's idea of happiness is in needing nothing from outside himself. In wanting nothing, he lacks nothing. He sits immobile, rapt in contemplation, free even of his own body. Or nearly free of it. If devout admirers bring him food he eats it; if not, he starves indifferently. Why be concerned? What is physical is an illusion to him. Contemplation is his joy and he achieves it through a fantastically demanding discipline, the accomplishment of which is itself a joy within him.

8   Is he a happy man? Perhaps his happiness is only another sort of illusion. But who can take it from him? And who will dare say it is more illusory than happiness on the installment plan?

9   But, perhaps because I am Western, I doubt such catatonic happiness, as I doubt the dreams of the happiness-market. What is certain is that his way of happiness would be torture to almost any Western man. Yet these extremes will still serve to frame the area within which all of us must find some sort of balance. Thoreau—a creature of both Eastern and Western thought—had his own firm sense of that balance. His aim was to save on the low levels in order to spend on the high.

10   Possession for its own sake or in competition with the rest of the neighborhood would have been Thoreau's idea of the low levels. The active dis-

cipline of heightening one's perception of what is enduring in nature would have been his idea of the high. What he saved from the low was time and effort he could spend on the high. Thoreau certainly disapproved of starvation, but he would put into feeding himself only as much effort as would keep him functioning for more important efforts.

Effort is the gist of it. There is no happiness except as we take on life-engaging difficulties. Short of the impossible, as Yeats put it, the satisfactions we get from a lifetime depend on how high we choose our difficulties. Robert Frost was thinking in something like the same terms when he spoke of "The pleasure of taking pains." The mortal flaw in the advertised version of happiness is in the fact that it purports to be effortless.   11

We demand difficulty even in our games. We demand it because without difficulty there can be no game. A game is a way of making something hard for the fun of it. The rules of the game are an arbitrary imposition of difficulty. When the spoilsport ruins the fun, he always does so by refusing to play by the rules. It is easier to win at chess if you are free, at your pleasure, to change the wholly arbitrary rules, but the fun is in winning within the rules. No difficulty, no fun.   12

The buyers and sellers at the happiness-market seem too often to have lost their sense of the pleasure of difficulty. Heaven knows what they are playing, but it seems a dull game. And the Indian holy man seems dull to us, I suppose, because he seems to be refusing to play anything at all. The Western weakness may be in the illusion that happiness can be bought. Perhaps the Eastern weakness is in the idea that there is such a thing as perfect (and therefore static) happiness.   13

Happiness is never more than partial. There are no pure states of mankind. Whatever else happiness may be, it is neither in having nor in being, but in becoming. What the Founding Fathers declared for us as an inherent right, we should do well to remember, was not happiness but the *pursuit* of happiness. What they might have underlined, could they have foreseen the happiness-market, is the cardinal fact that happiness is in the pursuit itself, in the meaningful pursuit of what is life-engaging and life-revealing, which is to say, in the idea of *becoming*. A nation is not measured by what it possesses or wants to possess, but by what it wants to become.   14

By all means let the happiness-market sell us minor satisfactions and even minor follies so long as we keep them in scale and buy them out of spiritual change. I am no customer for either puritanism or asceticism. But drop any real spiritual capital at those bazaars, and what you come home to will be your own poorhouse.   15

Understanding Meaning

1. How does the view "whoever dies with the most toys wins" fit with Ciardi's thoughts on materialism?
2. What seems to be Ciardi's purpose in this essay? How much of this definition is *persuasive?* What does he mean by the comment that "a nation is not measured by what it possesses or wants to possess, but by what it wants to become"?
3. How does Ciardi *compare* the Eastern mystic's concept of happiness with that of most Americans? Can happiness be achieved by being free of possessions or by owning them all?
4. How does advertising exploit the public hunger for happiness? Does advertising suggest, in Ciardi's view, that happiness can be purchased instead of earned?
5. *Critical Thinking:* Although he criticizes what he calls "the happiness-market," Ciardi does not condemn it. However, he advises readers to be cautious consumers. What does he warn readers against? What does he mean by his comment about dropping "any real spiritual capital"?

Evaluating Strategy

1. Ciardi admits that happiness is not easy to define, noting "the best one can do is to try to set some extremes to the idea and then work in toward the middle." Is this an effective method of defining abstract or elusive concepts?
2. Throughout the essay, Ciardi quotes Swift, Bernard DeVoto, and Frost. Is this an effective way of working toward the definition of a difficult subject? Does this add credibility to Ciardi's view?
3. *Other Modes:* How does Ciardi use *comparison* and *analysis* to develop his definition?

Appreciating Language

1. Ciardi uses simple but abstract words—*happiness, possessions, dream, illusion.* How does he define these terms and give them personal meaning?
2. How does Ciardi paraphrase the language of advertising to reveal its appeals to consumers?

Connections across the Disciplines

1. Does Ellen Goodman's essay "The Company Man" (page 181) illustrate the sense that happiness depends on material success?

2. Marie Winn's essay describes addiction to television (page 194). Do people spending hours watching other people live real lives suggest a loss of happiness, a passive willingness to abandon the challenge of work and experience by becoming compulsive voyeurs?

Writing Suggestions

1. Use Ciardi's technique of setting extremes and then working toward the middle to define an elusive or complex subject such as love, friendship, success, wealth, or beauty in a short essay.
2. *Critical Writing:* Write an essay based on Ciardi's observation that the founding fathers did not promise a right to happiness but a right to the *pursuit* of happiness. Do Americans today seem to believe they have a *right* to happiness? Discuss whether Americans feel cheated if they are not happy and whether this partly explains the epidemic of drug abuse and violence.
3. *Collaborative Writing:* Discuss Ciardi's essay with a group of students, and then write a few paragraphs reflecting the group's viewpoint on happiness. You may wish to address a single observation made by Ciardi, such as the partial nature of happiness or the idea that it must derive from a challenge met.

MARIE WINN

Marie Winn was born in Czechoslovakia and grew up in New York. After completing her education at Radcliffe College, Winn began a career in publishing, writing and editing a number of children's books. While working with children's literature, she explored the effects television has on childhood development. She has written extensively on children and television, publishing articles in the New York Times *and* Village Voice. *In 1977 she published an influential study* The Plug-In Drug: Television, Children and Family, *which was revised in 1985. Her other books include* Children without Childhood *(1983),* Unplugging the Plug-In Drug *(1987),* The Secret Life of Central Park *(1997), and* Red-Tails in Love: A Wildlife Drama in Central Park *(1998). In 2002 Winn published a 25th anniversary edition of* The Plug-In Drug *subtitled* Television, Computers, and Family Life.

TV Addiction

OVERVIEW: *In building her case that television has negative effects, Winn first defines the term "addiction" then argues that television, like drugs and alcohol, damages those who allow it to consume their lives.*

Cookies or Heroin?

1   The word "addiction" is often used loosely and wryly in conversation. People will refer to themselves as "mystery-book addicts" or "cookie addicts." E. B. White wrote of his annual surge of interest in gardening: "We are hooked and are making an attempt to kick the habit." Yet nobody really believes that reading mysteries or ordering seeds by catalogue is serious enough to be compared with addictions to heroin or alcohol. In these cases the word "addiction" is used jokingly to denote a tendency to overindulge in some pleasurable activity.

2   People often refer to being "hooked on TV." Does this, too, fall into the lighthearted category of cookie eating and other pleasures that people pursue with unusual intensity? Or is there a kind of television viewing that falls into the more serious category of destructive addiction?

3   Not unlike drugs or alcohol, the television experience allows the participant to blot out the real world and enter into a pleasurable and passive mental state. To be sure, other experiences, notably reading, also provide a temporary respite from reality. But it's much easier to stop reading and return to reality than to stop watching television. The entry into another world offered by reading includes an easily accessible return ticket. The

entry via television does not. In this way television viewing, for those vulnerable to addiction, is more like drinking or taking drugs—once you start it's hard to stop.

Just as alcoholics are only vaguely aware of their addiction, feeling that   4
they control their drinking more than they really do ("I can cut it out any time I want—I just like to have three or four drinks before dinner"), many people overestimate their control over television watching. Even as they put off other activities to spend hour after hour watching television, they feel they could easily resume living in a different, less passive style. But somehow or other while the television set is present in their homes, it just stays on. With television's easy gratifications available, those other activities seem to take too much effort.

A heavy viewer (a college English instructor) observes: 5

I find television almost irresistible. When the set is on, I cannot ignore it. I can't turn it off. I feel sapped, will-less, enervated. As I reach out to turn off the set, the strength goes out of my arms. So I sit there for hours and hours.

Self-confessed television addicts often feel they "ought" to do other   6
things—but the fact that they don't read and don't plant their garden or sew or crochet or play games or have conversations means that those activities are no longer as desirable as television viewing. In a way, the lives of heavy viewers are as unbalanced by their television "habit" as drug addicts' or alcoholics' lives. They are living in a holding pattern, as it were, passing up the activities that lead to growth or development or a sense of accomplishment. This is one reason people talk about their television viewing so ruefully, so apologetically. They are aware that it is an unproductive experience, that by any human measure almost any other endeavor is more worthwhile.

It is the adverse effect of television viewing on the lives of so many peo-   7
ple that makes it feel like a serious addiction. The television habit distorts the sense of time. It renders other experiences vague and curiously unreal while taking on a greater reality for itself. It weakens relationships by reducing and sometimes eliminating normal opportunities for talking, for communicating.

And yet television does not satisfy, else why would the viewer continue   8
to watch hour after hour, day after day? "The measure of health," wrote the psychiatrist Lawrence Kubie, "is flexibility . . . and especially the freedom to cease when sated." But heavy television viewers can never be sated with

their television experiences. These do not provide the true nourishment that satiation requires, and thus they find that they cannot stop watching.

9   A former heavy watcher, a filmmaker, describes a debilitating television habit:

> I remember when we first got the set I'd watch for hours and hours, whenever I could, and I remember that feeling of tiredness and anxiety that always followed those orgies, a sense of time terribly wasted. It was like eating cotton candy; television promised so much richness, I couldn't wait for it, and then it just evaporated into air. I remember feeling terribly drained after watching for a long time.

10   Similarly a nursery-school teacher remembers her own childhood television experience:

> I remember bingeing on television when I was a child and having that vapid feeling after watching hours of TV. I'd look forward to watching whenever I could, but it just didn't give back a real feeling of pleasure. It was like no orgasm, no catharsis, very frustrating. Television just wasn't giving me the promised satisfaction, and yet I kept on watching. It filled some sort of need, or had to do with an inability to get something started.

11   The testimonies of ex–television addicts often have the evangelistic overtones of stories heard at Alcoholics Anonymous meetings.

12   A handbag repair-shop owner says:

> I'd get on the subway home from work with the newspaper and immediately turn to the TV page to plan out my evening's watching. I'd come home and then we'd watch TV for the rest of the evening. We'd eat our dinner in the living room while watching, and we'd only talk every once in a while, during the ads, if at all. I'd watch anything, good, bad, or indifferent.
>
> All the while we were watching I'd feel terribly angry at myself for wasting all that time watching junk. I could never go to sleep until at least the eleven o'clock news, and then sometimes I'd still stay up for the late-night talk show. I had a feeling that I *had* to watch the news programs, even though most of the time nothing much was happening and I could easily find out what by reading the paper the next morning. Usually my wife would fall asleep on the couch while I was watching. I'd get angry at her for doing that. Actually, I was angry at myself.
>
> I had a collection of three years of back issues of different magazines, but I never got around to reading them. I never got around to sorting or labeling my collection of slides I had made when traveling. I only had time for televi-

sion. We'd take the telephone off the hook while watching so we wouldn't be interrupted! We like classical music, but we never listened to any, never!

Then one day the set broke. I said to my wife, "Let's not fix it. Let's just see what happens." Well, that was the smartest thing we ever did. We haven't had a TV in the house since then.

Now I look back and I can hardly believe we could have lived like that. I feel that my mind was completely mummified for all those years. I was glued to that machine and couldn't get loose, somehow. It really frightens me to think of it. Yes, I'm frightened of TV now. I don't think I could control it if we had a set in the house again. I think it would take over no matter what I did.

Heavy television viewers often make comparisons between their view-   13
ing habits and substance addictions. Several decades ago, a lawyer reported:

I watch TV the way an alcoholic drinks. If I come home and sit in front of the TV, I'll watch any program at all, even if there's nothing on that especially appeals to me. Then the next thing I know it's eleven o'clock and I'm watching the Johnny Carson show, and I'll realize I've spent the whole evening watching TV. What's more, I can't stand Johnny Carson! But I'll still sit there watching him. I'm addicted to TV, when it's there, and I'm not happy about the addiction. I'll sit there getting madder and madder at myself for watching, but still I'll sit there. I can't turn it off.

Nor is the television addict always blind to the dysfunctional aspects of   14
his addiction. A homemaker says:

Sometimes a friend will come over while I'm watching TV. I'll say, "Wait a second. Just let me finish watching this," and then I'll feel bad about that, letting the machine take precedence over people. And I'll do that for the stupidest programs, just because I *have* to watch, somehow.

In spite of the potentially destructive nature of television addiction, it is   15
rarely taken seriously in American society. Critics mockingly refer to television as a "cultural barbiturate" and joke about "mainlining the tube." A spectacle called *Media Burn* perfectly illustrates the feeling of good fun that often surrounds the issue of television addiction. The event, which took place in San Francisco when television was still a young medium, involved the piling up of forty-four old television sets in the parking lot of the Cow Palace, soaking them with kerosene, and applying a torch. According to the programs distributed before the event, everybody was supposed to

experience "a cathartic explosion" and "be free at last from the addiction to television."

16   The issue of television addiction takes on a more serious air when the addicts are our own children. A mother reports:

> My ten-year-old is as hooked on TV as an alcoholic is hooked on drink. He tries to strike desperate bargains: "If you let me watch just ten more minutes, I won't watch at all tomorrow," he says. It's pathetic. It scares me.

17   A number of years ago a mother described her six-year-old son's need to watch:

> We were in Israel last summer where the TV stations sign off for the night at about ten. Well, my son would turn on the set and watch the Arabic stations that were still on, even though he couldn't understand a word, just because he had to watch *something*.

18   Other signs of serious addiction come out in parents' descriptions of their children's viewing behavior:

> We used to have very bad reception before we got on Cable TV. I'd come into the room and see my eight-year-old watching this terrible, blurry picture and I'd say, "Heavens, how can you see? Let me try to fix it," and he'd get frantic and scream, "Don't touch it!" It really worried me, that he wanted to watch so badly that he was even willing to watch a completely blurred image.

19   Another mother tells of her eight-year-old son's behavior when deprived of television:

> There was a time when both TV sets were out for about two weeks, and Jerry reached a point where I felt that if he didn't watch something, he was really going to start climbing the walls. He was fidgety and nervous. He'd crawl all over the furniture. He just didn't know what to do with himself, and it seemed to get worse every day. I said to my husband, "He's having withdrawal symptoms," and I really think that's what it was. Finally I asked one of my friends if he could go and watch the Saturday cartoons at their house.

20   In the early 1980s Robin Smith, a graduate student at the University of Massachusetts in Amherst, conducted a research study on television addiction as part of a doctoral dissertation. Setting out to discover whether television viewing can truly be classified as an addiction according to a particular, narrow definition she had constructed from the work of various social

scientists, Smith sent out a questionnaire to 984 adults in Springfield, Massachusetts, in which they were asked to rate their own behavior in regard to television viewing. Using a number of statistical tests to analyze the responses, the author concluded that the results failed to confirm that television addiction exists. "Television addiction does not appear to be a robust phenomenon," Smith wrote in that poetic yet obscure way academics sometimes have of expressing things.

Striving to understand why television is so widely considered an addic-   21
tion, in the conclusion of her research paper Smith noted:

> . . . the popularity of television as "plug-in drug" is enduring. One possible source of this image lies in the nature of viewing experience. The only study to date that examines the nature of the viewing experience in adults found that television watching, of all life activities measured in the course of one week, was the least challenging, involved the least amount of skill, and was most relaxing.

If television viewing is so bereft of value by most measures of well-   22
being, and yet takes up the greatest part of people's leisure hours, it becomes moot whether it is defined as an addiction or simply a powerful habit. As psychologists Robert Kubey and Mihaly Csikszentmihalyi concluded in their book about the television experience: "A long-held habit becomes so ingrained that it borders on addiction. A person may no longer be watching television because of simple want, but because he or she virtually has to. Other alternatives may seem to become progressively more remote. What might have been a choice years earlier is now a necessity."

Robert Kubey explains further: "While television can provide relax-   23
ation and entertainment . . . it still rarely delivers any lasting fulfillment. Only through active engagement with the worlds we inhabit and the people in them can we attain for ourselves the rewards and meaning that lead to psychological well-being."

Understanding Meaning

1. How does Winn define "addiction"? How does addiction, in her view, differ from overindulgence in something pleasurable?
2. Describe the negative effects Winn sees in habitual television viewing.
3. How does the simple ease and accessibility of watching television versus going out to a movie contribute to making television so addictive?

4. One viewer Winn quotes states, "I had the feeling that I *had* to watch the news programs, that I *had* to know what was happening." Today are more people likely to feel almost obligated to watch television to be informed, to be a good citizen? Can the news be as dangerously addicting as entertainment shows?

5. *Critical Thinking:* Do you think that many of Winn's observations about television addiction describe people who feel compelled to spend hours on the Internet? Can cyberspace be just as addictive and just as harmful?

Evaluating Strategy

1. Why is it important for Winn to first define "addiction" before moving to her argument about television?

2. How effective is her use of interviews or case studies of television viewers? Is it important to hear from the "addicts" in their own words?

3. *Other Modes:* How much of this definition essay can be considered a *persuasive argument*? What role do *description* and *narration* play in developing the definition?

Appreciating Language

1. Winn quotes one viewer who reports that television leaves him "sapped, willless, enervated." How important are words like these to argue that television is addictive?

2. Winn repeatedly uses the word "sated." Look this up in a dictionary. Why is it a key word in defining an addiction?

3. *Critical Thinking:* Would some people object to applying the word "addiction" to an activity that is not life-threatening? Drugs and alcohol, after all, lead to disease and early death. Does using the term in other contexts weaken its impact?

Connections across the Discipline

1. Review Ann McClintock's "Propaganda Techniques in Today's Advertising" (page 396). Does this reveal another potential hazard for the addicted viewer, especially since the introduction of home shopping channels? Can people become addicted consumers, using credit cards and a telephone to buy what seems so appealing on the screen?

2. Compare Winn's observations about television addicts and Ritter's comments on computer hackers (page 185). Do both writers sense that communications technology can lead to isolation and a separation from reality?

Writing Suggestions

1. Write a short analysis of your own childhood experiences with television. How many hours did you watch a day? What were your favorite programs? Did television add or detract from your development? Did you forgo studying, playing with other children, reading, or spending time with your family to watch television?

2. *Collaborative Writing:* Working with a group of other students, write a paper instructing parents step-by-step how to monitor their children's viewing habits. How can parents prevent their children from becoming television addicts?

TERRY TEMPEST WILLIAMS

Terry Tempest Williams (1955–) was born in Utah, where her ancestors had lived for more than a century and a half. She received degrees in English and science education from the University of Utah, where she now teaches in a women's studies program. Williams also serves as Naturalist-in-Residence at the Utah Museum of Natural History in Salt Lake City. Her concern for nature is evident in her writing, which includes children's books, short stories about Utah, and several nonfiction books blending natural history and personal experience.

Yucca

OVERVIEW: *This essay from* Pieces of White Shell: A Journey to Navajoland *provides a personal definition of a plant, emphasizing its importance to the Navajo people of the Southwest. Notice how Williams blends several modes to demonstrate the significance of a common desert plant.*

1   One night the stars pulled me into a dream. A basket sat before me, coiled: around and around and around and around. It was striped with persimmon. I should not touch it. This much I knew. I knelt down closely and saw a woman's long black hair curled between stitches. I picked up a sprig of salt bush and rattled it above the hair strand. Suddenly, the woven bowl began to pulsate, writhe, until a snake uncoiled herself slowly. This is what I heard:

2

       Sha-woman, Sha-woman, hiss
       Sha-woman, Sha-woman, hiss
       Tongue, rattle, hiss
       Tongue, rattle, hiss
       Sha-woman, Sha-woman, hiss

3   She stopped. She raised her head and blew upward. I watched the breezes pull her vertically until she became a white desert torch. Yucca.

4   In the Navajo account of yucca's birth, Tracking Bear was a monster from whom there was no escape. He lived in a cave in the mountains. Monster Slayer, pursued by Tracking Bear, climbed a sheer wall. As he did so he grasped a fruit of the yucca in his left hand, and in his right a twig of hard oak. The monster feared these medicine rattles. Monster Slayer killed

Tracking Bear and cut off his claws and large canine teeth, taking the gall and windpipe as trophies. He then cut the head into three pieces: One became the broad-leaved yucca, one the narrow-leaved yucca, and one the mescal.

And so yucca appears evenly spaced across the land. They stand as sentinels with their flowering stalks rising from vegetative swords. They are shields for creatures who live near. Sundown strikes yucca. Desert candles flame.

I remember peering into a yucca flower at dusk and seeing a tiny moth scraping pollen from within. The little white-robed pilgrim rolled the pollen into a tight ball and carried it to another blossom. There I watched her pierce the ovary wall with her long ovipositor and lay a clutch of eggs among the ovules, much as a farmer in the spring scatters seeds along his furrows. She packed the sticky mass of pollen through the openings of the stigma. Moth larvae and seeds would now develop simultaneously, with the larvae feeding on developing yucca. She walked to the edge of the petals. With her last bit of strength, she glided into the darkness, carried away by grace. The larvae would eventually gnaw their way through the ovary wall and lower themselves to the ground to pupate until the yuccas bloomed again. Circles. Cycles. Yucca and moth.

Perhaps the moth was on her way to pollinate the Navajo mind as well, for yucca and Navajo are relatives. Yucca is the single most important non-cultivated plant to Indian peoples in the Southwest. It has been plaited into baskets, woven into mats, and wrapped around bundles. Early peoples walked with yucca bound around their feet. Sandals. Imagine the care extended to plants when they mean your survival.

In days of painted language, yucca leaves were soaked in warm water to soften. They were then beaten against the rocks for further pliancy. Fibers finely peeled—like corn silk, only stronger—were twisted into cordage with organic tension. This same process can be tried today with patience.

The children know yucca, *tsá-ászi´*, intimately. On the banks of the San Juan River we stood in a circle with yucca at the center.

"What is this?" I asked.

"Yucca!" they sang out in unison.

"And what story does it tell?"

I heard as many responses as there are yucca blossoms. But one common strand connecting their stories was soap.

"We call it soapweed because there's soap under there. . . . "

"Yes?"

16   "Yes. You find the root under here—they pointed to the body of the plant—cut off a piece, and slice it into four strips. Then you pound it with your hands and add warm water until it lathers up."

17   "Then what do you do?"

18   "We wash our hair with the suds."

19   Before I knew what was happening, two boys pulled the plant out from the sand. They cut off the root, sliced it into four strips, placed it on the sandstone, and began pounding it with a rock—just as they had said. It worked: The root was frothing with suds.

20   The boys didn't stop there. They moved to a desert pothole that was holding rainwater. Loren bent over the basin as Bryan washed his hair. The rest of the children gathered. This was a familiar sight and they laughed.

21   "Loren, you better watch out—tomorrow you'll come to school with hair hanging down your back!"

22   The lore of yucca supports this teasing. The Navajo say a yucca shampoo will make your hair long, shiny, and black. If there are doubts as to yucca magic, just look at the children.

23   On another occasion, the children warned me against using yucca.

24   "Why not?" I asked. My curiosity was up.

25   "Because it might give you warts." A wave of giggles rushed over them.

26   But on this day, things were different. After the boys had finished their demonstration, they handed me a fresh section of the root.

27   "Try it."

28   The girls disappeared and returned with a brush they had made from a bunch of rice grass. They began combing my hair. I sat toward the wind, unable to speak.

29   The ritual of bathing with yucca suds is woven into the Navajo Way. It has been said that the mound of earth upon which the basket for water and suds is placed commemorates the visit of two children to Changing Woman's home, where they witnessed her rejuvenation. Blessed yucca suds have the power to transform—to change the profane to sacred, the doubtful to controlled, the contaminated to the purified.

30   One of the Navajo ceremonies associated with yucca washings is *Kinaaldá*, Changing Woman's puberty rites. *Kinaaldá* is part of the Blessing Way, a Navajo rite that maintains harmony for the people by attracting the goodness and power of benevolent Holy People. Most Navajo use the word *kinaaldá* to refer to the "first menses," alluding to the ceremonial rather than the physical event.

31   *Kinaaldá* ushers the adolescent Navajo girl into womanhood and invokes blessings upon her, ensuring her health, prosperity, and well-being.

It is a festive occasion where the accounts of Changing Woman and her *Kinaaldá* are retold and reenacted.

The *Kinaaldá* started when White Shell Woman first menstruated. Nine days after her *Kinaaldá*, Changing Woman gave birth to twin boys: Monster Slayer and Child-of-the-waters. They were placed on the earth to kill the monsters. As soon as they had done this, their mother, Changing Woman, who was then living at Governador Knob, left and went to her home in the west, where she lives today.   32

After she moved to her home in the west, she created the Navajo people. When she had done this, she told these human beings to go to their original home, which was Navajo country. Before they left, she said, "After this, all the girls born to you will have periods at certain times when they become women. When the time comes, you must set a day and fix the girl up to be *Kinaaldá;* you must have these songs sung and do whatever else needs to be done at that time. After this period, a girl is a woman and will start having children."   33

That is what Changing Woman told the people she made in the west. She told them to go to their own country and do this.   34

And so *Kinaaldá* continues. A *Kinaaldá* may last anywhere from three to five days depending on the circumstances. Today, many families cannot afford this ceremony as it has become too expensive to hire a medicine man and provide food for friends and family. Even so, many young Navajo women have participated in this celebration. Traditionally, the singer or medicine man conducting the ceremony asks the mentoring woman, usually the girl's mother or aunt, to set out the basket containing the yucca roots. This is done usually before dawn of the last day of the ceremony. The roots have been carefully unearthed with two rocks found close by to aid in the crushing. The older woman ritualistically shreds the roots and pulverizes them. She then pours water into the basket, creating yucca suds so that the girl can bathe her hair. But first, the woman washes all the girl's jewelry—beads, bracelets, rings, and concha belt—and sets them on a blanket to dry. Then the girl kneels before the water, unfastens her hair tie, and begins to wash her hair with the same lather. The woman helps her, making certain she receives a good shampoo. All during the washing ritual "Songs of Dawn" are being sung and a ritual cake is being prepared.   35

The older woman takes the basket of soapweed water, *táláwosh*, to the west and empties it in a northerly direction. As soon as the singing stops, the young woman in *Kinaaldá* wrings out her hair and begins her last run to the east before dawn. Younger sisters and friends may follow her.   36

37   The breeze coming from her as she runs
The breeze coming from her as she runs
The breeze coming from her as she runs is beautiful.

38   The breeze coming from her as she runs
The breeze coming from her as she runs
The breeze coming from her as she runs is beautiful.

39   How many times have Navajo hands asked for the release of this root from the earth? How many times have these beaten roots been rubbed between flesh in warm water until heavy lather appeared? This source of soap, containing the compound saponin, has bathed skeins of yarn and skeins of hair, leaving both to glisten in desert sunlight.

40   Yucca is also edible. The children call yucca fruit "Navajo bananas." When boiled, it tastes much like summer squash, slightly sweet but with a twist of bitterness. But most of the yucca fruit is left in the heat to dry and wither. I have cut into its flesh many times and found exquisite symmetry. Six windows—once panes for seeds—become a chartreuse kaleidoscope.

41   The children look through yucca and see each other playing the ball and stick game, traditionally known as the "moccasin game."

42   "You play the game like this," they said. "You make a ball out of the yucca root with your hands, then everyone takes off their shoes and lines them up on either side of the yucca. One side takes the ball and hides it inside one of the shoes. The other team has to guess which shoe it's in. If they guess right it's their turn to hide the ball, but if they're wrong, the other side gets to cut off a yucca leaf. The side with the most yucca sticks at the end of the game wins."

43   Another story is told. A long, long time ago all creatures on earth, including insects, spoke as human beings. The Animal People gathered around the yucca and said, "Let's have a shoe game." A great hoopla rose from the crowd as everyone showed his favor for such an event.

44   "But how will we keep score?" asked a small beast.

45   "We will use the blades of yucca as counters," spoke another. And one hundred and two yucca sticks were pulled. A ball from the root of yucca was shaped, along with a stick for pointing.

46   "We will have the shoe game at a place called Tse′yaa Hodilhil," they said. And everyone ran, jumped, flew and crawled to the designated site.

47   Gopher dug two shallow furrows on either side. Four moccasins were placed in each groove and then covered with sand. Then it was asked among the herds, swarms, and flocks, "What shall we bet?"

A great stirring occurred in the animal assemblage as everyone offered opinions. Finally, all the diurnal beings said, "We will bet the earth to have continual sunlight." 48

The nocturnal beings stepped forward and said, "We will bet the sky to have perpetual darkness." 49

And so the bets were placed between day and night. 50

There were many, many Animal People on both sides. The diurnal creatures on the south, the nocturnal creatures on the north. Anticipation for the contest grew like midsummer corn. 51

The game began with one side hiding the ball in one of the four moccasins, then covering the moccasins up with sand. The other side began guessing with the indicator stick which shoe the ball was in. They were given three chances. If they guessed correctly it became their turn to hide the ball. If they were fooled, the opponents took a yucca counter. Back and forth, back and forth it went, with lots of laughter and singing. 52

The Animal People became so immersed in the shoe game that no one realized morning had come. They continued to play throughout the day and into the night placing their bets high, with neither side ever quite winning all one hundred and two yucca sticks. 53

They did things then just as people do today. Once they started something, they would not stop. The wager between day and night still continues. 54

The shoe game is played by Navajos with delight. Some call it Navajo gambling. But those who know the stories say it keeps Sun and Moon in balance. 55

After all the children have shared their own versions of the game, they are quick to tell you that "you must only play this game in winter." A botanist will tell you winter is the dormant season for yucca. Earth wisdom. 56

I brought out my pouch and took a slice, a circle of yucca. It had been aged by Sun. Once supple, now shriveled. Bitter, hard. What could this be? I mused over the possibilities. If I were home, it could be cucumber, zucchini, even eggplant. But here it could be peyote or datura, any number of powerful medicines. Where could they take me? I closed my eyes and slipped the yucca slice into my mouth. From a far-off place I could smell the smoke of piñyon. 57

Yucca. Plants. Navajo. Plants yield their secrets to those who know them. They can weep the colors of chokecherry tears, purplish-brown, into a weaver's hands. They can be backbones for baskets holding the blessings of *Kinaaldá*. Cedar bark and sage can purify; Indian paintbrush soothes an ailing stomach. Juniper ash water creates blue cornmeal. Petals of larkspur 58 are sprinkled in ceremony. Native plants are a repository. They hold our health. A Navajo medicine man relies on plants as we rely on pharmacies.

59   Edward S. Ayensu, director of the Office of Biological Conservation at the Smithsonian Institution, tells a story about an African herbalist who told his students to pay attention to the natural world, to listen and observe the behavior of animals such as lizards, snakes, birds, rodents, and insects.

60   To stress his point, the herbalist narrated a fight between two chameleons. As Ayensu describes it:

61   At the climax of the fight one of the chameleons passed out. The other quickly dashed into a thicket and came back with a piece of a leaf in its mouth. It forcibly pushed the leaf into the mouth of the unconscious lizard. In a matter of two or three minutes the defeated chameleon shook its body and took off.

62   The specific plant that saved the life of the chameleon was not disclosed to me. When I insisted on knowing, the teacher smiled and said, "This is a trade secret. It is a plant that can spring a dying person to life. Unless you became one of us I cannot tell you."

63   This is earth medicine, and it is all around us, delivered into the hands that trust it. What do we know?

64   Yucca. The desert torch burns and returns its ashes to crimson sand. A snake slithers across the way and recoils itself under a slickrock slab. This is what I heard:

65   Sha-woman, Sha-woman, hiss
Sha-woman, Sha-woman, hiss
Tongue, rattle, hiss
Tongue, rattle, hiss
Sha-woman, Sha-woman, hiss

66   Silence. A basket sits before me, coiled: around and around and around and around. It is striped with persimmon.

Understanding Meaning

1. What are the principal characteristics of the yucca plant?
2. How was the yucca plant created, according to Navajo legend?
3. Why is the plant so important to the Native Americans of the Southwest?

4. What traditions do the children reenact?
5. What special role does the yucca plant play in the lives of Navajo women?
6. *Critical Thinking:* Williams makes the statement that "yucca and Navajo are relatives." Could a similar essay define the importance of the potato to the pre-famine Irish or rice to the Chinese? Can American urban civilization be defined by oil or electricity?

Evaluating Strategy

1. Williams opens the essay with a dream. How does this help introduce the spiritual importance of yucca to the Navajo?
2. What role does Williams play in the essay? How does she use dialogue?
3. Near the end of her essay, Williams introduces comments by an official of the Smithsonian Institution. Is the inclusion of outside scientific authorities essential to her essay?
4. *Other Modes:* How does Williams blend *narration* and *description* in creating a definition of the yucca plant?

Appreciating Language

1. Underline the metaphors Williams uses to describe the yucca plant. How do they aid in creating a definition?
2. Look up the terms *nocturnal* and *diurnal.*

Connections across the Disciplines

1. How does Williams's role in the essay compare with that of N. Scott Momaday in "The Way to Rainy Mountain" (page 142)?
2. Does Williams's detailed observation of the yucca follow Dr. Agassiz's admonition to "look again, look again" in Samuel Scudder's essay "Take This Fish and Look at It" (page 47)?

Writing Suggestions

1. Write a brief essay defining an element central to the lives of a group of people. You might define a computer as the heart of a small business or coffee as the lifeblood of students during exam week. Provide details to illustrate the significance of this object or substance.

2. *Collaborative Writing:* Working with several students, ask each to select an item that is central to a group they know. If the yucca plant defines the Navajo, what would define students on your campus—soda, pizza, computer disks, sweatshirts? Ask each member of the group to supply a brief definition.

BLENDING THE MODES

THE ECONOMIST

The Economist *is a British weekly publication written expressly for business and government leaders, offering readers in-depth articles about international issues, science, the arts, finance, politics, and economics. In 1996 the* Economist *published this article about terrorism.*

What Is Terrorism?

OVERVIEW: *As you read this article, consider how difficult it is to define a politically charged term such as "terrorism." Would the British have considered George Washington a terrorist in 1776? Can the term be used to dismiss legitimate political activists? Do terrorists use patriotism and religion to mask criminal activities?*

JUNE 1914: a young man in Sarajevo steps up to a carriage and fires his pistol. Archduke Ferdinand dies. Within weeks, the first world war has begun. The 1940s: the French resistance kill occupying troops when and how they can. June 1944: at Oradour-sur-Glane, in central France, German SS troops take revenge, massacring 642 villagers. August 1945: the United States Air Force drops the world's first nuclear weapons. Some 190,000 Japanese die, nearly all of them civilians. Within days the second world war has ended.

    Which of these four events was an act of terrorism? Which achieved anything? Which, if any, will history judge as justified? And whose history? Terrorism is not the simple, sharp-edged, bad-guy phenomenon we all love to condemn. No clear line marks off politics from the threat of force, threat from use, use from covert or open war. Who is or is not a terrorist? The suicide bomber, the rebel guerrilla, the liberation front, the armed forces of the state?

    In practice, what act or person earns the label depends on who wants to apply it. To Ulster loyalists all IRA violence is terrorism; to Sinn Fein it is part of a legitimate war. To many Israelis, everyone from the suicide-bombers in Jerusalem or Ashkelon to the Hizbollah grenade-thrower in South Lebanon is a terrorist; to many Arabs during the 1982 Lebanon war, the worst terrorists in the Middle East were the—entirely legitimate, uniformed—Israel Defence Force.

1

2

3

4   If the concept is not to vanish into all-embracing fudge, two distinctions can be drawn, though habitually they are not. Terrorism is indeed about terror; not just violence, but its use to spread terror. And the violence is aimed specifically at civilians.

5   Classical terrorism, ideological rather than territorial, reveals the niceties. Recent decades saw West Germany's Baader-Meinhof gang and Red Army Fraction murder prominent businessmen such as Alfred Herrhausen and Jurgen Ponto (bosses of Germany's two largest banks, Deutsche and Dresdner respectively). Italy's Red Brigades murdered Aldo Moro, a former prime minister. Its far right in 1980 blew up a train in Bologna station, killing 84 people. Which of these was truly terrorism? Arguably, only the last. It was an act of indiscriminate violence to terrorise citizens at large; the others were discriminate assassinations to win publicity and display power.

6   Likewise, lobbing mortar-bombs into a British army base in South Armagh may have deadly results, but it is guerrilla warfare. Planting a bomb that kills a dozen diners in a restaurant is terrorism. The suicide bomber in Jerusalem was a terrorist; the Hizbollah fighter in South Lebanon attacking Israeli army patrols is not.

7   Even in the distinction between guerrilla warfare and terrorism, there are grey areas. The soldier in a tank is a military target. What about one in a jeep escorting civilian vehicles? Or returning on a bus from leave? A bus that may—and was, when a suicide bomber attacked it in Gaza last April—be carrying civilians too?

8   There are, in contrast, distinctions often made that ought not to be. What is or is not "terrorism" does not depend on the badness or goodness of the cause, nor on whether those espousing it have the chance to express their demands democratically. When President James Garfield was assassinated in America in the same year, 1881, that a Russian terrorist group blew up Tsar Alexander II, the Russians wrote an open letter condemning Garfield's killers and arguing that:

9   In a land where the citizens are free to express their ideas, and where the will of the people does not merely make the law but appoints the person who is to carry the law into effect, political assassination is the manifestation of despotism. . . . Despotism is always blameworthy and force can only be justified when employed to resist force.

10   Yet despotism does not justify throwing bombs into crowds (as the group sometimes did).

11   The fact is that a good cause may use terrorism just as a bad one may. South Africa has provided a clear example. The ending of white dominance

was a plainly good cause. For the most part, the African National Congress used mass demonstrations and industrial sabotage to advance its cause. But the men who shot up a white church congregation or planted a bomb outside a cinema were terrorists in the purest sense of the word.

Nor does the terrorists' ultimate success or failure alter the truth. Menachem Begin got to lead a country; Yasser Arafat may do; Velupillai Prabhakaran, who leads the Tamil Tigers, probably will not. None of that changes the fact that Deir Yassin (a massacre of Palestinian villagers by Israelis fighting to establish their state), the killing of 11 Israeli athletes at the Munich Olympics in 1972 and this year's Tamil Tiger bomb in Colombo were all acts of terror.   12

The Terror of the State

So much for the underdogs. Can there be terrorist governments too? The Americans certainly think so when they accuse Libya or Iran of supporting international terrorism. In the cold war, international terrorists were used to wage war by proxy: the East German regime provided safe houses for Baaders and Meinhofs; the modern era's most notorious terrorist, the gun-for-hire Carlos the Jackal, made his career in this world of state-sponsored terrorism.   13

All that was diplomacy by terror. Can a recognised government also be guilty of terrorism against its own people?   14

Yes. Stalin used terror systematically to consolidate his power—random murders of Communist-Party members and army officers in the 1930s, massacres and exiles of smaller ethnic groups throughout his rule. Much of Latin America practised state terrorism in recent decades. The brasshat regimes of the day faced left-wing, sometimes terrorist movements. Many fought back with terror. And not just through paramilitaries or unacknowledged death squads. The infamous massacre at El Mozote in El Salvador in 1981 was the work of that country's regular army. The unit that did it had a cheerful song of its own, "Somos Guerreros":   15

We are warriors,   16
Warriors all!
We are setting out to kill
A mountain of terrorists.

What in fact they killed was over 500 peasants; probably the worst "official" massacre in Latin America's recent history.   17

18   Can regular armies, in regular war, be guilty of terrorism? The answer, surely, is yes. Look at the Japanese rape of Nanking in 1937, when not hundreds or thousands but tens of thousands of civilians were murdered, to terrorise the rest of China. Then go a step further. Can the armies of proud democracies be guilty too? A century ago, the rich world, with the rules of war that it claimed to use, would have called attacking civilians impermissable. The modern world has other ideas. The Allied bombing of Germany was aimed at civilians in the hope of shattering morale: in short, terror. The fire bombing of Tokyo and the atomic weapons that vaporised Hiroshima and Nagasaki were arguably aimed at government morale, not that of Japan's population. Their victims did not notice the difference.

Who Kills and How?

19   What use, one can ask, is a definition so wide that it can go from Stalin to the American air force? There are two answers.

20   First, it is a reminder that terrorism, historically, has been the tool of the strong, not the weak. Medieval armies, having taken a besieged town, would slaughter some or all of the citizens to encourage other towns to surrender faster. During India's struggle for independence, by far the worst terror was the Amritsar massacre in 1919, when British-officered troops shot up a political gathering, and carried on shooting until the bullets ran out; 379 civilians died (and it worked: the rebellious province of Punjab returned to order). In contrast, discriminate assassination was the typical weapon of the 19th-century anarchist and nihilist.

21   By and large, true random terrorism has come in the past 30 years, as in the Bologna train bomb, the recent nerve-gassing of the Tokyo metro by a religious cult, or the Oklahoma City bomb; all three crimes were aimed at no matter whom for a purpose so vague or Utopian as to seem irrelevant, except to the deranged. Even in this period most—if not all—IRA killing was aimed at defined targets: soldiers, policemen, individual Protestant farmers in border areas. The Basque violence of ETA has often followed this pattern. Peru's Shining Path guerrillas are truer terrorists, but even they (mostly) prefer the tactics, honed by the Vietcong, of killing officials, not just (as in some infamous massacres) everyone in sight. Algeria's and Sri Lanka's terrorists today probably have the strongest claim to be called spreaders of true random terror.

22   The second thing one can learn from the wide definition of terrorism is that the phenomenon is neither uniquely wicked, nor—still less—uniquely deadly. People fight with the weapons they have: knives, Semtex, rifles,

fighter-bombers. All their users are alike convinced of their own righteousness, all kill and all their victims are equally dead. What they are not is equal in number. The Munich terrorists killed 11 Israelis; Israel's retaliation against the Lebanese town of Nabatiyeh, however justified, killed about 100 Arabs. The State Department has totted up the deaths due to international terrorism from 1968 through 1995. Its total, and it defines terrorism broadly, is 8,700. Twenty-four hours of air raids killed six times as many civilians at Dresden in 1945. One is a crime, says international law, the other a legitimate act of war.

The Response

Is all this mere word-play? It is not. It crucially affects responses to terrorism. 23

One true difference between a terrorist group and a government is that 24 the group is almost impossible to smash. You can destroy or seize a government's ability to make conventional war; you will never get every terrorist's last stick of dynamite or timing mechanism, and it requires wonderfully few terrorists to keep a civilised society on edge.

But many other imagined differences are less great than they might ap- 25 pear. It is a common error to suppose that because terrorism is not war, and because its weapons are not the full panoply of war, then the psychology of terrorists must be different too. Of course, there are plenty of curious specimens among terrorism's ranks: Carlos the Jackal, now in French hands, was not just any old gunman; or consider Abimael Guzman, an academic who until his capture in 1992 led Peru's Shining Path movement. Every terrorist must have personal devotion to the cause—he is, after all, risking his liberty, and often his life; not many reluctant army conscripts, drafted by a legitimate government, are likely [to] feel the same way. And plainly, say those who know them, the IRA and other groups include people who enjoy violence for its own sake.

But so do most armies. And most governments, once at war, can pro- 26 duce remarkable devotion to the national cause. In its own terms, a warring terrorist group, like a warring government, is "pursuing diplomacy by other means," even if its means of war are different. It too is subject to highs and lows, to war fatigue and collapses of morale, to premature celebration of a battle won as if it had been the war. It too can be threatened with a heavy hand; some of its members may be wooed with a lighter one.

Terrorists, like governments, may be rational: they are pursuing a policy 27 they hope will succeed. And the more it works, the more vigorously they will pursue it.

28   It is always hard, when terrorism is just one element in a complex pattern of events, to identify its impact. But the world is manifestly a different place because of acts of terror. In 1948, the Israelis blew up the King David hotel, the administrative centre of the British rulers of Palestine. The atrocity helped persuade the British to leave.

29   Often, terrorists help advance a general cause, but not their own particular aims. That may be the case with the IRA. Irish Republican terrorism helped dramatise the nationalist cause throughout periods of discriminatory Protestant rule. And Britain has made concessions to the nationalists. In the Anglo-Irish agreement of 1985, the British accepted the right of the Irish Republic to a say in a province of the United Kingdom; in the two governments' Downing Street declaration of 1993 Britain said it had "no selfish strategic or economic interest in Northern Ireland." It is hard to imagine any other government saying such things of its own accord. Yet whether it was the IRA that brought this about, or persistent pressure from the Irish government and peaceful nationalists in the north, is debatable. The leader of the biggest nationalist party in Northern Ireland, John Hume, argues that IRA terrorism has been the main obstacle to a peaceful settlement in Ulster. If so, the IRA may also have harmed the nationalist cause.

30   And sometimes, terrorists can advance both a general cause and themselves. The PLO's campaigns in the 1970s made the organisation the dominant representative of the Palestinians. They also helped solidify the Palestinians' own sense of their distinct identity, which until then had been relatively weak.

31   Just as terrorists make a difference to the world, so changes in the world make a difference to terrorists. It was not just their own weakness that led the British to quit India, or later Cyprus (whose EOKA gunmen, though damned as terrorists, were more like guerrilla fighters), or later still Kenya (where they faced a genuinely terrorist liberation movement). Weakness played its part, but so did a world view that said colonial empires had had their day. Much the same was true in South Africa. F. W. de Klerk, probably the last white president there, may not have been a more virtuous man than the architects of apartheid who preceded him. But he was and is a realist, who lived in different days and under different pressures.

32   In that case, a just cause plainly helped the terrorists. For Muslim countries the Palestinian cause was no less just. Western countries, guiltily aware of the horrors of Jewish history, disagreed, and it took 20 years of Israeli occupation and the *intifada*, the Palestinian uprising of 1987–90, to persuade them that the PLO too had a case. It is still not one that much impresses Americans; and though other westerners may have sympathy with Palestin-

ian dreams of statehood, any movement that still seeks a quite different thing, the destruction of Israel, on top will—very rightly—find that its bombers face a western world united behind the Jewish state.

Like the Rest of Us—Mostly

In all this, what is different about dealing with terrorism? The answer, perhaps unsurprisingly, is not very much. 33

Any government has its own interests, its own pressures, its concessions it can make and those it cannot. It fights its conventional wars with tanks and aircraft, its small-scale wars—partly terrorist, mostly not—with intelligence men and small arms. It cannot, usually, zap the terrorists' territory as it could that of a hostile state. But its psychology will be much the same in the two cases—and so will that of its enemies. The terrorist or suicide bomber or gunman or fighter or liberation hero is not different from other men (men, sic; rarely have women played any notable part, any more than they have in old-fashioned war). 34

With one notable exception: the nutters, whether with a cause or no evident cause at all. The American way-out redneck who thinks he has to plant a bomb, when he could vote for Pat Buchanan, is beyond any but a psychiatrist's reach. So too elitist solipsists like the Baader-Meinhof mob, convinced that murder was justified because they knew all the answers and it was society that was out of step. Among the almost causeless, Italy's far right may have sought instability, but for what? That was never clear. And no known concession could have led Japan's Aum Shinrikyo cult to put aside its chemistry set. 35

Is it coincidence that three of these four groups seem to specialise in the true terrorism, the random murder of civilians for terror's sake? Perhaps it is not. 36

Understanding Meaning

1. What makes defining "terrorism" difficult? Can one discuss highly-ideological political issues in the Middle East or Northern Ireland without appearing to take sides?
2. How does "terrorism" differ from assassinating political leaders?
3. What is the goal of terrorism?
4. Why did Russian terrorists condemn the assassination of an American president in the nineteenth century, even though they sought to assassinate the czar?
5. Has terrorism ever succeeded in changing political reality?

6. *Critical Thinking:* Does terrorism have more than one goal? In addition to terrorizing innocent civilians, does it hope to provoke retaliation that will inflict punishment on innocent civilians among the opposition, providing the terrorists sympathy, support, and new recruits?

Evaluating Strategy

1. "What Is Terrorism?" opens with four short historical examples, then poses a question. Is this an effective way of getting readers to think more critically about terrorism?
2. Is it important to give distant, historical examples of terrorism? Are current events so politically-charged that readers will have difficulty being objective?
3. *Other Modes:* What role do *narration, classification, division,* and *cause and effect* play in developing this definition?

Appreciating Language

1. Why is it important to use neutral and objective terms when writing about controversial issues?
2. The authors see a distinction between "assassination" and "terrorism." How do they explain the difference?
3. How important is connotation in writing about terrorism? Do you detect any bias in this article? Would Arabs, Israelis, Irish Republicans, Basque nationalists, Indians, or the British find anything objectionable in this article?

Connections across the Disciplines

1. Ellen Goodman uses a single extended example to define a "company man" (page 181). Is a single example effective in defining "terrorism"? Why or why not?
2. Martin Luther King Jr. (page 381) advocates passive resistance to achieve social change. Do fringe groups that cannot mobilize large populations to protest feel justified to use violence?

Writing Suggestions

1. Write a brief essay that defines terrorism in your own words and provides examples of terrorism.
2. *Collaborative Writing:* Work with a group of students and write a cause-and-effect essay that details the impact terrorism can have on a community and its leaders.

WRITING BEYOND THE CLASSROOM: TWO DEFINITIONS OF DEPRESSION

Definition is a critical feature of all professional writing. Professionals need common standards in order to communicate and operate efficiently. The way definitions are expressed depends on the writer's goal, the audience, and the discipline.

THE ENCYCLOPEDIA OF PSYCHOLOGY

This definition is taken from a specialized encyclopedia designed for mental health professionals. As a standard reference, it seeks to establish a common understanding of terms for people who must diagnose and treat patients with psychological problems.

DEPRESSION
The Concept of Depression

Depression is a term used to describe a mood, a symptom, and syndromes of affective disorders. As a mood, it refers to a transient state of feeling sad, blue, forlorn, cheerless, unhappy, and/or down. As a symptom, it refers to a complaint that often accompanies a group of biopsychosocial problems. In contrast, the depressive syndromes include a wide spectrum of psychobiological dysfunctions that vary in frequency, severity, and duration. Normal depression is a transient period of sadness and fatigue that generally occurs in response to identifiable stressful life events. The moods associated with normal depression vary in length but generally do not exceed 7 to 10 days. If the problems continue for a longer period and if the symptoms grow in complexity and severity, clinical levels of depression may be present. Clinical depression generally involves sleep disorders, eating disorders, anergia, hopelessness, and despair. Sometimes problems assume psychotic proportions, and the depressed individual may attempt suicide and/or may experience hallucinations, delusions, and serious psychological and motor retardation.

1

This definition, written by a practicing psychologist, appeared in a brochure distributed in the waiting room of a Milwaukee mental health clinic. It is directed to the general public and seeks to explain the nature of depression to people seeking help for psychological problems they may have difficulty understanding.

WHAT IS DEPRESSION?

1   Depression is <u>an internal state—a feeling of sadness, loss, "the blues," deep disappointment</u>. *When it is more severe, you may have feelings of irritability, touchiness, guilt, self-reproach, loss of self-esteem, worthlessness, hopelessness, helplessness, and even thoughts of death and suicide.* It may include such other feelings as <u>tearfulness, being sensitive and easily hurt, loss of interests, loss of sexual drive, loss of control in life, feeling drained and depleted, anger at yourself, and loss of the ability to feel pleasure.</u>

2   It may be accompanied by *physical symptoms* similar to the sense of profound loss, including:

3   * *loss of appetite,* often with weight loss, but sometimes we find increased eating
   * *insomnia or early morning waking,* often 2–4 times per night, nearly every day, but sometimes we see a need to sleep excessively
   * moving and speaking slows down, but sometimes we see *agitation*
   * *fatigue or loss of energy* nearly every day
   * *loss of concentration,* foggy and indecisive
   * sometimes it includes anxious and headachy feelings and also *frequent crying*

4   Besides the <u>physical sensations</u> and <u>emotions of depression</u>, depressed people may *withdraw, may brood or ruminate about problems,* have trouble remembering things, wonder if they would be better off dead, and become very concerned about bodily symptoms and pains. They may be grouchy, sulking, restless, and unwilling to interact with family and friends.

Understanding Meaning

1.   *The Encyclopedia of Psychology* is a reference text for mental health students and professionals. What is the purpose of its definition? How does its definition differ from the clinic's definition, aimed at the general public?

2. What role does definition play in the treatment of any disorder? How is addressing professionals different from addressing potential patients?
3. Which are the objective statements in both definitions? Do both definitions agree on the basic elements of depression?
4. How does the brochure address its readers differently from the encyclopedia?
5. *Other Modes:* What *persuasive* elements are used in the brochure?

Evaluating Strategy

1. The brochure by Don Rosenberg uses italics, underlining, and asterisks for highlighting. What functions do these have? Discuss their suitability.
2. How does the brochure direct its message to the public and potential patients?

Appreciating Language

1. Does the purpose of the definition dictate the tone of the language in these two examples? Does the encyclopedia's *description* focus on objective, observable symptoms? Does the brochure seem to focus on feelings and emotions?
2. Would the language of the encyclopedia appear cold and unfeeling to a patient seeking help with depression?

Writing Suggestions

1. Take a definition from the glossary section of a textbook, and write a version for a general audience of clients, consumers, or students.
2. Using information from the encyclopedia and brochure, write a definition of depression targeted to college students. Describe symptoms in terms students will readily identify.
3. *Collaborative Writing:* Discuss a common problem or issue with fellow students: job insecurity, lack of sleep, stressful family relationships, child care, or the fear of crime. Select a term you often overhear, and provide a clear definition for it. Have each member of the group list features of this term. Try to incorporate objective elements. Write the definition in two versions: one designed for an "official" publication such as the college catalog or textbook, the other for an informal handout.

STRATEGIES FOR WRITING DEFINITIONS

1. **Determine your purpose.** Does your definition seek to provide a common language to prevent confusion, or does it seek to persuade readers by altering their perceptions?

2. **Define your role.** Your definition can be based on personal observation and opinion or standard principles and methods followed in a specific discipline or profession.

3. **Consider your audience.** What knowledge base do your readers have? Your definition should offer recognizable examples in language they will understand. Determine what uses your audience has for this definition. Will readers have to base decisions on your definition?

4. **Make extended definitions relevant.** Extended definitions depend on examples, illustrations, and narratives. The items you include to explain your topic should be relevant and understandable to your audience.

5. **Review special needs of the discipline or writing situation.** Each discipline can have a distinct history, research methodology, and set of concerns. Make sure your definition respects any special interests and addresses special needs.

6. **Use or refer to existing definitions.** Instead of attempting to create your own definition, you can adopt an existing one. If you accept the American Psychological Association's definition of *obsession*, you can simply restate the definition for readers. In using existing definitions, acknowledge their sources. If you disagree with an existing or official definition, restate it and then demonstrate how your interpretation differs.

SUGGESTED TOPICS FOR WRITING DEFINITIONS
General Assignments

Write a definition on any of the following topics. Your definition will probably contain other modes, such as description, comparison, and narration. Choose your terminology carefully, and avoid using words with misleading connotations. When defining complex and abstract concepts, consider using John Ciardi's method of defining extremes and then working toward the middle.

- A successful professional in your career. Define a good defense attorney, computer programmer, nurse, or teacher.
- A good relationship

- Sexual harassment
- Addiction
- The perfect career
- An educated person
- A healthy lifestyle
- The level of insanity at which a person should not be held criminally liable for his or her actions
- Racism
- Self-respect

Writing in Context

1. Imagine you have been asked to write a brief brochure about college life to be distributed to disadvantaged high school students. The principal stresses that she fears many of her students lack independent study skills and the discipline needed to succeed in college. Define the characteristics of a good college student, stressing hard work.

2. You have been asked to participate in a panel on sexual harassment. In preparation, provide two definitions of sexual harassment: one expressing attitudes, feelings, and statements you have observed and heard from males on campus, the other from females. Try to be as objective as possible, and state any differences fairly.

This is a working draft of a paper written in response to the following assignment:

Invent a definition for a social issue or problem you have experienced. You may support your definition with factual research or personal observation. Make sure your paper clearly defines the subject and not simply describes it.

Disneyland Dads

1   Like half the members of my generation, I am the product of what used to be called a "broken home." My parents divorced when I was eight. I lived with my mother and saw my father on alternate weekends and two weeks during the summer.

2   My father, like many of his generation, was a classic Disneyland Dad. The Disneyland Dad is usually found at malls, little league fields, upscale pizza restaurants and ice cream parlors. He is usually accompanied by a child busily eating food forbidden by Mom, wearing new clothes, or playing with expensive toys. The Disneyland Dad dispenses cash like an ATM and provides an endless supply of quarters for arcade games. Whether they are motivated by guilt, frustration, or an inability to parent, Disneyland Dads substitute material items for fatherly advice, guidance, and discipline.

3   While my mother furnished the hands-on, day to day parenting, my father remained distant. My mother monitored my eating habits, my friends, my grades, even the programs I watched on television. But without daily contact with my mother, my father found it difficult to make decisions about my upbringing. He was afraid of contradicting Mom. So he showered me with gifts and trips. He expanded my wardrobe, gave me my first pieces of real jewelry, introduced me to Broadway shows, and took me to Disneyland — but he did not help me with school, teach me about the job market, give me insight into boys, or allow me to be nothing more than a spoiled consumer.

4   As I grew older, my relationship with my father became strained. Weekends with him were spent shopping, going to movies, playing tennis, and horseback riding — activities I loved, but activities that limited opportunities for anything but casual conversation.

Like most of my friends, I came to view my father as more of an   5
uncle than a parent. He was a beloved family figure, someone who
could be counted on for some extra cash, new clothes, a pizza. And
like most of my friends, I was troubled by the gulf that widened between my father and myself. I talked, argued, and made up with my
mother as I went through my teens. Both of us changed over the
years. But my father remained the same — the generous but distant
Disneyland Dad.

The Disneyland Dad is a neglected figure. While books and daytime   6
talk shows focus on the plight of single moms, few people offer advice
to the fathers. Men in our society are judged by success and conditioned to dispense tokens of their achievement to their children. We
kids of divorce want all the things the Disneyland Dad can offer, but
we really need his attention, his guidance, his experience, his mentoring. Someone has to help Disneyland Dads become fathers.

Questions for Review and Revision

1. What tone does the term "Disneyland Dad" have? Is it suitable for a serious essay? What connotations does it suggest?
2. Does this student really "define" or merely "describe" Disneyland Dads?
3. Does the paper include enough details to outline the qualities of a
   Disneyland Dad?
4. The student uses italics to highlight certain words. Do you find this an
   effective technique?
5. *Other Modes:* Where does the student use *narration* and *comparison* to develop the essay? Does the final paragraph state a *persuasive argument?*
6. Read the paper aloud. Can you detect awkward or vague passages that
   would benefit from revision?

Writing Suggestions

1. Invent a term that defines a personality type, and illustrate it using a parent, friend, or coworker as an example.
2. *Collaborative Writing:* Discuss this paper with several students, and collect ideas for a process paper that offers tips to teenage children on how
   to communicate with a Disneyland Dad.

DEFINITION CHECKLIST

Before submitting your paper, review these points.

1. Is your purpose clear—to inform or persuade?

2. Do you avoid defining a word with the same word, such as "a diffusion pump diffuses"?

3. Is your level of technical or professional language suited to your audience?

4. Does your definition provide enough information and examples so that readers can restate your thesis in their own words?

5. Are there existing definitions you can use for reference or contrast?

6. Do extended definitions contain illustrations, narratives, or comparisons that readers may either not recognize or misinterpret?

7. Do you state the essence of your definition in a short summary statement that readers can remember or highlight for future reference?

 Companion Web Site

See **http://sundance.heinle.com** for information on writing definitions.

 InfoTrac® College Edition

For additional reading go to InfoTrac College edition, your on-line research library, at **http://infotrac.thomsonlearning.com.**

*   Enter the search term "definition" using Keywords.
*   Enter the name of an author you read in this chapter using Keywords.
*   Enter a theme or idea your class discussed using Keywords.

Comparison and Contrast

INDICATING SIMILARITIES AND DIFFERENCES

WHAT IS COMPARISON AND CONTRAST?

Comparison and contrast answers the question: How are things alike or different? What distinguishes a gasoline engine from a diesel engine? Is it cheaper to buy or lease a car? What separates a misdemeanor from a felony? How does a bacterial infection differ from a viral one? What did Malcolm X and Martin Luther King Jr. have in common? Do men and women approach mathematics differently? All of these questions can be answered by comparing similarities and contrasting differences.

You have probably encountered essay questions that require comparison and contrast responses:

Compare the industrial output of the North and South at the outbreak of the Civil War. Which side was better equipped to prosecute a protracted conflict?

How do the rules of evidence differ in criminal and civil proceedings?

Which arrangement offers business owners greater protection of personal assets—full or limited partnerships?

Contrast Freud's dream theory with Jung's concept of the unconscious.

At the end of *The Great Gatsby*, Nick Carraway decides to return to the West because he is too "squeamish" for the East. What differences did Fitzgerald see between the East and West?

Outline the principal differences between warm- and cold-blooded animals.

Comparison and contrast writing is commonly used to organize research papers. You might compare two short stories by Edgar Allan Poe in an English course, explain the differences among methods of depreciation in accounting, or contrast conflicting theories of childhood development for psychology. Comparison and contrast writing is also used by engineers to explain the fuel efficiency of different engines, by real estate developers to explore potential building sites, and by social workers to determine the best method of delivering medical services to the homeless.

The Purposes of Comparison and Contrast

Writers use comparison and contrast for two purposes:

1. **To draw distinctions among related subjects.** In many instances comparison is used to eliminate confusion. Many people, for instance, mistake an *optician*, who makes and sells eyeglasses, for an *optometrist*, who performs eye examinations and prescribes lenses. Comparison can pair extended definitions to show readers the difference, for example, between air-cooled and water-cooled engines, African and Indian elephants, or cross-country and downhill skiing. When drawing distinctions, writers explain differences between similar subjects but do not choose one over the other. William Zinsser's essay "The Transaction" (page 240) contrasts the ways two writers work without endorsing either writer's method. The basic goal of drawing distinctions is to *inform readers of similarities and differences.*

2. **To recommend a choice between two things.** Television commercials compare competing products. Political campaign brochures urge voters to support a candidate over his or her rival. Articles in medical journals argue that one drug is more effective than another. Business proposals recommend one computer program or one security service over competitors. Government studies assert that one air-quality standard is preferable to another. In "A Tale of Two Sitcoms" (page 249), Steven Stark recommends *Home Improvement* as "a better reflection of who we are" than *Seinfeld*, despite its lesser success with critics. The basic purpose of stating recommendations is to *persuade readers to make a choice.*

Organizing Comparison and Contrast Papers

When developing a paper using comparison and contrast, you must be sure your subjects share enough common points for meaningful discussion. You can compare two sports cars, two action adventure films, or two diets. But comparing a sports car to an SUV, an action film to a comedy, or a diet to plastic surgery is not likely to generate more than superficial observations. The entries in this chapter focus on related subjects, such as the ways two writers work or the backgrounds of two Civil War generals.

In addition, comparisons have to be carefully limited, especially when comparing broad or complex subjects. For contrasting the differences between American and Chinese cultures, Yi-Fu Tuan (page 233) limits the essay to demonstrating the different ways Americans and Chinese view space and place. By exploring this limited topic in depth, Yi-Fu Tuan reveals more about Chinese culture in a page or two than a twenty-page essay would that attempts to cover religion, politics, economics, history, and marriage customs. If you are comparing two presidents, you might focus your comparison on their relations with the press, the way they handled crises, or their trade policies.

Perhaps the most frustrating problem students face while writing comparison and contrast papers is organizing ideas. Without careful planning, you may find yourself awkwardly switching back and forth between subjects. Your reader may have difficulty following your train of thought and may confuse one subject with another. Whether drawing distinctions or making recommendations, writers use two methods of organizing comparison and contrast.

Subject by Subject

The *subject-by-subject* method divides the paper into two sections. Writers state all the information about topic A and then discuss topic B. Usually, the actual comparisons are drawn in the second part of the paper, where B is discussed in relation to A. In a short paper about two types of life insurance, the writer first explains "whole life" insurance and then discusses "term" insurance and draws distinctions between the two types. Since the purpose is to make distinctions, the conclusion does not offer a recommendation:

WHOLE LIFE AND TERM INSURANCE

Most life insurance companies offer a variety of life insurance products, investments, and financial services. Two of the most common policies provided are whole life and term insurance.

Whole life insurance is the oldest and most traditional form of life insurance. Life insurance became popular in the nineteenth century as a way of protecting the buyer's dependents in the event of premature death. A purchaser would select a policy amount to be paid to his or her beneficiaries after his or her death. Payments called premiums were made on a yearly, quarterly, or monthly basis. As the policyholder paid premiums, the policy gained cash value. Part of the payment earned interest like money in a bank account. Insurance served as an investment tool, allowing people to save for retirement and giving them access to guaranteed loans. For a low interest fee, insurance holders could borrow against the cash value of their policies.

Term insurance, introduced in the twentieth century, serves the same basic purpose as whole life insurance, protecting the insured's dependents. Unlike whole life, however, no cash value accrues. In a sense the policyholder is "renting" insurance, buying only a death benefit. The advantage of term insurance is its low cost. Because there is no money set aside for investment, the premiums are lower. This allows a person to afford a larger policy. A term policy for $100,000 could be cheaper than a whole life policy for $50,000.

The type of insurance a person needs depends on his or her income, family situation, investment goals, savings, and obligations. Most investment counselors agree, however, that anyone with a spouse or children should have some form of life insurance protection.

Advantages and Disadvantages   The subject-by-subject method is best suited to short papers. A twenty-page report organized in this fashion would read much like two ten-page papers fastened together. It would be difficult for readers to remember enough of the first subject to appreciate how it differs from the second. This method, however, allows writers to compare abstract subjects with ease, especially when a subject has individual features the other does not share.

Point by Point

The *point-by-point* method organizes the comparison of A and B on a number of specific points. Following an introduction, A and B are discussed in a series of comparisons. Hotels, for example, have a number of common points: location, appearance, atmosphere, and room rates. In the following paper, the writer groups comments about the two hotels in each paragraph. For the recommendation, the writer states a clear preference in the opening and concluding paragraphs:

ST. GREGORY AND FITZPATRICK HOTELS

Campus organizations and academic conventions visiting the city hold special events in either the St. Gregory or Fitzpatrick. Both are large convention hotels, but for many reasons the St. Gregory is more desirable.

Opened in 1892, the St. Gregory is the oldest surviving hotel in the city. The Fitzpatrick is the newest, having opened just last spring. The St. Gregory has a commanding view of State Street. The Fitzpatrick is part of the $200 million Riverfront Centre.

The chief attraction of the St. Gregory is its famed domed lobby ornamented with carved mahogany and elaborate brass and marble fittings. Admiral Dewey was presented with the key to the city here following his victory in Manila Bay in 1898. In contrast, the sleek Fitzpatrick is noted for its sweeping thirty-story atrium. The open lobby is banked with massive video screens.

The main lounge of the St. Gregory is the Pump Room, a plush, turn-of-the-century Irish bar decorated with gilt-framed paintings of the Emerald Isle. The Fitzpatrick features two bars. Homerun, a sports bar, is popular with local students and young professionals. The Exchange is a smaller, quieter bar that is a favorite of visiting executives. Copiers, fax machines, and computers are available in the nearby executive center.

Both hotels offer a range of room rates. The cheapest rooms at the St. Gregory are $95 a night. Though small, they are comfortable. The Fitzpatrick has only a dozen single traveler rooms for $125. Double rooms at the St. Gregory range from $175 to $250, depending on size and decor. All Fitzpatrick double rooms are identical and cost $195. In addition to convention rates, the St. Gregory offers 20 percent student discounts. The Fitzpatrick does not offer student discounts.

Both hotels provide excellent convention services. Since most professors and academic delegates have access to university computers and fax machines, they prefer the historic elegance of the St. Gregory. Students especially appreciate discount rates and the availability of public transport to the university.

Advantages and Disadvantages   The point-by-point method is useful in organizing longer and more technical papers. The specific facts, statistics, and quotes about A and B appear side by side. Readers of a long report about two hotels organized in a subject-by-subject manner would be easily frustrated because instead of seeing room rates compared in the same paragraph, they might have to flip back a dozen pages. Point-by-point organization is helpful when addressing multiple readers who may be interested in only a portion of the paper. However, point-by-point papers about abstract subjects such as two films or two novels might be difficult to organize because many important details about one subject may have nothing in common with the other subject.

As you read the essays in this chapter, you may note that many writers blend both methods to develop their comparisons.

STRATEGIES FOR READING COMPARISON AND CONTRAST

When reading the comparison and contrast entries in this chapter, keep these questions in mind.

Meaning

1.   What is the writer's goal—to draw distinctions or to recommend a choice?
2.   What details does the writer present about each subject?

3. Who is the intended audience? Is the essay directed to a general or a specific reader?
4. Is the comparison valid? Is the writer comparing two subjects in a fair manner? Have any points been overlooked?
5. Does the author have an apparent bias?
6. If the comparison makes a recommendation, does the selection seem valid? What makes the chosen subject superior to the others? What evidence is offered?

Strategy

1. What is the basic pattern of the comparison—subject by subject or point by point? Do variations occur?
2. Does the author use a device to narrow the topic or to advance the comparison?
3. Does the writer make use of visual aids? Are they effective?

Language

1. Does the writer use connotations that ascribe positive or negative qualities to one or both of the items? How does the author describe the two subjects?
2. What do the diction, level of language, and use of technical terms reveal about the intended audience?
3. If suggesting a choice, how does the writer use language to highlight its desirability?

YI-FU TUAN

Yi-Fu Tuan (1930–) was born in China and later moved to the United States. Now a geography professor in Madison, Wisconsin, he has studied the cultural differences between America and his native country. He states that he writes "from a single perspective—namely that of experience." In this article published in Harper's, *he compares the way people in two cultures view their environments.*

Chinese Space, American Space

OVERVIEW: *Cultures as diverse as America's and China's have many points of difference. In attempting to provide insight into their differences in a brief essay, Yi-Fu Tuan focuses on the concept of space and location. Americans, he asserts, are less rooted to place and are future oriented. The Chinese, savoring tradition, are deeply tied to specific locations. Note that Yi-Fu Tuan devotes most of his essay to describing the less familiar Chinese houses and values.*

American space

Americans have a sense of space, not of place. Go to an American home in exurbia, and almost the first thing you do is drift toward the picture window. How curious that the first compliment you pay your host inside his house is to say how lovely it is outside his house! He is pleased that you should admire his vistas. The distant horizon is not merely a line separating earth from sky, it is a symbol of the future. The American is not rooted in his place, however lovely: his eyes are drawn by the expanding space to a point on the horizon, which is his future. [1 / thesis]

[American home]

By contrast, consider the traditional Chinese home. Blank walls enclose it. Step behind the spirit wall and you are in a courtyard with perhaps a miniature garden around a corner. Once inside his private compound you are wrapped in an ambiance of calm beauty, an ordered world of buildings, pavement, rock, and decorative vegetation. But you have no distant view: nowhere does space open out before you. Raw nature in such a home is experienced only as weather, and the only open space is the sky above. The Chinese is rooted in his place. When he has to leave, it is not for the promised land on the terrestrial horizon, but for another world altogether along the vertical, religious axis of his imagination. [2 / transition]

[Chinese home]

The Chinese tie to place is deeply felt. Wanderlust is an alien sentiment. The Taoist classic *Tao Te Ching* captures the ideal of rootedness in place with these words: "Though there may be another country in the neighborhood so close that they are within sight of each other and the crow- [3]

Chinese place

233

ing of cocks and barking of dogs in one place can be heard in the other, yet there is no traffic between them; and throughout their lives the two peoples have nothing to do with each other." In theory if not in practice, farmers have ranked high in Chinese society. The reason is not only that they are engaged in a "root" industry of producing food but that, unlike pecuniary merchants, they are tied to the land and do not abandon their country when it is in danger.

4   Nostalgia is a recurrent theme in Chinese poetry. An American reader of translated Chinese poems may well be taken aback—even put off—by the frequency, as well as the sentimentality, of the lament for home. To understand the strength of this sentiment, we need to know that the Chinese desire for stability and rootedness in place is prompted by the constant threat of war, exile, and the natural disasters of flood and drought. Forcible removal makes the Chinese keenly aware of their loss. By contrast, Americans move, for the most part, voluntarily. Their nostalgia for home town is really longing for a childhood to which they cannot return: in the meantime the future beckons and the future is "out there," in open space. When we criticize American rootlessness, we tend to forget that it is a result of ideals we admire, namely, social mobility and optimism about the future. When we admire Chinese rootedness, we forget that the word "place" means both a location in space and position in society: to be tied to place is also to be bound to one's station in life, with little hope of betterment. Space symbolizes hope; place, achievement and stability.

Final comments on American and Chinese values

Understanding Meaning

1. How does the author see a difference between "space" and "place"?
2. What do the traditional designs of American and Chinese homes reveal about cultural differences?
3. Why do the Chinese honor farmers?
4. What historical forces have shaped the Chinese desire for "rootedness"? How is American history different?
5. What negative aspects does Yi-Fu Tuan see in the Chinese sense of place?

Evaluating Strategy

1. The writer really devotes only a single paragraph to describing American concepts of space. Why? Is the essay out of balance? Discuss whether or not a comparison paper should devote half its space to each topic.

2. Is the author objective? Is it possible for a writer to discuss cultures without inserting a measure of bias?

Appreciating Language

1. What words does Yi-Fu Tuan use in describing the two cultures? Do they seem to differ in connotation?
2. Does the word *rootlessness* suggest something negative to most people? How does Yi-Fu Tuan define it?
3. Look up the word *wanderlust*. How does a German term suit an essay comparing American and Chinese cultures?

Connections across the Disciplines

1. Yi-Fu Tuan explores the differences between the Chinese and Americans by focusing on the structure of traditional homes. Bob Levey (page 236) reveals differences between men and women by describing their attitudes toward walking alone at night. How can concentrating on a single detail make a complex and abstract topic easier for readers to grasp?
2. Contrast the format of this standard essay with the use of bulleted points and columns in "Communication Styles: United States and Taiwan" (page 272). Why is structure important in developing a comparison?

Writing Suggestions

1. If you have lived in or visited another country or region within the United States, write a brief essay outlining how it differs from your home. Just as Yi-Fu Tuan used the concept of space to focus a short article, you may wish to limit your comparison to discussing eating habits, dress, attitudes to work, music, or dating practices.
2. *Collaborative Writing:* Ask a group of students about their attitudes toward rootlessness and place. Determine how often students have moved in their lives. How many have spent their entire lives in a single house or apartment? Write a few paragraphs outlining the attitudes expressed by the group.

BOB LEVEY

Robert Levey (1945–) is a popular Washington columnist and talk show host. Born in New York City, he attended the University of Chicago. After completing his bachelor's degree in 1966, he worked as a reporter for the Albuquerque Tribune. In 1967 he began working as a reporter and editor for the Washington Post. In 1981 he started writing his own column. Focusing on life in the nation's capital, he has commented on a range of serious and humorous topics, including road rage, sexual harassment, fashion, and celebrities.

Men vs. Women Over Walking at Night

OVERVIEW: *As you read this essay, consider how gender affects your decision to walk alone at night. Do men and women make unconscious, instinctual decisions that reflect their view of the world, their place in society, their security, and their view of the opposite sex?*

1   They didn't quite elect me an honorary woman, but female readers all over Beltwayland have been writing to thank me for The Allison Column.

2   In it, I recounted the story of Allison Smith and her once-trusty but now-suspect 1988 Toyota.

3   One night in January, long after dark, the car conked out deep in the heart of Rock Creek Park, near Park Road. Allison called her boyfriend, Todd Miller, on her cell phone. She asked what Todd thought she should do.

4   He suggested abandoning the car and walking the three-quarters of a mile up to Connecticut Avenue. There, Allison could find a bus or taxi to take her home, Todd said.

5   That advice rankled and scared Allison. She told Todd that no 5-foot-3, 105-pound woman should walk alone at night. She thought she'd be safer calling for help, locking the doors of the Toyota and waiting inside for the help to arrive.

6   After a few minutes, Todd took the hint, hopped in his car, went to the scene and rescued the damsel in distress.

7   But a big gender question hung heavily (and still hangs) over this story.

8   Do women feel more vulnerable than men, especially in situations where they're alone at night, especially in a place like Washington?

9   Do men not see this?

10   Female readers broke many land-speed records to tell me that the answer to both questions is yes.

"I live in Reston, and I used to watch my teenage son walk all over town   11
at night without fear," wrote Liza Bedian Covert.

"I used to think that my very young son has more privileges than I do.   12
Would I ever dare walk by myself through the woods or in the streets? Never.
Would I allow my daughter to do so? Of course not."

"I don't know if we will ever achieve equality in this particular category.   13
How sad."

"The added risk of late-night solo sojourns, and we all know this, is the   14
one of being sexually assaulted," wrote Cat Needham, a reader from Fairfax.
"It's an added dimension to person-on-person crime that men don't have any
awareness of."

Kathryn Concannon, a librarian, recommended a book called *Gift of*   15
Fear. The author, Gavin de Becker, "says that the intrinsic difference between men and women is that men are scared women will laugh at them
and women are scared men will kill them." She thinks this theory explains
the behavior of Allison and Todd on the night in question.

Barbara Ricker was one of many readers who worried about Allison's   16
taste in men.

When Todd didn't hop in his car to rescue Allison immediately, he waved   17
"a huge red warning flag," Barbara said. She urges Allison to "run from the
guy" and "don't look back."

On the other side of the ledger is Michael Fay, a reader from Spring-   18
field. While he didn't (and doesn't) wish any harm on Allison, he faults her
for not leveling with Todd.

Michael points out that Allison never said to Todd, "Come and pick me   19
up." She asked for his advice, not his direct action.

"Why can't women just tell us what they want?" Michael wonders.   20

Kim Flournoy noted that Allison might reduce her fear of walking at   21
night if she took self-defense classes.

"While they will never remove that eerie feeling of walking alone   22
through the park at night, they will give another option," Kim argues.

In case male readers think they're always on the same wavelength as   23
the women in their lives, Mary Beth O'Quinn served up a story that had me
nodding.

Mary Beth and her husband live in a row house on Capitol Hill, where   24
parking can be a huge headache. "When my husband comes home from
work, he drives by the house and keeps going in one direction until he finds
a parking space, even if it's eight blocks away," even at night, she writes.

"What do I do? Keep circling our block until someone leaves within one   25
block of our door. . . . He doesn't get it!"

26   Mary Beth's annoyance is widely shared by her fellow females. Cat Needham put it especially well.

27   "I can't tell you how frustrated, angry and powerless I feel as a woman sometimes," she said.

28   "It is so sad that we women have to be constantly on the defensive. Be alert! Be ready! Every woman should be able to experience [the freedom that men enjoy]. But no woman truly can."

Understanding Meaning

1.   What is the principal difference between men and women when it comes to walking alone at night?
2.   Do you find Todd insensitive or uncaring because he did not rush to assist a stranded woman?
3.   What do you think of the suggestion that women should take self-defense courses? Is this practical advice, or does it avoid the real issue of violence against women?
4.   Do men get it? Do they appreciate or dismiss women's concerns about security?
5.   *Critical Thinking:* Are women socialized to behave differently in public? Do they accept a limited freedom of movement? Do many women accept this limitation as natural? How many share the frustration and anger of the woman who noticed that her young son had more privileges than she did?

Evaluating Strategy

1.   To contrast the attitudes of men and women, why is it useful to include quotes from a number of people?
2.   In developing a comparison about a broad and complex topic such as gender differences, why does concentrating on a single small issue or incident help a writer focus his or her comments?
3.   *Critical Thinking:* By design newspaper columns have to be short and easy to read. Levey uses simple sentences and short paragraphs to make his writing easy to scan. What challenges does a columnist face when he or she wants to address a serious topic? Does a simple easy-to-read format lend itself to serious discussion?

Appreciating Language

1.   Levey uses a breezy simple style in his column. Do his tone and word choice suggest he is not serious about the issue of women's safety?

2. Why is it important for Levey to use direct quotations rather than paraphrases?

Connections across the Disciplines

1. Levey's article suggests that there are profound differences between men and women and their sense of freedom of movement. Consider Anna Quindlen's argument that women should be required to register for the draft (page 558). Are women fully equal in society? Do men and women have the same rights? Despite laws, policies, and changing attitudes about gender, are there some remaining differences between men and women?
2. Bruce Catton (page 244) compares the values of the North and South by comparing two generals. Would an essay about gender work well if only one man and one woman were discussed? Why or why not?

Writing Suggestions

1. Explore gender differences by writing comparison about some simple common activity. Your essay may be serious or humorous. Do men and women shop differently in supermarkets? Do you see gender differences in the cars they drive, the on-line screen names they invent for themselves, the way they address e-mail, talk to waiters or hail cabs?
2. *Collaborative Writing:* Discuss Levey's article with a group of students, then analyze your college campus. How safe is the environment? Do men and women move about equally, or do women feel more restricted or threatened?

WILLIAM ZINSSER

William Zinsser (1922–) was born in New York City and graduated from Princeton in 1944. He was a feature writer, drama editor, and film critic for the New York Herald Tribune. *He wrote columns for* Life *and the* New York Times. *In the 1970s Zinsser taught English at Yale. For seven years he served as general editor for the Book-of-the-Month Club. Zinsser has written many books on a variety of subjects, including jazz and baseball. But he is best known by college students for his books and articles on writing and study skills. His book* On Writing Well: An Informal Guide to Writing Nonfiction *and an article "College Pressures" have become standard reading for a generation of freshmen.*

The Transaction

OVERVIEW: *This article uses the point-by-point method to compare Zinsser's writing style with that of a popular writer. Zinsser organizes his article using interviewer questions as a device to contrast the responses of the two writers.*

1   A school in Connecticut once held "a day devoted to the arts," and I was asked if I would come and talk about writing as a vocation. When I arrived I found that a second speaker had been invited—Dr. Brock (as I'll call him), a surgeon who had recently begun to write and had sold some stories to magazines. He was going to talk about writing as an avocation. That made us a panel, and we sat down to face a crowd of students, teachers and parents, all eager to learn the secrets of our glamorous work.

2   Dr. Brock was dressed in a bright red jacket, looking vaguely bohemian, as authors are supposed to look, and the first question went to him. What was it like to be a writer?

3   He said it was tremendous fun. Coming home from an arduous day at the hospital, he would go straight to his yellow pad and write his tensions away. The words just flowed. It was easy. I then said that writing wasn't easy and it wasn't fun. It was hard and lonely, and the words seldom just flowed.

4   Next Dr. Brock was asked if it was important to rewrite. Absolutely not, he said. "Let it all hang out," and whatever form the sentences take will reflect the writer at his most natural. I then said that rewriting is the essence of writing. I pointed out that professional writers rewrite their sentences repeatedly and then rewrite what they have rewritten. I mentioned that E. B. White and James Thurber rewrote their pieces eight or nine times.

5   "What do you do on days when it isn't going well?" Dr. Brock was asked. He said he just stopped writing and put the work aside for a day when it

would go better. I then said that the professional writer must establish a daily schedule and stick to it. I said that writing is a craft, not an art, and that the man who runs away from his craft because he lacks inspiration is fooling himself. He is also going broke.

"What if you're feeling depressed or unhappy?" a student asked. 6 "Won't that affect your writing?"

Probably it will, Dr. Brock replied. Go fishing. Take a walk. Probably it 7 won't, I said. If your job is to write every day, you learn to do it like any other job.

A student asked if we found it useful to circulate in the literary world. 8 Dr. Brock said he was greatly enjoying his new life as a man of letters, and he told several stories of being taken to lunch by his publisher and his agent at Manhattan restaurants where writers and editors gather. I said that professional writers are solitary drudges who seldom see other writers.

"Do you put symbolism in your writing?" a student asked me. 9

"Not if I can help it," I replied. I have an unbroken record of missing 10 the deeper meaning in any story, play or movie, and as for dance and mime, I have never had any idea of what is being conveyed.

"I *love* symbols!" Dr. Brock exclaimed, and he described with gusto the 11 joys of weaving them through his work.

So the morning went, and it was a revelation to all of us. At the end 12 Dr. Brock told me he was enormously interested in my answers—it had never occurred to him that writing could be hard. I told him I was just as interested in *his* answers—it had never occurred to me that writing could be easy. (Maybe I should take up surgery on the side.)

As for the students, anyone might think we left them bewildered. But 13 in fact we probably gave them a broader glimpse of the writing process than if only one of us had talked. For there isn't any "right" way to do such intensely personal work. There are all kinds of writers and all kinds of methods, and any method that helps you to say what you want to say is the right method for you.

Some people write by day, others by night. Some people need silence, 14 others turn on the radio. Some write by hand, some by typewriter or word processor, some by talking into a tape recorder. Some people write their first draft in one long burst and then revise; others can't write the second paragraph until they have fiddled endlessly with the first.

But all of them are vulnerable and all of them are tense. They are driven 15 by a compulsion to put some part of themselves on paper, and yet they don't just write what comes naturally. They sit down to commit an act of literature, and the self who emerges on paper is far stiffer than the person who sat down to write. The problem is to find the real man or woman behind all the tension.

16   Ultimately the product that any writer has to sell is not the subject being written about, but who he or she is. I often find myself reading with interest about a topic I never thought would interest me—some scientific quest, perhaps. What holds me is the enthusiasm of the writer for his field. How was he drawn into it? What emotional baggage did he bring along? How did it change his life? It's not necessary to want to spend a year alone at Walden Pond to become deeply involved with a writer who did.

17   This is the personal transaction that's at the heart of good nonfiction writing. Out of it come two of the most important qualities that this book will go in search of: humanity and warmth. Good writing has an aliveness that keeps the reader reading from one paragraph to the next, and it's not a question of gimmicks to "personalize" the author. It's a question of using the English language in a way that will achieve the greatest strength and the least clutter.

18   Can such principles be taught? Maybe not. But most of them can be learned.

Understanding Meaning

1. What is the "transaction" suggested by the title?
2. What is the purpose of this comparison? What is Zinsser trying to say about the writing process?
3. Is Zinsser, who no doubt considers himself a "professional" writer, suggesting that his work is superior to the surgeon's? Is the surgeon an amateur?
4. Zinsser states that "ultimately the product that any writer has to sell is not his subject, but who he or she is." Do you agree with this assessment?
5. *Critical Thinking:* After reading this article, review your own writing habits. Can this article assist you to master techniques Zinsser admits cannot be "taught" but can be "learned"?

Evaluating Strategy

1. How effective is the device of using interviewer questions to organize the comparison? Does it put the professional writer and surgeon on an equal footing?
2. Zinsser describes the "Bohemian" dress of the doctor and his enthusiasm for entering literary circles. What does this suggest about Zinsser's attitude?
3. Is the comparison the heart of the essay or simply a device introducing Zinsser's comments about writing?

Appreciating Language

1. What language does Zinsser use to describe the surgeon? What impact does this have on the reader?
2. Zinsser calls writing "hard and lonely" and writers "solitary drudges." What was he attempting to express to the audience?

Connections across the Disciplines

1. Compare this essay with Peter Elbow's "Desperation Writing" (page 448). What do these writers suggest about the writing process?
2. Review Samuel Scudder's essay "Take This Fish and Look at It" (page 47). Is Zinsser, like Professor Agassiz, arguing that his profession demands hard work?

Writing Suggestions

1. Write a brief essay comparing two methods of accomplishing similar tasks: cooking, dieting, exercising, studying for exams, playing a sport, parenting, or managing employees.
2. *Collaborative Writing:* Have a number of students write a few paragraphs about their own writing practices. Remind the group to write honestly, to describe how they really write. Have each member read his or her statement to the group, and then discuss how writing styles could be improved to overcome common problems. Have one member of the group record the suggestions.

BRUCE CATTON

Bruce Catton (1899–1978) grew up listening to stories of Civil War veterans. His own college career was interrupted by service in the First World War. Catton went to work as a reporter for the Cleveland Plain Dealer *and later served as information director for several government agencies. His interest in history, especially the Civil War, never flagged. In 1953 his book* A Stillness at Appomattox *became a best-seller, and Catton received a Pulitzer Prize. He wrote several other books about the Civil War and edited* American Heritage *magazine for two decades.*

Grant and Lee

OVERVIEW: *Perhaps no other essay is as widely anthologized as a sample of comparison writing than Catton's "Grant and Lee," which first appeared in a collection,* The American Story. *Directed to a general audience, the essay seeks to contrast the two most famous generals of the Civil War.*

1   When Ulysses S. Grant and Robert E. Lee met in the parlor of a modest house at Appomattox Court House, Virginia, on April 9, 1865, to work out the terms for the surrender of Lee's Army of Northern Virginia, a great chapter in American life came to a close, and a great new chapter began.

2   These men were bringing the Civil War to its virtual finish. To be sure, other armies had yet to surrender, and for a few days the fugitive Confederate government would struggle desperately and vainly, trying to find some way to go on living now that its chief support was gone. But in effect it was all over when Grant and Lee signed the papers. And the little room where they wrote out the terms was the scene of one of the poignant, dramatic contrasts in American history.

3   They were two strong men, these oddly different generals, and they represented the strengths of two conflicting currents that, through them, had come into final collision.

4   Back of Robert E. Lee was the notion that the old aristocratic concept might somehow survive and be dominant in American life.

5   Lee was tidewater Virginia, and in his background were family, culture, and tradition . . . the age of chivalry transplanted to a New World which was making its own legends and its own myths. He embodied a way of life that had come down through the age of knighthood and the English country squire. America was a land that was beginning all over again, dedicated to nothing much more complicated than the rather hazy belief that all men had equal rights and should have an equal chance in the world. In such a

land Lee stood for the feeling that it was somehow of advantage to human society to have a pronounced inequality in the social structure. There should be a leisure class, backed by ownership of land; in turn, society itself should be keyed to the land as the chief source of wealth and influence. It would bring forth (according to this ideal) a class of men with a strong sense of obligation to the community; men who lived not to gain advantage for themselves, but to meet the solemn obligations which had been laid on them by the very fact that they were privileged. From them the country would get its leadership; to them it could look for the higher values—of thought, of conduct, of personal deportment—to give it strength and virtue.

Lee embodied the noblest elements of this aristocratic ideal. Through 6 him, the landed nobility justified itself. For four years, the Southern states had fought a desperate war to uphold the ideals for which Lee stood. In the end, it almost seemed as if the Confederacy fought for Lee; as if he himself was the Confederacy . . . the best thing that the way of life for which the Confederacy stood could ever have to offer. He had passed into legend before Appomattox. Thousands of tired, underfed, poorly clothed Confederate soldiers, long since past the simple enthusiasm of the early days of the struggle, somehow considered Lee the symbol of everything for which they had been willing to die. But they could not quite put this feeling into words. If the Lost Cause, sanctified by so much heroism and so many deaths, had a living justification, its justification was General Lee.

Grant, the son of a tanner on the Western frontier, was everything Lee 7 was not. He had come up the hard way and embodied nothing in particular except the eternal toughness and sinewy fiber of the men who grew up beyond the mountains. He was one of a body of men who owed reverence and obeisance to no one, who were self-reliant to a fault, who cared hardly anything for the past but who had a sharp eye for the future.

These frontier men were the precise opposite of the tidewater aristo- 8 crats. Back of them, in the great surge that had taken people over the Alleghenies and into the opening Western country, there was a deep, implicit dissatisfaction with a past that had settled into grooves. They stood for democracy, not from any reasoned conclusion about the proper ordering of human society, but simply because they had grown up in the middle of democracy and knew how it worked. Their society might have privileges, but they would be privileges each man had won for himself. Forms and patterns meant nothing. No man was born to anything, except perhaps to a chance to show how far he could rise. Life was competition.

Yet along with this feeling had come a deep sense of belonging to a na- 9 tional community. The Westerner who developed a farm, opened a shop, or set up in business as a trader, could hope to prosper only as his own community prospered—and his community ran from the Atlantic to the Pacific and from Canada down to Mexico. If the land was settled, with towns and highways and accessible markets, he could better himself. He saw his fate in terms of the nation's own destiny. As its horizons expanded, so did his. He had, in other words, an acute dollars-and-cents stake in the continued growth and development of his country.

10   And that, perhaps, is where the contrast between Grant and Lee becomes most striking. The Virginia aristocrat, inevitably, saw himself in relation to his own region. He lived in a static society which could endure almost anything except change. Instinctively, his first loyalty would go to the locality in which that society existed. He would fight to the limit of endurance to defend it, because in defending it he was defending everything that gave his own life its deepest meaning.

11   The Westerner, on the other hand, would fight with an equal tenacity for the broader concept of society. He fought so because everything he lived by was tied to growth, expansion, and a constantly widening horizon. What he lived by would survive or fall with the nation itself. He could not possibly stand by unmoved in the face of an attempt to destroy the Union. He would combat it with everything he had, because he could only see it as an effort to cut the ground out from under his feet.

12   So Grant and Lee were in complete contrast, representing two diametrically opposed elements in American life. Grant was the modern man emerging; beyond him, ready to come on the stage, was the great age of steel and machinery, of crowded cities and a restless burgeoning vitality. Lee might have ridden down from the old age of chivalry, lance in hand, silken banner fluttering over his head. Each man was the perfect champion of his cause, drawing both his strengths and his weaknesses from the people he led.

13   Yet it was not all contrast, after all. Different as they were—in background, in personality, in underlying aspiration—these two great soldiers had much in common. Under everything else, they were marvelous fighters. Furthermore, their fighting qualities were really very much alike.

14   Each man had, to begin with, the great virtue of utter tenacity and fidelity. Grant fought his way down the Mississippi Valley in spite of acute personal discouragement and profound military handicaps. Lee hung on in the trenches at Petersburg after hope itself had died. In each man there was an indomitable quality . . . the born fighter's refusal to give up as long as he can still remain on his feet and lift his two fists.

15   Daring and resourcefulness they had, too; the ability to think faster and move faster than the enemy. These were the qualities which gave Lee

the dazzling campaigns of Second Manassas and Chancellorsville and won Vicksburg for Grant.

Lastly, and perhaps greatest of all, there was the ability, at the end, to turn quickly from war to peace once the fighting was over. Out of the way these two men behaved at Appomattox came the possibility of a peace of reconciliation. It was a possibility not wholly realized, in the years to come, but which did, in the end, help the two sections to become one nation again . . . after a war whose bitterness might have seemed to make such a re-union wholly impossible. No part of either man's life became him more than the part he played in their brief meeting in the McLean house at Appomattox. Their behavior there put all succeeding generations of Americans in their debt. Two great Americans, Grant and Lee—very different, yet under everything very much alike. Their encounter at Appomattox was one of the great moments of American history.

16

Understanding Meaning

1. What does Catton see as the most striking differences between the two generals?
2. How did Grant and Lee differ in background and sense of allegiance?
3. What were the historical forces that shaped the two men?
4. What areas of similarity between the two does Catton detect?
5. *Critical Thinking:* Essentially Catton is telling the story of a confrontation between victor and vanquished, yet his account does not seem to depict the men as winner and loser. Catton does not dwell on what made Grant victorious or on the causes for Lee's defeat. What does this reveal about Catton's purpose?

Evaluating Strategy

1. How does Catton organize his comparison? Is this an effective method?
2. The Civil War was, in part, a battle over slavery. Catton does not mention this issue. Does his account appear to be ethically neutral, suggesting that neither the Union nor the Confederacy were morally superior in their war aims?

Appreciating Language

1. Does Catton appear to be neutral in his descriptions of the two men? What similes or metaphors does he use? Is the language balanced or biased?
2. What do the tone, level of language, and word choice suggest about Catton's intended audience?

Connections across the Disciplines

1. Catton uses words such as "nobility" and "virtue" to describe Robert E. Lee. How might an African-American writer such as Cornel West (page 37) respond to Catton's depiction of Lee's "daring" and "resourcefulness" as a defender of the Confederacy?
2. Compare Catton's discussion of two individuals with Yi-Fu Tuan's comparison of traditional Chinese and American homes (page 233). Does focusing on specifics such as these risk creating oversimplification and stereotypes? Can a single person fully represent a nation, a movement, or a political cause? Can a single building, product, or item fully represent a culture?

Writing Suggestions

1. Write an essay comparing two people in the same profession you have known. Compare two teachers, two bosses, two landlords, or two coworkers. Try to focus on their personalities rather than appearance. You may limit your discussion to a specific attitude, situation, or activity. For example, compare how two teachers dealt with troublesome students, how two bosses motivated employees, or how two landlords maintained their properties.
2. *Collaborative Writing:* Work with a group of students to write a short dramatic scene based on Catton's essay. Use set descriptions to establish the locale, and invent dialogue. Discuss with members of the group how Lee and Grant might have sounded. What words would they have chosen? How would their vocabulary indicate their different backgrounds and personalities?

STEVEN D. STARK

Steven D. Stark (1952–) graduated from Yale Law School and worked as an aide to Jimmy Carter before becoming a journalist. He has written a column for the Boston Globe *and lectured at Harvard Law School. His articles have appeared in the* New York Times, *the* Atlantic Monthly, *and the* Los Angeles Times. *Stark is a regular commentator on popular culture for National Public Radio. In 1997 he published* Glued to the Set: The 60 Television Shows That Made Us Who We Are Today.

A Tale of Two Sitcoms

OVERVIEW: *In this section from his recent book, Stark compares two popular television programs*—Home Improvement *and* Seinfeld. *As you read the essay, notice how Stark organizes his commentary.*

The popular shows of a decade are usually a lot alike. In many ways *Dallas* 1 and *Dynasty* were indistinguishable, and it would take Wyatt Earp himself to discern great differences between *Wagon Train* and *Gunsmoke*. In the late seventies, *Happy Days, Laverne and Shirley,* and *Three's Company* often seemed to form one long seamless web.

Yet sometimes, in eras of cultural conflict or confusion, no one type of 2 show can accurately capture the public mood. In the early 1970s, for example, *All in the Family* made a hero of a conservative traditionalist while *The Mary Tyler Moore Show* romanticized the life of a single career woman blazing new ground. In their own ways, both shows reflected their time and both were popular—often with the same viewers.

In much the same fashion, popular programming in the nineties offered 3 a contrast, as it struggled with an emerging question which had no clear answer: What does it mean to be a man in a postfeminist age? Two very different situation comedies which hit Number 1 in that decade tried to provide an answer. On the one hand, there was ABC's *Home Improvement*—the top-rated show for the 1993–94 season. And then, there was NBC's *Seinfeld*—which hit Number 1 the following season.

Even the reaction to both shows provided a sharp contrast. Critics regu- 4 larly lavished *Seinfeld* with praise for its postmodern plots; its technical innovations were hailed as breakthroughs; and the show was always an Emmy contender in several categories. Novelist Jay McInerney went so far in a 1996 issue of *TV Guide* to ask, "Is *Seinfeld* the Best Comedy Ever?" By comparison, *Home Improvement* was perhaps the quietest Number 1 in TV history, eliciting few critical comments and winning little more than a slew of (what else?) People's Choice awards, in which the public does the voting.

5   There were indeed surface similarities between the two shows. Both starred male comedians, who took their standup nightclub acts and transformed them for television. Both comedians wrote best-selling books once they hit it big, and both shows featured subplots about television itself. Both presented memorable supporting players, like Kramer of *Seinfeld*, or next-door neighbor Wilson of *Home Improvement*, whose full face is never shown over his fence. Both ran in prime time and in syndication over roughly the same period with similar ratings—though the one time *Seinfeld* was matched directly against *Home Improvement* in 1992–93, *Seinfeld* got plastered in the ratings.

6   Yet the differences between the shows were more revealing. *Home Improvement* was set in suburban Detroit, in the white-bread heartland. Though actually filmed in L.A., *Seinfeld* was a New York show which roughly approximated the lifestyles of influential New York critics and Madison Avenue types. *Home Improvement* was solidly suburban middle class; *Seinfeld* was a portrait of life in yuppie Upper Manhattan.

7   *Home Improvement* was a rather traditional family sitcom about a wife, three kids, and a bumbling Dad; the *Seinfeld* family of friends featured no children and no workplace either, at least in the traditional sense. With its "morality tale" quality, *Home Improvement* was cousin of *Leave It to Beaver* and *My Three Sons*—an anachronism in an era when wisecracking shows like *Friends* or *Murphy Brown* dispensed with nuclear families altogether.

8   By contrast, *Seinfeld* was closer to Jack Benny, or even Milton Berle. That was a remarkable turnaround for a medium which for much of its bland and homogeneous entertainment life took single Jews like Seinfeld, changed their names, converted them to Christianity, married them off to attractive WASP housewives, and moved them to the suburbs. New York *Newsday* once called *Seinfeld* "the most fully realized schlemiel in the history of television."

9   What encouraged programmers to take these chances was the way that cable television had atomized the viewing audience. Because of cable competition, network television was not the mass medium in 1995 that it was in 1975; it took far fewer viewers to make a hit. *Seinfeld* won the 1994–95 ratings race with a rating that two decades earlier wouldn't have even placed the show in the Top Twenty-five. Such a disintegration of the network audience meant that the networks no longer had to program for as large a mass to make money, and shows like *Seinfeld*—which appealed to upscale viewers—often were the results. By 1995, half the sitcoms on TV seemed to fea-

ture singles living in cities like New York, if only because these series appealed to viewers similarly situated who, in turn, appealed to advertisers because they have lots of discretionary income.

Yet even though television was finally acknowledging the nation's diversity, that didn't mean that shows like *Seinfeld* were realistic national self-portraits either. After all, the more that television sitcoms have moved in the direction of "realism," the less authentic they have often become. For all the praise that *All in the Family* received, Archie Bunker was a parody; even the witty comedy of *Mary Tyler Moore* hardly reflected a workplace anyone could recognize with honest assurance. Similarly, no one—not even an Upper East Sider—has hours every day to spend chatting with friends in a diner. Yet critics were fond of praising the realism of *Seinfeld*. "Men probably laughed louder than women at the episode in which Elaine discovered that her nipple was exposed on her Christmas card photo," wrote McInerney. "This stuff happens to all of us." Oh, really?

Seinfeld did have considerable strengths, however. The show was genuinely funny, a rare treat on prime-time television. Some of the series episodes, like the one on the "soup Nazi" or on losing a car in a parking lot, were inspired, and the supporting cast of Elaine, Kramer, and George was exceptional. "It's about nothing, everything else is about something; this, it's about nothing," said George in pitching his and Jerry's sitcom proposal to a network, as *Seinfeld* became a show within a show. Already, some of its lines have become pop culture classics: "I'm Cosmo Kramer, the Assman!"; "Not that there's anything wrong with that"; and "Master of your Domain."

Seinfeld was also a hit because it appealed to men more than did many other sitcoms, as it reflected a new adolescent sensibility sweeping America in the 1990s. Along with the comedy of David Letterman, the cartoon series *Beavis and Butt-Head*, megamovies like *Jurassic Park*, and syndicated radio talkmeisters Howard Stern and Don Imus, *Seinfeld* often echoed the world of 11-to-15-year-old boys. The radio style of Stern and Imus, for example, was that of the narcissistic class cutup in seventh grade: Both sat in a playhouse-like radio studio with a bunch of guys and horsed around for hours talking about sex, sports, and politics, all while laughing at their own loutish, subversive jokes.

Seinfeld shared a similar sensibility, albeit softened somewhat for television. Like a group of 14-year-olds, the men on *Seinfeld* seemed not to hold regular jobs, the better to devote time to "the gang." (One woman, Elaine, was allowed to tag along with the boys, much like those younger sisters who are permitted to hang out with their brothers.) Not only was every man in *Seinfeld*'s gang unmarried and pushing fortysomething, but it also was difficult to imagine any having a real relationship with any woman but his mother. Note how much more often parents of adult children appeared here than on other shows.

14   Or compare *Seinfeld* to its predecessor in its NBC Thursday night time slot, *Cheers*. If the men on that show didn't spend much time at work either, they did hang out in a traditional domain of adults—the tavern—and the hero, Sam Malone, spent many of his waking hours chasing women. Seinfeld, by contrast, was better known for sitting in a restaurant eating french fries with his pals. One of the most celebrated risqué *Seinfeld* episodes was about (what else?) masturbation, while others dealt with urinating in the shower or on couches. That's usually big stuff in the seventh grade, but not much beyond.

15   The *Seinfeld* evocation of early male adolescence did reflect deeper cultural strains. This country has always venerated "bad boys," from Huck Finn to Holden Caulfield. Moreover, many psychologists consider that pre-teen stage of life, when one is acutely aware of being powerless, as the time when individuals are most subversive of the society at-large. That senti-ment fit a nineties cultural mood as America became full of the defiant, op-positional anger that often characterizes the early adolescent—witness the tearing down of public figures with the ready help of the tabloid press, and the flocking to antiestablishment talk radio whereon humor grew more de-risive by the day. In a similar vein, one could imagine the whole *Seinfeld* cast of perpetual adolescents on the Clinton White House staff working with George Stephanopolous or Craig Livingstone. Yet boys will be boys: Maybe that's why much of the country viewed the Clinton administration's mis-steps as benignly as they viewed George Costanza's.

16   Because this country has always had tendencies that remind observers of a 14-year-old-boy, no one would blame *Seinfeld* alone for society's failure to grow up and take care of its real children; its current ambivalence about paternal authority; or its vulgarity and exhibitionist inclinations. Yet the show definitely played a role, along with its cultural cousins. In much the same way that *Roseanne* had domesticated tabloid television for the masses, *Seinfeld* did the same for sophomoric talk radio, as embodied by fellow Man-hattanites Stern and Imus.

17   By contrast, *Home Improvement* had the gentle ring of mainstream truth. It's no accident that 14-to-30-year-olds in a *TV Guide* poll voted Jill and Tim the TV parents most like their own. Naturally, that state of affairs some-times drew the critics' ire. "'*Home Improvement*' is a reactionary return, after 'Roseanne' and 'Married with Children' and all those Census Bureau re-ports, to the semi-extinct idea of a nuclear family whose members actually

like each other," wrote Chuck Eddy in a review of the show for *millen-ium pop.*

Unlike *Seinfeld, Home Improvement* was about grown-ups. Take the pre-   18
miere episode: Tim (the Toolman) Taylor, host of a cable show called *Tool Time,* wants to rewire his dishwasher to make it more powerful but ends up breaking it. When he goes to comfort his wife after she doesn't get a job, he inadvertently ends up making her feel worse. In just such a fashion *Home Improvement* was built around that preoccupation central to the zeitgeist of the nineties: If television once told us *Father Knows Best,* this show proved what it meant to be the best father and husband in an age of feminism and embattled male identity.

When Matt Williams and David McFadzean were developing the idea   19
for this show, they were both reading the work of noted linguist Deborah Tannen on male-female communication. "Her book deals with the fact that men and women speak different languages," Williams once remembered. "That right there is the piston that drives this television series. Jill and Tim will never do the same thing the same way, and both sides are valid." On another occasion, Williams noted:

> The biggest challenge for us is to take absurd situations, or extreme points of view or actions, and root them in some kind of truth. . . . If we do our job cor-rectly, those are the things the audience will never think twice about, because we've rooted them in some kind of behavioral truth.

And so the show went in the 1990s, quietly drawing better in rural than   20
urban areas, yet still doing well among professionals. Like Jerry Seinfeld, Tim Allen's persona became a new cultural icon—the postfeminist handy-man. His was a sitcom prototype with the qualities that many Americans in the 1990s held dear—low-key, predictable, intelligent but not particularly well-educated, with a little dirt under his fingernails. If he'd been a politi-cian in the nineties, he would have had little in common with Bill Clinton or Newt Gingrich—Washington insiders and policy preachers to the core. (Colin Powell would be another story.) For different reasons, Taylor also would have had little to talk about with Seinfeld, who never would have tuned in to *Tool Time,* much less own a hammer. (Like many Manhattanites, Seinfeld always seemed to prefer the movies to television anyway.)

Here, then, were two conflicting strains in the American character: *Sein-*   21
feld, a popular urban show about eccentric individualism and the flight from adulthood, versus *Home Improvement,* a popular suburban show about com-mitment and ultimately about family. The forces which create "the buzz"

in this country—the press, the public relations establishment, and Madison Avenue—simply loved *Seinfeld,* which tells us as much about their makeup and tastes as about the show itself. We also had our *Seinfeld*-esque White House.

22   The guess here, however, is that *Home Improvement* was still a better reflection of who we are, despite major social changes over decades. In the not-so-grand tradition of television, viewers still feel more comfortable with the Cleavers, the Andersons, and the Bradys than they do with the *Seinfeld* alternative. Viewers want happy, traditional families, even when they realize that a TV family and setting is idealized—or perhaps *especially* when they realize it. The perfect man for the nineties? It's OK to have that fling with the "bad boy"—who, after all, has always been part of the greater American family. But when it's time to settle down, he isn't the guy you're going to want to bring into your living rooms and bedrooms, night after night.

Understanding Meaning

1.   What similarities does Stark see between *Home Improvement* and *Seinfeld?* Why were their differences more revealing?
2.   How did the expansion of cable television affect the ratings of network programs?
3.   In Stark's view, what was the appeal of *Seinfeld* and *Home Improvement?* Did they appeal to different audiences or different attitudes within the viewers?
4.   How did *Seinfeld* and *Home Improvement* differ from previous sitcoms?
5.   *Critical Thinking:* Traditional sitcoms focused on family situations. In the 1990s, programs like *Murphy Brown, Friends,* and *Seinfeld* featured non-family groups of friends, neighbors, and coworkers. How does this reflect social changes and demographic trends?

Evaluating Strategy

1.   What method does Stark use in organizing his essay? What role do paragraph breaks play in signaling transitions?
2.   Stark concludes his comparison, stating, "The guess here, however, is that *Home Improvement* was still a better reflection of who we are. . . ." Should his choice be more strongly worded? Does using the word "guess" appear to weaken the merit of his judgment?
3.   Does Stark provide enough details about the two programs for readers unfamiliar with *Home Improvement* or *Seinfeld* to grasp their essential character?

Appreciating Language

1. Does Stark's choice of words in describing the programs reveal any preference or bias, favoring one show over the other?
2. *Critical Thinking:* Stark repeatedly comments on the "adolescent" nature of *Seinfeld* and its unmarried characters. Does this imply a bias, suggesting immaturity? Would another writer celebrate the characters' youth and freedom?

Connections across the Disciplines

1. "TV Movies in the First Decade of AIDS" (page 323) analyzes the way in which television confronted a controversial social issue. Can sitcoms address serious issues as well? Can you think of any examples?
2. *Critical Thinking:* The key figure in many family sitcoms—*Home Improvement, Father Knows Best, Leave It to Beaver, The Brady Bunch, Family Matters*—is often the father. How have TV fathers changed since the 1950s?

Writing Suggestions

1. Using this essay as a model, compare two popular soap operas, talk shows, or dramas. Outline both their similarities and their differences. Highlight reasons for their popularity, and describe their viewers.
2. Magazines, like television shows, often bear striking similarities. Examine issues of related magazines such as *Time* and *Newsweek* or *Cosmopolitan* and *Redbook*. Write an essay comparing the two magazines, focusing on what distinguishes them. Can you develop a profile of their intended readers? Do the magazines seem to target the same or different audiences? Review the advertisements as well as the articles.
3. *Collaborative Writing:* Discuss current sitcoms with a group of students, and develop a cause and effect essay detailing the impact you feel these programs have on young people. If members of the group disagree, consider writing contrasting statements.

MICHAEL BARONE

Michael Barone attended Harvard University and graduated from Yale Law School. He is a senior writer for U.S. News & World Report *and a frequent guest on many talk shows. For thirty years he has been the coauthor of the biannual* Almanac of American Politics. *He is also the author of* Our Country: The Shaping of America from Roosevelt to Reagan. *In 2001 he published* The New Americans: How the Melting Pot Can Work Again, *which compares today's African-American, Hispanic, and Asian minorities to the Irish, Italian, and Jewish immigrants who entered the American mainstream a century before.*

Irish and Blacks

OVERVIEW: *In this section from* The New Americans *Barone compares the experiences of today's African-American community with the Irish Catholics who migrated to America following the potato famine of the 1840s. As you read his comparison, consider the role of race. Does color create profound differences between minorities entering mainstream culture?*

1   To most Americans today, it is not immediately obvious that the black migrants who left the rural South for the industrial cities of the North starting in the 1940s resemble the Irish immigrants who left rural Ireland and crossed the ocean to the great cities of the Atlantic seaboard starting in the 1840s. Yet the resemblances are many.

2   Both the Irish and the blacks came from an old country where they were second-caste citizens—the Irish from "Britain's other island," the blacks from the segregated American South. Both were barred, because of their religion or their race, from government and politics. As tenant farmers many Irish and as sharecroppers many blacks were effectively excluded from the market economy. Both were ordinarily denied all but a rudimentary education. "The movement of the progressive societies," wrote the English legal historian Sir Henry Maine a century ago, "has hitherto been a movement from Status to Contract." That is to say, it was a movement from a society in which how you were treated depended on who you were—free or unfree, Protestant or Catholic, white or black—to a society in which how you were treated depended on voluntary agreements between you and others. But British-ruled Ireland and the segregated South were not progressive societies in Maine's sense. Irish Catholics in the 1840s and southern blacks in the 1940s lived in societies where on important matters they were defined by status, not contract. They could never escape the adverse consequences

of being Catholic or being black. They might be guaranteed subsistence by the owners of the land they worked, but they could expect to reap no other benefits: there was no reliable connection between effort and reward. Their subordinate status inevitably had an impact on their personal lives. Their males were demeaned and denied respect because of their subservient economic status, and fathers often deserted their families.

These were peoples whose experiences infected them with fatalism: they did not do things, things happened to them. But one aspect of their lives they controlled: their religion. The Irish had the Catholic Church, which was not controlled by the ruling Protestants; southern blacks had their own Protestant sects, with ministers who were not controlled by the ruling whites. For all their religious faith, violence and crime were common in their communities, with the ruling class indifferent to Irish-on-Irish or black-on-black crime. Yet in these difficult circumstances the Irish and blacks nevertheless managed to develop a protest politics of great strength and moral force, a movement in which their churches played leading roles, before their respective great migrations began. 3

Both began leaving the old country in large numbers in a moment of crisis, when their old way of life suddenly became unfeasible—with the outbreak of the potato famine in the 1840s and the introduction of the mechanical cotton picker and the onset of World War II in the 1940s. In the new country of the American North, both the Irish and blacks were unsophisticated rural people suddenly thrust in very large numbers into the nation's most sophisticated great cities. Both were noticeably different from others in these cities—different in appearance, different in accent and their use of language, different in behavior. Both met with discrimination. The Irish and blacks worked mostly at unskilled jobs and earned low incomes compared to others, though economically they were significantly better off than in the old country. Neither showed much entrepreneurial impulse; with no experience in economic activity, few started their own businesses. 4

Both groups were also in many ways fenced off from the larger society. For several generations, the Irish and blacks had continuing contact with the places from which they came, and few intermarried with other groups. To be sure, however, the consequences of intermarriage in America were very different: the children of Irish/non-Irish marriages often found their Irish identification obscured, while the children of black/white marriages to this day are almost invariably classified as black. 5

The Irish and blacks each created and dominated their own churches, the Irish within the hierarchical structure of the Catholic Church, where in America they usually encountered non-Irish Catholics, blacks in the more 6 entrepreneurial setting of churches that have had few if any non-black members.

7   Even in the new country, family ties among both groups proved to be weak; fatherlessness was common, as many men abandoned their wives and children or were victims of work accidents and crime. Crime rates among both groups were high, significantly higher than among other groups in the city, with crime becoming markedly more visible about a decade after the great migrations began. And about twenty years after the migrations started, large numbers of both groups took part in bloody urban riots—the draft riots of the 1860s and the urban riots of the 1960s. (More people died in the New York draft riot of 1863 than in the Watts riot of 1965 and the Detroit riot of 1967 combined.) Both groups had high rates of substance abuse—alcohol with the Irish, alcohol plus marijuana and crack cocaine with blacks.

8   Despite all these disadvantages, both groups produced many examples of excellence. The Irish and black communities produced many notable sports heroes and entertainment figures. Both, that is, put an indelible imprint on American popular culture long before they became fully interwoven into the fabric of American life.

9   With their traditions of peaceful protest and their sense of grievance against an unfair larger society, both groups looked to control of government as a means of advancement, and both excelled at politics. They built their own political organizations, modeled on their churches: the Irish, hierarchical political machines; blacks, ad hoc organizations assembled by charismatic local leaders. They were initially the object of competition between Democrats and Whigs or Republicans, but within about twenty years both became heavily, almost unanimously, Democratic. Both used politics to create large numbers of public sector jobs for their own people. In some cities where they were majorities—Boston and Jersey City for the Irish, Detroit and Washington for blacks—they created a predatory politics, which overloaded the public payroll and neglected to enforce the law, ultimately damaging the cities' private economies. But in other cities and in state and national politics, members of these groups also provided competent and constructive political leadership.

10   Convergence to the American mean—rising to levels of average income and education—was for both groups very slow. They were handicapped by the habit of mind that cherished grievances against a fundamentally unfair society whose rules they saw no reason to obey. This habit of mind, functional in the genuinely unfair status societies of Ireland and the American South, proved dysfunctional in the more ambiguous—partly fair, partly unfair—contract society of the northern American city. A continuing preoc-

cupation with religious, ethnic, or racial grievance persisted for many years, understandably so given the viciously discriminatory character of the old country and the continuing discrimination in the new. The Irish bemoaned "No Irish need apply" signs long after most had disappeared and insisted that Al Smith had been defeated in 1928 only because he was an Irish Catholic, though there is no reason to believe any Democrat could have won the White House that year. Blacks remained alert for signs of racism and discrimination even as these became less common, and many were fixated on charges of white mass killings of black children in Atlanta or the burning of black churches in the rural South, though the Atlanta killer turned out to be black and most of the churches were burned in accidents or by blacks.

But both groups, like almost all migrants and immigrants, had headed 11 to areas of rapid economic growth and partook of at least some of the benefits. Within fifty years of the initial migrations, there were many lace-curtain Irish and middle-class blacks. Discrimination held back many members of both groups, but so did the widespread fatherlessness, which tended to produce economic dependency and crime—the characteristics of a stubbornly persistent underclass. Still, dysfunctional habits of mind tend to grow weaker over the generations. America's elites, never much bothered by discrimination against the Irish, caustically scorned Irish cultural behavior and Irish patronage politics, to the point that Irish leaders felt obliged to pretend at least to adhere to the standards of the larger society. Over time, this presumably weakened the sense of grievance and the dysfunctional habits of mind brought over from the old country. Society addressed the ills of the Irish through private charities, the settlement house movement, temperance societies, and police forces, all of which tried to improve individuals' conduct and to help people conform to the standards of the larger society. The Irish rose to average levels of income and education by the 1950s, and in 1960 an Irish Catholic was elected president of the United States. The Irish had finally become interwoven into the fabric of American life.

In contrast, America's elites, who from the 1870s to the 1960s had gen- 12 erally ignored racism and segregation, in the early 1960s took a strong stand against discriminating against blacks—a great improvement over their predecessors' treatment of the Irish. Starting in the late 1960s and early 1970s, these elites championed programs of vast public spending and lenient law enforcement. These programs purposefully avoided trying to improve individuals' conduct and to help them conform to the standards of the larger society—that was called "blaming the victim"—and gave sanction to behaviors that resulted in the tripling of crime and welfare in the decade after 1965—trends that gravely harmed many black Americans. In the 1970s,

1980s, and 1990s, America's corporate, university, and media elites gave their imprimatur to the system of racial quotas, preferences, and set-asides that has strengthened the sense of grievance, racial consciousness, and, on elite campuses and in workplaces, the dysfunctional habit of mind which holds that the larger society is fundamentally unfair and that one has no obligation to obey it. These policies resulted from the same good motives that prompted civil rights laws and an end to legal segregation in the South. Unlike those measures, however, the new system had bad as well as good effects on black Americans and has probably retarded their movement toward becoming interwoven into the fabric of American life.

13   Nevertheless, there is much reason for optimism. In the 1990s the black middle class continued to expand, while crime and welfare dependency trended sharply downward. Moreover, as the experience of the Irish shows, this country is by its nature far readier than any other to interweave peoples of different background and sometimes dysfunctional behavior into the national fabric. It took 120 years for the Irish; it may not take as long for blacks.

Understanding Meaning

1. What are the major similarities between the Irish and African-American experience in Barone's view?
2. What role did religious institutions play in maintaining African-American and Irish identity?
3. How have the Irish and African-Americans achieved political power, especially in large cities?
4. What common problems faced both groups? Does Barone believe that some problems were self-inflicted?
5. Barone states that centuries of oppression generated a profound fatalism in both groups, making them suspicious of authority and antisocial. What elements helped erode this alienation?
6. *Critical Thinking:* Barone outlines numerous striking similarities but does not comment on skin color. Is race such a profound difference that it overwhelms whatever likenesses can be drawn between a group of whites and blacks?

Evaluating Strategy

1. Barone organizes his essay using a point-by-point approach. Would a subject-by-subject method work as well? Why or why not?

2. Does Barone have to devote more time to discussing Irish-American history? Are many Americans familiar with the discrimination Irish Catholics once faced?

3. In discussing such sweeping and complex issues, how does Barone use facts and details to support his thesis?

4. *Other Modes:* What role does *process* and *cause and effect* play in developing Barone's comparison?

Appreciating Language

1. How would you evaluate Barone's overall tone—judgmental, sympathetic, sarcastic, or encouraging? What words or phrases reflect his attitude?

2. Barone uses the phrase "blaming the victim." How does Barone interpret its meaning?

3. How does Barone define the terms "status" and "contract"?

4. Discuss the term "melting pot." How do different people respond to this word and the concept it represents?

Connections across the Disciplines

1. Barone compares immigrant experiences between ethnic groups. Bharati Mukherjee (page 262) compares the immigrant experience between two Indian sisters. How much of an immigrant's life in America depends not only on large social and political issues but also on personal attitudes and decisions?

2. Refer to the "Irish Need Apply" ad (page 599). Does this reveal that even when integrated into the melting pot, ethnic groups retain a special loyalty to their native land and culture?

Writing Suggestions

1. Write a comparison essay that explores the similarities of your generation and your parents'. Can you draw parallels between their goals, values, and attitudes and yours? Did common experiences shape their views of the world and themselves?

2. *Collaborative Writing:* Discuss Barone's essay with a group of students, then write a critique. What is the greatest difference between the Irish and African-American experience? Is it race or the difference between the industrial age and the information age?

BHARATI MUKHERJEE

Bharati Mukherjee was born in Calcutta and is now a distinguished professor at the University of California at Berkeley. In 1989 she became the first naturalized American citizen to win the National Book Critics Circle Award for Fiction for The Middleman and Other Stories. *Her other books include* Leave It to Me, The Holder of the World, Darkness, The Tiger's Daughter, Wife, Jasmine, *and* Desirable Daughters. *Much of her fiction and nonfiction commentary explores the diversity of immigrant experiences in the United States.*

Two Ways to Belong to America

OVERVIEW: *This essay appeared in the* New York Times *in 1996 when Congress was debating bills that would greatly limit the benefits granted to legal immigrants. The debate gave Bharati Mukherjee an opportunity to compare her experience as a naturalized citizen with that of her sister who, though living and working in America for decades, preferred to remain an Indian national.*

1   This is a tale of two sisters from Calcutta, Mira and Bharati, who have lived in the United States for some 35 years, but who find themselves on different sides in the current debate over the status of immigrants. I am an American citizen and she is not. I am moved that thousands of long-term residents are finally taking the oath of citizenship. She is not.

2   Mira arrived in Detroit in 1960 to study child psychology and pre-school education. I followed her a year later to study creative writing at the University of Iowa. When we left India, we were almost identical in appearance and attitude. We dressed alike, in saris; we expressed identical views on politics, social issues, love and marriage in the same Calcutta convent-school accent. We would endure our two years in America, secure our degrees, then return to India to marry the grooms of our father's choosing.

3   Instead, Mira married an Indian student in 1962 who was getting his business administration degree at Wayne State University. They soon acquired the labor certifications necessary for the green card of hassle-free residence and employment.

4   Mira still lives in Detroit, works in the Southfield, Michigan, school system, and has become nationally recognized for her contributions in the fields of pre-school education and parent-teacher relationships. After 36 years as a legal immigrant in this country, she clings passionately to her Indian citizenship and hopes to go home to India when she retires.

In Iowa City in 1963, I married a fellow student, an American of Canadian parentage. Because of the accident of his North Dakota birth, I bypassed labor-certification requirements and the race-related "quota" system that favored the applicant's country of origin over his or her merit. I was prepared for (and even welcomed) the emotional strain that came with marrying outside my ethnic community. In 33 years of marriage, we have lived in every part of North America. By choosing a husband who was not my father's selection, I was opting for fluidity, self-invention, blue jeans and T-shirts, and renouncing 3,000 years (at least) of caste-observant, "pure culture" marriage in the Mukherjee family. My books have often been read as unapologetic (and in some quarters overenthusiastic) texts for cultural and psychological "mongrelization." It's a word I celebrate.

Mira and I have stayed sisterly close by phone. In our regular Sunday morning conversations, we are unguardedly affectionate. I am her only blood relative on this continent. We expect to see each other through the looming crises of aging and ill health without being asked. Long before Vice President Gore's "Citizenship U.S.A." drive, we'd had our polite arguments over the ethics of retaining an overseas citizenship while expecting the permanent protection and economic benefits that come with living and working in America.

Like well-raised sisters, we never said what was really on our minds, but we probably pitied one another. She, for the lack of structure in my life, the erasure of Indianness, the absence of an unvarying daily core. I, for the narrowness of her perspective, her uninvolvement with the mythic depths or the superficial pop culture of this society. But, now, with the scapegoating of "aliens" (documented or illegal) on the increase, and the targeting of long-term legal immigrants like Mira for new scrutiny and new self-consciousness, she and I find ourselves unable to maintain the same polite discretion. We were always unacknowledged adversaries, and we are now, more than ever, sisters.

"I feel used," Mira raged on the phone the other night. "I feel manipulated and discarded. This is such an unfair way to treat a person who was invited to stay and work here because of her talent. My employer went to the I.N.S. and petitioned for the labor certification. For over 30 years, I've invested my creativity and professional skills into the improvement of *this* country's pre-school system. I've obeyed all the rules, I've paid my taxes, I love my work, I love my students, I love the friends I've made. How dare America now change its rules in midstream? If America wants to make new rules curtailing benefits of legal immigrants, they should apply only to immigrants who arrive after those rules are already in place."

9   To my ears, it sounded like the description of a long-enduring, comfortable yet loveless marriage, without risk or recklessness. Have we the right to demand, and to expect, that we be loved? (That, to me, is the subtext of the arguments by immigration advocates.) My sister is an expatriate, professionally generous and creative, socially courteous and gracious, and that's as far as her Americanization can go. She is here to maintain an identity, not to transform it.

10   I asked her if she would follow the example of others who have decided to become citizens because of the anti-immigration bills in Congress. And here, she surprised me. "If America wants to play the manipulative game, I'll play it too," she snapped. "I'll become a U.S. citizen for now, then change back to Indian when I'm ready to go home. I feel some kind of irrational attachment to India that I don't to America. Until all this hysteria against legal immigrants, I was totally happy. Having my green card meant I could visit any place in the world I wanted to and then come back to a job that's satisfying and that I do very well."

11   In one family, from two sisters alike as peas in a pod, there could not be a wider divergence of immigrant experience. America spoke to me—I embraced the demotion from expatriate aristocrat to immigrant nobody, surrendering those thousands of years of "pure culture," the saris, the delightfully accented English. She retained them all. Which of us is the freak?

12   Mira's voice, I realize, is the voice not just of the immigrant South Asian community but of an immigrant community of the millions who have stayed rooted in one job, one city, one house, one ancestral culture, one cuisine, for the entirety of their productive years. She speaks for greater numbers than I possibly can. Only the fluency of her English and the anger, rather than fear, born of confidence from her education, differentiate her from the seamstresses, the domestics, the technicians, the shop owners, the millions of hard-working but effectively silenced documented immigrants as well as their less fortunate "illegal" brothers and sisters.

13   Nearly 20 years ago, when I was living in my husband's ancestral homeland of Canada, I was always well-employed but never allowed to feel part of the local Quebec or larger Canadian society. Then, through a Green Paper that invited a national referendum on the unwanted side effects of "nontraditional" immigration, the Government officially turned against its immigrant communities, particularly those from South Asia.

14   I felt then the same sense of betrayal that Mira feels now. I will never forget the pain of that sudden turning, and the casual racist outbursts the Green Paper elicited. That sense of betrayal had its desired effect and drove me, and thousands like me, from the country.

Mira and I differ, however, in the ways in which we hope to interact with   15
the country that we have chosen to live in. She is happier to live in America
as expatriate Indian than as an immigrant American. I need to feel like a
part of the community I have adopted (as I tried to feel in Canada as well).
I need to put roots down, to vote and make the difference that I can. The
price that the immigrant willingly pays, and that the exile avoids, is the
trauma of self-transformation.

Understanding Meaning

1. What is the principal difference between the writer and her sister?
2. Why does the writer's sister prefer to remain an Indian national and not become an American citizen?
3. Can a person contribute to the American economy, society, and culture without becoming a citizen?
4. Why did Bharati Mukherjee become a citizen? How did that decision reflect
   her view of herself and of her position in American society?
5. Can you understand why the writer's sister feels "manipulated and discarded"
   by the suggestion that she should become a citizen? In your view, is her anger
   justified?
6. *Critical Thinking:* If your future career took you to France, would you consider
   becoming a French citizen or would you prefer to remain an American, even if
   you planned to live there for decades? Why? Would keeping your American
   citizenship show loyalty to your native country? If you renounced your American citizenship would you feel you were rejecting your homeland?

Evaluating Strategy

1. Do you feel the device of comparing two sisters is an effective way of exploring
   different immigrant experiences? By using a person she loves and respects to
   represent a different viewpoint, does the writer avoid seeming overly biased?
2. Bharati Mukherjee wrote this as an op-ed piece for a major newspaper. Do you
   think she was effective in sharing her observations with the general public?
   What challenges do writers face when trying to address a complex topic in a
   brief newspaper editorial?
3. *Other Modes:* Where does Bharati Mukherjee use *description, narration,* and *cause
   and effect* to develop her comparison?

Appreciating Language

1. Bharati Mukherjee uses the word "mongrelization," stating, "It's a word I celebrate." Look up *mongrelization* in a dictionary. What connotations does it have? If Mukherjee celebrates this word, what does it reveal about her values and attitudes?

2. Mukherjee refers to her sister as an "expatriate." What connotation does this word have? Is the word neutral or does it have positive or negative connotations?

Connections across the Disciplines

1. Review Bruce Catton's essay "Grant and Lee" (page 244). Do you see similar patterns in the way Catton and Mukherjee use two personalities to reflect two value systems? What problems can emerge if you attempt to use a single person to represent a value system, a philosophy, or a way of life?

2. Do the views of Armando Rendón (page 586) and Barbara Ehrenreich (page 592) reflect the views of Bharati Mukherjee and her sister? Why or why not?

Writing Suggestions

1. Use a comparison of two people to illustrate contrasting values. Compare two friends and their different attitudes about work or school. Contrast your spending habits with those of your mother. Compare the way you drive with your cousin's driving. Your essay may suggest that one person's values or methods are more desirable, or you may simply highlight their differences.

2. If you moved to another country to live and work, would you consider renouncing your American citizenship? Write an essay explaining your views.

3. *Collaborative Writing:* Discuss Bharati Mukherjee's essay with a group of students. Work together to develop a brief essay that outlines the pros and cons of becoming an American citizen. Only citizens can vote. Does the writer's sister deny herself the ability of choosing the leaders of the country she is living in? Ask members of the group if they have any friends or relatives who decided either to become citizens or retain their original nationality.

BLENDING THE MODES

LOUIS GATES JR.

Louis Gates Jr. was educated at Yale University and Clare College of the University of Cambridge. He currently chairs the Afro-American studies department at Harvard University and is the director of the W. E. B. Du Bois Institute for Afro-American Research. He has published a number of general and scholarly works, including The Signifying Monkey, Loose Canons: Notes of the Culture Wars *and* Thirteen Ways of Looking at a Black Man. *He is a regular contributor to the* New Yorker.

One Internet, Two Nations

OVERVIEW: *In this 1999 essay, Louis Gates Jr. compares white and African-American use of the Internet to make a persuasive argument. Note that he devotes little space to commenting on whites but instead concentrates his commentary on African-Americans.*

After the Stono Rebellion of 1739 in South Carolina—the largest uprising of slaves in the colonies before the American Revolution—legislators there responded by banishing two forms of communication among the slaves: the mastery of reading and writing, and the mastery of "talking drums," both of which had been crucial to the capacity to rebel.

For the next century and a half, access to literacy became for the slaves a hallmark of their humanity and an instrument of liberation, spiritual as well as physical. The relation between freedom and literacy became the compelling theme of the slave narratives, the great body of printed books that ex-slaves generated to assert their common humanity with white Americans and to indict the system that had oppressed them.

In the years since the abolition of slavery, the possession of literacy has been a cardinal value of the African-American tradition. It is no accident that the first great victory in the legal battle over segregation was fought on the grounds of education—of equal access to literacy.

Today, blacks are failing to gain access to the new tools of literacy: the digital "knowledge economy." And while the dilemma that our ancestors confronted was imposed by others, this cybersegregation is, to a large degree, self-imposed.

The Government's latest attempt to understand why low-income African-Americans and Hispanics are slower to embrace the Internet and the personal computer than whites—the Commerce Department study "Falling Through the Net"—suggests that income alone can't be blamed for the so-called digital divide. For example, among families earning $15,000 to $35,000 annually, more than 33 percent of whites own computers, compared with only 19 percent of African-Americans—a gap that has widened 64 percent over the past five years despite declining computer prices.

6   The implications go far beyond online trading and chat rooms. Net promoters are concerned that the digital divide threatens to become a 21st century poll tax that, in effect, disenfranchises a third of the nation. Our children, especially, need access not only to the vast resources that technology offers for education, but also to the rich cultural contexts that define their place in the world.

7   Today we stand at the brink of becoming two societies, one largely white and plugged in and the other black and unplugged.

8   One of the most tragic aspects of slavery was the way it destroyed social connections. In a process that the sociologist Orlando Patterson calls "social death," slavery sought to sever blacks from their history and culture, from family ties and a sense of community. And, of course, de jure segregation after the Civil War was intended to disconnect blacks from equal economic opportunity, from the network of social contacts that enable upward mobility and, indeed, from the broader world of ideas.

9   Despite the dramatic growth of the black middle class since affirmative action programs were started in the late 60's, new forms of disconnectedness have afflicted black America. Middle-class professionals often feel socially and culturally isolated from their white peers at work and in the neighborhood and from their black peers left behind in the underclass. The children of the black underclass, in turn, often lack middle-class role models to help them connect to a history of achievement and develop their analytical skills.

10   It would be a sad irony if the most diverse and decentralized electronic medium yet invented should fail to achieve ethnic diversity among its users. And yet the Commerce Department study suggests that the solution will require more than cheap PC's. It will involve content.

11   Until recently, the African-American presence on the Internet was minimal, reflecting the chicken-and-egg nature of Internet economics. Few investors have been willing to finance sites appealing to a PC-scarce community. Few African-Americans have been compelled to sign on to a medium that offers little to interest them. And educators interested in diversity have repeatedly raised concerns about the lack of minority-oriented educational software.

Consider the birth of the recording industry in the 1920's. Blacks began 12
to respond to this new medium only when mainstream companies like Columbia Records introduced so-called race records, blues and jazz discs
aimed at a nascent African-American market. Blacks who would never have
dreamed of spending hard-earned funds for a record by Rudy Vallee or Kate
Smith would stand in lines several blocks long to purchase the new Bessie
Smith or Duke Ellington hit.

New content made the new medium attractive. And the growth of Web 13
sites dedicated to the interests and needs of black Americans can play the
same role for the Internet that race records did for the music industry.

But even making sites that will appeal to a black audience can only go 14
so far. The causes of poverty are both structural and behavioral. And it is
the behavioral aspect of this cybersegregation that blacks themselves are
best able to address. Drawing on corporate and foundation support, we
can transform the legion of churches, mosques and community centers in
our inner cities into after-school centers that focus on redressing the digital divide and teaching black history. We can draw on the many examples
of black achievement in structured classes to re-establish a sense of social
connection.

The Internet is the 21st century's talking drum, the very kind of grass- 15
roots communication tool that has been such a powerful source of education
and culture for our people since slavery. But this talking drum we have not
yet learned to play. Unless we master the new information technology to
build and deepen the forms of social connection that a tragic history has
eroded, African-Americans will face a form of cybersegregation in the next
century as devastating to our aspirations as Jim Crow segregation was to
those of our ancestors. But this time, the fault will be our own.

Understanding Meaning

1. Why was attaining literacy an important part of the African-American struggle
   for liberty and equality?
2. What explains the reason why African-Americans have less interest in the
   Internet than their white counterparts?
3. Why does poverty fail to explain the failure of African-American families to
   provide their children with computers?
4. Why does Gates believe that it is important for African-Americans to use the
   Internet?
5. *Critical Thinking:* Do you think that the gulf between those plugged into the information age and those left out will be a major rift in the future? Will those,

male or female, black or white, who fail to embrace the new technology find themselves less able to compete in the marketplace?

Evaluating Strategy

1. Gates opens his essay with a historical narrative. Do you find this effective? Does it make sense to compare computers to talking drums?
2. Gates mentions "two nations" in his title but really only discusses one. In writing a comparison, is it necessary to devote equal attention to both items? Why or why not?
3. *Other Modes:* Note where Gates uses *narration, definition,* and *cause and effect* in creating this essay. Can you consider this comparison to be essentially a *persuasive argument?*

Appreciating Language

1. What tone does Gates adopt? Do any words suggest concern, anger, or disappointment? Do you find words and phrases that create a sense of urgency?
2. In writing about the Internet, does Gates seem to assume his readers are strangers to cyberspace or familiar with the Internet? Does he use any technical language or computer jargon?

Connections across the Disciplines

1. James Poniewozik's essay "What's Wrong with This Picture?" (page 317) points out that Hispanics are underrepresented in television. Does the disparity in Internet use between racial groups indicate a more important divide? Why or why not?
2. Consider John Brooks's "The Effects of the Telephone" (page 492). How did the telephone alter human existence? What impact will the Internet have on individuals, on society, and on our culture? Will there be winners and losers?

Writing Suggestions

1. Gates sees a growing divide between those who are plugged into the Internet and those who are not. Write a short comparison essay contrasting two other groups. You might describe the gulf between those who exercise and stay fit and those who let themselves go or between those who invest and those who spend. Indicate how these lifestyle choices affect people's futures.

2. *Collaborative Writing:* Using Gates's essay as a source, work with a group of students to prepare a short process paper outlining a method to encourage minorities to use the Internet. If you worked for a computer manufacturer or an Internet provider, what promotional campaign might appeal to minorities? How could new content attract ethnic groups who perceive cyberspace as white and alien?

WRITING BEYOND THE CLASSROOM

PEGGY KENNA
AND SONDRA LACY

Peggy Kenna and Sondra Lacy are communications specialists based in Arizona who work with foreign-born employees. In addition, they provide cross-cultural training to executives conducting international business. Kenna is a speech and language patholo-gist who specializes in accent modification. Kenna and Lacy have collaborated on a series of fifty-page booklets that compare American and foreign business organiza-tions, habits, behaviors, and negotiating styles. Widely sold in airports, these booklets give Americans tips on doing business overseas.

Communication Styles: United States and Taiwan

OVERVIEW: *This section from* Business Taiwan *contrasts American and Taiwanese styles of communicating. In designing their booklets for quick skimming, Kenna and Lacy use charts to highlight cultural differences.*

1   UNITED STATES

    TAIWAN

2   • *Frank*

    • *Subtle*

3   Americans tend to be very straight-forward and unreserved. The people of Taiwan often find them abrupt and not interested enough in human relationships.

    Frankness is not appreciated by the people of Taiwan. They particu-larly dislike unqualified negative statements.

4   • *Face saving less important*

    • *Face saving important*

5   To Americans accuracy is important but errors are tolerated. Admitting mistakes is seen as a sign of maturity. They believe you learn from failure and therefore encourage some risk taking.

    The Chinese do not like to be put in the position of having to admit a mis-take or failure. They also do not like to tell you when they don't understand your point.

6
7   Americans believe criticism can be objective and not personal, however, all criticism should be done with tact.

    You also should not admit too read-ily when you don't know something as it can cause you to lose face.

UNITED STATES

• *Direct eye contact*

Direct eye contact is very important to Americans since they need to see the nonverbal cues the speaker is giving. Nonverbal cues are a very important part of the American English language. Americans use intermittent eye contact when they are speaking but fairly steady eye contact when they are listening.

• *Direct and to the point*

Americans prefer people to say what they mean. Because of this they tend to sometimes miss subtle nonverbal cues. Americans are uncomfortable with ambiguousness and don't like to have to "fill in the blanks." They also tend to discuss problems directly.

• *"Yes" means agreement*

Americans look for clues such as nodding of the head, a verbal "yes" or "uh huh" in order to determine if their arguments are succeeding.

TAIWAN 8

• *Avoid direct eye contact* 9

Holding the gaze of another person is considered rude. 10

• *Indirect and ambiguous* 11

People in Taiwan dislike saying "no." 12
They may not tell you when they don't understand. They often hedge their answers if they know you won't like the answer. If they say something like, "We'll think about it," they may mean they aren't interested.

They dislike discussing problems 13
directly and will often go around the issue which can be frustrating for Americans.

The Chinese language (Mandarin) 14
is so concise that the listener needs to use much imagination to "fill in the gaps."

• *"Yes" means "I hear"* 15

People in Taiwan do not judge information given to them so they do not 16
indicate agreement or disagreement; they only nod or say "yes" to indicate they are listening to you.

The people of Taiwan believe 17
politeness is more important than frankness so they will not directly tell you "no." The closest they will come to "no" is "maybe."

Understanding Meaning

1. What appear to be the major differences between American and Taiwanese methods of communicating?
2. Why is it important for Americans to be sensitive about making direct eye contact with Taiwanese?
3. How do Americans and Taiwanese accept failure?
4. *Critical Thinking:* Why would this booklet be valuable to Americans visiting Taiwan on business? Does such a brief, to-the-point guide risk relying on stereotypes?

Evaluating Strategy

1. How easy is this document to read and review? How accessible would the information be if it were written in standard paragraphs?
2. What does the directness of the document reveal about the intended audience? Would it be suitable for a college classroom?

Appreciating Language

1. What language do the writers use in describing the Taiwanese? Do they attempt to be neutral, or does their word choice favor one nationality over another?
2. Kenna and Lacy suggest that many Taiwanese find Americans to be "abrupt." Is this a good word choice? Does the guide express common prejudices?

Connections across the Disciplines

1. Compare Kenna and Lacy's observations with those stated in Yi-Fu Tuan's "Chinese Space, American Space" (page 233). Do these authors make similar observations about American attitudes and behaviors? Do the authors explain differences in communication styles?
2. Kenna and Lacy observe how two nationalities communicate. Bob Levey (page 236) contrasts male and female perceptions about walking alone at night. Do gender differences generate as many barriers to communication as ethnic or cultural differences? Why or why not?

Writing Suggestions

1. Using Kenna and Lacy's entry as a source, write a short process paper instructing how an American should present an idea or product in Taiwan. Assume you are writing to sales representatives traveling to Taiwan for the first time. Provide step-by-step suggestions for how they should conduct themselves from the moment they enter a seminar room to make a presentation.

2. *Collaborative Writing:* Working with a group of students, discuss the differences between high school teachers and college instructors, then develop a chart contrasting their attitudes toward absenteeism, late homework, tests, and research papers.

STRATEGIES FOR WRITING COMPARISON AND CONTRAST

1. **Determine your purpose.** Is your goal to explain differences between two topics or to recommend one over the other? Do you want readers to be informed, or do you wish them to make a choice?
2. **Consider your audience.** Before you can compare two items, you may have to explain background information. Before comparing two treatments for arthritis, it may be necessary to explain the nature of the disease and to define basic terminology.
3. **Determine which method would best suit your topic.** A short, nontechnical paper might be best organized using the subject-by-subject method. Longer works with facts and statistics that should be placed side by side are better developed using the point-by-point method.
4. **Make use of transitional statements.** To prevent confusion in writing comparison, use transitional statements carefully. You may wish to invent labels or titles to clearly distinguish the different subjects you are examining.
5. **Use visual aids to guide your readers.** Careful paragraphing, page breaks, bold or italic headings, and charts can help readers follow your comparison and prevent confusion.

SUGGESTED TOPICS FOR COMPARISON AND CONTRAST WRITING
General Assignments

Write a comparative paper on one of the following topics. You may use either subject-by-subject or point-by-point methods of organization. Clearly determine your purpose. Is your goal to inform or recommend?

- High school versus college
- Your best and worst jobs
- Male and female student attitudes on dating/marriage/career/parenting
- The two most influential teachers you have known
- Two popular situation comedies
- Two computer programs you have worked with
- Your best and worst college courses
- Your parents' values and your own
- Two campus political organizations
- Two popular entertainers
- Two talk shows

Writing in Context

1. Imagine you have been asked by a British newsmagazine to write an article explaining the pro-and-con attitudes Americans have about a controversial topic such as gun control, capital punishment, or affirmative action. Your article should be balanced and objective and provide background information rather than express an opinion.
2. Write the text for a brief pamphlet directed to high school seniors comparing high school and college. You may wish to use a chartlike format.
3. Write a letter to a friend comparing the best and worst aspects of your college, dorm room, community, or job.
4. Examine a magazine on cars, computers, or entertainment. Write a letter to the editor comparing the magazine's best and worst features.
5. Compare two popular student clubs or restaurants for a review in the campus newspaper. Direct your comments to students interested in inexpensive entertainment.

STUDENT PAPER: COMPARISON AND CONTRAST

This is a draft of a comparison paper a student wrote after reading several articles comparing different cultures. In addition to fulfilling a composition assignment, she considered using these ideas for a talk or display for an upcoming Saint Patrick's Day celebration.

Parallel States: Israel and Ireland

Despite obvious historical and cultural differences, Israel and Ireland share striking similarities. Both are small — each has a population of about five million — yet significant nations. Israel is a narrow sliver of desert on the Mediterranean, a Middle Eastern country with negligible oil reserves. Ireland, an island on the fringe of Europe, is a neutral nation which played marginal roles in World War II and the Cold War.

Yet these nations have greater profiles than their larger and more powerful neighbors, largely because they represent homelands to vast Diaspora populations. More Jews live in America than Israel; more Irish live in America than Ireland. American Jews and Irish were significant supporters of the Zionist and Republican movements that helped establish the modern independent states.

3   Their recent emergence as sovereign states indicates a shared legacy of oppression and occupation. Although both the Jews and the Irish have cultures thousands of years old, Israel and Ireland did not achieve full independence until after the Second World War. Israel was recognized by the United Nations in 1948. Though partitioned in 1922, Ireland was not officially declared a republic until 1949, ending eight hundred years of British influence.

4   Since their creation, Israel and Ireland have endured decades of violence and terrorism. Both nations have labored to maintain democratic rights while preserving security for their citizenry.

5   Both nations have dual identities. On one hand, both Israel and Ireland were founded as Western-style Parliamentary democracies. Yet both are religious states. Israel is the Jewish homeland. Ireland is a Catholic nation. The religious authorities — the Catholic bishops and orthodox rabbis — believe citizens should accept their views on marriage, divorce, abortion, censorship, and civil customs. Secular forces, who view the religious orthodoxies as tradition-bound and male dominated, champion diversity and tolerance. Issues such as the role of women and gay rights evoke similar debates in Israel and Ireland as both nations struggle to reconcile their political and religious traditions.

6   In recent years both nations have engaged in a peace process to resolve long standing conflicts in contested areas. In both Northern Ireland and the West Bank the populations are split by religious, political, and cultural differences.

7   Recently the President of the United States, prompted by the large number of Jews and Irish in America, played a pivotal role in stimulating stalled peace talks. Negotiations in both regions were difficult to conduct because Israeli and Northern Irish politicians did not wish to recognize leaders of terrorist organizations.

8   By first inviting Yasser Arrafat and Gerry Adams to the White House, Bill Clinton helped transform their public images from terrorists to legitimate leaders so that other democratic leaders could negotiate with them without appearing to endorse violence.

9   Despite ongoing tensions in both regions, Israel and Ireland enjoy expanding tourism, particularly from millions of American Jews and Irish who enjoy visiting homelands that represent their heritage.

Questions for Review and Revision

1. Is the thesis of this essay too general? Does the paper provide genuine insights or merely list obvious observations? Would it be better to fully develop a single issue, such as the role of religion in the two countries?
2. Would a revised introduction and conclusion provide greater focus?
3. What audience does the student seem to address?
4. *Critical Thinking:* To be effective, does a comparison paper have to accomplish more than merely list similarities? Should there be a greater purpose?
5. How effectively does the student organize the comparison? What role does paragraph structure play?
6. Read the paper aloud. Do you detect any passages that could be revised to reduce wordiness and repetition?

Writing Suggestions

1. Write a 500-word essay comparing two nations, cities, or neighborhoods. Stress similarities of which most readers would be unaware.
2. *Collaborative Writing:* Discuss this paper with a group of students. Ask each member to suggest possible changes. Do they find common areas needing improvement?

COMPARISON AND CONTRAST CHECKLIST

Before submitting your paper, review these points.

1. Are your subjects closely related enough to make a valid comparison?

2. Have you identified the key points of both subjects?

3. Have you selected the best method of organizing your paper?

4. Is the comparison easy to follow? Are transitions clear?

5. Does the comparison meet reader needs and expectations?

6. Have you defined terms or provided background information necessary for readers to fully appreciate the comparison?

7. Is your thesis clearly stated and located where it will have the greatest impact?

Companion Web Site

See **http://sundance.heinle.com** for information on writing comparison and contrast.

InfoTrac® College Edition

For additional reading go to InfoTrac College edition, your on-line research library, at **http://infotrac.thomsonlearning.com**.

- Enter the search term "comparison" using Keywords.
- Enter the name of an author you read in this chapter using Keywords.
- Enter a theme or idea your class discussed using Keywords.

Analysis

MAKING EVALUATIONS

WHAT IS ANALYSIS?

Analysis moves beyond description and narration to make judgments or evaluations about persons, places, objects, ideas, or situations. A movie reviewer *describes* a new film and then *analyzes* it—critiquing the plot, acting, special effects, and social message. A historian *narrates* an event and then *evaluates* its lasting significance. Marketing executives *summarize* sales reports to *judge* the results of their advertising campaign. A psychiatrist *examines* a patient and then *diagnoses* the individual's mental condition.

Analysis often seeks to answer questions. Does aspirin prevent heart attacks? What are Vicki Shimi's chances for being elected governor? Is General Motors' new minivan fuel efficient? Does America have too many lawyers? Is addiction a disease? How effective were the poverty programs launched in the 1960s? What is the best way to remove asbestos from a public school? Is a defendant mentally competent to stand trial? Is the central figure of *Death of a Salesman*, Willy Loman, a victim of society or of his own delusions? The answers to all these questions require a careful gathering of information, critical thinking, and a clear presentation of the writer's thesis.

Analysis entails more than expressing an opinion or creating an impression. In an analytical paper, you cannot simply write, "I hated *A Streetcar Named Desire* because it was stupid," or "Welfare programs waste taxpayers' money." You must base your positions on observations and evidence. Why is the play stupid? What facts demonstrate that welfare programs are wasteful? When asked to write analytical papers, students often supply description and narration, summarizing a short story or describing a social problem. To keep your paper analytical, you can use the journalists' "five W's"— *Who? What? When? Where? Why?*—to develop your thesis. By answering questions, you are forced to find evidence and provide answers instead of simply retelling a story or describing a situation.

Subjective and Objective Analysis

The way writers develop analytical writing depends greatly on context. In many situations, writers rely wholly on personal observation and experience. Film critics, political columnists, book reviewers, fashion consultants, and social commentators tend to write subjective analysis. *Subjective analysis* is based on close observation and careful interpretation. The writer's points are supported by examples and illustrations he or she has chosen rather than by research. Subjective analysis is informed opinion. In a newspaper column, "The Handicap of Definition" (page 287), William Raspberry analyzes the negative impact of the popular definition of "blackness" accepted by many African American children:

> What we have here is a tragically limited definition of blackness, and it isn't only white people who buy it.
>
> Think of all the ways black children can put one another down with charges of "whiteness." For many of these children, hard study and hard work are "white." Trying to please a teacher might be criticized as acting "white." Speaking correct English is "white." Scrimping today in the interest of tomorrow's goals is "white." Educational toys and games are "white."
>
> An incredible array of habits and attitudes that are conducive to success in business, in academia, in the nonentertainment professions are likely to be thought of as somehow "white." Even economic success, unless it involves such "black" undertakings as numbers banking, is defined as "white."
>
> And the results are devastating.

After analyzing how children label activities as being "black" or "white," Raspberry explains how limited definitions lead to limited opportunities. Raspberry's article, written for a general audience, makes conclusions, although it provides no independent research such as surveys or interviews.

Objective analysis begins with close observations but seeks to answer questions through factual research. In objective analysis, the writer needs more than personal experience and anecdotal examples to support a position. In "What's Wrong with This Picture?" (page 317) James Poniewozik cites statistics documenting the disparity between the growing Hispanic population and the presence of Hispanic television characters:

> According to the 2000 Census, Hispanic Americans number 35 million, or 12.5% of the population, a nearly 58% jump since 1990. But on TV? A report by the advocacy group Children Now found that in prime time, the number of Hispanic characters dropped since last season, from 3% to 2%. (Blacks

make up 17%, the study found, Asian Americans 3% and Native Americans 0.2%; they are 12.3%, 3.6% and 0.9% of the population.) In all of prime time, Hispanics account for only 47 out of 2,251 characters. As for nonfiction TV, the Center for Media and Public Affairs found that Latino correspondents reported only 1.3% of all network evening-news stories in 2000.

Objective analysis is not limited to facts and statistics. Writers can balance numbers with interviews, personal examples, and anecdotal accounts. To dramatize the impact of overheard cell phone calls, Louis R. Mizell Jr. provides two cases of intercepted phone calls:

> Doctors and lawyers frequently discuss everyday business on cellular phones. In one case, a doctor was notified that a VIP patient had tested positive for AIDS. The information was intercepted, and before long, the VIP's medical status was common knowledge. In another case, a lawyer from Ohio reviewed a client's prenuptial agreement with a second lawyer who was using a cellular telephone. A teenage neighbor of the second lawyer intercepted the conversation. "Before long, the whole damn neighborhood knew about our secret wedding and my financial situation," said the angry groom-to-be.

The blending of statistics and personal interviews strengthens the analysis because the conclusions are drawn from more than one source of information.

The way writers develop their analytical writing is often influenced by their readers and their discipline. A widely respected restaurant critic will review a new cafe in wholly personal and subjective terms. But an engineer analyzing the structure of a hurricane-damaged bridge will use standard tests and procedures and will only provide conclusions clearly supported by scientific findings and observable detail. Kimberly Crawford, an attorney, analyzes the admissibility of surreptitious recordings of suspects by strictly studying Supreme Court rulings. Suppose the police arrest a man suspected of a bank robbery and place him in a cell with an officer posing as a fellow criminal. The officer engages the suspect in conversation, leading him to boast of his robbery. Could a recording of this admission be admitted as evidence in court, even though the Fifth Amendment of the Constitution protects citizens from self-incrimination? Crawford provides this analysis of the Constitution's guarantee against self-incrimination:

> To be successful, a challenge to the admissibility of surreptitiously recorded conversations based on the fifth amendment self-incrimination clause would have to establish that the conversations in question were the product of unlawful custodial interrogation. Because statements made to individuals not known

to the defendant as government actors do not normally amount to interrogation for purposes of the fifth amendment, this challenge is destined to fail.

Crawford is writing strictly as a legal analyst of the Constitution. A defense attorney concerned with defendant rights or an ethicist might analyze this issue in moral rather than legal terms.

Detailed Observation

Analysis requires close observation, critical thinking, and in some instances outside research. If you have not read Samuel Scudder's "Take This Fish and Look at It" (page 47), you might wish to review it. This essay demonstrates the value of close observation. Good analysis cannot rely on first impressions. Before you can analyze a short story or a poem, you will have to read the work several times. If you are thinking of evaluating how women are depicted in television commercials, you may wish to videotape two or three evenings' worth of commercials and watch them several times rather than relying on memory. The more you observe about your subject, the more likely you will move from superficial observation to detecting details you may have previously overlooked.

Critical Thinking for Writing Analysis

Analytical writing can be challenging. Even the best writers often fall into common traps called *logical fallacies* and make errors in judgment. Following these guidelines can help you improve your analytical writing skills:

1. **Ask questions to avoid summarizing.** The most common error students make is mistaking summary or description for analysis. Asking questions such as *why?* or *who?* can help you avoid simply retelling the plot of a story rather than analyzing it. For example, before starting to write an analysis of Hemingway's short story "Hills Like White Elephants," you might develop questions. Answering a question such as "Who is the stronger character, the man or the woman?" will guide you toward evaluating the story rather than supplying a two-page summary.
2. **Limit the scope of your analysis.** Unless you are willing to devote months to research, it would be difficult to gather sufficient material to fully analyze a subject such as day-care centers. You might restrict your topic to day-care centers in one neighborhood or focus on a single issue such as licensing requirements.

3. **Evaluate sources for bias.** If you were analyzing the use of animals in medical research, you would not want to base your judgments solely on information from an animal rights group. When evaluating controversial subjects, you may be unable to obtain objective information, but you can achieve a measure of balance by examining data provided by organizations with opposing viewpoints.

4. **Apply common standards.** Analyzing data from different sources will be accurate only if all the sources have the same standards and definitions. If you were analyzing juvenile delinquency, you might face a problem if each study examined has a different definition of just who is a delinquent.

5. **Distinguish between opinion and fact.** Opinions are judgments or inferences, not facts. Facts are reliable pieces of information that can be verified by studying other sources:

OPINION: John Smith is an alcoholic.

FACT: John Smith drinks two martinis at lunch and frequents nightclubs on weekends.

The factual statement relies on observation. The judgment of alcoholism is based on limited evidence and probably requires more support.

6. **Avoid hasty generalizations.** Generalizations should be based on adequate information, not a few instances that you may find dramatic or interesting. The fact that two friends had purses stolen in the Student Union last week and that your car was broken into this morning does not mean the college is in the grip of a crime wave. You would have to examine several months of police reports to determine if an actual increase in campus crime has occurred.

7. **Consider alternative interpretations.** Facts do not always indicate what they imply at first glance. A rise in reported cases of child abuse may not indicate increasing violence against children but instead better reporting. If a school has a low retention rate, does that indicate it is failing to address the needs of students or that it instead maintains such rigorous standards that only the best students graduate?

8. **Avoid "filtering" data.** If you begin with a preconceived thesis, you may consciously or unconsciously select evidence that supports your view and omit evidence that contradicts it. Good analysis is objective; it does not consist of simply collecting facts to support a previously held conviction.

9. **Do not assume that parts represent the whole.** Just because one or more patients respond favorably to a new drug does not mean that it will cure all people suffering from the same disease. In the extreme, because individual men and women die does not mean the human race will eventually become extinct.

10. **Do not assume that the whole represents each part.** If fifty percent of students on campus receive financial aid, it does not mean you can assume that half the English majors receive aid. The student population in any given department may be less or more than the college average.

11. **Avoid reasoning on false analogies.** Analogy or comparison essays often provide weak evidence because they overlook that no two situations are exactly alike. Avoid assuming, for example, that results from a study conducted in Japan provide valid evidence for researchers in the United States. Because airbags have been proven to save lives in car accidents does not mean they should be installed in airplanes.

STRATEGIES FOR READING ANALYSIS

As you read the analysis entries in this chapter, keep the following questions in mind.

Meaning

1. What is the author's purpose—to provide a personal opinion or an evaluation based on standard research methods?
2. What discipline is the writer operating in? What kinds of evidence and what analytical methods are presented?
3. Does the writer present sources for his or her information?
4. What does the original source of the entry indicate about the intended audience and discipline?
5. What is the most significant conclusion the author draws?

Strategy

1. Does the writer rely on close observation, surveys, statistics, or expert testimony?
2. How were the data collected? Does the writer cite sources and supply footnotes?
3. Did the writer consider alternative interpretations?
4. Does the entry appear to be biased? Does the writer present facts to support a preconceived theory?
5. Does the writer avoid the logical fallacies?

Language

1. Do the author's choice of words and use of connotations indicate bias?
2. What language does the writer use in discussing people or organizations that hold different beliefs?
3. Are standard terms defined?

WILLIAM RASPBERRY

William Raspberry was born in Mississippi and began his journalism career as a photographer and reporter for the Indianapolis Recorder *in 1956. In 1962 he began working for the* Washington Post. *He received the Capital Press Club's Journalist of the Year Award in 1965 for his coverage of the Watts riot in Los Angeles. In 1971 Raspberry began an urban affairs column for the* Washington Post *that has been nationally syndicated since 1977. William Raspberry was awarded the Pulitzer Prize for Distinguished Commentary in 1994.*

The Handicap of Definition

OVERVIEW: *In this* Washington Post *article Raspberry analyzes the effect that the definition of "blackness" has on African-American children. Typically, stereotypes are viewed as limiting definitions imposed on people. Raspberry suggests that in many instances young African-Americans accept negative stereotypes that limit their opportunities.*

I know all about bad schools, mean politicians, economic deprivation and racism. Still, it occurs to me that one of the heaviest burdens black Americans—and black children in particular—have to bear is the handicap of definition: the question of what it means to be black.   1

anticipates reader reaction

Let me explain quickly what I mean. If a basketball fan says that the Boston Celtics' Larry Bird plays "black," the fan intends it—and Bird probably accepts it—as a compliment. Tell pop singer Tom Jones he moves "black" and he might grin in appreciation. Say to Teena Marie or the Average White Band that they sound "black" and they'll thank you.   2

thesis

examines

But name one pursuit, aside from athletics, entertainment or sexual performance, in which a white practitioner will feel complimented to be told he does it "black." Tell a white broadcaster he talks "black" and he'll sign up for diction lessons. Tell a white reporter he writes "black" and he'll take a writing course. Tell a white lawyer he reasons "black" and he might sue you for slander.   3

What we have here is a tragically limited definition of blackness, and it isn't only white people who buy it.   4

analysis

Think of all the ways black children can put one another down with charges of "whiteness." For many of these children, hard study and hard work are "white." Trying to please a teacher might be criticized as acting "white." Speaking correct English is "white." Scrimping today in the interest of tomorrow's goals is "white." Educational toys and games are "white."   5

6   An incredible array of habits and attitudes that are conducive to success in business, in academia, in the nonentertainment professions are likely to be thought of as somehow "white." Even economic success, unless it involves such "black" undertakings as numbers banking, is defined as "white."

7   And the results are devastating. I wouldn't deny that blacks often are better entertainers and athletes. My point is the harm that comes from too narrow a definition of what is black.

8   <u>One reason black youngsters tend to do better at basketball, for instance, is that they assume they can learn to do it well, and so they practice constantly to prove themselves right.</u>

analysis why black youth succeed in sports

9   Wouldn't it be wonderful if we could infect black children with the notion that excellence in math is "black" rather than white, or possibly Chinese? Wouldn't it be of enormous value if we could create the myth that morality, strong families, determination, courage and love of learning are traits brought by slaves from Mother Africa and therefore quintessentially black?

10   There is no doubt in my mind that most black youngsters could develop their mathematical reasoning, their elocution and their attitudes the way they develop their jump shots and their dance steps: by the combination of sustained, enthusiastic practice and the unquestioned belief that they can do it.

11   In one sense, what I am talking about is the importance of developing positive ethnic traditions. Maybe Jews have an innate talent for communication; maybe the Chinese are born with a gift for mathematical reasoning; maybe blacks are naturally blessed with athletic grace. I doubt it. What is at work, I suspect, is assumption, inculcated early in their lives, that this is a thing our people do well.

12   Unfortunately, many of the things about which blacks make this assumption are things that do not contribute to their career success—except for that handful of the truly gifted who can make it as entertainers and athletes. And many of the things we concede to whites are the things that are essential to economic security.

13   So it is with a number of assumptions black youngsters make about what it is to be a "man": physical aggressiveness, sexual prowess, the refusal to submit to authority. The prisons are full of people who, by this perverted definition, are unmistakably men.

distorted and limited definition of "black"

14   But the real problem is not so much that the things defined as "black" are negative. The problem is that the definition is much too narrow.

Somehow, we have to make our children understand that they are intelli-   15
gent, competent people, capable of doing whatever they put their minds to   call for
and making it in the American mainstream, not just in a black subculture.   expanded
                                                                            definition
What we seem to be doing, instead, is raising up yet another generation   16
of young blacks who will be failures—by definition.

Understanding Meaning

1. What kind of analysis does Raspberry provide?
2. What do readers expect in a personal column? What standards for gathering
   and studying data do they require?
3. According to the author, how does the definition of "blackness," internalized
   by many young African-Americans, affect the development of many children?
4. *Critical Thinking:* Does Raspberry ignore other definitions of "blackness" encountered by African-American children, such as black literature they read in
   school and black politicians they see on television? If so, does it affect his
   thesis?

Evaluating Strategy

1. Raspberry opens his essay by briefly referring to other burdens hampering the
   success of African-American children. Why is this important?
2. What evidence does Raspberry provide readers to support his views?
3. *Other Modes:* How does Raspberry *define* popular concepts of "blackness"? How
   does he use *comparison* to other ethnic groups to illustrate how definitions
   shape people's self-concept?

Appreciating Language

1. How does Raspberry use connotations to shape his analysis?
2. Raspberry talks of an idea to "infect" black children and create a "myth" that
   morality is a "black" value. What is the impact of this language?

Connections across the Disciplines

1. How did Miss Bessie, Carl Rowan's teacher, help African-American children
   overcome negative stereotypes (page 137)?

2. Consider "What's Wrong with This Picture?" (page 317). What impact does popular culture have on shaping young people's image of themselves? Are some groups penalized by being ignored by popular culture and are others damaged by being depicted in negative stereotypes?

Writing Suggestions

1. Look back on your own childhood, and write a brief essay describing how you came to define yourself. Analyze how it helped or hindered your development.
2. Write an essay analyzing how stereotyped attitudes have led women, the elderly, the disabled, or others to define themselves.
3. *Collaborative Writing:* Working in a group of students, write your own lists of behaviors defined as "black," "white," "Asian," "male," or "female." Discuss these definitions, and then draft a short analysis of your views and experiences.

MICHAEL ZIELENZIGER

Michael Zielenziger is a reporter for the Knight-Ridder/Tribune News Service. Based in Tokyo, he has published numerous articles on Asian economic and political affairs. In addition, he has commented on a wide variety of social and cultural issues, ranging from Japanese wedding customs to Tokyo nightlife.

Black Is Beautiful: Tokyo Style

OVERVIEW: *As you read this article, consider the media images of African Americans distributed throughout the world. Does popular culture provide realistic representations of blacks and other minorities?*

TOKYO — They're bouncing to hip-hop music at health clubs, boogying all night to rhythm and blues at the Soul Train Cafe. Women are curling their hair into Afro style haircuts—called "wafferu" (waffle) hair—while their boyfriends are growing goatees or taking to tanning rooms to darken their complexion.

Suddenly black is very, very beautiful for some of Tokyo's trendiest youth.

From dance parties in Roppongi to cutting-edge videos on television, from rising demand for porkpie hats to a rush for "gangsta" fashion, a new focus on African-American music and culture is giving voice to a strain of rebelliousness in young Japanese, confronting the most serious economic stagnation in 50 years.

"When I listen to this music, I don't have to think," explained Takako Yamamoto, 20, as she danced with a boyfriend at a Tokyo soul club. "I don't have to deal with work or stress. I can just be free. Black people and black music are totally cool."

"It's a way of telling people you don't want to be part of the large corporate lifestyle," said Minako Suzuki Wilder, who admires the new black scene. "A lot of people in their 20s are not into working at old-fashioned companies, so they get into the black music and the hip-hop dancing, getting frizzy hair or an Afro haircut.

"It's new to us and it seems fun. People like the way the music helps you work out your stress."

Strains of black culture have long existed in Japan, often carried here by African-American soldiers who decide to stay on. Jazz bars permeated in the 1950s and black baseball players often have become popular.

8   But now a new generation of black culture has entered the Japanese mainstream.

9   The most obvious sign: the appearance last month of a new beer called "Dunk," whose name alone connotes the German word "dunkel," for dark beer, with allusions to basketball players jamming the ball through the hoop.

10   Dunk advertisements, which now plaster Tokyo's subways, employ three sequined-studded, sashaying Motown-style singers and a Japanese entertainer, Masayuki Suzuki, most noted for his efforts to look African-American. During the 1980s, Suzuki dressed in blackface and white gloves to belt out soul songs for a group known as "Shanels."

11   "We didn't need to have a focus group to see whether black is cool," said Kiyoshi Oguri, marketing researcher for Asahi Brewery, manufacturers of Dunk. "But when we see black people playing ball on TV, not only basketball but also on entertainment programs, we could see that would be the right focus for us. We didn't intentionally focus on black culture, but certainly there is a recognition that black is cool.

12   "We knew that black things were 'kakko-ii' (cool). It's hard to explain the reason that it's 'kakko-ii,' but we know it is there."

13   However, observers note that because the relatively insulated Japanese have not been exposed to African-American culture, they tend to go wild over stereotypes.

14   "They may be interested in the trappings, but really their interest in African-American culture is completely superficial," said Kako Kawachi, who teaches women's and African-American studies at the prestigious Waseda University.

15   She dismisses the black fashion trend as a fad that has not brought new students into her classes.

16   "It's very shallow," she said.

17   Still, the surge in interest in things black is creating opportunities for African-Americans in Japan.

18   "Really, it's paradise over here," said Thomas Paul, a hip-hop dance instructor and promoter, who earns nearly $4,000 a month teaching spin moves and twists at a health club. "People think we're really exotic, and most are really open to learning about the real hip-hop scene. A lot of folks come to check out my class just to experience real black culture."

19   His classes are a sea of twisting arms and sweat-drenched T-shirts as 20- and 30-year old Japanese, predominately women, try to mimic Paul's dance-steps and twirls. "Twist! 'Mawatte!' (Turn!) 'Tatte!' (Stand!)," Paul shouts at his students as they attempt to master his complex choreography.

While there aren't many blacks in Japan, those who land here find them- 20
selves among the most exotic, erotic and sought-after foreigners ever to set
foot in this homogeneous and somewhat insulated island nation.

"You can feel the difference in the air," said jazz saxophone star Branford 21
Marsalis, who recently concluded a three-week tour of Japan with his quar-
tet. "When I first came to Japan eight years ago, people stared at you and
thought you were strange. They really kept their distance and were sort of
standoffish."

"But now, people are totally into what we are doing," he explained after 22
a set at Tokyo's Blue Note jazz cafe. "They really listen to the music, and
after the shows, the people really want to meet and talk to you."

"The attitude has completely changed, and it's really great." 23

In a nation that consciously encourages its young people to forge cohe- 24
sive group identity, Japan always has produced its share of rebels who shun
the corporate blue suits. Twenty-something "greasers" with slicked-back,
duck-tail haircuts and leather jackets regularly dance on the weekends in
Yoyogi Park. The Varsity shop sells cheerleader costumes. Reggae bars and
salsa clubs beckoned the affluent and adventurous seeking a good time.

But the black trend, researchers say, signifies a clear disenchantment 25
with the rigidity and lack of individual expression in Japan.

"In Japanese society, you don't have many options; society is quite in- 26
flexible," said Akiko Togawa, a market researcher for Dentsu Eye. "Most
young Japanese don't see any successful entrepreneurs around them in
Japan."

"So when they see black people who have made it, despite the discrim- 27
ination in America, they see people who have successfully asserted their
individual identity. So in a way, it's a revolt against traditional Japanese
culture."

Valerie Koehn, a Tokyo-based designer and writer, says the rebellious 28
quality of hip-hop and rap music is what is generating more interest in
African-Americans and their culture. "It's the young people saying 'We
don't care what our parents did or what society demands of us. We don't
have to do that.' It's totally in your face."

Toshiaki Koike, 34, an executive with a debt-ridden construction com- 29
pany, says he prefers going to black music bars because "there's more energy. Times aren't good right now," he said, over the strains of a rap song at
the Soul Train Cafe. "But here I can get great energy from the music."

His friend Yamamoto said she really likes rap music and would love 30
to meet more African-Americans. But, as Kawachi, the black studies profes-

sor, indicated, this new fascination with black people might be more style than substance and does not necessarily mean all cultural biases have been conquered.

31   "I don't think I'd want to date one," Yamamoto said of African-Americans. "I'd be a little afraid."

Understanding Meaning

1. Why do young Japanese embrace hip-hop music and "gangsta" fashion? What does it represent to them? Why is black "cool"?
2. How have Japanese attitudes toward African Americans changed in the last decade?
3. What images of African Americans seem to have been exported to Japan?
4. How did Japan's recent recession influence the popularity of black culture?
5. *Critical Thinking:* American movies and television programs are viewed worldwide. Are people in other countries likely to develop distorted images of America?

Evaluating Strategy

1. Zielenziger includes numerous quotations in his essay. How effectively does he organize them?
2. Do the comments by Kako Kawachi, who dismisses the Japanese interest in black culture as a shallow fad, form an implied thesis?
3. How effective is the last quotation? What impact does it have on readers? What does it reveal about Japanese attitudes toward African Americans?

Appreciating Language

1. This is a news article, which is written to be skimmed rather than read. How do word choice, sentence structure, and paragraph length affect its readability?
2. What do Japanese words like "wafferu" for "waffle" and "kako-ii" for "cool" suggest about the influence of English in Japan?

Connections across the Disciplines

1. William Raspberry (page 287) argues that limited definitions of blackness have harmed African-American youth. How have definitions of blackness influ-

enced the Japanese? What does the woman's statement that she would be "afraid" of dating an African American reveal?

2. In "Spanglish," Janice Castro (page 177) discusses the confluence of Hispanic and American cultures. Is there a different interchange when the introduction of a new culture into an established one is based on media images rather than immigration?

Writing Suggestions

1. Write a brief essay outlining your view of the Japanese, based solely on their media image. How are the Japanese represented in movies and television programs? What are the positive and negative stereotypes?

2. *Collaborative Writing:* Discuss this article with a group of students. Note members' observations and reactions. Work together to draft a short statement analyzing the way in which American popular culture influences world opinion.

RICHARD BROOKHISER

Richard Brookhiser is the Senior Editor for the National Review *and a columnist for the* New York Observer. *He has written about politics, fashion, popular culture, and education. He is a frequent commentator on television. His books include* Founding Father: Rediscovering George Washington, The Way of the WASP, *and* Alexander Hamilton, American.

The Skinny

OVERVIEW: *In this essay Brookhiser analyzes the fashion industry's obsession with thin supermodels. As you read his article, which first appeared in the conservative magazine* National Review, *consider how images of thin women have affected you and women you know. Have fashion designers given the public a distorted and unobtainable image of beauty? Are males subjected to similar images?*

1   Shoshanna Lonstein was a peculiarly New York kind of celebrity. She was the teenage girlfriend of Jerry Seinfeld, when everyone watched his TV show. So well known was she in this role that even I, who neither watched the TV show nor went to Moomba (or any of the other then-fashionable spots she frequented), knew who she was. She quickly rose to the level of celebrity where she lost her last name, always appearing in print as "Shoshanna."

2   "Lonstein" became a discarded appendage, like Wojtyla, Windsor, or Lewinsky.

3   Gossip columnists often casually linked her with Monica, on the grounds that both women were young, Jewish, and known for their boyfriends. The comparison was grossly unfair to Miss Lonstein, for her lover was not our president, not her boss, and not married, while she, it soon became obvious, was not a dolt who couldn't get a job without Vernon Jordan's help. After Shoshanna and Jerry split up, she went into the fashion business and designed a line of clothes, which has found its niche.

4   She appeared in an ad in the *New York Times* in February, modeling one of her bathing suits. I did not recognize her at first (why would I, never having seen her on the beach?). But I was stopped cold by the ad. It was as startling as a story on peace in the Congo, or Clintons telling the truth. The four-inch high woman on my breakfast table had actual thighs, hips, and breasts. Her arms could not be passed through a napkin ring. Her face was round, without Tartar cheekbones, and her expression was neither sullen nor dead. She was, in short, a pretty version of a normal woman.

The ad was doubly provocative, running during Fashion Week, which celebrates one of the city's few thriving industries. Designers show their new collections, and New York asserts its parity with Paris and Milan. Once upon a time a fashion show meant Princess Grace looking at the latest offerings from Chanel. Now a big top rises in Bryant Park behind the public library, and the designers and supermodels (there are no more plain ol' models) get even more ink than they normally do. The buzz of the last Fashion Week was the war between the Brazilians and the Belgians. The allegedly "curvy" Brazilian supermodels, who dominated the catwalks a year ago, were replaced by wan waffle-eaters. After an interregnum of fleshiness, the heroin addict/pedophile victim has resumed her rightful place as the norm of female beauty.

That's what the fashion world was saying. But to the layman, the Brazilian/Belgian war recalled an argument between Stalinists and Trotskyites, who were both despotic murderers even if they squabbled about socialism in one country. Similarly, the cariocas may have one and a half more curves per torso than Magritte's nieces, but to the average unbiased student of women (i.e., to a man) they all look like survivors of the Donner party. Both sets of young women have mile-high gawksome legs, praying-mantis arms, and hips that would actually be comfortable in a modern coach-class airplane seat. Whether or not they have breasts detectable with a carpenter's level is a topographical detail, of interest only to fashionistas.

The only true exception proves the rule. Anna Nicole Smith has enjoyed a moment or two in the modeling sun. But she is a 38 DD ex-stripper. In what world, outside the fashion world, could she be considered a legitimate swing of the pendulum? Consider how other famous women, plumper than skeletons but smaller than Macy's Thanksgiving Parade balloons, are written of. A few years ago Alicia Silverstone, the lovely star of *Clueless*, reportedly put on a few pounds; so, more recently, has the supermodel Kate Moss. Neither one has heard the end of it. Jennifer Lopez presently rules the world with such assurance that she shucked her gun-toting lover, Sean "Puffy" Combs, without a blip in her box office. Yet every story about her (except in the *Times*, which still maintains a certain prudery) mentions her big butt. She doesn't have a "big" butt, she has a butt, but the world behaves as if she were a sexier version of the Venus of Willendorf.

It is inevitable that New York should be the battleground between normal women and fashion women. As a metropolis, we have, by definition, millions of normal women; as a capital of symbolism, we also have a disproportionate number of fashion women. Los Angeles, home of the movie industry, is another battleground. But starlets are occasionally required to play normal women. As a center of fashion, New York is a realm of will and taste unconstrained by reality.

9   Whose taste is being served? Conservative folk like to blame gay designers. The rag trade is a magnet for perverts: The late Gianni Versace probably hadn't had a normal sexual desire since the Marshall Plan. But there are also gay designers who like women, and like to make them look as good as prevailing standards will allow. The physics of fabric are probably more significant. It is easier to predict how cloth will fall on a model who looks like a hanger.

10   Feminists would blame the patriarchy. Certainly the archetypal fashion woman suggests an issue of control. Traditional pornographic delivery systems, from centerfolds to online images, are two-dimensional. Why not have two-dimensional women too?

11   But, sisters, I am afraid the real control freaks are women themselves. You can't become that thin without a lot of hard work. So too, if you work hard, you can become unhealthily thin. If you're not thin, how will anyone know that you're working? Kant believed that virtue could be demonstrated only by the performance of painful acts; who knew that the sage of Konigsberg would find his apotheosis in Bryant Park?

12   Meanwhile, walk the city streets the other 51 weeks of the year, and see the women (especially the poor women) sadly stuffing themselves with Fritos and oversized Cokes. They've given up on will; they just want consolation. Shoshanna has her opportunities cut out for her.

Understanding Meaning

1.   What made Shoshanna Lonstein a celebrity?
2.   Why did the public compare Lonstein to Monica Lewinsky? What differences does Brookhiser see?
3.   What caused Brookhiser to notice Shoshanna Lonstein's fashion ad? What made her ad, in Brookhiser's eyes, as startling as "a story of peace in the Congo"?
4.   What images dominate the fashion industry?
5.   Do you find the images of women in ads and commercials distorted or ideal?
6.   Why is New York the "battleground between normal women and fashion women"?
7.   *Critical Thinking:* Brookhiser comments that control is the key issue that fashion women represent. Do women control the fashion industry or does the fashion industry control women? What makes millions of women buy fashion magazines, aspire to be models, and design clothes most people can't wear?

Evaluating Strategy

1. Brookhiser opens the essay with a brief narrative about a single model. Is this an effective introduction to his analysis?
2. Brookhiser mentions a number of celebrities without defining them. What kind of knowledge does he assume his readers possess? What audience is Brookhiser addressing?
3. How much of Brookhiser's analysis is subjective? How much is objective?
4. *Other Modes:* Where does Brookhiser use *comparison, cause and effect,* and *description* to develop his analysis of the fashion industry?

Appreciating Language

1. What tone and style does Brookhiser adopt? Is he trying to entertain as well as inform his readers?
2. Brookhiser uses the term "fashionistas." What does this word suggest? What political connotations does it have?
3. Brookhiser describes fashion models as looking like "survivors of the Donner party" with "praying mantis arms." Are these images effective in revealing his point that models are abnormal? What other words and phrases does Brookhiser use to express his point of view?

Connections across the Disciplines

1. Consider John Ciardi's essay "What Is Happiness?" (page 189). How much of the desire to be thin reflects women's search for happiness? Brookhiser states that women eating junk food are seeking "consolation." How much of women's happiness seems to involve image?
2. Bob Levey's article about men and women walking alone at night (page 236) illustrates a striking difference between the sexes about a common activity. Consider the way men and women respond to fashion. Why don't men seem affected by the male models in *Gentlemen's Quarterly?* Why are there no male supermodels?

Writing Suggestions

1. Write a similar analysis of the images young men respond to. Do athletes, superheroes, and action heroes also give males negative messages? If girls starve themselves to look like models, do some boys become violent to appear masculine?

2. *Collaborative Writing:* Working with a group of students, develop a process paper giving parents a set of instructions on how they should approach their teenage daughters' reactions to the fashion industry. What should parents do if they notice their daughters developing unhealthy habits to look thin?

DARRELL HUFF

Darrell Huff was born in 1913 and received his B.A. and M.A. at the State University of Iowa in the 1930s. He published hundreds of articles in popular magazines and served as editor of Better Homes and Gardens *for several years. "How to Lie with Statistics" appeared in* Harper's *in 1950. His analysis of how statistics are misused remains a useful primer on what he calls "the secret language of statistics," which is used to "sensationalize, inflate, confuse, and oversimplify."*

How to Lie with Statistics

OVERVIEW: *Perhaps no other evidence is more misinterpreted or misunderstood than statistics. People often hear and repeat statistics without knowing their source or their true meaning. As you read Huff's article, consider why appreciating statistics is an important element of critical thinking.*

"The average Yaleman, Class of '24," *Time* magazine reported last year after reading something in the New York *Sun*, a newspaper published in those days, "makes $25,111 a year." 1

Well, good for him! 2

But, come to think of it, what does this improbably precise and salubrious figure mean? Is it, as it appears to be, evidence that if you send your boy to Yale you won't have to work in your old age and neither will he? Is this average a mean or is it a median? What kind of sample is it based on? You could lump one Texas oilman with two hundred hungry freelance writers and report *their* average income as $25,000-odd a year. The arithmetic is impeccable, the figure is convincingly precise, and the amount of meaning there is in it you could put in your eye. 3

In just such ways is the secret language of statistics, so appealing in a fact-minded culture, being used to sensationalize, inflate, confuse, and oversimplify. Statistical terms are necessary in reporting the mass data of social and economic trends, business conditions, "opinion" polls, this year's census. But without writers who use the words with honesty and understanding and readers who know what they mean, the result can only be semantic nonsense. 4

In popular writing on scientific research, the abused statistic is almost crowding out the picture of the white-jacketed hero laboring overtime without time-and-a-half in an ill-lit laboratory. Like the "little dash of powder, little pot of paint," statistics are making many an important fact "look like what she ain't." Here are some of the ways it is done. 5

6   *The sample with the built-in bias.* Our Yale men—or Yalemen, as they say in the Time-Life building—belong to this flourishing group. The exaggerated estimate of their income is not based on all members of the class nor on a random or representative sample of them. At least two interesting categories of 1924-model Yale men have been excluded.

7   First there are those whose present addresses are unknown to their classmates. Wouldn't you bet that these lost sheep are earning less than the boys from prominent families and the others who can be handily reached from a Wall Street office?

8   There are those who chucked the questionnaire into the nearest wastebasket. Maybe they didn't answer because they were not making enough money to brag about. Like the fellow who found a note clipped to his first pay check suggesting that he consider the amount of his salary confidential: "Don't worry," he told the boss. "I'm just as ashamed of it as you are."

9   Omitted from our sample then are just the two groups most likely to depress the average. The $25,111 figure is beginning to account for itself. It may indeed be a true figure for those of the Class of '24 whose addresses are known and who are willing to stand up and tell how much they earn. But even that requires a possibly dangerous assumption that the gentlemen are telling the truth.

10   To be dependable to any useful degree at all, a sampling study must use a representative sample (which can lead to trouble too) or a truly random one. If *all* the Class of '24 is included, that's all right. If every tenth name on a complete list is used, that is all right too, and so is drawing an adequate number of names out of a hat. The test is this: Does every name in the group have an equal chance to be in the sample?

11   You'll recall that ignoring this requirement was what produced the *Literary Digest's* famed fiasco. When names for polling were taken only from telephone books and subscription lists, people who did not have telephones or *Literary Digest* subscriptions had no chance to be in the sample. They possibly did not mind this underprivilege a bit, but their absence was in the end very hard on the magazine that relied on the figures.

12   This leads to a moral: You can prove about anything you want to by letting your sample bias itself. As a consumer of statistical data—a reader, for example, of a news magazine—remember that no statistical conclusion can rise above the quality of the sample it is based upon. In the absence of information about the procedures behind it, you are not warranted in giving any credence at all to the result.

The truncated, or gee-whiz, graph. If you want to show some statistical in- 13
formation quickly and clearly, draw a picture of it. Graphic presentation is
the thing today. If you don't mind misleading the hasty looker, or if you
quite clearly *want* to deceive him, you can save some space by chopping the
bottom off many kinds of graphs.

Suppose you are showing the upward trend of national income month 14
by month for a year. The total rise, as in one recent year, is 7 per cent. It
looks like this:

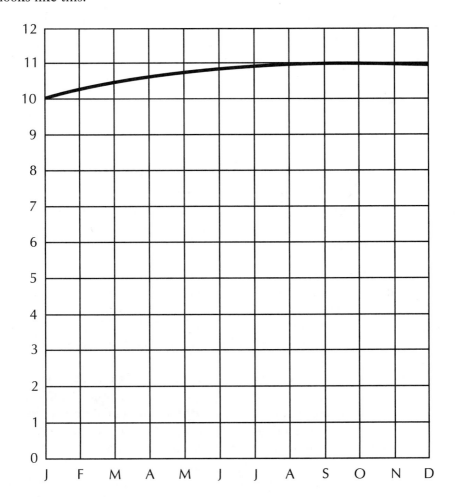

That is clear enough. Anybody can see that the trend is slightly upward. 15
You are showing a 7 per cent increase and that is exactly what it looks like.

16   But it lacks schmaltz. So you chop off the bottom, this way:

17   The figures are the same. It is the same graph and nothing has been falsi-
fied—except the impression that it gives. Anyone looking at it can just feel
prosperity throbbing in the arteries of the country. It is a subtler equivalent
of editing "National income rose 7 per cent" into " . . . climbed a whopping
7 per cent."

18   It is vastly more effective, however, because of that illusion of
objectivity.

19   *The souped-up graph.* Sometimes truncating is not enough. The trifling
rise in something or other still looks almost as insignificant as it is. You can
make that 7 per cent look livelier than 100 per cent ordinarily does. Simply
change the proportion between the ordinate and the abscissa. There's no
rule against it, and it does give your graph a prettier shape.

20   But it exaggerates, to say the least, something awful (see page 305).

21   *The well-chosen average.* I live near a country neighborhood for which I
can report an average income of $15,000. I could also report it as $3,500.

22   If I should want to sell real estate hereabouts to people having a high
snobbery content, the first figure would be handy. The second figure,
however, is the one to use in an argument against raising taxes, or the local
bus fare.

23   Both are legitimate averages, legally arrived at. Yet it is obvious that at
least one of them must be as misleading as an out-and-out lie. The $15,000-
figure is a mean, the arithmetic average of the incomes of all the families in
the community. The smaller figure is a median; it might be called the income of the average family in the group. It indicates that half the families
have less than $3,500 a year and half have more.

24   Here is where some of the confusion about averages comes from. Many
human characteristics have the grace to fall into what is called the "normal"
distribution. If you draw a picture of it, you get a curve that is shaped like a
bell. Mean and median fall at about the same point, so it doesn't make very
much difference which you use.

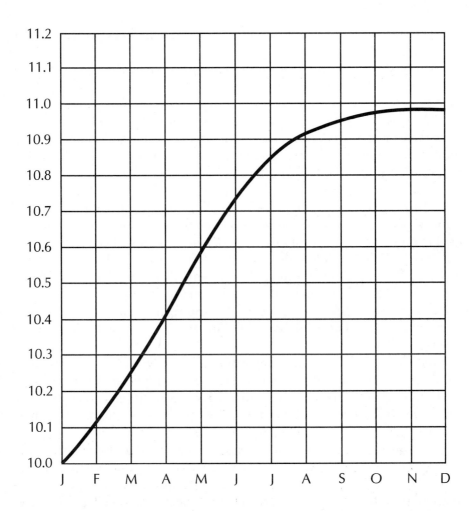

But some things refuse to follow this neat curve. Income is one of them. 25
Incomes for most large areas will range from under $1,000 a year to upward
of $50,000. Almost everybody will be under $10,000, way over on the left-
hand side of that curve.

One of the things that made the income figure for the "average Yale- 26
man" meaningless is that we are not told whether it is a mean or a median.
It is not that one type of average is invariably better than the other; it depends upon what you are talking about. But neither gives you any real information—and either may be highly misleading—unless you know which
of those two kinds of average it is.

In the country neighborhood I mentioned, almost everyone has less 27
than the average—the mean, that is—of $10,500. These people are all

small farmers, except for a trio of millionaire week-enders who bring up the mean enormously.

28   You can be pretty sure that when an income average is given in the form of a mean nearly everybody has less than that.

29   *The insignificant difference or the elusive error.* Your two children Peter and Linda (we might as well give them modish names while we're about it) take intelligence tests. Peter's IQ, you learn, is 98 and Linda's is 101. Aha! Linda is your brighter child.

30   Is she? An intelligence test is, or purports to be, a sampling of intellect. An IQ, like other products of sampling, is a figure with a statistical error, which expresses the precision or reliability of the figure. The size of this probable error can be calculated. For their test the makers of the much-used Revised Stanford-Binet have found it to be about 3 per cent. So Peter's indicated IQ of 98 really means only that there is an even chance that it falls between 95 and 101. There is an equal probability that it falls somewhere else—below 95 or above 101. Similarly, Linda's has no better than a fifty-fifty chance of being within the fairly sizeable range of 98 to 104.

31   You can work out some comparisons from that. One is that there is rather better than one chance in four that Peter, with his lower IQ rating, is really at least three points smarter than Linda. A statistician doesn't like to consider a difference significant unless you can hand him odds a lot longer than that.

32   Ignoring the error in a sampling study leads to all kinds of silly conclusions. There are magazine editors to whom readership surveys are gospel; with a 40 per cent readership reported for one article and a 35 per cent for another, they demand more like the first. I've seen even smaller differences given tremendous weight, because statistics are a mystery and numbers are impressive. The same thing goes for market surveys and so-called public-opinion polls. The rule is that you cannot make a valid comparison between two such figures unless you know the deviations. And unless the difference between the figures is many times greater than the probable error of each, you have only a guess that the one appearing greater really is.

33   Otherwise you are like the man choosing a camp site from a report of mean temperature alone. One place in California with a mean annual temperature of 61 is San Nicolas Island on the south coast, where it always stays in the comfortable range between 47 and 87. Another with a mean of 61 is in the inland desert, where the thermometer hops around from 15 to 104.

The deviation from the mean marks the difference, and you can freeze or roast if you ignore it.

The one-dimensional picture. Suppose you have just two or three figures to compare—say the average weekly wage of carpenters in the United States and another country. The sums might be $60 and $30. An ordinary bar chart makes the difference graphic: 34

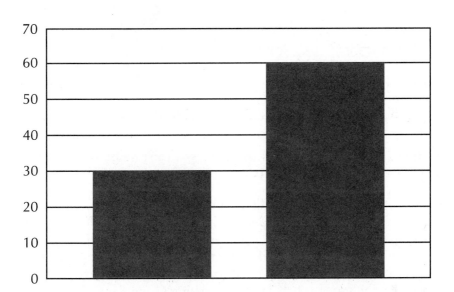

That is an honest picture. It looks good for American carpenters, but perhaps it does not have quite the oomph you are after. Can't you make that difference appear overwhelming and at the same time give it what I am afraid is known as eye-appeal? Of course you can. Following tradition, you represent these sums by pictures of money bags. If the $30 bag is one inch high, you draw the $60 bag two inches high. That's in proportion, isn't it? The catch is, of course, that the American's money bag, being twice as tall as that of the $30 man, covers an area on your page four times as great. And since your two-dimensional picture represents an object that would in fact have three dimensions, the money bags actually would differ much more than that. The volumes of any two similar solids vary as the cubes of their heights. If the unfortunate foreigner's bag holds $30 worth of dimes, the American's would hold not $60 but a neat $240: 35

36   You didn't say that, though, did you? And you can't be blamed, you're only doing it the way practically everybody else does.

37   *The ever-impressive decimal.* For a spurious air of precision that will lend all kinds of weight to the most disreputable statistics, consider the decimal.

38   Ask a hundred citizens how many hours they slept last night. Come out with a total of, say, 781.3. Your data are far from precise to begin with. Most people will miss their guess by fifteen minutes or more and some will recall five sleepless minutes as half a night of tossing insomnia.

39   But go ahead, do your arithmetic, announce that people sleep an average of 7.813 hours a night. You will sound as if you knew precisely what you are talking about. If you were foolish enough to say 7.8 (or "almost 8") hours it would sound like what it was—an approximation.

40   *The semi-attached figure.* If you can't prove what you want to prove, demonstrate something else and pretend that they are the same thing. In the daze that follows the collision of statistics with the human mind, hardly anybody will notice the difference. The semi-attached figure is a durable device guaranteed to stand you in good stead. It always has.

41   If you can't prove that your nostrum cures colds, publish a sworn laboratory report that the stuff killed 31,108 germs in a test tube in eleven seconds. There may be no connection at all between assorted germs in a test tube and the whatever-it-is that produces colds, but people aren't going to reason that sharply, especially while sniffling.

Maybe that one is too obvious and people are beginning to catch on. Here is a trickier version. [42]

Let us say that in a period when race prejudice is growing it is to your advantage to "prove" otherwise. You will not find it a difficult assignment. [43]

Ask that usual cross section of the population if they think Negroes have as good a chance as white people to get jobs. Ask again a few months later. As Princeton's Office of Public Opinion Research has found out, people who are most unsympathetic to Negroes are the ones most likely to answer yes to this question. [44]

As prejudice increases in a country, the percentage of affirmative answers you will get to this question will become larger. What looks on the face of it like growing opportunity for Negroes actually is mounting prejudice and nothing else. You have achieved something rather remarkable: the worse things get, the better your survey makes them look. [45]

The unwarranted assumption, or post hoc *rides again.* The interrelation of cause and effect, so often obscure anyway, can be most neatly hidden in statistical data. [46]

Somebody once went to a good deal of trouble to find out if cigarette smokers make lower college grades than non-smokers. They did. This naturally pleased many people, and they made much of it. [47]

The unwarranted assumption, of course, was that smoking had produced dull minds. It seemed vaguely reasonable on the face of it, so it was quite widely accepted. But it really proved nothing of the sort, any more than it proved that poor grades drive students to the solace of tobacco. Maybe the relationship worked in one direction, maybe in the other. And maybe all this is only an indication that the sociable sort of fellow who is likely to take his books less than seriously is also likely to sit around and smoke many cigarettes. [48]

Permitting statistical treatment to befog causal relationships is little better than superstition. It is like the conviction among the people of the Hebrides that body lice produce good health. Observation over the centuries had taught them that people in good health had lice and sick people often did not. *Ergo,* lice made a man healthy. Everybody should have them. [49]

Scantier evidence, treated statistically at the expense of common sense, has made many a medical fortune and many a medical article in magazines, including professional ones. More sophisticated observers finally got things straightened out in the Hebrides. As it turned out, almost everybody in those circles had lice most of the time. But when a man took a fever (quite [50] possibly carried to him by those same lice) and his body became hot, the lice left.

51   Here you have cause and effect not only reversed, but intermingled.

52   There you have a primer in some ways to use statistics to deceive. A well-wrapped statistic is better than Hitler's "big lie": it misleads, yet it can't be pinned onto you.

53   Is this little list altogether too much like a manual for swindlers? Perhaps I can justify it in the manner of the retired burglar whose published reminiscences amounted to a graduate course in how to pick a lock and muffle a footfall: The crooks already know these tricks. Honest men must learn them in self-defense.

Understanding Meaning

1.   Why do statistics impress people? What is their appeal in advertising?
2.   What are the principal methods used to create misleading statistics?
3.   Is Huff suggesting that advertisers deliberately lie, or is he suggesting that advertisers often do not understand the meaning of their own numbers?
4.   Armed with computers, many people love to construct elaborate graphs to include in their reports. What does Huff's article reveal about the reliability of many visual aids?
5.   *Critical Thinking:* What are the implications of Huff's observation that "A well-wrapped statistic is better than Hitler's 'big lie': it misleads, yet it can't be pinned onto you"? Can you think of examples of falsely stated statistics that have been used to influence the public?

Evaluating Strategy

1.   What impact does the title have?
2.   How effective are Huff's examples in communicating complex ideas to a general audience?
3.   How does Huff try to maintain reader interest while explaining a topic many readers find abstract, boring, or intimidating?

Appreciating Language

1.   What does Huff's choice of words suggest about the tone he is trying to establish?

2. What changes in language would you suggest making if the article were to be rewritten for inclusion in a textbook?

Connections across the Disciplines

1. Consider the lesson Samuel Scudder learned about close observation in "Take This Fish and Look at It" (page 47). Does Huff's article provide another lesson in critical thinking?
2. Consider recent statistics you have heard used in commercials or by politicians. Were any sources provided? Could you evaluate their validity?

Writing Suggestions

1. Select a statistic you have heard people cite. Write a brief essay analyzing why the statistic is popular. Do statistics that support a cause serve the same purpose as a slogan on a bumper sticker by providing a shorthand argument?
2. Imagine you plan to publish this article as a brochure for distribution. Write a brief analysis of the audience that would benefit most from its contents.
3. *Collaborative Writing:* Working with a group of students, use this writing exercise to learn more about statistics:

    Imagine that a school district has 1,000 teachers earning an average of $30,000 a year. After a bitter dispute, the school board agrees to provide teachers with a five percent raise. Discuss the impact of the following newspaper headlines:

    Teachers Get 5% Pay Hike
    Teachers Get $1,500 Raise
    Teachers Get $31.5 Million

    Write a short analysis of how presenting numbers in different forms can influence readers. Which statistic do members of the group feel to be the most accurate?

LOUIS R. MIZELL JR.

Louis R. Mizell Jr. was a special agent and intelligence officer for the U. S. State Department. He is now president of Mizell and Company, an international firm specializing in crime prevention. Mizell frequently appears on television commenting on home and personal security issues. He has published a series of books on personal safety. In 1998 he published Invasion of Privacy, *analyzing how modern technology has compromised personal privacy and security.*

Who's Listening to
Your Cell Phone Calls?

OVERVIEW: *Before reading this passage from* Invasion of Privacy, *consider how often you have used or have seen friends use a cell phone. Do people assume their conversations are private?*

1   More than forty million cellular phones are currently in use in the United States, and the numbers are dramatically increasing each year.

2   On any given day, thousands of eavesdroppers intercept, record, and listen to conversations made from cellular and so-called cordless phones. These eavesdroppers include curious neighbors, business competitors, stalkers, journalists, private investigators, and even espionage agents.

3   In California, spies for hire cruise the highways of Hollywood and the Silicon Valley, hoping to steal valuable trade secrets from executives talking on their car phones. Armed with radio scanners, tabloid reporters in New York monitor conversations of the rich, famous, and infamous, hoping to get a front-page scoop. In Florida, a ham operator monitoring the poolside conversations of a prominent lawyer got incredible inside information on three divorce cases.

4   Cellular telephone conversations can be easily monitored by anyone with a radio scanner, but it is a violation of state and federal law to do so intentionally. A 1993 law made it illegal to make or sell radio scanners that pick up cellular calls, but the law didn't make it illegal to own the old scanners. Furthermore, it is rather easy, although illegal, to modify a legal police scanner so that it will pick up cellular conversations.

5   The problem is that there are hundreds of thousands of the old radio scanners in circulation and an equal number of people who don't care about the law. "How are they going to catch me and how are they going to prove

it?" said one ham operator who listens to his neighbors' cellular conversations "just for the fun of it."

In truth, only a very small percentage of the people who have been 6 monitored ever learn that their calls were intercepted. An even smaller percentage of the perpetrators are ever caught. Curious kooks, corporate snoops, and spies for hire who use intercepted information are usually smart enough not to publicize where they got it.

"I really couldn't care less if someone listens to my conversations," said 7 a schoolteacher from Indiana. "I'm not discussing my love life or national security." One of the biggest problems concerning privacy and portable phones is that most people do not realize how even innocent information can be used by criminals and other opportunists. Another problem is that just because you don't care if someone is listening to your conversation, the person you are talking to might care very much.

Burglars are known to monitor the calls of people discussing evening or 8 weekend plans. Knowing that the occupants are going to be away, the burglars enter their homes.

Doctors and lawyers frequently discuss everyday business on cellular 9 phones. In one case, a doctor was notified that a VIP patient had tested positive for AIDS. The information was intercepted, and before long, the VIP's medical status was common knowledge. In another case, a lawyer from Ohio reviewed a client's prenuptial agreement with a second lawyer who was using a cellular telephone. A teenage neighbor of the second lawyer intercepted the conversation. "Before long, the whole damn neighborhood knew about our secret wedding and my financial situation," said the angry groom-to-be.

Stalking, or inappropriate pursuit, has become a dangerous epidemic in 10 the United States and is evolving into one of the most insidious threats to personal privacy. Many researchers estimate that more than two hundred thousand women, men, and children are currently being harassed, threatened, and endangered by stalkers.

Stalking may begin with an innocuous contact and then, through misin- 11 terpretation or delusion, the pursuer escalates to harassment, surveillance, threats, and sometimes murder.

I have been involved in seven cases and am aware of many more in 12 which stalkers intercepted cellular phone conversations and used the intelligence to harass their targets.

A jobless and toothless forty-one-year-old man, hooked on ampheta- 13 mines, became infatuated with a fifteen-year-old girl whom he first noticed at a state swimming competition. "He's really scary and keeps showing up wherever I go," explained the frightened swimmer. "It's like he always knows where I'm going to be."

14   The young lady had good reason to be scared; the man had a long history of bizarre and criminal behavior. On one occasion, he burglarized a home and fell asleep in a teenage girl's bed. The horrified family called the police who arrested the man and confiscated handcuffs and a number of stolen house keys.

15   Released on good behavior, the "nonviolent" criminal was once again free to victimize others. We can't prove what his ultimate plans were concerning our fifteen-year-old client, but we did prove that he had a scanner in his car and had recorded the swimmer's mother as she talked on various cell phones, including a car phone. Two of the taped conversations informed the stalker where his target would be. "I've got to pick my daughter up at McDonald's at 4:30," she mentioned to one friend. "The swim team is celebrating at the Hyatt tonight," she told her neighbor. Needless to say, the stalker showed up at both locations.

16   Eavesdropping on cellular phones is only one of the issues that worry privacy advocates. There is also concern that cellular phones will be used by police and sophisticated criminals to locate the caller.

17   Unbeknownst to most consumers, cellular phones are portable homing devices that allow police and others to pinpoint the caller's position. Police have used this tool to locate a wide range of criminals and kidnap victims. Privacy advocates worry that police will abuse this tool to spy on innocent citizens.

18   When a cellular phone is switched to the On position, it emits a low-power signal to the network to announce which cell site it is in. A cell site is a zone served by a single relay station and is generally several square miles in size. When a caller moves out of one cell site, the call is automatically switched to a different cell site.

19   By using a technique called triangulation, police are able to get a directional fix on the cellular signal and pinpoint the phone's cell site or location. This is the technique police used to locate the car owned by the slain father of basketball great Michael Jordan. Triangulation techniques have also been used by intelligence agencies to locate enemy radio sites and by ocean search-and-rescue teams to pinpoint the location of vessels.

20   There are dozens of cases in which triangulation techniques have assisted law enforcement worldwide.

21   When the Los Angeles police needed to locate O. J. Simpson during the now-famous highway chase, they received court-ordered help from a mobile

phone company and were able to locate the Ford Bronco by tracing its cellular phone radio signal. In Colombia, ruthless drug boss Pablo Escobar was finally located and shot dead by police after they traced his mobile telephone's radio signal. Police in the United States located fugitive lawyer Nicholas Bissell, Jr., in Nevada on November 26, 1996, after tracing calls he made on his cellular telephone. Bissell was running from the law after being convicted of fraud, embezzlement, and abuse of power.

Another advantage of cellular tracing from a law enforcement perspective is that cellular phones can tell police not only where a suspect is going but also where he has been.   22

A federal drug informant is accused of booby-trapping a briefcase in an unsuccessful attempt to kill a U.S. prosecutor. Using the informant's cellular phone records, prosecutors showed that he was in the same town on the same day where the would-be assassination kit was purchased.   23

Unlike hard-line telephones that most people have in their homes, customers pay for each local cellular call. The billing record for each cellular call shows the cell site from which it was made.   24

Privacy advocates recognize that cellular call tracing can be a great tool for law enforcement, but they argue that the bad will outweigh the good if police abuse their powers.   25

"Police have no right to know my location just because they reason that I might be relevant to some investigation," explained a law-abiding political science professor. "I want to make sure police cannot track and follow a person using a mobile phone unless they obtain a full wiretap warrant." At present, police only need a simple subpoena, which is easier to obtain than a wiretap warrant, to legally intercept cell phone signals.   26

"I bet the good professor would change his mind real quickly if his daughter were kidnapped," countered a police captain. "We don't have the time, the resources, or the inclination to snoop on law-abiding citizens. . . . We only use cellular tools to catch criminals," he protested. "Shouldn't we be more worried about the way rapists and burglars invade our privacy and less worried about taking crime-fighting weapons from the police?"   27

Understanding Meaning

1. Why are cell phones easy to monitor? What makes them different from traditional telephones?
2. Why have laws banning police scanners that can pick up cell calls failed to curb illegal monitoring?
3. How can even innocent calls expose people to risk?

4. How do cell phones work as homing devices? How can police use them to track people's movements?
5. *Critical Thinking:* Can anyone be sure that his or her legal, medical, or financial records are secure? Even if you never use a cell phone, can you be sure that conversations by your lawyer, doctor, or broker are not being monitored?

Evaluating Strategy

1. How effective is the evidence Mizell presents? Do you find it convincing? Do you think it will change people's use of cell phones?
2. *Other Modes:* How does Mizell use *narration* and *cause and effect* in developing his analysis?

Appreciating Language

1. Mizell uses words like "kook" in his essay. Does the use of slang make the essay easy to read, or does it detract from the seriousness of the subject?
2. Mizell's book is targeted to a wide audience. Do you find his style readable? Can you easily remember facts and details? Would the use of technical or legal terminology lend the article greater authority?

Connections across the Disciplines

1. Refer to Kimberly Crawford's article about recording suspects' conversations (page 344). How can society balance concerns for privacy with the need for police departments to investigate crime?
2. Review television commercials or print advertisements for cell phones. Do manufacturers explain how easily these devices can be monitored? Should cell phones come with clearer warnings?

Writing Suggestions

1. Write an essay analyzing how technology—cell phones, e-mail, computers, the Internet, security video cameras—have robbed citizens of their privacy. Is there any way to protect people from stalkers and hackers who might monitor phone calls or illegally access computer files and post the information on a Web page?
2. *Collaborative Writing:* Working with a group of students, review Mizell's article, and write a short process paper instructing consumers in cell phone use. Remind people to avoid discussing sensitive issues or providing information that could be used by burglars or stalkers.

JAMES PONIEWOZIK

James Poniewozik grew up in Michigan and received a degree in English from the University of Michigan, Ann Arbor. He attended the graduate fiction program at New York University. He has published articles in Fortune, Rolling Stone, New York, The New York Times Book Review, *and* Talk. *From 1997 to 1999 Poniewozik served as media critic and editor for* Salon.com. *In July 1999, he joined* Time *as a television and media writer.*

What's Wrong with This Picture?

OVERVIEW: *In this article, which first appeared in* Time, *Poniewozik analyzes the lack of Hispanic actors and characters on network television. Before you read the article, consider how television shaped your view of society when you were growing up. If a group of people is underrepresented on television, does it affect the way others view them, the way institutions respond to their needs, the way the larger society evaluates them?*

It was a proud moment for Hispanic Americans last week when NBC un- 1
veiled its fall schedule in New York City. The network showed a clip of a
rare TV show: a sitcom with a strong, charismatic Latino lead and broad audience appeal.

The bad news: the show was *Chico and the Man*, part of a reel of high- 2
lights from NBC's history. By and large, major Hispanic TV characters
are still just that, history—Freddie Prinze's Chico, Desi Arnaz's Ricky Ri-
cardo—even though Latinos are America's fastest-growing minority, now
roughly equal in number to African Americans. The disparity is not new,
but it has never been so embarrassingly glaring. According to the 2000 Census, Hispanic Americans number 35 million, or 12.5% of the population, a
nearly 58% jump since 1990. But on television? A report by the advocacy
group Children Now found that in prime time, the number of Hispanic
characters dropped since last season, from 3% to 2%. (Blacks make up 17%,
the study found, Asian Americans 3% and Native Americans 0.2%; they are
12.3%, 3.6% and 0.9% of the population.) In all of prime time, Hispanics account for only 47 out of 2,251 characters. As for nonfiction television, the
Center for Media and Public Affairs found that Latino correspondents reported only 1.3% of all network evening-news stories in 2000.

It wasn't supposed to be this way. After the N.A.A.C.P. and affiliated 3
groups attacked the lack of diversity on television and threatened boycotts
in 1999, the networks recast series, appointed diversity czars and instituted

minority recruitment and training programs. Last year, with the media and activists looking over the networks' shoulders, those efforts produced results—mostly African Americans plugged into ensembles. But there is no Latino *Cosby Show* or even *Steve Harvey Show*. Hispanics still have trouble getting parts other than the perp, the victim or that newly resurgent figure, the maid/nanny. (A rare exception was Esai Morales, recently added to *NYPD Blue* as Lieutenant Tony Rodriguez.) In the Latino actors' community, the scarcity of roles makes casting "like throwing meat to hungry dogs," says Lisa Vidal, who co-stars as a cop on Lifetime's police drama *The Division*. "Most of us don't want to play only the victim or the accused roles, but we have to pay the rent."

4   As for Latino producers, the diversity controversy provided brief entree. To a point. Jeff Valdez, producer of Nickelodeon's *The Brothers Garcia*, says he began to get calls from networks that had blown him off before. "So I pitched three shows and never got a return call," he says. "Now they can say they met with a real Hispanic and move on with their business."

5   Film director Gregory Nava (*El Norte*) did parlay that moment into a television deal, but not with a commercial network. CBS signed him to make *American Family*, a drama pilot starring Edward James Olmos, Sonia Braga and Raquel Welch, unusual in that it portrayed a Latino family whose kids are upscale strivers. CBS passed but let Nava shop it around. The show landed at PBS, which will air 13 episodes next season. Cable has filled in some of the breach too, notably on Showtime's *Resurrection Blvd.*, TV's first Hispanic drama, returning in June. Creator Dennis Leoni says the story, about a family with roots in the boxing world, "was the perfect metaphor of Latinos trying to fight, literally and figuratively, for a piece of the American Dream."

6   But network series remain dominated by white male writers inclined to write about what they know—themselves—and Hispanics are scarcely present in TV's executive suites. "Why can't they change the role of George to Jorge?" asks Ruben Blades, who played psychiatrist Max Cabranes on ABC's just canceled *Gideon's Crossing*. "One argument is, We can't use Latinos because they don't have the drawing power on a national scale. But how can you acquire power if you don't get that second or third important role?"

7   Viewed in the larger context of pop culture, the no-crossover argument seems downright archaic. We've gone from the Freddie Prinze era to the Freddie Prinze Jr. era. This year's movie action comedy *Spy Kids* took the No. 1 spot at the box office with a story about a family of spies who just happened to be Hispanic, but you would have had a hard time pitching the idea as a television series. Young whites had no problem embracing *Popstars*,

the WB reality show about a girl group, three of whose five members were Hispanic.

But these successes, and the Census figures, are not reflected in the fall 8 schedules unveiled last week, in which Latino actors are few and characters fewer. Network diversity executives insist that they're trying. H. Mitsy Wilson of Fox cites the network's outreach to minority groups and says, "Our goal is to place Hispanic writers on all shows." Says CBS senior vice president/diversity Josie Thomas: "We're working on it. There are opportunities for guest stars, recurring roles are still open. This isn't the end of the story."

Part of the problem may be the perception of Hispanics as a largely im- 9 migrant (and thus downscale) market, not interested in English-language shows. Spanish-language networks draw 35% of prime-time Hispanic viewers, but that leaves plenty to compete for. And television still at least pretends to reflect society at large. "A lot of these shows are set in New York and L.A.," says Clara Rodriguez, a sociology professor at Fordham University and editor of the anthology *Latin Looks: Images of Latinas and Latinos in the U.S. Media.* "We're representing the city as Hispanic-less."

But diversity goes beyond numbers. Changing George to Jorge doesn't 10 automatically add cultural depth. The question of what counts as a "real" Hispanic character is more complicated than it is for African or Asian Americans, whose physical characteristics help distinguish them. Light-skinned Hispanic actors can end up like Jewish actors have—relegated to playing other ethnicities. Arguably the most visibly Latino character announced last week was campy superhero Bat Manuel (Nestor Carbonell) on Fox's *The Tick.* On NBC's *UC: Undercover,* Jon Seda plays a cop named Jake Shaw; on, NBC's *Crossing Jordan,* Miguel Ferrer is Dr. Garrett Macy.

Is an "authentic" Hispanic portrayal one steeped in Hispanic culture? 11 Is it Ramon Estevez, aka Martin Sheen, playing Anglo President Josiah Bartlet on *The West Wing?* Does it even have to be played by a Hispanic actor? Spokeswoman Lisa Navarrete of the National Council of La Raza, which makes these distinctions every year when it gives out its ALMA awards in film, TV and music, says the answer is not cut and dried. (The group once even recognized non-Latino Nicholas Turturro for playing a Latino cop on *NYPD Blue.*) "We want [Hispanic] actors to be able to play Shakespeare and the whole gamut of roles," she says. "But we're also concerned about kids' self-esteem and self-image when they don't see themselves [on television]."

In fact, one of the few lights for Hispanics on English-language televi- 12 sion is children's television, especially Nickelodeon, which has two Hispanic family sitcoms, *The Brothers Garcia* and *Taina.* And Nick's *Dora the Explorer,* a cartoon for small children with a Latina heroine and a smattering of Spanish, also runs on CBS's Saturday morning, where it has proved a hit.

13   It doesn't hurt that children are the most racially diverse—and most Hispanic—segment of the population. Which suggests that the networks and their advertisers may be leaving money on the table. Marketing company Santiago & Valdes Solutions estimates the Hispanic market at $630 billion, and while English-language networks are facing a weak ad market, the Spanish-language Univision and Telemundo are expected to increase their ad sales from 10% to 25% this year. And they aim not just at the "Spanish-dominant" speakers but also bilingual youths. "They've grown up with Spanish music and Spanish stars," says Univision president Ray Rodriguez. "Young Hispanics are now embracing their heritage better." Next year, Univision will launch a second Spanish-language network, reaching 80% of American Hispanics and directly aiming at bilingual viewers currently watching English-language television.

14   There are a few signs that the major networks are paying attention too. CBS carries the Latin Grammys and in June begins broadcasting the soap opera *The Bold and the Beautiful* with a Spanish-language track, eyeing Univision and Telemundo's sizable telenovela audience. And last week, NBC signed a deal with Jennifer Lopez to do a music special next fall and develop a sitcom based on her childhood, even though the popular singer-actress is not expected to appear in it. The browning of TV is overdue. But it could just come about because of a different kind of diversity effort: the deep yearning to see more green.

Understanding Meaning

1.   What evidence does Poniewozik present to support his thesis that Hispanics are not represented in television?
2.   Hispanic actors and characters appeared on television long before African-Americans were represented. Desi Arnaz, the Cisco Kid, and Zorro were immensely popular in the 1950s. Why did television lose interest?
3.   What, if anything, will change Hollywood's attitude toward Hispanics?
4.   What role does language play? Are Hispanics dismissed by television executives because many assume that Hispanics don't watch English language shows and won't buy their sponsors' products?
5.   Poniewozik focuses his analysis on entertainment programs but notes that only 1.3% of network evening-news stories in 2000 were reported by Hispanics. Is this lack of representation even more important? If the news media ignores a community's interests, problems, leading figures, and culture, will traditional stereotypes remain unchallenged?

6. *Critical Thinking:* Does Poniewozik's article reveal a greater trend in our society? Accustomed to seeing diversity in white and black, have we failed to notice that the largest minority group in the twenty-first century will be Hispanic and that the Asian population is one of the fastest growing groups?

Evaluating Strategy

1. Poniewozik presents a number of statistics in his essay. Statistics can be powerful evidence but can bore and confuse readers. Does he use them effectively? Why is it important to present both statistics about Hispanic personalities on television and in census figures?
2. Poniewozik includes a number of quotes by experts, actors, producers, and scholars. What impact do they have? Do observations by others strengthen Poniewozik's analysis? Why or why not?
3. *Other Modes:* Where does Poniewozik use *comparison* and *cause and effect* to create his analysis?

Appreciating Language

1. What does Poniewozik mean by "real" and "authentic" Hispanic portrayals? Can you think of examples?
2. Poniewozik uses the terms "Latinos" and "Hispanics" interchangeably. Do these terms have different definitions?

Connections across the Disciplines

1. Review Darrell Huff's "How to Lie with Statistics" (page 301). In your view, does Poniewozik use his statistics objectively and accurately? Do they give a fair depiction of the media's treatment of Hispanics?
2. Consider the characters and conflicts that appear in "The Fender Bender" (page 56) and "My Ecumenical Father" (page 133). Could you envision these stories and situations as material that could make television shows? Would they appeal to the general public? Why or why not?

Writing Suggestions

1. Write your own analysis of how television depicts or fails to depict a group of people. How many handicapped, gay, Catholic, or Muslim characters appear on

television? Are some groups "overrepresented"? Does the number of upper income characters distort the public's view of American affluence?

2. *Collaborative Writing:* Discuss a few popular television shows with a number of students, and write a brief comparison paper contrasting people and characters who seem over- and underrepresented. Why does television seem to be populated by police officers and attorneys and not teachers and farmers? What kinds of female characters appear on television and which do not?

FRANK PILIPP
AND CHARLES SHULL

Frank Pilipp is an associate professor of German at the Georgia Institute of Technology. He has conducted research in modern European literature and film and is the author of The Novels of Martin Walser: A Critical Introduction. *Charles Shull is an associate professor of sociology at Lynchburg College in Virginia, where he teaches courses about AIDS. He served as president of an AIDS support group and assisted people with HIV. Pilipp and Shull collaborated to write an analysis of how movies made for television have treated the epidemic and its victims.*

TV Movies of the First Decade of AIDS

OVERVIEW: *First published in the* Journal of Popular Film and Television *in 1993, Pilipp and Shull's article analyzes the messages about AIDS contained in four television movies that appeared between 1985 and 1991.*

Among the media of popular culture, television, over the past decade, has hesitantly become a mouthpiece for reporting and responding to the AIDS epidemic.[1] In addition to documentary and news-related coverage, a small array of fictional accounts, that is full-length feature films spawned by the disease, have constituted a general, albeit basic, chronicle of the multifaceted dimensions of the epidemic. As a set, these movies both challenge *and* reinforce a number of basic values and stereotypes linked to nurturing, caretaking, parenting, and sexuality. Consequently, these movies generate an imagery of the first AIDS decade as multifarious and, perhaps, as confusing as the epidemic itself. Contrasting the presentations of the gay male AIDS protagonists and their families in the films *An Early Frost* (1985), *As Is* (1986), *Andre's Mother* (1990), and *Our Sons* (1991) should not only show the degree to which the AIDS epidemic has been a cultural catalyst and influenced American society but also how cultural values predetermine public and personal perceptions of such an issue as AIDS.

These films present the views of the AIDS issue[2] through images of those who are either "inside" or "outside" the social worlds of gay men and/ or of AIDS. This division reflects the parallel worlds of the "gay"/"straight" and AIDS involved/non-involved experiential worlds of contemporary American society. The films illustrate the tensions generated when a terminal illness forces strangers to acknowledge the experiences of the other; to confront, accept, and interact with a social (or medical) world alien to them.

The walls that divide these worlds have been built by the dynamics of fear: families fearing and rejecting those who are gay and/or AIDS infected and gay men fearing rejection by their families. That insider/outsider dichotomy has also been identified as the worlds of the *immune* and the *implicated*.[3] In a compelling manner, Goldstein illustrates how popular culture and the arts have reacted differently to the AIDS epidemic. He indicates that although the treatment or representation of AIDS in the arts reflects the insider perspective of the implicated, often the traumatized view of the artist himself, popular culture represents the unassailable refuge of the immune, the unaffected, and presumably non-infected, outside platform of the broad masses. Unquestionably this premise is well argued, though we must disagree with Goldstein's view that "TV movies about AIDS shy away from gay male protagonists" and that "the typical protagonist is a young, virtuous, and vulnerable woman" (28–29). Although this holds true for most of those films of the '80s that deal with terminal diseases in general[4] (which are generically indebted to the AIDS epidemic), the films to be discussed here all introduce single, white, professionally successful, gay, male protagonists experiencing AIDS.

3   On the other hand, Goldstein aptly comments:

4   In television, where demography is destiny, the person with AIDS is rarely an innocent everyman. . . . Adult males are usually represented as transgressors whose behavior places others in jeopardy; infected women are usually exempt from blame, but rendered nearly as helpless as their children. In these prime-time masques, it is not the person with AIDS who is victimized but those threatened or affected by the disease. Family and community occupy center stage, and the issue is not survival but cohesion: how to deal with a breach in the safety net. (21)

5   He suggests that in order to appeal to rather than appall the populace, television must resort to cautious and sensible treatment of the AIDS threat for, as one critic comments, "the social stigma surrounding homosexuality and intravenous drug use create a distance that precludes automatic sympathy."[5] Therefore TV movies redirect primary emphasis away from the anxieties, self-reproaches, and fears of the HIV-infected (or the world of homosexuals) and toward the reactions of those around him. Only secondarily do these movies focus on the AIDS epidemic as experienced by gay men—in fact, modes of contraction (or prevention for that matter) are mostly silenced and sex and drug use are not discussed.[6]

6   Unlike the independent theatrical releases *Parting Glances* (1986) and *Longtime Companion* (1990), the movies made for commercial television lack

any direct presentation of the linkage of their protagonists, usually gay couples, with other members of the gay community.[7] *Parting Glances* and *Longtime Companion*, however, are documentary-style investigations of the impact of the AIDS epidemic *specifically* upon the gay male community. Set in New York City, these two movies examine the issue through distinctly different approaches. Both of these movies must be seen from the point of view of the respective temporal context (i.e., knowledge about and impact of the AIDS crisis in 1986 vs. 1990). Both are rich with interwoven subtle and complex motifs presenting issues of the lives of gay men and of gay men dealing with AIDS during the 1980s.

Parting Glances uses a micro-level lens, limiting the action to a period of   7
twenty-four hours. Within that time, the impact of the epidemic is presented as a force that is a presence, a given that pervades and invades reality in the lives of the characters. Good-byes must be said; caretaking must be carried out; relationships must be resolved. Each must deal with the possibility of the death of friends and relationships. *Longtime Companion* reverses the view and, using a macro-level approach, scans across the first decade of the crisis, presenting the multi-faceted AIDS experiences and responses of gay men during those years. The viewer is shown how the disease reorganizes the lives of a network of friends. Friends die alone; partners take care of partners; some become AIDS activists; and each must deal with personal feelings about dying and death. Although the two movies apply a direct and exclusive approach in their focus on the gay community, their intentions do not seem notably different from that of those films made for television. Both force the viewer to confront (1) the social world of gay men; (2) the multiple dimensions of the destructiveness of AIDS; and (3) the complications of unresolved relationships.

An Early Frost is the first of the AIDS films made for TV, starring Aidan   8
Quinn as the infected Michael, Gena Rowlands as his caring mother, and Ben Gazzara as the prejudiced father. An eminently successful Ivy League law school graduate, Michael inhabits a luxurious house in Chicago with his lover, Peter. Diagnosed as having AIDS, Michael ejects Peter when Peter confesses infidelity during their two-year relationship and resorts to the support of his (Michael's) family in suburbia. His return forces his parents to deal with a double-barreled issue: their son's sexuality and his terminal disease. They are facing a diseased stranger. Additionally, the son now must break down the false image of himself that he has worked to maintain for his parents and that has helped the denial pattern of his parents to continue. Michael is the only "closeted" gay man in these films. Contrary to him, his lover, Peter, is said to be open to his parents/family. Michael's fear of dis-

closing himself is validated by his father's reaction of pure repulsion and hatred, perceiving it as a family shame having to call "a homosexual [with] this disease" his son and he relegates Michael to "his own kind." The father asks "How can a son of mine become a stranger?" This is a hollow question since it is unclear whether he is saying that his son is a stranger because he (Michael) is gay or because he (Michael) had not been honest with his parents. It is not entirely clear whether he is questioning Michael's sexuality, his own lack of perception, or his son's not telling him the truth.

9   Michael's revelations force both father and mother to realize that they do not know their son as an adult; they merely remember him as a child/teenager playing Chopin and running track. They have allowed him privacy as an adult but that choice means not having to ask too many questions about his life in the city.[8] After Michael's disclosures the film illustrates how the protagonist's "otherness" shatters the harmony of this representative middle-class family and meticulously traces the path as one by one family members and friends accept his strangeness. The film's strategy is such that it repeatedly pits two characters against each other in all possible (relevant) constellations in order to expound the views on the AIDS/gay-issue from various outsider perspectives. These views are shown both by the reactions of family members who know nothing about the disease, and even by the rescue squad who refuse to transport Michael to the hospital. The mother's fear and confusion is balanced by her unflagging understanding and love and her resolute demand for information from his doctor and for her husband's acceptance of Michael. Her reaction forms a sharp contrast with his pregnant sister's fear of possible transmission to her small son and unborn child and his father's fear when Michael moves to kiss his mother. Within the family only Michael's totally reasonable grandmother offers nothing but love and support pronouncing the film's message: "It's a disease, not a disgrace."

10   Two scenes reflect that Michael as a gay man knew about AIDS but was able to stand outside until his own illness transformed him into an insider. When Michael's doctor explains to him that someone can be a "carrier of the disease without actually showing the symptoms himself," Michael responds "You mean you can pass it on without actually getting it?"[9] Michael's anger at Peter's infidelity is an all too understandable reaction to the breaking of the safety bond that protected them from what was happening to others.

11   As an insider Michael comes into contact with the larger world of AIDS when he joins a hospital AIDS support group: mostly young—by inference, gay—white men, but also including a heterosexual male infected through a

prostitute, and a black male. There he is exposed to their fears and the humiliating reactions of others to their illness. Only the blackest of humors displayed by a fellow-patient, Victor (John Glover in a superb performance), grants the viewer temporary comic relief. Representing the popular stereotype of the effeminate, flamboyant homosexual man, this character is easy to laugh at, and to discount without taking him seriously as a man or acknowledging his sexuality. Yet the viewer is forced to acknowledge the humanness of Victor as he is seen dictating his will to Michael. When Michael sees Victor's belongings in a trash can after Victor's death, both Michael and the viewer are shown the deadly physical and social power of the disease as well as a forecast of Michael's future. The insider gay male messages also focus on the problem of accepting one's sexual orientation as part of one's individual identity and being accepted by others. Peter, who is open to his family, has criticized Michael for never admitting his homosexuality to his parents: "When are they going to find out who you really are? After you're dead?" Michael's difficulty becomes evident in a hospital conversation with his mother about his being gay. His statement "I haven't been unhappy" certainly is not a very strong self-affirmation.

The fear of the outsiders' reaction to Michael's "coming out" is one dy-   12
namic that drives this movie. Faced with the panicky reactions of those around him, most notably his father's, and in order to rid the latter of the burden of society's disapproval, while at the same time not wanting to burden Peter with his sickness, Michael attempts suicide. After Michael is rescued by his father, the ensuing, violently verbose altercation between father and son allows the father to break through his own fears and to demand that Michael fight, because the father does not want to see his life's work destroyed. Although this patriarchal reasoning is probably based on material values (the life-long struggle of the hard-working petit bourgeois may serve as an explanation for the prejudices rampant in this social class), the film's ending celebrates reconciliations all around. Sister and father have fully accepted Michael's fate. Yet Michael, the "contaminated stranger," has to leave the restored family order (reinforced by the final image of the parents in an endearing embrace) and return to "his own kind," to the world of gay men and AIDS where his family does not belong. Although he has gained acceptance within the social microcosm of his familial circle, he has to "win that case" alone. He is still the "other," the outcast who represents a threat, but an outsider who enjoys universal familial sympathy.

In *As Is*, Robert Carradine plays Rich, a gay man in New York City   13
newly diagnosed as having AIDS. Structurally far less complex than *An Early Frost,* this film, adapted from the play of the same title, shows Rich re-

turning to Saul (Jonathan Hadary), his lover of many years. Rich's new lover has left him; his catering business is gone; his health insurance company is trying to get out of covering his illness; he is nearly broke. In this film the viewer is shown the double insider experience from the narrow focus of two gay men struggling against the onslaught of the disease. Together the two recall friends who are sick or have already died of AIDS; remember their life together; and, ultimately, move apprehensively to face the future. Assuring Rich of his unconditional acceptance ("as is"), Saul finally succeeds in dissuading Rich from his intentions to commit suicide. The film ends on a didactic note when a hospice worker (Colleen Dewhurst), whose function as a narrative framing device has been adopted from the play, states that she is "angry with God" and that for the HIV infected "(i)t's a long way to finding acceptance."

14   This second film, like the first, "reads" much like a popular introduction to AIDS, presenting again the typical symptoms (persistent cough, weight-loss, night sweats, seizures, recurrent flu, swollen glands) and admitting medicine's ignorance and inability to cope with the problem. Like Peter in *An Early Frost*, Saul also has to face the possibility of being infected and getting sick. Contrary to the first film, *As Is* dispels popular misconceptions such as that the disease can be contracted through mere physical contact or by air. *As Is* also draws more attention to the diversity of AIDS victims. For example, among the patients of an AIDS crisis center we hear the story of a pregnant woman who contracted AIDS from her husband who "shot up." Nevertheless, the film seems to suggest that the disease originated in the gay male, thus reaffirming the social stigma imposed on homosexuality. Indeed homosexuality is shown to be accepted only by homosexuals, first and foremost by the loyal Saul or by minorities, such as Saul's Jewish father, whom we never meet, and Rich's actress friend, Lilly.

15   Outsider responses are minimal in this film as the parents of the two protagonists remain off-stage or are assumed to be dead. However, the open-minded approval of Saul's family is contrasted with the conservative and fearful attitude of Rich's brother (whose name is never used). Aware of but not entirely accepting Rich's life (he can never remember Saul's name), the brother is the only immediate family member to visit Rich in the hospital. He enters the room appearing frightened and ridiculous in gown and mask. Rich has become the doubly threatening "other" who represents a threat to his brother's outside, untainted rural—south Jersey—environment. Yet, in the end, brotherly love overrides fear and, breaking through his reservations—"Richie, you're my brother!"—the two characters finally embrace.

Andre's Mother, a film adapted from a play by Terrence McNally, displays   16
an unmistakable staginess with its monologues and its oftentimes too brisk
dialogues. The two central figures are Cal (Richard Thomas), the lover of
the deceased Andre, and Andre's mother (Sada Thompson) who still has
not accepted her late son's social-sexual identity.[10] The tension of the film
is created by Cal's fight for that acceptance from Andre's mother. The
events portrayed center on Andre's memorial service. There, for one last
time, the characters attest to their attachment to the admired, beloved, almost worshipped friend. The outsider AIDS dimension in this film is illustrated by Andre's mother, who does not understand the releasing of the
memorial balloons in Central Park as a symbol of a final "letting go," a ceremony that has become part of many AIDS memorials. Cal's behavior toward her shows the inside perspective of someone who has lived through
months of caretaking of a loved one during the illness. His own need for
resolution and closure of his anger and pain may explain his demands upon
the mother who has remained an outsider to her son's being gay and to his
disease.

Cal introduces the final scene when he attempts resolution of that   17
tension by forcing acknowledgment of what caused Andre's death: "Andre
died of AIDS." When he cries "I didn't kill him!" and reveals that he is
HIV-negative, he hopes to get the mother to accept and share his love for
the deceased Andre. In a vehement tirade of anger and tears about the walls
of denial—"how many of us . . . don't want to disappoint our mothers?"—
he demands her approval. Indeed, her aversion surprisingly turns to hesi-
tant affection (she returns Cal's embrace) and Cal earns her acceptance. In
this scene the musical score, "L'amero, Saro Costante" from Mozart's "Il
Re Pastore" underscores the theme of loyalty and commitment but also
contributes to the stylized ambiance of this film that never manages to con-
vincingly develop the motivation for the title character's change or Cal's ob-
sessive behavior. In sum, this short film deals with the two main characters
resolving tensions: coming to terms with the "other" and making peace
with themselves. Again, attitudes about gay men are reflected in the clash-
ing views of two families. Cal's sister and father are shown as accepting
Cal's sexuality, although the latter indicates minimal understanding, "a lack
of imagination on my part"; Cal's mother and Andre's father are shown as
rejecting it. Andre's mother is moving towards acceptance only as the
film ends.

Although the stage of physical deterioration of the AIDS victim was in-   18
timated in *As Is* and briefly illustrated in *Early Frost*, the TV movie *Our Sons*
is more graphic in revealing the suffering of the AIDS victim. Here the cen-

tral protagonist, twenty-eight-year-old Donald (Zeljko Ivanek), previously a successful architect in San Diego, is near death. In a fairly simple plot, his lover, James (Hugh Grant), enlists his own mother, Audrey (Julie Andrews), to help in reuniting Donald and his mother, Lou-Anne (Ann-Margaret), before death occurs. Audrey, a successful, liberal and open-minded, upper-class executive business woman, has to travel to Fayetteville, Arkansas, to confront the waitress Lou-Anne, who is presented as typifying the prejudices and ignorance of the lower-middle class in small-town America. Her frighteningly immature view that "homosexuality is an offense against God, man, and nature" seems like a learned prejudice. She is embittered that her son is "one of them," "a queer," and it takes all of Audrey's persuasive powers to induce her to return with her to visit the dying Donald. When she (all too quickly and quite predictably) overcomes her reluctance and visits Donald, she is controlled and unemotional, still blaming her son. The movie suggests that Lou-Anne's anger and denial begin to break only when Audrey makes the central statement, "Our sons are two of us" (as opposed to two of *them*). Those words seem to work wonders. Lou-Anne hastens to cleanse herself of the past by swimming nude in Audrey's pool; seeks reconciliation with Donald at his bedside in a touching, albeit somewhat pathetic scene; and stays with James and Donald until the end. The movie ends with Donald's coffin being carried onto the plane on which Lou-Anne takes off—into a cliché-glorious California sunset. Dedicated to all the United States AIDS victims, the movie, similar to *As Is*, pleads for emancipation from "centuries of rules and revulsions." [11]

19   This film, too, centers on the issue of overcoming prejudices about homosexuality by presenting the conflicting perspectives of the two single parents. Both mothers have already confronted the issues of their sons' homosexuality, which led to two distinctly different reactions. Lou-Anne drove Donald away so that she would not have to know anything about him and his life while Audrey accepted James's gay life-style. But that acceptance is revealed as having been superficial and non-confrontational. Audrey has always refrained from prying into her son's personal life and has chosen to ignore his homosexuality because, as James says, "(w)e know what we want to know." In parallel fashion, Donald has created a life without any family connection while James has never breached the wall of privacy and non-interference that he and his mother maintain. Just as both mothers have chosen not to know their sons as adult men, the sons have not forced their mothers to know. The crisis of the disease forces the walls to be broken.

20   This film minimally deals with the AIDS insider-outsider dichotomy. Here the mothers represent only slightly different AIDS knowledge pat-

terns, probably reflecting education levels more than anything else. Lou-Anne is fearful of even touching Donald and Audrey is surprised when James says that he and Donald have "been to twenty different funerals in the past eighteen months"; the sons are insiders, the mothers outsiders. Audrey's contact with Donald and James forces her to deal with her son as a gay man and with the possibility that he might also become sick and die. Part of this mother-son dynamic is her belated questioning about his HIV status and urging him to be tested. The fact that James has not been tested reflects an insider AIDS issue that troubles many gay men. That choice requires a personal confrontation with the possibility of being antibody positive, of having to deal with the probability of impending disease and death. James must break through his own very honest fear. He is able to face this when he and his mother begin to deal with each other as concerned adults.

Throughout these four films certain messages, images, and stereotypes are presented about AIDS and gay men. As for demographics, two images of the city are presented: one as a refuge for gay men where they can be free, anonymous, and create their lives as gay men, and another as a location of the AIDS infected.[12] On the other hand, in the rural, suburban settings where there are few gay men, the disease is perceived as an alien phenomenon. Naturally, this reinforces the classic American "city" myth. In reality, gay men do live in rural-suburban America and, even when the earliest of these films was released, most rural-suburban areas had their own indigenous AIDS populations. Bigotry, prejudice, and fear of gay men and AIDS have no geographical boundaries. On a medical level, mixed images of medical professionals illustrate the experiences of many AIDS patients. Some doctors (although not portrayed in these films) are still AIDS-phobic, although most others are both concerned and overworked. And, as these films indicate, some rescue squads, nurses, and other staff members have refused to treat AIDS patients, whereas most others have proven to be deeply compassionate in working with their patients.

As to the familial issues of acceptance, we can discern interesting generational and gender combination patterns. The two grandmothers presented in these films (both played by Sylvia Sidney) are accepting characters. In *An Early Frost* she reacts more to the disease issue than to the fact of having a gay grandson. In *Andre's Mother*, it is—ironically—the grandmother who accepts her grandson as he is. She is also a catalyst pushing her daughter to break through the wall of denial. Similarly, the two sisters presented in the movies both know about and accept their brothers being gay, although Michael's pregnant sister (*An Early Frost*) withdraws in fear because of AIDS. The mothers in the films have difficulties accepting their sons as men bonding with other men. Four mothers, two of them on camera, have known about and rejected their sons. However, the stereotypical female gender roles of nurturing and defending ultimately help all of them to overcome their fears. We only *hear* of cases in which this does not happen, e.g., the family that disowned its son who had AIDS (Victor in *An Early Frost*). That, on the other hand, is used by Michael's mother to reaffirm that this "is not going to happen to *our* son."

23   Men tend to have greater difficulties with acceptance than women. Grandfathers and brothers are absent in these films—with one nameless exception in *As Is*. Even Michael's brother-in-law (*An Early Frost*), who knows Michael is gay, is absent after Michael's return to his family and Cal's future brother-in-law (*Andre's Mother*), who is said to be supportive, is off camera. Like their wives, the fathers of the HIV-infected protagonists, as far as they are introduced, reflect minimal variation of the male parent struggling to accept his gay son. Michael's father in *An Early Frost* rejects but shifts towards more acceptance when his son agrees to fight the disease—like a man. In *Andre's Mother*, Cal's father accepts his son although Andre's father turns his back on his son completely. The absence of the other five fathers, for whatever reason, seems to emphasize the difficulties in presenting male parent acceptance of the gay son to viewers. Overall, the parental generation is shown struggling (presumably because of their own unfulfilled wishes for their sons) with acceptance.

24   Three variations of gay male interaction with the "straight world" occur in these films: There is the son who is open and accepted by his family (Peter, Saul, Cal, James, the lovers of the HIV-infected protagonists); the son who is open but not accepted or discussed (Rich, Andre, and Donald); and the son who lives in hiding from his family (Michael). An interesting pattern is that those gay men who are neither open to nor accepted by their families are the men stricken with AIDS. Those who are open to their families are uninfected[13] and are shown as supportive, nurturing, caretaking, and constant companions who are willing to sacrifice their energies and emotions for their partners. They choose, even insist on remaining with their partners, reaffirming the positive force of parental acceptance overcoming all stereotypes and fears. These caring characters present an interesting variation on the stereotype of gay men. Their model of personal and social responsibility may be the beginning of a new gay male image in film. On the other hand, however, all of the other characters who are shown as nurturers are women, which may one more time reinforce the general stereotype of gay men not really being "men."

25   In all the films a certain blame seems to be imputed to the biased parent, who perhaps did not provide sufficient understanding, openness, warmth,

and security for the son to breed the right "virtues." Because of this, the parent becomes partly responsible for the son's exodus to a life in an environment harboring "sin" and disease, away and separate from the mainstream, conservative middle-class values. The flight of the sons can be perceived as an escape from these values, from a world in which they are strangers. Their homosexuality and infection contaminate their identities and they become, much like Kafka's Gregor Samsa, estranged, almost metamorphosized (physically in some films) into a socially unacceptable "other." Usually, the family is unable to provide that much needed ultimate support for its sons; this can only be rendered by the respective lover, their "own kind." And, as in Samsa's case, sometimes only their deaths can restore the former identities as respectable sons and citizens.

Although scattered comments in these films mark the HIV virus as blind   26 to gender, race, or sexual orientation, this does not necessarily neutralize the false image of AIDS as a purely homosexual disease. In these films the virus is often seen as a punishment inflicted on the protagonists and their families for their breach with middle-class norms and values. By contrast, it is most striking that if the son's openness is reciprocated by the family's approval, he does not experience HIV infection. The conclusion lies at hand: Unflagging adherence to the solid values of parental or companion love and honesty, constancy and exclusiveness in love relationships, or simply, "doing the right thing" precludes contraction. Although this exhortation to middle-class conformism would weaken the otherwise socio-critical and emancipatory impact with regard to the implicated, these values are presented as larger than the issues that make the characters strangers to each other. These values and behaviors are shown to heal the wounds caused by that strangeness. Throughout these movies the terror of the destruction of AIDS leads most of the characters of both worlds to be involved with each other, to resolve tensions about sexuality or fear of rejection, to break the walls between them. Ultimately, however, and despite parental and sibling love overriding stereotypes and fears, the movies seem to suggest that these walls should have never been built.

NOTES

1.   For a detailed synopsis see Timothy E. Cook and David Colby, "The Mass-Mediated Epidemic: The Politics of AIDS on the Nightly Network News," in *AIDS: The Making of a Chronic Disease*, ed. Elizabeth Fee and Daniel M. Fox (Berkeley and Los Angeles: University of California Press, 1992) 84–122.

2. The term AIDS will be used here to refer both to the condition of infection with the human immunosuppressive virus (HIV infection) and to the condition of anyone experiencing the multiple disease pattern referred to as acquired immune depressive syndrome (AIDS).

3. Richard Goldstein, "The Implicated and the Immune: Responses to AIDS in the Arts and Popular Culture," in *A Disease of Society: Cultural and Institutional Responses to AIDS*, ed. Dorothy Nelkin, et al. (Cambridge: Cambridge UP, 1991) 17–42. Goldstein's dichotomy is somewhat simplified because it does not deal with the complexities that this epidemic has engendered, i.e., what happens when the disease process forces the two groups into a confrontation, which is precisely the central conflict of the films discussed here.

4. Unlike the independent, and mostly made-for-television "AIDS movies," the films in this category are all star-studded, major Hollywood productions and have been enormous box office hits—for example *Terms of Endearment* (1983), *Beaches* (1988), *Steel Magnolias* (1989), *Silence Like Glass* (1990), *Dying Young* (1991; the only film with a male victim), or *The Doctor* (1991). These films usually appeal to the whole gamut of emotions in the spectator, ranging from flighty and frivolous comedy to the tear-jerking drama of the young and innocent protagonist's slow decease. The audience strongly identifies with the "heroines" of these films, whereas in the "AIDS movies" the HIV-infected protagonist does not necessarily serve as a figure of identification.

5. Don Shewey, "In Memory of My Feelings," *Film Comment*, vol. 24, May/June 1990: 12.

6. Contrary to this squeamish treatment indigenous to American culture, the German film *A Virus Knows No Morals* (1986), a cynical black comedy by Rosa von Praunheim (Holger Mischwitzki), employs a casual directness and explicitness in its depiction of the world of gays.

7. Vice-versa, in *Parting Glances* the parents are all "off stage" and there is no indication of their acceptance or rejection, and *Longtime Companion* makes no mention of parents of any of the gay male protagonists.

8. In an earlier bantering table conversation, the parents question Michael about relationships to which Michael ambiguously jokes about not being celibate and the conversation is dropped. The parents are satisfied and Michael has successfully fended off any probing into his personal life.

9. This is a reflection of the lack of medical knowledge in 1985 about the incubation period of the virus. Justifiably scared that he may have been the transmitter, Peter refuses to be checked himself. In fact, any further discussion of the disquieting issue of "finding out" is strictly avoided.

10. Her somewhat dubious rationale is that approving of her son would mean "too terrible a criticism" of herself.

11. These words are uttered by James. Incidentally, it is somewhat surprising that when Audrey hears about Donald she does not immediately ask her son James about his own health, but rather the issue of finding out is saved for the end.

12. However, as Cal in *Andre's Mother* indicates, the choice of many gays to live in the "dreadful, anonymous city" is simply to spare their family the disappointment.

13. What is not mentioned, however, is that they may have to face infection in the future, depending on what transmission-risk behaviors they shared with their partners. Another issue glossed over is that Cal's negative HIV result does not guarantee that he will not later test positive. And finally, throughout these films no mention is made of transmission prevention or of safe sex techniques.

Understanding Meaning

1. What general impressions do the authors have about the films they describe?
2. How have commercial television movies about AIDS dealt with homosexuality? How have they differed from independently produced, theatrical releases?
3. Do Pilipp and Shull see these films educating the public or reinforcing common stereotypes about people with AIDS?
4. According to Pilipp and Shull's analysis, do television films present scientifically accurate information about the disease?
5. How are images of the city and the suburb presented in these films? What do they suggest about American values?
6. What seems to be the common message apparent in most of these television dramas about AIDS?
7. *Critical Thinking:* Commercial television is, after all, an entertainment medium. Can a movie made for television seriously address complex and controversial topics? Does the need to present characters people can identify with lead to a "good guys" and "bad guys" formula? Are stereotypes bound to emerge?

Evaluating Strategy

1. How do the authors provide readers with enough information about four films without turning the article into a series of plot summaries?
2. What analytical methods do the authors use? How important is detailed observation in their analysis?
3. How do the authors use direct quotes from characters in the films to dramatize their points? Is this an effective device?

Appreciating Language

1. This article appeared in a journal dedicated to film and television. Does it have technical terms that many readers would find confusing or unfamiliar?
2. How do the authors describe the attitudes expressed by characters in the films? Does their choice of words reveal a bias?
3. What do the authors mean by "the worlds of the *immune* and the *implicated*"?

Connections across the Disciplines

1. James Poniewozik describes the way Hispanics are depicted on television (page 317) and mentions "real" and "authentic" portrayals of Latinos and Latinas. Do writers and producers have a harder time determining which images of gays to present?

2. Elizabeth Kolbert's essay "Birth of a TV Show" (page 433) shows the lengthy process writers must go through in order to get an idea turned into a television program. Does such a cumbersome process cause writers to avoid controversial characters and situations?

3. *Critical Thinking:* How are gay characters different than ethnic characters? Do writers face different challenges in developing motion pictures and television programs?

Writing Suggestions

1. Select a recent made-for-television film, and write a short analysis of the social messages it seems to advocate. Do television films seek to reinforce widely held values or to challenge them?

2. *Collaborative Writing:* Discuss Pilipp and Shull's conclusions with a group of students. What opinions do members of the group have about the way television has treated people with AIDS? Has the media responded with intelligence and compassion or simply exploited the public's fears? Write a brief paper outlining the views of the group.

BLENDING THE MODES

PHILIP GOUREVITCH

Philip Gourevitch is a staff writer for the New Yorker *and a contributing editor for the newspaper* The Forward. *He has published articles in* Granta, Harpers, *and the* New York Review of Books. *His first book,* We Wish to Inform You That Tomorrow We Will Be Killed with Our Families: Stories from Rwanda *(1998), examined the African genocide that was largely ignored by the West. This book received numerous awards, including the National Book Critics' Circle Award for Nonfiction and the George Pope Book Award for Foreign Reporting.*

What They Saw at the Holocaust Museum

OVERVIEW: *Before you read this essay, consider what you know about the Holocaust, both the historical events and the way it is depicted in popular culture.*

The ticket line outside the United States Holocaust Memorial Museum in Washington forms two hours before opening time. Waiting amid the crowd, I try to read a magazine but a photograph stops me: bodies swirling in water, dead bodies, bloated and colorless, bodies so numerous that they jam against each other and clog the stream. The caption explains that these are the corpses of victims of the tribal genocide in Rwanda. 1

Looking up, I see a group of museum staffers arriving for work. On their maroon blazers, several wear the lapel buttons that sell for a dollar each in the museum bookstore, buttons printed with the slogans "Remember" and "Never Again." 2

I put away my magazine and go to the museum cafe for coffee. There, I meet Virginia Slemker of Dayton, Ohio, and her sister, Sue Thornbro of Sterling, Virginia. The women, both in their 50's, tell me they share a longstanding interest in the Holocaust, a chapter of history, they explain, that is full of associations in the contemporary world. 3

"Abortion comes into mind for me," Slemker says, "because there are so many that are being killed and, I think, because of the innocence of the victims." 4

5   Thornbro agrees. Like the Germans who allowed the Holocaust to happen, she says, today's Americans "don't want to go and see and know what's happening in the clinics."

6   The sisters describe themselves as Protestants who believe that the Bible is the literal truth, so I raise the question that has provoked intense theological debate in the past half century: Where was God during the Holocaust?

7   "I've thought about that," Slemker says. "You can't have a Santa Claus attitude toward God. He allows everything. He allows the tragedy and He allows the mountaintops. He was there. And some did come through, and that was him too. I don't know why. Ask God. Interview God."

8   "Sin brought it into the world," Thornbro says. "It was Adam who made the choice, and history will repeat itself. In America, we've been having religious freedom since we started, and now if you're a Christian, you're persecuted."

9   "You have a picture of Christ on your desk in the workplace," Slemker says, "you can get a lawsuit."

10   In the museum's permanent exhibition, I stand beside a video monitor displaying ghastly images of Jews brutalized and dismembered by Nazi doctors. "Pretty neat, huh?" I hear a teen say to his friend. "I mean, really sick."

11   Emerging from the gallery, I meet Michael Sien, 69-year-old retired dry cleaner from Cranbury, New Jersey, who is a survivor of the Warsaw ghetto and of four Nazi concentration camps. "The experience is torture," he says, "because I went through all these things." In the ghetto, his father was shot before his eyes; his mother and sister were killed at Treblinka; his wife, Ruth, who is with him at the museum, was hidden as a child by Polish farmers. "So I live through it again," Sien tells me. "And it hurts."

12   Sien's intimacy with the history displayed here is unimaginable for most visitors, the majority of whom are not Jewish and are too young to remember the events of midcentury. In visitor comment books outside the exhibition, one reads statements like "This was great" and "We really enjoyed learning about all of the horrible things that happened in Nazi Germany."

13   Near these books, I find a group of 13- and 14-year-olds from Watertown, Massachusetts, on their eighth-grade class trip to Washington. Their first reactions to the museum are single words: "Awesome . . . Intense . . . Creepy . . . Interesting . . . Graphic . . . Cool."

14   "The pictures are disgusting—it wasn't a joke," Robin Shea says. "But it seems like a long time ago because it was all black and white. It was a long time ago because, like, now we all get along together."

"It makes worries like what you wear today seem so stupid," reflects   15
Rebecca Neel.

The Watertown kids have a busy schedule in Washington—the Smith-   16
sonian, Arlington National Cemetery, Ford's Theater, the Presidential
monuments, the Federal Bureau of Investigation. Announcing this itiner-
ary, one of the students, Peter Vitello, remarks that the Holocaust museum
seems "out of place in Washington."

"Yeah," Rebecca says, "everything else is patriotic, but this sort of sub-   17
tly says war is stupid, so it's sort of subtly against the rest of Washington and
also fits in. It was fun."

Since its opening in April 1993, 3.5 million people have come to the   18
Holocaust Museum, more than twice the expected number. Despite com-
plaints of overcrowding, a survey found that 94 percent of the visitors describe their experience as "extremely favorable" or "very favorable," an approval rating most museum administrators can only dream of.

But what does it mean to have a "favorable" encounter with this chron-   19
icle of absolute evil?

At a time when those who carry the memory of the extermination of   20
European Jewry are passing into history, the Holocaust Museum was built
so that visitors would continue, in the words of the museum's motto, to
"bear witness" to the horrors of the Nazi past. The museum's overwhelming popularity testifies, however, to the great difference between bearing
direct witness to history and bearing witness to the documentary representation of historical events at half a century's remove.

The general public, after all, is not lining up each day to gain firsthand   21
experience of the Rwandan genocide or the "ethnic cleansing" in Bosnia.
Rather, as Nona Reiss, a 47-year-old homemaker from New City, New York,
tells me: "We know the atrocities that happen in the world right now. And
what are we doing? Sitting in a museum."

The children from the Vision Christian Academy, an apostolic church   22
school in Baltimore, knew nothing about the Holocaust before they came to
the museum, and none knew any Jews. These black fourth- and fifth-graders
have just spent an hour in "Daniel's Story," an exhibit that tells the fictional
story of a Jewish boy's ordeal during the Holocaust. They say it was a disturbing experience, that it made them sad, and scared, and sometimes angry.

Early on in "Daniel's Story," the first-person voice-over says: "Have you   23
ever been punished for something you didn't do? We were." The 8- and 9-
year-olds from Baltimore tell me they identify with Daniel because they
know what it's like to be forced to clean up their rooms or to have someone

threaten to steal their bicycles. They cannot really imagine the extremity of the Holocaust, which is so beyond their own experience, and their grasp of the history is uncertain at best.

24   "The Germans thought they had the right just to take over the country because the Jews were different," Marquita Cole says. "They were jealous because the Jews were almost ruling the country."

25   Like Virginia Slemker and Sue Thornbro, these children all say they believe in God, and again I ask how God could have allowed so many people to be killed so unjustly.

26   "They didn't pray," a boy named Antwaun Dillard declares.

27   "But many did pray," I say. "Right to their deaths."

28   "Then they weren't believing," Marquita says.

29   "Maybe," Chanel Steele suggests, "they did something wrong and they didn't repent."

30   "It's a 'jealous God,'" Antwaun says, quoting Exodus. "Terrible. He's jealous because people worship golden calves, idols."

31   The children recognize the injustice in "Daniel's Story" but they explain it away by presuming that the Jews were misguided in their faith. As their teacher, Deitre Lynn Allen, puts it: "I believe that the Jews are God's chosen people. But they don't recognize that Jesus Christ is the messiah, that He came already. If they had, I think the Lord could have heard their prayers a lot more. In a way, they were praying to a God that they don't really know."

32   Allen has told me that her school's trip to the Holocaust Museum is part of a "multicultural diversity program" to study other cultures and teach tolerance. But how, I ask her, can you teach tolerance if you teach that the tenets of another religion are wrong?

33   "It's similar to when we teach about Native Americans," she says. "Since we are a Christian school, we recommend that the children pray that the people of that country would come to know Jesus Christ, and that they pray for their needs."

34   Everyone I spoke with at the museum said they liked the place—everyone but a New Zealander who called it "one-sided Jewish propaganda," and even he seemed pleased that the museum was there to confirm his prejudices. In my encounters and in the comment books, I found that visitors often said they would never forget the museum. It occurred to me that the Holocaust maxim, "Remember," may be acquiring a new meaning with the passage of time. What we cannot remember directly, we must imagine through representation, and our response is less immediately to the event than to the medium that has conveyed it to us.

It is not the Holocaust that is suddenly such a huge popular draw, but   35
the Holocaust Museum and the Holocaust movie, *Schindler's List.* The creators of these artifacts, and many who celebrate them, tend to indulge in vainglorious rhetoric, claiming that an affirmative public response to representations of the Holocaust places today's secondhand witnesses firmly on the right side in the struggle of good against evil.

My conversations in Washington suggest that the public may not be so   36
easily led. The world is too much with us for anyone to conclude that genocide can be confined to a museum. The visitors I spoke with about the exhibitions talked more of the present than of the past, and their diverse reactions reflect the beliefs and attitudes they brought to the museum as much as anything they discovered within its walls.

At different moments in time, particular historical events and personal-   37
ities come to exert a special fascination on the public imagination. Today, the Holocaust is invoked but nobody speaks much of Napoleon; few read Gibbon's *History of the Decline and Fall of the Roman Empire;* references to the Roaring 20's, so popular in the hungry 80's, are rarely heard, and the ghost of Richard Nixon has come in from the cold. Such fashions in popular history invariably tell us more about our own times than about the piece of the past that is suddenly turned to as a mirror.

As Americans observe the bloody unravelings of the post-cold-war world,   38
the Holocaust Museum provides a rhetorical exercise in bearing witness to dehumanization and mass murder from a seemingly safe distance.

Understanding Meaning

1. What reactions do visitors have to the exhibits in the Holocaust Museum? Are people responding to the historical event itself, according to Gourevitch, or do they seem to make personal associations?
2. What has made the museum so popular with the public?
3. Does Gourevitch suggest that the museum has ultimately failed to do justice to the Holocaust? Do many visitors seem to walk away blaming the Jews for their fate? Does the museum live up to its motto of "bearing witness"?
4. Does including the Holocaust Museum in a rushed trip of national monuments in the nation's capital do it justice? Can young people really take away anything meaningful when they are hustled to Arlington, Ford's Theater, the FBI headquarters, and the Smithsonian in a single day?
5. Gourevitch states that people will not remember the event but the medium that presented the event to them. Do many of us "remember" historical events and people not through actual documents and artifacts but by Hollywood

movies, textbooks, and museums? Do we remember and respond to history or to images of history?

6. *Critical Thinking:* Gourevitch concludes his essay by commenting that different historical events and people fascinate the public at different times. When we look at history do we try to truly know what the past was like, or do we want and expect associations with our current lives? Why does slavery resonate with African Americans, the Holocaust with Jews, the Vietnam war with foreign policy makers? Would the public be interested in a story about an extinct ethnic group? Do scholars, writers, movie makers, and museum boards have to "sell" history by making it "relevant" to us today?

Evaluating Strategy

1. Gourevitch presents a number of quotations without commentary. Does allowing people to speak for themselves illustrate his thesis? Can a writer use too many quotations?

2. What objective facts does Gourevitch include to document the popularity of the museum?

3. *Other Modes:* Identify passages in which Gourevitch uses *comparison, cause and effect*, and *narration* to develop his analysis.

Appreciating Language

1. How would you characterize the tone and style of the essay? What does the author's choice of words reveal about his attitude toward the museum and its visitors?

2. Gourevitch quotes visitors who see the museum as being "cool" and "awesome." How do you react to these words? Does it simply reflect the language of the young, or does it reveal ignorance and insensitivity about an evil system that claimed the lives of millions?

3. Gourevitch analyzes the word "favorable." Do the visitors have the kind of "favorable" response to the museum the institution's planners hoped for? Is a "favorable" impression necessarily a beneficial or informed one?

Connections across the Disciplines

1. Review John Taylor Gatto's "Why Schools Don't Educate" (page 495). Do museums fail to educate or inform for the same reason?

2. Carl Sagan's "Why We Need to Understand Science" (page 563) is a powerful argument for better educational policies. Could a historian write a parallel ar-

ticle, "Why We Need to Understand History"? What does history teach us? Do past events have to be relevant to the present to be of value, or should the past be appreciated in its own context?

Writing Suggestions

1. Write a brief process paper instructing parents and teachers how children should be introduced to the Holocaust Museum. How can children who have never met a Jew and were born fifty years after the war ended appreciate the Holocaust?
2. *Collaborative Writing:* Discuss this essay with a group of students. Do you think that the United States could open a large national museum about slavery? What controversies would it arouse? Would even some African Americans be afraid to tackle such a project? Would some argue that building a museum about slavery would do more harm than good? Record the comments of the group and create a comparison listing pros and cons.

WRITING BEYOND THE CLASSROOM

KIMBERLY A. CRAWFORD, J.D.

Kimberly A. Crawford is an attorney specializing in criminal law and a legal instructor at the FBI Academy. In this article written for law enforcement officers, she analyzes the constitutionality of secretly recording suspects' conversations to gather evidence. Her article appeared in the FBI Law Enforcement Bulletin *in 1993.*

Surreptitious Recording of Suspects' Conversations

OVERVIEW: *Crawford's analysis focuses on the legality, not the morality or political implications, of using secret recordings to gather evidence about suspects. She addresses the needs of her audience, law enforcement professionals seeking direction on which investigative techniques they can legally use.*

1   Whether in a prison cell, interrogation room, or the back seat of a police car, suspects left seemingly unattended with a co-conspirator, friend, or total stranger often seize the opportunity to discuss or lament their current predicament. Very often, incriminating statements are made. Law enforcement officers who put themselves in a position to hear and record suspects' conversations, either by planting a listening device or by posing as a co-conspirator, friend, or stranger, are apt to obtain very valuable incriminating evidence.

2   Of course, in any subsequent prosecution, the government is likely to be confronted with a vehement constitutional and statutory attack to the admissibility of such damaging evidence. Specifically, the defense is likely to argue that the surreptitious recording of the suspects' conversations violated rights guaranteed by the fourth, fifth, and sixth amendments to the U.S. Constitution, as well as certain protections afforded individuals under Title III of the Omnibus Crime Control and Safe Streets Act[1] (hereinafter title III).

3   This article discusses the validity of these constitutional and statutory challenges. It then provides a review of court decisions that have dealt with the admissibility of such surreptitiously recorded conversations and related issues.

FIFTH AMENDMENT—
SELF-INCRIMINATION CLAUSE CHALLENGE

To be successful, a challenge to the admissibility of surreptitiously recorded   4
conversations based on the fifth amendment self-incrimination clause would
have to establish that the conversations in question were the product of unlawful custodial interrogation. Because statements made to individuals not
known to the defendant as government actors do not normally amount to
interrogation for purposes of the fifth amendment, this challenge is destined to fail.

The fifth amendment to the U.S. Constitution provides in part that "no   5
person . . . shall be compelled in any criminal case to be a witness against
himself. . . . "[2] Over two decades ago, the U.S. Supreme Court in *Miranda* v.
Arizona[3] held that custodial interrogation of an individual creates a psychologically compelling atmosphere that works against this fifth amendment
protection.[4] In other words, the Court in *Miranda* believed that an individual in custody undergoing police interrogation would feel compelled to respond to police questioning. This compulsion, which is a byproduct of most
custodial interrogation, directly conflicts with every individual's fifth amendment protection against self-incrimination.

Accordingly, the Court developed the now-familiar *Miranda* warnings as   6
a means to reduce the compulsion attendant in custodial interrogation. The
Miranda rule requires that these warnings be given to individuals in custody
prior to the initiation of interrogation. This rule, however, is not absolute.[5]

Stanley v. *Wainwright*[6] is one of the original cases to deal with a fifth   7
amendment challenge to the admissibility of surreptitiously recorded suspect conversations. In *Stanley,* two robbery suspects were arrested and
placed in the back seat of a police car. Unbeknownst to the suspects, one of
the arresting officers had activated a tape recorder on the front seat of the
car before leaving the suspects unattended for a short period of time. During that time, the suspects engaged in a conversation that later proved to be
extremely incriminating.

On appeal, the defense argued that the recording violated the rule in   8
Miranda, because the suspects were in custody at the time the recording
was made and placing of the suspects alone in the vehicle with the activated recorder was interrogation for purposes of *Miranda*. The Court of Appeals for the Fifth Circuit, however, summarily dismissed this argument
and found that the statements were spontaneously made and not the product of interrogation.

9   The Supreme Court later validated the rationale in *Stanley* with its decision in *Illinois* v. *Perkins*.[7] Although *Perkins* did not deal specifically with the issue of surreptitious recordings, the Court's analysis of *Miranda* is applicable to situations in which suspects' conversations with either private individuals or undercover government actors are recorded.

10   In *Perkins*, police placed an informant and an undercover officer in a cell block with Lloyd Perkins, a suspected murderer incarcerated on an unrelated charge of aggravated assault. While planning a prison break, the undercover officer asked Perkins whether he had ever "done" anyone. In response, Perkins described at length the details of a murder-for-hire he had committed.

11   When Perkins was subsequently charged with the murder, he argued successfully to have the statements that he made in prison suppressed, because no *Miranda* warnings had been given prior to his conversation with the informant and undercover officer. On review, however, the Supreme Court reversed the order of suppression.

12   Rejecting Perkins' argument, the Supreme Court recognized that there are limitations to the rule announced in *Miranda*. The Court expressly declined to accept the notion that "*Miranda* warnings are required whenever a suspect is in custody in a technical sense and converses with someone who happens to be a government agent."[8] Rather, the Court concluded that not every custodial interrogation creates the psychologically compelling atmosphere that *Miranda* was designed to protect against. When the compulsion is lacking, so is the need for *Miranda* warnings.

13   The Court in *Perkins* found the facts at issue to be a clear example of a custodial interrogation that created no compulsion. Pointing out that compulsion is "determined from the perspective of the suspect,"[9] the Court noted that Perkins had no reason to believe that either the informant or the undercover officer had any official power over him, and therefore, he had no reason to feel any compulsion. On the contrary, Perkins bragged about his role in the murder in an effort to impress those he believed to be his fellow inmates. *Miranda* was not designed to protect individuals from themselves.

14   Applying this rationale to the surreptitious recording of suspects' conversations while they are in the back seat of a police car, a prison cell, or an interrogation room, it is clear that *Miranda* warnings are unnecessary if the suspect is conversing with someone who either is, or is presumed by the suspect to be, a private individual. Because suspects in this situation would have no reason to believe that the person to whom they are speaking has any official power over them, they have no reason to feel the compulsion that *Miranda* was designed to protect against.

SIXTH AMENDMENT—
RIGHT-TO-COUNSEL CHALLENGE

Because of its limited application, a successful challenge to the admissibility of surreptitiously recorded suspect conversations based on the sixth amendment right to counsel will require the convergence of certain factors. Specifically, the defense must be able to establish that the suspect's right to counsel had attached and that the government took deliberate steps to elicit information from the suspect about a crime with which the suspect had been previously charged.

Right to Counsel Attaches
at Critical Stage

The sixth amendment to the U.S. Constitution guarantees that "[i]n all criminal prosecutions, the accused shall . . . have the Assistance of Counsel for his defense." [10] The U.S. Supreme Court has interpreted the sixth amendment as guaranteeing not merely the right to counsel but, more importantly, the right to the *effective assistance* of counsel.[11] To be effective, an attorney must be permitted to form a relationship with the accused some time prior to trial,[12] and the government cannot needlessly interfere with that relationship.[13]

Although the right to counsel would be meaningless if the suspect and attorney were not permitted to form a relationship some time prior to trial, the Supreme Court has held that it is not necessary to allow this relationship to form simply because the individual becomes a suspect in a case.[14] Instead, the Court has found that the sixth amendment guarantee of the effective assistance of counsel is satisfied if the attorney and suspect are permitted to form their relationship once the prosecution has reached a critical stage.[15] The Court has defined the critical stage as the filing of formal charges (i.e., an indictment or information) or the initiation of adversarial judicial proceedings.[16]

Thus, a necessary first step in a successful sixth amendment challenge to the admissibility of a surreptitiously recorded conversation is to establish that the right to counsel had attached at the time of the recording. If the suspect was neither formally charged nor subjected to adversarial judicial proceedings at the time the recorded conversation took place, the sixth amendment challenge will fail.

15

16

17

18

Deliberate Elicitation by the Government

19   If successful in establishing that the suspect's right to counsel had attached at the time a surreptitious recording took place, the defense will also have to prove that the conversation in question was the result of deliberate elicitation on the part of the government. The Supreme Court has determined that simply placing suspects in situations where they are likely to incriminate themselves does not, in and of itself, constitute a sixth amendment violation.[17] Rather, there must be some deliberate attempt on the part of the government to elicit information from the suspect.[18] It is the act of deliberate elicitation that creates the sixth amendment violation.

20   In *Kuhlmann* v. *Wilson*,[19] the Supreme Court held that placing an informant in a cell with a formally charged suspect in an effort to gain incriminating statements did not amount to deliberate elicitation on the part of the government. In doing so, the Court made the following statement:

21   'Since the Sixth Amendment is not violated whenever—by luck or happenstance—the State obtains incriminating statements from the accused after the right to counsel has attached,' a defendant does not make out a violation of that right simply by showing that an informant, either through prior arrangement or voluntarily, reported his incriminating statements to the police. Rather, the defendant must demonstrate that the police and their informant took some action, *beyond merely listening*, that was designed deliberately to elicit incriminating remarks.[20] (emphasis added)

22   As a result of the Supreme Court's decision in *Kuhlmann*, the mere placing of a recorder in a prison cell, interrogation room, or police vehicle will not constitute deliberate elicitation by the government. Instead, to raise a successful sixth amendment challenge, the defense has to show that someone acting on behalf of the government went beyond the role of a mere passive listener (often referred to by the courts as a "listening post") and actively pursued incriminating statements from the suspect.

Right to Counsel Is Crime-Specific

23   Even if it can be established that the government deliberately elicited and recorded incriminating conversations from a suspect after the right to counsel had attached, a sixth amendment challenge to the admissibility of those recordings will not succeed if the conversations in question pertained to crimes with which the suspect had not yet been charged at the time of the

recording. Because the sixth amendment is crime-specific, a suspect only has the right to the assistance of counsel with respect to the crimes formally charged against him.[21] Consequently, the surreptitious recording of a conversation with a formally charged suspect that pertains to some unrelated, uncharged offense, will not violate the sixth amendment, regardless of whether there is deliberate elicitation on the part of the government.

FOURTH AMENDMENT— RIGHT-TO-PRIVACY CHALLENGE

Another constitutional attack waged against the admissibility of surreptitiously recorded conversations is the claim that monitoring and recording these conversations violates the suspects' fourth amendment right of privacy. However, if the recorded conversations take place in government space, whether it be a prison cell, interrogation room, or back seat of a police car, the fourth amendment challenge is bound to fail unless law enforcement officers give suspects specific assurances that their conversations will be private. 24

The fourth amendment to the U.S. Constitution guarantees the right of the people to be secure from unreasonable searches and seizures.[22] As it is used in the fourth amendment, the term "search" includes any governmental action that intrudes into an area where there is an expectation of privacy that is both subjectively and objectively reasonable.[23] To be objectively reasonable, an expectation of privacy must be one that society as a whole is willing to recognize and protect.[24] 25

Thus, to be successful, a fourth amendment challenge to the surreptitious recording of suspects' conversations would have to establish that the suspects expected their conversations to be private and that society as a whole recognizes those expectations as reasonable. Although sometimes willing to accept suspects' assertions that they believed their conversations were private,[25] courts generally reject the notion that the suspects' beliefs were objectively reasonable. 26

For example, in *Ahmad A.* v. *Superior Court*,[26] the California Court of Appeals confronted a fourth amendment challenge to the admissibility of a surreptitiously recorded conversation between the defendant and his mother. The defendant, a juvenile arrested for murder, asked to speak with his mother when advised of his constitutional rights. The defendant and his mother were thereafter permitted to converse in an interrogation room with 27 the door closed. During the surreptitiously recorded conversation that ensued, the defendant admitted his part in the murder.

28   Reviewing the defendant's subsequent fourth amendment challenge, the California court noted that at the time the mother and her son were permitted to meet in the interrogation room, "no representations or inquiries were made as to privacy or confidentiality."[27] Finding the age-old truism "Walls have ears" to be applicable, the court held that any subjective expectation that the defendant had regarding the privacy of his conversation was not objectively reasonable.

29   Several Federal and State courts have adhered to the rationale announced in *Ahmad A.* and have concluded that any expectation of privacy a suspect may foster in a conversation occurring in government space is objectively unreasonable.[28] While some courts predicate their conclusion on an arrest having taken place, thereby reducing the suspects' expectations of privacy,[29] other courts have taken the position that the lack of an expectation of privacy in government space is not dependent on an arrest.[30]

30   This latter position is demonstrated by the holding of the U.S. Court of Appeals for the 11th Circuit in *United States* v. *McKinnon*.[31] In *McKinnon*, law enforcement officers stopped the vehicle in which the defendant was riding for failing to abide traffic laws. Once stopped, the driver of the vehicle was asked to submit to a sobriety test. After successfully completing the test, officers asked the driver whether they could search his vehicle for drugs. Upon receiving consent, the officers invited the driver and defendant to sit in the back seat of the police car until the search was completed.

31   Accepting the officers' invitation, defendant and the driver sat in the police car and engaged in an incriminating conversation that was surreptitiously recorded. Cocaine was found during the search of the vehicle, and both the defendant and driver were subsequently arrested. Following their arrest, the defendant and driver were again placed, seemingly unattended, in the back seat of the police car, where they once again engaged in an incriminating conversation.

32   Conceding the admissibility of the post-arrest statements, the defendant argued that prior to arrest, he had an expectation of privacy in his conversation that was violated by the surreptitious recording. The court, however, found "no persuasive distinction between pre-arrest and post-arrest situation"[32] and refused to suppress the recordings. In support of its decision, the court in *McKinnon* cited several cases in which surreptitious recordings of conversations were found to be admissible against visitors and guests of arrestees and other individuals not under formal arrest at the time of the recorded conversations.[33]

Specific Assurances

Although courts generally find no reasonable expectation of privacy in sus-   33
pects' conversations occurring in government space, specific assurances offered by officers that such conversations will be private may generate a valid
fourth amendment claim. As previously noted, in the case of *Ahmad A.*, the
court was particularly impressed by the fact that "no representations or inquiries were made as to privacy or confidentiality." [34]

A reasonable inference to be drawn from this case is that the resulting   34
expectations would have been reasonable, had there been some representations or inquiries regarding privacy that were met with assurances. This
inference is supported by the case of *People* v. *Hammons*,[35] in which a California court found that law enforcement officers' actions had fostered the
suspects' expectations of privacy, and therefore, the expectations were
reasonable.[36]

Consequently, when placing suspects together with co-conspirators,   35
friends, or strangers for the purpose of surreptitiously recording a conversation, law enforcement officers should be careful not to give the suspects any
specific assurances that their conversations will be private. To do so would
likely create a reasonable expectation of privacy in their subsequent conversations that would be protected by the fourth amendment.

TITLE III—STATUTORY CHALLENGE

The only statutory attack based on Federal law likely to be raised regarding   36
the surreptitious recording of suspects' conversations is that the recording
violates Title III of the Omnibus Crime Control and Safe Streets Act.[37] Because title III protects only oral conversations in which there is a reasonable
expectation of privacy, such challenges are resolved by reference to fourth
amendment analysis.

To be protected under title III, oral communications must be "uttered   37
by a person exhibiting an expectation that such communication is not subject to interception under circumstances justifying such expectation." [38] In
other words, the statute only affords protection to oral conversations uttered
under conditions indicating that there was a reasonable expectation of privacy. Consequently, the warrantless surreptitious recording of suspects' oral
conversations does not violate title III where the suspects lack a fourth
amendment expectation of privacy in those conversations.[39]

CONCLUSION

38   The surreptitious recording of suspects' conversations is an effective investigative technique that, if done properly, can withstand both constitutional and statutory challenges. Law enforcement officers contemplating the use of this technique should keep the following points in mind:

39   1.   Because the technique does not amount to "interrogation" for purposes of *Miranda*, it is not necessary to advise suspects of their constitutional rights and obtain a waiver prior to using this technique.

40   2.   To avoid a sixth amendment problem, this technique should not be used following the filing of formal charges or the initial appearance in court, unless the conversation does not involve a government actor, the conversation involves a government actor who has assumed the role of a "listening post," or the conversation pertains to a crime other than the one with which the suspect has been charged.

41   3.   To avoid both fourth amendment and title III concerns, suspects should not be given any specific assurances that their conversations are private.

42   In addition, State and local law enforcement officers should consult with their legal advisors prior to using this investigative technique. This will ensure compliance with State statutes or local policies that may be more restrictive than the Federal law discussed in this article.

NOTES

1.   18 U.S.C. §§ 2510 *et seq.* Defendants may also claim that the surreptitious recording of their conversations violated State eavesdropping statutes. Although many State eavesdropping statutes closely follow title III, law enforcement officers should consult their State statute before using this technique, because some State laws are more restrictive than title III.

2.   U.S. Const. amend. V.

3.   394 U.S. 436 (1966).

4.   *Id.* at 467.

5.   *See, e.g., Berkemer* v. *McCarty*, 468 U.S. 420 (1984), wherein the Supreme Court held *Miranda* inapplicable to traffic stops. *See also, New York* v. *Quarles*, 467 U.S. 649 (1984), which recognizes a public safety exception to *Miranda*.

6.   604 F.2d 379 (5th Cir. 1979), *cert. denied*, 100 S.Ct. 3019.

7.   110 S.Ct. 2394 (1990).

8.   *Id.* at 2397.

9.   *Id.* in *Perkins*, the Supreme Court used the words coercion and compulsion interchangeably.

10. U.S. Const. amend. VI.

11. *Cuyler* v. *Sullivan*, 100 S.Ct. 1708 (1980).

12. *United States* v. *Wade*, 338 U.S. 218 (1967).

13. In *Weatherford* v. *Bursey*, 429 U.S. 545 (1977), the Supreme Court held that some interference with the right to counsel may be justified.

14. *United States* v. *Gouveia*, 104 S.Ct. 2292 (1984).

15. *Massiah* v. *United States*, 377 U.S. 201 (1964).

16. *Id.*

17. *Kuhlmann* v. *Wilson*, 106 S.Ct. 2616 (1986).

18. *Id.*

19. *Id.*

20. *Id.* at 2630.

21. *Hoffa* v. *United States*, 377 U.S. 201 (1964).

22. U.S. Const. amend. IV.

23. *Katz* v. *United States*, 389 U.S. 347 (1967).

24. *Oliver* v. *United States*, 104 S.Ct. 1735 (1984).

25. Most courts reject this notion as well. In *United States* v. *Harrelson*, 754 F.2d 1153 (5th Cir. 1985), *cert. denied*, 106 S.Ct. 277 (1985), the Court found that "one who expects privacy under the circumstances of a prison visit is, if not actually foolish, exceptionally naive." *Id.* at 1169.

26. 263 Cal. Rptr. 747 (Cal.App. 2 Dist. 1989), *cert. denied*, 11 S.Ct. 102 (1991).

27. *Id.* at 751.

28. *See, e.g., United States* v. *McKinnon*, 985 F.2d 525 (11th Cir. 1993) *cert. pending* (filed 1/7/93 No. 92-8963); *United States* v. *Harrelson*, 754 F.2d 1153 (5th Cir. 1985), *cert. denied*, 106 S.Ct. 277 (1985); *United States* v. *Sallee*, (unreported; 1991 WL 352613 N.D. Ill. 1991); *State* v. *McAdams*, 559 So.2d 601 (Fla.App. 5th Dist. 1990); *People* v. *Marland*, 355 N.W. 2d 378 (Mich.App. 1984).

29. *See, e.g., Brown* v. *State*, 349 So.2d 1196 (Fla.App. 4th Dist. 1977), *cert. denied*, 98 S.Ct. 1271 (1978).

30. *See, e.g., United States* v. *McKinnon*, 985 F.2d 525 (11th Cir. 1993), *cert. pending* (filed 1/7/93 No. 92-8963); and *State* v. *Hussey*, 469 So.2d 346 (La. Ct. App. 2d Cir. 1985), reconsideration denied, 477 So.2d 700 (La. 1985).

31. 985 F.2d 525 (11th Cir. 1993).

32. *Id.* at 528.

33. *Id.*

34. 263 Cal Rptr. 747 (Cal.App. 2 Dist. 1989), *cert. denied*, 111 S.Ct. 102 (1991).

35. 5 Cal. Rptr.2d 317 (Cal.App. 1st Dist. 1991).

36. *See also, State* v. *Calhoun*, 479 So.2d 241 (Fla.App. 4th Dist. 1985).

37. U.S.C. §§ 2510 *et seq.*

38. 18 U.S.C. § 2510(2).

39. *See, e.g., United States* v. *Harrelson*, 754 F.2d 1153 (1985), *cert. denied*, 106 S.Ct. 277 (1986).

Understanding Meaning

1. What is the purpose of Crawford's analysis? Why does her audience need this information?

2. How does she analyze the Fourth, Fifth, and Sixth Amendments?

3. What rights do criminals have in custody? Do they surrender all pretense of privacy when they are arrested?
4. *Critical Thinking:* Does the surreptitious recording of suspects' conversations threaten privacy and democracy or protect it? Would you approve of using this technique to gather evidence that would establish the guilt of a child molester or a terrorist? Should the technique be used to secure evidence against people accused of "victimless" crimes?

Evaluating Strategy

1. Does citing specific cases help readers understand what is constitutional and what is not?
2. How is Crawford's analysis organized?
3. Crawford concludes the article with a list of suggestions. What does this imply about the needs of her readers?

Appreciating Language

1. How much legal terminology does the writer use? What does this reveal about her audience?
2. What language does Crawford use to describe suspects? What does this suggest about suspects?

Connections across the Disciplines

1. How does Crawford's professional role as attorney shape her writing? Compare her article to the one written by physician Oliver Sacks (page 86). What similarities do you see?
2. Compare this article with the FBI report on Lee Harvey Oswald (page 97). What do these entries reveal about writing in law enforcement?

Writing Suggestions

1. Write a short essay analyzing your view of secretly recording suspects' conversations. Should police officers advise suspects that anything they say in private may be held against them? Is surreptitious recording a violation of people's rights? How would you feel if the person who admitted killing a friend of yours was acquitted because his or her statements could not be entered into evidence?

2. *Collaborative Writing:* Working with a group of students, consider the following scenario. A student suspects his or her lover of being unfaithful and installs a recording device in the lover's apartment that transmits clear evidence that this person is engaging in unsafe practices with multiple partners. Discuss the ethics of this situation. Have a member of the group record responses, and as a group review the list and each write a brief analysis. Does a consensus exist? Do the responses indicate gender differences?

STRATEGIES FOR WRITING ANALYSIS

1. **Determine your purpose.** Does your analysis seek to explain the parts of a complex object, issue, condition, or situation, or does it seek to identify a reason, a cause, or a solution to a problem? Persuasive analysis requires greater attention to context.
2. **Define your role.** Are you expressing personal opinion supported by facts and examples of your own choosing, or are you following the dictates of a specific discipline? When writing in a professional role, use standard methods and tools of analysis. If you use unconventional methods, explain your rationale, and be prepared for criticism.
3. **Consider your audience.** In addition to evaluating your readers' knowledge base, you should consider their perceptual world. Are your readers likely to be receptive or hostile to your conclusions? What kind of evidence will most impress them?
4. **Limit your subject.** Analysis requires close study, and an ill-defined topic likely will lead to confusion.
5. **Gather appropriate sources, data, and information.** The strength of your analysis will depend on the quantity and quality of the information you examine. Avoid making judgments on limited data. Evaluate the sources of your data for possible flaws, oversights, or bias.
6. **Be open to alternative interpretations.** Do not make general statements based on data without entertaining alternative interpretations. Consider possible data you may have overlooked.
7. **Apply the rules of critical thinking, and avoid the logical fallacies.**

SUGGESTED TOPICS FOR WRITING ANALYSIS
General Assignments

Write an analysis on any of the following topics. Your analysis will require careful thinking, observation, and possibly outside research. Remember to avoid the logical fallacies and to qualify your remarks.

- Affordable student housing (Define "affordable" in your area.)
- Current movies (Use the newspaper listings as a source.)
- Status of women in your college's faculty and administration
- The principal problem facing fellow students
- The political climate on your campus

- Airport security
- Your generation's attitude toward the Vietnam War, the Civil Rights movement, or any other historical event
- Racial profiling
- The effect of divorce on children
- America's role in international affairs

Writing in Context

1. Assume you have been asked by the campus newspaper to analyze how students feel about abortion, gun control, or another controversial issue. Design a method to gather and analyze data. Indicate what methods you would use, such as focus groups, surveys, or personal interviews.

2. Analyze the image of women, the elderly, black males, businessmen, or any other group presented in popular television shows. Include as many examples as possible in your analysis.

3. Analyze editions of the largest newspaper in your area to determine the amount of attention given to international events versus domestic news. Explain your research methods—the number of editions reviewed and the methods of measurement (number of articles or amount of space).

This paper was written in response to the following assignment:

> Analyze the meaning or significance of a common personal trait, event, social phenomenon, prevailing attitude, or widespread problem. Support your thesis with examples, and provide readers with a clear description of your subject.

Nostalgia: Why We Need and Love the Past

1 I met my current girlfriend at a '70s party. That night the usual Irish decor of O'Donoghue's Pub was obscured by posters of Farrah Fawcett and Burt Reynolds. Men in white suits and girls in disco dresses bounced and twirled to the whining voices of the Bee-Gees and the moans of Donna Summer. Winners of the dance competition received timely prizes — eight-track tapes, lava lamps, mood rings, and Studio 54 T-shirts.

2 Twenty-five years ago my parents, new hires at rival law firms, met at a '50s party. It was the 1970s and my Mom, who normally tried to look like Jaclyn Smith (the brunette on "Charlie's Angels"), cut a striking figure in her poodle skirt and saddle shoes. A fading Polaroid shows her leaning against my Dad in his teen angel leather jacket, his hair greased up into an early Elvis do.

3 Nostalgia is not new. Snapshots my grandfather took in England during World War II show a group of B-17 pilots partying in riding boots and silk scarves, imitating the pilots of the First World War. No doubt in 1917 doughboys tried to impress French girls by impersonating Teddy Roosevelt's Rough Riders.

4 Why this appeal of the past? Why does every generation seem to find a previous era more interesting, more glamorous, more adventurous, more fun? In part, there is simply the desire to be young again. The forty-fifty somethings look back twenty years to a time when they were young, attractive, and idealistic — a time when their lives were new and their options open. To the teens and twenty-somethings this former era offers safety.

5 In the past we can play and feel secure. We can look back on the Seventies, the Fifties, even the Thirties because we survived them. We

358

find previous decades "simpler" and "better" because they existed before current problems. The 1970s seem simpler and more innocent because AIDS, cyberstalking, and crack were unknown. We forget, however, that the Seventies meant Cold War, Watergate, inflation, mass unemployment, and gas lines. Back in the Seventies, people like my parents could escape the malaise of the Carter era by dressing up like Fifties teens and dancing to do-wop music. No doubt, in their eagerness to find the perfect skirt, locate the right nail polish, and fix their hair to look like Annette Funicello's they forgot that the simpler and nicer era of the Fifties meant segregation, sexual hypocrisy, air raid drills, McCarthyism, and war in Korea.

Nostalgia — that longing for the past — has deleterious elements.   6
It can trivialize problems and distort our view of history. It can mar our ability to think critically. Looking back on the Sixties, certain figures like Martin Luther King Jr. and John F. Kennedy emerge as icons. We forget they were controversial in their time and that intelligent men and women of good will opposed them. The complexity of Vietnam and the Civil Rights marches are blurred because we can look back and easily see in hindsight the right course the nation should have taken.

What we really look for in nostalgia is peace and direction. In the   7
past we can side with the winners, forgetting how stressful and fearful those times were. The Seventies parties evoke a time when all sexually transmitted diseases were curable with a penicillin shot, when feminism meant reading Fear of Flying, and people assumed racism would evaporate in a decade or two because the Love Boat was integrated. In reliving that era and trying to dance like younger and thinner Travoltas, we forget that the crowds who jammed the discos then lived in an era when imports were filling the parking lots, factories were closing, and experts predicted America was doomed to become a second-class nation owned by Japanese bankers and Arab sheiks.

Maybe I am reading too much into nostalgia, seeing a harmless   8
pastime as some kind of brain-deadening addiction. I just hope that in our desire to find the perfect costume, remember who won the Academy Award in 1978, or which team won the most Super Bowls in the Eighties we learn a little something about our past. Maybe in looking back and dressing up, we can think about the progress women and minorities have made. We might even imagine what it was like to

write without computers, conduct research without the Internet, and live without cable TV.

Questions for Review and Revision

1. What does the student see as the principal reasons people enjoy pretending to be in another era?
2. How does the student open the paper? Does the opening quickly demonstrate the writer's subject?
3. How is the essay organized? How effective is the paragraph structure?
4. *Critical Thinking:* Could this student provide a more in-depth analysis of nostalgia? Does this paper do more than simply describe nostalgia? Can you think of other ideas this essay might explore?
5. Do you see any paragraphs that could be deleted or should be expanded?
6. Read the paper aloud. How effectively does the choice of words establish the writer's tone and style?

Writing Suggestions

1. Write an essay analyzing a current fad, trend, or common behavior. Include key details, and suggest the cause or significance of your subject.
2. *Collaborative Writing:* Discuss this essay with a group of students, and work together to develop a statement on nostalgia. What current examples of nostalgia can your group identify? Do you see nostalgia as a harmless pastime or something with negative implications?

ANALYSIS CHECKLIST

Before submitting your paper, review these points.

1. Is the topic clearly limited?

2. Is your approach appropriate for the writing context?

3. Do you present enough evidence?

4. Have you evaluated sources for inaccuracy or bias?

5. Have you avoided errors in logic?

6. Are your research methods clearly explained?

7. Do you clearly present the results of your analysis?

8. Have you considered alternative interpretations?

 Companion Web Site

See **http://sundance.heinle.com** for information on writing analysis.

 InfoTrac® College Edition

For additional reading go to InfoTrac College edition, your on-line research library, at **http://infotrac.thomsonlearning.com.**

- Enter the search term "analysis" using Keywords.
- Enter the name of an author you read in this chapter using Keywords.
- Enter a theme or idea your class discussed using Keywords.

7

Division and Classification

WHAT ARE DIVISION AND CLASSIFICATION?

Division helps readers understand complex subjects by separating them into parts. *Classification,* often used to aid decision making, rates subjects by placing them on a scale of different categories.

Division

If you enter a hospital, you will probably see signs directing you to different departments: cardiology, radiology, psychiatry, and pediatrics. Hospitals are divided into specific services. Universities consist of separate colleges, such as business and liberal arts. American literature can be divided into courses by historical era (nineteenth- and twentieth-century American writers), by genre (American poetry and American drama), or by special interest (women's literature and science fiction). Corporations place personnel into different departments: design, production, maintenance, marketing, sales, and accounting.

Division makes complicated subjects easier to comprehend and work with. For example, the human body is overwhelmingly intricate. In order to understand how it functions, medical disciplines divide it into systems: digestive, respiratory, nervous, muscular-skeletal, reproductive, and others. By studying individual systems, medical students come to a fuller understanding of how the whole body operates. Crime is such a vast social problem that writers discuss it in terms of traditional divisions—robbery, car theft, homicide, and fraud—or invent their own categories, dividing crime by causes: power, greed, identity, and revenge. People use the term *depression* to express everything from minor disappointment to suicidal despair. In order to inform patients about the variety of depressive illnesses, a mental health brochure divides the disorder into specific types:

Bereavement—a 2–8 week process of grieving with sad and empty feelings after the death of someone important to you. May linger for much longer after loss of parent, child, or partner, but tends to gradually improve over time. You should observe steady readjustment to your changed world and resumption of social activities and pleasures.

Adjustment Reaction—a period of up to 6 months after a major stressful event during which depressed mood, or hopeless feelings are more intense than normal and interfere with daily social and school or work activities. Like BEREAVEMENT, it is often helped by brief crisis therapy or family therapy.

Major Depression—depressed mood or loss of interests with a variety of the symptoms and feelings of depression discussed earlier, lasting at least 2 weeks. Major depression ranges from mild cases with few symptoms to severe cases (known as "*clinical depression*") marked by a persistent bleak outlook which may lead to thoughts of escape through suicide. Depression may begin to lift after several weeks or may become chronic, lasting 2 years or more.

In this case division presents readers with a series of definitions. Division writing can also organize a set of narratives, descriptions, processes, or persuasive arguments.

Critical Thinking for Writing Division

Dividing any subject can be challenging. Would it make more sense to explain American politics to a foreign visitor in terms of political parties or specific issues? Would you group used cars by year, by price, or by model? When writing division, follow these guidelines:

1. **Avoid oversimplifying your subject.** You have no doubt seen magazine articles announcing three kinds of bosses, four types of marriages, or five methods of childrearing. Writers often invent descriptive or humorous labels, warning you to avoid "the toxic controller" or advising you how to negotiate with the "whiny wimp." Although these divisions can be amusing and insightful, they can trivialize or oversimplify a subject. Not all people or situations can neatly fit into three or four types. *When discussing complex topics, inform readers of possible exceptions to your categories.*

2. **Select a method of division that includes all parts of the whole.** If you divide college students into four types, for example, make sure everyone on campus is included in one of the groups. Eliminate potential gaps. You cannot simply divide students into Protestants, Catholics, and Jews if some are agnostics or Muslims. Every member or part of the whole must be accounted for.

3. **Make sure individual parts fit only one category.** If you were to divide businesses by geographical region—North, South, East, and West—how would you handle a company with operations on both coasts? If items can fit in more than one category, your method of division is not suited to your subject. It might be better to discuss businesses in terms of their gross sales, products, or size rather than location.

4. **Avoid categories that include too many differences.** If you were examining people of different ages, it could make sense to write about people in groups from age thirty to forty or fifty to sixty. But a category of age sixty to seventy would include both working and retired people, both those still paying into Social Security and those receiving benefits. It might be more accurate to break this group into people who are age sixty to sixty-five and those who are older than sixty-five.

Classification

Like division, classification breaks a complex subject into parts. But for classification, the categories are ranked or rated according to a single standard. In medicine, for example, burns are classified first-, second-, and third-degree based on the amount of tissue damage. Teachers grade tests according to the number of correct answers. Insurance companies set rates based on their clients' history of loss. Motion pictures are judged G, PG, PG13, R, NC17, and X based on depictions of sex and violence.

Perhaps no more serious an incident occurs in society than when an individual causes the death of another. In addressing this issue, the law identifies a range of situations in which a fatality occurs and ranks them from the most to least objectionable:

Felonious homicide. The wrongful killing of a human being, of any age or either sex, without justification or excuse in law; of which offense there are two degrees, manslaughter and murder.

Homicide by misadventure. The accidental killing of another, where the slayer is doing a lawful act, unaccompanied by any criminally careless or reckless conduct. . . .

Homicide by necessity. A species of justifiable homicide, because it arises from some unavoidable necessity, without any will, intention, or desire, and without any inadvertence or negligence in the party killing, and therefore without any shadow of blame.

Classification helps people to make decisions and to direct actions. Classifications can set prices, establish salaries, and in some cases save lives.

The importance of classification is demonstrated by the use of triage in emergency medicine. When a hospital is flooded with accident victims, doctors place patients into three categories: those who will die with or without immediate medical attention, those who will survive without emergency care, and those who will survive only if treated without delay. The last group is given priority to ensure that doctors do not waste time on the dying or those with minor injuries.

Critical Thinking for Writing Classification

As with division writing, classification requires careful planning. To avoid common problems, follow these guidelines:

1. **Avoid confusing division with classification.** Perhaps the most frequent mistake students make in classification writing papers is simply dividing a subject into parts. *Classification not only divides a subject into parts but also rates the parts on a scale.*
2. **Establish a clearly defined standard of measurement.** To successfully teach writing, for example, an English professor must provide students with a clear understanding of what distinguishes an A paper from a B paper. Even if you are making up your own categories, each one should be clearly defined so readers understand what distinguishes one from the other.
3. **Do not mix standards.** You can classify automobiles, for instance, from the cheapest to the most expensive, from the safest to the most dangerous, or from the most fuel efficient to the least fuel efficient. But you cannot write a classification essay that rates cars as being safe, fuel efficient, or expensive since many cars could be both expensive and fuel efficient.
4. **Arrange categories in order.** Organize the categories so they follow a ladder-like pattern, such as judging items from the best to the worst, the cheapest to the most expensive, or the newest to the oldest.
5. **Provide enough categories to include all parts of the whole.** If you were to classify cars as being either American or foreign, how would you account for Toyotas produced in the United States or Chryslers assembled in Mexico?

STRATEGIES FOR READING DIVISION AND CLASSIFICATION

As you read the division and classification entries in this chapter, keep the following questions in mind.

Meaning

1. What is the writer trying to explain by dividing or classifying his or her topic? Does the division or classification help you understand the subject better than a simple description would?
2. Do the divisions risk oversimplifying the subject?
3. Do the classification essays have a clearly defined standard?
4. Do the standards seem fair? Do they adequately measure what they claim to evaluate?

Strategy

1. How does the writer introduce or set up the division or classification?
2. How does the author use definitions and examples to create distinct categories?
3. Does the writer use standard divisions and classifications accepted by a particular discipline or profession, or does he or she invent new ones?
4. Does the writer use division or classification to explain a topic, or is it used as a device to recommend one item over another?

Language

1. What does the level of language reveal about the writer's discipline and intended audience?
2. What words does the author use to describe or define standards of classification? Do you detect a bias?

RUSSELL BAKER

Russell Baker (1925–) was born in Virginia and raised in New Jersey and Maryland. After serving in World War II, he attended Johns Hopkins University. After graduating in 1947, Baker became a reporter for a Baltimore newspaper. In the 1950s he joined the staff of the New York Times *and covered the White House and the State Department. In 1962 he began writing "Observer," a column that now appears in hundreds of newspapers. In the 1980s he published two autobiographical books,* Growing Up *and* The Good Times. *Many of his columns appeared in the collection* There's a Country in My Cellar *in 1990.*

The Plot Against People

OVERVIEW: *In this humorous piece, Baker invents three categories of common objects we encounter. As you read the essay, notice how Baker uses* definition, description, *and* example.

Inanimate objects are classified into three major categories—those that don't work, those that break down and those that get lost.   1

thesis

The goal of all inanimate objects is to resist man and ultimately to defeat him, and the three major classifications are based on the method each object uses to achieve its purpose. As a general rule, any object capable of breaking down at the moment when it is needed most will do so. The automobile is typical of the category.   2

explains categories

With the cunning typical of its breed, the automobile never breaks down while entering a filling station with a large staff of idle mechanics. It waits until it reaches a downtown intersection in the middle of the rush hour, or until it is fully loaded with family and luggage on the Ohio Turnpike.   3

category #1

Thus it creates maximum misery, inconvenience, frustration and irritability among its human cargo, thereby reducing its owner's life span.   4

Washing machines, garbage disposals, lawn mowers, light bulbs, automatic laundry dryers, water pipes, furnaces, electrical fuses, television tubes, hose nozzles, tape recorders, slide projectors—all are in league with the automobile to take their turn at breaking down whenever life threatens to flow smoothly for their human enemies.   5

examples

Many inanimate objects, of course, find it extremely difficult to break down. Pliers, for example, and gloves and keys are almost totally incapable of breaking down. Therefore, they have had to evolve a different technique for resisting man.   6

category #2

7   <u>They get lost.</u> Science has still not solved the mystery of how they do it, and no man has ever caught one of them in the act of getting lost. The most plausible theory is that they have developed a secret method of locomotion which they are able to conceal the instant a human eye falls upon them.

8   It is not uncommon for a pair of pliers to climb all the way from the cellar to the attic in its single-minded determination to raise its owner's blood pressure. Keys have been known to burrow three feet under mattresses. Women's purses, despite their great weight, frequently travel through six or seven rooms to find a hiding space under a couch.

9   Scientists have been struck by the fact that things that break down virtually never get lost, while things that get lost hardly ever break down.

examples

10   A furnace, for example, will invariably break down at the depth of the first winter cold wave, but it will never get lost. A woman's purse, which after all does have some inherent capacity for breaking down, hardly ever does; it almost invariably chooses to get lost.

11   Some persons believe this constitutes evidence that inanimate objects are not entirely hostile to man, and that a negotiated peace is possible. After all, they point out, a furnace could infuriate a man even more thoroughly by getting lost than by breaking down, just as a glove could upset him far more by breaking down than by getting lost.

12   Not everyone agrees, however, that this indicates a conciliatory attitude among inanimate objects. Many say it merely proves that furnaces, gloves and pliers are incredibly stupid.

13   <u>The third class of objects—those that don't work—is the most curious of all.</u> These include such objects as barometers, car clocks, cigarette lighters, flashlights and toy train locomotives. It is inaccurate, of course, to say that they never work. They work once, usually for the first few hours after being brought home, and then quit. Thereafter, they never work again.

category #3

examples

14   In fact, it is widely assumed that they are built for the purpose of not working. Some people have reached advanced ages without ever seeing some of these objects—barometers, for example—in working order.

15   Science is utterly baffled by the entire category. There are many theories about it. The most interesting holds that the things that don't work have attained the highest state possible for an inanimate object, the state to which things that break down and things that get lost can still only aspire.

16   They have truly defeated man by conditioning him never to expect anything of them, and in return they have given man the only peace he receives from inanimate society. He does not expect his barometer to work, his electric locomotive to run, his cigarette lighter to light or his flashlight to illuminate, and when they don't, it does not raise his blood pressure.

conclusion

He cannot attain that peace with furnaces and keys and cars and wom-   17
en's purses as long as he demands that they work for their keep.

Understanding Meaning

1. What is Baker's purpose?
2. How have objects "defeated" people?
3. Are there objects that you frankly do not expect to work?
4. *Critical Thinking:* Humor is often based on acute observation. What is Baker saying about the lives of Americans, who often measure their success or happiness by the number of objects they possess? Do all the things we yearn to have truly enrich or merely complicate our lives?

Evaluating Strategy

1. Why is the essay's introduction important? Is it effective in setting up the body of the essay?
2. How important are the examples Baker uses to define each category? Can readers relate to these?
3. Baker creates three categories. Would the humor of the essay wear thin if he invented four, five, or six categories? Is there a limit to audience attention when reading for entertainment?

Appreciating Language

1. Baker uses the third person to describe people's experiences with objects. Would a first person approach, emphasizing his personal encounters with things, have the same effect?
2. *Critical Thinking:* Throughout this 1968 essay Baker uses male references— "man" and "he." Would a modern editor insist on nonsexist language? Would you suggest making changes? Why or why not?

Connections across the Disciplines

1. Compare this essay to Martin Luther King Jr.'s "The Ways of Meeting Oppression" (page 381) and Judith Viorst's "Friends, Good Friends—Such Good Friends" (page 375). How do the authors organize their essays? What transitional devices do they use to separate each item?

2. Consider John Brook's essay about the telephone (page 492). What can the study of common objects reveal about our culture, civilization, and values? Do objects come to define us?

Writing Suggestions

1. Write a short essay, using Baker's as a model, to humorously classify college courses, professors, local restaurants, garages, or stores. Define each type clearly, and illustrate with examples.
2. *Collaborative Writing:* Discuss Baker's essay with a group of students, and work together to create a short, humorous, updated version that includes CDs, computers, e-mail, answering machines, and VCRs.

MARY MEBANE

Mary Mebane (1933–) received a doctorate in English from the University of North Carolina. She teaches English at the University of South Carolina at Columbia. Mebane is the author of a play, Take a Sad Song, *and two autobiographical books,* Mary *and* Mary Wayfarer. *In 1982 she received a National Endowment for the Arts Creative Writing Fellowship. Much of her work has focused on the experience of African Americans in the South.*

Black Wasn't Beautiful

OVERVIEW: *This section from Mebane's autobiography* Mary *(1981) details the four options that dark-complexioned African-American women faced in the segregated South. Attending a black college in the 1950s, Mebane encountered a rigid system of discrimination in which lighter-skinned African Americans considered themselves superior to those with darker skin.*

In the fall of 1951 during my first week at North Carolina College, a black school in Durham, the chairman's wife, who was indistinguishable from a white woman, stopped me one day in the hall. She wanted to see me, she said.

When I went to her office, she greeted me with a big smile. "You know," she said, "you made the highest mark on the verbal part of the examination." She was referring to the examination that the entire freshman class took upon entering the college. In spite of her smile, her eyes and tone of voice were saying, "How could this black-skinned girl score higher on the verbal than some of the students who've had more advantages than she? It must be some sort of fluke." I felt it, but I managed to smile my thanks and back off. For here at North Carolina College, social class and color were the primary criteria used in deciding status. The faculty assumed light-skinned students were more intelligent, and they were always a bit nonplussed when a dark-skinned student did well, especially if she was a girl.

I don't know whether African men recently transported to the New World considered themselves handsome or, more important, whether they considered African women beautiful in comparison with native American Indian women or immigrant European women. But one thing I know for sure: By the twentieth century, really black skin on a woman was considered ugly in this country. In the 1950s this was particularly true among those who were exposed to college. Black skin was to be disguised at all costs. Since a black face is rather hard to disguise, many women took refuge in ludicrous makeup.

4   I observed all through elementary and high school, in various entertainments, the girls were placed on the stage in order of color. And very black ones didn't get into the front row. If they were past caramel-brown, to the back row they would go. Nobody questioned the justice of this—neither the students nor the teachers.

5   Oddly enough, the lighter-skinned black male did not seem to feel so much prejudice toward the black black woman. It was no accident, I felt, that Mr. Harrison, the eighth-grade teacher, who was reddish-yellow himself, once protested to the science and math teacher about the fact that he always assigned sweeping duties to Doris and Ruby, two black black girls. Mr. Harrison said to them one day in the other teacher's presence, "You must be some bad girls. Every day I come down here you all are sweeping." The science and math teacher got the point and didn't ask them to sweep any more. Uneducated black males, too, sometimes related very well to the black black woman. They had been less indoctrinated by the white society around them.

6   Because of the stigma attached to having dark skin, a black black woman had to do many things to find a place for herself. One possibility was to attach herself to a light-skinned woman, hoping that some of the magic would rub off on her. A second was to make herself sexually available, hoping thereby to attract a mate. Third, she could resign herself to a more chaste life-style—either (for the professional woman) teaching and work in established churches or (for the uneducated woman) domestic work and zealous service in "holy and sanctified" churches.

7   Lucy had chosen the first route. Lucy was short, skinny, short-haired and black black, and thus unacceptable. So she made her choice. She selected Patricia, the lightest-skinned girl in the school, as her friend and followed her around. Patricia and her friends barely tolerated Lucy, but Lucy smiled and doggedly hung on, hoping that those who noticed Patricia might notice her also. Though I felt shame for her behavior, even then I understood.

8   A fourth avenue open to the black black woman is excellence in a career. Since in the South the field most accessible to such women is education, a great many of them prepared to become teachers. But here, too, the black black woman had problems. Grades weren't given to her lightly in school, nor were promotions on the job. She had to pass examinations with flying colors or be left behind. She had to be overqualified for a job because otherwise she didn't stand a chance of getting it—and she was competing only with other blacks.

The black woman's training would pay off in the 1970s. With the arrival 9
of integration, the black black woman would find, paradoxically enough,
that her skin color in an integrated situation was not the handicap it had
been in an all-black situation. But it wasn't until the middle and late 1960s,
when the post-1945 generation of black males arrived in college, that I
noticed any change in the situation at all. *He* wore an Afro and *she* wore
an Afro, and sometimes the only way you could tell them apart was when
his Afro was taller than hers. Black had become beautiful. It was then that
the dread I felt at dealing with the college-educated black male began to
ease. Even now, though, when I have occasion to engage in any transaction with a college-educated black man, I gauge his age. If I guess he was
born after 1945, I feel confident that the transaction will turn out all right. If
he probably was born before 1945, my stomach tightens, I find myself taking shallow breaths, and I try to state my business and escape as soon as
possible.

When the grades from the first quarter at North Carolina College came 10
out, I had the highest average in the freshman class. The chairman's wife
called me into her office again. We did a replay of the same scene we had
played during the first week of the term. She complimented me on my
grades. Then she reached into a drawer and pulled out a copy of the freshman English final examination. She asked me to take the exam over again.

At first I couldn't believe what she was saying. I had taken the course 11
under another teacher; and it was so incredible to her that I should have
made the highest score in the class that she was trying to test me again personally. For a few moments I knew rage so intense that I wanted to take my
fists and start punching her. I have seldom hated anyone so deeply. I handed
the examination back to her and walked out.

Understanding Meaning

1. What caused the African-American community to discriminate against those
   with dark skin?
2. What evidence of discrimination does Mebane offer?
3. Briefly describe the four options dark-skinned women faced.
4. How did gender affect people's attitudes toward dark-skinned women?
5. What changes occurred in the 1970s?
6. *Critical Thinking:* What other examples of discrimination *within* a group can you
   think of? Have some members of ethnic groups attempted to distance themselves from those seen as less desirable by mainstream society, hence the conflict, for example, between "lace curtain Irish" and "shanty Irish"? Do women

discriminate against other women they see as less attractive, less respectable, too traditional, or too radical?

Evaluating Strategy

1. Mebane begins and ends the piece with a narrative. How effective is this device?
2. *Other Modes:* Where does Mebane use *comparison* and *contrast* within her essay?

Appreciating Language

1. How does Mebane describe the differences among African Americans?
2. What does her word choice reveal about her attitudes toward those who discriminated against her?

Connections across the Disciplines

1. Compare Mebane's account of discrimination *within* the black community with Nathan McCall's essay (page 61), which discusses black-white racial conflict. How did these experiences shape the writers' attitudes? How did they respond to discrimination?
2. Martin Luther King Jr.'s essay (page 381) suggests three ways oppressed people respond to their condition. Does this essay suggest a fourth way? Do oppressed people often build a separate society mirroring the values of their oppressors?

Writing Suggestions

1. Write an essay describing a situation in which you were unfairly classified because of your race, age, appearance, or occupation.
2. *Collaborative Writing:* Discuss Mebane's essay with a small group of students. How often is discrimination internalized? Have members of the group offer examples they have witnessed or experienced. After taking notes, work together to write a brief division or classification paper stating the reasons for this behavior.

JUDITH VIORST

Judith Viorst (1936–) is best known for the columns she writes for Redbook. *She has published several children's books, including* Alexander and the Terrible, Horrible, No Good, Very Bad Day *(1982) and* Sad Underwear and Other Complications *(1995). She has also written a number of collections of light verse, including* It's Hard to Be Hip Over Thirty and Other Tragedies of Modern Life *(1970),* How did I Get to Be Forty and Other Atrocities *(1984), and* Suddenly Sixty and Other Shocks of Later Life *(2000). She has also published a novel,* Murdering Mr. Monti: A Merry Little Tale of Sex and Violence *(1994).*

Friends, Good Friends — and Such Good Friends

OVERVIEW: *Before reading this essay, consider the friends you have had in your life. Did they belong to different types? Were school friends different from neighborhood friends or friends met through relatives?*

Women are friends, I once would have said, when they totally love and support and trust each other, and bare to each other the secrets of their souls, and run—no questions asked—to help each other, and tell harsh truths to each other (no, you can't wear that dress unless you lose ten pounds first) when harsh truths must be told. 1

Women are friends, I once would have said, when they share the same 2 affection for Ingmar Bergman, plus train rides, cats, warm rain, charades, Camus, and hate with equal ardor Newark and Brussels sprouts and Lawrence Welk and camping.

In other words, I once would have said that a friend is a friend all the 3 way, but now I believe that's a narrow point of view. For the friendships I have and the friendships I see are conducted at many levels of intensity, serve many different functions, meet different needs and range from those as all-the-way as the friendship of the soul sisters mentioned above to that of the most nonchalant and casual playmates.

Consider these varieties of friendship: 4

1. Convenience friends. These are women with whom, if our paths 5 weren't crossing all the time, we'd have no particular reason to be friends: a next-door neighbor, a woman in our car pool, the mother of one of our children's closest friends or maybe some mommy with whom we serve juice and cookies each week at the Glenwood Co-op Nursery.

6   Convenience friends are convenient indeed. They'll lend us their cups and silverware for a party. They'll drive our kids to soccer when we're sick. They'll take us to pick up our car when we need a lift to the garage. They'll even take our cats when we go on vacation. As we will for them.

7   But we don't, with convenience friends, ever come too close or tell too much; we maintain our public face and emotional distance. "Which means," says Elaine, "that I'll talk about being overweight but not about being depressed. Which means I'll admit being mad but not blind with rage. Which means that I might say that we're pinched this month but never that I'm worried sick over money."

8   But which doesn't mean that there isn't sufficient value to be found in these friendships of mutual aid, in convenience friends.

9   2. Special-interest friends. These friendships aren't intimate, and they needn't involve kids or silverware or cats. Their value lies in some interest jointly shared. And so we may have an office friend or a yoga friend or a tennis friend or a friend from the Women's Democratic Club.

10   "I've got one woman friend," says Joyce, "who likes, as I do, to take psychology courses. Which makes it nice for me—and nice for her. It's fun to go with someone you know and it's fun to discuss what you've learned, driving back from the classes." And for the most part, she says, that's all they discuss.

11   "I'd say that what we're doing is *doing* together, not being together," Suzanne says of her Tuesday-doubles friends. "It's mainly a tennis relationship, but we play together well. And I guess we all need to have a couple of playmates."

12   I agree.

13   My playmate is a shopping friend, a woman of marvelous taste, a woman who knows exactly *where* to buy *what*, and furthermore is a woman who always knows beyond a doubt what one ought to be buying. I don't have the time to keep up with what's new in eyeshadow, hemlines and shoes and whether the smock look is in or finished already. But since (oh, shame!) I care a lot about eyeshadow, hemlines and shoes, and since I don't *want* to wear smocks if the smock look is finished, I'm very glad to have a shopping friend.

14   3. Historical friends. We all have a friend who knew us when . . . maybe way back in Miss Meltzer's second grade, when our family lived in that three-room flat in Brooklyn, when our dad was out of work for seven months, when our brother Allie got in that fight where they had to call the police, when our sister married the endodontist from Yonkers and when, the morning after we lost our virginity, she was the first, the only, friend we told.

The years have gone by and we've gone separate ways and we've little   15
in common now, but we're still an intimate part of each other's past. And so
whenever we go to Detroit we always go to visit this friend of our girlhood.
Who knows how we looked before our teeth were straightened. Who knows
how we talked before our voice got un-Brooklyned. Who knows what we
ate before we learned about artichokes. And who, by her presence, puts us
in touch with an earlier part of ourself, a part of ourself it's important never
to lose.

"What this friend means to me and what I mean to her," says Grace, "is   16
having a sister without sibling rivalry. We know the texture of each other's
lives. She remembers my grandmother's cabbage soup. I remember the way
her uncle played the piano. There's simply no other friend who remembers
those things."

4. Crossroads friends. Like historical friends, our crossroads friends are   17
important for *what was*—for the friendship we shared at a crucial, now past,
time of life. A time, perhaps, when we roomed in college together; or
worked as eager young singles in the Big City together; or went together, as
my friend Elizabeth and I did, through pregnancy, birth and that scary first
year of new motherhood.

Crossroads friends forge powerful links, links strong enough to endure   18
with not much more contact than once-a-year letters at Christmas. And out
of respect for those crossroads years, for those dramas and dreams we once
shared, we will always be friends.

5. Cross-generational friends. Historical friends and crossroads friends   19
seem to maintain a special kind of intimacy—dormant but always ready to
be revived—and though we may rarely meet, whenever we do connect, it's
personal and intense. Another kind of intimacy exists in the friendships
that form across generations in what one woman calls her daughter-mother
and her mother-daughter relationships.

Evelyn's friend is her mother's age—"but I share so much more than I   20
ever could with my mother"—a woman she talks to of music, of books and
of life. "What I get from her is the benefit of her experience. What she
gets—and enjoys—from me is a youthful perspective. It's a pleasure for
both of us."

I have in my own life a precious friend, a woman of 65 who has lived very   21
hard, who is wise, who listens well; who has been where I am and can help
me understand it; and who represents not only an ultimate ideal mother to
me but also the person I'd like to be when I grow up.

In our daughter role we tend to do more than our share of self-revelation;   22
in our mother role we tend to receive what's revealed. It's another kind of

pleasure—playing wise mother to a questing younger person. It's another very lovely kind of friendship.

23   6. Part-of-a-couple friends. Some of the women we call our friends we never see alone—we see them as part of a couple at couples' parties. And though we share interests in many things and respect each other's views, we aren't moved to deepen the relationship. Whatever the reason, a lack of time or—and this is more likely—a lack of chemistry, our friendship remains in the context of a group. But the fact that our feeling on seeing each other is always, "I'm *so* glad she's here" and the fact that we spend half the evening talking together says that this too, in its own way, counts as a friendship.

24   (Other part-of-a-couple friends are the friends that came with the marriage, and some of these are friends we could live without. But sometimes, alas, she married our husband's best friend; and sometimes, alas, she *is* our husband's best friend. And so we find ourself dealing with her, somewhat against our will, in a spirit of what I'll call *reluctant* friendship.)

25   7. Men who are friends. I wanted to write just of women friends, but the women I've talked to won't let me—they say I must mention man-woman friendships too. For these friendships can be just as close and as dear as those that we form with women. Listen to Lucy's description of one such friendship:

26   "We've found we have things to talk about that are different from what he talks about with my husband and different from what I talk about with his wife. So sometimes we call on the phone or meet for lunch. There are similar intellectual interests—we always pass on to each other the books that we love—but there's also something tender and caring too."

27   In a couple of crises, Lucy says, "he offered himself for talking and for helping. And when someone died in his family he wanted me there. The sexual, flirty part of our friendship is very small, but *some*—just enough to make it fun and different." She thinks—and I agree—that the sexual part, though small, is always *some*, is always there when a man and a woman are friends.

28   It's only in the past few years that I've made friends with men, in the sense of a friendship that's *mine*, not just part of two couples. And achieving with them the ease and the trust I've found with women friends has value indeed. Under the dryer at home last week, putting on mascara and rouge, I comfortably sat and talked with a fellow named Peter. Peter, I finally decided, could handle the shock of me minus mascara under the dryer. Because we care for each other. Because we're friends.

8. There are medium friends, and pretty good friends, and very good   29
friends indeed, and these friendships are defined by their level of intimacy.
And what we'll reveal at each of these levels of intimacy is calibrated with
care. We might tell a medium friend, for example, that yesterday we had a
fight with our husband. And we might tell a pretty good friend that this
fight with our husband made us so mad that we slept on the couch. And we
might tell a very good friend that the reason we got so mad in that fight that
we slept on the couch had something to do with that girl who works in his
office. But it's only to our very best friends that we're willing to tell all, to
tell what's going on with that girl in his office.

The best of friends, I still believe, totally love and support and trust   30
each other, and bare to each other the secrets of their souls, and run—no
questions asked—to help each other, and tell harsh truths to each other
when they must be told.

But we needn't agree about everything (only 12-year-old girl friends   31
agree about *everything*) to tolerate each other's point of view. To accept
without judgment. To give and to take without ever keeping score. And to
be there, as I am for them and as they are for me, to comfort our sorrows, to
celebrate our joys.

Understanding Meaning

1. What was Viorst's original view of women friends? How did she define them?
2. How do convenience friends differ from special-interest friends? Are they both
   superficial relationships in many ways? Why or why not?
3. Viorst states that she did not want to include men in her article, but her female
   friends insisted that man-woman friendships should be included. Does this
   reflect a social change? Do you think women today have more friendships with
   men, especially in the workplace, than their mothers or grandmothers did?
4. *Critical Thinking:* Viorst writes almost exclusively about female friendship. Do
   you think that men, too, have the same type of friends—convenience friends,
   special interest friends, historical friends, etc.? Are male friendships different?

Evaluating Strategy

1. Viorst divides friends into types rather than classifying them from best friends
   to acquaintances. Does her approach make more sense? Can friendships
   change? Can a convenience friend become over time your best friend?

2. Viorst mentions other women in her essay. Does this make her observations more effective? If she limited her commentary to only her friends, would the essay be as influential?

3. *Other Modes:* Where does Viorst use *description* and *comparison* to develop her essay?

4. *Critical Thinking:* Viorst wrote this essay in 1977. Since then has technology created new communities and new friendships? Should on-line friends be included?

Appreciating Language

1. This essay first appeared in *Redbook.* Is there anything in her word choices or tone that indicate she was writing to a female audience?

2. Consider the words we use to describe people we include in our lives: *friend, acquaintance, colleague, partner, pal.* Do men and women define these words differently?

Connections across the Disciplines

1. Louis Gates Jr.'s "One Internet: Two Nations" (page 268) argues that African Americans are not entering cyberspace. Does this suggest that blacks are not developing a new source of friendship?

2. Jonathan Ritter describes computer hackers (page 185) as self-involved recluses who only relate to fellow hackers. Would they be examples of special-interest friends?

Writing Suggestions

1. Write a short essay about the types of friendships you have developed. Have you maintained many friendships that began in childhood? Why or why not?

2. Write a classification essay categorizing people who only take from friends, those who share with friends, and those who only seem to give in relationships. Provide examples of each type.

3. *Collaborative Writing:* Discuss Viorst's essay with a group of students. Do her comments seem to apply exclusively to women's friendships? Why or why not? Write a brief comparison paper contrasting the different ways men and women develop friendships. Is one gender more competitive? Do men or women seem to have or need more friends?

MARTIN LUTHER KING JR.

Martin Luther King Jr. (1929–1968) was a leading figure in the Civil Rights movement in the 1950s and 1960s. A noted minister, King blended his deeply felt religious values and his sense of political and social justice. He created the Southern Christian Leadership Conference, organized many demonstrations, and lobbied for voting rights. In 1964 he received the Nobel Peace Prize. He was assassinated in 1968.

The Ways of Meeting Oppression

OVERVIEW: *In this section from his 1958 book* Stride toward Freedom, *King classifies three ways oppressed people have responded to oppression. King uses classification to rate which response is the most effective and concludes his comments persuading readers to accept his choice.*

Oppressed people deal with their oppression in three characteristic ways. 1
One way is acquiescence: The oppressed resign themselves to their doom. They tacitly adjust themselves to oppression, and thereby become conditioned to it. In every movement toward freedom some of the oppressed prefer to remain oppressed. Almost 2,800 years ago Moses set out to lead the children of Israel from the slavery of Egypt to the freedom of the promised land. He soon discovered that slaves do not always welcome their deliverers. They become accustomed to being slaves. They would rather bear those ills they have, as Shakespeare pointed out, than flee to others that they know not of. They prefer the "fleshpots of Egypt" to the ordeals of emancipation.

There is such a thing as the freedom of exhaustion. Some people are so 2
worn down by the yoke of oppression that they give up. A few years ago in the slum areas of Atlanta, a Negro guitarist used to sing almost daily: "Been down so long that down don't bother me." This is the type of negative freedom and resignation that often engulfs the life of the oppressed.

But this is not the way out. To accept passively an unjust system is to 3
cooperate with that system; thereby the oppressed become as evil as the oppressor. Noncooperation with evil is as much a moral obligation as is cooperation with good. The oppressed must never allow the conscience of the oppressor to slumber. Religion reminds every man that he is his brother's keeper. To accept injustice or segregation passively is to say to the oppressor that his actions are morally right. It is a way of allowing his conscience to fall asleep. At this moment the oppressed fails to be his brother's keeper. So acquiescence—while often the easier way—is not the moral way. It is the

way of the coward. The Negro cannot win the respect of his oppressor by acquiescing; he merely increases the oppressor's arrogance and contempt. Acquiescence is interpreted as proof of the Negro's inferiority. The Negro cannot win the respect of the white people of the South or the peoples of the world if he is willing to sell the future of his children for his personal and immediate comfort and safety.

4   A second way that oppressed people sometimes deal with oppression is to resort to physical violence and corroding hatred. Violence often brings about momentary results. Nations have frequently won their independence in battle. But in spite of temporary victories, violence never brings permanent peace. It solves no social problem; it merely creates new and more complicated ones.

5   Violence as a way of achieving racial injustice is both impractical and immoral. It is impractical because it is a descending spiral ending in destruction for all. The old law of an eye for an eye leaves everybody blind. It is immoral because it seeks to humiliate the opponent rather than win his understanding; it seeks to annihilate rather than to convert. Violence is immoral because it thrives on hatred rather than love. It destroys community and makes brotherhood impossible. It leaves society in monologue rather than dialogue. Violence ends by defeating itself. It creates bitterness in the survivors and brutality in the destroyers. A voice echoes through time saying to every potential Peter, "Put up your sword."* History is cluttered with the wreckage of nations that failed to follow this command.

6   If the American Negro and other victims of oppression succumb to the temptation of using violence in the struggle for freedom, future generations will be the recipients of a desolate night of bitterness, and our chief legacy to them will be an endless reign of meaningless chaos. Violence is not the way.

7   The third way open to oppressed people in their quest for freedom is the way of nonviolent resistance. Like the synthesis in Hegelian philosophy, the principle of nonviolent resistance seeks to reconcile the truths of two opposites—the acquiescence and violence—while avoiding the extremes and immoralities of both. The nonviolent resister agrees with the person who acquiesces that one should not be physically aggressive toward his opponent; but he balances the equation by agreeing with the person of violence that evil must be resisted. He avoids the nonresistance of the former and the violent resistance of the latter. With nonviolent resistance, no indi-

---

*The apostle Peter had drawn his sword to defend Christ from arrest. The voice was Christ's, who surrendered himself for trial and crucifixion (John 18:11).

vidual or group need submit to any wrong, nor need anyone resort to violence in order to right a wrong.

It seems to me that this is the method that must guide the actions of the Negro in the present crisis in race relations. Through nonviolent resistance the Negro will be able to rise to the noble height of opposing the unjust system while loving the perpetrators of the system. The Negro must work passionately and unrelentingly for full stature as a citizen, but he must not use inferior methods to gain it. He must never come to terms with falsehood, malice, hate, or destruction.

Nonviolent resistance makes it possible for the Negro to remain in the South and struggle for his rights. The Negro's problem will not be solved by running away. He cannot listen to the glib suggestion of those who would urge him to migrate en masse to other sections of the country. By grasping his great opportunity in the South he can make a lasting contribution to the moral strength of the nation and set a sublime example of courage for generations yet unborn.

By nonviolent resistance, the Negro can also enlist all men of good will in his struggle for equality. The problem is not a purely racial one, with Negroes set against whites. In the end, it is not a struggle between people at all, but a tension between justice and injustice. Nonviolent resistance is not aimed against oppressors but against oppression. Under its banner consciences, not racial groups, are enlisted.

Understanding Meaning

1. Briefly describe the three ways people respond to oppression, according to King. Do you know of a fourth or fifth way? Do people, for instance, respond to oppression by blaming each other?
2. Humility is a Christian value. How does King, a minister, argue that humble acceptance of injustice is immoral?
3. King admits that nations have won freedom through violence, but why does he reject it for African Americans?
4. *Critical Thinking:* King defines the third way as a blend or synthesis of the first two. Why does he argue that this last manner is the most successful? What are its advantages?

Evaluating Strategy

1. Why does King use classification to suggest a solution instead of writing a direct persuasive argument?

2. How does King use his religious values as a way of arguing the desirability of his choice?
3. What transition statements does King use to direct his readers?

Appreciating Language

1. How does King define the difference between "acquiescence" and "nonviolent resistance"?
2. What do King's use of biblical analogies and reference to Hegelian philosophy reveal about his intended audience?

Connections across the Disciplines

1. In attempting to define happiness, John Ciardi (page 189) suggests the best way is to define the outer boundaries and work toward the center. Does King use this device in classifying or ranking responses to oppression?
2. Manning Marable (page 578) and Shelby Steele (page 582) argue whether or not African Americans should be compensated for slavery. How important is it for African Americans to come to terms with past oppression in order to make progress?

Writing Suggestions

1. Use King's essay as a model to write your own classification paper revealing the way people generally respond to a common issue or problem—the death of a loved one, the loss of a job, the discovery that a partner has been unfaithful, or being victimized. Rank the responses from the least effective to the most effective.
2. *Collaborative Writing:* Discuss King's classification with a group of students. How many people suffering oppression appear to be following his "third way"? Have a member of the group take notes, then work together to draft a short paper dividing or classifying, if possible, your group's responses.

JAMES AUSTIN

Dr. James Austin (1925–) graduated from Harvard Medical School and is a specialist in neurology. He devoted more than twenty years to research on the brain. While serving as professor and chairman of the Department of Neurology at the University of Colorado Medical School, he received the American Association of Neuropathologists Prize. Austin has also earned a reputation as a writer with an ability to make complicated scientific issues understandable to general readers.

Four Kinds of Chance

OVERVIEW: *James Austin has written widely on the role of chance or luck in scientific discovery. In this article, written for the* Saturday Review *(1974), he classifies the four kinds of chance that occur in scientific research. Luck, he explains, is not as simple as drawing a winning hand in poker. As you read the article, consider how many of the varieties of chance you have experienced.*

What is chance? Dictionaries define it as something fortuitous that happens 1 unpredictably without discernable human intention. Chance is unintentional and capricious, but we needn't conclude that chance is immune from human intervention. Indeed, chance plays several distinct roles when humans react creatively with one another and with their environment.

We can readily distinguish four varieties of chance if we consider that 2 they each involve a different kind of motor activity and a special kind of sensory receptivity. The varieties of chance also involve distinctive personality traits and differ in the way one particular individual influences them.

Chance I is the pure blind luck that comes with no effort on our part. If, 3 for example, you are sitting at a bridge table of four, it's "in the cards" for you to receive a hand of all 13 spades, but it will come up only once in every 6.3 trillion deals. You will ultimately draw this lucky hand—with no intervention on your part—but it does involve a longer wait than most of us have time for.

Chance II evokes the kind of luck Charles Kettering had in mind when 4 he said: "Keep on going and the chances are you will stumble on something, perhaps when you are least expecting it. I have never heard of anyone stumbling on something sitting down."

In the sense referred to here, Chance II is not passive, but springs from 5 an energetic, generalized motor activity. A certain basal level of action "stirs up the pot," brings in random ideas that will collide and stick together in fresh combinations, lets chance operate. When someone, *anyone*, does swing into motion and keeps on going, he will increase the number of collisions between events. When a few events are linked together, they can then be exploited to have a fortuitous outcome, but many others, of course, cannot. Kettering was right. Press on. Something will turn up. We may term this the Kettering Principle.

6   In the two previous examples, a unique role of the individual person was either lacking or minimal. Accordingly, as we move on to Chance III, we see blind luck, but in camouflage. Chance presents the clue, the opportunity exists, but it would be missed except by that one person uniquely equipped to observe it, visualize it conceptually, and fully grasp its significance. Chance III involves a special receptivity and discernment unique to the recipient. Louis Pasteur characterized it for all time when he said: "Chance favors only the prepared mind."

7   Pasteur himself had it in full measure. But the classic example of his principle occurred in 1928, when Alexander Fleming's mind instantly fused at least five elements into a conceptually unified nexus. His mental sequences went something like this: (1) I see that a mold has fallen by accident into my culture dish; (2) the staphylococcal colonies residing near it failed to grow; (3) the mold must have secreted something that killed the bacteria; (4) I recall a similar experience once before; (5) if I could separate this new "something" from the mold, it could be used to kill staphylococci that cause human infections.

8   Actually, Fleming's mind was exceptionally well prepared for the penicillin mold. Six years earlier, while he was suffering from a cold, his own nasal drippings had found their way into a culture dish, for reasons not made entirely clear. He noted that nearby bacteria were killed, and astutely followed up the lead. His observations led him to discover a bactericidal enzyme present in nasal mucus and tears, called lysozyme. Lysozyme proved too weak to be of medical use, but imagine how receptive Fleming's mind was to the penicillin mold when it later happened on the scene!

9   One word evokes the quality of the operations involved in the first three kinds of chance. It is *serendipity*. The term describes the facility for encountering unexpected good luck, as the result of: accident (Chance I), general exploratory behavior (Chance II), or sagacity (Chance III). The word itself was coined by the Englishman-of-letters Horace Walpole, in 1754. He used it with reference to the legendary tales of the Three Princes of Serendip (Ceylon), who quite unexpectedly encountered many instances of good fortune on their travels. In today's parlance, we have usually watered down *serendipity* to mean the good luck that comes solely by accident.

We think of it as a result, not an ability. We have tended to lose sight of the element of sagacity, by which term Walpole wished to emphasize that some distinctive personal receptivity is involved.

There remains a fourth element in good luck, an unintentional but sub-   10
tle personal prompting of it. The English Prime Minister Benjamin Disraeli summed up the principle underlying Chance IV when he noted that "we make our fortunes and we call them fate." Disraeli, a politician of considerable practical experience, appreciated that we each shape our own destiny, at least to some degree. One might restate the principle as follows: *Chance favors the individualized action.*

In Chance IV the kind of luck is peculiar to one person, and like a per-   11
sonal hobby, it takes on a distinctive individual flavor. This form of chance is one-man-made, and it is as personal as a signature. . . . Chance IV has an elusive, almost miragelike, quality. Like a mirage, it is difficult to get a firm grip on, for it tends to recede as we pursue it and advance as we step back. But we still accept a mirage when we see it, because we vaguely understand the basis for the phenomenon. A strongly heated layer of air, less dense than usual, lies next to the earth, and it bends the light rays as they pass through. The resulting image may be magnified as if by a telescopic lens in the atmosphere, and real objects, ordinarily hidden far out of sight over the horizon, are brought forward and revealed to the eye. What happens in a mirage then, and in this form of chance, not only appears farfetched but indeed is farfetched.

About a century ago, a striking example of Chance IV took place in the   12
Spanish cave of Altamira.[1] There, one day in 1879, Don Marcelino de Sautuola was engaged in his hobby of archaeology, searching Altamira for bones and stones. With him was his daughter, Maria, who had asked him if she could come along to the cave that day. The indulgent father had said she could. Naturally enough, he first looked where he had always found heavy objects before, on the *floor* of the cave. But Maria, unhampered by any such preconceptions, looked not only at the floor but also all around the cave with the open-eyed wonder of a child! She looked up, exclaimed, and then he looked up, to see incredible works of art on the cave ceiling! The magnificent colored bison and other animals they saw at Altamira, painted more than 15,000 years ago, might lead one to call it "the Sistine Chapel of Prehistory." Passionately pursuing his interest in archaeology, de Sautuola, to

---

[1]The cave had first been discovered some years before by an enterprising hunting dog in search of game. Curiously, in 1932 the French cave of Lascaux was discovered by still another dog.

his surprise, discovered man's first paintings. In quest of science, he happened upon Art.

13   Yes, a dog did "discover" the cave, and the initial receptivity was his daughter's, but the pivotal reason for the cave paintings' discovery hinged on a long sequence of prior events originating in de Sautuola himself. For when we dig into the background of this amateur excavator, we find he was an exceptional person. Few Spaniards were out probing into caves 100 years ago. The fact that he—not someone else—decided to dig that day in the cave of Altamira was the culmination of his passionate interest in his hobby. Here was a rare man whose avocation had been to educate himself from scratch, as it were, in the science of archaeology and cave exploration. This was no simple passive recognizer of blind luck when it came his way, but a man whose unique interests served as an active creative thrust—someone whose own actions and personality would focus the events that led circuitously but inexorably to the discovery of man's first paintings.

14   Then, too, there is a more subtle manner. How do you give full weight to the personal interests that imbue your child with your own curiosity, that inspire her to ask to join you in your own musty hobby, and that then lead you to agree to her request at the critical moment? For many reasons, at Altamira, more than the special receptivity of Chance III was required—this was a different domain, that of the personality and its actions.

15   A century ago no one had the remotest idea our caveman ancestors were highly creative artists. Weren't their talents rather minor and limited to crude flint chippings? But the paintings at Altamira, like a mirage, would quickly magnify this diminutive view, bring up into full focus a distant, hidden era of man's prehistory, reveal sentient minds and well-developed aesthetic sensibilities to which men of any age might aspire. And like a mirage, the events at Altamira grew out of de Sautuola's heated personal quest and out of the invisible forces of chance we know exist yet cannot touch. Accordingly, one may introduce the term *altamirage* to identify the quality underlying Chance IV. Let us define it as the facility for encountering unexpected good luck as the result of highly individualized action. Altamirage goes well beyond the boundaries of serendipity in its emphasis on the role of personal action in chance.

16   Chance IV is favored by distinctive, if not eccentric, hobbies, personal life-styles, and modes of behavior peculiar to one individual, usually invested with some passion. The farther apart these personal activities are from the area under investigation, the more novel and unexpected will be the creative product of the encounter.

Understanding Meaning

1. What are the four categories of chance?
2. What is meant by "blind" or "dumb" luck? Give some examples from your own life.
3. What is the Kettering Principle? Would Edison's famous trial-and-error experiments to discover a filament for the incandescent lightbulb fit this kind of chance?
4. How does the Pasteur principle differ from the Kettering Principle?
5. How did the dog's discovery of a cave differ from "blind luck" or Chance I?
6. *Critical Thinking:* How often have you discovered things by chance? What role has chance played in your career and education? Does understanding Austin's four kinds of chance enhance your ability to be "lucky" in the future? Can you "make your own kind of luck"?

Evaluating Strategy

1. What principle does Austin use to divide chance into four categories?
2. What examples does Austin use to illustrate each type? Are they accessible by a general audience?
3. Would a chart aid in explaining the four types of chance?
4. *Other Modes:* How does Austin make use of *definition* and *narration* in developing his classification essay?

Appreciating Language

1. How much technical language does Austin include?
2. *Critical Thinking:* Is part of Austin's task in this article to invent new terms to create categories of chance? Do most of our words for chance—"luck," "fortune," "lot"—all suggest the same meaning?

Connections across the Disciplines

1. Relate this article to Carl Sagan's "Why We Need to Understand Science" (page 563) and Darrell Huff's "How to Lie with Statistics" (page 301). Do all these articles suggest a prevailing lack of critical thinking skills?
2. Would any of Austin's types of chance favor scientists researching a problem such as the Ebola virus (page 73)? Why or why not?

Writing Suggestions

1. List a number of instances in your life you considered lucky. Using Austin's four categories, write a paper categorizing your experiences. Have you ever gotten past Chance I?

2. *Collaborative Writing:* Discuss the role of chance with a group of students. Do many people use the idea of chance to dismiss the accomplishments of others? Do people use luck as an excuse for not trying? Talk about these issues, and then collaborate on a short paper suggesting how Austin's concept of chance should be taught to children.

JOHN HOLT

John Holt (1923–1985) was the author of several books about children and education, including How Children Fail *and* How Children Learn. *Having taught in grade and high schools for fourteen years, Holt became a critic of the American educational system. He created and edited* Growing Without Schooling, *a magazine dedicated to home schooling.*

Three Kinds of Discipline

OVERVIEW: *In this section from his book* Freedom and Beyond *(1972), Holt classifies three types of discipline that occur in children's lives. Most people assume that discipline comes only from authority figures, such as parents and teachers. Holt reveals that discipline also comes from a child's environment.*

A child, in growing up, may meet and learn from three different kinds of 1
disciplines. The first and most important is what we might call the Discipline of Nature or of Reality. When he is trying to do something real, if he does the wrong thing or doesn't do the right one, he doesn't get the result he wants. If he doesn't pile one block right on top of another, or tries to build on a slanting surface, his tower falls down. If he hits the wrong key, he hears the wrong note. If he doesn't hit the nail squarely on the head, it bends, and he has to pull it out and start with another. If he doesn't measure properly what he is trying to build, it won't open, close, fit, stand up, fly, float, whistle, or do whatever he wants it to do. If he closes his eyes when he swings, he doesn't hit the ball. A child meets this kind of discipline every time he tries to *do* something, which is why it is so important in school to give children more chances to do things, instead of just reading or listening to someone talk (or pretending to). This discipline is a good teacher. The learner never has to wait long for his answer; it usually comes quickly, often instantly. Also it is clear, and very often points toward the needed correction; from what happened he can not only see that what he did was wrong, but also why, and what he needs to do instead. Finally, and most important, the giver of the answer, call it Nature, is impersonal, impartial, and indifferent. She does not give opinions, or make judgments; she cannot be wheedled, bullied, or fooled; she does not get angry or disappointed; she does not praise or blame; she does not remember past failures or hold grudges; with her one always gets a fresh start, this time is the one that counts.

2   The next discipline we might call the Discipline of Culture, of Society, of What People Really Do. Man is a social, a cultural animal. Children sense around them this culture, this network of agreements, customs, habits, and rules binding the adults together. They want to understand it and be a part of it. They watch very carefully what people around them are doing and want to do the same. They want to do right, unless they become convinced they can't do right. Thus children rarely misbehave seriously in church, but sit as quietly as they can. The example of all those grownups is contagious. Some mysterious ritual is going on, and children, who like rituals, want to be part of it. In the same way, the little children that I see at concerts or operas, though they may fidget a little, or perhaps take a nap now and then, rarely make any disturbance. With all those grownups sitting there, neither moving nor talking, it is the most natural thing in the world to imitate them. Children who live among adults who are habitually courteous to each other, and to them, will soon learn to be courteous. Children who live surrounded by people who speak a certain way will speak that way, however much we may try to tell them that speaking that way is bad or wrong.

3   The third discipline is the one most people mean when they speak of discipline—the Discipline of Superior Force, of sergeant to private, of "you do what I tell you or I'll make you wish you had." There is bound to be some of this in a child's life. Living as we do surrounded by things that can hurt children, or that children can hurt, we cannot avoid it. We can't afford to let a small child find out from experience the danger of playing in a busy street, or of fooling with the pots on the top of a stove, or of eating up the pills in the medicine cabinet. So, along with other precautions, we say to him, "Don't play in the street, or touch things on the stove, or go into the medicine cabinet, or I'll punish you." Between him and the danger too great for him to imagine we put a lesser danger, but one he can imagine and maybe therefore wants to avoid. He can have no idea of what it would be like to be hit by a car, but he can imagine being shouted at, or spanked, or sent to his room. He avoids these substitutes for the greater danger until he can understand it and avoid it for its own sake. But we ought to use this discipline only when it is necessary to protect the life, health, safety, or well-being of people or other living creatures, or to prevent destruction of things that people care about. We ought not to assume too long, as we usually do, that a child cannot understand the real nature of the danger from which we want to protect him. The sooner he avoids the danger, not to escape our punishment, but as a matter of good sense, the better. He can learn that faster than we think. In Mexico, for example, where people drive their cars with a good deal of spirit, I saw many children no older than five or four walking

unattended on the streets. They understood about cars, they knew what to do. A child whose life is full of the threat and fear of punishment is locked into babyhood. There is no way for him to grow up, to learn to take responsibility for his life and acts. Most important of all, we should not assume that having to yield to the threat of our superior force is good for the child's character. It is never good for *anyone's* character. To bow to superior force makes us feel impotent and cowardly for not having had the strength or courage to resist. Worse, it makes us resentful and vengeful. We can hardly wait to make someone pay for our humiliation, yield to us as we were once made to yield. No, if we cannot always avoid using the discipline of Superior Force, we should at least use it as seldom as we can.

There are places where all three disciplines overlap. Any very demanding human activity combines in it the disciplines of Superior Force, of Culture, and of Nature. The novice will be told, "Do it this way, never mind asking why, just do it that way, that is the way we always do it." But it probably *is* just the way they always do it, and usually for the very good reason that it is a way that has been found to work. Think, for example, of ballet training. The student in a class is told to do this exercise, or that; to stand so; to do this or that with his head, arms, shoulders, abdomen, hips, legs, feet. He is constantly corrected. There is no argument. But behind these seemingly autocratic demands by the teacher lie many decades of custom and tradition, and behind that, the necessities of dancing itself. You cannot make the moves of classical ballet unless over many years you have acquired, and renewed every day, the needed strength and suppleness in scores of muscles and joints. Nor can you do the difficult motions, making them look easy, unless you have learned hundreds of easier ones first. Dance teachers may not always agree on all the details of teaching these strengths and skills. But no novice could learn them all by himself. You could not go for a night or two to watch the ballet and then, without any other knowledge at all, teach yourself how to do it. In the same way, you would be unlikely to learn any complicated and difficult human activity without drawing heavily on the experience of those who know it better. But the point is that the authority of these experts or teachers stems from, grows out of their greater competence and experience, the fact that what they do *works*, not the fact that they happen to be the teacher and as such have the power to kick a student out of the class. And the further point is that children are always and everywhere attracted to that competence, and ready and eager to submit themselves to a discipline that grows out of it. We hear constantly that children will never do anything unless compelled to by bribes or threats. But in their private lives, or in extracurricular activities in school, in sports, music,

4

drama, art, running a newspaper, and so on, they often submit themselves willingly and wholeheartedly to very intense disciplines, simply because they want to learn to do a given thing well. Our Little-Napoleon football coaches, of whom we have too many and hear far too much, blind us to the fact that millions of children work hard every year getting better at sports and games without coaches barking and yelling at them.

Understanding Meaning

1. What lessons in discipline do children learn from experience?
2. How does Holt *define* discipline? Is learning about limits of experience in the physical world, such as the effect of gravity, a kind of discipline?
3. Does Holt's Discipline of Culture indicate that parents should make sure their children participate in adult activities, such as attending concerts and religious services?
4. What is Holt's opinion of parental authority and direction? When does he feel that strict discipline is justified?
5. *Critical Thinking:* What does Holt's view of discipline reveal about his attitude toward children? How much discipline can children learn on their own? Is strict discipline from parents and teachers effective? Would some people view Holt as being permissive?

Evaluating Strategy

1. How does Holt organize his classification?
2. How effective are the titles, which he capitalizes, for defining each type of discipline?
3. *Other Modes:* Where does Holt include *definition* and *narration* in his essay?

Appreciating Language

1. What connotations does the word *discipline* have?
2. How does Holt's word choice reveal his bias toward and against the different types of discipline?

Connections across the Disciplines

1. How does the structure of Holt's essay compare to that of Martin Luther King Jr.'s (page 381)? Are both writers really using classification as a means to persuade readers?

2.   Review Mary Mebane's essay (page 371), and analyze the kinds of discipline she faced in childhood.

Writing Suggestions

1.   Holt wrote this essay before the tide of school violence and teenage homicide dominated the media. In an era when many public schools require students to wear uniforms and parents are concerned about teenage pregnancy and gangs, would many reject Holt's views? Write an essay expressing your views.
2.   *Collaborative Writing:* Working with a group of students, discuss the issue of rearing and disciplining children. Consider your own childhood. If any of the members are parents, ask their honest opinion of Holt's essay. Take notes on the comments, and work together to write a *definition* of good childhood discipline.

ANN MCCLINTOCK

Ann McClintock (1946–) attended Temple University in Philadelphia and later completed an advanced degree from the University of Pennsylvania. Before becoming a freelance writer and editor, McClintock served as the director of occupational therapy at Ancora State Hospital in New Jersey. McClintock, who often speaks before many community groups, has studied the effects advertising has had on American society and values.

Propaganda Techniques in Today's Advertising

OVERVIEW: *Before reading this essay, consider the way advertising has affected your life and values. Have you purchased items you only learned about from ads and commercials? What commercials have you found most appealing? Do you notice that commercials have a powerful influence on children and young people?*

1 Americans, adults and children alike, are being seduced. They are being brainwashed. And few of us protest. Why? Because the seducers and the brainwashers are the advertisers we willingly invite into our homes. We are victims, content—even eager—to be victimized. We read advertisers' propaganda messages in newspapers and magazines; we watch their alluring images on television. We absorb their messages and images into our subconscious. We all do it—even those of us who claim to see through advertisers' tricks and therefore feel immune to advertising's charm. Advertisers lean heavily on propaganda to sell products, whether the "products" are a brand of toothpaste, a candidate for office, or a particular political viewpoint.

2 *Propaganda* is a systematic effort to influence people's opinions, to win them over to a certain view or side. Propaganda is not necessarily concerned with what is true or false, good or bad. Propagandists simply want people to believe the messages being sent. Often, propagandists will use outright lies or more subtle deceptions to sway people's opinions. In a propaganda war, any tactic is considered fair.

3 When we hear the word "propaganda," we usually think of a foreign menace: anti-American radio programs broadcast by a totalitarian regime or brainwashing tactics practiced on hostages. Although propaganda may seem relevant only in the political arena, the concept can be applied fruitfully to the way products and ideas are sold in advertising. Indeed, the vast majority of us are targets in advertisers' propaganda war. Every day, we are

bombarded with slogans, print ads, commercials, packaging claims, billboards, trademarks, logos, and designer brands—all forms of propaganda. One study reports that each of us, during an average day, is exposed to over *five hundred* advertising claims of various types. This saturation may even increase in the future since current trends include ads on movie screens, shopping carts, videocassettes, even public television.

What kind of propaganda techniques do advertisers use? There are   4
seven basic types:

1. *Name Calling*   Name calling is a propaganda tactic in which nega-   5
tively charged names are hurled against the opposing side or competitor. By using such names, propagandists try to arouse feelings of mistrust, fear, and hate in their audiences. For example, a political advertisement may label an opposing candidate a "loser," "fence-sitter," or "warmonger." Depending on the advertiser's target market, labels such as "a friend of big business" or "a dues-paying member of the party in power" can be the epithets that damage an opponent. Ads for products may also use name calling. An American manufacturer may refer, for instance, to a "foreign car" in its commercial—not an "imported" one. The label of foreignness will have unpleasant connotations in many people's minds. A childhood rhyme claims that "names can never hurt me," but name calling is an effective way to damage the opposition, whether it is another car maker or a congressional candidate.

2. *Glittering Generalities*   Using glittering generalities is the opposite of   6
name calling. In this case, advertisers surround their products with attractive—and slippery—words and phrases. They use vague terms that are difficult to define and that may have different meanings to different people: *freedom, democratic, all-American, progressive, Christian,* and *justice.* Many such words have strong, affirmative overtones. This kind of language stirs positive feelings in people, feelings that may spill over to the product or idea being pitched. As with name calling, the emotional response may overwhelm logic. Target audiences accept the product without thinking very much about what the glittering generalities mean—or whether they even apply to the product. After all, how can anyone oppose "truth, justice, and the American way"?

The ads for politicians and political causes often use glittering generali-   7
ties because such "buzz words" can influence votes. Election slogans include high-sounding but basically empty phrases like the following:

"He cares about people." (That's nice, but is he a better candidate than his opponent?)

"Vote for progress." (Progress by *whose* standards?)

"They'll make this country great again." (What does "great" mean? Does "great" mean the same thing to others as it does to me?)

"Vote for the future." (What kind of future?)

"If you love America, vote for Phyllis Smith." (If I don't vote for Smith, does that mean I don't love America?)

8   Ads for consumer goods are also sprinkled with glittering generalities. Product names, for instance, are supposed to evoke good feelings: *Luvs* diapers, *New Freedom* feminine hygiene products, *Joy* liquid detergent, *Loving Care* hair color, *Almost Home* cookies, *Yankee Doodle* pastries. Product slogans lean heavily on vague but comforting phrases: Kinney is "The Great American Shoe Store," General Electric "brings good things to life," and Dow Chemical "lets you do great things." Chevrolet, we are told, is the "heartbeat of America," and Chrysler boasts cars that are "built by Americans for Americans."

9   3. *Transfer*   In transfer, advertisers try to improve the image of a product by associating it with a symbol most people respect, like the American flag or Uncle Sam. The advertisers hope that the prestige attached to the symbol will carry over to the product. Many companies use transfer devices to identify their products: Lincoln Insurance shows a profile of the president; Continental Insurance portrays a Revolutionary War minuteman; Amtrak's logo is red, white, and blue; Liberty Mutual's corporate symbol is the Statue of Liberty; Allstate's name is cradled by a pair of protective, fatherly hands.

10   Corporations also use the transfer technique when they sponsor prestigious shows on radio and television. These shows function as symbols of dignity and class. Kraft Corporation, for instance, sponsored a "Leonard Bernstein Conducts Beethoven" concert, while Gulf Oil is the sponsor of *National Geographic* specials and Mobil supports public television's *Masterpiece Theater.* In this way, corporations can reach an educated, influential audience and, perhaps, improve their public image by associating themselves with quality programming.

11   Political ads, of course, practically wrap themselves in the flag. Ads for a political candidate often show either the Washington Monument, a Fourth of July parade, the Stars and Stripes, a bald eagle soaring over the mountains, or a white-steepled church on the village green. The national anthem or "America the Beautiful" may play softly in the background. Such appeals to Americans' love of country can surround the candidate with an aura of patriotism and integrity.

12   4. *Testimonial*   The testimonial is one of advertisers' most-loved and most-used propaganda techniques. Similar to the transfer device, the testi-

monial capitalizes on the admiration people have for a celebrity to make the product shine more brightly—even though the celebrity is not an expert on the product being sold.

Print and television ads offer a nonstop parade of testimonials: here's 13 William Shatner for Priceline.com; here's basketball star Michael Jordan eating Wheaties; a slew of well-known people (including rap star LL Cool J and the rock group Aerosmith) advertise clothing from the Gap; and Jerry Seinfeld assures us he never goes anywhere without his American Express card. Testimonials can sell movies, too; newspaper ads for films often feature favorable comments by well-known reviewers. And, in recent years, testimonials have played an important role in pitching books; the backs of paperbacks frequently list complimentary blurbs by celebrities.

Political candidates, as well as their ad agencies, know the value of tes- 14 timonials. Barbra Streisand lent her star appeal to the presidential campaign of Bill Clinton, while Arnold Schwarzenegger endorsed George Bush. Even controversial social issues are debated by celebrities. The nuclear-freeze debate, for instance, starred Paul Newman for the pro side and Charlton Heston for the con.

As illogical as testimonials sometimes are (Pepsi's Michael Jackson, for 15 instance, is a health-food adherent who does not drink soft drinks), they are effective propaganda. We like the *person* so much that we like the *product* too.

5. *Plain Folks* The plain folks approach says, in effect, "Buy me or 16 vote for me. I'm just like you." Regular folks will surely like Bob Evans's Down on the Farm Country Sausage or good old-fashioned Countrytime Lemonade. Some ads emphasize the idea that "we're all in the same boat." We see people making long-distance calls for just the reasons we do—to put the baby on the phone to Grandma or to tell Mom we love her. And how do these folksy, warmhearted (usually saccharine) scenes affect us? They're supposed to make us feel that AT&T—the multinational corporate giant— has the same values we do. Similarly, we are introduced to the little people at Ford, the ordinary folks who work on the assembly line, not to bigwigs in their executive offices. What's the purpose of such an approach? To encourage us to buy a car built by these honest, hard-working "everyday Joes" who care about quality as much as we do.

Political advertisements make almost as much use of the "plain folks" 17 appeal as they do of transfer devices. Candidates wear hard hats, farmers' caps, and assembly-line coveralls. They jog around the block and carry their own luggage through the airport. The idea is to convince voters that the candidates are average people, not the elite—not wealthy lawyers or executives but common citizens.

18   6. *Card Stacking*   When people say that "the cards were stacked against me," they mean that they were never given a fair chance. Applied to propaganda, card stacking means that one side may suppress or distort evidence, tell half-truths, oversimplify the facts, or set up a "straw man"—a false target—to divert attention from the issue at hand. Card stacking is a difficult form of propaganda both to detect and to combat. When a candidate claims that an opponent has "changed his mind five times on this important issue," we tend to accept the claim without investigating whether the candidate had good reasons for changing his mind. Many people are simply swayed by the distorted claim that the candidate is "waffling" on the issue.

19   Advertisers often stack the cards in favor of the products they are pushing. They may, for instance, use what are called "weasel words." These are small words that usually slip right past us, but that make the difference between reality and illusion. The weasel words are underlined in the following claims:

> "<u>Helps control</u> dandruff symptoms." (The audience usually interprets this as *stops* dandruff.)
> "Most dentists <u>surveyed</u> recommend sugarless gum for their patients <u>who chew gum</u>." (We hear the "most dentists" and "for their patients," but we don't think about how many were surveyed or whether the dentists first recommended that the patients not chew gum at all.)
> "Sticker price $1,000 lower than <u>most comparable</u> cars." (How many is "most"? What car does the advertiser consider "comparable"?)

20   Advertisers also use a card stacking trick when they make an unfinished claim. For example, they will say that their product has "twice as much pain reliever." We are left with a favorable impression. We don't usually ask, "Twice as much pain reliever as what?" Or advertisers may make extremely vague claims that sound alluring but have no substance: Toyota's "Oh, what a feeling!"; Vantage cigarettes' "The taste of success"; "The spirit of Marlboro"; Coke's "the real thing." Another way to stack the cards in favor of a certain product is to use scientific-sounding claims that are not supported by sound research. When Ford claimed that its LTD model was "400% quieter," many people assumed that the LTD must be quieter than all other cars. When taken to court, however, Ford admitted that the phrase referred to the difference between the noise level inside and outside the LTD. Other scientific-sounding claims use mysterious ingredients that are never explained as selling points: "Retsyn," "special whitening agents," "the ingredient doctors recommend."

21   7. *Bandwagon*   In the bandwagon technique, advertisers pressure, "Everyone's doing it. Why don't you?" This kind of propaganda often suc-

ceeds because many people have a deep desire not to be different. Political ads tell us to vote for the "winning candidate." Advertisers know we tend to feel comfortable doing what others do; we want to be on the winning team. Or ads show a series of people proclaiming, "I'm voting for the Senator. I don't know why anyone wouldn't." Again, the audience feels under pressure to conform.

In the marketplace, the bandwagon approach lures buyers. Ads tell us   22 that "nobody doesn't like Sara Lee" (the message is that you must be weird if you don't). They tell us that "most people prefer Brand X two to one over other leading brands" (to be like the majority, we should buy Brand X). If we don't drink Pepsi, we're left out of "the Pepsi generation." To take part in "America's favorite health kick," the National Dairy Council asks us, "Got Milk?" And Honda motorcycle ads, praising the virtues of being a follower, tell us, "Follow the leader. He's on a Honda."

Why do these propaganda techniques work? Why do so many of us buy   23 the products, viewpoints, and candidates urged on us by propaganda messages? They work because they appeal to our emotions, not to our minds. Often, in fact, they capitalize on our prejudices and biases. For example, if we are convinced that environmentalists are radicals who want to destroy America's record of industrial growth and progress, then we will applaud the candidate who refers to them as "treehuggers." Clear thinking requires hard work: analyzing a claim, researching the facts, examining both sides of an issue, using logic to see the flaws in an argument. Many of us would rather let the propagandists do our thinking for us.

Because propaganda is so effective, it is important to detect it and un-   24 derstand how it is used. We may conclude, after close examination, that some propaganda sends a truthful, worthwhile message. Some advertising, for instance, urges us not to drive drunk, to become volunteers, to contribute to charity. Even so, we must be aware that propaganda is being used. Otherwise, we have consented to handing over to others our independence of thought and action.

Understanding Meaning

1. How does McClintock define the word "propaganda"?
2. McClintock refers to consumers as "brainwashed victims." Do you agree or disagree? Do people exhibit a kind of denial, not wishing to admit that they have been manipulated into buying products they don't need?
3. Can you list commercials and ads that engage in "name calling," "glittering generalities," and "transfer"?

4. Endorsements by famous athletes such as Michael Jordan often appear in commercials. Why did advertisers drop Magic Johnson after he announced he was HIV-positive? Which current celebrities do advertisers embrace and which ones do they avoid?
5. *Critical Thinking:* Imagine you want to raise money for the homeless, encourage people to exercise, introduce a line of environmentally safe products, or market computer software that will help handicapped people. Would you feel compelled to use some of these propaganda techniques to get attention? Can ads be honest? Should McClintock present positive advertising techniques?

Evaluating Strategy

1. McClintock opens her essay with a definition of "propaganda." Why is it important to clearly define a subject before attempting to break it into parts?
2. What methods does McClintock use in organizing her essay?

Appreciating Language

1. Consider the word "propaganda." What connotations does it have? How might an advertising executive or television sponsor react to this word?
2. What words does McClintock use to describe ads and advertisers? Circle words that have strong connotations.
3. What is a "buzz word"? Can you think of current examples?

Connections across the Disciplines

1. Refer to Carl Sagan's "Why We Need to Understand Science" (page 563) and Darrell Huff's "How to Lie with Statistics" (page 301). Do both articles support the need for critical thinking for people to make intelligent choices as citizens and consumers?
2. McClintock depicts people as "brainwashed victims" who are bombarded with ads. How do her comments support Marie Winn's observations in "TV Addiction" (page 194)? Do the passive viewers of television allow themselves to become uncritical consumers?
3. Review the fund-raising ad (page 599). Do you see any propaganda techniques at work?

Writing Suggestions

1. Watch an evening of network television and analyze the commercials you see. How many use the techniques McClintock describes? Write a short analysis of your findings.

2. Examine the ads in a popular magazine. Do you find one advertising technique more popular than another? Write a brief essay detailing the nature of the ads you find.

3. *Collaborative Writing:* Working with a group of students, discuss McClintock's essay. Transform McClintock's article into a short process paper telling consumers how to apply critical thinking to ads and commercials. What questions should consumers ask before buying products?

BLENDING THE MODES

NORTHROP FRYE

Northrop Frye (1912–1991) was born in Quebec and received a degree in philosophy and English from Victoria College. He studied theology at Emmanuel College in Toronto and was ordained by the United Church of Canada in 1936. Frye obtained a master's degree from Oxford and took a teaching position at Victoria College. Frye published a number of books of literary criticism, including Anatomy of Criticism *(1957),* The Well-Tempered Critic *(1962), and* The Critical Path *(1971).*

Our Three Languages

OVERVIEW: *In this section from* The Educated Imagination, *Frye classifies language into three levels of use. Notice how he uses an extended example of placing a person on a remote island to illustrate how we use language.*

1 Suppose you're shipwrecked on an uninhabited island in the South Seas. The first thing you do is to take a long look at the world around you, a world of sky and sea and earth and stars and trees and hills. You see this world as objective, as something set over against you and not yourself or related to you in any way. And you notice two things about this objective world. In the first place, it doesn't have any conversation. It's full of animals and plants and insects going on with their own business, but there's nothing that responds to you: it has no morals and no intelligence, or at least none that you can grasp. It may have a shape and a meaning, but it doesn't seem to be a human shape or a human meaning. Even if there's enough to eat and no dangerous animals, you feel lonely and frightened and unwanted in such a world.

2 In the second place, you find that looking at the world, as something set over against you, splits your mind in two. You have an intellect that feels curious about it and wants to study it, and you have feelings or emotions that see it as beautiful or austere or terrible. You know that both these attitudes have some reality, at least for you. If the ship you were wrecked in was a Western ship, you'd probably feel that your intellect tells you more about what's really there in the outer world, and that your emotions tell you more about what's going on inside you. If your background were Oriental, you'd be more likely to reverse this and say that the beauty or terror was what was

really there, and that your instinct to count and classify and measure and pull to pieces was what was inside your mind. But whether your point of view is Western or Eastern, intellect and emotion never get together in your mind as long as you're simply looking at the world. They alternate, and keep you divided between them.

The language you use on this level of the mind is the language of con- 3 sciousness or awareness. It's largely a language of nouns and adjectives. You have to have names for things, and you need qualities like "wet" or "green" or "beautiful" to describe how things seem to you. This is the speculative or contemplative position of the mind, the position in which the arts and sciences begin, although they don't stay there very long. The sciences begin by accepting the facts and the evidence about an outside world without trying to alter them. Science proceeds by accurate measurement and description, and follows the demands of the reason rather than the emotions. What it deals with is there, whether we like it or not. The emotions are unreasonable: for them it's what they like and don't like that comes first. We'd be naturally inclined to think that the arts follow the path of emotion, in contrast to the sciences. Up to a point they do, but there's a complicating factor.

That complicating factor is the contrast between "I like this" and "I 4 don't like this." In this Robinson Crusoe life I've assigned you, you may have moods of complete peacefulness and joy, moods when you accept your island and everything around you. You wouldn't have such moods very often, and when you had them, they'd be moods of identification, when you felt that the island was a part of you and you a part of it. That is not the feeling of consciousness or awareness, where you feel split off from everything that's not your perceiving self. Your habitual state of mind is the feeling of separation which goes with being conscious, and the feeling "this is not a part of me" soon becomes "this is not what I want." Notice the word "want": we'll be coming back to it.

So you soon realize that there's a difference between the world you're 5 living in and the world you want to live in. The world you want to live in is a human world, not an objective one: it's not an environment but a home; it's not the world you see but the world you build out of what you see. You go to work to build a shelter or plant a garden, and as soon as you start to work you've moved into a different level of human life. You're not separating only yourself from nature now, but constructing a human world and separating it from the rest of the world. Your intellect and emotions are now both engaged in the same activity, so there's no longer any real distinction between them. As soon as you plant a garden or a crop, you develop the conception of a "weed," the plant you don't want in there. But you can't say that "weed" is either an intellectual or an emotional conception because it's both at once. Further, you go to work because you feel you have to, and because you want something at the end of the work. That means that the important categories of your life are no longer the subject and the object, the watcher and the things being watched: the important categories are what you have to do and what you want to do—in other words, necessity and freedom.

6   One person by himself is not a complete human being, so I'll provide you with another shipwrecked refugee of the opposite sex and an eventual family. Now you're a member of a human society. This human society after a while will transform the island into something with a human shape. What that human shape is, is revealed in the shape of the work you do: the buildings, such as they are, the paths through the woods, the planted crops fenced off against whatever animals want to eat them. These things, these rudiments of city, highway, garden and farm, are the human form of nature, or the form of human nature, whichever you like. This is the area of the applied arts and sciences, and it appears in our society as engineering and agriculture and medicine and architecture. In this area we can never say clearly where the art stops and the science begins, or vice versa.

7   The language you use on this level is the language of practical sense, a language of verbs or words of action and movement. The practical world, however, is a world where actions speak louder than words. In some ways it's a higher level of existence than the speculative level, because it's doing something about the world instead of just looking at it, but in itself it's a much more primitive level. It's the process of adapting to the environment, or rather of transforming the environment in the interests of one species, that goes on among animals and plants as well as human beings. The animals have a good many of our practical skills: some insects make pretty fair architects, and beavers know quite a lot about engineering. In this island, probably, and certainly if you were alone, you'd have about the ranking of a second-rate animal. What makes our practical life really human is a third level of the mind, a level where consciousness and practical skill come together.

8   This third level is a vision or model in your mind of what you want to construct. There's that word "want" again. The actions of man are prompted by desire, and some of these desires are needs, like food and warmth and shelter. One of these needs is sexual, the desire to reproduce and bring more human beings into existence. But there's also a desire to bring a social human form into existence: the form of cities and gardens and farms that we call civilization. Many animals and insects have this social

form too, but man knows that he has it: he can compare what he does with what he can imagine being done. So we begin to see where the imagination belongs in the scheme of human affairs. It's the power of constructing possible models of human experience. In the world of the imagination, anything goes that's imaginatively possible, but nothing really happens. If it did happen, it would move out of the world of imagination into the world of action.

We have three levels of the mind now, and a language for each of them, which in English-speaking societies means an English for each of them. There's the level of consciousness and awareness, where the most important thing is the difference between me and everything else. The English of this level is the English of ordinary conversation, which is mostly monologue, as you'll soon realize if you do a bit of eavesdropping, or listening to yourself. We can call it the language of self-expression. Then there's the level of social participation, the working or technological language of teachers and preachers and politicians and advertisers and lawyers and journalists and scientists. We've already called this the language of practical sense. Then there's the level of imagination, which produces the literary language of poems and plays and novels. They're not really different languages, of course, but three different reasons for using words.

Understanding Meaning

1. According to Frye, what are the three levels of language?
2. What do these levels of language reveal about how we think and how we interact with the world?
3. How does language separate human beings from other animals?
4. *Critical Thinking:* How does this classification of language help you understand the role of language in human thought? At what age do we acquire or use each level? Do some people function at one level more than others in thinking and communicating?

Evaluating Strategy

1. Frye originally delivered this essay as a radio lecture designed for a general audience. Does his use of the deserted island create concrete examples readers can visualize?
2. What methods does Frye use to explain each level? What other modes does he include in this essay?

Appreciating Language

1. Would high school students be able to understand this classification? Are there words requiring definitions or references that are remote? How might you revise it for a tenth-grade English class?
2. What does Frye mean by the "objective" world?

Connections across the Disciplines

1. Relate Frye's essay to Ann McClintock's "Propaganda Techniques in Today's Advertising" (page 396). What role does language play in creating messages to influence consumers?
2. Examine "Interrogation of Lee Harvey Oswald" (page 97). What level of language did the FBI agent use in this report? Why?

Writing Suggestions

1. Follow up on Frye's example of being shipwrecked on an uninhabited island, and classify the ways personality types would confront their situation—those who would seek immediate escape by fashioning a raft; those who would seek food and shelter; those who might pray; those who would not cope; and so forth.
2. *Collaborative Writing:* Discuss Frye's levels of language with a group of other students, and then work together to write a short process paper explaining how to incorporate his ideas into a unit on critical thinking.

WRITING BEYOND THE CLASSROOM

BLACK'S LAW DICTIONARY

Black's Law Dictionary *is a standard reference used by attorneys, paralegals, administrators, and law enforcement personnel. Like any dictionary, it serves to define terms.*

Homicide

OVERVIEW: *When reading this entry, which includes a classification, pay attention to the specialized use of language. Note that the authors stress that the word "homicide" is neutral and does not even imply that a crime has been committed. Notice how television and movies have distorted the complexities of this legal issue.*

Homicide. The killing of one human being by the act, procurement, or [1] omission of another. A person is guilty of criminal homicide if he purposely, knowingly, recklessly or negligently causes the death of another human being. Criminal homicide is murder, manslaughter or negligent homicide. Model Penal Code, §210.1; 18 U.S.C.A. §1111 et seq. *See* Manslaughter; Murder.

Homicide is not necessarily a crime. It is a necessary ingredient of the [2] crimes of murder and manslaughter, but there are other cases in which homicide may be committed without criminal intent and without criminal consequences, as, where it is done in the lawful execution of a judicial sentence, in self-defense, or as the only possible means of arresting an escaping felon. The term "homicide" is neutral; while it describes the act, it pronounces no judgment on its moral or legal quality. People v. Mahon, 77 Ill.App.3d 413, 395 N.E.2d 950, 958. *See Excusable homicide; Justifiable homicide, below.*

CLASSIFICATION

Homicide is ordinarily classified as "justifiable," "excusable," and "felo- [3] nious." For the definitions of these terms, and of some other compound terms, see *below.*

4   *Culpable homicide.* Described as a crime varying from the very lowest culpability, up to the very verge of murder.

5   *Excusable homicide.* The killing of a human being, either by misadventure or in self-defense. Such homicide consists of a perpetrator's acting in a manner which the law does not prohibit, such as self-defense or accidental homicide. Law v. State, 21 Md.App. 13, 318 A.2d 859, 869. The name itself imports some fault, error, or omission, so trivial, however, that the law excuses it from guilt of felony, though in strictness it judges it deserving of some little degree of punishment. It is of two sorts,—either *per infortunium,* by misadventure, or *se defendendo,* upon a sudden affray. Homicide *per infortunium* is where a man, doing a lawful act, without any intention of hurt, unfortunately kills another; but, if death ensues from any unlawful act, the offense is manslaughter, and not misadventure. Homicide *se defendendo* is where a man kills another upon a sudden affray, merely in his own defense, or in defense of his wife, child, parent, or servant, and not from any vindictive feeling. *See* Self-defense; also *Justifiable homicide, below.*

6   *Felonious homicide.* The wrongful killing of a human being, of any age or either sex, without justification or excuse in law; of which offense there are two degrees, manslaughter and murder.

7   *Homicide by misadventure.* The accidental killing of another, where the slayer is doing a lawful act, unaccompanied by any criminally careless or reckless conduct. The same as "homicide *per infortunium.*" *See* Manslaughter.

8   *Homicide by necessity.* A species of justifiable homicide, because it arises from some unavoidable necessity, without any will, intention, or desire, and without any inadvertence or negligence in the party killing, and therefore without any shadow of blame. *See* Self-defense.

9   *Homicide per infortunium.* Homicide by misfortune, or accidental homicide; as where a man doing a lawful act without any intention of hurt, accidentally kills another; a species of excusable homicide. *See* Negligent homicide.

10 *Homicide se defendendo.* Homicide in self-defense; the killing of a person in self-defense upon a sudden affray, where the slayer had no other possible (or, at least, probable) means of escaping from his assailant. A species of excusable homicide. *See* Self-defense.

11 *Justifiable homicide.* Such as is committed intentionally, but without any evil design, and under such circumstances of necessity or duty as render the act proper, and relieve the party from any shadow of blame; as where a sheriff lawfully executes a sentence of death upon a malefactor, or where the killing takes place

in the endeavor to prevent the commission of felony which could not be otherwise avoided, or, as a matter of right, such as self-defense or other causes provided for by statute. *See* Self-defense; also *Excusable homicide, above.*

Negligent homicide. Criminal homicide constitutes negligent homicide when it is committed negligently. Model Penal Code, §210.4. *See* Negligent homicide; also *Vehicular homicide, below.*   12

Reckless homicide. See that title.   13

Vehicular homicide. The killing of a human being by the operation of an automobile, airplane, motorboat or other motor vehicle in a manner which creates an unreasonable risk of injury to the person or property of another and which constitutes a material deviation from the standard of care which a reasonable person would observe under the same circumstances.   14

Understanding Meaning

1. Does it surprise you to learn that homicide may not be a crime? Do most people equate that term with "murder"?
2. What does the law regard as the most serious, most criminal forms of homicide?
3. Provide your own examples of felonious homicide, homicide by misadventure, and homicide by necessity.
4. *Critical Thinking:* What values seem to play a role in determining what is excusable and what is criminal homicide?

Evaluating Strategy

1. How well organized is this entry? Is it easy to follow?
2. How important are the examples used to support the definitions?

Appreciating Language

1. What do the tone, style, and word choice reveal about the intended audience?
2. How might you reword this entry for a general audience?

Connections across the Disciplines

1. How does the writing style of this entry compare to Kimberly Crawford's article written for the *FBI Law Enforcement Journal* (page 344)?

2. How does the style differ from the chart developed for *Communication Styles: United States and Taiwan* (page 272)?

Writing Suggestions

1. Select one of the types of homicide listed in the entry, and provide a fictional example in a brief narrative.
2. *Collaborative Writing:* Discuss the types of homicide listed in the entry with fellow students, and ask members to provide their own version of justifiable homicide. Work together to create a definition.

Textbooks and reference works often use division and classification to explain concepts, processes, objects, or conditions.

Kinds of Sentences

OVERVIEW: *This section from a grammar handbook explains four types of sentences by classifying them according to number of and type of clauses. Independent clauses contain a subject and verb and make a complete statement:* I drive to school. *Dependent clauses contain a subject and verb but do not make a complete statement and are not a sentence:* Because I drive to school.

7E KINDS OF SENTENCES

Independent clauses appear alone or in combinations—with other independent clauses or with dependent clauses. One method of classifying sentences is based on the number and kinds of clauses in a single construction. According to this classification system, there are four categories of sentences: simple, compound, complex, and compound-complex. [1]

(1) Simple sentence

A **simple sentence** is made up of only one independent clause. The sentence may contain modifiers and compound elements (for example, compound subjects and verbs); but it may not contain more than one subject-predicate structure. [2]

Cigarette smoke contains carbon monoxide. [3]
For most college students, computers and calculators have become essential. [4]
The Rhône flows south through France and then empties into the Mediterranean. [5]

413

(2) Compound sentence

6   A **compound sentence** is made up of two or more independent clauses. The primary ways to coordinate independent clauses are with commas and coordinating conjunctions (*and, but, or, for, nor, so, yet*) and with semicolons.

7   For centuries, Brittany was an independent state, but now the area is part of France.

8   The restaurant was dark, the air was filled with smoke, and the music was deafening.

9   Socrates wrote nothing; his thoughts are known only through the works of Plato and Xenophon.

(3) Complex sentence

10   A **complex sentence** is made up of one independent clause and one or more dependent clauses—adverb, adjective, or noun.

11   Although most rifle experts have 20/20 vision, pistol experts are often very near-sighted.

12   The game involves three contestants who spin a roulette wheel.

13   Whoever could solve the riddle of the Sphinx would be spared her wrath.

(4) Compound-complex sentence

14   A **compound-complex sentence** is made up of two or more independent clauses and one or more dependent clauses.

15   London's Great Exhibition, which opened in 1851, was designed to show human progress; it brought together in the "Crystal Palace" industrial displays remarkable for their day.

16   Alchemists believed that they could change lesser metals into gold, and although they failed, they helped establish the science of chemistry.

17   The fathom once was the distance that a Viking could encompass in a hug; a gauge was the distance that lay between the wheels of a Roman chariot; an acre was an area that could be plowed in one day by a team of two oxen.

Understanding Meaning

1. Provide an example of each sentence type.
2. How does understanding the four types of sentences help with writing?

Evaluating Strategy

1. How effective is the method of organizing this information?
2. Do the visual effects such as bold print, underscores, numerals, and italics assist readers?
3. *Other Modes:* How are the different sentence types *defined?*

Appreciating Language

1. What does the level of language assume about the readers, who are mostly college students?
2. Are these terms initially misleading? Does "simple" suggest a short or easily read sentence? Would the term "complex sentence" lead you to expect a long, complicated statement?

Connections across the Disciplines

1. Compare this entry to that from *Black's Law Dictionary* (page 409). How important are visual effects in reference books?
2. Compare this explanation with one available in your own grammar book. What are the differences? Is one easier to read than the other?

Writing Suggestions

1. Rewrite this entry for a junior high school audience.
2. Analyze your own use of sentences by reviewing one of your previous papers. How often do you use each type?

STRATEGIES FOR DIVISION AND CLASSIFICATION WRITING

1. **Determine which mode you will use.** Which method will best suit your purpose: dividing your subject into subtopics or measuring subtopics against a common standard?
2. **Select an effective method of division.** If you were writing about improving the public schools, for example, it might be more effective to divide the paper by discipline, discussing how to improve math skills, writing ability, and knowledge of geography rather than improving elementary schools, junior high schools, and high schools.
3. **Avoid divisions that oversimplify or distort meaning.** Your paper should aid in helping readers grasp a complex subject without trivializing or misstating the issues. You may wish to qualify your division and explain to readers that exceptions and situations may exist where the division may not apply.
4. **Avoid overlapping categories.** When writing both division and classification make sure the categories are distinct. Do not separate cars into "domestic, foreign, and antique models" because antique cars would clearly have to belong to the first two groups.
5. **Use a single, clearly defined standard to classify subjects.** Classification relies on a clearly stated standard that is used to measure all the items you discuss. Avoid mixing standards. In some instances you may have to explain or justify why you are using a particular standard.
6. **In classification writing, make sure all topics fit into *one* category.** In a properly written classification paper, every unit should fit only one category. For example, a term paper is either an A− or a B+. In addition, make sure no items are left over that cannot be logically placed.

SUGGESTED TOPICS FOR DIVISION AND CLASSIFICATION WRITING
General Assignments

Write a division essay on any of the following topics. Your division may make use of standard categories or ones you invent. Remember to clearly state the way you are dividing your subject. Each subject or example should be supported with definitions, brief narratives, or descriptions.

- Dates you have had
- Student housing on campus and off

- Baseball, basketball, or football teams
- Popular music
- Careers for women

Write a classification essay on any of the following topics. Make sure to use a single method of rating the subtopics, from best to worst, easiest to hardest, or least desirable to most desirable, for example.

- Jobs you have had
- Student services, including health, police, food, etc.
- Vacation destinations
- Bosses or professors you have known
- Talk shows or news programs

Writing in Context

1. Assume you have been asked by a national magazine to write about students' political attitudes. You may develop your essay by division or classification. You can discuss politics in general terms of liberal and conservative or restrict your comments on students' attitudes toward a particular issue, such as abortion, capital punishment, or health care.
2. Write a humorous paper about campus fashion by dividing students into types. Invent titles or labels for each group, and supply enough details so readers can readily fit the people they meet into one of your categories.

STUDENT PAPER: DIVISION AND CLASSIFICATION

This paper was written in response to the following assignment:

> Write a 500-word paper classifying people, objects, or issues you have observed on campus. Make sure that you choose meaningful divisions and describe each category fully.

Hispanics on Campus

1   Students, faculty, and administrators tend to refer to "Hispanics" as if all Latino and Latina students belonged to a single homogeneous group. Actually, there are four distinct groups of Hispanic students. Outsiders may only see slight discrepancies in dress and behavior, but there are profound differences which occasionally border on suspicion and hostility. Their differences are best measured by their attitude toward and their degree of acceptance of mainstream American values and culture.

2   The least assimilated and most alien group of these students are politically active immigrants or children of immigrants. These are the students who sponsored the recent protest against Western Civilization courses. Most of them were born in Mexico or Puerto Rico. English is their second language and a perceived cultural barrier. Because of this, they tend to see European culture as oppressive, an arbitrary hurdle blocking their progress. They are keenly sensitive to negative stereotypes of Hispanics and resent media portrayals of bandits, drug dealers, and gang members.

3   Equally alien to American culture but less politically active are the foreign students from Latin America. Whether they are from Mexico, Chile, or Argentina, they speak excellent English. Many have lived or studied in Europe. As citizens of their native countries, they have no insecurities about their ethnic identities and seem willing to mix socially with Americans, but only if they share the same class values. Unlike the immigrants, they consider themselves linked to European culture. Many speak French and German in addition to Spanish and

Italian. Often they seem to feel more at home with foreign students from Europe than either Americans or other Hispanic students.

The most assimilated and largest group of Hispanic students are second and third generation Latinos and Latinas. Few speak more than a few Spanish phrases. Many pronounce their names with an Anglo accent, so that they say "Rammer-ez" for Rameriz. They interact with all students and consider themselves Americans. Their parents work for IBM, sell real estate, or own restaurants. These students are not politically active. They use the terms "Chicano," "Latino," and "Spanish" interchangeably. Although many participate in Hispanic cultural activities on campus, they generally avoid political rallies. Only a few consider themselves radical, and some, especially the Cuban-Americans, are extremely conservative.

4

There is a group of Hispanics who are so assimilated into mainstream American culture that I call them invisible. Because of intermarriage, many Hispanics have last names like O'Brien, Edelman, and Kowalski. My father is third generation Irish. While working on an engineering project in Mexico, he met my mother, who ironically had an Irish grandmother. I was born in San Diego but spent almost every summer in Cancun with my aunt. I speak and write Spanish. I subscribe to Mexican magazines. I serve on numerous Hispanic organizations. But because of my blonde hair and my last name, Callaghan, I am frequently viewed as an outsider by Hispanics who don't speak Spanish.

5

Questions for Review and Revision

1. What's the student's thesis?
2. How does the student define her standard of measurement?
3. What value does this classification have in understanding Hispanic students?
4. Is each class of students clearly defined? Can you think of any students you know who would not fit in one of the categories?
5. Does the student include enough examples or descriptions to fully explain each category of students?
6. Read the essay aloud. Can you detect weak or awkward passages that need revision?

Writing Suggestions

1. Using this paper as a model, write a similar classification paper about students on your campus. Classify students by academic performance, school spirit, support of athletic teams, or involvement in campus activities or politics. Remember to use a single standard or method of evaluation.

2. *Collaborative Writing:* Discuss this essay with other students. Do students in other ethnic groups fit a pattern similar to the Hispanics at the writer's college? Work together to select a group, and write a short paper that classifies them into different types.

DIVISION AND CLASSIFICATION CHECKLIST

Before submitting your paper, review these points.

1. Have you clearly defined your goal—to write a division or classification paper?

2. Do you make meaningful divisions or classifications, or does your paper oversimplify a complex subject?

3. Are your categories clearly defined?

4. Do you avoid overlapping categories?

5. Do you use parallel patterns to develop categories and items?

6. In classification, do you use a single standard of evaluation?

7. Do all the parts of your subject clearly fit into a single category? Are there any items left over?

 Companion Web Site

See **http://sundance.heinle.com** for information on writing division and classification.

 InfoTrac® College Edition

For additional reading go to InfoTrac College edition, your on-line research library, at **http://infotrac.thomsonlearning.com**.

- Enter the search term "division" using Keywords.
- Enter the search term "classification" using Keywords.
- Enter the name of an author you read in this chapter using Keywords.
- Enter a theme or idea your class discussed using Keywords.

8

Process

EXPLAINING HOW THINGS WORK AND GIVING DIRECTIONS

WHAT IS PROCESS?

Process writing shows how things work or how specific tasks are accomplished. The first type of process writing is used to demonstrate how a complex procedure takes place. Biology textbooks describe how the heart operates by separating its actions into a series of steps. This chain-of-events explanation also can illustrate how an engine works, how inflation affects the economy, how the IRS audits an account, or how police respond to a 911 call. Process writing is a directed form of narration that explains how a procedure or event occurs.

The second type of process writing instructs readers how to complete a specific task. Recipes, owners' manuals, textbooks, and home repair articles provide readers with step-by-step directions to bake a cake, rotate tires, set up a stereo system, write a research paper, lose weight, or fix a leaking roof. These instructions are challenging to create because writers may be unable to determine how much background information to provide and may easily forget a critical piece of information.

Explaining How Things Work

Just as division writing seeks to explain an abstract or complex subject by separating it into smaller categories, process writing separates the workings of complicated operations into distinct steps. In her essay "Birth of a TV Show: A Drama All Its Own" (page 433), Elizabeth Kolbert explains the process of how a writer's idea or concept becomes a television program:

> At the start of the season, executives from each of the networks—CBS, NBC, ABC and Fox—listen to hundreds of writers pitch new sitcoms. The fortunate few dozen advance to the next step: writing scripts for the prospective shows. After examining those scripts, the networks narrow their choices

to 8 or 10, for which pilot episodes will be filmed. From these pilots, they will eventually make four or five new sitcoms.

In writing explanations such as this, it is important to consider the knowledge base of your readers. You may have to define technical terms; make use of illustrative analogies, such as comparing the heart to a pump; and tell brief narratives so readers will understand the process. Some writers will use an extended analogy, comparing a nuclear power plant to a tea kettle or a computer virus to a brush fire. One of the challenges of explanatory writing can be deciding which details to leave out and where to make separations.

Critical Thinking for Writing Explanations

1. **Study the process carefully.** Note principal features that need emphasis. Identify areas that are commonly confused or might be difficult for readers to understand.
2. **Determine how much background information is needed.** Your readers may require, for example, a basic knowledge of how normal cells divide before being able to comprehend the way cancer cells develop. In some instances, you may have to address common misconceptions. If you were to explain criminal investigation methods, you first might have to point out how actual police operations differ from those depicted on television.
3. **Determine the beginning and end of the process.** In some cases the process may have an obvious beginning and end. Leaves emerge from buds, flower, grow, turn color, and fall off. But the process of a recession may have no clear-cut beginning and no defined end. If you were to write a paper about the process of getting a divorce, would you stop when the final papers are signed or continue to discuss alimony and child visitation rights? When does a divorce end?
4. **Separate the process into logical stages.** Readers will naturally assume all the stages are equally significant unless you indicate their value or importance. Minor points should not be overemphasized by being isolated in separate steps.
5. **Alert readers to possible variations.** If the process is subject to change or alternative forms, present readers with the most common type. Indicate, either in the introduction or in each stage, that exceptions or variations to the pattern of events exist.
6. **Use transitional phrases to link the stages.** Statements such as *at the same time, two hours later,* and *if additional bleeding occurs* help readers follow explanations.
7. **Stress the importance of time relationships.** Process writing creates a slow-motion effect that can be misleading if the chain of events naturally occurs

within a short period. You can avoid this confusion by opening with a "real time" description of the process:

> The test car collided with the barrier at thirty-five miles an hour. In less than a tenth of a second the bumper crumpled, sending shock waves through the length of the vehicle as the fenders folded back like a crushed beer can. At the same instant sensors triggered the air bag to deploy with a rapid explosion so that it inflated before the test dummy struck the steering wheel.

The rest of the paper might repeat this process for four or five pages, slowly relating each stage in great detail.

8. **Use images, details, narratives, and examples to enrich the description of each stage.** Give readers a full appreciation of each stage by describing it in details they can grasp. Avoid long strings of nonessential, technical language. Use comparisons and narratives to provide readers with clear pictures of events and situations.

9. **Review the final draft for undefined technical terms.** Use a level of language your readers understand. Include technical terms only when necessary, and define ones your readers may not know or may find confusing.

Giving Directions

Directions are step-by-step instructions guiding readers to accomplish a specific goal or task. Process writing can include advice such as how to buy a house or negotiate a loan. In "Desperation Writing" (page 448), Peter Elbow offers students this initial advice about writing under stress:

> Just write and keep writing. . . . Just write and keep writing. It will probably come in waves. After a flurry, stop and take a brief rest. But don't stop too long. Don't think about what you are writing or what you have written or else you will overload the circuit again. Keep writing as though you are drugged or drunk. Keep doing this till you feel you have a lot of material that might be useful; or, if necessary, till you can't stand it any more—even if you doubt that there's anything useful there.

When giving instructions, you may find it helpful to add visual aids such as bold type, capital letters, and underlining, as well as pictures, graphs, and charts. Visual aids are commonly used in documents that must be read quickly or referred to while working. A recipe printed in standard paragraphs instead of lists and numbered steps would be extremely difficult to follow while one were cooking. The instructions for cleaning car battery terminals on page 472 illustrate how directions can be arranged for quick, accurate reading.

Critical Thinking for Writing Directions

1. **Consider your readers carefully.** Determine your readers' current knowledge. They may need background information to understand the process. Readers may also have misconceptions that must be cleared up.
2. **Make sure the directions are self-contained.** A recipe, for example, should list *all* the ingredients, appliances, and instructions needed. *Readers should not be directed to another source for information to complete the process.*
3. **Consider using numbered steps.** Readers find it easier to follow numbered steps and can mark their places if interrupted.
4. **Provide complete instructions.** Do not tell readers to "put the cake in the oven for thirty minutes or until done." Someone baking the cake for the first time has no idea what the cake is supposed to look like at that point—should it be evenly browned, or can the center remain soft? When is it "done"?
5. **Warn readers of possible events they may misinterpret as mistakes.** If, at some point in the process, the mixture readers are working with suddenly changes color or a machine they are operating makes excess noise, they may assume they have made a mistake and stop. If a person assembling a desk discovers the legs are wobbly, he or she may assume the product is defective. If this is normal, if the legs tighten up when the drawers are installed, let readers know what to expect.
6. **Give negative instructions.** Tell readers what not to do, especially if you know people have a tendency to misuse materials, skip difficult steps, or substitute cheaper materials.
7. **Warn readers of any hazards to their safety, health, property, or the environment.** Warnings about dangerous chemicals, fire hazards, and electrical shocks should be clearly stated and placed in large print. *In giving instructions to customers and employees, you are assuming a legal liability.*

STRATEGIES FOR READING PROCESS

As you read the process entries in this chapter, keep these questions in mind.

Meaning

1. What is the writer's goal, to explain or instruct?
2. Is the goal clearly stated?
3. What are the critical steps in the process?
4. What errors should readers avoid?

Strategy

1. What is the nature of the intended audience?
2. How much existing knowledge does the writer assume readers have? Are terms explained?
3. What are the beginning and ending points of the process? Are these clearly defined?
4. How are steps or stages separated? Are the transitions clear?
5. Does the writer use paragraph breaks, numbers, bold type, and other visual prompts? Are these skillfully used?
6. Are instructions easy to follow?
7. Does the writer demonstrate the significance of the process or the value of his or her advice?

Language

1. Are technical terms clearly defined and illustrated?
2. Does the writer use language that creates clear images of what is being explained?

MORTIMER ADLER

Mortimer Adler (1902–2001) was born in New York City. He taught psychology at Columbia University then moved to Chicago, where he taught the philosophy of law for more than twenty years. He resigned from the University of Chicago in 1952 to head the Institute for Philosophical Research in San Francisco. His books include How to Read a Book *and* Philosopher at Large: An Intellectual Autobiography. *Adler became famous as an editor of the* Encyclopedia Britannica *and leader of the Great Books Program of the University of Chicago. This program encouraged adults from all careers to read and discuss classic works. This essay first appeared in the* Saturday Review of Literature *in 1940.*

How to Mark a Book

OVERVIEW: *Before reading Adler's essay, consider your own reading habits. Do you read with a pen in your hand? Do you scan a work first or simply begin with the first line? Do you take notes? Do you have problems remembering what you read?*

You know you have to read "between the lines" to get the most out of anything. I want to persuade you to do something equally important in the course of your reading. I want to persuade you to "write between the lines." Unless you do, you are not likely to do the most efficient kind of reading. 1   introduction

I contend, quite bluntly, that marking up a book is not an act of mutilation but of love. 2   thesis

You shouldn't mark up a book which isn't yours. Librarians (or your friends) who lend you books expect you to keep them clean, and you should. If you decide that I am right about the usefulness of marking books, you will have to buy them. Most of the world's great books are available today, in reprint editions, at less than a dollar. 3   disclaimer

There are two ways in which one can own a book. The first is the property right you establish by paying for it, just as you pay for clothes and furniture. But this act of purchase is only the prelude to possession. Full ownership comes only when you have made it a part of yourself, and the best way to make yourself a part of it is by writing in it. An illustration may make the point clear. You buy a beefsteak and transfer it from the butcher's icebox to your own. But you do not own the beefsteak in the most important sense until you consume it and get it into your bloodstream. I am arguing that books, too, must be absorbed in your bloodstream to do you any good. 4   defines "full ownership"

Confusion about what it means to *own* a book leads people to a false reverence for paper, binding, and type—a respect for the physical thing— 5

427

the craft of the printer rather than the genius of the author. They forget that it is possible for a man to acquire the idea, to possess the beauty, which a great book contains, without staking his claim by pasting his bookplate inside the cover. Having a fine library doesn't prove that its owner has a mind enriched by books; it proves nothing more than that he, his father, or his wife, was rich enough to buy them.

6   There are three kinds of book owners. The first has all the standard sets and best-sellers—unread, untouched. (This deluded individual owns wood-
pulp and ink, not books.) The second has a great many books—a few of them read through, most of them dipped into, but all of them as clean and shiny as the day they were bought. (This person would probably like to make books his own, but is restrained by a false respect for their physical appearance.) The third has a few books or many—every one of them dog-eared and dilapidated, shaken and loosened by continual use, marked and scribbled in from front to back. (This man owns books.)

7   Is it false respect, you may ask, to preserve intact and unblemished a beautifully printed book, an elegantly bound edition? Of course not. I'd no more scribble all over a first edition of *Paradise Lost* than I'd give my baby a set of crayons and an original Rembrandt! I wouldn't mark up a painting or a statue. Its soul, so to speak, is inseparable from its body. And the beauty of a rare edition or of a richly manufactured volume is like that of a painting or a statue.

8   But the soul of a book *can* be separated from its body. A book is more like the score of a piece of music than it is like a painting. No great musician confuses a symphony with the printed sheets of music. Arturo Toscanini reveres Brahms, but Toscanini's score of the C-minor Symphony is so thoroughly marked up that no one but the maestro himself can read it. The reason why a great conductor makes notations on his musical scores—marks them up again and again each time he returns to study them—is the reason why you should mark your books. If your respect for magnificent binding or typography gets in the way, buy yourself a cheap edition and pay your respects to the author.

9   Why is marking up a book indispensable to reading? First, it keeps you awake. (And I don't mean merely conscious; I mean wide awake.) In the
second place, reading, if it is active, is thinking, and thinking tends to express itself in words, spoken or written. The marked book is usually the thought-through book. Finally, writing helps you remember the thoughts you had, or the thoughts the author expressed. Let me develop these three points.

If reading is to accomplish anything more than passing time, it must be active. You can't let your eyes glide across the lines of a book and come up with an understanding of what you have read. Now an ordinary piece of light fiction, like say, *Gone with the Wind*, doesn't require the most active kind of reading. The books you read for pleasure can be read in a state of relaxation, and nothing is lost. But a great book, rich in ideas and beauty, a book that raises and tries to answer great fundamental questions, demands the most active reading of which you are capable. You don't absorb the ideas of John Dewey the way you absorb the crooning of Mr. Vallee. You have to reach for them. That you cannot do while you're asleep.

10

defines "active reading"

If, when you've finished reading a book, the pages are filled with your notes, you know that you read actively. The most famous active reader of great books I know is President Hutchins, of the University of Chicago. He also has the hardest schedule of business activities of any man I know. He invariably reads with a pencil, and sometimes, when he picks up a book and pencil in the evening, he finds himself, instead of making intelligent notes, drawing what he calls "caviar factories" on the margins. When that happens, he puts the book down. He knows he's too tired to read, and he's just wasting time.

11

But, you may ask, why is writing necessary? Well, the physical act of writing, with your own hand, brings words and sentences more sharply before your mind and preserves them better in your memory. To set down your reaction to important words and sentences you have read, and the questions they have raised in your mind, is to preserve those reactions and sharpen those questions.

12

why write?

Even if you wrote on a scratch pad, and threw the paper away when you had finished writing, your grasp of the book would be surer. But you don't have to throw the paper away. The margins (top and bottom, as well as side), the end-papers, the very space between the lines, are all available. They aren't sacred. And, best of all, your marks and notes become an integral part of the book and stay there forever. You can pick up the book the following week or year, and there are all your points of agreement, disagreement, doubt, and inquiry. It's like resuming an interrupted conversation with the advantage of being able to pick up where you left off.

13

And that is exactly what reading a book should be: a conversation between you and the author. Presumably he knows more about the subject than you do; naturally, you'll have the proper humility as you approach him. But don't let anybody tell you that a reader is supposed to be solely on the receiving end. Understanding is a two-way operation; learning doesn't con-

14

reading as conversation

sist in being an empty receptacle. The learner has to question himself and question the teacher. He even has to argue with the teacher, once he understands what the teacher is saying. And marking a book is literally an expression of your differences, or agreements of opinion, with the author.

15   There are all kinds of devices for marking a book intelligently and fruitfully. Here's the way I do it:

uses numbered
steps and
italics for easy
reading

1. *Underlining:* of major points, of important or forceful statements.
2. *Vertical lines at the margin:* to emphasize a statement already underlined.
3. *Star, asterisk, or other doo-dad at the margin:* to be used sparingly, to emphasize the ten or twenty most important statements in the book. (You may want to fold the bottom corner of each page on which you use such marks. It won't hurt the sturdy paper on which most modern books are printed, and you will be able to take the book off the shelf at any time and, by opening it at the folded-corner page, refresh your recollection of the book.)
4. *Numbers in the margin:* to indicate the sequence of points the author makes in developing a single argument.
5. *Numbers of other pages in the margin:* to indicate where else in the book the author made points relevant to the point marked; to tie up the ideas in a book, which, though they may be separated by many pages, belong together.
6. *Circling of key words or phrases.*
7. *Writing in the margin, or at the top or bottom of the page, for the sake of:* recording questions (and perhaps answers) which a passage raised in your mind; reducing a complicated discussion to a simple statement; recording the sequence of major points right through the book. I use the end-papers at the back of the book to make a personal index of the author's points in the order of their appearance.

16   The front end-papers are, to me, the most important. Some people reserve them for a fancy bookplate. I reserve them for fancy thinking. After I have finished reading the book and making my personal index on the back end-papers, I turn to the front and try to outline the book, not page by page, or point by point (I've already done that at the back), but as an integrated structure, with a basic unity and an order of parts. This outline is, to me, the measure of my understanding of the work.

17   If you're a die-hard anti-book-marker, you may object that the margins, the space between the lines, and the end-papers don't give you room enough. All right. How about using a scratch pad slightly smaller than the page-size of the book—so that the edges of the sheets won't protrude? Make your index, outlines, and even your notes on the pad, and then insert these sheets permanently inside the front and back covers of the book.

Or, you may say that this business of marking books is going to slow up 18 your reading. It probably will. That's one of the reasons for doing it. Most of us have been taken in by the notion that speed of reading is a measure of our intelligence. There is no such thing as the right speed for intelligent reading. Some things should be read quickly and effortlessly, and some should be read slowly and even laboriously. The sign of intelligence in reading is the ability to read different things according to their worth. <u>In the case of good books, the point is not to see how many of them you can get through, but rather how many can get through you—how many you can make your own.</u> A few friends are better than a thousand acquaintances. If this be your aim, as it should be, you will not be impatient if it takes more time and effort to read a great book than it does a newspaper.

goal of reading good books

You may have one final objection to marking books. You can't lend them 19 to your friends because nobody else can read them without being distracted by your notes. Furthermore, you won't want to lend them because a marked copy is a kind of intellectual diary, and lending it is almost like giving your mind away.

If your friend wishes to read your *Plutarch's Lives, Shakespeare,* or *The* 20 *Federalist Papers,* tell him gently but firmly to buy a copy. You will lend him your car or your coat—but your books are as much a part of you as your head or your heart.

conclusion

Understanding Meaning

1. In Adler's view, when do you really *own* a book? What makes a book truly yours? What makes a book like a steak?
2. What does Adler mean by the "soul" of a book? How does respecting it differ from respecting its "body"?
3. Why is it important, in Adler's view, to write as you read?
4. *Critical Thinking:* This essay was first published more than sixty years ago. Are Adler's suggestions any different than the study skills you may have learned in high school or college?

Evaluating Strategy

1. What audience is Adler addressing?
2. *Other Modes:* Where does Adler use *comparison, description,* and *classification* in developing this essay?

3. Adler provides seven suggestions that are stated in italics and numbered. If this advice were written in a standard paragraph, would it be as effective? Why or why not?

Appreciating Language

1. The *Saturday Review of Literature* had a general but highly literary readership, much like that of today's *New Yorker* or *Vanity Fair.* Does the tone and style of the article seem suited to this audience?
2. Are there any words, phrases, references, or expressions in this sixty-year-old article that need updating?

Connections across the Disciplines

1. Consider Samuel Scudder's "Take This Fish and Look at It" (page 47) and Carl Sagan's "Why We Need to Understand Science" (page 563). Can Adler's article be seen as a call for critical thinking? Do too many people simply let the words flow past their eyes without interacting with the text by asking questions, looking for meaning, and examining and measuring ideas?
2. Marie Winn (page 194) criticizes television as a passive medium, one that encourages people to simply absorb images without thought. Ann McClintock (page 396) outlines propaganda techniques used in advertising. Can Adler's principles be applied to watching television and examining ads?

Writing Suggestions

1. Using Adler's seven suggestions, write a brief one-page guide on active reading directed to high school students.
2. *Collaborative Writing:* Adler presents tips for active reading. Work with a group of students and discuss their experiences in studying for examinations. Record your ideas and suggestions, and then write a well-organized list of tips to help new students develop successful study skills.

ELIZABETH KOLBERT

> *Elizabeth Kolbert (1961–) was born in New York City and received a degree in English from Yale University. After college she began working for the* New York Times, *eventually heading the newspaper's office in Albany, New York. She has reported on the last two presidential campaigns as well as on the role of media in politics and culture. She also contributes to the* Times's *"Metro Matters" column.*

Birth of a TV Show: A Drama All Its Own

OVERVIEW: *Most readers are familiar only with the finished products of television—the shows that appear on the screen. In this essay, Kolbert explains the behind-the-scenes process that winnows hundreds of ideas down to the few that eventually become shows.*

It was supposed to be "Grease" updated for the 1990's and packaged for television. Every week, a bunch of high school students would grapple with—and make wisecracks about—issues of life and love. Occasionally they would break into song. 1

The idea for this musical sitcom belonged to Marta Kauffman and David Crane, who have been writing together for 16 years. A few months ago, they pitched it to a group of high-ranking ABC executives here. The reaction was immediate. 2

"As soon as a couple of words left our mouths, their eyes glazed over," said Ms. Kauffman. 3

"It was like all the blood drained from the room," said Mr. Crane. 4

THE WINNOWING PROCESS

It is now the height of "development season" in the television business, a period that's not really a season, and is only rarely about development. Stretching from early fall through late spring, it is a time when writers like Ms. Kauffman and Mr. Crane watch most of their cherished ideas turned into scrap. 5

At the start of the season, executives from each of the networks—CBS, NBC, ABC and Fox—listen to hundreds of writers pitch new sitcoms. The fortunate few dozen advance to the next step: writing scripts for the pro- 6 spective shows. After examining those scripts, the networks narrow their choices to 8 or 10, for which pilot episodes will be filmed. From these pilots, they will eventually make four or five new sitcoms.

7   Ideas for dramatic series are winnowed similarly, except that even fewer dramas are made. By the time the networks' fall schedules are fixed, sometime in mid-May, roughly 99 out of 100 of the new series that were proposed will have been relegated to oblivion.

8   From the networks' perspective, the point of development season is to obtain, for the least amount of money, the shows that are most likely to succeed. A network pays nothing for a pitch. It pays anywhere from $50,000 to $100,000 for a script. And it pays up to $1.2 million for a pilot. (The writers and producers don't see all of this money; the cast, the crew and the studios they all work for get a cut.)

9   Over the last few years, the big broadcast networks have lost viewers and dollars to cable channels. So network budgets have shrunk and the number of pilot orders has been cut almost in half. For the people who produce television shows, the stakes and the pressure are now much higher every time they approach a network with an idea or a script or a pilot episode. Even a cherished spot on the fall schedule means little by itself. The networks' new cost-consciousness dictates that new shows are often given just a few weeks (and in the case of CBS's "South of Sunset," only one) to find an audience or be canceled.

10   For writers and producers (and Mr. Crane and Ms. Kauffman are both), development season is a time of unremitting insecurity. Mr. Crane compared the process of vying for a network time slot to entering a beauty pageant and donning a bathing suit.

11   "You feel like Miss New Jersey," he said over lunch the other day at the commissary at Warner Brothers, the studio where the team works.

12   In their not-infrequent encounters with rejection, Ms. Kauffman and Mr. Crane are probably fairly typical of television writers here, except they are a lot more successful at getting their shows on the air.

13   Four years ago, the pair created the popular HBO series "Dream On," which is still in production. (That show, which incorporates nudity and profanity above and beyond "N.Y.P.D. Blue," could not have been made for a broadcast network.)

LOOKING AHEAD TO FALL

14   "Dream On" was followed by "The Powers That Be," which lasted for a season on NBC. Last fall the Crane-Kauffman team, along with a third part-

ner, Kevin Bright, produced "Family Album" on CBS, which got the ax after just six episodes.

The set for "Family Album" had barely been dismantled before it was   15
time to start developing ideas for the next fall. Ms. Kauffman, Mr. Crane and Mr. Bright agreed to let a reporter observe the progress of these projects through the scheduling process in May.

"Once 'Family Album' was done, we said, 'O.K., what are we going to   16
do next?'" recalled Leslie Moonves, the president of Warner Brothers Television, which has more than 25 other writers working to get pilots on the air. "We do this with all our producers. We analyze what their strengths are, what kind of shows they write. In the meantime, we are gathering acorns at the various networks, trying to get a bidding war going on, trying to get some excitement about them."

Because of the success of "Dream On," a comedy about a sex-obsessed   17
man who thinks in film clips, Ms. Kauffman and Mr. Crane are, in Mr. Moonves's words, a "hot commodity." All four networks are eager to work with them, though not necessarily on the shows they want to work on.

After several consultations with Warner, Ms. Kauffman and Mr. Crane   18
decided to pitch three sitcoms for the fall: the musical, a show about six people in their 20's making their way in Manhattan and a series about a Staten Island teen-ager with a fertile fantasy life. In an effort to maximize their chances, they examined each network's style—although it might not seem so, people in the industry think the four networks have distinguishable tastes and preferences—and which time slots might be available at each. They decided to pitch the high-school musical to ABC, the teen-age show to Fox and the young-adult show to NBC.

"We felt cutting-edge-wise, Fox and NBC probably right now were bet-   19
ter for them," Mr. Moonves said.

ABC, perhaps still cringing from the response to its last musical ven-   20
ture, "Cop Rock," turned down the show it was pitched. Fox ordered a script. NBC was so eager to work with the pair again that, in an unusual move, it agreed to shoot a pilot, even though no script was in hand.

A NETWORK CONCESSION

Explaining the network's concession to Ms. Kauffman and Mr. Crane, War-   21
ren Littlefield, the president of NBC Entertainment, said, "You have to make a substantial commitment to be in business with them." If the net-

work eventually decides not to make a pilot episode, it will pay a substantial penalty. (Hundreds of thousands of dollars is typical in such cases.)

22   Ms. Kauffman and Mr. Crane met at Brandeis University, where they both wanted to be actors. After college, they moved to New York and began writing musical comedies together instead. Some of these musicals, including "A . . . My Name Is Alice," and "Upstairs at O'Neal's," ran Off Broadway. Posters for the shows now hang in their shared office at Warner Brothers, above their desks, which face each other.

23   "We actually don't get tired of each other," Ms. Kauffman said of the arrangement.

24   "Annoyed sometimes," Mr. Crane interjected.

25   After all these years of writing together, the two have come to sound alike, and their conversation has the easy, interrupt-each-other quality one expects from a married couple, which they are not. Ms. Kauffman is married to a composer, Michael Skloff, who has written the opening music for some of their television shows.

EXPLORING TEEN-AGERS

26   To prepare for writing the script for the NBC pilot, Ms. Kauffman interviewed several of the twentysomething babysitters who care for her two young children. For the Fox show, she and Mr. Crane rented an armful of teen-age movies, including "Risky Business" and "Say Anything." They started to watch the Fox series "Beverly Hills 90210," trying to discern what it had that attracted so many teen-agers. ("The actors are all very good looking," was Ms. Kauffman's conclusion.)

27   For the last several weeks the pair have been sitting across from each other, doing what television producers must often do: trying to write funny dialogue for two different sets of characters. From the way they talk about the characters—Harry is the lead in the Fox script, Rachel and Monica are important figures in the NBC script—it is clear they have been spending a lot of time with their creations. "Monica is sick of dating," Ms. Kauffman said knowingly, as if referring to a close friend. "She feels like if she has to eat another Caesar salad, she's going to die."

28   The Fox script was due first, late last month. As the deadline approached, there was a crunch. They weren't satisfied with the opening of the script and decided to rewrite it. The script was too long and had to be cut. On an easel in their office, Ms. Kauffman and Mr. Crane wrote themselves a

message in black letters: "Write Faster." After some second thoughts, they crossed out "faster" and replaced it with "better."

CHANGES REQUESTED

Fox told the pair recently that it liked the script and wanted to shoot a pilot,   29
but with some changes. The main character will grow up a little—he will be a junior in high school instead of a freshman, as originally planned—and a few family members, including his father, will be dropped. (As to how they will account for the absence of the father, Mr. Crane said, "Ask us in a few weeks.")

Pending approval of the script they just sent to NBC, Ms. Kauffman   30
and Mr. Crane are gearing up to shoot two pilots by the end of April. Mr. Crane described their mood as "harried, happy and anxious."

Casting is the next step, and much of the shows' future depends on   31
finding the right actors. This is especially true for the Fox show, which requires a dynamic young man for the lead. Ms. Kauffman and Mr. Crane are convinced that somewhere out there, the next Michael J. Fox is waiting. Now all they need to do is find him.

Understanding Meaning

1. What chances do writers have of seeing their ideas become television shows?
2. How has cable television altered the process of network production?
3. What motivates writers to work in a medium that offers so few opportunities for success? How do they cope with rejection?
4. *Critical Thinking:* What does this process reveal about the nature of television? Americans usually despair about the sameness or shallowness of network television. Could the process be altered to include more types of viewer evaluations besides ratings?

Evaluating Strategy

1. How effective is the opening example? Does it make a good introduction to the process?
2. Kolbert uses a single writing team to explain the process. Is this an effective strategy? Does it humanize or "dramatize" a commercial endeavor? Would readers care as much about writers if they remained faceless workers?

3. *Other Modes:* Indicate where Kolbert uses *example*, *narration*, and *comparison* to develop her explanation.

Appreciating Language

1. What tone and style does Kolbert use? What does her choice of words reveal about her attitude toward the writers? Toward television?
2. Note places where Kolbert introduces and defines television terms. How effective are her definitions?

Connections across the Disciplines

1. How do Steven Stark's observations in "A Tale of Two Sitcoms" (page 249) relate to those made by Kolbert?
2. Does this process explain how television confronts controversial social issues? Refer to Pilipp and Shull's "TV Movies in the First Decade of AIDS" (page 323).

Writing Suggestions

1. Using Kolbert's article as a model, write a short essay that explains a process you encountered in a job—the way department stores purchase clothing; the way libraries order new books; the way restaurants plan menus; the way car dealers sell automobiles, and so forth.
2. *Collaborative Writing:* Work with a group of students, and discuss their attitudes about network television. Craft a short essay explaining the ideal process for selecting ideas for new television shows.

ARMOND D. BUDISH

Armond D. Budish is an attorney and consumer-law reporter. He practices law in Ohio, where he writes columns on consumer issues for the Cleveland Plain Dealer. *He has also published articles in* Family Circle *magazine. His book* How to Beat the Catastrophic Costs of Nursing Home Care *was published in 1989, and his latest book is* Avoiding the Medicaid Trap *(1996).*

Fender Benders: Legal Do's and Don't's

OVERVIEW: *As you read this article, notice how Budish makes use of numbered steps and bold type to make this* Family Circle *article easy to skim.*

The car ahead of you stops suddenly. You hit the brakes, but you just can't stop in time. Your front bumper meets the rear end of the other car. *Ouch!* 1

There doesn't seem to be any damage, and it must be your lucky day because the driver you hit agrees that it's not worth hassling with insurance claims and risking a premium increase. So after exchanging addresses, you go your separate ways. 2

Imagine your surprise when you open the mail a few weeks later only to discover a letter from your "victim's" lawyer demanding $10,000 to cover car repairs, pain and suffering. Apparently the agreeable gentleman decided to disagree, then went ahead and filed a police report blaming you for the incident and for his damages. 3

When automobiles meet by accident, do you know how to respond? Here are 10 practical tips that can help you avoid costly legal and insurance hassles. 4

1. Stop! It's the Law.

No matter how serious or minor the accident, stop immediately. If possible, don't move your car—especially if someone has been injured. Leaving the cars as they were when the accident occurred helps the police determine what happened. Of course, if your car is blocking traffic or will cause another accident where it is, then move it to the nearest safe location. 5

For every rule there are exceptions, though. If, for example, you are rear-ended at night in an unsafe area, it's wisest to keep on going and notify the police later. There have been cases in which people were robbed or assaulted when they got out of their cars. 6

439

2. Zip Loose Lips.

7   Watch what you say after an accident. Although this may sound harsh, even an innocent "I'm sorry" could later be construed as an admission of fault. Also be sure not to accuse the other driver of causing the accident. Since you don't know how a stranger will react to your remarks, you run the risk of making a bad situation worse.

8   Remember, you are not the judge or jury; it's not up to you to decide who is or is not at fault. Even if you think you caused the accident, you might be wrong. For example: Assume you were driving 15 miles over the speed limit. What you probably were not aware of is that the other driver's blood-alcohol level exceeded the legal limits, so he was at least equally at fault.

3. Provide Required Information.

9   If you are involved in an accident, you are required in most states to give your name, address and car registration number to: any person injured in the accident; the owner, driver or passenger in any car that was damaged in the accident; a police officer on the scene. If you don't own the car (say it belongs to a friend or your parents), you should provide the name and address of the owner.

10   You must produce this information even if there are no apparent injuries or damages and even if you didn't cause the accident. Most states don't require you to provide the name of your insurance company, although it's usually a good idea to do so. However, *don't* discuss the amount of your coverage—that might inspire the other person to "realize" his injuries are more serious than he originally thought.

11   What should you do if you hit a parked car and the owner is not around? The law requires you to leave a note with your name, and the other identifying information previously mentioned, in a secure place on the car (such as under the windshield wiper).

4. Get Required Information.

12   You should obtain from the others involved in the accident the same information that you provide them with. However, if the other driver refuses to co-operate, at least get the license number and the make and model of the car to help police track down the owner.

5. Call the Police.

13   It's obvious that if it's a serious accident in which someone is injured, the police should be called immediately. That's both the law and common sense. But what if the accident seems minor? Say you're stopped, another car taps you in the rear. If it's absolutely clear to both drivers that there is no damage or injury, you each can go your merry way. But that's the exception.

14   Normally, you should call the police to substantiate what occurred. In most cities police officers will come to the scene, even for minor accidents, but if they won't, you and the other driver should go to the station (of the city

where the accident occurred) to file a report. Ask to have an officer check out both cars.

If you are not at fault, be wary of accepting the other driver's suggestion 15
that you leave the police out of it and arrange a private settlement. When you submit your $500 car-repair estimate several weeks later, you could discover that the other driver has developed "amnesia" and denies being anywhere near the accident. If the police weren't present on the scene, you may not have a legal leg to stand on.

Even if you *are* at fault, it's a good idea to involve the police. Why? Be- 16
cause a police officer will note the extent of the other driver's damages in his or her report, limiting your liability. Without police presence the other driver can easily inflate the amount of the damages.

6. Identify Witnesses.

Get the names and addresses of any witnesses, in case there's a legal battle 17
some time in the future. Ask bystanders or other motorists who stop whether they saw the accident; if they answer "yes," get their identifying information. It is also helpful to note the names and badge numbers of all police officers on the scene.

7. Go to the Hospital.

If there's a chance that you've been injured, go directly to a hospital emer- 18
gency room or to your doctor. The longer you wait, the more you may jeopardize your health and the more difficult it may be to get reimbursed for your injuries if they turn out to be serious.

8. File a Report.

Every driver who is involved in an automobile incident in which injuries 19
occur must fill out an accident report. Even if the property damage is only in the range of $200 to $1,000, most states require that an accident report be filed. You must do this fairly quickly, usually in 1 to 30 days. Forms may be obtained and filed with the local motor vehicle department or police station in the city where the accident occurred.

9. Consider Filing an Insurance Claim.

Talk with your insurance agent as soon as possible after an accident. He or 20
she can help you decide if you should file an insurance claim or pay out of your own pocket.

For example, let's say you caused an accident and the damages totaled 21
$800. You carry a $250 deductible, leaving you with a possible $550 insurance claim. If you do submit a claim, your insurance rates are likely to go up, an increase that will probably continue for about three years. You should compare that figure to the $550 claim to determine whether to file a claim or to pay the cost yourself. (Also keep in mind that multiple claims sometimes make it harder to renew your coverage.)

10. Don't Be Too Quick to Accept a Settlement.

22   If the other driver is at fault and there's any chance you've been injured, don't rush to accept a settlement from that person's insurance company. You may not know the extent of your injuries for some time, and once you accept a settlement, it's difficult to get an "upgrade." Before settling, consult with a lawyer who handles personal injury cases.

23   When you *haven't* been injured and you receive a fair offer to cover the damage to your car, you can go ahead and accept it.

Understanding Meaning

1. What problems can motorists run into if they are careless about handling even minor accidents?
2. What are some of the most important things you should do if involved in a fender bender?
3. Why should you go to the hospital even if you have what appears to be a minor injury?
4. *Critical Thinking:* Should this article be printed as a pamphlet and distributed to drivers' education classes? Have you known anyone who has encountered difficulties that could have been avoided if he or she had followed the writer's advice?

Evaluating Strategy

1. How does Budish arouse reader attention in the opening?
2. How effective are the numbered steps? Would the article lose impact if printed in standard paragraphs?
3. How easy is this article to remember? Can you put it down and recall the main points?

Appreciating Language

1. This article was written for *Family Circle*. Does the level of language appear targeted to a female audience?
2. Why does Budish, who is an attorney, avoid legal terminology?
3. Does Budish's language create concrete images that make strong impressions to dramatize his subject?

Connections across the Disciplines

1. Budish provides tips in numbered points. Could Louis Mizell's article "Who's Listening to Your Cell Phone Calls?" (page 312) be restated in a list of steps instructing consumers on the safe use of cell phones?
2. How does Budish's article relate to Ramon "Tianguis" Pérez's "The Fender-Bender" (page 56)?

Writing Suggestions

1. Using this article as a model, provide the general public with a similar list of tips to prevent heart disease, deter muggers, prepare children for school, save money for retirement, or a topic of your choice.
2. *Collaborative Writing:* Work with a group of students to provide tips for new students on campus. Use peer review to make sure you do not overlook details in your student guide.

MARVIN HARRIS

Marvin Harris (1927–2001) was born in Brooklyn and received degrees from Columbia University. After teaching at Columbia for many years, Harris moved to the University of Florida, where he served as a graduate research professor in anthropology. Harris conducted research in Harlem, Africa, South America, and Asia. He published several scholarly works but is best known for books written to general readers such as Cows, Pigs, Wars, and Witches: The Riddles of Culture *and* Cannibals and Kings: The Origins of Cultures. *Much of Harris's work focused on how people's basic needs for food and shelter influence their culture.*

How Our Skins Got Their Color

OVERVIEW: *In this essay from* Our Kind: Who We Are, Where We Came From, Where We Are Going *(1988), Harris explains how human beings developed different skin colors. In reading this account, determine how he addresses a topic laden with controversy.*

1   Most human beings are neither very fair nor very dark, but brown. The extremely fair skin of northern Europeans and their descendants, and the very black skins of central Africans and their descendants, are probably special adaptations. Brown-skinned ancestors may have been shared by modern-day blacks and whites as recently as ten thousand years ago.

2   Human skin owes its color to the presence of particles known as melanin. The primary function of melanin is to protect the upper levels of the skin from being damaged by the sun's ultraviolet rays. This radiation poses a critical problem for our kind because we lack the dense coat of hair that acts as a sunscreen for most mammals. Hairlessness exposes us to two kinds of radiation hazards: ordinary sunburn, with its blisters, rashes, and risk of infection; and skin cancers, including malignant melanoma, one of the deadliest diseases known. Melanin is the body's first line of defense against these afflictions. The more melanin particles, the darker the skin, and the lower the risk of sunburn and all forms of skin cancer. This explains why the highest rates for skin cancer are found in sun-drenched lands such as Australia, where light-skinned people of European descent spend a good part of their lives outdoors wearing scanty attire. Very dark-skinned people such as heavily pigmented Africans of Zaire seldom get skin cancer, but when they do, they get it on depigmented parts of their bodies—palms and lips.

3   If exposure to solar radiation had nothing but harmful effects, natural selection would have favored inky black as the color for all human populations. But the sun's rays do not present an unmitigated threat. As it falls on the skin, sunshine converts a fatty substance in the epidermis into vita-

444

min D. The blood carries vitamin D from the skin to the intestines (technically making it a hormone rather than a vitamin), where it plays a vital role in the absorption of calcium. In turn, calcium is vital for strong bones. Without it, people fall victim to the crippling diseases rickets and osteomalacia. In women, calcium deficiencies can result in a deformed birth canal, which makes childbirth lethal for both mother and fetus.

Vitamin D can be obtained from a few foods, primarily the oils and livers of marine fish. But inland populations must rely on the sun's rays and their own skins for the supply of this crucial substance. The particular color of a human population's skin, therefore, represents in large degree a trade-off between the hazards of too much versus too little solar radiation: acute sunburn and skin cancer on the one hand, and rickets and osteomalacia on the other. It is this trade-off that largely accounts for the preponderance of brown people in the world and for the general tendency for skin color to be darkest among equatorial populations and lightest among populations dwelling at higher latitudes. 4

At middle latitudes, the skin follows a strategy of changing colors with the seasons. Around the Mediterranean basin, for example, exposure to the summer sun brings high risk of cancer but low risk for rickets; the body produces more melanin and people grow darker (i.e., they get suntans). Winter reduces the risk of sunburn and cancer; the body produces less melanin, and the tan wears off. 5

The correlation between skin color and latitude is not perfect because other factors—such as the availability of foods containing vitamin D and calcium, regional cloud cover during the winter, amount of clothing worn, and cultural preferences—may work for or against the predicted relationship. Arctic-dwelling Eskimos, for example, are not as light-skinned as expected, but their habitat and economy afford them a diet that is exceptionally rich in both vitamin D and calcium. 6

Northern Europeans, obliged to wear heavy garments for protection against the long, cold, cloudy winters, were always at risk for rickets and osteomalacia from too little vitamin D and calcium. This risk increased sometime after 6000 B.C., when pioneer cattle herders who did not exploit marine resources began to appear in northern Europe. The risk would have been especially great for the brown-skinned Mediterranean peoples who migrated northward along with the crops and farm animals. Samples of Caucasian skin (infant penile foreskin obtained at the time of circumcision) exposed to sunlight on cloudless days in Boston (42°N) from November through February produced no vitamin D. In Edmonton (52°N) this period extended from October to March. But further south (34°N) sunlight was effective in producing vitamin D in the middle of the winter. Almost all 7 of Europe lies north of 42°N. Fair-skinned, nontanning individuals who could utilize the weakest and briefest doses of sunlight to synthesize vitamin D were strongly favored by natural selection. During the frigid winters, only a small circle of a child's face could be left to peek out at the sun through the heavy clothing, thereby favoring the survival of individuals with translucent patches of pink on their cheeks characteristic of many northern Europeans. . . .

8   If light-skinned individuals on the average had only 2 percent more children survive per generation, the changeover in their skin color could have begun five thousand years ago and reached present levels well before the beginning of the Christian era. But natural selection need not have acted alone. Cultural selection may also have played a role. It seems likely that whenever people consciously or unconsciously had to decide which infants to nourish and which to neglect, the advantage would go to those with lighter skin, experience having shown that such individuals tended to grow up to be taller, stronger, and healthier than their darker siblings. White was beautiful because white was healthy.

9   To account for the evolution of black skin in equatorial latitudes, one has merely to reverse the combined effects of natural and cultural selection. With the sun directly overhead most of the year, and clothing a hindrance to work and survival, vitamin D was never in short supply (and calcium was easily obtained from vegetables). Rickets and osteomalacia were rare. Skin cancer was the main problem, and what nature started, culture amplified. Darker infants were favored by parents because experience showed that they grew up to be freer of disfiguring and lethal malignancies. Black was beautiful because black was healthy.

Understanding Meaning

1. What is Harris's thesis?
2. What is the "natural" color for human skin?
3. What caused people to develop different complexions?
4. What role did sunlight play in human evolution?
5. *Critical Thinking:* What impact could this scientific explanation of skin color have on debates about race and discrimination? Can biological aspects of humanity be separated from social, cultural, political, or psychological attitudes?

Evaluating Strategy

1. How does Harris organize his essay?
2. What research does Harris use to support his views?

3. *Other Modes:* Where does Harris use *narration, comparison,* and *definition* in his explanation?

Appreciating Language

1. How does Harris define *melanin?*
2. Does Harris's selection of words describing color contain connotations that suggest a bias? Is his essay wholly objective? How often does he use words such as *white* and *black?*
3. Would the average newspaper reader be able to understand this essay? What does the level of language suggest about the intended audience?

Connections across the Disciplines

1. Does this article lend more support to the argument made by Carl Sagan in "Why We Need to Understand Science" (page 563)? Can an understanding of science help people cope with social, gender, and cultural conflicts?
2. Would this essay make a good preface to an essay about racial prejudice such as Nathan McCall's "The Lesson" (page 61)?

Writing Suggestions

1. Using this essay for background information, draft a brief explanation about skin color for an elementary school brochure on race relations. Use easily understood language, and employ comparisons and short narratives to explain scientific principles. Avoid words that may have negative connotations.
2. *Critical Writing:* Write an essay analyzing the effect reading this essay had on you. Did it affect your attitudes toward people of different races? Does the knowledge that all humans probably once shared the same complexion change the way you view yourself?
3. *Collaborative Writing:* Discuss Harris's essay with a group of students. What value does a scientific explanation of skin color have in addressing racial problems? Would it be beneficial to share this information with children? Record members' reactions, and create a short statement about the importance of understanding the origins of skin color. If members disagree, consider developing pro and con responses.

PETER ELBOW

Peter Elbow (1935–) was educated at Williams College, Brandeis, Harvard, and Oxford. A noted director of college writing programs, Elbow started a highly acclaimed "Workshop in Language and Thinking" at Bard College. He has published numerous articles about writing and several books including Writing without Teachers *and* Writing with Power.

Desperation Writing

OVERVIEW: *In this section from* Writing without Teachers *(1973), Peter Elbow offers advice to students writing under stress. Facing deadlines, many students feel almost paralyzed, unable to even start an assignment. Elbow presents his recommendations in the form of a process.*

1   I know I am not alone in my recurring twinges of panic that I won't be able to write something when I need to, I won't be able to produce coherent speech or thought. And that lingering doubt is a great hindrance to writing. It's a constant fog or static that clouds the mind. I never got out of its clutches till I discovered that it was possible to write something— not something great or pleasing but at least something usable, workable— when my mind is out of commission. The trick is that you have to do all your cooking out on the table: Your mind is incapable of doing any inside. It means using symbols and pieces of paper not as a crutch but as a wheelchair.

2   The first thing is to admit your condition: Because of some mood or event or whatever, your mind is incapable of anything that could be called thought. It can put out a babbling kind of speech utterance, it can put a simple feeling, perception or sort-of-thought into understandable (though terrible) words. But it is incapable of considering anything in relation to anything else. The moment you try to hold that thought or feeling up against some other to see the relationship, you simply lose the picture— you get nothing but buzzing lines or waving colors.

3   So admit this. Avoid anything more than one feeling, perception, or thought. Simply write as much as possible. Try simply to steer your mind in the direction or general vicinity of the thing you are trying to write about and start writing and keep writing.

4   Just write and keep writing. (Probably best to write on only one side of the paper in case you should want to cut parts out with scissors—but you

probably won't.) Just write and keep writing. It will probably come in waves. After a flurry, stop and take a brief rest. But don't stop too long. Don't think about what you are writing or what you have written or else you will overload the circuit again. Keep writing as though you are drugged or drunk. Keep doing this till you feel you have a lot of material that might be useful; or, if necessary, till you can't stand it any more—even if you doubt that there's anything useful there.

Then take a pad of little pieces of paper—or perhaps 3 × 5 cards—and simply start at the beginning of what you were writing, and as you read over what you wrote, every time you come to any thought, feeling, perception, or image that could be gathered up into one sentence or one assertion, do so and write it by itself on a little sheet of paper. In short, you are trying to turn, say, ten or twenty pages of wandering mush into twenty or thirty hard little crab apples. Sometimes there won't be many on a page. But if it seems to you that there are none on a page, you are making a serious error—the same serious error that put you in this comatose state to start with. You are mistaking lousy, stupid, second-rate, wrong, childish, foolish, worthless ideas for no ideas at all. Your job is not to pick out *good* ideas but to pick out ideas. As long as you were conscious, your words will be full of things that could be called feelings, utterances, ideas—things that can be squeezed into one simple sentence. This is your job. Don't ask for too much. 5

After you have done this, take those little slips or cards, read through them a number of times—not struggling with them, simply wandering and mulling through them; perhaps shifting them around and looking through in various sequences. In a sense these are cards you are playing solitaire with, and the rules of this particular game permit shuffling the unused pile. 6

The goal of this procedure with the cards is to get them to distribute themselves in two or three or ten or fifteen different piles on your desk. You can get them to do this almost by themselves if you simply keep reading through them in different orders; certain cards will begin to feel like they go with other cards. I emphasize this passive, thoughtless mode because I want to talk about desperation writing in its pure state. In practice, almost invariably at some point in the procedure, your sanity begins to return. It is often at this point. You actually are moved to have thoughts or—and the difference between active and passive is crucial here—to *exert* thought; to hold two cards together and *build* or *assert* a relationship. It is a matter of bringing energy to bear. 7

So you may start to be able to do something active with these cards, and begin actually to think. But if not, just allow the cards to find their own piles with each other by feel, by drift, by intuition, by mindlessness. 8

9   You have now engaged in the two main activities that will permit you to get something cooked out on the table rather than in your brain: writing out into messy words, summing up into single assertions, and even sensing relationships between assertions. You can simply continue to deploy these two activities.

10   If, for example, after the first round of writing, assertion-making, and pile-making, your piles feel as though they are useful and satisfactory for what you are writing—paragraphs or sections or trains of thought—then you can carry on from there. See if you can gather each pile up into a single assertion. When you can, then put the subsidiary assertions of that pile into their best order to fit with that single unifying one. If you *can't* get the pile into one assertion, then take the pile as the basis for doing some more writing out into words. In the course of this writing, you may produce for yourself the single unifying assertion you were looking for; or you may have to go through the cycle of turning the writing into assertions and piles and so forth. Perhaps more than once. The pile may turn out to want to be two or more piles itself; or it may want to become part of a pile you already have. This is natural. This kind of meshing into one configuration, then coming apart, then coming together and meshing into a different configuration—this is growing and cooking. It makes a terrible mess, but if you can't do it in your head, you have to put up with a cluttered desk and a lot of confusion.

11   If, on the other hand, all that writing *didn't* have useful material in it, it means that your writing wasn't loose, drifting, quirky, jerky, associative enough. This time try especially to let things simply remind you of things that are seemingly crazy or unrelated. Follow these odd associations. Make as many metaphors as you can—be as nutty as possible—and explore the metaphors themselves—open them out. You may have all your energy tied up in some area of your experience that you are leaving out. Don't refrain from writing about whatever else is on your mind: how you feel at the moment, what you are losing your mind over, randomness that intrudes itself on your consciousness, the pattern on the wallpaper, what those people you see out the window have on their minds—though keep coming back to the whateveritis you are supposed to be writing about. Treat it, in short, like ten-minute writing exercises. Your best perceptions and thoughts are always going to be tied up in whatever is really occupying you, and that is also where your energy is. You may end up writing a love poem—or a hate poem—in one of those little piles while the other piles will finally turn into a lab report on data processing or whatever you have to write about. But you couldn't, in your present state of having your head shot off, have written that report without also writing the poem. And the report will have some of the juice of the poem in it and vice versa.

Understanding Meaning

1. What is Elbow's purpose?
2. What problems does Elbow want students to overcome?
3. Do you find this advice helpful? Would you use it?
4. *Critical Thinking:* What does Elbow's essay reveal to you about the writing process? Why is it important to see writing as a process and not merely a product?

Evaluating Strategy

1. Does the opening adequately demonstrate the need for this process?
2. Are the stages or steps clearly defined?
3. How does Elbow signal transitions?

Appreciating Language

1. Elbow writes of ideas that are "lousy" and "stupid" but still have value. What is he trying to indicate to students with these word choices?
2. Judging by the language, what audience, what type of student, is this essay targeted to?

Connections across the Disciplines

1. How do Elbow's comments about writing compare to William Zinsser's (page 240)?
2. Do you think the reading skills Mortimer Adler (page 427) describes can help people become better writers as well?

Writing Suggestions

1. Experiment with the freewriting process Elbow describes. Select a topic, and write nonstop for at least ten minutes. Afterward underline the ideas you came up with while writing.
2. *Collaborative Writing:* Talk about writing with other students. Discuss working methods. Take notes on the tips you feel are helpful. Work with others to craft these into a process essay.

ANNE WEISBORD

Anne Weisbord has a master's in education and served as director of Career Services at Hahnemann University in Philadelphia before beginning a career as a private career counselor. Widely published, she has appeared on radio and television providing advice on careers, job search strategies, and interviewing. In this article, written for Nurse Extra, *Weisbord tells nurses how to write effective résumés.*

Resumes That Rate a Second Look

OVERVIEW: *Although directed to nurses, Weisbord's advice applies to most professionals. As you read the article, notice how her terse, to-the-point phrases mirror the kind of writing found on most résumés.*

1   In today's business and professional environment—in which healthcare positions can be eliminated STAT—every nurse should have a resume ready to send to potential employers.

2   The purpose of the resume is to get you a job interview. Employers use resumes to screen out undesirable, or less desirable, candidates. Your resume should summarize your skills and experience, and convince employers of the value they will gain in hiring you. It's an advertisement for yourself, and as with all ads, it should generate interest and motivate the reader.

3   Before you prepare your resume, take a few moments to consider your marketable skills. Identify the strengths and accomplishments that are relevant to the position you are seeking, and present them as succinctly and as clearly as possible. You'll need to organize all of this information in no more than two pages, in an easy-to-read, attractive format. Beyond this, there are really no hard-and-fast rules about writing resumes.

4   Let's look at the standard components of the traditional resume that presents your relevant nursing background in reverse chronological order.

5   1. **Personal identification.** You need include only your name, degree, and your professional certification, address, and phone number. Omit date of birth, marital status, and health; these can be discriminatory factors in hiring.

6   2. **Career objective.** This is optional. If you know *exactly* what you want to do, you can use a phrase that describes the type and level of position you are seeking. An objective might be "Nurse Coordinator in Pediatrics," or "Nurse Manager, ICU." However, if you would consider a variety of positions, skip the objective and use only a summary.

3. **Summary.** Describe your background in a few punchy sentences. This is the   7
   "hook" that will pique the reader's interest in the rest of the resume.
4. **Professional experience.** List names, places, job titles, and dates of em-   8
   ployment. Link your experience to your summary or objective. Stress accomplishments, and emphasize responsibilities that will impress the potential
   employer. Use brief phrases with vivid verbs and nouns to describe the skills
   essential to each position. Omit obvious duties. Emphasize accomplishments
   with bullets.

     As you go back into your work history, present fewer details. When you   9
   first became a nurse, you naturally had fewer responsibilities. Devote more
   space to higher-level, more professional duties.
5. **Education.** If you are a recent graduate with little nursing experience, put ed-   10
   ucation before professional experience. Always list the most recent school, degree or certificate program and work backward. Do include honors or academic
   awards. Don't list high school. If you have a college degree, the employer will
   assume you earned a high-school diploma.
6. **Professional certification(s).** List certifications in reverse chronological or-   11
   der, or organize them according to specialty areas.
7. **License(s).** List only the state and title of each professional license. Don't give   12
   your license number(s). You will be asked to provide them later in the interview process.
8. **Activities.** No one will hire you for a healthcare position based on your interest   13
   in golf or coin collecting, but volunteer community involvement shows positive personal characteristics. Be careful about listing political or religious activities. Your reader may have biases against your persuasions.

Remember that your resume serves as a first impression of you. To a   14
potential employer, your coffee-stained copy or your misspellings say
something about your attention (or lack of attention) to detail, your neatness, and even your attitude. Also, modesty is not an asset in a resume. Toot
your own horn!

Understanding Meaning

1. Summarize Weisbord's key points on résumés.
2. What is the purpose of a résumé? Why does this seemingly obvious fact need
   to be explained? Do many people have misconceptions about résumés?
3. What information does Weisbord suggest omitting? Why?
4. *Critical Thinking:* What is the context of a résumé? How does this document
   reflect the roles of writer, audience, and discipline?

Evaluating Strategy

1. How effective is the format of Weisbord's article?
2. Weisbord tells readers "there are really no hard-and-fast rules about writing resumes." Why is this important?
3. How does her article mirror the document she is training readers to write?

Appreciating Language

1. How effective are Weisbord's style and choice of words? Is the article readable?
2. How does Weisbord's emphasis on verbs, "*Describe* your background . . ." and "*List* names, places . . ." (italics added), reflect the kind of language found on most résumés?

Connections across the Disciplines

1. Review Monica Ramos's résumé (page 159). Does it follow Weisbord's advice?
2. Can a résumé provide talking points for an interview? Review Eugene Raudsepp's "Seeing Your Way Past Interview Jitters" (page 455).

Writing Suggestions

1. If you have not written a résumé already, draft one adopting Weisbord's advice.
2. *Collaborative Writing:* Meet with a group of students, and review each other's résumés. Select the best features you discover, and then write a brief process essay explaining step by step how to create an effective résumé.

EUGENE RAUDSEPP

Eugene Raudsepp is president of Princeton Creative Research Inc., based in New Jersey. An expert on job interviewing techniques, Raudsepp created this article for Machine Design *(1993), a magazine read widely by engineers and industrial managers.*

Seeing Your Way
Past Interview Jitters

OVERVIEW: *This article, directed toward engineers, instructs candidates to use a psychological technique called visualization to improve their performance during job interviews.*

It is not unusual to experience a mild attack of nerves before a job inter- 1
view. But there are engineers whose interview jitters are intense enough to
be harmful. They have such overwhelming apprehension and fear that they
either become tongue-tied or proceed to talk themselves out of the job.
Even many capable and articulate engineers act stiff and awkward in interviews, often fidgeting or sitting on the edge of the chair.

When we're anxious, we frequently become self-conscious spectators 2
of our own behavior during interviews, observing and judging our every utterance and movement. This makes us not only more anxious and less convincing, but also divides our attention.

Excessive self-consciousness is particularly true among engineers who 3
go to interviews with a do-or-die attitude. Trying too hard to succeed increases tension and reduces effectiveness. "The self-imposed pressure of
trying to ace an interview can make some people focus too much on how
they look and act," says Steven Berglas, a psychiatry instructor at Harvard
Medical School. He feels that those who are overly conscious of their
grooming, speech, body language, and other interviewing behavior frequently "suppress those elements of their personality that won them the interview in the first place."

Perfectionist engineers particularly experience high anxiety during job 4
interviews. Because they have a strong need to do well and have such inflated
expectations of their own performance, any real or imaginary deviation from
their self-imposed high, and often unrealistic, standards triggers excessive
nervousness and self-critical ruminations. From one slight, innocuous mistake they automatically assume the entire interview will turn out badly.

This anticipation often drives them to behaviors and statements that 5
would seem self-sabotage to an innocent bystander.

455

REDUCING TENSION

6   Although you may feel your blood pressure rise, palms moisten, and stomach tighten before an important interview, you can control these reactions.

7   According to H. Anthony Medley, author of *Sweaty Palms: The Neglected Art of Being Interviewed*, there are four sound reasons why you have nothing to fear but fear itself, and they can help you keep an interview in perspective:

8   1. The interview centers on the subject you know best: yourself.
    2. If you've done your homework, you have a decided advantage: You know more about the interviewer's company than it knows about you.
    3. Interviewers expect job candidates to be a bit nervous.
    4. You have nothing to lose. You didn't have the job offer before the interview, so if you don't have it afterward, you're no worse off.

9   Some interview failures may be inevitable. Most engineers have experienced at least one. The important point is to refrain from exaggerating the importance of an interview situation. Also, if possible, generate several interviews; don't pin your hopes on just one. A winning-at-all-costs attitude seldom wins a job offer.

10   It is detrimental to adopt a confrontational stance with the interviewer. If you feel overly tense or belligerent, it is helpful to pretend that the interviewer is a good friend. A little make-believe can go a long way toward calming hostile feelings.

11   One interesting method of lessening interview stress is suggested by Lawrence Darius, president of Corporate Communication Skills Inc., New York. He is convinced that one of the more effective ways to overcome interview jitters is to separate yourself from your performance. "Just as an actor or actress creates the character in a script, you must try to create a character for the position you're seeking," he explains. "You probably have an image of the ideal engineer or, better yet, of the perfect candidates for the job. How do they differ from you? How do they walk, talk, and act?"

12   Daralee Schulman, a New York City–based career counselor, teaches her clients to relax before an interview by doing this exercise: "Visualize a serene and beautiful scene, perhaps a moonlit beach, while becoming aware of the rhythm of your breathing. On each breath in, think 'I am' and on each breath out, think 'calm.' Ten repetitions of 'I am calm' breathing done in the reception area before an interview can ease your tension." A "reliving" of a past interview in which you did well boosts your self-confidence, too.

A more advanced and exceedingly effective breathing technique is of-   13
fered by Dan Lang, who conducts stress-reducing workshops in New York.
First, exhale totally, imagining that you are relaxing all your tension. Next,
close your mouth and place your right thumb on your right nostril so that it
is completely closed. Then slowly and deeply inhale and exhale through
your left nostril a couple of minutes, or 25 to 30 times. This enables you to
tap into the right hemisphere of your brain, particularly the limbic part that
governs emotions. You will experience an immediate reduction of fear and
anxiety resulting in a more relaxed, in-charge feeling.

THE POWER OF VISUALIZATION

Many top athletes experience almost overwhelming stress before important   14
events. However, most of them have learned—through the new sports psychology of visualization—how to manage performance anxiety, improve
concentration, and enhance athletic performance.

Tennis champion Chris Evert, for example, used to carefully and re-   15
peatedly visualize every detail of an upcoming championship match in her
mind's eye. She pictured her opponent's style and form, and then visualized
how she would counter and respond to every possible maneuver or tactic.

Golf great Jack Nicklaus programs his "bio-computer" for success this   16
way: "I never hit a shot, even in practice, without having a sharp, in-focus
picture of it in my head. It's like a color movie. First, I 'see' the ball where I
want it to finish. I 'see' the ball going there: its path, trajectory, and shape.
The next scene shows me making the kind of swing that will turn the previous image into reality."

There are significant emotional parallels between sports and job inter-   17
views. Through visualizing your ideal interview performance, you can build
confidence and reduce anxiety to manageable levels.

Visualization of a successful interview is impressed upon the memory.   18
When the actual event happens, there is complete confidence of success, as
if one had done it before with a positive outcome.

Understanding Meaning

1. Does Raudsepp suggest engineers suffer from more anxiety at interviews than
    other professionals?
2. Describe the process of visualization in your own words. Why does it work?

3. Why does "trying too hard" often defeat a candidate interviewing for a job?
4. What does Raudsepp tell engineers not to do?
5. *Critical Thinking:* Could these techniques aid students facing an oral exam or essay test? Could visualizing your completed paper help in the writing process?

Evaluating Strategy

1. How effective are the examples Raudsepp uses for support?
2. How does Raudsepp reinforce his views with quotes from other authorities? Why is this important in giving advice?

Appreciating Language

1. What kind of language does Raudsepp use in explaining psychological techniques to engineers? How might this article be stated if written for a psychology journal?
2. Do the tone and style of the article help ease a reader's anxiety about facing a job interview? Explain.

Connections across the Disciplines

1. Refer to Anne Weisbord's article about résumé writing (page 452). Would visualization assist a job applicant in highlighting his or her key strengths? Could reviewing a well-stated résumé help prepare an applicant for an interview by reinforcing his or her accomplishments?
2. Could visualization assist writers? Refer to Peter Elbow's "Desperation Writing" (page 448). Could visualizing the completed document help inspire and guide someone writing under stress?

Writing Suggestions

1. Write a narrative essay about a job interview you have had. At the end provide a brief analysis of your performance. Could it have been better?
2. *Collaborative Writing:* Discuss job interview experiences with a group of students. Ask the members about the toughest questions they were asked. Have the members suggest possible answers. Collect the comments, and collaborate on a process paper: "How to Handle Tough Questions in a Job Interview."

LIZ GRINSLADE

Liz Grinslade is vice president of MSI Healthcare, a national executive search firm that specializes in locating professionals for health care providers. In this 1993 article published in Healthcare Financial Management, *she tells executives how to evaluate a job opportunity.*

Evaluating a Job Opportunity

OVERVIEW: *Grinslade's advice is directed toward health care professionals but applies to almost anyone considering a job offer. Her article is important because for some people taking the wrong job can do more damage to their careers than not being hired.*

For financial managers, as well as other job candidates, the decision to accept or reject a position offered during the job hunting process can be a difficult one. However, if eight basic areas are investigated and considered, the decision to accept or reject an offer can be made more easily. During the job interview, the job candidate should try and obtain information that will help answer the following questions:

1. Will the work be fulfilling and challenging?
2. What skills are necessary to be successful at the job? If the skills are not already possessed, can they readily be developed?
3. Is the facility stable? Is the position stable?
4. Is the management philosophy acceptable?
5. Is there good chemistry between the job candidate and the hiring manager and prospective coworkers?
6. Is the location satisfying?
7. Will there be opportunities for continuing growth and new challenges?
8. Is the compensation fair and equitable?

The answers to these questions can lead a job candidate to the right decision.

What skills are necessary to be successful at the job? If the skills are not already possessed, can they readily be developed? The candidate should consider the scope of responsibilities of the position, as well as the expectations of others, including the facility's administrator, board of directors, and hiring manager. The candidate should try and determine if these expectations are realistic. One way to gather relevant information is to ask what was liked and

459

what was disliked about the performance of the employee previously in the position.

5   Lynn Boltuch, business office director at Mount Sinai Medical Center of Greater Miami, Miami, Florida, suggests that job applicants try to ascertain whether a company is genuinely anxious to hire someone who can make changes to improve operations. Has the company identified specific problems in a department that need to be solved? If the company is seeking a turnaround specialist, will the person hired be given the autonomy, resources, and support needed to make necessary changes? How many layers of management will be involved in making decisions? What are the administrator's overall goals for the position? Are schedules established for implementation of change and does meeting the schedule seem feasible? Are staffing levels adequate?

6   *Is the facility stable? Is the position stable?* Employers expect a job applicant to inquire about a facility's current financial condition. (For independent verification, a Medicare cost report on U.S. healthcare facilities is available for $75 through the Center for Healthcare Industry Performance Studies—CHIPS—in Columbus, Ohio.) If recent financial reports have not been positive, consider the trend. Is the facility's financial position cyclical and approaching an upswing or does an ongoing downslide seem probable? While asking about the financial picture, the job candidate should note not only what the hiring manager says but also the confidence level of his or her response.

7   There are other aspects of stability that should be explored. For instance, the candidate should try to ascertain why the position is open. Has someone been promoted within the system or has there been a "revolving door" of CFOs who could not work with the administrator or the board? What are the market conditions? Are there two other competing hospitals of similar or larger size in the immediate service area? And how tough is the managed care environment?

8   *Is the management philosophy acceptable? Is there good chemistry between the job candidate and the hiring manager and prospective coworkers?* Overall job satisfaction may rest with the answers to these questions. To assess the management philosophy, the candidate should inquire about the priorities for the position and how they should be accomplished. Job candidates should be able to adapt to new ways of doing things and, just as important, organizations should be open to employees' suggestions for change.

9   The job candidate also should ask other staff members, such as the chief operating officer or director of personnel, about the administrator's management style. How does the administrator react in different situations? Is he

or she emotional and erratic? Does he or she avoid confrontations at all costs? Boltuch says one factor that determines how well a job candidate will enjoy working with a hiring manager is noting how the manager makes the candidate feel upon entering the office for the first interview. Did the manager make the candidate feel at ease or "on display"?

When it comes to evaluating the chemistry between the candidate   10 and the management team and other coworkers, the candidate should make a point of meeting as many people he or she would come in contact with in a position as soon as possible. Meeting off-site is preferable. A lot more can be learned over a casual lunch than in a potential coworker's office. "Gut" feelings should be given strong consideration when evaluating the position.

Is the location satisfying? If accepting the position means moving to an-   11 other city, the job candidate should make a list of important considerations, including climate, affordability, quality of school systems, proximity to family and friends, potential cultural and recreational activities, and educational opportunities. The needs of the candidate's spouse should not be forgotten.

Cost of living also can be a significant factor to weigh in making a deci-   12 sion. Using the cost-of-living index, produced by the American Chamber of Commerce Researchers Association, the candidate can compare the relative cost of living in a city. The index is updated quarterly and is available at most libraries.

Will there be opportunities for continuing growth and new challenges? By ask-   13 ing about the organizational structure of a facility, a potential career path can be outlined. Are there higher positions within the company that can be pursued in the future? Have specific situations been mentioned where individuals have been promoted internally? Does the organization provide tuition reimbursement for advanced degrees? Does the organization support/ pay for membership in professional associations? In addition to paying for membership, does the organization also allow for time off to attend meetings or serve as a volunteer on committees? All of these factors can indicate the potential for future advancement.

Is the compensation fair and equitable? The candidate should gather infor-   14 mation about competitive salary structures from mentors, human resource departments, executive recruiters, and professional associations. HFMA periodically surveys and publishes salary data for CFOs and patient accounts managers. But money is only one of many factors to consider.

The old "rule of thumb" requiring a certain percentage of increase in   15 compensation to change jobs is no longer valid. Many healthcare financial professionals accept lateral salary moves or even lower salaries to gain valuable experience from a particular position. Opting for a higher salary at the expense of quality of life or job satisfaction can be a poor tradeoff.

Understanding Meaning

1. What key issues should people consider before accepting a job?
2. In their eagerness to accept jobs, what problems can people create for themselves?
3. What questions should an applicant ask about the employer?
4. Why does Grinslade suggest that a high salary is sometimes worth passing over?
5. *Critical Thinking:* Does Grinslade's article suggest that many people, including skilled professionals, are too passive in the job process? Do people fail to interview their potential employers? Are they too trusting? Do you think many people feel they will be perceived as being rude or ungrateful if they seem critical of an organization offering them a job?

Evaluating Strategy

1. How effectively is the article organized? Are points easy to follow?
2. How does Grinslade use transitions?
3. Grinslade offers sources for gaining further information. Do many other writers fail to do this?

Appreciating Language

1. This article is directed to financial managers in the health care industry. Would it require much rewriting to be reprinted in a sales, engineering, or computer magazine?
2. Grinslade uses clichés such as "rule of thumb" and "'gut' feelings." Are these appropriate phrases in this context?

Connections across the Disciplines

1. Review the 3M want ad (page 157) and Monica Ramos's résumé (page 159). What questions should Ramos consider before accepting a job with 3M?
2. Does selecting the right job differ from selecting the right business opportunity? Can any of the points Charles Jamison offers entrepreneurs in "Why My Business Failed" (page 464) assist a job seeker?

Writing Suggestions

1. Have you ever been burned by a job that did not work out? Were you hired only to find that the company was facing bankruptcy or that you would not receive the equipment or resources needed to do the job? Write a narrative essay about your experience.

2. *Collaborative Writing:* Meet with a group of students, and discuss experiences, both good and bad, with job opportunities. Take notes, and write a process essay similar to Grinslade's offering advice on evaluating job offers. You may wish to target your essay to college students seeking part-time or summer jobs.

BLENDING THE MODES

C H A R L E S   N .   J A M I S O N   J R .

Charles N. Jamison Jr. became the first African-American vice president at Ted Bates Advertising. With ten years' experience in advertising and a doctorate in psychology, Jamison was well-equipped to launch his own ad agency. He teamed up with Kathryn Leary, who also worked at Bates, to create Jamison and Leary. Backed by their former employer and armed with powerful contacts, the team did well. Jamison and Leary landed major accounts such as Bacardi, NYNEX, and the Alvin Ailey dance company. Employing a dozen people, the firm was generating $5 million in billings when it began to fail.

Why My Business Failed

OVERVIEW: *In this "reverse success" story, a talented entrepreneur provides advice to people hoping to achieve success. This article appeared in* Black Enterprise *(1994), a magazine aimed at African-American executives and business owners. Notice how Jamison uses* narrative, description, cause and effect, *and* analysis *to develop his guidelines.*

1   For nearly five years I ran an advertising agency, Jamison & Associates Advertising Inc. (originally Jamison & Leary Advertising).

2   Starting out, I believed that I knew a lot about making advertising work. I proved to myself that I was right.

3   During our glory years, we did work for such large clients as Bacardi, General Foods, PepsiCo, TIAA-CREF, NYNEX, Dow Jones & Co. Inc., and M&M/MARS, as well as for black clients like *Emerge* magazine, Yaska Shoes Ltd. and the Alvin Ailey American Dance Theater. We did video, television, radio and print. We sold a lot of goods, services and tickets. We even won a CEBA (Communication Excellence in Black Advertising) our second year out.

4   The agency is closed now. A victim of the most recent recession. Bankrupt. Chapter 7. History. Past tense.

5   What I learned, somewhat painfully, was that knowing how to create effective advertising doesn't necessarily mean that you're going to know how to run an advertising business. During a recession, which is what we ran into, it's easy to say that the economic climate is the cause of a business' demise. But there is usually more to the story than the most obvious an-

swer. Along the way, I learned some things that I wish I had known before I got started. If you're thinking about running a business, I've got 10 tips to consider that may prove helpful to you along the way.

1. Be sure to have more than one major backer. When we started the 6 agency, we put all our chips in the same basket. We launched the business as an arm of Bates, our employer at the time.

We capitalized on Bates' entry into strategically focused market research. 7 Bates already had a Hispanic ad agency. So, it seemed natural to build a business that offered psychosocial data on African Americans. This information would give Bates clear-cut ways to predict how cultural differences among blacks affect the buying habits of different segments of the market.

Ironically, just as our agency was about to turn profitable, Bates dis- 8 solved the relationship. The reason was no one's fault and had nothing to do with either side's respect for the other. I still do business with Bates (now Backer Spielvogel & Bates). It was simply that Saatchi and Saatchi, which had purchased Bates, had a different set of business priorities.

Despite all this, our agency survived for four more years. But the loss of 9 that early backing definitely affected our ability to weather the financial storms to come.

The motto of all this? Never assume that all the business givens will 10 stay that way, and be sure to line up a diverse set of backers early on in starting your firm.

2. Sell something people want to buy. When I went into business, I be- 11 lieved that my agency would provide a necessary and potentially profitable service in the marketplace.

I spent nearly a decade in large general-market advertising agencies 12 learning how to develop award-winning strategic advertising. I also have a Ph.D. in psychology, where my primary research had been on black culture. Furthermore, I had sole access to a large database on black consumer preferences, attitudes and media behavior.

I was convinced that if I had an opportunity to present a story to a client 13 about their product or service, then they would have to give us the business. I had been on enough new-business pitches to know how this works. How could we miss?

It didn't work. We made pitch after pitch presenting data to marketing 14 managers about the black consumer presence within their brand products. Instead of giving me the business, they would (a) praise me for giving them better insight into and a more sophisticated understanding of the black consumer market, and (b) tell me that despite this compelling story, they didn't feel the need to target this consumer base.

15   For instance, one packaged-goods marketing manager told us our presentation made a lot of sense. But when we tried to follow up, we were told that the company had "other priorities."

16   After a while, I realized that I was trying to sell a very good product that, for whatever reason, few people wanted. Sure, I got some business, but nowhere near the amount I had expected.

17   My advice to you is to realize the real potential for what it is you have to offer and adjust your actions and perceptions accordingly. In other words, do the same kind of in-depth research on your marketplace and industry as you would on the clients you want to land.

18   We looked at the tremendous growth in targeted black advertising and assumed we could expand the marketplace even further. What we failed to see was that most of the African-American ad agencies were not growing much. There was a ceiling on the amount of total business out there. Rather than relying solely on breaking new ground with companies that did not yet have carefully targeted black ad campaigns, we should have been trying to take existing business away from other black ad agencies.

19   3. Pick your partner carefully, and be sure you both have a similar approach to doing business. This one should come as no surprise given that my agency changed from a two-person firm into a one-person operation. But what I have to say may be a surprise.

20   Business isn't about making money. Oh yes, that's part of it, but not even the most important part. No, business is about power, decision-making power, control-over-your-destiny power.

21   If you take on a partner or are invited to be one, make sure that you have a clear understanding of the power relationship between you.

22   Those businesses where the power definitions are clear between the partners have a better chance of maximizing those partners' efforts to ensure the survival of the business, instead of continually putting the business through internecine bouts.

23   What happened to me and my partner? We had the same *goals* for the agency, but two radically different *approaches* to running an agency.

24   For example, we had different philosophies about landing new business. My partner believed that to get business one had to socialize and make contacts. It was something she did very well. In contrast, I believed, during the formal presentation process, you had to create a legitimate reason for the company to need your services. This was something I did very well.

25   What we encountered in working together was simply a clash in styles. Plus, we both believed strongly that our individual approach to landing clients was the *right* way.

Of course, successful agencies have been built on both approaches to   26
landing new business. But because we had a new business with limited resources, it was difficult to try to take the agency in two different directions
at the same time.

The problem here is that it's not easy to discover beforehand what con-   27
trol your potential partner really wants over the direction of the business.
Ordinary conversation may give you some clues about how each of you
views the process of doing business and a feel for one another's goals and
values. But coming to a clear understanding of the issues of power and control requires straightforward discussion. You need to be direct with each
other *before* you form a partnership.

To understand what someone wants out of a business you must really   28
get to know a potential partner. Details about his or her upbringing, family
life, social style, fears, expectations, business philosophy and priorities are
all key.

The success of your venture will require a productive balance of pow-   29
ers—and way of doing things—between the two of you.

4. Never stop marketing your business. The breakup in our partner-   30
ship happened during 1990 and 1991, just before the recession and the
really tough times hit. Nonetheless, my partner and I were so distracted
dealing with interpersonal issues that we had no time for marketing to new
clients.

The result was that during the year the partnership was splitting up,   31
I managed to pitch only two pieces of major business, instead of the
12 pitches I had been making before. Needless to say, this had a big impact
on total billings.

My advice to you: Market, market, market. No matter how well you've   32
done before or how well you're doing now, keep that new business coming
in the door.

5. Don't hire your friends to work for you. Boy, that sounds cold. But   33
does it sound less cold to lay off, or even worse, fire a friend?

When you hire a friend, you are less likely to make strictly business de-   34
cisions about that person, and any time this happens, you've put yourself in
a compromising situation.

Objectivity helps an effective boss get his employees to produce great   35
work, but there is nothing objective about friendship. For instance, I should
have laid people off at the first stroke of losing business. But because I had
personal ties with some friends I had hired, I kept them on payroll even
during tough times.

And speaking about being a boss . . .   36

37   6. Don't be a manager. Be a boss. I was a very good people person when I worked in corporate America. I helped a lot of coworkers get through problems and issues in their lives and they liked working with me. So, naturally, I thought those skills were necessary when I started doing my own thing.

38   Yes. And no.

39   Being a good capitalist means keeping your eyes on the prize. How is what I am doing today going to help the business be more profitable tomorrow than it was yesterday?

40   In any business dealings, there will be distractions that can keep you from focusing on that prize.

41   As a boss with a small business to run, you have no one to fall back on if someone has problems, plus you can't afford the time to support someone emotionally. Trying to be a "good guy" also breaks down your authority, and it wastes energy you could be putting into running your company better.

42   If someone has a personal problem, don't make it your problem. If the problem is affecting productivity and there is a work-related solution to it, implement it. If someone's problems interfere with his or her getting the job done and there is no way that the job can be restructured to provide a solution, replace that person as quickly as possible.

43   7. Charge what you are worth. This primarily concerns those in the service industry where pricing can be somewhat variable.

44   Calculate what your contribution is to your client's bottom line and then charge accordingly. Many people will want your services at reduced fee because they perceive you as hungry or as offering a service that can be derived from other sources. This perception may also be influenced negatively if you are black.

45   If our agency had charged our clients what the value of our services were really worth, we would have been profitable before the tough times hit. You also need to charge a rate that takes into consideration what it costs you to service a particular client. Some accounts required so many agency man hours that we wound up not getting paid for the actual amount of overhead we were investing.

46   In other words, set your fees high enough to reflect what those services really cost you to provide. Be prepared to make a case for why your charges are what they are, and stick to it. Obviously, I am not suggesting inflexibility. You should make adjustments in what you would charge a *Fortune* 500 company, compared with a mom-and-pop store. But keep in mind, all clients will demand your best work, no matter what price you agree on.

8. Turn down bad clients. You won't know whether someone is going to be a good or bad client until you start working with them. However, as soon as you recognize that you've landed a bad client, get rid of them—no matter how much cash you are letting walk out the door.

Recognizing them is a lot easier when you're supplying goods and products as opposed to services. In the product industries, a bad client is someone who doesn't pay within 30 days.

In the service industry, someone who's paying within 30 days could still create havoc in your business. How? By placing demands on the business that, in the process of fulfilling the work requirements, end up poisoning your work environment.

This position can take a variety of forms, but let me mention one example so you get the flavor. We had a packaged-goods client with top executives who had a need for control. Every time we would work on this client's account, these executives would pit one of our staffers against another. Each person who was working on the account would end up getting criticized to another staffer working on the account. The result was that they were demoralizing my people.

Everyone in your company can get tangled up in it when there is a client who is consciously trying to manipulate egos.

All the usual ways of stopping any intentional miscommunications are done routinely in large companies through written reports. In a small business, few have the time to write "CYA" memos.

Why would any client try to undermine your business in this way? The worst clients create trouble so that they either can get more services for free or can justify not paying for services already rendered.

If you want to learn from my experience, save yourself the mental anguish. Resign the account and keep your sanity.

9. Make sure you save for a rainy day. The advice here is tricky. Once you start a business, you must realize that the business is not you, and that as soon as you bring other people into the venture, it takes on a life all its own. Like any newborn, it has an insatiable appetite and will take all the nurturing you have to offer. That nurturance comes in two forms: capital and psychic energy.

You run a significant risk of losing your shirt when you start a business, and it's essential never to forget that. However, as I learned the hard way, taking all of your personal cash and pouring it into your business is ill-advised, no matter how much you are on the verge of making it. Just as ill-advised is pouring so much of yourself into the enterprise that you have no life outside the office.

57   Therefore, prepare for every contingency, even failure. That's not a defeatist attitude; it's a realistic strategy. Even generals preparing for battle leave themselves a way out so that they can fight again another day. Making sure that you can play the game another day—by having some money put away as well as by keeping your emotional options open—means that a failed business can be thought of as a single chapter in your life, rather than your entire story.

58   10. Know what you want to do with your life the day after. The day after what?

59   The day after you realize that your business is either a success or a failure. If the business is a true success, then for all intents and purposes, it can run without you, which means you'll need something else to do next. If it's a failure, then you don't have to worry about it anymore, which could leave a big hole in your day-to-day life.

60   Either way, you'll have time on your hands. I know because I had prepared no contingency plans in case something happened to my business. As a result of my lack of personal disaster planning, despite all the setbacks, I kept automatically looking for more business for our agency to do, rather than heading out to hunt for a marketing job on someone else's payroll.

61   The moral of this story is: If you know what you want to do the day after, you're giving yourself an alternative that will have meaning over and above what you derive from being associated with your business.

62   Trust me. That's a good idea.

63   These 10 confessions represent the personal knowledge I gained from being an entrepreneur. Now that I know them, I am ready to write a happier ending to the book of my business life. Hopefully, you can learn something from them, too.

Understanding Meaning

1. What appear to have been the chief *causes* for the demise of Jamison & Associates?
2. What lessons did Jamison feel he learned about running a business versus creating advertising?
3. What advice does Jamison offer about selecting partners and employees?
4. Jamison tells readers to "be a boss." What are the elements of a good boss?
5. *Critical Thinking:* Many of Jamison's statements are negative, telling readers what not to do. Does this emphasis on avoiding mistakes suggest that he feels many people who dream of opening their own businesses are naive? What does it take to start and maintain a business? What do people often overlook?

Evaluating Strategy

1. What impact does the title have in a magazine dedicated to success and achievement?
2. How effective is the opening *narration?*
3. How does Jamison use *analysis* to diagnose the forces that caused his business to fail?
4. What would make this article easier to read?

Appreciating Language

1. Jamison uses tips like "save for a rainy day." Does this homey language work in this article?
2. What tone comes across in this essay? Does it convey any sense of bitterness or blame seeking?

Connections across the Disciplines

1. Jamison tells readers to look beyond their business ventures. Whether they succeed or fail, entrepreneurs should, he says, consider their lives beyond their careers. How does this relate to John Ciardi's "What Is Happiness?" (page 189)? Do all of these writers suggest that happiness or success cannot be measured solely in dollars?
2. Liz Grinslade provides advice on selecting a job (page 459). How much more important is it to consider a business opportunity, especially one requiring substantial personal investment?

Writing Suggestions

1. Write a similar essay in which you offer advice to readers based on a failure you have experienced. Tell readers, for example, how to avoid paying too much for a car, renting the wrong apartment, losing a lawsuit, or failing a college course.
2. *Collaborative Writing:* Discuss with a number of students the pros and cons of owning a business. Take notes, and then work together to write a set of instructions making use of comparison to demonstrate the advantages and disadvantages of working for yourself instead of someone else.

WRITING BEYOND THE CLASSROOM

LUCILLE TREGANOWAN

Auto expert Lucille Treganowan (1930–) operates Transmissions by Lucille, a chain of repair shops in Pittsburgh, Pennsylvania. She also appears on the popular PBS tele-vision series Lucille's Car Care Clinic. *In 1996 she published a book on auto repair,* Lucille's Car Care, *written in collaboration with Gina Catanzarite, the producer of her television series.*

Cleaning Battery Terminals

OVERVIEW: *As you read the following instructions from* Lucille's Car Care, *think about whether or not you would find it easy to follow them. Do they seem clear and detailed enough for someone who has never performed this procedure before?*

1   Corrosion around the battery terminals affects the way electrical currents are conducted, and if the corrosion is severe it can even prevent the car from starting. Sometimes you'll be able to see a kind of whitish powder de-velop on the terminals, but most problems are caused by corrosion you *can't* see at the contact surfaces between the terminal and the post.

2   You will need:

3   A ½-inch or ⅝-inch box wrench or an open-end wrench from your tool kit or a small ratchet wrench designed specifically for side terminals. Use a 10M (metric measurements) wrench for imports.

4   screwdriver or battery cable terminal puller

5   battery terminal cleaner brush

6   rag

7   water and baking soda solution

8   petroleum jelly

9   NOTE: *Never* smoke cigarettes or use anything that might spark around a bat-tery. To avoid electrical shock, perform the following procedure in the fol-lowing sequence:

10 1.   Use the wrench to loosen the nuts on the battery terminals at the end of the ca-ble. Be sure to note which is the negative terminal and which is the positive ter-minal. They will be clearly marked, and the positive cable is almost always red.

2. Use the battery cable terminal puller to remove the negative terminal. If you   11
    do not own this tool, use your fingers to work the cable back and forth until
    it is loosened, or insert a screwdriver underneath the terminal and gently pry
    it up.
3. Use the battery terminal cleaner brush to scrub the inside of the hole in the   12
    terminal. Brush until the surface is shiny like new metal. Then fit the other
    side of the tool over the battery post and rotate it until the metal shines.
4. Dip a rag in the water/baking soda solution and clean the top of the battery, re-   13
    moving metal particles that were brushed off the terminal and posts.
5. Repeat Step 2 through 4 with the positive terminal.   14
6. Return the terminals to the proper posts, positive *first*, then negative. Tighten   15
    the bolts until you cannot turn the terminal any more.
7. Apply a light coating of petroleum jelly to the outside of the terminals to fight   16
    future corrosion buildup.

Understanding Meaning

1. Why is it important to make sure that a car's battery terminals are clean?
2. What is the point of the warning note that precedes the numbered list of
    instructions?
3. Why is it important to note "which is the negative terminal and which is the
    positive terminal"?
4. Why is the final step to apply petroleum jelly to the cleaned terminals?

Evaluating Strategy

1. Why do you think these instructions begin with a list of items one will need to
    perform the task? Would they be harder or easier to follow without this open-
    ing list?
2. How effectively organized are the instructions? Can they be quickly
    understood?
3. How do numbered points and typeface variations affect the way you read these
    instructions?

Appreciating Language

1. What do the level of diction and word choice suggest about the intended
    audience?
2. Does the author successfully avoid overly technical language that some readers
    might find difficult?

Writing Suggestions

1. Write a set of instructions on first aid, car or home repair, or campus security to be read in an emergency. Use visual aids and short, direct sentences to communicate in as few words as possible.

2. *Collaborative Writing:* Analyze the effectiveness of these instructions with a group of students. Have members read the instructions, and then close their books. One person should refer to the instructions and quiz the group on the steps. Note how much people remembered, and identify areas that more than one person forgot. Based on your group's experiences, work collaboratively to write a short analysis, suggesting changes for greater readability if needed.

STRATEGIES FOR PROCESS WRITING

1. **Define your goal—to explain or to instruct.** Is your purpose to explain how something takes place, or do you seek to instruct readers how to accomplish a specific task?

2. **Evaluate your audience's existing knowledge.** How much does your audience know about the subject? Do any common misconceptions need to be clarified? What terms should be defined?

3. **Define clear starting and ending points.** When does this process begin? What is the end? Readers must have a clear concept of the beginning and end, especially in instructions.

4. **Separate the process into understandable stages or steps.** To explain a process, it is important to break it down into a chain of separate events that makes the process understandable without distorting it. When giving instructions, do not include too many operations in a single step.

5. **Number steps for clarity in the instructions.** Instructions are easier to follow if organized in numbered steps. If interrupted, readers can easily mark their places and later resume the process without confusion.

6. **Consider using visual aids.** Large print, capital letters, bold or italic type, and underlining can highlight text. Graphs, drawings, diagrams, and other visual aids can be beneficial to reinforce both explanatory writing and instructions.

7. **Measure readability of instructions.** Instructions, especially directions people will have to refer to while working, should communicate at a glance. Short sentences and wide spacing between steps are used in cookbooks and repair manuals so a person working in a kitchen or garage can read the text at a distance.

8. **Test your writing.** Because it is easy to skip steps when explaining a process you are familiar with, it is important to have other people read your writing. Other readers can be objective and easily detect missing information.

SUGGESTED TOPICS FOR PROCESS WRITING
General Assignments

Write a process paper on any of the following topics. Assume you are writing for a general, college-educated audience. You may develop your explanation using narratives, comparisons, and definitions. Explain the process as a clearly stated chain of events. Draw from your own experiences.

- How the university processes student applications
- The operation of an appliance such as a microwave, refrigerator, or washing machine

- The process of a disease or disability
- The way small children learn to talk
- The method your employer used in training
- The stages of childbirth
- How a computer virus "infects" a computer
- The way corporations market a new product
- The way the body loses fat through diet or exercise
- How networks select television programs

Write a process paper giving directions to complete a specific task. You may wish to place your instructions in numbered steps rather than standard paragraphs. Remember to highlight any safety hazards.

- How to protect your computer against viruses
- How to purchase a new or used car at the best price
- How to deter a mugger or attacker
- How to quit smoking
- How to find a job
- How to handle sexual harassment on campus or in a job
- How to prepare for an IRS audit
- How to operate a drill press, microscope, or other piece of industrial or scientific equipment
- How to treat a second-degree burn
- How to teach children the importance of saving money

Writing in Context

1. Imagine you have been selected to write a section for a student handbook instructing freshmen how to register for classes. Write a step-by-step paper giving complete instructions. Give exact room numbers, times, and locations. You may wish to refer to a campus map. When you complete a draft of your paper, review it carefully to see if you have left out any pieces of essential information.
2. Select a process you learned on a job, and write instructions suitable for training a new employee. Consider how your job may have changed. Give trainees the benefit of your experience, and add tips that might not be included in the standard job descriptions. Warn readers, for instance, of common problems that arise.
3. Select a process from one of your textbooks, and rewrite it for a sixth-grade class. Simplify the language, and use analogies sixth graders would understand.

STUDENT PAPER: PROCESS

This paper was written in response to the following assignment:

Write a 500-word process paper providing directions to accomplish a specific task. You may include graphs, charts, diagrams, or numbered steps.

Securing Your Home

Homeowners frequently think of security only when planning a vacation. Leaving home for a week or two, they install additional locks, set timers to trigger lights, purchase sophisticated monitoring systems, alert neighbors, and hope their homes will not be robbed in their absence. But most homes are not burglarized while their owners are thousands of miles away. And most burglaries do not occur in the dead of night. Most houses are robbed before 9 p.m., often while their owners are near or inside the residence. Your house is more likely to be robbed while you are grilling in the backyard or watching a football game than when you are on a cruise or camping trip.

Although it is impossible to make any home "burglar proof," there are some actions you can take to protect your home and property:

1. **Document your assets**

   Make a list of your valuables. Photograph or videotape each room in your home. Keep receipts of major purchases. Store these and other records in a safe deposit box so you can prove any losses. Review your insurance policies to see if special items such as furs, artwork, or coin collections are covered.

2. **Identify valuables**

   Engrave computers, televisions, cameras, stereos, and VCR's with your name or an identifying number. Police often discover stolen property but have no way of contacting the owners.

3. **Always lock your doors**

   Nothing attracts a thief more than an open garage or unlatched screen door. Lock up even when you plan to visit a neighbor for "just a minute." That "minute" can easily become half an hour, plenty of time for a burglary to occur. Don't leave doors open if you are going to be upstairs or in the basement.

4. ***Install only security systems you will use***

   Many homeowners invest in expensive, high-tech systems that are so cumbersome they leave them off most of the time. A cheap alarm system used twenty-four hours a day provides more protection than a state of the art system used randomly.

5. ***Trim shrubbery around entrances and windows***

   Don't provide camouflage for burglars. Thieves can easily conceal themselves behind foliage while jimmying doors and windows.

6. ***Network with neighbors***

   Let neighbors know if you expect deliveries, house guests, or contractors. Thieves have posed as moving crews, casually looting a house and loading a truck while neighbors look on.

7. ***Store valuables in attics and basements***

   Thieves are reluctant to venture beyond the ground floor, which usually offers numerous exits in case of detection.

3   Finally, call the police the moment you discover that a burglary has occurred. If you return home and find evidence of a break-in — **do not go inside!** The thieves, who might be armed, could still be on the premises. Go to a neighbor's and call the police. Never attempt to confront a burglar yourself. No personal possession is worth risking death or a disabling injury.

Questions for Review and Revision

1. The student offers seven directions. Would these be easier to recall if emphasized by the subtitle "Seven Tips to Keep Your Home Secure"?
2. What misconceptions does the student address?
3. How important is the final warning?
4. The student writes in the second person, directly addressing the readers. Would the paper be less effective if written in third person?
5. Do the level of language, diction, and tone suit the intended audience?
6. Read the paper aloud. Is this document easy to read and easy to remember? Could revisions increase its clarity?

Writing Suggestions

1. Using this paper as a model, write a set of instructions directed to a general audience about improving the performance of your car, installing a

new computer program, planning a trip or a wedding, losing weight, choosing a pet, preparing for a job interview, or another topic of your choice.

2. *Collaborative Writing:* Discuss this paper with other students. Using some of its ideas, work together to write a brief set of instructions on securing a dorm room or an apartment.

PROCESS CHECKLIST

Before submitting your paper, review these points.

1. Is the process clearly defined?

2. Do you supply background information that readers need?

3. Is the information easy to follow? Is the chain of events or the steps logically arranged?

4. Could the text be enhanced by large print, bold or italic type, diagrams, or charts?

5. Are your instructions complete? Do readers know when one step is over and another begins?

6 Do your instructions alert readers to normal changes they might mistake for errors?

7. Are hazards clearly stated?

8. Did you use peer review to test your document?

 Companion Web Site

See **http://sundance.heinle.com** for information on writing process.

 InfoTrac® College Edition

For additional reading go to InfoTrac College edition, your on-line research library, at **http://infotrac.thomsonlearning.com.**

- Enter the search term "process" using Keywords.
- Enter the search terms "how to" using Keywords.
- Enter the name of an author you read in this chapter using Keywords.
- Enter a theme or idea your class discussed using Keywords.

Cause and Effect

DETERMINING REASONS
AND PREDICTING RESULTS

WHAT IS CAUSE AND EFFECT?

What led to the stock market crash of 1929? Why did the *Hindenburg* explode? What caused the Soviet Union to collapse? How did Microsoft corner the software market? How will budget cuts affect education? Would a handgun ban lower street crime? Can a Supreme Court ruling prevent frivolous lawsuits? The answers to these questions call for the use of *cause and effect*, writing that either seeks to establish reasons why something occurred or to predict future results.

Historians devote much of their time to determining the causes of events. Did Lenin cause the Russian Revolution, or did the revolution create Lenin? Why did Hitler rise to power? What led to the women's movement of the 1970s? Historians also consider the ramifications of current events and speculate about the future. Will another oil crisis occur? How will a change in American foreign policy affect chances for peace in the Middle East?

Nearly all professions and disciplines engage in cause-and-effect reasoning. Marketers try to determine why a product succeeded. Engineers work to discover why a test engine failed. Medical researchers measure the results of a new drug. City planners predict the effect a major earthquake would have on emergency services. Educators consider if curriculum changes will improve Scholastic Aptitude Test scores. Federal Aviation Administration (FAA) investigators examine wreckage to establish why a plane crashed.

Many of the research papers you will be assigned in college and the letters and reports you write in your future career will be developed using cause and effect. Identifying the reasons why something occurred can be formidable. Determining future outcomes, no matter how much data are examined or how many experiments are conducted, can remain largely guesswork.

Deduction and Induction

Writers often formulate cause-and-effect papers using deduction and induction. *Deduction* is a form of logic in which a *major premise* or general rule is applied to a *minor premise* or specific instance in order to reach a *conclusion*. You may be familiar with this classic example of deduction:

MAJOR PREMISE: All cows are mammals.
MINOR PREMISE: Bessie is a cow.
CONCLUSION: Bessie is a mammal.

This illustration, though famous, fails to show the practical value of deduction. Other examples should give you an idea of how often we use deduction:

MAJOR PREMISE: All full-time students are eligible for financial aid.
MINOR PREMISE: Sandra Lopez is a full-time student.
CONCLUSION: Sandra Lopez is eligible for financial aid.

MAJOR PREMISE: The student health plan is only available to California residents.
MINOR PREMISE: Amy Kwan is a resident of New York.
CONCLUSION: Amy Kwan cannot join the student health plan.

Deduction can be used to solve problems and answer questions: Are dental exams deductible on my income tax? Can I sublet my apartment? Will the college give me a refund if I drop a class in the fourth week? All of these questions form a minor premise. The IRS rules, apartment leases, and college policies you consult for answers serve as major premises.

Deduction can be used to help determine both causes and effects. Was a plane crash caused by a defective part?

MAJOR PREMISE: FAA regulations consider this part defective if three bolts are missing.
MINOR PREMISE: One bolt was missing from this part.
CONCLUSION: This part was not defective.

How will an increase in bus fares affect ridership?

MAJOR PREMISE: Bus ridership declines with fare increases.
MINOR PREMISE: The city authorized a fifty-cent fare increase.
CONCLUSION: Bus ridership will decline.

Problems occur with deductive reasoning if the major and minor premises are not precisely stated. The statement that "All full-time students are eligible for financial aid" might be clearer if it included a definition of who is considered a full-time student: "All students taking twelve credits are eligible for financial aid." Other problems arise if the major premise is subject to interpretation. A warranty for snow tires might refuse to cover "improper use." Is off-road driving considered "improper"? How much damage can be considered "normal wear and tear"? Some major premises may prove to be false or require qualification:

Major Premise: Democrats are antibusiness.

Are *all* Democrats antibusiness? What is meant by *antibusiness?*

Major Premise: Gun control reduces crime.

Can this be proven? Could a drop in crime in a city that passed gun control be caused by other factors—a decrease in unemployment, a shift in population, or more effective policing?

Induction, unlike deduction, does not open with a major premise. Instead it presents and interprets data and then makes a conclusion:

$$
\begin{array}{ccccc}
X & X & X & X & X \\
 & X & X & X & X \\
X & X & X & X & X \\
 & X & X & X & X \\
 & & X & X & X \\
\end{array}
$$

X = Data
Inductive Leap → Conclusion

The *X*'s in the diagram could represent stolen cars, the number of computers sold last month, blood tests of patients taking a new fertility drug, satellite photographs, interviews with consumers, or evidence collected at a crime scene. Based on a review of the evidence, a conclusion is drawn: car thefts are increasing in the suburbs, the new fertility drug damages red blood cells, coastline erosion is worse than last year, the consumers' major complaint is poor service, or the murder suspect is a Caucasian female with O-positive blood and dyed hair.

As these examples illustrate, effective induction requires a large body of valid evidence to achieve reasonable conclusions. Ford Motor Company would have to interview more than a handful of Taurus owners to determine customer satisfaction. Medical researchers must rule out other reasons for damaged red blood cells. As the diagram notes, the movement from specific details to conclusion requires an *inductive leap*. No matter how much evidence is discovered and examined, no absolute assurance can be made that the conclusion is totally true.

The best demonstration of inductive reasoning takes place in a courtroom. In a criminal case the prosecutor tells members of the jury that if they examine all the evidence they will conclude that the defendant is guilty *beyond a reasonable doubt*. The defense attorney will attempt to raise doubt by providing alternative interpretations and by introducing conflicting evidence. He or she will tell the jury that *reasonable doubt* exists and that not enough evidence has been found to reach a conclusion of guilt.

Establishing Causes

By the 1920s surgeons and physicians began noticing that many of their patients with lung cancer were heavy smokers. An observable association was discovered but not clear proof of a cause-and-effect relationship. Not all lung cancer patients smoked, and millions of smokers were free of the disease. Though scientists were concerned, they had no evidence that smoking *caused* cancer. In fact, throughout the 1930s and 1940s cigarette ads featured endorsements by doctors who claimed that the calming effect of nicotine reduced stress and prevented stomach ulcers. It was not until 1964 that researchers assembled enough data to convince the surgeon general of the United States to proclaim cigarette smoking a health hazard.

In some instances causes can be established through investigation and research. Doctors can diagnose an infection as the cause of a fever. Accountants can study financial records to discover why a company lost money. But many controversial issues remain subject to debate for decades. Why are American schools failing to educate children? John Taylor Gatto (page 495) examined the issue, determining that television and schools have detrimental effects on children's lives:

> Two institutions at present control our children's lives—television and schooling, in that order. Both of these reduce the real world of wisdom, forti-

tude, temperance, and justice to a never-ending, nonstop abstraction. In centuries past, the time of a child and adolescent would be occupied in real work, real charity, real adventures, and the real search for mentors who might teach what one really wanted to learn.

When evaluating a writer attempting to establish a cause, consider the amount of evidence, the degree of objective analysis, and the willingness to qualify assertions.

Predicting Results

In 1936 the *Literary Digest* predicted that Alf Landon would defeat Franklin Roosevelt in his bid for a second term as president. The editors based their prediction on a detailed telephone survey. By randomly selecting names from phone books and asking people whom they planned to vote for, the surveyors assumed they would get an accurate prediction. Their responses from men and women, government employees and business executives, Italians and Jews, farmers and factory workers, and young and old strongly indicated a preference for Landon. But their research failed to accurately predict the outcome of the election because the survey method did not measure a significant population. In 1936 many Americans could not afford telephones, and these economically deprived voters tended to favor Roosevelt.

Predicting future outcomes can be challenging because evidence may be difficult to collect or may be subject to various interpretations. In addition, numerous unforeseen factors can take place to alter expected events. A school board that determines to close schools because of a declining birth rate may fail to account for an influx of immigrants or the closure of private schools that would place more students into the public system.

In "Swept Away" (page 514), Jodi Jacobson asserts that global warming will dramatically affect the climate in the next century:

> Most scientists now agree that a global warming has begun. Its causes are by now depressingly familiar: Greenhouse gases generated by human activity are accumulating in the atmosphere and trapping the sun's radiant heat. These gases include carbon dioxide and nitrous oxides from the combustion of wood and fossil fuels, chlorofluorocarbons (used as a refrigerant and in industrial applications), and methane (from ruminant animals and rice paddies). Meanwhile, population pressures in the Third World are forcing wholesale forest clearing for fuel, farmland and living space. The result is fewer trees left to recapture the chief greenhouse gas, carbon dioxide.

Jacobson continues to predict that global warming will cause the polar ice caps to melt. The rising oceans will flood cities, consume islands, and devastate low-lying deltas.

Jocelyn Tomkin, on the other hand, dismisses these grim predictions. Tomkin's article "Hot Air" (page 525) cautions that the effects of global warming may not be severe. In fact, no global warming may be happening at all:

> The observational evidence that global warming is actually increasing is very shaky. Some researchers claim to see an increase in global warming of about 0.8 degree since 1860. Although average temperatures since then have increased by this much, it's doubtful that the rise reflects carbon-dioxide-induced global warming.
>
> The large year-to-year fluctuations of average temperature . . . mean that the behavior of average global temperature is somewhat like that of a stock market index. Spotting a "real" temperature trend is like deciding if one is in a bull or a bear market. . . .
>
> Moreover, natural causes, rather than the increase in carbon dioxide, are a more likely explanation of the temperature increase. Most of the rise took place prior to 1940, *before* the main increase in the carbon-dioxide level.

When examining writing that predicts future effects, consider the amount of evidence presented, the recognition of other factors that may affect results, and the use of critical thinking.

CRITICAL THINKING FOR CAUSE-AND-EFFECT WRITING

When writing cause-and-effect essays, avoid these common traps, many of which are known as logical fallacies.

1. **Avoid mistaking a time relationship for a cause** (post hoc ergo propter hoc). If your brakes fail after taking your car into the dealer for an oil change, does that mean the mechanics are to blame? Can the president take credit for a drop in unemployment six months after signing a labor bill? Because events occur in time, it can be easy to assume an action that precedes another is a cause. The mechanics may have not touched your brakes, which were bound to wear out with or without an oil change. A drop in unemployment could be caused by a decline in interest rates or an upsurge in exports and may have nothing to do with a labor bill. *Do not assume events were caused by preceding events.*

2. **Do not mistake an effect for a cause.** Early physicians saw fever as a cause of disease rather than as an effect or symptom. If you observe that children with poor reading skills watch a lot of television, you might easily assume that television interferes with their reading. In fact, excessive viewing could be a symptom. Because they have trouble reading, they watch television.

3. **Do not confuse associations with causes.** For years researchers argued that marijuana use led to heroin addiction. The evidence was clear. Nearly every heroin addict interviewed admitted to starting with marijuana. But since most addicts also drank beer, smoked cigarettes, chewed gum, and attended high school, this association could not alone be considered proof. Associations can be compelling and command attention, but they are not proof of a cause-and-effect relationship.

4. **Anticipate unexpected changes.** Many researchers qualify their predictions with the statement "all things being equal, we can anticipate . . ." But conditions never remain frozen. An increase in sales following a major ad campaign could be caused by a competitor going out of business or a drop in unemployment rather than by television commercials.

5. **Avoid "slippery slope" interpretations.** Do not assume that changes will start a trend that will snowball without restraint. If the government allows euthanasia for the terminally ill, you cannot argue that eventually all the elderly and handicapped will be put to death.

6. **Realize that past performance, though an important factor, cannot predict future results.** During the oil crisis of the 1970s, the price of oil soared from $10 to $40 a barrel. Alarmists predicted financial disaster when Americans would have to pay $50–$100 a barrel for oil to run cars and to fuel industry. But the dramatic price escalation was short-lived. Price increases spurred exploration for new oil fields and launched conservation efforts. Soon the world was awash in surplus oil, and prices dropped to precrisis levels. *Past trends cannot be assumed to continue into the future.*

STRATEGIES FOR READING CAUSE AND EFFECT

When reading the cause-and-effect entries in this chapter, keep these questions in mind.

Meaning

1. Is the writer seeking to establish a cause or to predict results?
2. What is the source of the evidence? A writer opposed to atomic power citing only studies commissioned by an antinuclear group is not as credible as one who presents data collected by neutral organizations.

3. Are alternative interpretations possible? Does a rise in the number of people receiving food stamps mean an increase in poverty, or does it reflect better government assistance?

Strategy

1. Does the writer mistake a symptom for a cause? A survey revealing that ninety percent of batterers in domestic violence cases are abusing alcohol might lead to a call for more treatment centers. In fact alcohol abuse and domestic violence may both result from unemployment.
2. Does the writer assume past trends will continue into the future?
3. Does the essay rest on unproven assumptions?
4. Does the writer demonstrate skills in critical thinking?
5. Does the author use narratives or comparisons to demonstrate his or her conclusions?

Language

1. Does the author's choice of words indicate bias?
2. How does the writer introduce technical terms? Are definitions supplied?
3. What do the tone and style of the entry suggest about the intended audience?

MAYA ANGELOU

Maya Angelou (1928–) was born in Stamps, Arkansas. She overcame a childhood marked by poverty and abuse to develop her talents in a range of artistic endeavors. She became a professional dancer and taught modern dance in Italy and Israel. She also acted in productions of Medea *and* Mother Courage *and appeared in several films and television programs, most notably,* Roots. *She is most recognized for her wide body of writing. She has published several children's books, including* My Painted House, My Friendly Chicken, *and* Me *(1994) and* Kofi and His Magic *(1996). Her collections of poetry include* Oh Pray My Wings Are Gonna Fit Me Well *(1975) and* And Still I Rise *(1996). Angelou is best known for her autobiographical books, which include* I Know Why the Caged Bird Sings *(1970).*

Why Blacks Are Returning to Their Southern Roots

OVERVIEW: *In this article, first published in* Ebony *in 1990, Angelou explores the reasons why many African Americans are returning to the South, a region of the country their ancestors had left to seek greater freedom and opportunity in the North.*

1

opens with a question

Stamps, Arkansas, is a little larger than the page upon which its name is printed, yet it looms in my thoughts wider than the Steppes of Russia or Africa's Sahara Desert. Why does a small town, a whistle stop, a red dirt burg of 5,000 souls, a hamlet I left forever over 40 years ago, weigh so heavily on my present-day 1990, big-city, internationally wise, sophisticated mind? The answer to that multi-phased question is because Stamps is located in the American South and I am an African-American. The answer to the question "Why are so many young Black people moving South today?" is that the American South sings a siren song to all Black Americans. The melody may be ignored, despised or ridiculed, but we all hear it.

2

After generations of separation and decades of forgetfulness, the very name brings back to our memories ancient years of pain and pleasure.

3

why blacks moved North

At the turn of the century many African-Americans left the South, left the Southern soul-crushing prejudice and prohibition and moved North to Chicago and New York City, West to Los Angeles and San Diego. They were drawn by the ready promise of better lives, equality, fair play and good old American four-star freedom. Their expectations were at once fulfilled and at the same time dashed to the ground and broken into shards of disappointment.

The sense of fulfillment arose from the fact that there were chances to exchange the dull drudgery of sharecrop farming for protected work under unionized agreements. Sadly, for the last 30 years those jobs have been decreasing as industry became increasingly computerized. And the atmosphere which the immigrants imagined as free of racial prejudice was found to be discriminatory in ways different from the Southern modes and possibly even more humiliating. The great writer, John Oliver Killens, has said, "Macon, Georgia, is down South. New York City is up South."   4

disappointment in the North

A small percentage of highly skilled and fully educated Blacks found and clung to rungs on the success ladder, but <u>most unskilled and undereducated Black workers were spit out by the system like so many un-digestible watermelon seeds.</u>   5

<u>They began to find their lives minimalized and their selves as persons trivialized.</u> Many members of that early band of 20th century pilgrims must have yearned for the honesty of Southern landscapes; even if they were the targets of hatemongers who wanted them dead, they were at least credited with being alive. Northern Whites with their public smiles of liberal acceptance and their private behavior of utter rejection wearied and angered the immigrants.   6

alienation

They stayed, however, in big-city hovels, crowded into small tenements and flowing out to the mean and quickly criminal street. They bore and raised children who were sent South each summer to visit grandparents, third cousins, double-second cousins and extended families. Those children grew up mainly in the large Northern cities, with memories of now dead Southern summers and fish fry, Saturday barbecues and the gentle manners of Southern upbringing. These are the people who are coming to the South to live. They often find that their Southern relatives have died or have themselves been transplanted to Detroit or Cleveland, Ohio. Still they come to live in Atlanta ("Y'all like Hot Lanta?") and New Orleans, quickly learning to call the historic city by its rightful name of "N'Awlins." <u>The returnees shop for churches with the same diligence they used to search for boutiques. What they find is the old-time religion made modern by young voices, young preachers and young music. Surrounded by the ancient healing, they find that they can come home again.</u>   7

reason for happiness

<u>They return and find or make their places in the land of their foreparents. They find and make friends under the shade of trees their ancestors left decades earlier. Many find themselves happy, without being able to explain the emotion. I think it is simply that they feel generally important.</u>   8

identity in South

Southern themes will range from a generous and luscious love to a cruel and bitter hate, but no one can ever claim that the South is petty. Even in   9

conclusion

little Stamps, Arkansas, Black people walk with an air which implies, "When I walk in, they may like me or dislike me, but everybody knows I'm here."

Understanding Meaning

1. What does Angelou mean by the term "siren song"?
2. Why did many African Americans leave the South decades ago?
3. Did African Americans achieve their goals in the North?
4. How did Northern racism differ from Southern racism?
5. *Critical Thinking:* What pulls African Americans back to the South? Is it economic opportunity or something else? Do other ethnic groups tend to glamorize or sentimentalize their homelands, even if their ancestors left to escape oppression and poverty? Does this explain the Irish romanticism about the Emerald Isle or the popularity of a musical such as *Fiddler on the Roof*, which depicts Jewish life in Czarist Russia?

Evaluating Strategy

1. This article was published in an African-American magazine. Does this explain why Angelou does not have to provide a great deal of background information? What can she assume her readers know about the African-American experience in the South?
2. *Other Modes:* Where does Angelou use *description, comparison,* and *narration* to develop her essay?

Appreciating Language

1. Angelou quotes John Oliver Killens's observation that "Macon, Georgia, is down South. New York City is up South." What does the word "South" mean in this context? What connotations did the word "South" have in the past? Have events and circumstances changed our view of the South?
2. Angelou describes the "public smiles of liberal acceptance" that African Americans encountered in the North. What does this term suggest?

Connections across the Disciplines

1. Review Michael Patrick MacDonald's "Returning to Southie" (page 67). Here a young Irish American is drawn back to a slum marked by poverty, drugs, and

corruption. Why do many people feel a need to return to their past, even a past filled with negative experiences they wanted to escape?

2. Michael Barone's "Irish and Blacks" (page 256) describes the mass migration of African Americans from the South to the North. In many ways, were African Americans an immigrant people?

Writing Suggestions

1. Write a cause-and-effect essay that explains why people return to some aspect of their past. Why do people love to watch reruns of TV shows they watched as children? Why do people enjoy homecomings? Do you know people who romanticize negative past experiences? Do you find yourself feeling nostalgic about a low-paying job or small apartment you once hated?

2. *Collaborative Writing:* Working with a group of students, write a brief comparison paper contrasting the way people deal with their past. Do some individuals or groups embrace their roots while others deny it, hoping to erase where they came from?

JOHN BROOKS

John Brooks (1920–1993) published his first novel, The Big Wheel, *in 1949. His second novel,* The Man Who Broke Things, *appeared in 1958. Brooks's nonfiction book about corporations in the 1980s,* The Takeover Game, *became a best-seller. Brooks, who served as a trustee of the New York Public Library for fifteen years, contributed articles to the* New Yorker *for four decades.*

The Effects of the Telephone

OVERVIEW: *In this brief essay, Brooks outlines how the telephone has shaped human lives and perceptions. Before reading this article, consider what your life would be like without a telephone. How much do you depend on the phone?*

1   What has the telephone done to us, or for us, in the hundred years of its existence? A few effects suggest themselves at once. It has saved lives by getting rapid word of illness, injury, or famine from remote places. By joining with the elevator to make possible the multistory residence or office building, it has made possible—for better or worse—the modern city. By bringing about a quantum leap in the speed and ease with which information moves from place to place, it has greatly accelerated the rate of scientific and technological change and growth in industry. Beyond doubt it has crippled if not killed the ancient art of letter writing. It has made living alone possible for persons with normal social impulses; by so doing, it has played a role in one of the greatest social changes of this century, the breakup of the multigenerational household. It has made the waging of war chillingly more efficient than formerly. Perhaps (though not provably) it has prevented wars that might have arisen out of international misunderstanding caused by written communication. Or perhaps—again not provably—by magnifying and extending irrational personal conflicts based on voice contact, it has caused wars. Certainly it has extended the scope of human conflicts, since it impartially disseminates the useful knowledge of scientists and the babble of bores, the affection of the affectionate and the malice of the malicious.

2   But the question remains unanswered. The obvious effects just cited seem inadequate, mechanistic; they only scratch the surface. Perhaps the crucial effects are evanescent and unmeasurable. Use of the telephone involves personal risk because it involves exposure; for some, to be "hung up on" is among the worst of fears; others dream of a ringing telephone and wake up with a pounding heart. The telephone's actual ring—more, per-

haps, than any other sound in our daily lives—evokes hope, relief, fear, anxiety, joy, according to our expectations. The telephone is our nerve-end to society.

In some ways it is in itself a thing of paradox. In one sense a metaphor   3
for the times it helped create, in another sense the telephone is their polar opposite. It is small and gentle—relying on low voltages and miniature parts—in times of hugeness and violence. It is basically simple in times of complexity. It is so nearly human, re-creating voices so faithfully that friends or lovers need not identify themselves by name even when talking across oceans, that to ask its effects on human life may seem hardly more fruitful than to ask the effect of the hand or the foot. The Canadian philosopher Marshall McLuhan—one of the few who have addressed themselves to these questions—was perhaps not far from the mark when he spoke of the telephone as creating "a kind of extra-sensory perception."

Understanding Meaning

1. What does Brooks see as the dominant effects of the telephone? Have there been negative consequences?
2. Why does Brooks see the telephone as "a thing of paradox"?
3. *Critical Thinking:* What lessons about the telephone can be applied to the Internet? Does cyberspace connect people in more ways than the typical one-on-one connection a telephone provides?

Evaluating Strategy

1. Most people have grown up with telephones. Many carry cell phones in pockets and purses. How does Brooks prompt readers to question something they take for granted? Could you imagine writing a similar essay about cars, ballpoint pens, or supermarkets?
2. *Critical Thinking:* Brooks states that the telephone and elevator made the highrise and the modern city possible. Does this suggest that it can be difficult to isolate a single cause? Do technological and social changes intertwine and interact to create unintended results?

Appreciating Language

1. Brooks calls the telephone "nearly human." How does he personalize a communications instrument, linking it to human emotions?

2. Brooks avoids technical language in his essay. Would the introduction of scientific terminology weaken his essay?
3. Consider Brooks's observation that the "telephone is our nerve-end to society." Does the telephone link you to others, to the world? Can we think of phone lines as nerves, making our society and economy function by transmitting information?

Connections across the Disciplines

1. Henry Louis Gates Jr. writes about the power of the Internet (page 268). Will cyberspace be the new "nerve-end to society" in the twenty-first century?
2. Marie Winn (page 194) sees television as a largely negative influence on children. Do you think the telephone benefits childhood development because it is interactive? Or does the telephone simply encourage young people to gossip rather than read or do homework?

Writing Suggestions

1. Using Brooks's article as a model, write your own essay explaining the effects of another common invention. How did the modern newspaper or the Sears catalog change life in the nineteenth century? How did shopping malls, freeways, and suburbs shape life in the twentieth century?
2. *Collaborative Writing:* Work with a group of students to discuss the effects computers have on children and society. Develop a list of positive and negative effects and write a brief essay comparing the benefits and dangers.

JOHN TAYLOR GATTO

John Taylor Gatto taught in New York City public schools for twenty-five years and was named the city's Teacher of the Year three times. He has published several books about public education, including Dumbing Us Down, The Exhausted School, *and* The Empty Child. *Since leaving teaching, Gatto has become a public speaker, addressing audiences at the White House and NASA's Goddard Space Flight Center.*

Why Schools Don't Educate

OVERVIEW: *In this section of a speech Gatto presented after receiving an award, he outlines the effects television and schools have had on children. As you read his list, consider if there could be other causes for the symptoms he describes.*

Two institutions at present control our children's lives—television and schooling, in that order. Both of these reduce the real world of wisdom, fortitude, temperance, and justice to a never-ending, nonstop abstraction. In centuries past, the time of a child and adolescent would be occupied in real work, real charity, real adventures, and the real search for mentors who might teach what one really wanted to learn. A great deal of time was spent in community pursuits, practicing affection, meeting and studying every level of the community, learning how to make a home, and dozens of other tasks necessary to becoming a whole man or woman.

But here is the calculus of time the children I teach must deal with:

Out of the 168 hours in each week, my children must sleep fifty-six. That leaves them 112 hours a week out of which to fashion a self.

My children watch fifty-five hours of television a week, according to recent reports. That leaves them fifty-seven hours a week in which to grow up.

My children attend school thirty hours a week; use about eight hours getting ready, going, and coming home; and spend an average of seven hours a week in homework—a total of forty-five hours. During that time they are under constant surveillance, have no private time or private space, and are disciplined if they try to assert individuality in the use of time or space. That leaves twelve hours a week out of which to create a unique consciousness. Of course my kids eat, too, and that takes some time—not much, because we've lost the tradition of family dining. If we allot three hours a week to evening meals we arrive at a net amount of private time for each child of nine hours.

6   It's not enough. It's not enough, is it? The richer the kid, of course, the less television he watches, but the rich kid's time is just as narrowly proscribed by a broader catalogue of commercial entertainments and his inevitable assignment to a series of private lessons in areas seldom of his choice.

7   And these things are, oddly enough, just a more cosmetic way to create dependent human beings, unable to fill their own hours, unable to initiate lines of meaning to give substance and pleasure to their existence. It's a national disease, this dependency and aimlessness, and I think schooling and television and lessons—the entire Chatauqua idea—have a lot to do with it.

8   Think of the things that are killing us as a nation: drugs, brainless competition, recreational sex, the pornography of violence, gambling, alcohol, and the worst pornography of all—lives devoted to buying things—accumulation as a philosophy. All are addictions of dependent personalities and that is what our brand of schooling must inevitably produce.

9   I want to tell you what the effect is on children of taking all their time—time they need to grow up—and forcing them to spend it on abstractions. No reform that doesn't attack these specific pathologies will be anything more than a facade.

10   1.   The children I teach are indifferent to the adult world. This defies the experience of thousands of years. A close study of what big people were up to was always the most exciting occupation of youth, but nobody wants to grow up these days, and who can blame them. Toys are us.

11   2.   The children I teach have almost no curiosity, and what little they do have is transitory; they cannot concentrate for very long, even on things they choose to do. Can you see a connection between the bells ringing again and again to change classes, and this phenomenon of evanescent attention?

12   3.   The children I teach have a poor sense of the future, of how tomorrow is inextricably linked to today. They live in a continuous present; the exact moment they are in is the boundary of their consciousness.

13   4.   The children I teach are ahistorical; they have no sense of how the past has predestined their own present, limiting their choices, shaping their values and lives.

14   5.   The children I teach are cruel to each other; they lack compassion for misfortune, they laugh at weakness, they have contempt for people whose need for help shows too plainly.

15   6.   The children I teach are uneasy with intimacy or candor. They cannot deal with genuine intimacy because of a lifelong habit of preserving a secret self inside an outer personality made up of artificial bits and pieces, of behavior bor-

rowed from television or acquired to manipulate teachers. Because they are not who they represent themselves to be, the disguise wears thin in the presence of intimacy, so intimate relationships have to be avoided.

7. The children I teach are materialistic, following the lead of schoolteachers who   16
    materialistically "grade" everything—and television mentors who offer every-
    thing in the world for sale.

8. The children I teach are dependent, passive, and timid in the presence of new   17
    challenges. This timidity is frequently masked by surface bravado or by anger
    or aggressiveness, but underneath is a vacuum without fortitude.

I could name a few other conditions that school reform will have to   18
tackle if our national decline is to be arrested, but by now you will have
grasped my thesis, whether you agree with it or not. Either schools, television, or both have caused these pathologies. It's a simple matter of arithmetic. Between schooling and television, all the time children have is eaten
up. That's what has destroyed the American family; it no longer is a factor in
the education of its own children.

Understanding Meaning

1. How, in Gatto's view, are television and schools linked in children's lives?
2. How has television affected children's views of the world?
3. Gatto states that schoolchildren are "cruel" and "passive." Can one be both
    cruel and passive? Can pent-up energy and stunted creativity lead children to
    express themselves in bursts of selfish violence?
4. Gatto observes that children are materialistic. How much of this is caused by
    television and how much by the values of their parents?
5. Do Gatto's observations explain why many people advocate school choice and
    home schooling?
6. *Critical Thinking:* Gatto remarks that "children live in a continuous present"
    without a sense of past and future. Is this a natural attribute of childhood or
    something induced by television? Doesn't television teach children something
    about history, even if simplified and distorted?

Evaluating Strategy

1. How effective is Gatto's use of numbered steps?
2. All of Gatto's eight points open with "The children I teach . . ." Is this repeti-
    tion suited to a speech? Does it help hammer home his ideas to a listening au-
    dience? Does it seem less effective in print?
3. What risk does a writer run in criticizing children? How might parents respond?

Appreciating Language

1. Gatto uses the word *ahistorical*. How would you define this term?
2. Gatto calls "being devoted to buying things" the "worst pornography of all." Is "pornography" an effective word choice?

Connections across the Disciplines

1. Does the school system Gatto describes explain the reactions Philip Gourevitch noted when he talked to children at the Holocaust Museum (page 337)? Would Gatto call the children who had never heard of the Holocaust "ahistorical"?
2. Marie Winn (page 194) comments extensively about the impact television has on children. Do her observations match Gatto's?
3. Compare Gatto's experiences as a teacher with the student experiences described by Samuel Scudder (page 47) and Carl T. Rowan (page 137). How did Dr. Agassiz, a noted Harvard scientist, and Miss Bessie, a black teacher in the segregated South of the 1940s, teach? Could others like them rescue today's schoolchildren?

Writing Suggestions

1. Write your own essay detailing the effects television has had on your generation or your children's. Do your observations match Gatto's?
2. Write a brief narrative about an elementary school experience that truly taught you something. Did it occur in the context of the traditional classroom?
3. *Collaborative Writing:* Discuss Gatto's article with a group of students. Record their observations about school reform. Select the major ideas you come up with and write a letter to the school board suggesting ways to improve education.

BLENDING THE MODES

BRENT STAPLES

Brent Staples (1951–) was born in Chester, Pennsylvania, and graduated from Widener University in 1973. He received a doctorate in psychology from the University of Chicago in 1982. After writing for several Chicago publications, he joined the New York Times in 1985 and became a member of its editorial board in 1990. He has also contributed articles to Ms. *and* Harper's. *In 1994 he published a memoir,* Parallel Time: Growing Up in Black and White, *recalling a childhood of poverty and violence.*

Black Men and Public Space

OVERVIEW: *In this* Harper's *article Staples recounts the effects he has had on white pedestrians. As a black male, he realized he had the power to cause fellow citizens to alter their behavior by simply walking in their direction.*

My first victim was a woman—white, well-dressed, probably in her early 1 twenties. I came upon her late one evening on a deserted street in Hyde Park, a relatively affluent neighborhood in an otherwise mean, impoverished section of Chicago. As I swung onto the avenue behind her, there seemed to be a discreet, uninflammatory distance between us. Not so. She cast back a worried glance. To her, the youngish black man—a broad 6 feet 2 inches with a beard and billowing hair, both hands shoved into the pockets of a bulky military jacket—seemed menacingly close. After a few more quick glimpses, she picked up her pace and was soon running in earnest. Within seconds she disappeared into a cross street.

That was more than a decade ago. I was 22 years old, a graduate student 2 newly arrived at the University of Chicago. It was in the echo of that terrified woman's footfalls that I first began to know the unwieldy inheritance I'd come into—the ability to alter public space in ugly ways. It was clear that she thought herself the quarry of a mugger, a rapist, or worse. Suffering a bout of insomnia, however, I was stalking sleep, not defenseless wayfarers. As a softy who is scarcely able to take a knife to a raw chicken—let alone hold one to a person's throat—I was surprised, embarrassed, and dismayed all at once. Her flight made me feel like an accomplice in tyranny. It also made it clear that I was indistinguishable from the muggers who occasionally seeped into the area from the surrounding ghetto. That first encounter, and those that followed, signified that a vast, unnerving gulf lay between nighttime pedestrians—particularly women—and me. And I soon gathered that being perceived as dangerous is a hazard in itself. I only needed to turn a corner into a dicey situation, or crowd some frightened, armed person in a foyer somewhere, or make an errant move after being pulled over by a policeman. Where fear and weapons meet—and they often do in urban America—there is always the possibility of death.

3   In that first year, my first away from my hometown, I was to become thoroughly familiar with the language of fear. At dark, shadowy intersections, I could cross in front of a car stopped at a traffic light and elicit the *thunk, thunk, thunk, thunk* of the driver—black, white, male, or female—hammering down the door locks. On less traveled streets after dark, I grew accustomed to but never comfortable with people crossing to the other side of the street rather than pass me. Then there were the standard unpleasantries with policemen, doormen, bouncers, cabdrivers, and others whose business it is to screen out troublesome individuals *before* there is any nastiness.

4   I moved to New York nearly two years ago and I have remained an avid night walker. In central Manhattan, the near-constant crowd cover minimizes tense one-on-one street encounters. Elsewhere—in SoHo, for example, where sidewalks are narrow and tightly spaced buildings shut out the sky—things can get very taut indeed.

5   After dark, on the warrenlike streets of Brooklyn where I live, I often see women who fear the worst from me. They seem to have set their faces on neutral, and with their purse straps strung across their chests bandolier-style, they forge ahead as though bracing themselves against being tackled. I understand, of course, that the danger they perceive is not a hallucination. Women are particularly vulnerable to street violence, and young black males are drastically overrepresented among the perpetrators of that violence. Yet these truths are no solace against the kind of alienation that comes of being ever the suspect, a fearsome entity with whom pedestrians avoid making eye contact.

6   It is not altogether clear to me how I reached the ripe old age of 22 without being conscious of the lethality nighttime pedestrians attributed to me. Perhaps it was because in Chester, Pennsylvania, the small, angry industrial town where I came of age in the 1960s, I was scarcely noticeable against a backdrop of gang warfare, street knifings, and murders. I grew up one of the good boys, had perhaps a half-dozen fistfights. In retrospect, my shyness of combat has clear sources.

As a boy, I saw countless tough guys locked away; I have since buried 7
several, too. They were babies, really—a teenage cousin, a brother of 22, a
childhood friend in his mid-twenties—all gone down in episodes of bravado
played out in the streets. I came to doubt the virtues of intimidation early on.
I chose, perhaps unconsciously, to remain a shadow—timid, but a survivor.

The fearsomeness mistakenly attributed to me in public places often 8
has a perilous flavor. The most frightening of these confusions occurred in
the late 1970s and early 1980s, when I worked as a journalist in Chicago.
One day, rushing into the office of a magazine I was writing for with a deadline story in hand, I was mistaken for a burglar. The office manager called
security and, with an ad hoc posse, pursued me through the labyrinthine
halls, nearly to my editor's door. I had no way of proving who I was. I could
only move briskly toward the company of someone who knew me.

Another time I was on assignment for a local paper and killing time be- 9
fore an interview. I entered a jewelry store on the city's affluent Near North
Side. The proprietor excused herself and returned with an enormous red
Doberman pinscher straining at the end of a leash. She stood, the dog extended toward me, silent to my questions, her eyes bulging nearly out of
her head. I took a cursory look around, nodded, and bade her good night.

Relatively speaking, however, I never fared as badly as another black 10
male journalist. He went to nearby Waukegan, Illinois, a couple of summers
ago to work on a story about a murderer who was born there. Mistaking the
reporter for the killer, police officers hauled him from his car at gunpoint
and but for his press credentials would probably have tried to book him. Such
episodes are not uncommon. Black men trade tales like this all the time.

Over the years, I learned to smother the rage I felt at so often being 11
taken for a criminal. Not to do so would surely have led to madness. I now
take precautions to make myself less threatening. I move about with care,
particularly late in the evening. I give a wide berth to nervous people
on subway platforms during the wee hours, particularly when I have exchanged business clothes for jeans. If I happen to be entering a building
behind some people who appear skittish, I may walk by, letting them clear
the lobby before I return, so as not to seem to be following them. I have
been calm and extremely congenial on those rare occasions when I've been
pulled over by the police.

And on late-evening constitutionals I employ what has proved to be an 12
excellent tension-reducing measure: I whistle melodies from Beethoven and
Vivaldi and the more popular classical composers. Even steely New Yorkers
hunching toward nighttime destinations seem to relax, and occasionally they

even join in the tune. Virtually everybody seems to sense that a mugger wouldn't be warbling bright, sunny selections from Vivaldi's *Four Seasons*. It is my equivalent of the cowbell that hikers wear when they know they are in bear country.

Understanding Meaning

1. What is Staples's thesis? What is he saying about race, class, crime, prejudice, and fear in our society?
2. What is Staples's attitude toward the way women responded to his presence? What causes their reactions?
3. Staples reports that both African-American and white drivers locked their doors when they encountered him. What is he saying about racial perceptions and fear?
4. How do you interpret the conclusion? Would people be reassured by a black man whistling classical music? What does this say about prejudice, racial profiling, and stereotyping? What else would make a black man appear less threatening—singing spirituals, carrying the *Wall Street Journal*, walking a poodle? Why?
5. *Critical Thinking:* Would a white man walking through an African-American neighborhood produce similar results? Would residents respond differently than if he were black? Would a Hispanic, an Asian, an orthodox Jew produce similar or different results?

Evaluating Strategy

1. What is the impact of the first sentence?
2. Staples shifts the chronology several times. How does he prevent readers from becoming confused? How important are transitional statements and paragraph breaks in maintaining a coherent essay?
3. *Other Modes:* How does Staples use *narration, comparison,* and *example* in developing his essay?

Appreciating Language

1. Staples avoids using words such as "racist," "prejudice," and "stereotype" in his essay. Do words like these tend to be inflammatory and politically charged? Would they detract from his message?
2. What do the tone and style of the essay suggest about the response Staples hoped to achieve from his readers? Do you sense he was trying to reach white or African-American readers?

Connections across the Disciplines

1. Bob Levey (page 236) discusses the differences between men and women walking alone at night. Does walking alone expose us to society? When walking alone are we likely to be judged by our age, gender, or race? Do we become a symbol or a representative of a group rather than an individual?

2. Maya Angelou (page 488) comments on the "public smiles of liberal acceptance" blacks encountered in the North. Do these "public smiles" extend to black men walking down a street? Why or why not?

Writing Suggestions

1. Write an essay narrating your own experiences in public space. You can explore how you cause others to react to your presence or how location affects your behavior. What happens when you cross the campus late at night, drive alone, or enter a high crime neighborhood? Would the police and public see you as a likely victim or a probable perpetrator?

2. *Collaborative Writing:* Discuss this essay with a group of students. Consider if a white man in shabby clothing or a black man in a business suit would provoke the same or different responses in white pedestrians. Is class or race the defining factor in producing fear? Is age an issue? Has the public been influenced to see young black men as threatening? Would a middle-aged black man provoke different reactions? Why or why not? Develop an outline for a sociological experiment measuring people's reaction to a variety of test figures engaged in the same actions. Write a process paper explaining how your group might conduct the experiment and evaluate the results.

OPPOSING VIEWPOINTS: THE "ABUSE EXCUSE"

ALAN M. DERSHOWITZ

Alan Dershowitz (1938–) was born in Brooklyn and graduated from Yale Law School in 1962. He was a law clerk for Supreme Court Justice Arthur Goldberg and joined the faculty of Harvard Law School in 1964. As a defense attorney, he has participated in many high profile cases, representing Claus von Bulow, Mike Tyson, and O. J. Simpson. His recent books include Chutzpah, Contrary to Popular Opinion, The Abuse Excuse, *and* Reasonable Doubts.

The "Abuse Excuse" Is Detrimental to the Justice System

OVERVIEW: *In this essay Alan Dershowitz argues that attorneys and defendants who use abuse as an excuse for violent acts damage the justice system by endorsing vigilante behavior.*

1   The "abuse excuse"—the legal tactic by which criminal defendants claim a history of abuse as an excuse for violent retaliation—is quickly becoming a license to kill and maim. More and more defense lawyers are employing this tactic and more and more jurors are buying it. It is a dangerous trend, with serious and widespread implications for the safety and liberty of every American.

2   Among the recent excuses that have been accepted by at least some jurors have been "battered woman syndrome," "abused child syndrome," "rape trauma syndrome," and "urban survival syndrome." This has encouraged lawyers to try other abuse excuses, such as "black rage." For example, the defense lawyer for Colin Ferguson—the black man convicted in March 1995 of killing white commuters on the Long Island Railroad on December 7, 1993—has acknowledged that his black rage variation on the insanity defense "is similar to the utilization of the battered woman's syndrome, the post-traumatic stress syndrome and the child abuse syndrome in other cases to negate criminal accountability."

THE DANGER OF VIGILANTISM

On the surface, the abuse excuse affects only the few handfuls of defen-   3
dants who raise it, and those who are most immediately impacted by an ac-
quittal or reduced charge. But at a deeper level, the abuse excuse is a symptom of a general abdication of responsibility by individuals, families, groups,
and even nations. Its widespread acceptance is dangerous to the very tenets
of democracy, which presuppose personal accountability for choices and
actions. It also endangers our collective safety by legitimating a sense of
vigilantism that reflects our frustration over the apparent inability of law enforcement to reduce the rampant violence that engulfs us.

At a time of ever-hardening attitudes toward crime and punishment, it   4
may seem anomalous that so many jurors—indeed, so many Americans—
appear to be sympathetic to the abuse excuse. But it is not anomalous at all,
since the abuse excuse is a modern-day form of vigilantism—a recognition
that since official law enforcement does not seem able to prevent or punish
abuse, the victim should be entitled to take the law into his or her own hands.

In philosophical terms, the claim is that society has broken its "social   5
contract" with the abused victim by not according him or her adequate protection. Because it has broken that social contract, the victim has been returned to a "state of nature" in which "might makes right" and the victim is
entitled to invoke the law of the jungle—"kill or be killed." Indeed, these
very terms were used in a 1994 Texas case in which one black youth [Dai-
mion Osby] killed two other blacks in a dangerous urban neighborhood. The
result was a hung jury.

But vigilantism—whether it takes the old-fashioned form of the lynch   6
mob or the new-fashioned form of the abuse victim's killing her sleeping
husband—threatens the very fabric of our democracy and sows the seeds of
anarchy and autocracy. The abuse excuse is dangerous, therefore, both in
its narrow manifestation as a legal defense and in its broader manifestation
as an abrogation of societal responsibility.

AFFIRMATIVE ACTION IN THE JUSTICE SYSTEM

The other characteristic shared by these defenses is that they are often "po-   7
litically correct," thus reflecting current trends toward employing different
criteria of culpability when judging disadvantaged groups. In effect, these

abuse-excuse defenses, by emphasizing historical discrimination suffered by particular groups, seek to introduce some degree of affirmative action into our criminal-justice system.

8   These abuse-excuse defenses are the daily fare of the proliferating menu of TV and radio talk shows. It is virtually impossible to flip the TV channels during the daytime hours without seeing a bevy of sobbing women and men justifying their failed lives by reference to some past abuse, real or imagined. Personal responsibility does not sell soap as well as sob stories. Jurors who watch this stuff begin to believe it, despite its status as junk science. The very fact that Sally Jessy Raphael and Montel Williams repeat it as if it were gospel tends to legitimate it in the minds of some jurors. They are thus receptive to it in the courtroom, especially when the defendant is portrayed as sympathetic, and his dead victim is unsympathetic. William Kunstler is quick to point to public-opinion polls that show that "two-thirds of blacks and almost half the whites surveyed recognize the validity of our [black rage] theory of Mr. Ferguson's defense."

MOST VICTIMS DO NOT COMMIT VIOLENCE

9   But neither public-opinion polls nor TV talk shows establish the empirical or normative validity of such abuse-excuse defenses. The basic fallacy underlying each of them is that the vast majority of people who have experienced abuses—whether it be sexual, racial, or anything else—do not commit violent crimes. Thus the abuse excuse neither explains nor justifies the violence. A history of abuse is not a psychological or a legal license to kill. It may, in some instances, be relevant at sentencing, but certainly not always.

10   Lest it be thought that the abuse excuse is credited only by radical defense lawyers, lay jurors, and talk-show-watching stay-at-homes, a quotation from the attorney general of the United States illustrates how pervasive this sort of thinking is becoming. In April 1993, Janet Reno was quoted as commenting on urban riots as follows: "An angry young man who lashes out in violence because he never had a childhood might do the right thing," and when the "right thing" is in contradiction with the law, "you try to get the law changed." I wonder if the angry young man's innocent victim agrees that the violence directed against his shop was the "right thing" and that the law protecting his property should be "changed."

The worst consequence of these abuse excuses is that they stigmatize   11
all abuse victims with the violence of the very few who have used their victimization as a justification to kill or maim. The vast majority of abuse victims are neither prone to violence nor to making excuses.

Understanding Meaning

1. How does Dershowitz define "the abuse excuse"?
2. Does Dershowitz believe that victims do not have the right to retaliate?
3. Do those who use abuse as an excuse for their violent behavior demean the
    majority of victims who do not seek revenge?
4. *Critical Thinking:* Does the abuse excuse extend throughout society? Do em-
    ployees, students, and parents give excuses rather than take responsibility for
    their actions? Have we become a nation of victims?

Evaluating Strategy

1. What examples does Dershowitz use as illustrations of the abuse excuse?
2. Dershowitz places his thesis at the opening of the essay. Is this effective? Can
    you think of situations in which it would be better to place the thesis at the
    conclusion?

Appreciating Language

1. Dershowitz is an attorney. How many legal terms does he use in the essay?
    What does this reveal about his intended audience?
2. Consider the term "abuse excuse." Is this phrase so glib that it risks trivializing
    a serious problem?

Connections across the Disciplines

1. How does the abuse excuse relate to Martin Luther King Jr.'s observation
    (page 381) that people often respond to oppression with violence?
2. John Taylor Gatto (page 495) observes that schoolchildren are passive and
    cruel and seem to lack a sense of focus and responsibility. Does the "abuse ex-
    cuse" seem like an extension of this behavior?

Writing Suggestions

1. Write an essay expressing your own view of the abuse excuse. Do people seem to dodge or deny responsibility for their actions by making excuses? Has almost every type of criminal or uncivil behavior been excused as the result of some mental or emotional disorder or an abusive past?

2. *Collaborative Writing:* Discuss this essay with a group of students. Have a member record comments of the group. Write an essay expressing your group's view of Dershowitz's essay. If the members disagree, consider writing pro and con statements.

LESLIE ABRAMSON

Leslie Abramson first achieved national attention by defending Erik Menendez, who was accused of conspiring with his brother to murder their wealthy parents. Born in New York, she worked as a public defender for seven years before entering private practice in Los Angeles. Twice named Trial Lawyer of the Year by the Los Angeles Criminal Courts Bar Association, Abramson is a frequent commentator on Court TV. In 1997 she published The Defense Is Ready: Life in the Trenches of Criminal Law, *which recounts her experiences as a defense attorney.*

The Abuse Defense Balances the Justice System

OVERVIEW: *In this article, Abramson argues that victims are fully justified in using past abuse as a factor in their defense when charged with a crime of retaliation. As you read her essay, consider how Alan Dershowitz would regard her position.*

I never learned about "male justice" in school.   1

During my education in the New York City public schools, the City Uni-   2
versity of New York and the University of California, Los Angeles, School
of Law, I was taught the noble fictions of our justice system. I was told that
American justice is equal for all. I was instructed that the accused always is
presumed innocent until proven guilty, and that the prosecution bears the
burden of proving that guilt beyond a reasonable doubt.

By the end of my first year of practice I also had learned that much of   3
what I'd been taught was naive. Most important, I discovered that the racism and sexism deforming so many of our institutions also infect the courts,
producing a double standard of justice.

Much has been written about racism's insidious role in our criminal-   4
justice system. But the recent cases of O.J. Simpson [acquitted of murder
in October 1995], Lyle and Erik Menendez [charged with murdering their
parents, their trial resulted in hung juries in January 1994], and Lorena Bob-
bitt [acquitted of maiming her husband in January 1994] have opened a public debate on how gender bias influences the way we perceive crime, criminal responsibility and justice.

509

JUSTICE FOR "WRONGED" MEN
AND ABUSED WOMEN

5   "Texas justice" was what we criminal lawyers used to call cases in which a man was acquitted after killing his wife and her lover in *flagrante delicto*. It mattered not if the victims were unarmed or asleep when the "wronged" man blew them away in his fit of jealous rage. No one went to the talk shows to decry the "heat of passion" defense employed by men expressing their possessory rights over the women of their choice—including the right to kill. Of course, no such right to kill was expressly provided in the written law, but the unwritten law—what might be called the male bill of rights— was implicitly understood by sympathetic male jurors.

6   The law of macho, of course, does not extend to women and children who kill. They rarely kill, but when they do, they don't do it out of wounded pride or from affronts to their sexuality or in the anger of the rejected. The forces that drive them to act are fear and terror, the motivations of the weak, the oppressed, the tortured and the broken. And they are scorned and ridiculed and hated for it.

7   We guiltily admire the successful barroom brawler, the fastest gun, the aggressive forechecker, the crushing lineman. The law of self-defense as currently codified in most states recognizes this, and is a male version of survival—two physical and emotional equals duking it out or facing off *High Noon* style, pistols at the ready. Burning beds, parents united in abuse in their family den—these are not the images our male legislators had in mind when the criminal codes were written.

8   We've learned a lot since then about the psychology of abusive relation-ships, about the cruelty, oppression and inescapability of child abuse and molestation, about the terror that marks virtually every moment for the vic-tims of chronic domestic violence. Despite this knowledge, the media, the self-anointed pundits and the self-promoting denizens of the law schools' ivory towers sanctimoniously declare their outrage when an abused person recounts a life of torment to explain why he or she succumbed at last to ter-ror and struck out at the abuser. These critics label such explanations the "abuse excuse." They lament our loss of "personal responsibility."

9   This male model of justice pervades the public consciousness and ex-plains why many people say they would sympathize with O.J. Simpson even if they believe he killed Nicole Brown Simpson and Ronald Goldman. It wouldn't matter, they say, even if they believed that these killings fol-lowed years in which this strong, physically fit professional athlete beat and

emotionally abused his five-foot-eight 125-pound wife. O.J. Simpson may indeed be innocent, as he is now legally presumed to be. What makes much of his support in the community troubling, however, is that it derives not from this presumption, but from the undercurrent of entitlement that the killing of an ex-wife engenders.

A CASE OF PSYCHOLOGICAL ABUSE

The best and worst example of this double standard was graphically displayed to me in a case I handled a decade ago. My client, then a woman of fifty, had been raped on her way home from work years before and traumatized by the experience. Twenty years later she married a widower with a four-year-old daughter—and a shadowy past. Only after marrying this wealthy, domineering man did my client discover that he had produced his widowerhood by shooting his unarmed first wife to death as she spoke to a friend on the telephone while his infant daughter slept in the next room. He was convicted of manslaughter, served less than two years in prison and regained custody of the little girl upon his release.   10

During the course of their ten-year marriage the husband's highest form of amusement was to play the role of my client's former rapist by sneaking up on her from behind and grabbing her. He was the textbook battering husband, jealous, possessive, controlling his wife's every movement and human contact, belittling, explosively angry, sexually demanding. Finally, after a period of especially frequent outbursts, he threatened to do to my client what he had done to his first wife. She shot him, once, in the head while he was sleeping. She ran screaming down the hallway, called the police, confessed her crime. At her first trial she was convicted of second-degree murder and sentenced to five years to life in state prison. Her conviction was reversed on appeal due to prosecutorial and judicial misconduct.   11

That's when I entered the case. In her second trial, we presented evidence of the extreme psychological impairment this woman suffered. The jury hung; subsequently, she pleaded guilty to manslaughter and the judge granted her probation. At the sentencing hearing, the male deputy D.A. took my client's hand and said: "I want to apologize to you for that first conviction. You are not a murderer. I just didn't understand."   12

Score one for equal justice.   13

Understanding Meaning

1. What is Abramson's thesis? How would you restate it in your own words?
2. What does Abramson mean by "male justice"?
3. Why does Abramson believe that the justice system was unbalanced, favoring men over women? Does the justice system give men special entitlements?
4. *Critical Thinking:* Does Abramson see any risk of an "abuse excuse" encouraging vigilante justice? How should society deal with those who act violently in response to abuse?

Evaluating Strategy

1. Abramson includes personal experiences in her essay. Does this give her writing greater credibility? Does firsthand experience provide powerful support?
2. What appeals does Abramson use to support her thesis?
3. Abramson provides several examples to support her thesis. Do you find them effective?

Appreciating Language

1. Abramson uses the term "abuse defense" rather than "abuse excuse." Consider the connotations these words have for readers. How does Abramson use language to justify use of the abuse defense?
2. *Critical Thinking:* How do word choice and connotation affect the way people view criminal cases? When does a "defendant" become an "accused killer," and how do those accused of crimes use the word "victim" to defend their actions?

Connections across the Disciplines

1. William Raspberry (page 287) comments on the negative self-definitions some African-American children develop, such as viewing hostility to authority as a sign of masculinity. Can these social and psychological forces, imposed on people at a young age, be viewed as a kind of abuse?
2. Michael Barone (page 256) states that both the Irish-American and African-American populations were involved in crime and violence, caused by poverty and discrimination. Should greater emphasis be placed on eradicating the social conditions that breed crime rather than on excusing criminals?

Writing Suggestions

1. Write an essay stating your opinion on the use of the abuse defense. Support your thesis with examples of situations in which people's past abuse should or should not be considered a justifiable defense for violent behavior.

2. *Collaborative Writing:* With a group of students, discuss a recent criminal case in which the abuse excuse was used as a defense. Have a member record comments. Write an essay advocating your group's opinion. If members have differing views, consider drafting pro and con versions.

JODI JACOBSON

Jodi Jacobson is a senior researcher at the World Watch Institute, an environmental organization that monitors the impact human activity has on the planet. She is also the author of Environmental Refugees: A Yardstick of Habitability.

Swept Away

OVERVIEW: *In this* World Watch *(1989) article, Jodi Jacobson describes the effects global warming will have in the future. Theorists claim that pollution is causing atmospheric changes that will trap heat and slowly cause the earth to become warmer. Climate changes will alter weather patterns and plant growth and raise ocean levels as the polar ice caps melt. Read Jacobson's account of the effects of global warming, and then read Jocelyn Tomkin's opposing piece.*

1   "Don't buy land in New Orleans," warns John Milliman of the Woods Hole Oceanographic Institution in Massachusetts. The scientist's comment stems from his knowledge of how sea level rise—an expected consequence of global warming—will affect the habitability of low-lying coastal regions around the world. In the 21st century, waves now breaking on the shores of Louisiana's coast could be lapping at the doors of homes in the Big Easy. Miami is another case in point. The first settlements in this city were built on what little high ground could be found, but today most of greater Miami lies at or just above sea level on swampland reclaimed from the Everglades. Water for its three million residents is drawn from the Biscayne aquifer that flows only feet below the city streets. That the city exists and prospers is due to what engineers call a "hydrologic masterwork" of natural and artificial systems that hold back swamp and sea.

2   Against a three-foot rise in ocean levels, which is expected by the year 2050, the city's only defense would be a costly system of sea walls and dikes. But that might not be enough to spare the city from insidious assault. Fresh water floats atop salt water, so as sea levels rise the water table would be pushed three feet closer to the surface. The elaborate pumping and

drainage system that currently maintains the integrity of the highly porous aquifer could be overwhelmed. Roads would buckle, bridge abutments sink, and land revert back to swamp.

Miami's experience would not be unique. Large cities around the world—New Orleans, New York, Venice, Bangkok and Taipei, to name a few—would face the prospect of inundation by invading seas. For each, the choice would be fight or flight.

Protecting infrastructure and water supplies of coastal cities, not to mention saving shorelines and wetlands, will require many billions of dollars, perhaps even more than most well-off nations could afford. Sea levels have only gone up several inches over the past century, but their rise is sure to accelerate in the coming decades as global warming sets in motion an expansion of ocean volume and a melting of mountain glaciers and polar icecaps. While some universal increase in sea level is now inevitable, the rate and extent of change depends on preemptive action adopted by society today.

THE EXPANDING OCEAN

Most scientists now agree that a global warming has begun. Its causes are by now depressingly familiar: greenhouse gases generated by human activity are accumulating in the atmosphere and trapping the sun's radiant heat. These gases include carbon dioxide and nitrous oxides from the combustion of wood and fossil fuels, chlorofluorocarbons (used as a refrigerant and in industrial applications), and methane (from ruminant animals and rice paddies). Meanwhile, population pressures in the Third World are forcing wholesale forest clearing for fuel, farmland and living space. The result is fewer trees left to recapture the chief greenhouse gas, carbon dioxide.

It is now all but certain that the delicate balance between incoming sunlight and reflected heat that keeps the earth at a relatively constant average temperature has been upset. What is not certain is just how much higher the temperature will go, and how quickly the increase will take place. Estimates based on current trends project that an average global rise of between three and eight degrees Fahrenheit can be expected within the next 40 years.

As temperatures rise the waters of the earth will expand. Glaciers and icecaps will melt. Still higher sea levels may occur if the warming breaks loose such large frozen ice masses as the West Antarctic sheet. If correct, the predicted temperature changes would escalate sea level by five to seven feet over the next century. Some climatologists now estimate that the rate of increase will accelerate after 2050, reaching about an inch per year.

8   The heat and dryness of the summer of 1988 drew attention to the withering effects global warming could have on agricultural productivity, but its most lasting legacy could well be the displacement of peoples, the abandonment of entire delta regions, and the destruction of vital coastal ecosystems caused by inundation.

AN UNAFFORDABLE BILL

9   China's 1,500-mile-long Great Wall is considered the largest construction project ever carried out, but it may soon be superseded in several countries by modern-day analogues: the "Great Seawalls." If nothing is done to slow global warming, then building structures to hold back the sea will become essential, but their multi-billion dollar price tags may be higher than even some well-to-do countries can afford.

10   Nowhere is the battle against the sea more actively engaged than in the Netherlands. The Dutch are perhaps best known for their achievements in building a nation on the deltas of the Meuse, Rhine and Schedule rivers. And well they should be: Without the carefully maintained stretches of dikes (250 miles long) and sand dunes (120 miles) built by Holland's engineers to hold back the sea, more than half the country would be under water.

11   As the engineers know, the ocean doesn't relinquish land easily. In early 1953, a storm surge that hit the delta region caused an unprecedented disaster. More than 100 miles of dikes were breached, leading to the inundation of 600 square miles of land and the deaths of more than 1,800 people. In response, the Dutch government put together the Delta Plan, a massive public works project that took two decades and the equivalent of 6 percent of the country's gross national product each year to complete.

12   The Dutch continue to spend heavily to keep their extensive system of dikes and pumps in shape, and are now protected against storms up to those with a probability of occurring once in 10,000 years. But, due to sea level rise, maintaining this level of safety may require additional investments of up to $10 billion by 2040.

13   Large though these expenditures are, they are trivial compared with what the United States, with more than 19,000 miles of coastline, will have to spend to protect Cape Cod, Long Island, the Maryland, Massachusetts and New Jersey shores, North Carolina's Outer Banks, most of Florida, the bayous of Louisiana, the Texas Gulf Coast and the San Francisco Bay Area.

Even so, industrial countries are in a far better financial position to pro- 14
tect their coastal regions than are developing nations. Bangladesh, for instance, can ill afford to match the Dutch mile for mile in seawalls. But its
danger is no less real. The cyclones originating in the Bay of Bengal before
and after the monsoon season already devastate the southern part of Bangladesh on a regular basis. Storm surges 18 feet higher than normal can
reach as far as 125 miles inland and cover a third of the country.

In addition to lifting the ocean's level, global warming is likely to in- 15
crease the frequency of these tropical storms. When added to the ongoing
alteration of the Bengal Delta's natural processes by human activity, these
conditions may wreak so much damage that Bangladesh as it is known today may virtually cease to exist.

SUBSIDING AWAY

Low-lying delta regions, vulnerable even to slight increases in sea level, 16
will be among the first land areas lost to inundation. Residents of these regions are joined in activities that amount to a lowering of defenses. By over-
pumping groundwater and interfering with the natural ground-building that
rivers achieve through sedimentation, they are causing the land to sink. In a
vicious circle, the more populated these regions become, the more likely
this subsidence—and the more devastating and immediate the hike in the
level of the sea.

Under natural conditions, deltas are in a state of dynamic equilibrium, 17
forming and breaking down in a continuous pattern of accretion and subsidence. Over time, these sediments accumulate to form marshes and
swamps. But regional and local tectonic effects, along with compaction,
cause the land to subside by as much as 4 inches a year if additional sediments are not laid down.

Channeling, diverting or damming rivers can greatly reduce the amount 18
of sediment that reaches a delta. Where humans interfere with river systems, sediment either shoots past lowlands and is borne out to sea, as with
the Mississippi River, or it is blocked upriver, as with the Nile. When this
happens, sediment accumulation does not offset subsidence. The result is
more severe shoreline erosion and a relative increase in sea water levels.
Subsidence also occurs where subterranean stores of water or oil are drained.
In Bangkok, Thailand, net subsidence has reached 5 inches per year due to
a drop in the water table caused by excessive withdrawals of groundwater
over the past three decades.

19   In Louisiana, reduced sedimentation along with extensive tapping of groundwater and underground stores of oil and gas have accelerated the disintegration of the Mississippi Delta. That state now loses more land to subsidence and sea level rise on an annual basis—50 square miles per year—than any other state or country in the world.

20   According to Woods Hole's Milliman, the combined effects of sea level rise and subsidence in Bangladesh and Egypt, whose populations are concentrated on deltas, threaten the homes and livelihoods of some 46 million people.

21   To arrive at that figure Milliman's research team started with two estimates of sea level rise: a minimum of 5 inches by 2050 and 11 inches by 2100, and a maximum of 31 inches by 2050 and 85 inches by 2100. They then calculated the effects under three scenarios.

22   Under the "best case" scenario, the researchers assume the minimum rise in sea level and a delta region in equilibrium. The second scenario, called the "worst case," assumes the maximum rate of sea level rise and the complete damming or diversion of the river system draining into the delta. As mentioned, the resulting subsidence must then be added to the absolute rise in sea level. The third scenario is referred to as the "really worst case." It assumes that excessive groundwater pumping from irrigation and other uses accelerates subsidence.

23   To calculate the economic implications of these three cases on both Egypt and Bangladesh, Milliman and his colleagues assumed present-day conditions, such as the estimated share of total population now living in areas that would be inundated and the share of economic activity that is derived from them. Continued settlement and population growth in these areas will only make for more environmental refugees.

SEVEN FEET FROM DISASTER

24   Milliman's calculations bode poorly for Bangladesh, which is nothing more than the world's largest deltaic plain. The Bengal Delta, built at the confluence of the Ganges, Brahmaputra and Meghna rivers, occupies about 80 percent of Bangladesh's total area. Much of the remainder is water. As a result, the nation's inhabitants are subject to annual floods from the rivers and from ocean storm surges.

25   Just how severely sea level rise will affect Bangladesh depends in part on the pace at which damming and channeling proceeds on the three giant rivers and their tributaries. Although annual flooding is severe and can dam-

age crops grown on the flood plains, large areas of the delta region suffer drought for the rest of the year. The diversion of river water to parched fields leaves Bangladesh in its present predicament: sedimentation is decreasing and subsidence is increasing.

The Woods Hole researchers have also concluded that the increasing 26 withdrawal of groundwater in Bangladesh is exacerbating subsidence. Between 1978 and 1985, there was at least a sixfold increase in the number of wells drilled in the country. Sediment samples suggest that the withdrawal of well water may have doubled the natural rate of subsidence.

Taking these factors into account, Milliman and his colleagues estimate 27 Bangladesh is going to experience the "really worst case" scenario. The effect of sea level rise will be as much as 82 inches along the coast by 2050, in which event it's likely 18 percent of the habitable land will be under water. More than 17 million people would become environmental refugees. The 57-inch rise in the worst case wouldn't spare the nation: 16 percent of its land would be lost.

By the year 2100, the really worst case scenario would have progressed 28 to the point that 38 million Bangladeshis will be forced to relocate. The social and economic effects will be jarring. Because nearly a third of the country's gross national product is generated within the land area that will be lost, an already poor country will have to accommodate its people on a far smaller economic base. Coastal mangrove forests, upon which 30 percent of the country's population depends to some extent for its livelihood, will be the first victims of advancing seas and extensive river diversion.

Where will those displaced by rising seas go? Moving further inland, 29 millions of refugees will have to compete with the local populace for scarce food, water and land, perhaps spurring regional clashes. Moreover, existing tensions between Bangladesh and its large neighbor to the west, India, are likely to heighten as the trickle of environmental refugees from the former becomes a torrent.

UP THE NILE

Egypt's habitable area is even more densely populated than that of Bangla- 30 desh. By and large, Egypt is desert except for the thin ribbon of productive land along the Nile River and its delta. Egypt's millions crowd onto less than 4 percent of the country's land, leading to a population density there of 700 people per square mile.

31   Milliman's study points out that because the Nile has already been dammed—which means most of the sediment that would offset subsidence of the delta is trapped upstream—only the "worst" and "really worst" cases are relevant for Egypt. Consequently, local sea level rise would range between 16 and 22 inches by 2050, rendering up to 19 percent of Egypt's good land uninhabitable.

32   If the increase is 22 inches, more than 8.5 million people would be forced to relinquish their homes to the sea, and Egypt would lose 16 percent of its gross national product. By 2100, local sea level rise will range between 101 and 131 inches, submerging up to 26 percent of habitable land and affecting an equal portion—24 percent—of both population and domestic economic output.

33   While neither Bangladesh nor Egypt is likely to influence the global emission of greenhouse gases or sea level rise, they do wield considerable control over local sea levels. The development policies they choose in the near future will have a significant effect on the future of their deltas and the people who live on them.

ECOSYSTEMS AT RISK

34   Coastal swamps and marshes are areas of prodigious biological productivity. The ecological and economic benefits derived from areas such as Louisiana's wetlands are inestimable. Nearly two-thirds of the migratory birds using the Mississippi flyway make a pitstop in those wetlands, while existing marshlands and barrier islands buffer inland areas against devastating hurricane surges. Marshes not only hold back the intrusion of the Gulf of Mexico's salt water into local rivers but are a major source of fresh water for coastal communities, agriculture and industry. Louisiana's wetlands supply 25 percent of the U.S. seafood catch and support a $500-million-a-year recreational industry devoted to fishing, hunting and birding.

35   What was laid down over millions of years by the slow deposit of silt washed off of land from the Rockies to the Appalachians could be jeopardized in a little over a century. Louisiana's famous bayous and marshland may be overrun by the year 2040, when the Gulf of Mexico surges up to 33 miles inland. With the delicate coastal marsh ecology upset, fish and wildlife harvests would decline precipitously and a ripple effect would flatten the coastal economy. Communities, water supplies and infrastructure will all be threatened.

According to U.S. Environmental Protection Agency estimates, erosion,   36
inundation and salt water intrusion could reduce the area of coastal wetlands in the United States by 30 to 80 percent if today's projections of sea
level rise are realized. Vital wetlands such as the Mississippi Delta and
Chesapeake Bay regions would be irreparably damaged. No one has yet calculated the immense economic and ecological costs of such a loss for the
United States, much less extrapolated it to the global level.

Were it not for the enormous pressure human encroachment puts on   37
them, coastal swamps and marshes might have a chance to handle rising
seas by reestablishing upland. But heavy development of beach resorts and
other coastal areas throughout the United States means that few wetlands
have the leeway to "migrate."

Highly productive mangrove forests throughout the world will also be   38
lost to the rising tide. Mangroves are the predominant type of vegetation on
the deltas along the Atlantic coast of South America. On the north coast of
Brazil active shoreline retreat is possible because there is little human settlement; the mangroves can possibly adapt. In the south, however, once-
extensive mangroves have been depleted or hemmed in by urban growth,
especially near Rio de Janeiro in Brazil. No more than 40 square miles of
mangroves remain where once thousands of square miles stood. As sea level
rises, these remaining areas will disappear.

MODERN-DAY ATLANTIS

In 2100, cartographers will likely be redrawing the coastlines of many coun-   39
tries. They may also make an important deletion: By that year, if current
projections are borne out, the Maldives will have been washed from the
earth. The small nation, made up of a series of 1,190 islands in atolls, is
nowhere higher in elevation than six feet. A mean sea level rise of equal
height would submerge the entire country. With a three-foot rise, well
within the expected increase of the next century, a storm surge would, in
the words of President Maumoon Abdul Gayoom, be "catastrophic and possibly fatal." Other such endangered places include the Pacific islands of
Kiribati, Tuvalu and the Marshalls.

By 2050, the Florida Keys "will no longer exist," according to Elton J.   40
Gissendanner, past executive director of the Florida Department of Natural
Resources. Loss of the Keys will displace thousands of permanent residents
and wipe out a tourist industry that brings 100,000 people to the area each

year. Approximately 70 percent of Florida's residents live right on the mainland coast, but no study has been done to determine how many will become environmental refugees.

41   Although increases in sea level will occur gradually over the next several decades—accelerating in 2030, when the greenhouse effect is expected to really kick in—the issue has already sparked a number of current debates.

42   For one, should society continue on its current path and accept sea level rise as inevitable, or should it change consumption patterns for fossil fuels and chemicals to mitigate a global warming? How long should local and national governments wait before investing heavily to defend their shores against a future threat, especially when other needs are pressing? When will it be too late? Conversely, should they seek to protect these areas at all? How can coastal residential and resort development be allowed to continue if the land is projected to disappear within a few decades? And who should provide insurance against catastrophe to those living in high-risk areas? Perhaps most important, who will help the Third World cope with the massive dislocations envisioned?

43   The industrial nations, heavily reliant on the burning of fossil fuels over the past century, are primarily responsible for initiating global warming. But, today virtually every citizen of every nation engages in activities that make the problem worse. Meanwhile, development strategies currently being adopted by many poorer countries—water projects that lead to subsidence, policies that encourage deforestation, and development programs based on fossil-fuel-intensive technologies—are likely to exacerbate, rather than abate, the warming and its effects.

44   If current trends persist, global warming and the subsequent rise in sea level will accelerate. If, on the other hand, concerted action is taken now—to raise energy efficiency and curtail overall fossil fuel use, to find substitutes for chlorofluorocarbons and other industrial chemicals that aggravate the greenhouse effect, to stem the tide of deforestation that destroys carbon-fixing trees—then sea level rise can be kept to a minimum.

45   President Gayoom of the Maldives frames the situation in blunt terms: "The predicted effects of the change are unnerving. . . . Reconstruction, rehabilitation and strengthening of coastal defense systems could turn out to be crippling for most affected countries." When the economic and environmental consequences are added in, no citizen of the planet is likely to remain unaffected.

Understanding Meaning

1. What is global warming?
2. What causes these changes, according to Jacobson?
3. How will global warming affect the planet? When will these changes occur?
4. How will governments be forced to respond to changes wrought by global warming?
5. *Critical Thinking:* What proof does Jacobson offer that these changes are likely to take place? How difficult is it to predict the future? What changes could alter the impact of global warming?

Evaluating Strategy

1. Jacobson begins the essay with a quote warning against buying land in New Orleans. Is this an effective attention getter, or does it risk being too sensational?
2. How does Jacobson explain complex scientific theories to a general audience?

Appreciating Language

1. How much technical language does Jacobson use? What does this reveal about her intended audience?
2. How does Jacobson use language to dramatize her view of the effects of global warming?

Connections across the Disciplines

1. How does this article support the argument made by Carl Sagan's "Why We Need to Understand Science" (page 563)?
2. *Critical Thinking:* Read Jocelyn Tomkin's refuting article (page 525). How does this article change your way of viewing Jacobson's assertions?

Writing Suggestions

1. Consider Jacobson's worst-case scenario. In your opinion, could the nations of the world cope with the slow rise of the oceans? Would the expenditure be much more than that spent on armaments? Write a short essay explaining how governments could respond to the crisis Jacobson describes.

2. *Collaborative Writing:* Discuss this essay with a group of students. Are they accustomed to reading articles full of gloom, predicting dire events in the future? Do writers overstate their cases to capture attention? Discuss instances where past predictions have been proven wrong. Work together to write a short paper outlining the issues raised in your group. You can develop the paper using comparison or cause and effect.

JOCELYN TOMKIN

Jocelyn Tomkin is an astronomer at the University of Texas at Austin. He wrote this article for Reason *(1993), a publication of the Reason Foundation based in Los Angeles. Tomkin argues that the effects of a rise in carbon dioxide are overstated. Instead of seeing global warming as an environmental threat, Tomkin asserts it "has been an essential ingredient in the evolution of life on earth."*

Hot Air

OVERVIEW: *Read Tomkin's article after studying the preceding essay by Jodi Jacobson. As you read Tomkin's piece, refer to Jacobson's. Which writer seems better at applying critical thinking skills?*

In his best-selling book, *Earth in the Balance,* Vice President Al Gore speculates that global warming caused by the greenhouse effect will throw "the whole global climate system . . . out of whack," dramatically reducing rainfall in parts of the world already troubled by drought, melting the polar icecaps, raising ocean levels, and devastating low-lying countries such as Bangladesh, India, Pakistan, Egypt, Indonesia, Thailand, and China. "In the lifetimes of people now living, we may experience a 'year without winter,'" Gore writes. "We are carelessly initiating climate changes that could well last for hundreds or even thousands of years."

Do such predictions have a basis in reality? Central to this question is the greenhouse effect. Contrary to the impression given by the mainstream media, the greenhouse effect is not of recent origin; it has been around for billions of years. But the link between this indisputable phenomenon and Gore's doomsday scenarios is tenuous at best. To understand why, you have to know something about the mechanics of the greenhouse effect.

The sun bathes the earth in sunshine. Some of the sunshine is reflected straight back into space, either by clouds or by the earth's surface. The remainder is absorbed by the earth's surface and thus heats it. Predictions about global warming hinge on the question of where this heat goes. Answering this question requires a brief trip into the world of electromagnetic radiation—light in all its forms, both visible and invisible.

All bodies radiate heat. A simple physical law says that the cooler a body is, the longer the wavelength at which it radiates its heat. The hot plate of a stove, for example, glows an orange-red when it's running at full blast. But turn it down, and as it cools it radiates its heat at longer and longer wavelengths, until it cools to the point where it's radiating exclusively in the infrared. To the eye it now appears to be off, although it is still too hot to touch.

5   Even everyday objects at everyday temperatures are busy radiators of heat in the infrared. A block of ice at melting point, for instance, has a temperature of 273 degrees Kelvin and is a raging furnace compared to a block of ice at absolute zero. (The Kelvin temperature scale is the same as the Celsius scale, except its zero is absolute zero, instead of the freezing point of water.) The earth itself continually radiates heat from both its dayside and its nightside. The balance between sunshine's heating effect and the cooling effect of the radiation the earth pours back into space allows the planet's surface to maintain a roughly constant temperature (apart from diurnal and seasonal variations).

6   But the earth's surface, with an average temperature of 288 degrees Kelvin, is much cooler than the sun's, with a temperature of 5,800 degrees Kelvin. So while the sun pumps most of its heat into space in the form of user-friendly visible light, the earth returns this heat to space in the form of much-longer-wavelength, invisible, infrared radiation. A greenhouse gas is a gas that is transparent at visible wavelengths but opaque at infrared wavelengths. It thus admits sunshine but blocks the escape of the earth's infrared radiation, thereby warming the planet's surface. As a rule, gases whose molecules have three or more atoms, such as carbon dioxide, are greenhouse gases, while gases whose molecules have only two atoms, such as oxygen, are not.

7   Among the greenhouse gases, carbon dioxide gets the lion's share of attention because its concentration is increasing, largely due to industrial activity. But it is actually a minor player. If the concentration of carbon dioxide in the atmosphere doubled, the blocking of the earth's infrared radiation would rise from 150 to 154 watts per square meter, an increase of roughly 3 percent. This means that the increasing level of carbon dioxide in the atmosphere is not matched by a corresponding increase in the greenhouse effect.

8   Over the last 100 years, for example, the level of carbon dioxide has increased by 25 percent, while the greenhouse effect has increased by around 1 percent. (This 1-percent figure assumes that other things have stayed equal in the meantime, but in the real world "other things" are usually not so obliging, so the actual behavior of the greenhouse effect during this time is unknown. Nonetheless, its variation has been much closer to 1 percent than to 25 percent.)

9   Ordinary water vapor is actually the main contributor to the greenhouse effect. The balance between the natural processes of evaporation, which

pumps water vapor into the atmosphere, and condensation into clouds, which squeezes it out, sets the level of water vapor in the atmosphere.

This means that the greenhouse effect and global warming are an integral part of the biosphere. They have been around at least since the formation of the first oceans and must therefore have preceded mankind's appearance by a few billion years. Indeed, if there were no global warming, if the earth's atmosphere were perfectly transparent at infrared wavelengths, the planet's average surface temperature would be a brisk zero degrees Fahrenheit, instead of the pleasant 59 degrees that we enjoy. Global warming has been an essential ingredient in the evolution of life on the earth.

Yet the illusion that carbon dioxide is the dominant greenhouse gas is extremely widespread. In an impromptu, totally nonscientific survey, I asked 10 of my fellow astronomers, "What is the major greenhouse gas?" Six said carbon dioxide. One added, "But isn't water vapor in there?" Two said water vapor. And one said, "Don't know."

Evidently a surprisingly large number of astronomers think that carbon dioxide is the major greenhouse gas, despite the fact that astronomers need to know how the earth's atmosphere stamps its spectral imprint on the radiation from heavenly bodies and what gases are responsible. In scientific disciplines that do not deal with the earth's atmosphere on a professional basis, the illusion that carbon dioxide is the major greenhouse gas is probably even more prevalent. Among the general public it must be well-nigh universal.

But even if carbon dioxide is a minor greenhouse gas, its level is increasing. Doesn't this mean global warming is increasing? Yes. But the real question is at what level, and is it significant compared to the changes in global warming that take place independent of mankind's activities? Will it cause an 8-degree increase during the next century, as predicted in the most alarming scenarios, or will there be a much more gradual, and mostly beneficial, increase of 1 degree or so?

We cannot answer this question by means of mere calculation, because our theoretical understanding of the biosphere is too incomplete. The *immediate* result of increased carbon dioxide is, indeed, an increase of global warming. The slightly higher average temperature leads to increased evaporation from the oceans, which leads to a further increase in global warming because water vapor is also a greenhouse gas. But this is far from the end of the story.

More water vapor in the atmosphere leads to increased cloudiness over the earth as a whole. This means more sunshine is reflected straight back into space and so never reaches the earth's surface. This, in turn, means less heating of the earth's surface and hence lower temperatures.

16   We don't know which one of these opposing mechanisms wins, so we don't know if the increase in the greenhouse effect is amplified or dampened by the time it feeds through to global warming. The availability of faster computers promises that during the next decade we will be able to get a better grip on these factors and many other, more complicated ones that are currently neglected.

17   In the meantime, the observational evidence that global warming is actually increasing is very shaky. Some researchers claim to see an increase in global warming of about 0.8 degree since 1860. Although average temperatures since then have increased by this much, it's doubtful that the rise reflects carbon-dioxide-induced global warming.

18   The large year-to-year fluctuations of average temperature—which are in the neighborhood of 1 degree—mean that the behavior of average global temperature is somewhat like that of a stock market index. Spotting a "real" temperature trend is like deciding if one is in a bull or a bear market. It's not impossible, but no bell rings when one trend ends and a new one begins.

19   Moreover, natural causes, rather than the increase in carbon dioxide, are a more likely explanation of the temperature increase. Most of the rise took place prior to 1940, *before* the main increase in the carbon-dioxide level.

20   Some climatologists interpret this pre-1940 temperature increase as an after-effect of the so-called Little Ice Age, a period of unusual worldwide cold that prevailed from 1600 to 1850. If we look at the 50 years or so from 1940 to the present, which have seen the major part of the increase in carbon-dioxide concentration, the increase in average global temperatures has been only 0.2 degree. This small increment is within the noise of natural variation. Although the level of carbon dioxide in the atmosphere is increasing, it does not seem to be affecting global temperatures much.

21   In examining the historical record, we also have to consider the urban heat island effect. The buildings and pavement of a city give it a microclimate slightly warmer than that of the surrounding countryside. As cities have grown, their heat islands have grown with them, so their weather stations, which tend to be in downtown locations, have been more and more prejudiced in favor of higher temperatures.

22   Phoenix is a dramatic example. Between 1960 and 1990, as its population grew from 650,000 to 2.1 million, its mean annual temperature heated up by 5 degrees, almost in lockstep with the population increase.

23   Climatologists who have tried to quantify the urban heat island's influence on the global temperature record estimate that it accounts for somewhere in the neighborhood of 0.2 degree of the 0.8-degree increase seen

since 1860. And when Kirby Hanson, Thomas Karl, and George Maul of the National Oceanic and Atmospheric Administration conducted a study of the U.S. temperature record that took into account the urban heat island effect, they found no long-term warming. They confirmed the temperature rise prior to 1940 but found that temperatures have fallen since then.

Another consideration is that most of the earth's surface is covered with   24
water. Temperature data over the oceans is extremely sparse, so the record of the earth's historic average temperature over both land and water is much vaguer than the land record. The recent advent of satellites with the capability to measure global temperatures accurately over both land and sea may solve the problem, but so far their time base is limited to a few years. However, global measurements by satellite of atmospheric (as distinct from surface) temperatures over the last decade show no sign of increasing temperatures.

Far more than historical evidence, the hullabaloo about global warming   25
is based on predictions by computer models. The global climate modeler gives his computer some basic facts, plus a program that recognizes the relevant physical processes and principles insofar as we know them and insofar as they can be calculated. With luck, the computer arrives at a climate not unlike that of the earth. Then the model gets a retroactive "tuning," so that its average global temperature is right.

A calculation of the greenhouse effect and associated global warming is   26
one step in the procedure. Assuming a doubling of atmospheric carbon dioxide, these models predict an increase in global warming of somewhere between 3 degrees and 8 degrees during the next century.

When they are judged by their verifiable accomplishments, however,   27
these computer models are not very impressive. They predict that the temperatures at the poles are lower than those at the equator, and they predict that it's hotter in summer than in winter. But they are weak on specifics. One model predicts an annual rainfall in the central Sahara that is the same as Ireland's.

Clearly, these global climate models are still in a primitive stage of development. They neglect many important factors—both known, such as the   28
poleward transport of heat from the equatorial regions by ocean currents and the atmosphere, and unknown. When it comes to telling us things we don't know already, such as trends in global warming during the next century, they are not far removed from the crystal-ball school of climatology.

Alarmists such as the vice president are impatient with people who   29
point this out. Gore writes: "If, when the remaining unknowns about the en-

vironmental challenge enter the public debate, they are presented as signs that the crisis may not be real after all, it undermines the effort to build a solid base of support for the difficult actions we must soon take. . . . The insistence on complete certainty about the full details of global warming—the most serious threat that we have ever faced—is actually an effort to avoid facing the awful, uncomfortable truth: that we must act boldly, decisively, comprehensively, and quickly, even before we know every last detail of the crisis."

30   But one of the "details" we still don't know is whether we are in fact facing a crisis requiring drastic action. The burden of proof is on the alarmists. They have failed to meet it.

Understanding Meaning

1. How does Tomkin define global warming?
2. When did the process of global warming begin, according to Tomkin?
3. What is the principal element causing the greenhouse effect?
4. What are the opposing effects of the greenhouse effect? Does Tomkin suggest outcomes?
5. *Critical Thinking:* What problems does Tomkin cite in making accurate predictions about global warming? In Tomkin's view, does enough evidence exist to make a prediction?

Evaluating Strategy

1. What impact does the article's opening have? Does Tomkin's questioning of Al Gore directly suggest that Jacobson's views lack credibility?
2. Tomkin is writing to a general audience about complex issues. Does his analogy of measuring climatic changes to making judgments about the stock market serve to enlighten or confuse readers?

Appreciating Language

1. What level of scientific language does Tomkin use? What does this reveal about his readers?
2. How does Tomkin refer to those he calls "alarmists"? Does he see them as fellow scientists making honest errors in judgment or as determined ideologues?

Connections across the Disciplines

1. Does Tomkin's article suggest that some environmentalists are motivated by political rather than scientific considerations?
2. Compare Tomkin's and Jacobson's articles. Is one writer more interested in making a political point than a scientific one?

Writing Suggestions

1. Consider the pro and con arguments by Jacobson and Tomkin. Which author's article, in your opinion, is more persuasive? Write an essay that defends your point of view.
2. *Collaborative Writing:* Discuss the two articles with a group of students, and decide which author is correct. If you feel you do not know enough about the topic to decide, make a list of information you would need before making a judgment. Work together to draft a brief analysis of your group's views on the subject.

THOMAS JEFFERSON ET AL.

During the hot summer of 1776, the Second Continental Congress met in Philadelphia. Following a call for a resolution of independence from Britain, John Adams, Thomas Jefferson, Benjamin Franklin, Robert Livingston, and Roger Sherman were charged with drafting a declaration. Jefferson wrote the original draft, which was revised by Adams and Franklin before being presented to the entire Congress. After further changes, the Declaration of Independence was adopted and signed.

The Declaration of Independence

OVERVIEW: *The Declaration of Independence presents a theory of government greatly influenced by the concept of natural rights espoused by Locke and Rousseau and then provides evidence that the British have failed to respect these rights. Notice that most of the declaration is a list of grievances or causes for the colonies to seek independence.*

1   *In Congress, July 4, 1776. The unanimous Declaration of the thirteen united States of America,*

2   When in the Course of human events, it becomes necessary for one people to dissolve the political bands which have connected them with another, and to assume among the powers of the earth, the separate and equal station to which the Laws of Nature and of Nature's God entitle them, a decent respect to the opinions of mankind requires that they should declare the causes which impel them to the separation.

3   We hold these truths to be self-evident, that all men are created equal, that they are endowed by their Creator with certain unalienable Rights, that among these are Life, Liberty and the pursuit of Happiness.

4   That to secure these rights, Governments are instituted among Men, deriving their just powers from the consent of the governed,

5   That whenever any Form of Government becomes destructive of these ends, it is the Right of the People to alter or to abolish it, and to institute new Government, laying its foundation on such principles and organizing its powers in such form, as to them shall seem most likely to effect their Safety and Happiness. Prudence, indeed, will dictate that Governments long established should not be changed for light and transient causes; and

accordingly all experience hath shown, that mankind are more disposed to suffer, while evils are sufferable, than to right themselves by abolishing the forms to which they are accustomed. But when a long train of abuses and usurpations, pursuing invariably the same Object evinces a design to reduce them under absolute Despotism, it is their right, it is their duty, to throw off such Government, and to provide new Guards for their future security.

Such has been the patient sufferance of these Colonies; and such is now 6 the necessity which constrains them to alter their former Systems of Government. The history of the present King of Great Britain is a history of repeated injuries and usurpations, all having in direct object the establishment of an absolute Tyranny over these States. To prove this, let Facts be submitted to a candid world.

He has refused his Assent to Laws, the most wholesome and necessary 7 for the public good.

He has forbidden his Governors to pass Laws of immediate and press- 8 ing importance, unless suspended in their operation till his Assent should be obtained; and when so suspended, he has utterly neglected to attend to them.

He has refused to pass other Laws for the accommodation of large dis- 9 tricts of people, unless those people would relinquish the right of Representation in the Legislature, a right inestimable to them and formidable to tyrants only.

He has called together legislative bodies at places unusual, uncomfort- 10 able, and distant from the depository of their public Records, for the sole purpose of fatiguing them into compliance with his measures.

He has dissolved Representative Houses repeatedly, for opposing with 11 manly firmness his invasions on the rights of the people.

He has refused for a long time, after such dissolutions, to cause others 12 to be elected; whereby the Legislative powers, incapable of Annihilation, have returned to the People at large for their exercise; the State remaining in the mean time exposed to all the dangers of invasion from without, and convulsions within.

He has endeavoured to prevent the population of these States; for that 13 purpose obstructing the Laws for Naturalization of Foreigners; refusing to pass others to encourage their migrations hither, and raising the conditions of new Appropriations of Lands.

He has obstructed the Administration of Justice, by refusing his Assent 14 to Laws for establishing Judiciary powers.

He has made Judges dependent on his Will alone, for the tenure of 15 their offices, and the amount and payment of their salaries.

16   He has erected a multitude of New Offices, and sent hither swarms of Officers to harrass our people, and eat out their substance.

17   He has kept among us in times of peace, Standing Armies without the Consent of our legislatures.

18   He has affected to render the Military independent of and superior to the Civil power.

19   He has combined with others to subject us to a jurisdiction foreign to our constitution, and unacknowledged by our laws; giving his Assent to their Acts of pretended Legislation:

20   For quartering large bodies of armed troops among us:

21   For protecting them, by a mock Trial, from punishment for any Murders which they should commit on the Inhabitants of these States:

22   For cutting off our Trade with all parts of the world:

23   For imposing Taxes on us without our Consent:

24   For depriving us in many cases, of the benefits of Trial by Jury:

25   For transporting us beyond Seas to be tried for pretended offences:

26   For abolishing the free System of English Laws in a neighbouring Province, establishing therein an Arbitrary government, and enlarging its Boundaries so as to render it at once an example and fit instrument for introducing the same absolute rule in these Colonies:

27   For taking away our Charters, abolishing our most valuable Laws, and altering fundamentally the Forms of our Governments:

28   For suspending our own Legislatures, and declaring themselves invested with power to legislate for us in all cases whatsoever.

29   He has abdicated Government here, by declaring us out of his Protection and waging War against us.

30   He has plundered our seas, ravaged our Coasts, burnt our towns, and destroyed the lives of our people.

31   He is at this time transporting large Armies of foreign Mercenaries to compleat the works of death, desolation and tyranny, already begun with circumstances of Cruelty & perfidy scarcely paralleled in the most barbarous ages, and totally unworthy the Head of a civilized nation.

32   He has constrained our fellow Citizens taken Captive on high Seas to bear Arms against their Country, to become the executioners of their friends and Brethren, or to fall themselves by their Hands.

33   He has excited domestic insurrections amongst us, and has endeavoured to bring on the inhabitants of our frontiers, the merciless Indian Savages, whose known rule of warfare, is an undistinguished destruction of all ages, sexes and conditions.

In every stage of these Oppressions We have Petitioned for Redress in the most humble terms: Our repeated Petitions have been answered only by repeated injury. A Prince, whose character is thus marked by every act which may define a Tyrant, is unfit to be the ruler of a free people.

Nor have We been wanting in attentions to our Brittish brethren. We have warned them from time to time of attempts by their legislature to extend an unwarrantable jurisdiction over us. We have reminded them of the circumstances of our emigration and settlement here. We have appealed to their native justice and magnanimity, and we have conjured them by the ties of our common kindred to disavow these usurpations, which, would inevitably interrupt our connections and correspondence. They too have been deaf to the voice of justice and consanguinity. We must, therefore, acquiesce in the necessity, which denounces our Separation, and hold them, as we hold the rest of mankind, Enemies in War, in Peace Friends.

We, therefore, the Representatives of the united States of America, in General Congress, Assembled, appealing to the Supreme Judge of the world for the rectitude of our intentions, do, in the Name, and by Authority of the good People of these Colonies, solemnly publish and declare, That these United Colonies are, and of Right ought to be, Free and Independent States; that they are Absolved from all Allegiance to the British Crown, and that all political connection between them and the State of Great Britain, is and ought to be totally dissolved; and that as Free and Independent States, they have full Power to levy War, conclude Peace, contract Alliances, establish Commerce, and to do all other Acts and Things which Independent States may of right do.

And for the support of this Declaration, with a firm reliance on the protection of divine Providence, we mutually pledge to each other our Lives, our Fortunes and our sacred Honor.

Understanding Meaning

1. What are the principal causes for the Congress to declare independence?
2. Why do Jefferson and the other authors argue that these grievances cannot be resolved in any other fashion?
3. *Critical Thinking:* When was the last time you read the Declaration of Independence? Do some items strike you as relevant to current conditions? Should Americans be more familiar with a document that helped create their own country and establish its values?

Evaluating Strategy

1. How does the Declaration of Independence use induction and deduction?
2. How much space is devoted to the list of causes? Is enough evidence provided to support severing ties with Britain?
3. The causes are placed in separate paragraphs rather than combined. What impact does this have?

Appreciating Language

1. How does the document refer to the king?
2. This document was drafted in 1776. How readable is it today? How has language changed in two hundred years?

Connections across the Disciplines

1. The opening of the Declaration of Independence asserts that the "pursuit of happiness" is a right. How does this concept relate to the search for happiness described by John Ciardi (page 189)? Do Americans believe they have a right to be happy?
2. Compare the Declaration of Independence to Albert Einstein's letter to President Roosevelt (page 596). What characteristics do many of the world's most important writings seem to have?

Writing Suggestions

1. Write a personal analysis of the Declaration of Independence. What do you think is the most significant feature of the document? What does the phrase "Life, Liberty and the pursuit of Happiness" mean to you?
2. *Collaborative Writing:* Discuss the declaration with a group of students. Does the current government reflect the ideals of Jefferson? How has America changed since 1776? For further discussion, look up the original draft, which contained a passage denouncing slavery, a passage Jefferson had to delete to pacify southern delegates. Develop a statement with other students expressing your opinion of the Declaration of Independence's importance in the twenty-first century.

Cause-and-effect writing is often used in manuals, textbooks, training guides, and consumer information packets. Hewlett-Packard includes this troubleshooting guide in the owner's manual of a laser printer.

Solving Printer Operation Problems

OVERVIEW: *As you examine the cause-and-effect guide, consider the intended audience and the use of a chart. How easy would this information be to follow if written in standard paragraphs?*

Use the following steps to help solve problems you experience with your   1
printer. If you need more help, refer to the service and support information. . . . That chapter will guide you in getting help from your dealer or, if necessary, contacting Hewlett-Packard for help.

SYMPTOM	POSSIBLE CAUSE	SOLUTION	
The printer does not respond when you send a print job from software.	The printer's parallel cable is loose.	Check the connections on the printer and on the computer. Make sure the cable on the printer is not attached upside-down (some cables have a flexible plastic sleeve that allows an improper connection).	2
		Secure the cable to the computer with screws and to the printer with the wire clips.	3
	The parallel cable is defective.	Try your cable on another system with a print job that you know works.	4

5	**The printer does not respond when you send a print job from software, continued.**	The printer is malfunctioning.	If the printer is in Intelligent Off mode, press the front panel button to turn on the Ready light. Then press it again to print a self test page. If the self test page prints, the printer is working correctly.
6			If all the lights are on, there is a hardware error. Disconnect the printer from its power source and wait 15 minutes. Then reconnect it. If all four lights come back on, contact your HP authorized service representative. . . .
7		You did not select the correct printer through your software.	Check your software's printer selection menu to see if you selected the HP LaserJet 4L printer.
8		Your software or your printer is not yet configured for the correct printer port.	Check your software's configuration menu to make sure it is accessing the correct printer port.
9			If your computer has more than one parallel port, make sure you are connected to the correct one.
10		The printer is not connected to power, or the power source is not active.	Check your power cord, switches, and fuses.
11		You did not reset the printer after clearing a paper jam.	Press the front panel button, or open and close the top printer door to reset the printer after a jam.

The printer does not respond when you send a print job from software, continued.	The printer's top door or rear door is open.	Make sure both doors are closed securely.	12
	The printer is connected to a switch box, and the switch box is not set up to receive data from your printer.	Check the switch box setting.	13
The Error light is on steadily.	The printer's top door is open, or the toner cartridge is not installed completely.	Open the door, reinstall the toner cartridge, then close the door firmly.	14
The Error light is blinking.	There was a memory error in your print job.	Press the front panel button to resume printing. (There may be some data loss.)	15
		Change your page to make it less complex, or add optional printer memory.	16
The Paper light is on steadily.	The paper cassette is empty.	Load more paper into the paper cassette.	17
The Paper light is blinking.	There is a paper jam.	See . . . instructions on how to clear paper jams.	18
Both the Data light and the Ready light are on steadily.	There is unprinted data in the printer. (Your software did not send an "end of job" command.)	Briefly press the front panel button to print the rest of the data.	19
The Data light is blinking.	The printer is in Manual Feed mode and the manual feed slot is waiting for paper.	Insert a piece of paper into the manual feed slot.	20

21	***All the printer's lights are off.***	The printer is in Intelligent Off mode.	Briefly press the front panel button to activate the Ready light. If the Ready light does not come on, check the power cord and your power source. If the printer still does not respond, contact your local HP authorized service representative. . . .
22	***All the printer's lights are on.***	The printer has a hardware error.	Disconnect the printer from its power source and wait 15 minutes. Then reconnect it. If all four lights come back on, contact your HP authorized service representative. . . .
23	***The printer is feeding multiple sheets or jams frequently.***	The paper does not meet HP's specifications for print media (embossed, damaged, too slick or too rough, too much moisture, wrong weight).	Try another kind of paper. See the paper specifications. . . .
24		The paper is sticking together.	Take the paper out of the cassette and fan it to separate the sheets.
25		The paper cassette is too full.	Remove some of the paper.
26		The printer may need service.	Contact your HP authorized service representative. . . .

The printer jams when you attempt a manual feed.	You removed and reinserted your paper while trying to do a manual feed.	Once the printer senses that the paper is in the manual feed slot (you feel it grab the corner), do not remove it and reinsert it. This causes the printer to pull the paper through the paper path too late, and results in a paper jam. Let the printer automatically realign the paper to straighten it in the paper path.

Understanding Meaning

1. What causes the "Paper light" to blink?
2. When should you call a service representative?
3. What should you try when the printer jams or feeds multiple sheets?

Evaluating Strategy

1. How readable is this guide? Is it clearly stated?
2. What impact does the format have?
3. *Critical Thinking:* What would be the best way for technical writers to test their owner's manual before printing and shipping it to hundreds of thousands of consumers worldwide?

Appreciating Language

1. Does any of the wording seem confusing to you? Could this set of instructions be read by nontechnical consumers?
2. Why do all the solution statements open with verbs?

Connections across the Disciplines

1. Compare these instructions with "Cleaning Battery Terminals" (page 472). Do they share common features?

2. Compare these instructions with "Communications Styles: United States and Taiwan" (page 272). When are chartlike presentations of text acceptable?

Writing Suggestions

1. Write a similar cause-and-effect chart about a product you are familiar with.
2. *Collaborative Writing:* Discuss with a small group manuals you have encountered as students or consumers. What problems and frustrations do people report having? Work together to write a list of causes of reader confusion. You may place these in a chart.

STRATEGIES FOR CAUSE-AND-EFFECT WRITING

1. **Determine your goal.** Are you attempting to explain a cause or to predict future outcomes?
2. **Evaluate your readers' needs.** What evidence does your reader require in order to accept your conclusions? Are government statistics more impressive than the testimony of experts? Does any background information or do any definitions need to be presented?
3. **Offer logical, acceptable evidence.** Present support that comes from reliable sources readers will accept. Present evidence in a clearly organized manner. Use brief narratives or analogies to dramatize data.
4. **Review your use of deduction or induction.** Does your major premise contain unproven assumptions? Is it clearly stated, or is it subject to different interpretations? Does your inductive leap move beyond reasonable doubt? Do you provide enough evidence to support your inductive conclusion?
5. **Qualify assertions and conclusions.** A writer who admits that alternative interpretations or conflicting evidence exists can appear more credible to readers than one who narrowly insists he or she has the only possible conclusion.
6. **Evaluate sources.** Do not allow yourself to automatically assume everything you read is valid. Experts have made errors of judgment. Read books, articles, and studies carefully. Look for signs of bias, unproven assumptions, or mistakes in logic. Look for what is missing.
7. **Use other modes to organize information.** It may be beneficial to use a narrative, comparison, extended definition, or division and classification to present your cause-and-effect thesis.

SUGGESTED TOPICS FOR CAUSE-AND-EFFECT WRITING
General Assignments

Write a cause-and-effect paper on any of the following topics. Your paper may use other modes to organize and present evidence. Cause-and-effect papers usually require research. It is possible to use cause and effect in less formal papers, in which you offer personal experience and observations as examples. However, the more objective facts you can cite, the stronger your writing will be.

Write a paper explaining the cause(s) of the following topics:

- Teenage pregnancy
- Sexual harassment

- Divorce
- The success or failure of a local business
- The victory or defeat of a political candidate

Write a paper predicting the effects of the following topics:

- The information superhighway
- Immigration
- Harsher drunk-driving laws
- An aging population
- The death of a spouse or loved one

Writing in Context

1. Analyze in a short essay a recent event on campus, in your community, or at your place of work. Examine what caused this event to take place. If several causes exist, you may use division to explain them or classification to rank them from the most important to the least important.
2. Write a letter to the editor of the campus newspaper predicting the effects of a current policy change, incident, or trend in student behavior.
3. Imagine a job application asks you to write a 250-word essay presenting your reasons for choosing your career. Write a one-page essay that lists your most important reasons. As you write, consider how an employer would evaluate your response.

This paper was written by a student who is active in a campus environmental movement. She intended to use the essay both to fulfill a composition assignment and as an article for the college newspaper.

Can the Devon Be Saved?

For decades the back cover of the college catalog featured a photo- 1
graph of a stone bridge crossing the Devon River. Fund raising brochures and alumni publications often include pictures of students ad-
miring Devon Falls on the north side of the campus. The river is as
much associated with the college as Old Main and the hundred-year-old
library clock tower. The Devon's grassy banks have been popular places
for students to relax, picnic, read, or sunbathe. The Devon has been one
of the college's main draws. Campus visitors are universally drawn by
the sound of water rushing over massive boulders to the river bank.

Now massive development has come to the Devon River. The uni- 2
versity has approved building a 300-room dorm along the river, clearing ten acres of woodland for the building and parking lot. Upriver,
the county's largest subdivision, Devoncrest, nears completion. Some
200 condominiums and 450 apartments will be occupied by next
spring. The surge in population will greatly increase the amount of
sewage flowing into the fifty-seven-year-old treatment plant at English
Beach. In addition, new storm sewers will feed more water into the
river, as will runoff from the new parking lots being built on the banks.

The Riverwest project on the opposite shore will have even a 3
greater impact on the Devon. Three high-rise office towers and a new
shopping mall with parking for 800 cars will occupy a half-mile strip
of newly cleared riverbank. Designed on an incline, the mall parking
lots will send rainwater cascading into the river, eroding the denuded
riverbank. Already mud slides have shorn ten feet off the edge. In
winter tons of snow will likely be plowed from the new parking lots
and dumped into the river.

This development will cause the narrow Devon River to flood in 4
the spring. Five years ago the state erected a series of levees to pro-

545

tect the marshes from floods and possible oil spills. These levees protect the bird sanctuary very effectively, but they limit the marshland's ability to act like a mammoth sponge which previously absorbed much of the spring runoff.

5   As a result, we can expect flooding as more water enters the river near the new parking lots. Mud slides will add to the problem. The sewage treatment plant, located on the flood plain, may easily be overwhelmed and release raw sewage into the bay. Sewage spills could contaminate beaches and have a dramatic effect on fishing, boating, and tourism. The value of beach property could plummet.

6   In our rush to capitalize on the beauty of our river, we are threatening the bay which generates jobs and income. We must lobby the university and developers to take steps now to limit runoff from parking lots and to plant fresh vegetation to prevent further erosion of the riverbanks. If steps are not taken now, the new condos and office towers will overlook nothing but a stream of mud and debris.

Questions for Review and Revision

1. How effective is the introduction? Does the student assume readers are familiar with the locale and the importance of the river?
2. This essay was directed to a local audience. How would it have to be revised for a wider readership unfamiliar with the campus?
3. What transitional devices does the student use? Could you suggest improvements?
4. *Other Modes:* How much of this essay contains *argument and persuasion?*
5. How does the student describe the river? Do words and connotations dramatize the importance of the river? Could added details create more striking images of the predicted environmental damage?
6. Read the paper aloud. Could revisions or reorganization clarify the writer's purpose?

Writing Suggestions

1. Using this student's essay as a model, write a cause-and-effect paper detailing results of an environmental, technological, or social change in your area. For example, how has a new computer system improved record keeping? Has a change in employee benefits affected morale?

2. *Collaborative Writing:* Discuss with a group of students the causes or effects of new construction, a new trend, or a new technological development. Brainstorm to list effects, both positive and negative. Create an essay listing the significant changes that may occur. You may divide the paper into two lists, detailing the beneficial and the detrimental results.

CAUSE-AND-EFFECT CHECKLIST

Before submitting your paper, review these points.

1. Is your thesis clearly stated?

2. Are causes clearly stated, logically organized, and supported by details?

3. Are conflicting interpretations disproven or acknowledged?

4. Are effects supported by observation and evidence? Do you avoid sweeping generalizations and unsupported conclusions?

5. Do you anticipate future changes that might alter predictions?

6. Do you avoid making errors in critical thinking, especially errors such as making hasty generalizations and confusing time relationships for cause and effect?

7. Have you tested your ideas through peer review?

 Companion Web Site

See **http://sundance.heinle.com** for information on writing cause and effect.

 InfoTrac® College Edition

For additional reading go to InfoTrac College edition, your on-line research library, at **http://infotrac.thomsonlearning.com**.

- Enter the search term "cause" using Keywords.
- Enter the search term "effect" using Keywords.
- Enter the search terms "cause and effect" using Keywords.
- Enter the name of an author you read in this chapter using Keywords.
- Enter a theme or idea your class discussed using Keywords.

10

Argument and Persuasion

WHAT IS ARGUMENT AND PERSUASION?

We are bombarded by argument and persuasion every day. Newspaper editorials encourage us to change our opinions about abortion, gun control, or public financing of religious schools. Sales brochures convince us to invest in stocks or buy life insurance. Fund-raising letters ask us to contribute to homeless shelters or the local symphony. Billboards, magazine ads, and television commercials urge us to buy automobiles and soft drinks. Political candidates solicit our votes. Public service announcements warn us against smoking and drunk driving.

As a student you have to develop persuasive arguments in essays and research papers to demonstrate your skills and knowledge. After graduation you will need a persuasive résumé and cover letter to secure job interviews. In your career you will have to impress clients, motivate employees, justify decisions, and propose new ideas to superiors with well-stated arguments and persuasive appeals.

Arguments are assertions designed to convince readers to accept an idea, adopt a solution, or change their way of thinking. Writers use reason and facts to support their arguments, often disproving or disputing conflicting theories or alternative proposals in the process. Attorneys prepare written arguments stating why a client has a valid claim or deserves a new trial. Scientists present the results of experiments to argue for new medical treatments or to disprove current assumptions. Economists assemble data to support arguments to raise or lower interest rates. In "Why We Need to Understand Science" (page 563), Carl Sagan urges his readers to appreciate the need for greater education in science. To impress his audience, he prepares a broad-based argument, demonstrating how science and technology are essential in solving current and future problems:

> We live in a society exquisitely dependent on science and technology, in which hardly anyone knows anything about science and technology. This is a

clear prescription for disaster. It's dangerous and stupid for us to remain ignorant about global warming, say, or ozone depletion, toxic and radioactive wastes, acid rain. Jobs and wages depend on science and technology. If the United States can't manufacture, at high quality and low price, products people want to buy, then industries will drift out of the United States and transfer a little prosperity to another part of the world. Because of the low birthrate in the '60s and '70s, the National Science Foundation projects a shortage of nearly a million professional scientists and engineers by 2010. Where will they come from? What about fusion, supercomputers, abortion, massive reductions in strategic weapons, addiction, high-resolution TV, airline and airport safety, food additives, animal rights, superconductivity, Midgetman versus rail-garrison MX missiles, going to Mars, finding cures for AIDS and cancer? How can we decide national policy if we don't understand the underlying issues?

The way writers present evidence depends on their discipline or profession. Each field has specific methods and standards of presenting evidence and stating arguments.

The audience plays a critical role in the way writers shape an argument, especially when they suspect that readers hold alternative viewpoints or be prejudiced against them or the groups they represent. In directing an argument to readers, writers often use *persuasion*, making emotional or dramatic statements that stir people's passions and beliefs. Advertisers use sex appeal to sell everything from toothpaste to cars. Commercials for charities flash 800-numbers over images of starving children to motivate people to make donations. In creating persuasive arguments, you should consider the perceptual world of your readers (page 13).

Persuasive Appeals

Writers traditionally use three basic appeals to convince readers to accept their ideas or take action: logic, emotion, and ethics. Because each appeal has advantages and disadvantages, writers generally use more than one.

LOGIC supports a point of view or proposed action through reasoned arguments and a presentation of evidence:

Test results Findings established by experiments or standard research methods.

Statistics Data represented by numbers and percentages.

Expert testimony Opinions or statements made by respected authorities.

Eyewitness testimony   Statements by those who experienced or witnessed events and situations.

Surveys   Measurements of public opinion or sample audiences.

Logic is widely used in academic, business, and government reports.

Advantages: Provides evidence needed for major decisions, especially group decisions.

Disadvantages: Can demand a high degree of reader attention and specialized knowledge.

EMOTION uses images, sensations, or shock appeals to lead people to react in a desired manner. Emotional appeals call on people's deeply felt needs and desires:

Creativity   The desire for recognition by self-expression.

Achievement   The need to attain money, fame, or fulfillment.

Independence   The drive to be unique, to stand out, and to be individual.

Conformity   The desire to be part of a group, to be included, and to be *in*.

Endurance   To achieve satisfaction by bearing burdens others could not or feeling successful by simply surviving.

Fear   To resist, avoid, or defeat threats to the self or society, such as cancer, crime, or terrorism.

Emotional appeals are found most frequently in public relations, marketing, and advertising.

Advantages: Produces immediate results.

Disadvantages: Has limited impact, can backfire, and provides limited factual support for readers to share with others.

ETHICS use shared values to influence people. Ethics may call on reasoning but do not rest wholly on logical analysis of data. Like emotional appeals, ethics reflect deeply held convictions rather than personal motivations.

Religion   The desire to follow the rules and behavior espoused by one's faith, such as to be a good Christian or practicing Jew.

Patriotism   The urge to place one's country before personal needs: "Ask not what your country can do for you; ask what you can do for your country."

Standards   The desire to be a good citizen, a good lawyer, or a good parent, to express the higher ideals of a community, profession, or family role.

Humanitarianism   A secular appeal to help others, save the environment, protect the weak, or to be a "citizen of the world."

Ethical appeals form the basis of many sermons, editorials, and political speeches.

Advantages: Can be very powerful, especially if the writer is addressing an audience with the same value system.

Disadvantages: Depends on readers who accept the principles espoused by the writer. A Muslim cleric's appeal, for example, may have little impact on Catholics or atheists.

To be effective, writers frequently mix factual detail with emotionally charged human interest. An article on homeless children might use the story of a single child to arouse sympathy, then provide statistics to illustrate the severity of the problem, and, finally, outline possible solutions.

Appealing to Hostile Readers

Perhaps most challenging is attempting to persuade a hostile audience, readers you anticipate having negative attitudes toward you, the organization you represent, or the ideas you advocate. Although no technique will magically convert opponents into supporters, you can overcome a measure of hostility and influence those who may still be undecided with a few approaches:

1. **Openly admit differences.** Instead of attempting to pretend no conflict exists, openly state that your view may differ from that of your readers. This honest admission can win a measure of respect.

2. **Responsibly summarize opposing viewpoints.** By fairly restating your opponents' views, you force readers to agree with you and demonstrate impartiality.

3. **Avoid making judgmental statements.** Do not label your opponents' ideas with negative language. Use neutral terms to make distinctions. If you call your ideas intelligent and your readers' naive, you will have difficulty getting people to accept your points because in the process they will have to accept your insults as being valid.

4. **Point to shared values, experiences, and problems.** Build common bridges with your readers by demonstrating past cooperation and common goals.

5. **Ask your readers to keep an open mind.** Don't demand or expect to convert readers. But almost everyone will agree to try to be open-minded and receptive to new ideas.
6. **Work to overcome negative stereotypes.** Play the devil's advocate, and determine what negative stereotypes your readers might have about you and your ideas. Then work to include examples, references, and evidence in your paper to counter negative assumptions.

CRITICAL THINKING FOR WRITING ARGUMENT AND PERSUASION

Perhaps no other form of writing demands more critical thinking than argument and persuasion. When using logical, emotional, and ethical appeals, avoid the common traps or fallacies writers often fall into:

- **Absolute statements**   Although it is important to convince readers by making a strong impression, avoid making absolute claims that can be dismissed with a single exception. If you state "all lawyers are honest," a reader has only to think of a single dishonest attorney to repudiate your argument. A qualified claim can make a strong impression and leave room for exceptions: "The legal profession is known for its high standards of ethical conduct."
- *Non sequitur* **(it does not follow)**   Avoid making assertions based on irrelevant evidence: "Bill Smith was a great football coach—he'll make a great mayor." Although a coach may possess leadership and skills in strategy, he may lack the political knowledge and diplomatic skills needed in government.
- **Begging the question**   Do not assume what has to be proved: "Nancy is lying because she never tells the truth." Asserting that Nancy never tells the truth offers no evidence that she is lying.
- **False dilemma**   Do not offer or accept only two alternatives to a problem: "Either employees must take a wage cut, or the company will go bankrupt." This statement ignores other possible solutions such as raising prices, lowering production costs, or increasing sales.
- **False analogy**   Comparisons make very weak arguments: "Crack cocaine should be legalized since Prohibition did not work." Alcohol and crack cocaine are not like substances. Alcohol has been consumed by humans for thousands of years. Crack cocaine has never been socially acceptable to most Americans.
- **Red herring**   Resist the temptation to dodge the real issue by drawing attention to something controversial: "How can you endorse the budget proposal of a congressman indicted for soliciting bribes?" Corruption charges alone do not invalidate a politician's policies.

- **Borrowed authority**   Avoid assuming that an expert in one field can be accepted as an authority in another: "Senator Johnson is convinced Dallas will win by ten points." A respected senator may have no more insight into the National Football League than a cab driver or a hairdresser. Celebrity endorsements are common examples of borrowed authority.
- *Ad hominem* **(attacking the person)**   Attack ideas, not the people who advocate them: "The only people who oppose gun control are paranoid Nazis and Uzi-toting drug dealers." The merits of the issue and not the personalities have to be discussed to create a convincing argument.

STRATEGIES FOR READING ARGUMENT AND PERSUASION

When reading the argument and persuasion entries in this chapter, keep these questions in mind:

Meaning

1. What is the author's thesis? What does he or she want readers to accept?
2. How credible is the thesis? Does it make sense? Are alternatives discussed?
3. How does the writer characterize those who advocate differing views? Does the writer appear to have an unfair bias?

Strategy

1. Which appeals are used—logic, emotion, or ethics?
2. Do the appeals seem to work with the intended audience?
3. Are the factual details interesting, believable, and effective?
4. Are emotional appeals suitable, or do they risk backfiring or distorting the issue?
5. Are the logical fallacies avoided?
6. Does the writer appear to anticipate rejection or approval?

Language

1. What role does connotation play in shaping arguments using logical, emotional, or ethical appeals?
2. What does the author's choice of words suggest about the intended audience?
3. Does word choice indicate a bias?

SCOTT SIMON

Scott Simon is a war correspondent and reporter, but he is best known to listeners of National Public Radio as the host of "Weekend Edition with Scott Simon."

Why Even Pacifists Support This War

OVERVIEW: *This essay appeared shortly after the September 11, 2001, terrorist attacks against the World Trade Center and the Pentagon. As you read Simon's argument, consider if subsequent events have altered the thoughts and emotions the attacks produced. Is the idea of a war against terrorism as popular now as it was in late 2001? Why or why not?*

1

introduction

Pacifists often commit the same mistake as generals: They prepare for the last war, not the next one.

2

Many of the peace activists I have seen trying to rouse opposition to to-day's war against terrorism remind me of a Halloween parade. They put on old, familiar-looking protest masks—against American imperialism, oppression and violence—that bear no resemblance to the real demons haunting us now.

3

appeal of pacifism

Pacifism has never been exactly popular. But when I became a Quaker as an adolescent in the late 1960s, pacifism seemed to offer a compelling alternative to the perpetuity of brute force. Mahatma Gandhi had overthrown an empire, and Martin Luther King had overturned a racial tyranny with nonviolent marches, fasts and boycotts that were nervy, ennobling and effective.

4

Pacifism seemed to offer a chance for survival to a generation that had been stunted by the fear of nuclear extinction.

5

Simon's roles as Quaker and war reporter

I worked as a war reporter, but I never saw a conflict between this and being a Quaker. If my reporting was sometimes drawn more to human de-tails than to the box-score kind of war coverage, those details struck me as critical to explaining war. I never covered a conflict—whether in Central America, the Caribbean, Africa or the Middle East—that seriously shook my religious convictions.

6

In fact, most conflicts seemed to prove how war was rotten, wasteful and useless. El Salvador's civil war killed 70,000 people over nine years. It was hard to see how the political compromise that ended the conflict could not have been reached after just six months.

7

fatal flaw of pacifism

But in the 1990s, I covered the Balkans. In Sarajevo, Srebrenica and Ko-sovo, I confronted the logical flaw (or perhaps I should say the fatal flaw) of non-violent resistance: All the best people can be killed by all the worst ones.

554

I had never believed that pacifism had all the answers; neither does militarism. About half of all draft age Quakers enlisted in World War II, believing that whatever wisdom pacifism had to give the world, it could not defeat the murderous schemes of Adolf Hitler and his cohorts.

8

Quakers and Hitler

It seems to me that in confronting the forces that attacked the World Trade Center and the Pentagon, American pacifists have no sane alternative now but to support war. I don't consider this reprisal or revenge, but self-defense: protecting the world from further attacks by destroying those who would launch them.

9

thesis

Some peace activists, their judgment still hobbled by shock, seem to believe that the attacks against New York and Washington were natural disasters: terrible, unpredictable whirlwinds that struck once and will not reoccur.

10

flawed view of pacifists

This is wrong. We know now that there has been an ongoing violent campaign aimed at bringing down diverse nations, with none being more gloriously speckled than the United States. People who try to hold certain American policies or culture responsible are trying to decorate the crimes of psychotics with synthetic political significance.

11

attacks critics

In 1933, the Oxford Student Union conducted a famous debate over whether it was moral for Britons to fight for king and country. The exquisite intellects of that leading university reviewed the many ways in which British colonialism exploited and oppressed the world. They cited the ways in which vengeful demands made of Germany in the wake of World War I had helped to kindle nationalism and fascism. They saw no moral difference between Western colonialism and world fascism.

12

historical example

The Oxford Union ended that debate with this famous proclamation: "Resolved, that we will in no circumstances fight for king and country."

13

Von Ribbentrop sent back the good news to Germany's new chancellor, Hitler: The West will not fight for its own survival. Its finest minds will justify a silent surrender.

14

impact of pacifism on tyrants

In short, the best-educated young people of their time could not tell the difference between the deficiencies of their own nation, in which liberty and democracy were cornerstones, and a dictatorship founded on racism, tyranny and fear.

15

And what price would those who urge reconciliation today pay for peace?

16

Should Americans impose a unitary religious state, throw women out of school and work and rob other religious groups of their rights so that we have the kind of society the attackers accept? Do pacifists really want to live in the kind of world that the terrorists who hit the World Trade Center and Pentagon would make?

17

Pacifists do not need any lectures about risking their lives to stop wickedness. Quakers resisted slavery by smuggling out slaves when even Abra-

18

ham Lincoln tried to appease the Confederacy. Pacifists sneaked refugee Jews out of Germany when England and the U.S. were still trying to placate Hitler. Many conscientious objectors have served bravely in gritty and unglamorous tasks that aided the U.S. in time of war.

19   But those of us who have been pacifists must admit that it has been our blessing to live in a nation in which other citizens have been willing to risk their lives to defend our dissent.

20   The war against terrorism does not shove American power into calls on America's military strength in a global crisis in which peaceful solutions are not apparent.

21   Only American (and British) power can stop more killing in the world's skyscrapers, pizza parlors, embassies, bus stations, ships and airplanes. Pacifists, like most Americans, would like to change their country in a thousand ways. And the blasts of Sept. 11 should remind American pacifists that they live in that one place on the planet where change—in fact, peaceful change

conclusion   —seems most possible.

22   It is better to sacrifice our ideals than to expect others to die for them.

Understanding Meaning

1. What is Simon's thesis? Can you restate it in your own words?
2. Why did Simon originally support the philosophy of pacifism? Who were his models?
3. After covering the war in the Balkans, Simon states he discovered the logical flaw of nonviolent resistance. What is the fatal flaw of pacifism?
4. Did Simon fully abandon his view of nonviolent resistance?
5. How important were Simon's religious views in shaping his attitude toward pacifism?
6. *Critical Thinking:* During World War I Clarence Darrow remarked that pacifists always spoke with a German accent. American Nazis opposed the United States entering the Second World War. People who protested the war in Vietnam were often condemned as Communists. Can pacifists oppose a conflict without being assumed to have sympathies with America's opponents?

Evaluating Strategy

1. What role does autobiography play in Simon's argument?
2. What historical examples does Simon provide to illustrate the weaknesses of pacifism?
3. Simon draws many comparisons between World War II and the war on terrorism. Are these analogies effective in supporting his thesis?

4. What audience is Simon addressing? Who would likely be persuaded by his essay? How might opponents respond to his characterization of pacifists?

Appreciating Language

1. Simon uses the term "Halloween parade" to describe pacifists who oppose the war on terrorism. Do you find this phrase effective?
2. Simon states that some pacifists treated the attacks on the United States as if they were "natural disasters." What does he mean by using this term? What is he suggesting about the pacifist reaction to the events of September 11, 2001?

Connections across the Disciplines

1. Anna Quindlen (page 558) argues that women should be required to register for the draft. Have the terrorist attacks changed many people's attitudes about the military, defense spending, the CIA, and public service?
2. Compare Scott Simon's article with Jonathan Schell's description of Ground Zero (page 117). How have other people reacted? Do some focus on taking action against the terrorists, while others concentrate on healing and recovery?

Writing Suggestions

1. Consider your own attitude about war. Is military action, in your view, ever justified? Write a letter to the editor of your local paper clearly defining your views. You may provide historical or theoretical examples to distinguish between acceptable and unacceptable uses of force.
2. *Collaborative Writing:* Discuss Simon's article with a number of students. Take a poll to see if you agree or disagree with his opinion. Write a statement that reflects the views of your group. If members disagree, consider writing a comparison paper outlining pro and con views or a classification paper that charts the range of viewpoints your group has expressed.

ANNA QUINDLEN

Anna Quindlen (1952–) graduated from Barnard College in 1974 and began working as a reporter in New York. After writing articles for the New York Post, *she took over the "About New York" column for the* New York Times. *In 1986 she started her own column, "Life in the Thirties." Her collected articles were published in* Living Out Loud *in 1988. She has written numerous op-ed pieces for the* Times *on social and political issues. In 1992 she received the Pulitzer Prize. The following year she published another collection of essays,* Thinking Out Loud: On the Personal, the Political, the Public, and the Private. *Quindlen has also written three novels,* Object Lessons, One True Thing, *and* Black and Blue.

Uncle Sam and Aunt Samantha: It's Simple Fairness: Women as Well as Men Should be Required to Register for the Draft

OVERVIEW: *Although women now serve in many combat roles in the military, unlike males, they are not required to register for the draft on their eighteenth birthday. As you read this article, consider if registering for the draft should be an obligation shared by both sexes. Does exempting women from the draft give them a separate, less significant status, even in peacetime?*

1   One out of every five new recruits in the United States military is female. The Marines gave the Combat Action Ribbon for service in the Persian Gulf to 23 women. Two female soldiers were killed in the bombing of the USS Cole.

2   The Selective Service registers for the draft all male citizens between the ages of 18 and 25.

3   What's wrong with this picture?

4   As Americans read and realize that the lives of most women in this country are as different from those of Afghan women as a Cunard cruise is from maximum-security lockdown, there has nonetheless been little attention paid to one persistent gender inequity in U.S. public policy. An astonishing anachronism, really: while women are represented today in virtually all fields, including the armed forces, only men are required to register for the military draft that would be used in the event of a national-security crisis.

Since the nation is as close to such a crisis as it has been in more than   5
60 years, it's a good moment to consider how the draft wound up in this particular time warp. It's not the time warp of the Taliban, certainly, stuck in
the worst part of the 13th century, forbidding women to attend school or
hold jobs or even reveal their arms, forcing them into sex and marriage. Our
own time warp is several decades old. The last time the draft was considered seriously was 20 years ago, when registration with the Selective Service was restored by Jimmy Carter after the Soviet invasion of, yep, Afghanistan. The president, as well as the Army chief of staff, asked at the time for
the registration of women as well as men.

Amid a welter of arguments—women interfere with esprit de corps,   6
women don't have the physical strength, women prisoners could be sexually assaulted, women soldiers would distract male soldiers from their mission—Congress shot down the notion of gender-blind registration. So did
the Supreme Court, ruling that since women were forbidden to serve in
combat positions and the purpose of the draft was to create a combat-ready
force, it made sense not to register them.

But that was then, and this is now. Women have indeed served in com-   7
bat positions, in the Balkans and the Middle East. More than 40,000 managed to serve in the Persian Gulf without destroying unit cohesion or failing because of upper-body strength. Some are even now taking out targets
in Afghanistan from fighter jets, and apparently without any male soldier's
falling prey to some predicted excess of chivalry or lust.

Talk about cognitive dissonance. All these military personnel, male and   8
female alike, have come of age at a time when a significant level of parity
was taken for granted. Yet they are supposed to accept that only males will
be required to defend their country in a time of national emergency. This is
insulting to men. And it is insulting to women. Caroline Forell, an expert
on women's legal rights and a professor at the University of Oregon School
of Law, puts it bluntly: "Failing to require this of women makes us lesser
citizens."

Neither the left nor the right has been particularly inclined to consider   9
this issue judiciously. Many feminists came from the antiwar movement and
have let their distaste for the military in general and the draft in particular
mute their response. In 1980 NOW released a resolution that buried support for the registration of women beneath opposition to the draft, despite
the fact that the draft had been redesigned to eliminate the vexing in-
equities of Vietnam, when the sons of the working class served and the
sons of the Ivy League did not. Conservatives, meanwhile, used an equal-

opportunity draft as the linchpin of opposition to the Equal Rights Amendment, along with the terrifying specter of unisex bathrooms. (I have seen the urinal, and it is benign.) The legislative director of the right-wing group Concerned Women for America once defended the existing regulations by saying that most women "don't want to be included in the draft." All those young men who went to Canada during Vietnam and those who today register with fear and trembling in the face of the Trade Center devastation might be amazed to discover that lack of desire is an affirmative defense.

10   Parents face a series of unique new challenges in this more egalitarian world, not the least of which would be sending a daughter off to war. But parents all over this country are doing that right now, with daughters who enlisted; some have even expressed surprise that young women, in this day and age, are not required to register alongside their brothers and friends. While all involved in this debate over the years have invoked the assumed opposition of the people, even 10 years ago more than half of all Americans polled believed women should be made eligible for the draft. Besides, this is not about comfort but about fairness. My son has to register with the Selective Service this year, and if his sister does not when she turns 18, it makes a mockery not only of the standards of this household but of the standards of this nation.

11   It is possible in Afghanistan for women to be treated like little more than fecund pack animals precisely because gender fear and ignorance and hatred have been codified and permitted to hold sway. In this country, largely because of the concerted efforts of those allied with the women's movement over a century of struggle, much of that bigotry has been beaten back, even buried. Yet in improbable places the creaky old ways surface, the ways suggesting that we women were made of finer stuff. The finer stuff was usually porcelain, decorative and on the shelf, suitable for meals and show. Happily, the finer stuff has been transmuted into the right stuff. But with rights come responsibilities, as teachers like to tell their students. This is a responsibility that should fall equally upon all, male and female alike. If the empirical evidence is considered rationally, if the decision is divested of outmoded stereotypes, that's the only possible conclusion to be reached.

Understanding Meaning

1. Why does Quindlen believe that women should be required to register with the Selective Service?

2. Why, in Quindlen's view, have feminists failed to focus on this example of gender inequality?
3. Does exempting women from the draft, in Quindlen's reasoning, result from a traditional belief that women are delicate and require special protections?
4. Should military service be a social responsibility shared by all citizens?
5. Quindlen points out that one of five recruits is female. How does this support her argument for requiring both women and men to register?
6. *Critical Thinking:* Would drafting women in time of war make sense for a reason other than equality? Now that many women are entering fields critical to the military such as health care, computers, aviation, and other occupations, would it not double the pool of talent the country needs to wage war in a high-tech world?

Evaluating Strategy

1. Quindlen mentions her own children. Does the fact that she is willing to have her own daughter register support her argument?
2. How effective is the list of opening facts? Do these statistics anticipate reader objections that women should not have to register for the draft?
3. *Other Modes:* Where does Quindlen use *narration, comparison,* and *cause and effect* to build her argument?

Appreciating Language

1. Look up the word "anachronism." Is this an effective word for Quindlen to use to characterize the "men only" requirement?
2. Quindlen is writing about a serious issue but includes statements like "What's wrong with this picture?" and "yep." Do these informal expressions weaken her argument in your view? Why or why not?

Connections across the Disciplines

1. Bob Levey (page 236) writes about the different ways men and women perceive walking alone at night. Would these gender differences affect the way men and women would act in a combat zone or other hostile territory?
2. Scott Simon (page 554) comments on the decision men have made in the past about serving in wars. If women are exempt from having to be drafted in both popular and unpopular wars, does it diminish their social status? If men are facing the choices of serving in the military, going to jail, or leaving the country

and women are exempt, does the draft limit women to the status of bystander? Why or why not?

Writing Suggestions

1. Write an editorial for your campus newspaper clearly stating your views on whether women should be required to register for the draft.
2. Quindlen writes specifically about registering for the Selective Service. Many nations have a national service program that requires young people to devote a year or two to military or social service. Do you think every citizen should serve the country in some capacity, be that defending the nation or teaching disadvantaged children how to read? Write a persuasive essay arguing for or against a national service plan.

CARL SAGAN

Carl Sagan (1934–1996) was born in New York City and educated at the University of Chicago, where he received his doctorate in 1960. A widely published astronomer, Sagan became known to American television audiences through a popular series called Cosmos. An expert on the atmospheres of Venus, Mars, and Titan, he was also noted for his ability to explain scientific issues to a general audience.

Why We Need to Understand Science

OVERVIEW: *This article originally appeared in the popular magazine* Parade *(1993). As you read the article, notice how Sagan moves from humorous narrative to a serious argument, supported by facts, that Americans are woefully lacking in their knowledge of science.*

As I got off the plane, he was waiting for me, holding up a sign with my name on it. I was on my way to a conference of scientists and TV broadcasters, and the organizers had kindly sent a driver. 1

"Do you mind if I ask you a question?" he said as we waited for my bag. "Isn't it confusing to have the same name as that science guy?" 2

It took me a moment to understand. Was he pulling my leg? "I *am* that science guy," I said. He smiled. "Sorry. That's my problem. I thought it was yours too." He put out his hand. "My name is William F. Buckley." (Well, his name wasn't *exactly* William F. Buckley, but he did have the name of a contentious TV interviewer, for which he doubtless took a lot of good-natured ribbing.) 3

As we settled into the car for the long drive, he told me he was glad I was "that science guy"—he had so many questions to ask about science. Would I mind? And so we got to talking. But not about science. He wanted to discuss UFOs, "channeling" (a way to hear what's on the minds of dead people—not much it turns out), crystals, astrology. . . . He introduced each subject with real enthusiasm, and each time I had to disappoint him: "The evidence is crummy," I kept saying. "There's a much simpler explanation." As we drove on through the rain, I could see him getting glummer. I was attacking not just pseudoscience but also a facet of his inner life. 4

And yet there is so much in real science that's equally exciting, more mysterious, a greater intellectual challenge—as well as being a lot closer to the truth. Did he know about the molecular building blocks of life sitting out there in the cold tenuous gas between the stars? Had he heard of the 5 footprints of our ancestors found in 4-million-year-old volcanic ash? What about the raising of the Himalayas when India went crashing into Asia? Or how viruses subvert cells, or the radio search for extraterrestrial intelligence or the ancient civilization of Ebla? Mr. "Buckley"—well-spoken, intelligent, curious—had heard virtually nothing of modern science. He *wanted* to know about science. It's just that all the science got filtered out before it reached him. What the society permitted to trickle through was mainly pretense and confusion. And it had never taught him how to distinguish real science from the cheap imitation.

6   All over America there are smart, even gifted, people who have a built-in passion for science. But that passion is unrequited. A recent survey suggests that 94 percent of Americans are "scientifically illiterate."

A PRESCRIPTION FOR DISASTER

7   We live in a society exquisitely dependent on science and technology, in which hardly anyone knows anything about science and technology. This is a clear prescription for disaster. It's dangerous and stupid for us to remain ignorant about global warming, say, or ozone depletion, toxic and radioactive wastes, acid rain. Jobs and wages depend on science and technology. If the United States can't manufacture, at high quality and low price, products people want to buy, then industries will drift out of the United States and transfer a little prosperity to another part of the world. Because of the low birthrate in the '60s and '70s, the National Science Foundation projects a shortage of nearly a million professional scientists and engineers by 2010. Where will they come from? What about fusion, supercomputers, abortion, massive reductions in strategic weapons, addiction, high-resolution TV, airline and airport safety, food additives, animal rights, superconductivity, Midgetman versus rail-garrison MX missiles, going to Mars, finding cures for AIDS and cancer? How can we decide national policy if we don't understand the underlying issues?

8   I know that science and technology are not just cornucopias pouring good deeds out into the world. Scientists not only conceived nuclear weapons; they also took political leaders by the lapels, arguing that *their* nation—whichever it happened to be—had to have one first. Then they arranged to manufacture 60,000 of them. Our technology has produced thalidomide, CFCs, Agent Orange, nerve gas, and industries so powerful they can ruin

the climate of the planet. There's a *reason* people are nervous about science and technology.

And so the image of the mad scientist haunts our world—from Dr. Faust to Dr. Frankenstein to Dr. Strangelove to the white-coated loonies of Saturday morning children's TV. (All of this doesn't inspire budding scientists.) But there's no way back. We can't just conclude that science puts too much power into the hands of morally feeble technologists or corrupt, power-crazed politicians and decide to get rid of it. Advances in medicine and agriculture have saved more lives than have been lost in all the wars in history. Advances in transportation, communication, and entertainment have transformed the world. The sword of science is double-edged. Rather, its awesome power forces on all of us, including politicians, a new responsibility—more attention to the long-term consequences of technology, a global and transgenerational perspective, an incentive to avoid easy appeals to nationalism and chauvinism. Mistakes are becoming too expensive.

Science is much more than a body of knowledge. It is a way of thinking. This is central to its success. Science invites us to let the facts in, even when they don't conform to our preconceptions. It counsels us to carry alternative hypotheses in our heads and see which best match the facts. It urges on us a fine balance between no-holds-barred openness to new ideas, however heretical, and the most rigorous skeptical scrutiny of everything—new ideas *and* established wisdom. We need wide appreciation of this kind of thinking. It works. It's an essential tool for a democracy in an age of change. Our task is not just to train more scientists but also to deepen public understanding of science.

HOW BAD IS IT?

Very bad. "It's Official," reads one newspaper headline: "We Stink in Science." Less than half of all Americans know that the Earth moves around the Sun and takes a year to do it—a fact established a few centuries ago. In tests of average 17-year-olds in many world regions, the U.S. ranked dead last in algebra. On identical tests, the U.S. kids averaged 43 percent and their Japanese counterparts 78 percent. In my book, 78 percent is pretty good—it corresponds to a C+, or maybe even a B−; 43 percent is an F. In a chemistry test, students in only two of 13 nations did worse than the U.S. Compared to us, Britain, Singapore, and Hong Kong were so high they were almost off-scale, and 25 percent of Canadian 18-year-olds knew just as much chemistry as a select 1 percent of American high school seniors (in their second chemistry course, and most of them in "advanced" programs). The best of 20 fifth-grade classrooms in Minneapolis was outpaced by every one of the 20 classrooms in Sendai, Japan, and 19 out of 20 in Taipei, Taiwan. South Korean students were far ahead of American students in all aspects of mathematics and science, and 13-year-olds in British Columbia (in Western Canada) outpaced their U.S. counterparts across the boards (in some areas they did better than the Koreans). Of the U.S. kids, 22 percent say they dislike school; only 8 percent of the Koreans do. Yet two-thirds of Americans, but only a quarter of the Koreans, say they are "good at mathematics."

WHY WE'RE FLUNKING

12   How do British Columbia, Japan, Britain, and Korea manage so much better than we do? During the Great Depression, teachers enjoyed job security, good salaries, respectability. Teaching was an admired profession, partly because learning was widely recognized as the road out of poverty. Little of that is true today. And, so, science (and other) teaching is too often incompetently or uninspiringly done, its practitioners, astonishingly, having little or no training in their subjects—sometimes themselves unable to distinguish science from pseudoscience. Those who do have the training often get higher-paying jobs elsewhere.

13   We need more money for teachers' training and salaries, and for laboratories—so kids will get hands-on experience rather than just reading what's in the book. But all across America, school-bond issues on the ballot are regularly defeated. U.S. parents are much more satisfied with what their children are learning in science and math than are, say, Japanese and Taiwanese parents—whose children are doing so much better. No one suggests that property taxes be used to provide for the military budget, or for agriculture, or for cleaning up toxic wastes. Why just education? Why not support it from general taxes on the local and state levels? What about a special education tax for those industries with special needs for technically trained workers?

14   American kids don't do enough schoolwork. The average high school student spends 3.5 hours a week on homework. The total time devoted to studies, in and out of the classroom, is about 20 hours a week. Japanese *fifth*-graders average 33 hours a week.

But most American kids aren't stupid. Part of the reason they don't study   15
hard is that they've received few tangible benefits when they do. Competency (that is, actually knowing the stuff) in verbal skills, mathematics, and science these days doesn't increase earnings for average young men in their first eight years out of high school—many of whom take service rather than industrial jobs.

In the productive sectors of the economy, though, the story is different.   16
There are furniture factories, for example, in danger of going out of business—not because there are no customers but because few entry-level workers can do simple arithmetic. A major electronics company reports that 80 percent of its job applicants can't pass a *fifth*-grade math test—and that's an American, not a Korean, fifth-grade test. The United States is already losing some $25 billion a year (mainly in lost productivity and the cost of remedial education) because workers, to too great a degree, can't read, write, count, or think. Parents should know that their children's livelihoods may depend on how much math and science they know. Now, while the kids are in school, is the time for them to learn. Parents might encourage their schools to offer—and their kids to take—comprehensible, well-taught advanced science courses. They might also limit the amount of mind-numbing TV their children watch.

WHAT WE CAN DO

Those in America with the most favorable view of science tend to be young,   17
well-to-do, college-educated white males. But three-quarters of new American workers between now and 2001 will be women, nonwhites, and immigrants. Discriminating against them isn't only unjust, it's also self-defeating. It deprives the American economy of desperately needed skilled workers.

Black and Hispanic students are doing better in standardized science   18
tests now than in the late 1960s, but they're the only ones who are. The average math gap between white and black U.S. high school graduates is still huge—two to three grade levels; but the gap between white U.S. high school graduates and those in, say, Japan, Canada, Great Britain, or Finland is more than *twice* as big. If you're poorly motivated and poorly educated, you won't know much—no mystery here. Suburban blacks with college-educated parents do just as well in college as suburban whites with college-educated parents. Enrolling a poor child in a Head Start program doubles his or her chances to be employed later in life; one who completes an Up-

ward Bound program is four times as likely to get a college education. If we're serious, we know what to do.

19   What about college and university? There are obvious steps similar to what should be done in high schools; salaries for teachers that approach what they could get in industry; more scholarships, fellowships, and laboratory equipment; laboratory science courses required of everyone to graduate; and special attention paid to those traditionally steered away from science. We should also provide the financial and moral encouragement for academic scientists to spend more time on public education—lectures, newspaper and magazine articles, TV appearances. This requires scientists to make themselves understandable and fun to listen to. To me, it seems strange that some scientists, who depend on public funding for their research, are reluctant to explain to the public what it is that they do. Fortunately, the number of scientists willing to speak to the public—and capably—has been increasing each year. But there are not yet nearly enough.

20   Virtually every newspaper in America has a daily astrology column. How many have a daily science column? When I was growing up, my father would bring home a daily paper and consume (often with great gusto) the baseball box scores. There they were, to me dry as dust, with obscure abbreviations (W, SS, SO, W-L, AB, RBI), but they spoke to him. Newspapers everywhere printed them. I figured maybe they weren't too hard for me. Eventually I too got caught up in the world of baseball statistics. (I know it helped me in learning decimals, and I still cringe a little when I hear that someone is "batting a thousand." But 1.000 is not 1,000. The lucky player is batting one.)

21   Or take a look at the financial page. Any introductory material? Explanatory footnotes? Definitions of abbreviations? None. It's sink or swim. Look at those acres of statistics! Yet people voluntarily read the stuff. It's not beyond their ability. It's only a matter of motivation. Why can't we do the same with math, science, and technology?

22   By far the most effective means of raising interest in science is television. There's lots of pseudoscience on TV, a fair amount of medicine and technology, but hardly any science—especially on the three big commercial networks, whose executives think science programming means ratings declines and lost profits, and nothing else matters. Why in all America is there no TV drama that has as its hero someone devoted to figuring out how the universe works?

23   Stirring projects in science and technology attract and inspire youngsters. The number of science Ph.D.s peaked around the time of the Apollo program and declined thereafter. This is an important potential side-effect

of such projects as sending humans to Mars, or the Superconducting Super-collider to explore the fine structure of matter, or the program to map all human genes.

Every now and then, I'm lucky enough to teach a class in kindergarten or the first grade. Many of these children are curious, intellectually vigorous, ask provocative and insightful questions, and exhibit great enthusiasm for science. When I talk to high school students, I find something different. They memorize "facts." But, by and large, the joy of discovery, the life behind those facts, has gone out of them. They're worried about asking "dumb" questions; they're willing to accept inadequate answers; they don't pose follow-up questions; the room is awash with sidelong glances to judge, second-by-second, the approval of their peers. Something has happened between first and 12th grade, and it's not just puberty. I'd guess that its partly peer pressure *not* to excel (except in sports); partly that the society teaches short-term gratification; partly the impression that science or math won't buy you a sports car; partly that so little is expected of students; and partly that there are so few role models for intelligent discussion of science and technology or for learning for its own sake.

But there's something else. Many adults are put off when youngsters pose scientific questions. Children ask why the Sun is yellow, or what a dream is, or how deep you can dig a hole, or when is the world's birthday or why we have toes. Too many teachers and parents answer with irritation or ridicule, or quickly move on to something else. Why adults should pretend to omniscience before a 5-year-old, I can't for the life of me understand. What's wrong with admitting that you don't know? Children soon recognize that somehow this kind of question annoys many adults. A few more experiences like this, and another child has been lost to science.

There are many better responses. If we have an idea of the answer, we could try to explain. If we don't, we could go to the encyclopedia or library. Or we might say to the child: "I don't know the answer. Maybe no one knows. Maybe when you grow up, you'll be the first to find out."

But mere encouragement isn't enough. We must also give children the tools to winnow the wheat from the chaff. I'm haunted by the vision of a generation of Americans unable to distinguish reality from fantasy, hopefully clutching their crystals for comfort, unequipped even to frame the right questions or to recognize the answers. I want us to rescue Mr. "Buckley" and the millions like him. I also want us to stop turning out leaden, incurious, unimaginative high school seniors. I think America needs, and deserves, a citizenry with minds wide awake and a basic understanding of how the world works.

28   Public understanding of science is more central to our national security than half a dozen strategic weapons systems. The sub-mediocre performance of American youngsters in science and math, and the widespread adult ignorance and apathy about science and math, should sound an urgent alarm.

Understanding Meaning

1. What is the difference between pseudoscience and science?
2. Why is American "scientific illiteracy" dangerous?
3. Why are people, in Sagan's view, disinterested in science?
4. What does Sagan persuade readers to accept? What must be done to improve our nation's understanding of science?
5. What does Sagan mean when he says that science is more than "knowledge" but "a way of thinking"? What is the difference?
6. *Critical Thinking:* Sagan argues that the media has portrayed science in a way children find unappealing. What image of scientists did you develop as a child? Were scientists depicted as less glamorous than police officers or lawyers?

Evaluating Strategy

1. How important is the opening narrative? What does it suggest about Sagan's intended readers?
2. What factual appeals does Sagan make?
3. How does he attempt to make his concerns about science relevant to general readers?
4. How does he present statistics? Are they understandable?

Appreciating Language

1. What level of language does Sagan use? How does it differ from that expected in a scientific paper or textbook?
2. How does Sagan use language to arouse reader concern about scientific illiteracy?

Connections across the Disciplines

1. How does Richard Preston's "Ebola River" (page 73) dramatize the need for scientific education and research?

2. Sagan argues that science is driven by facts and truth. How does Sagan's argument relate to Samuel Scudder's nineteenth-century article (page 47)?

Writing Suggestions

1. Write a short essay arguing that Americans lack a general knowledge of an important topic—science, mathematics, the Constitution, the environment, or their own bodies.
2. *Collaborative Writing:* Discuss Sagan's article with a group of students. What impressions of science and scientists did the group have in childhood? Write a brief, persuasive, open letter to parents encouraging them to invest more in their children's knowledge of science. You may use facts from Sagan's article for support.

BLENDING THE MODES

NAT HENTOFF

Nat Hentoff (1925–) was born in Boston. The author of more than twenty-five books, Hentoff is also known for his numerous articles in the Village Voice, New Yorker, *and the* Washington Post. *A committed liberal, he has been outspoken on issues ranging from drug testing and the draft to racism and abortion. Although considered a leftist, Hentoff has criticized those on the Left who have advocated suppressing what they call "hate speech."*

Should This Student Have Been Expelled?

OVERVIEW: *In this 1991 article from the* Village Voice, *Hentoff persuades readers to accept "hate speech," no matter how offensive it is, as "speech" and therefore protected by the Constitution. As you read Hentoff's essay, notice how he uses* definition, narration, *and* comparison *to build his argument.*

> *The day that Brown denies any student freedom of speech is the day I give up my presidency of the university.*
> —Vartan Gregorian, president of Brown University,
>
> February 20, 1991

1   Doug Hann, a varsity football player at Brown, was also concentrating on organizational behavior and management and business economics. On the night of October 18, 1990, Hann, a junior, was celebrating his twenty-first birthday, and in the process had imbibed a considerable amount of spirits.

2   At one point, Hann shouted into the air, "Fuck you, niggers!" It was aimed at no one in particular but apparently at all black students at Brown. Or in the world. A freshman leaned out a dormitory window and asked him to stop being so loud and offensive.

3   Hann, according to reporters on the *Brown Daily Herald*, looked up and yelled, "What are you, a faggot?" Hann then noticed an Israeli flag in the dorm. "What are you, a Jew?" he shouted. "Fucking Jew!"

Hann had achieved the hat trick of bigotry. (In hockey, the hat trick is   4
scoring three goals in a game.) In less than a minute, Hann had engaged in
racist, anti-Semitic, and homophobic insults.

He wasn't through. As reported by Smita Nerula in the *Brown Daily*   5
Herald, the freshman who had asked Hann to cool it recruited a few people
from his dorm "and followed Hann and his friends."

"This resulted in a verbal confrontation outside of Wayland Arch. At   6
this time, [Hann] was said to have turned to one of the freshman's friends, a
black woman, and shouted, 'My parents own your people.'"

To the Jewish student, or the student he thought was Jewish, Hann   7
said, "Happy Hanukkah."

There are reports that at this juncture Hann tried to fight some of the   8
students who had been following him. But, the *Brown Daily Herald* reports,
he "was held back by one of his friends, while [another] friend stretched his
arm across the Wayland Gates to keep the students from following Hann."

John Howard Crouch—a student and Brown chapter secretary of the   9
American Civil Liberties Union there—tells me that because Hann had
friends restraining him, "nobody seriously expected fighting, regardless of
anyone's words."

Anyway, there was no physical combat. Just words. Awful words, but   10
nothing more than speech. (Nor were there any threats.)

This was not the first time Hann's graceful drunken language had sur-   11
faced at Brown. Two years before, in an argument with a black student at a
fraternity bar, Hann had called the student a "nigger." Thereupon he had
been ordered to attend a race relations workshop and to get counseling for
possible alcohol abuse. Obviously, he has not been rehabilitated.

Months went by after Hann's notorious birthday celebration as Brown's   12
internal disciplinary procedures cranked away. (To steal a phrase from Robert Sherrill, Brown's way of reaching decisions in these matters is to due
process as military music is to music. But that's true of any college or university I know anything about.)

At last, the Undergraduate Disciplinary Council (five faculty or admin-   13
istration members and five students) ruled that Doug Hann was to leave the
university forevermore. Until two years ago, it was possible for a Brown student to be dismissed, which meant that he or she could reapply after a
decent period of penance. But now, Brown has enshrined the sentence of
expulsion. You may go on to assist Mother Teresa in caring for the dying or
you may teach a course in feminism to 2 Live Crew, but no accomplishments, no matter how noble, will get you back into Brown once you have
been expelled.

14   Doug Hann will wander the earth without a Brown degree for the rest of his days.

15   The president of Brown, Vartan Gregorian—formerly the genial head of the New York Public Library—had the power to commute or even reverse the sentence. But the speech code under which Hann was thrown out had been proposed by Gregorian himself shortly after he was inaugurated in 1989, so he was hardly a detached magistrate.

16   On January 25, 1991, Vartan Gregorian affirmed, with vigor, the expulsion decision by the Undergraduate Disciplinary Council.

17   Hann became a historic figure. Under all the "hate speech" codes enacted around the country in recent years, he is the first student to actually be expelled for violating one of the codes.

18   The *New York Times* (February 12) reported that "Howard Ehrlich, the research director of the National Institute Against Prejudice and Violence, said that he did not know of any other such expulsions, but that he was familiar with cases in which students who had harassed others were moved to other dormitories or ordered to undergo counseling."

19   But that takes place in *educational* institutions, whose presidents recognize that there are students who need help, not exile.

20   At first, there didn't seem to be much protest among the student body at Brown on free speech grounds—except for members of the Brown chapter of the ACLU and some free thinkers on the student paper, as well as some unaffiliated objectors to expelling students for what they say, not for what they do. The number of these dissenters is increasing, as we shall see.

21   At the student paper, however, the official tone has changed from the libertarian approach of Vernon Silver, who was editor-in-chief last semester. A February 13 *Brown Daily Herald* editorial was headed: *"Good Riddance."*

22   It began: "Doug Hann is gone, and the university is well to be rid of him."

23   But President Gregorian has been getting a certain amount of flack and so, smiting his critics hip and thigh, he wrote a letter to the *New York Times*. Well, that letter (printed on February 21) was actually a press release, distributed by the Brown University News Bureau to all sorts of people, including me, on February 12. There were a few changes—and that *Brown Daily Herald* editorial was attached to it—but Gregorian's declaration was clearly not written exclusively for the *Times*.

24   Is this a new policy at the *Times*—taking public relations handouts for the letters page?

Next week I shall include a relentlessly accurate analysis of President   25
Gregorian's letter by the executive director of the Rhode Island ACLU. But
first, an account of what Gregorian said in that letter to the *Times*.

President Gregorian indignantly denies that Brown has ever expelled   26
"anyone for the exercise of free speech, nor will it ever do so." Cross his
heart.

He then goes into self-celebration: "My commitment to free speech and   27
condemnation of racism and homophobia are well known. . . .

"The university's code of conduct does not prohibit speech; it prohibits   28
actions."

Now watch this pitiable curve ball: 29

"Offence III [of the Brown code]—which deals with harassment—   30
prohibits inappropriate, abusive, threatening, or demeaning actions based
on race, religion, gender, handicap, ethnicity, national origin, or sexual
orientation."

In the original press release, Gregorian underlined the word *actions*.   31
There, and in the letter to the *Times*—lest a dozing reader miss the point—
Gregorian emphasizes that "The rules do not proscribe words, epithets, or
slanders, they proscribe behavior." Behavior that "shows flagrant disrespect
for the well-being of others or is unreasonably disruptive of the University
community."

Consider the overbreadth and vagueness of these penalty-bearing pro-   32
visions. What are the definitions of "harassment," "inappropriate," "demeaning," "flagrant," "disrespect," "well-being," "unreasonably"?

Furthermore, with regard to Brown's termination of Doug Hann with   33
extreme prejudice, Gregorian is engaging in the crudest form of Orwellian
newspeak. Hann was kicked out for *speech*, and only speech—not for *actions*, as Gregorian huffily insists. As for behavior, the prickly folks whose
burning of the American flag was upheld by the Supreme Court were indeed engaged in behavior, but that behavior was based entirely on symbolic
speech. So was Hann's. He didn't punch anybody or vandalize any property.
He brayed.

Art Spitzer, legal director of the ACLU's National Capital Area affiliate,   34
wrote a personal letter to Gregorian:

"There is a very simple test for determining whether a person is being   35
punished for his actions or his speech. You just ask whether he would have
received the same punishment if he had spoken different words while engaging in the same conduct.

"Thus, would your student have been expelled if he had gotten drunk   36
and stood in the same courtyard at the same hour of the night, shouting at

the same decibel level, 'Black is Beautiful!' 'Gay is Good!' or 'Go Brown! Beat Yale!' or even 'Nuke Baghdad! Kill Saddam!'?"

37   "I am confident," Spitzer said, that "he would not have been expelled for such 'actions.' If that is correct, it follows that *he was expelled for the unsavory content of his speech*, and not for his actions. I have no doubt that you can understand this distinction. (Emphasis added.)

38   "Now, you are certainly entitled to believe that it is appropriate to expel a student for the content of his speech when that content is sufficiently offensive to the 'university community.' . . .

39   "If that is your position, why can't you deliver it forthrightly? Then the university community can have an open debate about which opinions it finds offensive, and ban them. Perhaps this can be done once a year, so that the university's rules can keep pace with the tenor of the times—after all, it wouldn't do to have outmoded rules banning procommunist or blasphemous speech still on the books, now that it's 1991. Then students and teachers applying for admission or employment at Brown will know what they are getting into.

40   "Your recent statements, denying the obvious, are just hypocritical. . . ."

41   And what did the *New York Times*—in a stunningly fatuous February 21 editorial—say of Vartan Gregorian's sending Doug Hann into permanent exile? "A noble attempt both to govern and teach."

42   The *Times* editorials should really be signed, so that the rest of the editorial board isn't blamed for such embarrassments.

Understanding Meaning

1.   What events led to Hann's expulsion? Why does Hentoff call him "a historic figure"?
2.   Can one make both a "commitment to free speech" and a "condemnation of racism"?
3.   What are "hate speech" codes? Does it strike you as odd that no one seemed offended by Hann's use of the infamous "f-word"? Is obscenity less disturbing than racial slurs?
4.   Would comments about Irish drunks or Italian gangsters be considered "hate speech"?
5.   *Critical Thinking:* How do you separate "speech" from "action"? Does the concept of free speech, for instance, allow us to insult a person without facing the legal consequences that would arise from a physical assault?

Evaluating Strategy

1. Hentoff opens his article with a quote from the president of Brown University. How does this set up the rest of his argument?
2. Label where Hentoff uses logical, emotional, and ethical appeals.
3. Do you find Hentoff's inclusion of the press release effective?
4. *Other Modes:* Where does Hentoff use *narration, comparison,* and *definition?*

Appreciating Language

1. Hentoff refers to Hann's activity as a "hat trick of bigotry"—scoring racist, anti-Semitic, and homophobic insults in one outburst. Does the use of this hockey term suggest mockery? Would "triple threat" have different connotations?
2. What tone does Hentoff create with comments about military music and statements such as "Doug Hann will wander the earth without a Brown degree for the rest of his days"? How serious does he take the issue of "hate speech" and those who condemn it?

Connections across the Disciplines

1. Consider Kimberly Crawford's article (page 344). How can a statement made to a friend lead to criminal prosecution? Should secretly recorded conversations be used as evidence?
2. *Critical Thinking:* Consider the impact the word "nigger" had on Nathan McCall (page 61). When speech has a devastating effect on people, does it become "action" as opposed to simple "expression of ideas"?

Writing Suggestions

1. Assume you were a student at Brown University during the Hann controversy. Write a letter to the editor of the college paper arguing whether or not Hann should be expelled. Support your argument with more than one persuasive appeal.
2. *Collaborative Writing:* Discuss the concept of "hate speech" with a group of students. Ask group members to consider the fate of Doug Hann. Should he have been expelled? Is "hate speech" protected by the Bill of Rights? Record comments, and write a brief argument for or against disciplining students for expressing racist comments.

OPPOSING VIEWPOINTS: REPARATIONS FOR SLAVERY

MANNING MARABLE

Manning Marable is the founding director of the Institute for Research in African American Studies at Columbia University. He attended Earlham and received his doctorate from the University of Maryland in 1976. His books include Black Liberation in Conservative America, Speaking Truth to Power: Essays on Race, Radicalism and Resistance, The Crisis of Color and Democracy *and* What Black America Thinks: Race, Ideology, and Political Power.

An Idea Whose Time Has Come: Whites Have a Moral Obligation to Recognize Slavery's Legacy

OVERVIEW: *In recent years people have sought compensations for past injustices. Congress awarded $20,000 to each Japanese American interned during World War II. Korean women forced into sexual slavery during the war have sought restitution from the Japanese government. Germany has paid billions of dollars to survivors of the Holocaust. Many writers, including Manning Marable, believe that African Americans should be compensated for centuries of slavery and discrimination.*

1   In 1854 my great-grandfather, Morris Marable, was sold on an auction block in Georgia for $500. For his white slave master, the sale was just "business as usual." But to Morris Marable and his heirs, slavery was a crime against our humanity. This pattern of human-rights violations against enslaved African Americans continued under Jim Crow segregation for nearly another century.

2   The fundamental problem of American democracy in the 21st century is the problem of "structural racism": the deep patterns of socioeconomic inequality and accumulated disadvantage that are coded by race, and constantly justified in public discourse by both racist stereotypes and white indifference. Do Americans have the capacity and vision to dismantle these structural barriers that deny democratic rights and opportunities to millions of their fellow citizens?

3   This country has previously witnessed two great struggles to achieve a truly multicultural democracy.

The First Reconstruction (1865–1877) ended slavery and briefly gave 4
black men voting rights, but gave no meaningful compensation for two centuries of unpaid labor. The promise of "40 acres and a mule" was for most
blacks a dream deferred.

The Second Reconstruction (1954–1968), or the modern civil-rights 5
movement, outlawed legal segregation in public accommodations and gave
blacks voting rights. But these successes paradoxically obscure the tremendous human costs of historically accumulated disadvantage that remain
central to black Americans' lives.

The disproportionate wealth that most whites enjoy today was first con- 6
structed from centuries of unpaid black labor. Many white institutions, including Ivy League universities, insurance companies and banks, profited
from slavery. This pattern of white privilege and black inequality continues
today.

Demanding reparations is not just about compensation for slavery and 7
segregation. It is, more important, an educational campaign to highlight the
contemporary reality of "racial deficits" of all kinds, the unequal conditions
that impact blacks regardless of class. Structural racism's barriers include
"equity inequity," the absence of black capital formation that is a direct
consequence of America's history. One third of all black households actually have negative net wealth. In 1998 the typical black family's net wealth
was $16,400, less than one fifth that of white families. Black families are de-
nied home loans at twice the rate of whites.

Blacks remain the last hired and first fired during recessions. During 8
the 1990–91 recession, African Americans suffered disproportionately. At
Coca-Cola, 42 percent of employees who lost their jobs were black. At Sears,
54 percent were black. Blacks have significantly shorter life expectancies, in
part due to racism in the health establishment. Blacks are statistically less
likely than whites to be referred for kidney transplants or early-stage cancer
surgery.

In criminal justice, African Americans constitute only one seventh of all 9
drug users. Yet we account for 35 percent of all drug arrests, 55 percent of
drug convictions and 75 percent of prison admissions for drug offenses.

White Americans today aren't guilty of carrying out slavery and segrega- 10
tion. But whites have a moral and political responsibility to acknowledge
the continuing burden of history's structural racism.

A reparations trust fund could be established, with the goal of closing 11
the socioeconomic gaps between blacks and whites. Funds would be targeted specifically toward poor, disadvantaged communities with the greatest need, not to individuals. Let's eliminate the racial unfairness in capital
markets that perpetuates black poverty. A national commitment to expand

black homeownership, full employment and quality health care would benefit all Americans, regardless of race.

12   Reparations could begin America's Third Reconstruction, the final chapter in the 400-year struggle to abolish slavery and its destructive consequences. As Malcolm X said in 1961, hundreds of years of racism and labor exploitation are "worth more than a cup of coffee at a white cafe. We are here to collect back wages."

Understanding Meaning

1. What is Marable's thesis? Restate it in your own words.
2. Marable states that white wealth was "first constructed from centuries of unpaid black labor." How does one explain the wealth obtained by Carnegie, Ford, Edison, and Rockefeller—people who started with modest means? Did they indirectly benefit from the legacy of slavery?
3. Marable does not suggest paying funds to individuals. Would such funds make reparations more effective in resolving racial discrimination? Why or why not?
4. According to Marable, what is the moral obligation of whites?
5. Hasn't America already devoted billions to achieving Marable's goal of "closing the socioeconomic gaps between whites and blacks"? Although the term "reparation" was not used, didn't affirmative action seek to undo the legacy of slavery and discrimination?
6. *Critical Thinking:* Marable discusses this issue in terms of white and black. As America becomes more diverse, will this argument resonate with the growing number of Asians and Hispanics? Do the millions of Americans whose ancestors immigrated after slavery ended have a sense of moral responsibility for the past wrongs committed against African Americans?

Evaluating Strategy

1. Marable opens his essay with a personal narrative. Does this effectively dramatize a historical issue?
2. What facts does Marable include to demonstrate the lasting effects of slavery?
3. How effective is the Malcolm X quotation that ends the essay? Does it leave you with a lasting impression? Why or why not?

Appreciating Language

1. How does Marable define the term "structural racism"?

2. What does the term "reparations" mean? How does it frame the debate about African Americans and poverty?

Connections across the Disciplines

1. In "Why Schools Don't Educate" John Taylor Gatto (page 495) states that American children are "ahistorical"—they lack a concept of the past. Marable argues that slavery reparations would educate people about a historical injustice. What challenges would such an attempt at education encounter? Would people be able to appreciate the historical wrong or focus on current politics?
2. Michael Barone (page 256) compares the experiences of blacks and the Irish. Both, he claims, faced poverty, discrimination, and self-destructive habits. But is slavery different than poverty that voluntary immigrants have experienced? Are there lasting effects of slavery that will require special resolutions?

Writing Suggestions

1. After reading Shelby Steele's article (page 582), consider your own views on reparations for slavery and write a persuasive letter to the editor arguing for or against reparations.
2. *Collaborative Writing:* Working with a group of students, consider this aspect of reparations—who should pay? Should West African tribes who sold other Africans into slavery be held liable? Should the British government bear some measure of responsibility since most of the slaves were imported during the colonial era? Since the government did not own slaves, can Congress appropriate money or should only those families or institutions that owned slaves have to pay?

SHELBY STEELE

Shelby Steele is a research fellow at the Hoover Institution who specializes in race relations. He received a degree in political science from Coe College and a doctorate in English from Southern Illinois University. His 1990 book The Content of Our Character: A New Vision of Race in America *received the National Book Critic's Circle Award. His most recent book is* A Dream Deferred: The Second Betrayal of Black Freedom in America. *He has published articles in the* Wall Street Journal *and the* New York Times. *Steele has appeared on numerous television programs, including* Sixty Minutes *and* Nightline.

A Childish Illusion: Reparations Enshrine Victimhood, Dishonoring Our Ancestors

OVERVIEW: *Shelby Steele opposes the payment of reparations for slavery, arguing that it reflects what he calls a "crippling sense of entitlement." The problem, he asserts, is not white responsibility but black responsibility.*

1   My father was born in the last year of the 19th century. His father was very likely born into slavery, though there are no official records to confirm this. Still, from family accounts, I can plausibly argue that my grandfather was born a slave.

2   When I tell people this, I worry that I may seem conceited, like someone claiming a connection to royalty. The extreme experience of slavery—its commitment to broken-willed servitude—was so intense a crucible that it must have taken a kind of genius to survive it. In the jaws of slavery and segregation, blacks created a life-sustaining form of worship, rituals for every human initiation from childbirth to death, a rich folk mythology, a world-famous written literature, a complete cuisine, a truth-telling comic sensibility and, of course, some of the most glorious music the world has ever known.

3   Like the scion of an aristocratic family, I mention my grandfather to stand a little in the light of the black American genius. So my first objection to reparation for slavery is that it feels like selling our birthright for a pot of porridge. There is a profound esteem that comes to us from having overcome four centuries of oppression.

4   This esteem is an irreplaceable resource. In Richard Wright's *Black Boy*, a black elevator operator makes pocket money by letting white men kick

him in the behind for a quarter. Maybe reparations are not quite this degrading, but when you trade on the past victimization of your own people, you trade honor for dollars. And this trading is only uglier when you are a mere descendent of those who suffered but nevertheless prevailed.

I believe the greatest problem black America has had over the past 30   5
years has been precisely a faith in reparational uplift—the idea that all the injustice we endured would somehow translate into the means of uplift. We fought for welfare programs that only subsidized human inertia, for cultural approaches to education that stagnated skill development in our young and for affirmative-action programs that removed the incentive to excellence in our best and brightest.

Today 70 percent of all black children are born out of wedlock. Sixty-   6
eight percent of all violent crime is committed by blacks, most often against other blacks. Sixty percent of black fourth graders cannot read at grade level. And so on. When you fight for reparational uplift, you have to fit yourself into a victim-focused, protest identity that is at once angry and needy. You have to locate real transformative power in white society, and then manipulate white guilt by seducing it with neediness and threatening it with anger. And you must nurture in yourself, and pass on to your own children, a sense of aggrieved entitlement that sees black success as an impossibility without the intervention of white compassion.

The above statistics come far more from this crippling sense of entitle-   7
ment than from racism. And now the demand for reparations is yet another demand for white responsibility when today's problem is a failure of black responsibility.

When you don't know how to go forward, you find an excuse to go back-   8
ward. You tell yourself that if you can just get a little justice for past suffering, you will feel better about the challenges you face. So you make justice a condition of your going forward. But of course, there is no justice for past suffering, and to believe there is only guarantees more suffering.

The worst enemy black America faces today is not white racism but   9
white guilt. This is what encourages us to invent new pleas rather than busy ourselves with the hard work of development. So willing are whites to treat us with deference that they are a hard mark to pass up. The entire civil-rights establishment strategizes to keep us the wards of white guilt. If these groups had to rely on black money rather than white corporate funding, they would all go under tomorrow.

An honest black leadership would portray our victimization as only a   10
condition we faced, and nurture a black identity around the ingenuity by which we overcame it. It would see reparations as a childish illusion of per-

fect justice. I can't be repaid for my grandfather. The point is that I owe him a great effort.

Understanding Meaning

1. Why does Steele, who is probably a descendent of a slave, object to reparations?
2. How does Steele look back on slavery? What legacies does he see?
3. Marable (page 578) argues that whites need to recognize past injustices. Steele believes the real problem is white guilt, not white racism. Do both writers sense that white attitudes ultimately shape the destiny of African Americans?
4. According to Steele, what are the greatest problems African Americans face?
5. *Critical Thinking:* Steele notes that he can't be repaid for his grandfather. Reparations for victims of the Holocaust, for example, are limited to survivors, not their offspring. Is it fair for descendants to be compensated if the generation of victims died without redress? Should Native American tribes be compensated for lands lost in the nineteenth century?

Evaluating Strategy

1. Like Marable (page 578), Steele opens his essay with a narrative about an ancestor who was a slave. How effective is this device? Is it necessary to establish his authority to speak on a controversial issue such as slavery?
2. What statistics does Steele present? How important are they in supporting his thesis?
3. How does Steele attempt to shift the focus away from reparations to African-American responsibility?

Appreciating Language

1. Steele uses the term "entitlement." What does the word mean? Why, in his view, is it "crippling"?
2. *Critical Thinking:* Steele uses the term "victimhood." In recent years words and phrases such as "victimization," "victimhood," and "blaming the victim" have become popular. What is a "victim"? Do people use the designation of "victim" to justify actions or demand compensation?

Connections across the Disciplines

1. Consider the racial hatred Nathan McCall describes in "The Lesson" (page 61). Would reparations for slavery lessen or increase racial hostility?

Marable calls for education (page 578). Could a program of reparations educate whites as well as empower blacks? Why or why not?

2. Philip Gourevich (page 337) suggests that the Holocaust Museum has not provided visitors with the lessons the founders intended. Can policies addressing slavery truly help people understand its legacy?

Writing Suggestions

1. Write a persuasive paper outlining how public schools should address the legacy of slavery. How should textbooks present the issue? Can it be taught without bias? What, if anything, do all Americans need to know about slavery?

2. *Collaborative Writing:* Working with a group of students, discuss the arguments of Marable (page 578) and Steele. Imagine that your group wants to poll students in your school to determine their attitudes about slavery reparations. Write a process paper detailing how you would conduct a poll. How would you word questions to avoid bias? What background information would you present before asking students to give their opinions? What would be the most effective way of conducting a poll to make sure it accurately reflected campus attitudes?

OPPOSING VIEWPOINTS: CULTURAL IDENTITY

ARMANDO RENDÓN

Armando Rendón (1939–) was raised in San Antonio, Texas. He is currently vice president of ATM Systems, a Chicago-based counseling firm. He has published articles in the Washington Post *and* Civil Rights Digest. *Rendón also wrote a film script,* El Chicano. *In 1971 he published* Chicano Manifesto, *which outlined his views of the place of Mexicans in American society.*

Kiss of Death

OVERVIEW: *In this section of* Chicano Manifesto, *Rendón argues the importance of Hispanics to resist assimilation into mainstream American society and maintain their language and culture to avoid being "sucked into the vacuum of the dominant society."*

1   I nearly fell victim to the Anglo. My childhood was spent in the West Side barrio of San Antonio. I lived in my grandmother's house on Ruiz Street just below Zarzamora Creek. I did well in the elementary grades and learned English quickly.

2   Spanish was off-limits in school anyway, and teachers and relatives taught me early that my mother tongue would be of no help in making good grades and becoming a success. Yet Spanish was the language I used in playing and arguing with friends. Spanish was the language I spoke with my *abuelita*, my dear grandmother, as I ate *atole* on those cold mornings when I used to wake at dawn to her clattering dishes in the tiny kitchen; or when I would cringe in mock horror at old folk tales she would tell me late at night.

3   But the lesson took effect anyway. When, at the age of ten, I went with my mother to California, to the San Francisco Bay Area where she found work during the war years, I had my first real opportunity to strip myself completely of my heritage. In California the schools I attended were all Anglo except for this little mexicanito. At least, I never knew anyone who admitted he was Mexican and I certainly never thought to ask. When my name was accented incorrectly, Réndon instead of Rendón, that was all right; finally I must have gotten tired of correcting people or just didn't bother.

I remember a summertime visit home a few years after living on the West Coast. At an evening gathering of almost the whole family—uncles, aunts, nephews, nieces, my *abuelita*—we sat outdoors through the dusk until the dark had fully settled. Then the lights were turned on; someone brought out a Mexican card game, the *Lotería El Diablito,* similar to bingo. But instead of rows of numbers on a pasteboard, there were figures of persons, animals, and objects on cards corresponding to figures set in rows on a pasteboard. We used frijoles (pinto beans) to mark each figure on our card as the leader went through the deck one by one. The word for tree was called: *Arbol!* It completed a row; I had won. Then to check my card I had to name each figure again. When I said the word for tree, it didn't come at all as I wanted it to; AR-BOWL with the accent on the last syllable and sounding like an Anglo tourist. There was some all-around kidding of me and good-natured laughter over the incident, and it passed.

But if I had not been speaking much Spanish up until then, I spoke even less afterward. Even when my mother, who speaks both Spanish and English fluently, spoke to me in Spanish, I would respond in English. By the time I graduated from high school and prepared to enter college, the break was nearly complete. Seldom during college did I admit to being a Mexican-American. Only when Latin American students pressed me about my surname did I admit my Spanish descent, or when it proved an asset in meeting coeds from Latin American countries.

My ancestry had become a shadow, fainter and fainter about me. I felt no particular allegiance to it, drew no inspiration from it, and elected generally to let it fade away. I clicked with the Anglo mind-set in college, mastered it, you might say. I even became editor of the campus biweekly newspaper as a junior, and editor of the literary magazine as a senior—not bad, now that I look back, for a tortillas-and-beans Chicano upbringing to beat the Anglo at his own game.

The point of my "success," of course, was that I had been assimilated; I had bought the white man's world. After getting my diploma I was set to launch out into a career in newspaper reporting and writing. There was no thought in my mind of serving my people, telling their story, or making anything right for anybody but myself. Instead I had dreams of Pulitzer Prizes, syndicated columns, foreign correspondent assignments, front-page stories—that was for me. Then something happened.

A Catholic weekly newspaper in Sacramento offered me a position as a reporter and feature writer. I had a job on a Bay Area daily as a copyboy at the time, with the opportunity to become a reporter. But I'd just been married, and there were a number of other reasons to consider: there'd be a variety of assignments, Sacramento was the state capital, it was a good town in which to raise a family, and the other job lacked promise for upward mobility. I decided to take the offer.

9   My wife and I moved to Sacramento in the fall of 1961, and in a few weeks the radicalization of this Chicano began. It wasn't a book I read or a great leader awakening me, for we had no Chávezes or Tijerinas or Gonzálezes at the time; and it was no revelation from above. It was my own people who rescued me. There is a large Chicano population in Sacramento, today one of the most activist in northern California, but at the time factionalized and still dependent on the social and church organizations for identity. But together we found each other.

10   My job soon brought me into contact with many Chicanos as well as with the recently immigrated Mexicans, located in the barrios that Sacramento had allocated to the "Mexicans." I found my people striving to survive in an alien environment among foreign people. One of the stories I covered concerned a phenomenon called Cursillos de Cristiandad (Little Courses in Christianity), intense, three-day group-sensitivity sessions whose chief objective is the re-Christianization of Catholics. To cover the story properly I talked my editor into letting me take a Cursillo.

11   Not only was much revealed to me about the phony gilt lining of religion which I had grown up believing was the Church, but there was an added and highly significant side effect—cultural shock! I rediscovered my own people, or perhaps they redeemed me. Within the social dimension of the Cursillo, for the first time in many years I became reimmersed in a tough, *macho ambiente* (an entirely Mexican male environment). Only Spanish was spoken. The effect was shattering. It was as if my tongue, after being struck dumb as a child, had been loosened.

12   Because we were located in cramped quarters, with limited facilities, and the cooks, lecturers, priests, and participants were men only, the old sense of *machismo* and *camarada* was revived and given new perspective. I was cast in a spiritual setting which was a perfect background for reviving my Chicano soul. Reborn but imperfectly, I still had a lot to learn about myself and my people. But my understanding deepened and renewed itself as the years went by. I visited bracero camps with teams of Chicanos; sometimes with priests taking the sacraments; sometimes only Chicanos, offering advice or assistance with badly needed food and clothing, distributed through a bingo-game technique; and on occasion, music for group singing provided by a phonograph or a guitar. Then there were barrio organization work; migrant worker programs; a rural self-help community development

project; and confrontation with antipoverty agencies, with the churches, with government officials, and with cautious Chicanos, too.

In a little San Francisco magazine called *Way*, I wrote in a March 1966 13 article discussing "The Other Mexican-American":

> The Mexican-American must answer at the same time: Who am I? and Who 14 are we? This is to pose then, not merely a dilemma of self-identity; but of self-in-group-identity. . . . Perhaps the answer to developing a total Mexican-American concept must be left in the hands of the artist, the painter, the writer, and the poet, who can abstract the essence of what it is to be Mexican in America. . . . When that understanding comes . . . the Mexican-American will not only have acculturized himself, but he will have acculturized America to him.

If anyone knew what he was talking about when he spoke of the 15 dilemma of who he was and where he belonged, it was this Chicano. I very nearly dropped out, as so many other Mexican-Americans have, under the dragging pressure to be someone else, what most of society wants you to be before it hands out its chrome-plated trophies.

And that mystique—I didn't quite have it at the time, or the right word 16 for it. But no one did until just the last few years when so many of us stopped trying to be someone else and decided that what we want to be and to be called is Chicano.

I owe my life to my Chicano people. They rescued me from the Anglo 17 kiss of death, the monolingual, monocultural, and colorless Gringo society. I no longer face a dilemma of identity or direction. That identity and direction have been charted for me by the Chicano—but to think I came that close to being sucked into the vacuum of the dominant society.

Understanding Meaning

1. What kind of childhood did Rendón have?
2. What represented his early success? What does Rendón mean by the statement "I had bought the white man's world"? What were his goals?
3. What is the "Anglo kiss of death"?
4. How did Rendón respond to people who mispronounced his name?
5. What led to Rendón's "radicalization"?
6. The Chicanos Rendón encountered were the poor of the barrios and bracero camps. Would his sense of identity be different if the Mexicans he encountered in California were affluent professionals and entrepreneurs?

7. *Critical Thinking:* Rendón describes the Gringo society as "monolingual, mono-cultural, and colorless." Does he overlook the diversity of cultures in mainstream America, which includes Jews, the Irish, Italians, Germans, Greeks, Russians, and the French? Is this the perception that immigrants have of any culture, such as that all Mexicans or Nigerians seem alike?

Evaluating Strategy

1. What tone is established in the first sentence? Does the use of the word "victim" indicate hostility?
2. Rendón includes a quote from one of his articles. Is this an effective device? Would it be better to simply restate his ideas within "Kiss of Death"?
3. *Other Modes:* How does Rendón use *narration*, *description*, and *comparison* in developing "Kiss of Death"?

Appreciating Language

1. What does the term "kiss of death" mean to you? Do you associate it with the Bible or Hollywood images of the Mafia?
2. Rendón uses several Spanish words without providing definitions in English. What does this suggest about his idea of America becoming "acculturized" to the Mexican American?
3. Rendón uses both "Mexican-American" and "Chicano." What definitions of these terms are you familiar with? Do "Latino" and "Hispanic" have different meanings and connotations?
4. What does Rendón mean by "cautious Chicanos"?

Connections across the Disciplines

1. How might Rendón view the Chicano police officer described by Ramon "Tianguis" Pérez in "The Fender-Bender" (page 56)? Might he see this officer as a "cautious Chicano"?
2. How does Rendón's concept of cultural identity compare with the concerns of William Raspberry (page 287)?

Writing Suggestions

1. Write your own version of a "kiss of death" you have escaped in your own life. Perhaps you nearly lost yourself or compromised your future by taking a job or

entering a relationship you found initially appealing but now view as an error. Your essay should emphasize how you altered your sense of identity.

2. Write a short essay analyzing your role in society. Do you see yourself as an individual in a collective society or as part of a group within society? Do others view you as a member of an ethnic group, one of the handicapped, or a product of your neighborhood or generation? Does an in-group identity provide support or heighten your sense of alienation from the greater society?

3. *Collaborative Writing:* Discuss Rendón's essay with a group of students, and ask each one to briefly respond to the notion of an "Anglo Kiss of Death." How do members of the group define this? Do they feel it is appropriate or unnecessarily harsh? Does it presume that mainstream American society is a malevolent force? Work together to write a few paragraphs expressing the views your group raises. You may organize your statement by using *comparison* or *division/classification.*

BARBARA EHRENREICH

Barbara Ehrenreich (1941–) was born in Butte, Montana and attended Reed College in Oregon, where she received a bachelor's degree in chemical physics. In 1968 she completed a doctorate in cell biology at Rockefeller University in New York. While in graduate school, she became active in political and social issues such as education, low-income housing, and the war in Vietnam. She has published numerous articles in Time, Ms, Mother Jones, New Republic, *and the* Nation, *as well as several collections of essays.*

Cultural Baggage

OVERVIEW: *Unlike Armando Rendón who embraces his ethnic heritage, Barbara Ehrenreich refuses to accept an ethnic identity, calling herself one of "the race of 'none.'"*

1 An acquaintance was telling me about the joys of rediscovering her ethnic and religious heritage. "I know exactly what my ancestors were doing 2,000 years ago," she said, eyes gleaming with enthusiasm, "and *I can do the same things now.*" Then she leaned forward and inquired politely, "And what is your ethnic background, if I may ask?"

2 "None," I said, that being the first word in line to get out of my mouth. Well, not "none," I backtracked. Scottish, English, Irish—that was something, I supposed. Too much Irish to qualify as a WASP; too much of the hated English to warrant a "Kiss Me, I'm Irish" button; plus there are a number of dead ends in the family tree due to adoptions, missing records, failing memories and the like. I was blushing by this time. Did "none" mean I was rejecting my heritage out of Anglo-Celtic self-hate? Or was I revealing a hidden ethnic chauvinism in which the Britannically derived serve as a kind of neutral standard compared with the ethnic "others"?

3 Throughout the 60's and 70's, I watched one group after another— African-Americans, Latinos, Native Americans—stand up and proudly reclaim their roots while I just sank back ever deeper into my seat. All this excitement over ethnicity stemmed, I uneasily sensed, from a past in which their ancestors had been trampled upon by *my* ancestors, or at least by people who looked very much like them. In addition, it had begun to seem almost un-American not to have some sort of hyphen at hand, linking one to more venerable times and locales.

4 But the truth is, I was raised with none. We'd eaten ethnic foods in my childhood home, but these were all borrowed, like the pasties, or Cornish

592

meat pies, my father had picked up from his fellow miners in Butte, Mont. If my mother had one rule, it was militant ecumenism in all matters of food and experience. "Try new things," she would say, meaning anything from sweetbreads to clams, with an emphasis on the "new."

As a child, I briefly nourished a craving for tradition and roots. I immersed myself in the works of Sir Walter Scott. I pretended to believe that the bagpipe was a musical instrument. I was fascinated to learn from a grandmother that we were descended from certain Highland clans and longed for a pleated skirt in one of their distinctive tartans.

But in "Ivanhoe," it was the dark-eyed "Jewess" Rebecca I identified with, not the flaxen-haired bimbo Rowena. As for clans: Why not call them "tribes," those bands of half-clad peasants and warriors whose idea of cuisine was stuffed sheep gut washed down with whisky? And then there was the sting of Disraeli's remark—which I came across in my early teens—to the effect that his ancestors had been leading orderly, literate lives when my ancestors were still rampaging through the Highlands daubing themselves with blue paint.

Motherhood put the screws on me, ethnicitywise. I had hoped that by marrying a man of Eastern European-Jewish ancestry I would acquire for my descendants the ethnic genes that my own forebears so sadly lacked. At one point, I even subjected the children to a seder of my own design, including a little talk about the flight from Egypt and its relevance to modern social issues. But the kids insisted on buttering their matzohs and snickering through my talk. "Give me a break, Mom," the older one said. "You don't even believe in God."

After the tiny pagans had been put to bed, I sat down to brood over Elijah's wine. What had I been thinking? The kids knew that their Jewish grandparents were secular folks who didn't hold seders themselves. And if ethnicity eluded me, how could I expect it to take root in my children, who are not only Scottish-English-Irish, but Hungarian-Polish-Russian to boot?

But, then, on the fumes of Manischewitz, a great insight took form in my mind. It was true, as the kids said, that I didn't "believe in God." But this could be taken as something very different from an accusation—a reminder of a genuine heritage. My parents had not believed in God either, nor had my grandparents or any other progenitors going back to the great-great level. They had become disillusioned with Christianity generations ago—just as, on the in-law side, my children's other ancestors had shaken their Orthodox Judaism. This insight did not exactly furnish me with an "identity," but it was at least something to work with: we are the kind of people. I realized—whatever our distant ancestors' religions—who do *not* believe, who do not carry on traditions, who do not do things just because someone has done them before.

10   The epiphany went on: I recalled that my mother never introduced a procedure for cooking or cleaning by telling me, "Grandma did it this way." What did Grandma know, living in the days before vacuum cleaners and disposable toilet mops! In my parents' general view, new things were better than old, and the very fact that some ritual had been performed in the past was a good reason for abandoning it now. Because what was the past, as our forebears knew it? Nothing but poverty, superstition and grief. "Think for yourself," Dad used to say. "Always ask why."

11   In fact, this may have been the ideal cultural heritage for my particular ethnic strain—bounced as it was from the Highlands of Scotland across the sea, out to the Rockies, down into the mines and finally spewed out into high-tech, suburban America. What better philosophy, for a race of migrants, than "Think for yourself"? What better maxim, for a people whose whole world was rudely inverted every 30 years or so, than "Try new things"?

12   The more tradition-minded, the newly enthusiastic celebrants of Purim and Kwanzaa and Solstice, may see little point to survival if the survivors carry no cultural freight—religion, for example, or ethnic tradition. To which I would say that skepticism, curiosity and wide-eyed ecumenical tolerance are also worthy elements of the human tradition and are at least as old as such notions as "Serbian" or "Croatian," "Scottish" or "Jewish." I make no claims for my personal line of progenitors except that they remained loyal to the values that may have induced all of our ancestors, long, long ago, to climb down from the trees and make their way into the open plains.

13   A few weeks ago, I cleared my throat and asked the children, now mostly grown and fearsomely smart, whether they felt any stirrings of ethnic or religious identity, etc., which might have been, ahem, insufficiently nourished at home. "None," they said, adding firmly, "and the world would be a better place if nobody else did, either." My chest swelled with pride, as would my mother's, to know that the race of "none" marches on.

Understanding Meaning

1. Why does Ehrenreich have difficulty defining her heritage?
2. Does Ehrenreich see something negative in embracing one's ethnic roots?
3. *Critical Thinking:* Armando Rendón (page 586) suggests that he avoided the "vacuum of the dominant society" that would have erased his identity. Does Ehrenreich suggest that embracing "nothingness" is liberating, freeing one from cultural mind-sets, Old World limitations, bias, and inhibiting traditions?

Evaluating Strategy

1. What is Ehrenreich's thesis? How would you restate it in your own words?
2. How effective is the opening narrative?
3. *Other Modes:* Where does Ehrenreich use *comparison* and *narration* to develop her essay?

Appreciating Language

1. What do the tone and style of this essay suggest about the intended audience?
2. What words does Ehrenreich use to describe those who embrace their cultural heritage?

Connections across the Disciplines

1. Review "My Ecumenical Father" (page 133). Is there a difference between embracing the "race of none" and being ecumenical—identifying with one's own culture while respecting that of others?
2. Consider Nathan McCall's "The Lesson" (page 61). Is ethnic status something some people cannot escape? Is it forced on them by bigots?

Writing Suggestions

1. Write an essay explaining your attitude about your own ethnic identity. Persuade readers to accept your view of identity. Do you embrace a culture or celebrate being "none"?
2. *Collaborative Writing:* Discuss Ehrenreich's essay with a group of students. Do they share her views on race and identity, or do they see it as a form of denial? Does the "race of none" risk masking racial injustice and oppression? Record members' comments, and work to create a response. If members have differing opinions, draft opposing essays.

WRITING BEYOND THE CLASSROOM

ALBERT EINSTEIN

Albert Einstein (1879–1955) was born in Ulm, Germany. He completed a doctorate at the University of Zurich in 1905. He developed his noted theory of relativity at this time and held several teaching positions in physics. His work soon received international attention. In 1921 Einstein was awarded the Nobel Prize in Physics. Nazi persecution forced him to leave Germany, and he took a teaching position at Princeton. As noted in the Introduction, Einstein's reputation led Leo Szilard to ask him to alert the United States government about the possibility of nuclear weapons.

Letter to President Roosevelt, August 2, 1939

OVERVIEW: *As you read the letter, consider the problem Einstein and the other scientists, for whom English was a second language, faced in explaining an abstract scientific theory to a political official.*

1
Albert Einstein
Old Grove Rd.
Nassau Point
Peconic, Long Island

August 2nd, 1939

2 F. D. Roosevelt,
President of the United States,
White House
Washington, D.C.

Sir:

3   Some recent work by E. Fermi and L. Szilard, which has been communicated to me in manuscript, leads me to expect that the element uranium may be turned into a new and important source of energy in the immediate future. Certain aspects of the situation which has arisen seem to call for watchfulness and, if necessary, quick action on the part of the Administration. I believe therefore that it is my duty to bring to your attention the following facts and recommendations:

In the course of the last four months it has been made probable— 4
through the work of Joliot in France as well as Fermi and Szilard in America—that it may become possible to set up a nuclear chain reaction in a large mass of uranium, by which vast amounts of power and large quantities of new radium-like elements would be generated. Now it appears almost certain that this could be achieved in the immediate future.

This new phenomenon would also lead to the construction of bombs, 5
and it is conceivable—though much less certain—that extremely powerful bombs of a new type may thus be constructed. A single bomb of this type, carried by boat and exploded in a port, might very well destroy the whole port together with some of the surrounding territory. However, such bombs might very well prove to be too heavy for transportation by air.

The United States has only very poor ores of uranium in moderate 6
quantities. There is some good ore in Canada and the former Czechoslovakia, while the most important source of uranium is Belgian Congo.

In view of this situation you may think it desirable to have some perma- 7
nent contact maintained between the Administration and the group of physicists working on chain reactions in America. One possible way of achieving this might be for you to entrust with this task a person who has your confidence and who could perhaps serve in an inofficial capacity. His task might comprise the following:

a) to approach Government Departments, keep them informed of the 8
further development, and put forward recommendations for Government action, giving particular attention to the problem of securing a supply of uranium ore for the United States;

b) to speed up the experimental work, which is at present being carried 9
on within the limits of the budgets of University laboratories, by providing funds, if such funds be required, through his contacts with private persons who are willing to make contributions for this cause, and perhaps also by obtaining the co-operation of industrial laboratories which have the necessary equipment.

I understand that Germany has actually stopped the sale of uranium 10
from the Czechoslovakian mines which she has taken over. That she should have taken such early action might perhaps be understood on the ground that the son of the German Under-Secretary of State, von Weizäcker, is attached to the Kaiser-Wilhelm-Institut in Berlin where some of the American work on uranium is now being repeated.

Yours very truly, 11
Albert Einstein

Understanding Meaning

1. What does Einstein want the president to realize?
2. What specific recommendations does Einstein urge Roosevelt to carry out?
3. *Critical Thinking:* How does Einstein end the letter? Does the mere mention of Germany and nuclear research appear alarming? Remember that in August 1939 Hitler had already taken the Rhineland and Czechoslovakia. That month he was stepping up pressures on Poland. Within a month World War II would begin.

Evaluating Strategy

1. What appeals does Einstein use?
2. How does Einstein suggest that the president accept his recommendations?
3. Does Einstein assume his name alone will command attention? Is that why he uses first person in the letter?

Appreciating Language

1. What level of language does Einstein use? How does he explain physics in common terms?
2. Is the tone of this letter alarmist?

Connections across the Disciplines

1. How would this letter provide added support to Carl Sagan's "Why We Need to Understand Science" (page 563)?
2. Compare this letter to the fund-raising ad on page 599. How are they similar in attempting to make a persuasive argument in a brief statement?

Writing Suggestions

1. Write a persuasive letter to the president or other official to persuade him or her to follow your recommendations on a subject you feel is important.
2. *Collaborative Writing:* Discuss the letter with some students. Did Einstein manage to communicate effectively? Is this a lost art today? Work together to write a persuasive essay on the need for experts to communicate with the public and officials.

THE IRISH AMERICAN PARTNERSHIP

The Irish American Partnership is a nonprofit organization supported by Irish-American politicians and business executives. Tip O'Neill, former Speaker of the House, and the retired commandant of the U.S. Marine Corps, General Paul X. Kelley, were among the founding members. The organization raises funds to support job training and business development programs in both the Republic of Ireland and Northern Ireland.

Irish Need Apply

OVERVIEW: *This advertisement appeared in Irish-American magazines and newspapers. The headline is a variation of the infamous "No Irish Need Apply" notices that greeted many Irish immigrants seeking work. Well into the twentieth century, want ads in American newspapers included this statement as a standard feature, often abbreviating it to "N.I.N.A."*

Irish need apply.

Ireland needs us. [1] [2]

Unemployment above 20 percent. Young people forced to leave their homeland [3] to find hope and work. Parents saying goodbye to their children everyday.

Ireland is a small island of abundant beauty but scarce financial [4] resources. To survive and grow, this land of 5 million needs our help.

There are 44 million of us of Irish descent in America. We overcame [5] our own struggles, and found comfort and prosperity in our new land.

Now it is time for us to apply that same determination to help those [6] back home. Through the Irish American Partnership. The Partnership is a unique organization committed to peace and economic recovery in Ireland, North and South.

The Partnership needs you to support its work. Work like 600 jobs for [7] people in Tralee, Ballymun, and West Belfast. Financial aid for graduate students in science and technology. Management training for Irish youth in U.S. companies.

(Continued)

8   *(Continued from previous page)*
　　　Ireland has much to build on. Breathtaking beauty. A proud, educated, motivated work force. Some 375 American companies on its soil.

9   　　　Above all, Ireland has us— deeply loyal Irish Americans able to help those in need.

10   　　　Just fill out the coupon, and return it with a contribution to the Irish American Partnership. The needs are too great to ignore. Apply yourself.

☐ Yes, I want to apply. I want to support the Irish American Partnership.
Enclosed is my contribution for
☐ $35 ☐ $50 ☐ $100 $_____ (amt.)
☐ I am not ready to contribute. Please send me more information.
Call toll-free 1-800-722-3893 or fill out and mail to:
Irish American Partnership, 4 Faneuil Hall Marketplace, Boston, MA 02109

Name (please print)

Address

City　　　　　　　　State　　　　　　　　Zip

The Irish American Partnership is a non-profit organization supported by American business executives and endorsed by political, religious, and business leaders in Ireland, North and South. Its mission is a strong, healthy, peaceful Ireland through economic development, job creation, and education.

11   # The Irish American Partnership

Understanding Meaning

1. How effective is the headline in getting attention? Would people of other ethnic groups recognize the historical allusion?
2. What appeals are used?
3. How much factual support is included in the ad? Why is factual support needed?
4. Is an emotional appeal to an ethnic loyalty to the "Old Sod" evident?

Evaluating Strategy

1. Ads must communicate in a glance. How effective is this ad?
2. *Critical Thinking:* How does this ad fit a problem/solution pattern?

Appreciating Language

1. What level of language is used? What words would strike the reader?
2. How does word choice reinforce the use of appeals?

Connections across the Disciplines

1. How does this ad compare to the 3M ad on page 157?

2. How does an ad such as this, calling on Irish Americans to support Irish causes, relate to the issues of cultural identity raised by Rendón, Rowan, Pérez, and others you may have read in this book?

Writing Suggestions

1. Invent a similar organization raising money to help a group you identify with. Consider your readers carefully in devising your appeal.
2. *Collaborative Writing:* Working with a group of students, discuss the implied ethical appeal in this ad—that those who have achieved prosperity have an obligation to help others. Do middle-class African Americans or prominent Hispanics have a similar obligation? Work together to write a persuasive letter or ad urging people to "take care of their own."

STRATEGIES FOR WRITING ARGUMENT AND PERSUASION

1. **Determine your purpose.** Clearly establish your thesis, and define what ideas you want readers to accept and what actions you want them to take. Do not try to communicate too many separate actions in one document.
2. **Evaluate your readers carefully.** Examine the perceptual world of your audience. Do barriers to your message exist that must be overcome? What information do your readers need in order to accept your ideas?
3. **Determine which appeals will be effective.** Recognize the advantages and disadvantages of each appeal, and consider blending more than one.
4. **Craft your introductions and conclusions carefully.** Your opening paragraphs must arouse interest and prepare readers for your argument or appeal. Your conclusion should end with a statement that will reinforce acceptance of your ideas or the taking of recommended action.
5. **Present factual detail in ways readers can understand.** In presenting facts and statistics, use methods such as analogies and narratives to dramatize their significance.
6. **Do not mistake propaganda for persuasion.** Do not assume that hurling accusations, using questionable facts, or employing shock tactics will make your argument or appeal successful. People dislike feeling manipulated, and often potential supporters will find overstated appeals objectionable and offensive.

SUGGESTED TOPICS FOR WRITING ARGUMENT AND PERSUASION
General Assignments

Write a persuasive argument to a general audience on one of the following topics. You may use one or more appeals. You can frame your paper in the form of an essay, a letter, a flyer, or an advertisement.

- Community and police relations
- The drinking age
- The way colleges prepare or fail to prepare graduates for the job market
- Censorship
- Affirmative Action
- Labor unions
- Welfare programs
- Out-of-wedlock births

- Sexual harassment
- A national sales tax

Select one of the following issues, and craft a persuasive essay targeted to one of the audiences listed.

Issues: Medicare reform, distribution of condoms in public schools, school prayer, bilingual education, recycling, gun control, legalization of drugs
Audiences: Suburban residents, retired schoolteachers, small-business owners, an organization of minority police officers, inner-city health care providers

Writing in Context

1. Imagine you have become close to a highly respected member of your community. This person is well regarded by your family and may have a key role in your future. He or she invites you to join an organization that actively supports a view on abortion that is opposite to yours. Write a letter persuading this person to accept your reasons for declining the offer. Try to make your disagreement known without creating animosity.

2. Write a letter to the editor of the campus newspaper about an issue that you have heard discussed but that no one else seems willing to raise. Urge the community to pay attention.

This paper was written in response to the following assignment:

> Write a 500–750-word persuasive essay about a current social or political issue. Avoid writing about subjects such as abortion or capital punishment unless you can provide a new or unique angle. Document use of any outside sources.

Why a Black Student Union?

1   Before any controversial issue can be discussed, there is usually a certain amount of misinformation to deal with. This is clearly the case with the Black Student Union. Many students have voiced concern and written letters to the editor since the college paper revealed that $540,000 was being allocated to the Union (Kane 1). The article stated that $52,000 was going to salaries, making the Black Student Union the only student organization with a paid staff.

2   First of all, the bulk of the money allocated to the Union is dedicated to renovating the building, which is university property. Constructed in 1962, the building has not had major repairs since 1974. Roof leaks, first reported to the administration three years ago, have led to substantial and costly damage. In addition, it is the only building that was not retrofitted with new heating and air conditioning systems in 1996 (CSU 22). Also, the building still does not comply with the Americans with Disabilities Act. Wheelchair ramps must be installed by court order (CSU 23).

3   Second, no one at the Union receives a salary for student activities. Five graduate students are paid to tutor remedial classes. Given the lack of space in the cramped Academic Support Center, use of the Black Student Union makes sense and creates more openings in the Center. Many non-black students attend classes and remedial seminars at the Union. Less than half the graduates of the Internet course last semester were African-American (Kane 2).

4   But there are other objections to the Union. Why should blacks have their own facility? Many on campus see the presence of a black student union as a kind of self-imposed apartheid. The Union has also been criticized for being the center of racially hostile militancy.

The Black Student Union hardly threatens to impose a new kind 5
of segregation. We live in integrated dorms, attend integrated classes,
participate in integrated sports, and serve on mostly white and Asian
academic committees. The few hours a week a student might spend
at the BSU hardly threatens racial isolation — any more than the
women's center risks ending co-education or the Newman Center pits
Catholics against Protestants. From my own observations, I see little
evidence of the radical and extremist politics union opponents mention. The most popular event the Black Student Union holds is Career
Week when black students line up to meet representatives from AT&T,
IBM, Bank One, and 3M. Most students are concerned about academic
performance and career options rather than radical politics. True, the
Union has sponsored some controversial speakers, but so has the university itself. Much of the "extremist literature" cited in a campus editorial is not distributed by the Union. The Union receives a lot of free
literature in the mail, which has been traditionally displayed in the
lobby. When it was brought to the attention of the board that some of
the pamphlets were anti-Semitic, members took quick steps to screen
incoming publications and discard "hate literature."

The real purpose of the Union is to assist African-Americans to 6
succeed on campus. Comprising less than 5% of the student body,
blacks easily feel alienated, particularly those who graduated from
predominately black high schools. According to Dean Smith, "Since
only one of eight black males entering a university will graduate, it is
imperative that we seek remedies to support their academic achievement and professional advancement" (12). Many black students have
difficulty forming friendships and joining organizations. Often there
were only a handful of college-bound students in their schools. To survive, they had to isolate themselves, studying alone to avoid associating with peers resentful of their dedication to academics. Outcasts in
high school, these students find college bewildering. They are not accustomed to participating in class or working in groups. They often
discover that they are woefully unprepared for college. Coming from
schools with 50–75% dropout rates, many suffered from "social promo-
tion." They discover that their A's and B's are only equal to C's and
D's in better suburban schools. The Black Student Union offers African-
American students a place to relax, interact with older students, and
work to make the university a more hospitable place to minorities.

7   Given the history of discrimination and disadvantage faced by African-Americans, the Union can be a positive asset. Is it a crutch, an undeserved luxury? No one can deny that black students feel handicapped on campus. No one complains about the cost of wheelchair ramps and elevators which benefit a handful of physically disabled students. Why should we ignore the crippling legacy of racism?

Works Cited

CSU Facilities Report: 1999 Sacramento: State University Budget Office, 1999.
Kane, Kelly. "BSU Funding Furor." *Campus Times* May 24, 1999, 1–2.
Smith, Dean. *Black Males in Crisis.* New York: Random House, 1998.

Questions for Review and Revision

1. What is the student's thesis?
2. What negative assumptions does the student seek to address? How does he counter them?
3. What audience does the writer appear to address? What appeals does the student use?
4. How much of the paper is driven by responding to opponents' criticisms? Is this a useful device?
5. How effective is the conclusion? Does comparing disabled students to African-Americans make a valid point? Would you suggest an alternative ending?
6. Read the paper aloud. Are there passages that should be deleted or expanded? Do the tone and style suit the writer's purpose?

Writing Suggestions

1. Using this paper as a model, write a similar essay taking a position on a current campus controversy. Assume you are addressing a hostile audience. Respond to their objections without criticizing or demeaning those who disagree with your thesis.
2. *Collaborative Writing:* Discuss this paper with a group of students. Have a member record comments by the group. Work together to write a short statement approving or disapproving of the concept of establishing separate student unions. If members disagree, consider writing pro and con versions.

ARGUMENT AND PERSUASION CHECKLIST

Before submitting your paper, review these points.

1. Is your message clearly defined?

2. Does your paper meet readers' needs? Do you provide the support they need in order to accept your thesis?

3. Do you support your views with adequate evidence?

4. Do you anticipate reader objections and alternative points of view?

5. Do you balance the strengths and weaknesses of logical, ethical, and emotional appeals?

6. Do you avoid overstated, sentimental, or propagandistic appeals?

7. Do you avoid preaching to the converted? Will only those who already agree with you accept your arguments?

8. Do you make it easy for undecided readers to accept your position without feeling manipulated or patronized?

9. Have you tested your argument with peer review?

Companion Web Site

See **http://sundance.heinle.com** for further information on writing argument and persuasion.

InfoTrac® College Edition

For additional reading go to InfoTrac College edition, your on-line research library, at **http://infotrac.thomsonlearning.com.**

- Enter the search term "persuasion" using Keywords.
- Enter the search term "argument" using Keywords.
- Enter the name of an author you read in this chapter using Keywords.
- Enter a theme or idea your class discussed using Keywords.

Appendix

WHAT IS DOCUMENTATION?

Many of the papers you will write in college require documentation—*a systematic method of acknowledging borrowed words and ideas.* Several of the entries in *The Sundance Reader* are documented: "TV Movies of the First Decade of AIDS" (page 323), "Surreptitious Recording of Suspects' Conversations" (page 344), and "Why a Black Student Union?" (page 604) cite the use of outside sources. Academic disciplines, publications, and professions have specific methods of documenting sources. When assigned a documented paper, make sure you understand the system your instructor expects.

WHY DOCUMENT SOURCES?

Whatever their discipline or topic, writers document outside sources for three main reasons:

1. *To avoid charges of plagiarism. Plagiarism* (derived from the Latin word for "kidnapping") refers to stealing or using the words, ideas, or artistic work of others without giving them credit. Some students find it difficult to believe that copying a few paragraphs from *The World Book* or using statistics found on a Web site can be considered a "crime." But using sources without credit is a theft of intellectual property. Most colleges have strict policies about plagiarism. Instructors routinely fail students who plagiarize papers. Many universities expel students who submit plagiarized assignments. Charges of plagiarism have ruined the careers of famous scholars and diminished the reputation of political figures. Hollywood studios, screenwriters, novelists, rock singers, and rap stars have been sued for stealing ideas, words, or lyrics of other artists. As a writer, you can protect yourself from charges of plagiarism by noting outside sources. *Accurate documentation clearly distinguishes your work from that of others so no one can accuse you of cheating.*

2. *To support a thesis.* Citing sources not only protects you from charges of cheating but makes your writing more effective. To convince readers to accept your thesis, it is important to provide them with evidence. In court, lawyers prove cases by presenting eyewitnesses, expert testimony, and exhibits. As a writer, you can persuade readers to accept your point of view if you provide proof. *The more controversial your thesis, the more readers will demand supporting evidence from credible sources.*

3. *To help readers learn more.* Your citations not only protect you from plagiarism and strengthen your argument but show readers where they can obtain additional information by listing periodicals, books, and Web sites.

WHEN TO DOCUMENT

Students are often confused about what they have to document.

What Not to Document

First, you do not have to document all the sources you use. Even if you look up something in an encyclopedia or on a Web site, you do not have to note its use if the information belongs to what researchers call "the realm of common knowledge":

1. *Common expressions or famous quotations.* You don't need to list the Bible or your edition of Shakespeare if you simply check the wording of a quotation by Jesus or Hamlet. If you refer to statements readers are familiar with, such as Martin Luther King Jr.'s "I have a dream" or John F. Kennedy's "Ask not what your country can do for you—ask what you can do for your country," you don't have to note their original source. *Less familiar statements, especially controversial ones, must be documented.*

2. *Common facts not subject to change and available in numerous sources.* You don't have to list *The Encyclopedia Britannica* as a source if you use it to look up where George Washington was born, when *Death of a Salesman* opened on Broadway, when Malcolm X died, or the height of Mount Everest. General facts such as these are not subject to change and are readily available in hundreds of books, almanacs, biographies, textbooks, and Web sites. No one will accuse you of stealing information that is considered standard and widely known by millions of people. *Facts subject to change or dispute such as the population of Denver, the number of people on death row, or income tax regulations must be documented.*

What to Document

In almost every other case, you must acknowledge the use of sources:

1. *Direct quotations.* Whenever you copy word-for-word the spoken or written words of others, you must use quotation marks or extracts to distinguish them from your own text; you must also indicate the source.
2. *Indirect quotations or paraphrases.* Even if you don't copy information but restate the author's ideas in your own words, you must acknowledge the source. Changing a few words in a quotation or summarizing several pages in a paragraph does not alter the fact that you are making use of ideas and information from another source. Although you don't use quotation marks, you need to indicate that you have borrowed from an outside source.
3. *Specific facts, statistics, and numbers.* Facts will only be acceptable to readers if they know where they came from. If you state, "Last year eighteen innocent men were sentenced to death for crimes they did not commit," readers will demand the source of this number.
4. *Graphs, charts, photographs, and other visual aids.* Indicate the source of any visual aid you reproduce in your paper. If you create your own graphics based on statistics, you must indicate their source.

USING QUOTATIONS

Direct quotations should be used sparingly. Remember, the goal of your paper is to express your thoughts and opinions, not present a collection of other people's ideas. There are times, however, when direct quotations can be powerful additions to your essay. Use direct quotations:

1. When presenting a significant statement by an authority or eyewitness.
2. When the statement is unique or memorable.
3. When the idea conflicts with the mainstream of thought or common knowledge.
4. When the original statement is well-written and more compelling than a paraphrase or summary.
5. When readers may doubt a controversial point of view or question that a certain person made the statement.

Direct quotations have to be integrated into the text of an essay in a clear, sensible manner and be documented.

1. Indicate short direct quotations (1–4 lines) by placing them in quotation marks followed by a parenthetical citation:

> According to Lester Armstrong, "The university failed to anticipate the impact of state budget cuts" (17).

Indicate long direct quotations (more than 4–5 lines) by placing them in indented paragraphs without quotation marks. Indent ten spaces on the left side and introduce with a colon:

> According to Lester Armstrong, higher education suffered greatly during the recession:

> > The university failed to anticipate the impact of state budget cuts. As a result, construction on the new stadium was halted. Twenty-five administrators were laid off. Plans to expand the computer labs, bilingual programs, and adult night school were scrapped. The library budget was slashed by 24%, and two daycare centers were closed. The century-old Main Hall, which was scheduled for an extensive refurbishing, was given only cosmetic repairs and painting. (17)

2. Link direct quotations with your text. Avoid isolated quotations:

Incorrect

> Children are greatly affected by violence on television. "By the time a child graduates from high school, he or she has witnessed over 18,000 homicides on television" (Smith 10). Young people come to view violence, even murder, as a reasonable method of resolving conflicts.

Blend direct quotations into your text by introducing them:

Revised

> Children are greatly affected by violence on television. "By the time a child graduates from high school," Jane Smith notes, "he or she has witnessed over 18,000 homicides on television" (10). Young people come to view violence, even murder, as a reasonable method of resolving conflicts.

3. You may edit quotations to eliminate redundant or irrelevant material. Indicate deleted words by inserting *ellipsis* (three spaced periods) in brackets:

Original Text

> George Washington, who was heading to New York to confer with his leading advisors, agreed to meet with Franklin in Philadelphia on June 10th.

Edited Quote

As Smith notes, "George Washington [. . .] agreed to meet with Franklin in Philadelphia on June 10th" (12).

Deletions should only remove unneeded information; they should not alter the meaning of the text by removing qualifications or changing a negative statement into a positive one. It is unethical to alter a quotation, "We should, only if everything else fails, legalize drugs" to read, "We should [. . .] legalize drugs."

4. Insert words or other information to prevent confusion or avoid grammatical errors. For instance, if a direct quote refers to a Frank Bush by his last name and you are concerned readers will confuse him with President Bush, you may insert his first name, even though it does not appear in the original text.

Original Text

Hoping to ease tensions in the Middle East, Bush called for UN peacekeepers to patrol the West Bank.

Quotation

"Hoping to ease tensions in the Middle East, [Frank] Bush," according to *Newsweek*, "called for UN peacekeepers to patrol the West Bank" (14).

If you delete words or phrases, you may have to insert words to prevent a grammar error:

Original Text

Poe and other writers of his generation were influential in shaping a new, truly American literature.

Quotation

According to Sydney Falco, "Poe [. . .] [was] influential in shaping a new, truly American literature" (64).

USING PARAPHRASES

Paraphrases are indirect quotes. You must document your use of sources, even when you do not copy the text word by word. If you read two or three pages of a history book and summarize its points in a single paragraph, document your use of that source. Although you did not directly reproduce any words or sentences, the ideas you present are not your own and should be documented:

Original Text

More than 10,000 of New York's 29,000 manufacturing firms had closed their doors. Nearly one of every three employables in the city had lost his job. An estimated 1,600,000 New Yorkers were receiving some form of public relief. Many of those fortunates who had kept their jobs were "underemployed," a euphemism for the fact that they worked two or three days a week or two weeks a month—or, if they worked full time, were paid a fraction of their former salaries; stenographers, earning $35 to $40 per week in 1928, were averaging $16 in 1933; Woolworth's was paying full-time salesladies $6 per week.

Robert Caro, The Power Broker 323–324

Paraphrase

The Depression devastated New York City. A third of the manufacturers shut down operations, and over a million and half New Yorkers were on relief. Those with jobs saw their hours cut and their salaries slashed (Caro 323–324). Conditions in Chicago, Los Angeles, and San Francisco were similar.

Parenthetical references should be placed immediately after the paraphrased material at an appropriate pause or at the end of the sentence.

USING MLA DOCUMENTATION

The MLA style, developed by the Modern Language Association, is the preferred documentation method used in language and literature courses. In the MLA system, outside sources are listed alphabetically at the end of the paper in a "Works Cited" list and parenthetical citations are placed after direct quotations and paraphrases. For complete details refer to *The MLA Handbook for Writers of Research Papers*, 5th edition, by Joseph Gibaldi.

Building a Works Cited List

List all sources you refer to under the title "Works Cited" at the end of your paper. Items should be alphabetized by authors' last names or the first significant word of titles if no author is listed.

Sample formats

A book by a single author:

Smith, John. *The City*. New York: Putnam Press, 2002.

A book by two authors:

Smith, John, and Naomi Wilson. *The New Suburb*. New York: Western Publishing, 2001.

> *(Only the first author is listed last name, first name.)*

A book with three or more authors:

Smith, John, et al. *Urban Housing*. Chicago: Chicago UP, 2000.

> *(University Press is abbreviated as UP.)*

A work in an anthology:

Miller, Arthur. *Death of a Salesman. American Literature 1945–2000*. Ed. Keisha Sahn and Wilson Goodwin. New York: Dial Press, 2001. 876–952.

An encyclopedia article:

"Miller, Arthur." *The World Book*. 1998 ed.

> *(Volume and page numbers are not needed in encyclopedia references.)*

A periodical article with a single author:

Smith, John. "Urban Planning Today." *American Architect*. 25 Oct. 1999: 24–29.

A newspaper article without an author:

"Mideast Crisis Boils Over." *The Washington Post*. 22. May 2002: 54+.

> *(If an article starts on one page, then skips to others, list the first page with a plus sign.)*

A television program:

"Oil Boom." Narr. Morley Safer. *Sixty Minutes*. CBS. WCBS, New York. 27 Jan. 2002.

> *(Include both network and local station with date of broadcast.)*

An on-line article:

Wilkins, Robert. "Reflections on Milton." *Michigan Literary Review*. 9.2 (1998). 22. Feb. 2002 <http://www.umichigan.edu/english/litreview.html>>

> *(Include both date of access and full electronic address.)*

A corporate or organizational Web site:

New York Drama Guild. Reviews. 30 Aug. 2002. <http://www.nydg.org/reviews
.html>>

(Cite specific pages where possible rather than home pages.)

Article on CD-Rom:

"Albania." The Oxford Encyclopedia of Education. 3rd. ed. CD-ROM. Oxford:
Oxford UP, 2001.

An e-mail:

Hennessey, Richard. "Re: Urban Planning Conference." E-mail to Sean Brugha.
22 June 2001.

(Provide name of writer, title of message in quotation marks, recipient, and date.)

In-text Citations

As you include direct quotations and paraphrases in your paper, cite their
use with parenthetical notations. These citations should be brief but accurate. If you mention an author or source in your text, you only need to add a
page number:

Winston Hachner has noted, "The Internet has provided us with a dilemma
of choice" (874).

(Note: Place the period after the parenthetical citation.)

If you do not mention the source, include the author's last name or title
with page numbers:

The Internet has given us more choices than we can process (Hachner 874).
The sheer volume of information can overwhelm, confuse, and strangle businesses accustomed to defined channels of communication ("Internet" 34–35).

Sources without page references do not require parenthetical notes if cited
in the text:

During a *Sixty Minutes* interview in 2002, Randall Pemberton argued, "A terrorist attack in cyberspace can cripple our economy."

You can avoid long, cumbersome parenthetical notes by citing titles or several authors in the text:

As stated in the *Modern Directory of Modern Drama*, "August Wilson has
emerged as one of the nation's most powerful dramatic voices" (13). Jacobson

and Marley view him as a dominant force in shaping the country's perceptions of the African-American experience (145–146).

USING APA DOCUMENTATION

The APA style, developed by the American Psychological Association, is the preferred documentation method used in social sciences, including psychology, sociology, political science, and history. In the APA style, outside sources are listed alphabetically at the end of the paper in a "References" list and parenthetical citations are placed after direct quotations and paraphrases. For complete details refer to *The Publication Manual of the American Psychological Association*, 5th edition.

Building a References List

List all sources you refer to under the title "References" at the end of your paper. Items should be alphabetized by authors' last names or the first significant word of titles if no author is listed.

Sample formats

A book by a single author:

Smith, J. (2002). *The city*. New York: Putnam Press.

(Only authors' last names and initials listed; only first word in title is capitalized.)

A book by two authors:

Smith, J. & Wilson, N. (2001). *The new suburb*. New York: Western Publishing.

(Both authors listed by last name, initial.)

A book with six or more authors:

Smith, J., Wilson, S., Franco, W., Kolman, R., Westin, K., Dempsey, F., et al. (2000). *Urban housing*. Chicago: Chicago University Press.

A work in an anthology:

Miller, A. (2001). Depression in the adolescent male. In J. P. Meyers, J. Reed, & R. Rank (Eds.), *The psychology of youth: Problems and solutions* (pp. 87–99). New York: The Dial Press.

(Quotation marks not used in titles of articles and other shorter works.)

An encyclopedia article:

Depression. (1998). In *The world book* (Vol. 13, pp. 324–325). Chicago: World Book.

A periodical article with a single author:

Smith, J. (1999, October 25). Urban planning today. *American Architect.* 24–29.

A newspaper article without an author:

Mideast crisis boils over. (2002, May 22). *The Washington Post,* pp. 54, 58, 78, 89–92.

> *(If an article starts on one page, then skips to others, list all pages.)*

A television program:

Paulus, G. (Executive Producer). (2002, January 27). The mind. [Television series]. New York: WNET.

An on-line article:

Wilkins, R. (1998, March). Reflections on depression. *Michigan Science Review.* 9, 116–123. Retrieved October 23, 2001, from <http://www.umichigan.edu/science/scireview.html>

> *(Include both date of access and full electronic address.)*

A corporate or organizational Web site without dates:

New York City Health Department. (n.d.). Bioterriorism. Retrieved May 12, 2002, from <http://www.nychd.org/bioterrorism.html>

> *(Cite specific pages where possible rather than home pages.)*

Article on CD-Rom:

Albania. (2001) *Oxford Encyclopedia of Education.* 3rd. ed. [CD-ROM]. Oxford: Oxford University Press.

An e-mail:

E-mail and other correspondence are not included in References but listed within the text by referring to the writer and date.

In-text Citations

When you include quotations and paraphrases in your paper, cite their use with parenthetical notations listing author and year. These citations should be brief but accurate:

Hachner (2002) has noted, "The Internet has provided us with a dilemma of choice" (p. 12).

(Note: Place the period after the parenthetical citation.)

Wellman (2000) compares two common therapies for treating depression.

(Note: No page references cited for paraphrases.)

For sources without authors, include the titles in the text or a parenthetical citation:

The *Psychology Year in Review* (2002) presents new theories on addiction. A recent article reveals a genetic predisposition to narcotic dependence ("Genetic Maps," 2002).

(Include only years even if day and month are available.)

If a work has three, four, or five authors, cite all authors by only last names in the first reference:

Bodkin, Lewis, Germaine, and Neimoller (2001) dispute commonly held views of addiction.

In subsequent references, cite only the first author:

Bodkin et al. (2001) found no single factor in determining predisposition to alcoholism.

For works with six or more authors, cite only the first author in first and subsequent references:

Bryant et al. (2001) analyzed census figures to determine demographic changes.

STRATEGIES FOR AVOIDING COMMON PROBLEMS

1. *Use outside sources sparingly.* A good essay is not a collection of quotations and paraphrases. The focus of your paper should be your thesis, supporting ideas, and commentary. Avoid using long direct quotations that can be summarized in short paraphrases. *The fact that you find many interesting sources in the library or on the Internet does not mean that you should include everything you find in your paper. Be selective.*

2. *Take careful notes and collect documentation information when you locate valuable sources.* Make sure you copy direct quotations carefully word for word and do not distort their meaning by taking ideas out of context. Place direct quotations in quotation marks. If you photocopy a book or periodical, make sure you record the author's name and all publication information needed to document

the sources. If you print an article from the Internet, make sure you record the full Web site address and the date.

3. *Select sources carefully.* Avoid sources that appear biased, outdated, or poorly presented. Remember that all the books, periodicals, and Web sites were created by human beings who may be misinformed or prejudiced. Avoid basing your entire paper on a single source. Do not assume that all sources are of equal value. Use critical thinking skills to measure the significance of the sources you locate.

4. *Comment on the quality and quantity of sources.* Let readers know the results of your research. If sources are limited, outdated, or fragmentary, explain this situation to readers. If you find conflicting evidence or theories, objectively summarize the differences and justify your decisions in selecting sources. Don't assume direct quotations can speak for themselves. Don't insert sources into your essay without commenting on their value and demonstrating how they support your thesis.

5. *Clearly distinguish your ideas from those of others.* Accurate documentation, transitional statements, and paragraph breaks can help readers understand which ideas are solely yours and which originate from outside sources.

6. *Blend quotations and paraphrases into your text to avoid awkward shifts.* There should be smooth transitions between your ideas and those of others.

7. *Be sure to use the documentation system your instructor expects.*

Credits

Abramson, Leslie, "Unequal Justice" from *Newsweek*, July 24, 1994. Copyright © 1994 Newsweek, Inc. All rights reserved. Reprinted by permission.

Adler, Mortimer, "How to Mark a Book" first appeared in *Saturday Review*, July 6, 1940, vol. 22, pp. 11–12. Reprinted *Reader's Digest* August 1940, vol. 37, pp. 70–72. From *How To Read a Book* by Mortimer J. Adler. Copyright © 1940 by Mortimer J. Adler © renewed 1967 by Mortimer J. Adler. © 1972 by Mortimer J. Adler and Charles Van Doren. Reprinted with permission of Simon & Schuster, Inc.

Angelou, Maya, "Why Blacks Are Returning to Their Southern Roots" first appeared in *Ebony Magazine*, April 1990, vol. 45, no. 6, pg. 44(3), published by Johnson Publishing Company. Copyright © 1990 Maya Angelou. Reprinted by permission the Helen Brann Agency, Inc.

Austin, James, "Four Kinds of Chance" from *Chase, Chance and Creativity: The Lucky Art of Novelty* by James Austin. Copyright © 1978 by Columbia University Press. Reprinted with the permission of the publisher.

Baker, Russell, "The Plot Against People" from *The New York Times*, June 18, 1968. Copyright © 1968 by The New York Times. Reprinted by permission.

Barone, Michael, "Irish and Blacks" from *The New Americans: How the Melting Pot Can Work Again* by Michael Barone, pp. 17–22. Copyright © 2001 by Michael Barone, Published by Regnery Publishing.

Brookhiser, Richard, "The Skinny" from *National Review*, March 19, 2001, vol. 53, issue 5, pp. 59–60. Copyright © 2001 National Review, Inc. Reprinted by permission.

Brooks, John, "The Effects of the Telephone" from *Telephone: The First Hundred Years*, pp. 8–9. Published by Harper & Row, 1976.

Budish, Armond D., "Fender Benders Do's and Don't's" as appeared in *Family Circle*, July 19, 1994. Reprinted by permission of the author.

Burciaga, José Antonio, "My Ecumenical Father" from *Drink Cultura* by José Antonio Burciaga. Copyright © 1993. Reprinted by permission of Cecilia P. Burciaga, Joshua Odell Editions.

Capote, Truman, "Out There" from *In Cold Blood*, pp. 1–3. Copyright © 1965 Truman Capote and renewed 1993 by Alan U. Schwartz. Used by permission of Random House, Inc.

Grinslade, Liz, "Evaluating a Job Opportunity" from *Healthcare Financial Management* June 1993, pp. 116–118. Copyright © 1993 Healthcare Financial Management Association.

Harris, Marvin, "How Our Skins Got Their Color" from *Our Kind*. Copyright © 1989 by Marvin Harris. Reprinted by permission of Harper Collins Publishers, Inc.

Hedges, Chris, "Gaza Diary" from *Harper's Magazine*, October 2001. Copyright © 2001 by Harper's Magazine. All rights reserved. Reproduction from the October issue by special permission.

Hentoff, Nat, "Should This Student Have Been Expelled?" From *The Village Voice*, 1991. Copyright © V.V. Publishing Corporation. Reprinted by permission of *The Village Voice*.

Hewlett-Packard, "Solving Printer Problems" from *LaserJet 4 User's Manual*. Copyright © 1995 Hewlett Packard Company. Reproduced by permission.

Holt, John, "Three Kinds of Discipline," from *Freedom and Beyond* Second Edition, pp. 90–94. Reprinted by permission from *Freedom and Beyond* by John Holt. Copyright © 1995 by John Holt. Published by Boynton/Cook, a subsidiary of Reed Elsevier Inc., Portsmouth, NH.

"Homicide" definition from *Black's Law Dictionary*, Sixth Edition. Reprinted by permission of West Group.

Huff, Darrell, "How to Lie With Statistics" from *Harper's Magazine*, August 1950. Copyright © 1950 by *Harper's Magazine*. All rights reserved. Reproduced from the August issue by special permission.

Irish American Partnership, "Irish Need Apply." Reprinted by permission of the Irish American Partnership.

Jacobson, Jodi, "Swept Away" from *World Watch*, January/February 1989. Copyright © 1989, Worldwatch Institute. Reprinted by permission of the Worldwatch Institute.

Jamison, Charles N., Jr., "Why My Business Failed" from *Black Enterprise Magazine*, June 1994. Copyright © 1994. Reprinted with permission, Black Enterprise Magazine. New York, NY. All rights reserved.

Kenna, Peggy, and Sondra Lacy, "Communication Styles: United States and Taiwan" from *Business Taiwan* by Peggy Kenna and Sondra Lacy. Copyright © 1994. Used with permission by NTC/Contemporary Publishing Group.

King, Martin Luther, Jr., "The Ways of Meeting Oppression." from *Stride Toward Freedom* by Martin Luther King, Jr. Reprinted by arrangement with the Heirs to the Estate of Martin Luther King Jr., c/o Writers House, Inc., as agent for the proprietor. Copyright © 1958 by Martin Luther King, Jr. Copyright renewed 1968 by Coretta Scott King.

Kolbert, Elizabeth, "Birth of a TV Show," from The *New York Times*, March 8, 1994. Copyright © 1994 by The New York Times. Reprinted by permission.

Levey, Bob, "Men vs. Women Over Walking at Night" from *The Washington Post*, March 12, 2001, p. C09. Copyright © 2001, The Washington Post. Reprinted with permission.

Raspberry, William, "The Handicap of Definition" from *The Washington Post*. Copyright © 1982 Washington Post Writers Group.

Raudsepp, Eugene, "Seeing Your Way Past Interview Jitters" from *Machine Design*, April 9, 1994. Reprinted by permission of the author.

Rendón, Armando, "Kiss of Death" from *Chicano Manifesto*. Reprinted by Ollin Books. Copyright © 1996 Armando B. Rendón. Reprinted by permission of the author.

Ritter, Jonathan, "The World View of a Computer Hacker," from *Canadian Content*, edited by Neil Waldman and Sarah Norton, Harcourt Brace and Company, Canada, 1996. Reprinted by permission of author.

Rosenberg, Don D., "What Is Depression?" Reprinted by permission of the author.

Rowan, Carl T., "Unforgettable Miss Bessie" from *Reader's Digest*, March 1985. Reprinted with permission. Copyright © 1985 by The Reader's Digest Assn., Inc.

Sacks, Oliver, "The Man Who Mistook His Wife for a Hat" from *The Man Who Mistook His Wife for a Hat* by Oliver Sacks. Reprinted with the permission of Simon & Schuster Adult Publishing Group. Copyright © 1970, 1981, 1983, 1984, 1985 by Oliver Sacks.

Sagan, Carl, "Why We Must Understand Science" Copyright © 1989 by Carl Sagan. Originally published in *Parade Magazine*, Sept. 10, 1989. Reprinted by permission of The Estate of Carl Sagan.

Schell, Jonathan, "Letter From Ground Zero." From *The Nation*, October 15, 2001 vol. 723, issue 11, p. 7. Reprinted with permission from *The Nation*.

Simon, Scott, "Why Even Pacifists Support This War" from *Wall Street Journal*, October 11, 2001. Reprinted by permission of the author.

Simpson, Eileen, "Dyslexia" from *Reversals*. Copyright © 1979, 1991 by Eileen Simpson. Reprinted by permission of Georges Borchardt, Inc., for the author.

Staples, Brent, "Black Men and Public Space," originally titled "Just Walk on By: A Black Man Ponders His Power to Alter Public Space" in *Harper's Magazine*, 1986. Reprinted by permission of the author.

Stark, Steven D., "A Tale of Two Sitcoms," pages 282–287 from *Glued to the Set: The 60 Television Shows and Events That Made Us Who We Are Today*. Reprinted with permission of The Free Press, an imprint of Simon & Schuster Adult Publishing Group. Copyright © 1997 by Steven D. Stark.

Steele, Shelby, "A Childish Illusion . . . Or a Childish Illusion of Justice? Reparations enshrine victimhood, dishonoring our ancestors" from *Newsweek*, August 27, 2001, pg. 23. Copyright © 2001 Newsweek, Inc. All rights reserved. Reprinted by permission.

3M Pharmaceutical Products, Sales Representative Want Ad, in *New Orleans Times Picayune*, July 31, 1994. Reprinted by permission of 3M Pharmaceutical Products.

Tomkin, Jocelyn, "Hot Air Reason" from *Reason Magazine*, March 1993. Copyright © 1993 by the Reason Foundation.

Index